Educational Psychology:
Effective Teaching, Effective Learning

Third Edition

Stephen N. Elliott
University of Wisconsin–Madison

Thomas R. Kratochwill
University of Wisconsin–Madison

Joan Littlefield Cook
University of Wisconsin–Whitewater

John F. Travers
Boston College

Boston   Burr Ridge, IL   Dubuque, IA   Madison, WI   New York   San Fransico   St. Louis
Bangkok   Bogotá   Caracas   Lisbon   London   Mardrid
Mexico City   Milan   New Delhi   Seoul   Singapore   Sydney   Taipei   Toronto

McGraw-Hill Higher Education

*A Division of The **McGraw-Hill** Companies*

EDUCATIONAL PSYCHOLOGY: EFFECTIVE TEACHING, EFFECTIVE LEARNING,
THIRD EDITION

This book is printed on acid-free paper.

1 2 3 4 5 6 7 8 9 0 VNH/VNH 0 9 8 7 6 5 4 3 2 1 0

ISBN 0–697–37540–4

Editorial director: *Jane E. Vaicunas*
Sponsoring editor: *Beth Kaufman*
Editorial coordinator: *Teresa N. Wise*
Senior marketing manager: *Daniel M. Loch*
Project manager: *Mary E. Powers*
Production supervisor: *Enboge Chong*
Coordinator of freelance design: *Rick Noel*
Senior photo research coordinator: *Carrie K. Burger*
Supplement coordinator: *Stacy A. Patch*
Compositor: *Carlisle Communications, Ltd.*
Typeface: *Berling 10/12 Cases–10/12 Officina*
Printer: *Von Hoffmann Press, Inc.*

Cover/interior designer: *Christopher Reese*
Cover image: © *Tony Stone Images*
Photographer: *Reza Estakhrian*
Photo research: *Shirley Lanners*

The credits section for this book begins on page 618 and is considered an extension of the copyright page.

Library of Congress Cataloging-in-Publication Data

Educational psychology : effective teaching, effective learning /
    Stephen N. Elliott .... [et al.]. — 3rd ed.
        p.   cm.
    Includes bibliographical references (p.   ) and indexes.
    ISBN 0–697–37540–4
    1. Educational psychology.   2. Learning, Psychology of.
3. Effective teaching.   I. Elliott, Stephen N.
LB1051.T6695 2000
370.15—dc21   99–18631
                                                      CIP

www.mhhe.com

Dedication

To my parents, Bob and Jean, for their enduring love and support.

Stephen N. Elliott

In loving memory of my parents, Rudy and Marian Kratochwill.

Thomas R. Kratochwill

To my family.

Joan Littlefield Cook

To my wife, Barbara, whose love, support, and encouragement have been a source of inspiration through the years.

John F. Travers

BRIEF CONTENTS

CONTENTS

SECTION 1

The Development of Students 25

The Case of Marsha Warren 26

CHAPTER two

Cognitive and Language Development 28

CHAPTER three

Psychosocial and Moral Development   70

CHAPTER four

Diversity in the Classroom: Culture, Class, and Gender   109

CHAPTER five

Exceptional Students   147

SECTION 2

Learning Theories and Implications for Practice 199

The Case of Mark Siegel 200

CHAPTER SIX

Behavioral Psychology and Learning   202

CHAPTER seven

Cognitive Psychology and the Construction of Knowledge   245

CHAPTER eight

Thinking Skills and Problem-Solving Strategies   292

CHAPTER nine

Motivation and Student Learning   331

SECTION 3

Effective Teaching and the Evaluation of Learning 373

The Case of Melissa Williams 374

CHAPTER ten

Classroom Management: Creating Effective Learning Environments 376

CHAPTER eleven

Assessment of Students' Learning Using Teacher-Constructed Methods   419

CHAPTER twelve

Standardized Tests and Behavior Rating Scales   473

CHAPTER thirteen

Effective Teaching Strategies and the Design of Instruction   519

Stephen N. Elliott received his doctorate from Arizona State University and is currently a professor of educational psychology and a senior research associate in the Wisconsin Center for Education Research at the University of Wisconsin–Madison. Dr. Elliott is on the faculty of the School Psychology Program and teaches courses in professional issues and practices, educational psychology, and research methods and technical writing. He codirects two federal grants concerning the effectiveness and the use of testing accommodations and performance assessments for students with disabilities. He frequently consults with educators on the assessment and instruction of children in grades K–12. Dr. Elliott's work has focused on the assessment of children's social skills and related problem behaviors, and the development of alternative assessment methods for evaluating academic performance. Dr. Elliott's scholarly and professional contributions are widely recognized by his colleagues. In 1984, he received the Lightner Witmer Award from the American Psychological Association for early career research contributions, and in 1996 he earned the Van Hise Outreach Teaching Award for outstanding teaching at UW–Madison.

Thomas R. Kratochwill received his doctorate in educational psychology from the University of Wisconsin–Madison, where he is currently the director of the Educational and Psychological Training Center. He is an active researcher and contributor to scientific psychological literature. Dr. Kratochwill's research has received recognition from national and state organizations including Division 16 of the American Psychological Association, the Arizona State Psychological Association, and the Wisconsin Psychological Association. In addition, he has been associate editor of *Behavior Therapy, The Journal of Applied Behavior Analysis, School Psychology Review,* and a guest editor of *Behavioral Assessment.* Dr. Kratochwill was selected as the founding editor of the APA Division 16 journal *Professional School Psychology* (now *School Psychology Quarterly*) from 1984 to 1992.

Joan Littlefield Cook received her doctorate in developmental psychology from Peabody College of Vanderbilt University. Her research focuses on understanding differences between more-successful versus less-successful problem solvers, helping children improve problem-solving skills, and using technology to foster problem-solving skills. Dr. Littlefield Cook taught educational psychology, child development, cognition and classroom learning, problem solving, and measurement and evaluation to college students. In 1991, she won the Wisconsin Student Association's "Top 100 Educators" award at UW–Madison.

John F. Travers received his doctorate from Boston College, where he is a professor of educational psychology and child psychology. In a faculty of more than eight hundred, Dr. Travers has been selected as one of the outstanding teachers and has been honored as Teacher of the Year. He is the author or coauthor of fourteen books in the fields of education and child psychology. Writing, teaching, and community service involving children and schools have been constant themes in his professional career.

Teaching and learning are complex and exciting processes that bring people together in ways that can change their lives. Educational psychologists have been keen observers of the interactions between teachers and learners for nearly a century and have provided many insights into what makes for *effective teaching and effective learning*. In this third edition of *Educational Psychology,* we have created a book that emphasizes how the theoretical and applied work of educational psychologists can help educators achieve their goals of effective teaching and learning. This emphasis on the application of educational psychology will be most evident as you read about the real-life experiences of teachers with classroom challenges woven throughout our chapters. It will also be very clear as you examine nearly one hundred of our TIPS—Teaching Interaction Principles and Strategies—and the practical suggestions we have for improving *communication, motivation, time usage, assessments,* and ultimately *students' learning.*

Individuals entering the education profession are often both excited and anxious, and they may have many questions and ideas about teaching and learning. What shall I teach? How shall I teach it? Will students like me? How will I discipline students who misbehave? Even experienced teachers approach that first class meeting of a new year with similar, though perhaps less intense, feelings and concerns, because education and students constantly change. We recognize you have questions about teaching and learning. We believe **educational psychology** can help answer many of these questions today and provide you insights that will facilitate answering your own questions tomorrow!

ABOUT OUR BOOK

Educational psychology textbooks provide insights into the teaching-learning process and student behavior, as well as research data, theories, and illustrations, all concerned with actual classroom application of psychological principles. Consequently, individuals taking an educational psychology course and reading an educational psychology textbook should enter a classroom and other teaching-learning situations with greater confidence in their ability to teach and their understanding of the learning process.

To accomplish these goals, we have presented the basic principles of effective teaching and effective learning in a book that has a *balanced (cognitive and behavioral) theoretical orientation.* Becoming a successful teacher depends to a considerable extent upon acquiring an understanding of students, of how they learn, and of the most effective means of teaching. Since teaching is reaching, that is, reaching students, we—the authors of *Educational Psychology: Effective Teaching, Effective Learning*—have attempted to present the latest and most pertinent data available, to apply those theories that best explain particular classroom situations, and to consistently illustrate with classroom examples how these theories and data "work." In this way, we provide readers with a practical and useful book, based largely on empirical research, that will provide knowledge and guidance now and in the future when teaching others is their priority!

Organization of the Text

Writing an educational textbook that is both practical and useful demands that certain decisions be made. What is to be presented and how is it to be organized? Answering these questions forced us to select and organize the most pertinent and critical information around core concepts of educational psychology as applied to effective teaching. The book starts with an introduction to the teaching-learning enterprise and then focuses first on students, then on learning, and ultimately on teaching. We believe that this organization helps the reader to focus on the learner and development, the learner and learning, and the learner and teaching, with classroom management and assessment being important parts of effective teaching. Thus, the book stresses the interactions between students as learners and teachers and contextualizes these interactions in an increasingly diverse social and technological environment called school. Chapter 13, focusing on effective teaching, is a culmination of the book and emphasizes that the content and themes (communication, learning, motivation, time, and assessment) of the previous chapters are the "building blocks" to effective teacher-student interactions.

NEW TO THIS EDITION

A dynamic field such as educational psychology must incorporate vital facts into heuristic theories as well as offer educators information and teaching suggestions for the changes that any society inevitably experiences. More children of widely different backgrounds are entering our classrooms; therefore, educators must be prepared to recognize and understand the values, beliefs, and behaviors of diverse students and their families. *Teachers must be prepared to apply findings from educational psychology research to enhance their teaching-learning interactions.* Thus, with this third edition of *Educational Psychology: Effective Teaching, Effective Learning,* we have added two new features, **TIPS** and **Case Studies.**

TIPS stands for **T**eaching **I**nteraction **P**rinciples and **S**trategies and are brief summaries of key teaching principles and related instructional actions. Our TIPS focus on five themes that teachers have told us permeate their lives: *communication, learning, motivation, time,* and *assessment.*

The **case studies** found throughout this text are designed to provide rich and frequent opportunities for readers to see connections between the concepts and strategies they are reading about and the practice of teaching. Case studies are comprised of five components: a *Case Description* located in the opening pages of each section, a chapter-opening *Case Box* relating the case to the specific focus of each chapter, *Case Notes* embedded within each chapter, *Case Reflections* at the end of each chapter, and a *Teachers' Case Conference* located on the closing pages of each section.

In Chapter 1, readers are introduced to our three cases which focus on a teacher and his or her interactions with students. Each case is then expanded on in one of the sections of the book. In the opening of Section 1, "The Development of Students," readers study the case of Marsha Warren, an experienced third-grade teacher who has a heterogeneous class of students, some of whom challenge her. Then throughout each of the four chapters in this section, readers will find case notes where we offer *observations, hypotheses, and possible actions* designed to illustrate how the content of each chapter applies to Marsha Warren and her class. In Section 2, "Learning Theories and Implications for Practice," readers are introduced to the case of Mark Siegel, a fourth-grade teacher who is puzzled by the learning problems of one of his students and also challenged by the student's parent to do more to help the child. The four chapters in this section afford many perspectives on learning. Finally, in Section 3, "Effective Teaching and the Evaluation of Learning," readers meet Melissa Williams, a novice seventh-grade teacher at a high-achieving school who is feeling pressure to maintain the superior end-of-year test scores that the previous teacher had accomplished with similar students. The four chapters in this section result in numerous case notes that document ideas for successfully solving the problems confronting Melissa. These three case studies and their treatment throughout the text illustrate how students can apply knowledge from this course to their future teaching challenges.

SUPPLEMENTARY MATERIALS FOR THE INSTRUCTOR

We have worked with the publisher and some very talented individuals led by Joan Littlefield Cook, to put together a quality set of supplementary materials to assist instructors and students who use this text. These include the following.

Instructor's Manual and Test Item Bank

The key to this teaching package was created by Joan Littlefield Cook, one of the text's authors. This flexible planner provides a variety of useful tools to enhance your teaching efforts, reduce your workload, and increase your enjoyment of teaching. For each chapter of the text, the manual provides an outline, overview, learning objectives, and key terms. These items also are contained in the Student Study Guide. The manual contains lecture suggestions, classroom activities, discussion questions, integrative essay questions, suggestions for using the Educational Psychology video series, a film list, and a transparency guide.

The instructor's manual also includes sections on "Using the Cases" and "Big Ideas" in Educational Psychology". The first section is to help you use the cases (the ones in the text as well as other suggested for every chapter) as contexts for students to identify concepts, and as contexts for applying the text information to solve realistic classroom problems. The "Big Ideas" section helps students identify important text concepts, state them as teaching and learning principles, and develop specific teaching and learning strategies. Both the principles and strategies are tied to the five themes of the text (assessment, communication, learning, motivation, and time) to help students organize their knowledge around these themes.

The comprehensive test bank includes more than one thousand multiple-choice and true/false questions that are keyed to the text and learning objectives. Computerized test banks are also available.

Student Study Guide

This guide for students was also created by Joan Littlefield Cook. For each chapter of the text, the student is provided with an outline, an overview, learning objectives, key terms, a guided review, study questions (with answers provided for self-testing), and integration and application questions. The study guide begins with a section on developing good study habits, to help students study more effectively and efficiently. The "Using the Cases" and "Big Ideas in Education" section from the Instructors Manual are modified for the Study Guide.

Videotapes

The final component of the supplementary materials package for *Educational Psychology* is its newest and most exciting component: an integrative series of videotapes. These videotapes draw upon the book's knowledge base and bring to life the content from each of the major sections of the text. The videotapes provide students with opportunities to observe a variety of classroom practices and to hear from some of the leading educational psychology researchers in the country. Please ask your local McGraw-Hill sales representative for other instructional resources to accompany this book.

ACKNOWLEDGEMENTS

The authors also wish to thank the following colleagues for their guidance in developing the 3rd edition:

Frank D. Adams
> *Wayne State College*

James Applefield
> *Watson School of Education*
> *University of North Carolina–*
> *Wilmington*

Roger F. Bass
> *Carthage College*

Marcy Blackburn
> *Cameron University*

Lyn Boulter
> *Catawba College*

Preston A. Britner
> *University of Connecticut*

Randy L. Brown
> *University of Central Oklahoma*

Kay S. Bull
> *Oklahoma State University*

Jean Buller
> *Pacific Union College*

Sheryl Cohn
> *City University of New York Borough*
> *of Manhattan Community College*

Thomas Dougherty
> *Tarleton State University*

David S. Dungan
> *Emporia State University*

Beverly Dupre
> *Southern University at New Orleans*

Lani Van Dusen
> *Utah State University*

William L. Franzen
> *University of Missouri–St. Louis*

Eleanor Hanold
> *University of Wisconsin-Milwaukee*

Vickie Harry
> *Clarion University of Pennsylvania*

Robert Hohn
> *University of Kansas*

Debra L. Hollister
> *Valencia Community College*

George Ladd
> *Boston College*

LaVerne Logan
> *Viterbo College*

Robert Lucking
> *Old Dominion University*

Susan M. Miller
> *Texas A&M University–Commerce*

Joyce S. Natzke
> *Wisconsin Lutheran College*

Joe Olmi
> *University of Southern Mississippi*

Ann J. Pace
> *University of Missouri*

Peggy Perkins
> *University of Nevada–Las Vegas*

Gary D. Phye
> *Iowa State University*

Timothy Reagan
> *University of Connecticut*

Lisa M. Reboy
> *Emporia State University*

Michelle Rowe
> *St. Joseph's University, Pennsylvania*

Louis Smith
University of West Alabama

Judith A. Stechly
West Liberty State College

Gary R. Taylor
University of Arkansas

Mary Wellman
Rhode Island College

David O. Wendler
Martin Luther College

Janet Whitley-Valadez
Tarleton State University

Ann K. Wilson
Buena Vista University

Jody Wolfe
West Virginia University

Barbara N. Young
Middle Tennessee State University

Special appreciation is extended to Ann C. Gutenberger for her editorial work on several chapters. In addition, a special thanks is extended to Karen O'Connell for her word processing of the many drafts of this work. Finally, a thanks goes out to all the folks at McGraw-Hill for their important work on this text. Two of the McGraw-Hill team, Beth Kaufman and Kate Scheinman, in particular deserve special recognition for their strong support, encouragement, and ideas about ways to communicate effectively with teachers-to-be. I don't think we would have made it without these two team members!

Happy reading and learning!

Educational Psychology and Effective Teaching Interactions

A famous scholar—Francis Bacon— once said that some books are to be tasted, others to be swallowed, and some to be chewed and digested. There are two reasons why we hope you will decide to "chew and digest" your educational psychology book. First, the story of educational psychology is exciting, and we have tried to maintain that excitement by having you interact with the theories, studies and tips for becoming a skilled teacher. Second, we have attempted to avoid a mere recitation of facts; *we want you to apply this knowledge in your search for excellence.* Enjoy.

It's an exciting time to teach and be involved in the development of students. Good teachers are needed in every classroom to improve the quality of education for a diverse population of students in our schools. Much is expected of our schools—and teachers—and, despite dramatic headlines that may claim otherwise, much has been accomplished. For example, the 27th Annual Phi Delta Kappa/Gallup poll of the public's attitudes toward the public schools clearly indicated that parents rated the school in their community much higher than they rated the nation's schools. Thus, it seems parents were quite satisfied with the teachers and schools they knew. Nevertheless, much remains to be done, and you may soon be in a position—as a teacher, an administrator, or a psychologist—to advance these positive feelings. We believe that knowledge central to the discipline of educational psychology can be a major contributor to your success as an educator.

In this first chapter, we'll begin by defining educational psychology and introducing you to five major themes that characterize educational psychology research and practice. Then we will examine characteristics of effective teaching: what it is, how to achieve it, how to maintain it. Good teaching doesn't just happen; you must be part artist and part scientist. But you'll be happy to know that your efforts will be well worth it. All the research we have reviewed points to one inescapable conclusion: *Effective teachers can, indeed, make a difference in their students' lives!*

Aside from the personal and professional knowledge that you need to be a successful teacher, issues arise that you'll have to address as an educator. For example, how should I best meet the diverse needs of my class? What does the new research on motivation say that can guide me in thinking about instructional and assessment strategies? We'll present several of these issues and ask you to examine their possible meaning for both you and your students. Finally, we'd like to suggest ways and means for you to use the ever-expanding knowledge base of educational psychology as a tool for improving your effectiveness as a teacher, a parent, or an administrator.

EDUCATIONAL PSYCHOLOGY: A DEFINITION AND KEY CONCEPTS

It seems too simple to say that educational psychology is the psychology of learning and teaching, and yet a majority of educational psychologists spend their time studying ways to describe and improve learning and teaching. After reviewing the historical literature in educational psychology, Glover and Ronning (1987, p. 14) suggested that educational psychology includes topics that span human development, individual differences, measurement, learning, and motivation and is both a data-driven and a theory-driven discipline. Thus, our definition of **educational psychology** is the application of psychology and psychological methods to the study of development, learning, motivation, instruction, assessment, and related issues that influence the interaction of teaching and learning. This definition is broad because the potential applications of educational psychology to the learning process are immense!

Today educational psychology is a vital discipline that is contributing to the education of teachers and learners. For example, Jerome Bruner, an enduring figure in educational psychology, recently noted the need to rethink our ideas of development, teaching, and learning and the interactions among them. Specifically, Bruner (1996) urged educators and psychologists to see children as thinkers, and stated:

> No less than the adult, the child is thought of as holding more or less coherent "theories" not only about the world but about her own mind and how it works. These naive theories are brought into congruence with those of parents and teachers not through imitation, not through didactic instruction, but by discourse,

EDUCATIONAL PSYCHOLOGY

A discipline bridging two fields, education and psychology, that is primarily interested in the application of psychological methods to the study and practice of teaching and learning.

collaboration, and negotiation.... This model of education is more concerned with interpretation and understanding than with the achievement of factual knowledge or skilled performance. (1996, p. 57)

These words reflect many of the goals of this book: Think of educational psychology as a vital tool that can be of immeasurable help in planning, delivering, and evaluating teaching. To illustrate how the science of educational psychology can help teachers, we'd like to identify some key concepts and their relationship to instruction and learning. Much more will be said about each of these concepts as you work your way through this book.

Understanding the Meaning of Teaching

The first key concept is the need to understand what it means to teach. We hope that as a result of reading this chapter and others, such as Chapter 10, you will have a better grasp of "life in the classroom." You must, however, have a basis from which to make decisions about teaching.

Knowledge of Students

The second core concept is the belief that to teach skillfully, you must have as much knowledge about students as possible: their needs, characteristics, and differences. Section 1 of this book introduces you to the developmental lives of children. Chapter 2 is devoted to tracing the cognitive and language development of children, while Chapter 3 focuses on their psychosocial and moral development. Reflecting the diversity in our classrooms, Chapter 4 examines the impact of culture, class, and gender on teaching and learning.

If you become a regular classroom teacher, you will come into contact with one or more students who are exceptional. There are many different types of exceptional students, including the gifted and talented, as well as students experiencing sensory handicaps, communication disorders, physical and health impairments, behavior disorders, learning disabilities, and mental retardation. Chapter 5 provides valuable information about the typical characteristics of students who are exceptional.

Understanding the Learning Process

A priority in educational psychology is understanding the learning process, that is, the procedures and strategies that students use to acquire new information. Chapter 6 focuses on behavioral explanations of learning and provides numerous examples of how this theoretical explanation of learning can be translated into classroom practice. Chapters 7 and 8 turn to more cognitive analyses of learning, mirroring current concerns with "teaching for understanding." These chapters have been written to help you turn students into better thinkers and problem solvers by presenting many techniques and "tips" that have proven helpful. Motivation, the subject of Chapter 9, is so essential that we can safely state that without it, learning will not occur.

Understanding Instructional Strategies

A fourth key concept is the function of instruction, beginning with the objectives that teachers wish to attain. Chapters 10 and 11 concentrate on those instructional strategies that research has shown to be effective. Learning, however, does not occur in a vacuum. You must understand the best circumstances in which learning can occur. Consequently, these chapters present in some detail successful strategies for managing a classroom, focusing on those techniques shown by both theory and research to be effective.

Understanding Assessment Strategies

Educational psychologists have been instrumental in providing techniques that teachers can use to determine how successful students have been in attaining new knowledge and skills. Today, perhaps more than ever, assessing students' knowledge and skills is a central issue in schools. From a teacher's perspective, two of the most relevant purposes of assessment are (a) to identify students who need educational or psychological assistance, and (b) to provide information to teachers that will help them develop instructional programs to facilitate all students' functioning. Assessment involves the use of many tools and a basic knowledge of measurement. These topics are examined in detail in Chapters 12 and 13.

So You Want to Teach

Why, exactly, have you decided to teach? You've probably been attracted to teaching and education by one, or several, of the following reasons: You enjoy working with young people; you like a particular subject; or you enjoy being in an environment where people want to learn. No matter which of these reasons you select, you undoubtedly have reached one firm conclusion: *You want to be the best teacher you can possibly be.* We want to help you achieve that goal.

Telling you what to do is the easy part. For example, you must have clear objectives in mind when you step into the classroom, so you must know precisely what you want students to learn. But to do that means you must have an accurate idea of what's appropriate for the age and level of your students, so you must understand their developmental characteristics. Then you begin to select materials and methods, using your knowledge of learning to select those that best meet the needs of your students. Finally, you want to determine how students are doing, so you assess their knowledge and skills. In other words, you must be a constant problem solver. But how can you smoothly and efficiently reach this level of performance? Let's attempt to answer this question by looking at several concerns of beginning teachers.

Questions That Teachers Ask

In late August or early September, after a restless night, tens of thousands of teachers across the country (both novice and experienced) wake up and wonder what the first day of school will bring. One way of shedding light on the excitement of the first day of school is to examine several questions that novice teachers typically ask.

- *Will I be able to maintain discipline in my classroom?* The inevitable question, almost always number one on any list of teachers' questions, deserves an honest answer—a resounding "Yes, if you are a good communicator and knowledgeable of class management tactics." How do you establish a classroom atmosphere that is both friendly enough to encourage open discussion, but also regulated enough so that the rights of all students are respected? Section 3 of this book presents the techniques of successful classroom management. This will give you a good idea of the basic principles of organization and also help you to think about multiple instructional strategies.

- *When are students ready for new learning experiences?* As you read through chapters 2, 3, 4, and 5, you'll frequently see reference to *developmentally appropriate material and methods.* In other words, what you use (subject matter, for example) and how they use it, will be powerful determinants of students' achievement. You must know your students well so that you select materials that interest them and use

Reflective teachers have clearly defined objectives, keep their students actively involved, and constantly check their students' progress.

methods that appeal to their learning styles. Section 2 of this book is designed to familiarize you with the developmental changes that students experience as they change from year to year. In this way, you have a developmental framework that guides you in identifying and meeting your students' needs.

- *Are specific teaching techniques better suited to some students than to others?* For example, do some students learn best when they are required to discover things for themselves with guidance; and do others learn best when they receive direct instruction? The simple answer is yes. Recognizing the individual preferences of students and matching them with a specific technique requires observational skill, instructional agility, and just plain hard work. But we can assure you—it's worth it. You'll find that students learn more easily, achieve to a higher level, and are quite contented when they do.

Analyzing *your* work in *your* classroom in this way—an honest and objective self-analysis—identifies you as a **reflective teacher.** Although we don't know as much as we would like about reflective teachers, we do know that reflective teachers learn from their experiences and speculate about the implications for their future teaching (Calderhead, 1996). Their speculation leads them to determine if they achieved their goals (was my classroom management better this week than last?), if their techniques not only worked but were fair (did I rely on threats and punishment too much?), and if the assumptions they made were accurate (was what my students learned worth it?).

Tapping these levels of reflection is difficult—teachers are so busy that it takes genuine effort to find the time for reflection. Yet we know that teachers possess enormous stores of knowledge about students, teaching, and learning. The reason we mention this subject here is to urge you, in spite of the demands on your time, to *think* about your teaching; become a reflective teacher for your own good, the good of your students, and the good of teaching in general.

REFLECTIVE
TEACHERS
Teachers who think about their teaching.

- *Does a knowledge of learning help in the classroom?* You will find that being comfortable with the various interpretations of learning is enormously valuable. In a very real sense, knowing how students learn directs the kinds of instructional techniques you'll use with your students. How do students process information? What do we know about their thinking? How do they solve problems? Will understanding the fundamentals of memory enable you to help your students retain their learning and transfer it to other subjects? When you pose these very practical questions about learning, the answer seems obvious. In fact, perhaps the question should be phrased: Can any teacher be effective without a knowledge of learning? Section 2 of this book will address these questions.

These practical questions have direct classroom application, and we'll use them to guide us in much of our work together. But, first, let's examine the qualities of excellent teachers.

Qualities of Outstanding Teachers

Ernest Boyer, former U.S. commissioner of education and president of the Carnegie Foundation for the Advancement of Teaching, reflected on features that characterized outstanding teachers. Reflecting on the outstanding teachers that he knew, Boyer (1990) identified several characteristics that he believed made them highly effective.

- They employed language clearly and efficiently, an important observation since words swirl around classrooms in an almost unending current. If teachers present their ideas in colorful, exciting writing, and express themselves precisely in their oral language, students have superb models from which to learn. These teachers talked *to* their students, not *at* them.

- They were well informed and comfortable with the history and frontiers of their disciplines, so they provided students not only with facts but also with a way of thinking that served them well in a complex world. For example, the science teacher who presents basic genetic facts and then goes on to show how this knowledge can lead to the future cure of serious diseases breathes real life into what may seem to students to be remote, abstract facts.

- They related what they know to their learners so that students become aware of the beauty, the power, and the application of knowledge.

Research on teaching and learning also supports Boyer's observations. Much of this research is reviewed in Chapter 10, but it is important to introduce some of it as a foundation to this book. For example, carefully designed research consistently has revealed several key behaviors that are associated with good teaching (Calfee & Berliner, 1996). These include lesson clarity, instructional variety, task involvement, use of praise, consistent classroom guidelines, and periodic feedback. Let's examine each of these briefly.

Lesson Clarity

Simply put, lesson clarity means that students understand you. If you organize material carefully, give precise directions, link the present lesson to past work, use instructional strategies that are appropriate for students' ages and cognitive levels, you'll be one of those instructors who maintain the attention of students and communicate effectively.

Effective teachers use a variety of instructional techniques to encourage meaningful learning.

Instructional Variety

Effective teachers use instructional variety. In other words, dynamic teachers experiment, evaluate, read the feedback from students, and switch techniques when a lesson seems to be stalled. They also are alert to the signals their students are giving and use these clues to change from recitation to discussion, from seatwork to physical activity.

Task Involvement

Good teachers are acutely aware of their students' task orientation and engagement in the learning process (Calfee & Berliner, 1996). Good teachers display a remarkable ability to keep students actively involved with a task, which is one of the most significant predictors of students' academic success. Ideally students should be *actively* engaged with a task if learning is to occur. Just sitting at a desk surrounded by books, either at school or at home, and daydreaming is not engagement with a task.

Praise Carefully

Be careful how you use praise, which means that praise can be a mixed blessing. **Noncontingent praise** is praise that is not linked to a specific behavior. Also, don't let a student's personal qualities, rather than achievement, be the occasion for praise. You'll find this becomes self-defeating when the student discerns the hollow nature of the praise. In their own way, students are astute readers of human nature. They can't be fooled indefinitely. Consequently, empty praise inevitably produces a challenge to their self-esteem and begins to erode appreciation of honest achievement.

NONCONTINGENT PRAISE
Praise that is not linked to specific behavior.

Consistent Classroom Guidelines

Good teachers avoid double standards—what is right for the pupil (politeness, punctuality) is right for the teacher. Teachers who refuse to use threats and intimidation know that students cannot learn or acquire self-discipline in a tense, hostile environment. Instead, they try to understand the purpose of misbehavior to establish a relationship based on trust and mutual respect. Teachers who treat their students as "nearly equal" gain their respect and establish relationships that lead to honest dialogue and fewer problems. Remember: *Emphasize the positive* and refuse to take misbehavior personally.

Periodic Feedback

Students need to know how well they are doing and what they need to improve on. Effective teachers provide students frequent feedback about their work efforts and performances. Therefore, assessment of student learning plays a central role in providing students meaningful information on what they are doing well and what they need to work on more. Good assessment is central to the communications needed to guide and reinforce learning.

Summarizing, we can say that to become a skilled teacher, you need to do the following:

- *Try to understand your students' behavior, their problems, and their solutions from their perspective.* It's hard work, but you will find it well worth your time. You will find Chapters 2, 3, 4, and 5 particularly helpful for this task.

- *Create a learning environment that encourages motivation, learning, and transfer of that learning to other activities, both in and out of the classroom.* Chapters 6, 7, 8, 9, 10 and 11 provide much information on this objective.

- *Use instructional techniques that lead to problem-solving activities for students.* Teach for understanding; don't be satisfied with the repetition of factual information. Chapters 8 and 10 provide many examples of activities that will help accomplish this objective.

- *Establish a positive learning environment; monitor it carefully to avoid problems and to facilitate learning.* In Chapters 10 and 11 you'll find suggestions to help you maintain the type of classroom atmosphere you desire.

- *Provide students frequent feedback about their effort and their actual performances.* Tests and other forms of assessment play a key role in feedback to students and other educational stakeholders. These topics are the focus of Chapters 11 and 12.

Figure 1.1 illustrates several of the complex behaviors that define good teaching.

FIGURE 1.1

Desirable Teacher Behavior

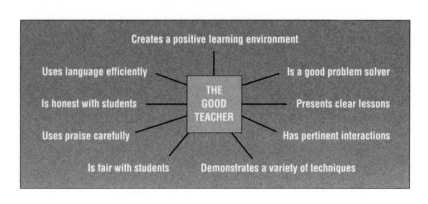

WHAT TEACHERS NEED TO KNOW

When you first enter a classroom, you'll have already acquired considerable knowledge about the characteristics of students, how to teach, and what to teach. You have acquired this knowledge over many years from personal experiences and formal education. You need this basic knowledge the minute you enter the classroom, which isn't to say that you won't add to it as you gain teaching experience and probably take graduate courses to pursue your goal of being the best teacher you can be.

Before we discuss the various types of knowledge that you need, remember that all of these ideas about children, about subject matter, and about teaching are filtered through your network of personal beliefs (Calderhead, 1996). For example, how do you think students learn? Your answer will have a lot to do with the methods and materials you select, as well as how you interact with your students. Do you have any underlying assumptions about teaching? For example, do you believe good teaching is a matter of presenting pertinent facts to students, or do you think good teaching is a matter of guiding students in their learning?

Let's turn to some specific examples of the kinds of knowledge that teachers need and use in their quest for "good teaching," while keeping in mind the uniqueness of all the learners we might interact with in a classroom. As Alexander (1996) noted:

> One of the most powerful and consistent findings to emerge from the research in cognitive psychology over the past several decades is the realization that what knowledge learners possess is a powerful force in what information they attend to, how that information is perceived, what learners judge to be relevant or important, and what they understand and remember. Truly, one's knowledge base is a scaffold that supports the construction of all future learning. (p. 89)

In analyzing the basic data teachers need, our first consideration should be the knowledge base of teaching. In a thoughtful essay, Good (1990) identified several topics with which you should be comfortable enough to use almost automatically in assessing your teaching. These include pertinent data from developmental psychology, motivation, classroom management, teacher expectations, and learning and learning strategies (topics that are at the heart of this book).

If you are familiar with this rich teacher knowledge base, you can then use it while your lesson is in progress. For example, in the middle of your lesson, you might decide that things aren't going as well as you had anticipated and you determine that motivation may be the reason, or that the strategy you had decided on just isn't reaching your students. You can then make changes during the lesson. You can do this, however, only if you are completely at ease with your ideas about your students, about the subjects you're teaching, and the various ways of teaching.

We'll use three categories to sort out the kinds of information you'll need to become an outstanding teacher: **teaching (pedagogical) knowledge** (managing the classroom, instructional techniques, etc.), **subject matter knowledge** (facts, structures, beliefs, etc.), and **teaching subject matter knowledge** (how you make a subject understandable to others).

Teaching Knowledge

Teaching knowledge refers to how the basic principles and strategies of a subject are best acquired and retained. Some refer to this as *pedagogical knowledge.* Questions like the following are about pedagogical knowledge. Am I sufficiently prepared in this subject to know the best way to introduce it? What is the best way to teach its core elements? What

TEACHING
(PEDAGOGICAL)
KNOWLEDGE
How best to present a subject.

SUBJECT MATTER
KNOWLEDGE
Basic content to be taught.

TEACHING
SUBJECT MATTER
KNOWLEDGE
Principles and strategies applicable to a particular subject.

Effective teachers constantly broaden their knowledge to enrich their students' learning.

is the best way to evaluate my students? To answer these questions, you must have usable knowledge about teaching, learning, and students (Borko & Putnam, 1996). Each of these three categories tells a story in itself, a story that helps to refine your personal skills.

For example, *classroom management* is critical, but keep in mind that positive classroom functioning depends on many things, perhaps most importantly on your personality. What style of management are you most comfortable with? You'll soon discover what's best for you, and once that happens you'll steadily improve your management strategies. But, unfortunately, that's not your only consideration. You'll have to adapt to the philosophy of your school, and to the wishes of your principal, a very real force to be reckoned with. For example, in the course of writing this book, one of us visited a school where the principal casually remarked that when she went by a classroom, she liked to "hear the clock ticking." The management style in this school is quite different from that of another school in which the principal wants to hear the hum of activity as a sign of learning. Your task then is to keep a group of twenty to twenty-five students working together and focused on classroom tasks within the boundaries established by your unique personality, your students' needs, and the overarching philosophy of the school.

Another aspect of teaching knowledge is that of *instructional strategies,* that is, how you structure activities in your classroom (Borko & Putnam, 1996). Although some teaching techniques will appeal more to you than others, you'll find that you need an arsenal of strategies to meet the widely varied needs of your students. At this point, you may well ask, "Why?" "Why can't I just use what works for me?" The answer to these questions cuts to the heart of what makes a good teacher. Different subjects demand different strategies; would you use the same methods for teaching algebra as you would in teaching Hamlet? Also, if you're to be a facilitator of meaningful learning for your students, you'll find yourself using many different approaches to reach them.

Our final concern regarding teaching knowledge relates to *learners and learning*. As a result of observations and your own education, you no doubt have certain ideas about how students think and learn, and how you can use these ideas to further their learning. Students are active problem solvers who will take the data available, and with your guidance and their own view of the world will give learning their own interpretations based on your efforts, their personalities, their home situation, their friends, and their own personal bank of experiences. As you can see, this constructivist view of learning sees learning as a student-mediated process. We'll have much more to say about this process and the topic of constructivism throughout the book.

Subject Matter Knowledge

Subject matter knowledge refers to a teacher's comprehension of a subject when compared with that of a specialist. How comfortable am I with this subject? Can I answer students' questions accurately and in a relaxed manner? For example, think of recent events that have captured our headlines:

- *The Human Genome Project* has resulted in the discovery of the genes that cause cystic fibrosis and Huntington's disease, and researchers are closing in on the elusive genetic causes of breast cancer.

- The Hubble telescope has sent back a series of amazing pictures of the universe.

- The Mars probe has resulted in a series of remarkable pictures, detailing facts about its surface.

- Astronauts walk in space as if it were the natural thing for us all to do.

- Computer technology is opening new vistas that are as startling as they are ingenious.

On and on it goes, almost as if knowledge that has been forced below our level of consciousness has burst through restraining barriers and, as if to make up for lost time, has exploded before our eyes. Students, in the midst of this marvel of discoveries, have a unique opportunity to acquire learning that will shape their future as never before.

We're not concerned here with how you teach a particular subject, but with your knowledge of the various subjects. Our focus is to urge you not to be content with the basic facts and information of a subject. Rather, acquire familiarity with the ideas, facts, and concepts of a subject, and how they are organized. In other words, know the basic ideas of a subject, and how these ideas are "put together." Try to keep up with the results of current research. What seems to be essential here is that you should know more than the facts of a subject; you should understand how facts and ideas interrelate, and what they mean for truly understanding the subject (Borko & Putnam, 1996).

Does your knowledge of a subject affect how you teach it? Subject matter knowledge cuts both ways. If you feel shaky about material, you may attempt to brush by it quickly. Conversely, if you have depth of knowledge, you may do too much with your pupils. However, research indicates that knowledgeable teachers can better detect student difficulties and seize opportunities for meaningful learning. Teachers who are less knowledgeable in subject matter may avoid presenting critical material if they are uncomfortable with it, and thus their students will not see the whole picture (Dill, 1990).

Nevertheless, it all comes down to one fundamental question: *How much and what should teachers know of what they teach* (Shulman, 1986, p. 26)? The best advice is to know as much as possible about your subject, to present it as dynamically as possible, and to be prepared to answer all kinds of questions about what you teach.

Teaching Subject Matter Knowledge

Teaching subject matter knowledge refers to the most appealing manner in which you organize and present content—telling, guiding, and using texts, computers, media, or workbooks. According to Shulman (1986, p. 9), teaching subject matter knowledge means

> *the ways of representing and formulating the subject that make it comprehensible to others, and an understanding of what makes the learning of specific topics easy or difficult: the conceptions and preconceptions that students of different ages and backgrounds bring with them to the learning of those most frequently taught topics and lessons.*

For example, assume that you are teaching one of Faulkner's stories and your students are having difficulty. What do you do? Do you yourself turn to the story and attempt to clarify themes, or do you search for an outside interpretation?

To help you organize your thoughts about how to teach various subjects, think about the following questions that help to shape your personal style (H. Grossman, 1990):

- *Why are you teaching what you're teaching?* In other words, what do you think is important for your students to know? Your decisions on what to teach will influence the objectives you want your students to achieve, the teaching strategies you'll use, and the materials you'll select (texts, videos, computer programs, etc.).

- *What are your students' typical understandings and misunderstandings of a subject?* For example, students usually understand that George Washington was our first president and the "father of our country." Don't count on them understanding the complex reasons that led to our involvement in Vietnam. They may understand fractions, but totally misunderstand the division of fractions.

- *How much do you know about curriculum and curricular materials?* Do you know the range of materials—texts and other instructional materials—available for teaching a particular topic? You should also understand how the topics and ideas of a subject are organized horizontally (within a course or grade level) and vertically (kindergarten through grade 12).

- *Have you thought about the strategies and representations you could use for particular topics?* Our concern here is that you give considerable attention to the best way of representing a particular subject or topic. What model, illustration, demonstration, example, or simulation is best suited for the needs of your students? Do you have to adapt your model to satisfy the individual differences in your class?

What Does All of This Mean for You?

If you remember one guiding principle, you'll be able to relate the various kinds of teacher knowledge to your daily classroom work: *Your task is to help students learn as much as they can.* To be more specific, here are several principles of learning, agreed upon by almost all educational psychologists, that will help you to use your knowledge most effectively. In fact, this list serves as an advanced organizer for much of what we cover in depth in the remaining twelve chapters in this book.

Be sure you know what you want to accomplish; that is, keep clearly defined objectives in sight at all times. In this way, you recognize the stages in any task that are necessary for mastery. If you're comfortable with the subject you're teaching, you're also aware of the progressive stages that students need to master. For example, pupils can't do long division until they can add, subtract, and do short division.

Encourage as much student activity as possible. Students will be—should be—engaged in multiple activities, ranging from reading a text with comprehension, to discussing topics in class, to searching for materials for their research projects. As they become engaged, provide reinforcement, but be sure it is both specific and deserved. Students need encouragement; just be sure it is appropriate, and don't use praise carelessly.

Guard against student anxiety, which can have many causes: pressure from home, pressure from you, pressure from competition. Frequently monitor the classroom atmosphere so that it remains challenging but not overwhelming. Remember that tried-and-true cliche: Match the mix; that is, use teaching techniques and materials that are appropriate for the level (emotional as well as cognitive) of your students.

Teach for understanding, and encourage the use of learning strategies. What do we mean by "understanding"? To answer this question, Perkins and Blythe (1994, pp. 5–6) stated that understanding is being able to do a variety of thought-demanding things with a topic—explaining, finding evidence and examples, applying, and representing the topic in new ways. For example, why do skates need to be sharp if you are to skate well? What are the pros and cons of a superpower's invasion of a small country to restore order?

Remember that students very often don't understand what they learn. They master facts, but their comprehension lags far behind. Changing these conditions is a difficult task for many reasons, but far too often we're more interested in how students do on standardized tests, on how many sheer facts they have mastered. In a complex and technological society, we simply can't afford this type of thinking any longer. As Bruer (1994) reminded us:

> The world didn't need Isaac Newton to know **that** apples fell off trees. It did need Newton to give us a general theory that explains **why** apples fall off trees. Knowing why apples fall off trees has allowed us to go to the moon and to see television images of the planets. Knowing why leads to other discoveries, new applications, and further refinements. (p. 17)

We hope you share our belief that teachers and schools that teach and assess *understanding as an outcome of instruction* can make a significant difference in students' lives. To accomplish this, however, we believe that teachers must be part scientist and part artist. Let's examine this idea for a moment. Following are definitions of artist and scientist found in *Merriam Webster's Collegiate Dictionary,* 10th edition.

artist: *a skilled performer*

scientist: *a scientific [knowledgeable] investigator*

By permission. From Merriam-Webster's Collegiate® Dictionary, Tenth Edition ©1998 by Merriam-Webster, Incorporated.

Teaching as an Art and Science

You must know your subject, which implies that you grasp not only the material that you currently are presenting in class, but also the core of the subject, and what researchers are discovering at the frontiers of the discipline. In an age devoted to empirical research, you'll find yourself doing independent study to prevent personal obsolescence. You don't want to plead ignorance on too many of your students' questions.

You, and any teacher, will avoid such work unless you like your subject and enjoy interacting with students. To devote hours of study beyond the demands of duty requires a commitment to a discipline and the company of the young, both of which can be provocative masters. You have already made a commitment that reflects a love of study and pleasure in working with youth. These categories actually mirror two basic themes that are at the heart of this book: the teacher as a professional and the teacher as a person.

Musing about the art of teaching, Cohen (1992) described the lives of five veteran secondary school teachers and concluded that common to them all was a passion and

ARTIST
A skilled performer.

SCIENTIST
A logical investigator.

Interacting with students in a variety of situations is an integral part of teaching.

enthusiasm for the subjects they taught. Particularly interesting was her finding that they were not locked into any single teaching style. They had developed their own unique and, for them, effective styles, which they constantly modified. In many ways, they never lost the perspective of a novice: always wanting to try something new, to seek constantly for improvement. As Cohen noted, they were "originals." These innovative, flexible teachers undoubtedly performed as artists in their classrooms.

Considering teaching strictly as an art, however, is too limiting. Given the knowledge that we have acquired about the nature of instruction and about the methods of inquiry into any discipline, we should explore the notion that teaching also be considered a science.

You'll find that you, knowingly or not, adopt—and adapt—the scientific method in your work. You'll adopt the role of experimenter as you try new instructional methods and classroom procedures (even something as simple as changing the seating arrangement). A quick rundown on your role of teacher-as-scientist will include the following four steps:

1. *Identifying the problem.* You must decide exactly what you want your students to learn.

2. *Formulating a logical series of steps to reach a goal.* You'll decide not only which topic to present but how you'll do it.

3. *Gathering the data.* You'll conclude just what student behavior is to be assessed and then the best means of measuring it.

4. *Interpreting the data.* You'll judge if your students' performance has achieved the desired goal.

By following the "scientific method" in instruction and by your involvement at various levels of scientific inquiry, you'll act as a scientist: you'll identify objectives, devise strategies, gather and evaluate their data, and communicate their results.

Thus, teaching is both art and science, a needed combination for today's changing classrooms and for enacting effective teaching-learning interactions.

IMPORTANT TOPICS IN EDUCA-TIONAL PSYCHOLOGY TODAY

One of the ways educational psychology has maintained its strength and vitality is by addressing problems that have broad national implications for teachers, schools, and education in general. At this point there are several topics involving schools and teaching that we'd like you to think about. These topics include constructivism, student diversity, and out-of-school influences on students' learning. These three topics may demand your input, not only as a classroom teacher concerned with local matters, but also as a professional educator or budding researcher concerned with the quality of teaching in our schools. Consequently, these topics are examined in several chapters in this book.

Constructivism

A quiet, yet dynamic change in both instructional theory and practice has been emerging in many classrooms of America, a change called **constructivism.** Simply put, constructivism means that students construct their own understanding of the world. We're not talking about some simple change in a teaching technique but, rather, the way we think about knowledge acquisition and the assessment of that knowledge (Brooks & Brooks, 1993). Think about it for a moment. If students construct their own understanding, what does this imply for the teacher's role? One immediate conclusion is that anyone who thinks "teaching is telling" is sadly mistaken. Shuell (1996, p. 743) has neatly summarized the meaning of constructivism:

> *The learner does not merely record or remember the material to be learned. Rather, he or she constructs a unique mental representation of the material to be learned and the task to be performed, selects information perceived to be relevant, and interprets that information on the basis of his or her existing knowledge and existing needs. In the process, the learner adds information not explicitly provided by the teacher whenever such information is needed to make sense of the material being studied. This process is an active one in which the learner must carry out various operations on the new materials in order for it to be acquired in a meaningful manner.*

The two key words here are *active* and *meaning.* Learners don't just sit there and copy what's put on the board or told to them. They take their own knowledge—that enormous reservoir of personal experiences they have accumulated in their lives—and interpret this new material according to what's in their reservoir.

Have you ever wondered why, when you're in a class with many others like you, and you're all subjected to the same lesson, lecture, or reading material, your answers to the same questions can differ greatly? Let's admit at the start that differences in attitude, motivation, and attention are all at work, but a major reason for the differences lies in the way that *you,* with your special knowledge, interpreted the material. You took in the material through your personal filter of experiences and constructed your understanding of it in light of your exclusive network of knowledge. You stamped your own meaning on the material.

As you can imagine, different interpretations of constructivism have arisen. The basic distinction to keep in mind is between those who believe that the individual alone—each student—constructs meaning (often referred to as individual or psychological constructivism). Others argue that individuals in a social situation—each student in the class, influenced by peers, home, and so on—construct meaning (often referred to as social constructivism). These distinctions are spelled out in detail in Chapter 2 when we analyze the works of two of the greatest psychologists of the twentieth century, Jean Piaget and Lev Vygotsky (Cobb & Yackel, 1996).

To enhance your understanding of constructivism, let's examine two classes who are studying the opening of the American West. One teacher has the class read the chapter that includes the Battle of Big Horn. The teacher then summarizes the chapter and indicates the important points to be remembered. He then gives them time to write an essay about the battle, telling them to "get their facts straight." Finally, he tells his students that they will be tested tomorrow.

CONSTRUCTIVISM
Current belief that students construct their own understanding of their world.

The second teacher has also prepared carefully and decided that this era in our history is too exciting to be restricted to text reading. She comes to class and poses a problem for her students. "I want you to assume that Custer, although critically wounded, survives the battle. He then has to stand trial for his leadership and the decisions he made leading up to and during the battle." The students are told to use all the sources they want, and to discuss the feeling of the country and the political climate of the times.

We trust you can see how the teacher who understands that students construct their own meanings will adopt different techniques in the classroom. Teachers who follow a constructivist pathway often do the following:

- Wrap their teaching in a cloak of problems for their students, problems that are real, meaningful, and age-appropriate.

- Use their students' perspectives to interpret their responses and solutions, that is, take into account such important variables as cognitive level, home experiences, and motivation.

- Know that their students' responses reflect their current level of understanding.

- Accept the conflicts and confusion that initially accompany the search for meaning.

More about constructivistic approaches to instruction and learning will be discussed later, but let's now turn to the issue of student diversity.

Student Diversity in the Classroom

Another topic that more and more educational psychologists are addressing in their research and practice is the **diversity** of students in schools today. Psychologists, for more than a century, have been interested in individual differences, but today more attention is being given to how schools can accommodate differences in ability, race, ethnicity, regional origin, family makeup, gender, and sexual orientation so that all students have opportunities to learn.

Developmental contextualism, popularized by Richard Lerner (1991), provides a rationale for recognizing and capitalizing on the richness and diversity of students' backgrounds. It also incorporates recent research relating to *cultural constructivism,* which means that students use the particular environment around them to construct their own worldview. Developmental contextualism attempts to analyze and understand development in the light of the multiple levels of interactions between individuals and their environments. That is, all students' characteristics, psychological as well as biological, interact with the environment (the context in this theory). *Context* is an inclusive term that attempts to portray the complexity of students' backgrounds by identifying four major forces of development:

1. The *physical settings* through which your students move, such as the home, classroom, and workplace.

2. *Social influences,* such as students' families, peers, and significant others.

3. The *personal characteristics* of students, such as physical appearance, temperament, and language fluency.

4. The *influence of time,* that is, change brought about by the sheer chronology of living; to put it simply, the longer we're able to survive, the more changes we experience.

These forces are illustrated in Figure 1.2.

Consequently, the crucial element in learning and development is the changing relationship between the complexity students bring to the classroom and a multilayered context (school, home, peers, etc.). If you think about this deceptively simple statement,

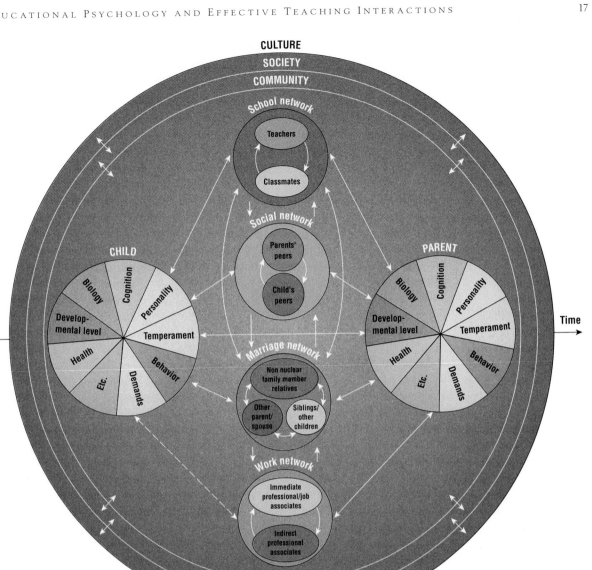

FIGURE 1.2 A Developmental Contextual Model of Person–Context Interaction

From R. Lerner, "Changing organism-context relations as the basic process of development: A developmental contextual perspective," *Developmental Psychology,* Volume 27(1), pp. 27–32. Copyright ©1991, by the American, Psychological Association. Reprinted with permission.

you can appreciate the need to study teaching, learning, and development from many different perspectives. For example, consider what's going on with students. The genes provide a blueprint that is passed on to the cells, tissues, and organs of the body, influencing the growth of such widely divergent growth features as brain development and temperament, to name only two. On the other hand, the intricate and involved layers of the context, ranging from family to peers to schools and to the wider social sphere, simultaneously weave their networks of influence. Simple explanations? Hardly. What is needed is a perspective equally as intricate as the behavior it attempts to clarify. As Lerner (1991, p. 31) noted:

The revised understanding of what constitutes the basic process of human development brings to the fore the cutting-edge importance of continued empirical focus on individual differences, on contextual variations, and on changing person-context relations. Nothing short of these emphases can be regarded as involving scientifically adequate developmental analysis of human life.

Out-of-School Influences

OUT-OF-SCHOOL INFLUENCES

Forces outside of the classroom that affect learning.

A natural outgrowth of developmental contextualism is the concern that educational psychologists have expressed about **out-of-school influences** that act decisively on students' learning. Educational psychologists have traditionally focused on those forces that are directly related to the classroom and school (instructional techniques, time-on-task, etc.), but now the time has come to adopt a broader perspective. Understanding the wellsprings of students' achievement demands that we know more about their lives beyond the classroom. What do we know about their families, their peers, their socioeconomic circumstances, and their cultural setting? It's becoming increasingly clear that *all* of these influences can play a significant role in motivating students to study and achieve in school.

In a recent survey of nine high schools involving about 20,000 students, Steinberg (1996) concluded that school is only *one* influence that affects what students learn and how well they do on tests of that learning. For example, the existence of differences in ethnic groups was the most important finding: Asian students outperform whites, blacks, and Latinos. Initially thinking that Asian students might believe that academic success correlated closely with out-of-school success, that is, there is a "payoff" for academic success, Steinberg was surprised this wasn't the case. *All* students believed that doing well in school would have a payoff. The students actually differed, however, in their belief that failing in school would have negative consequences. The Asian students clearly felt that poor academic performance would definitely and negatively affect their future. Non-Asian students didn't share this belief, with black and Latino students not really believing that doing poorly in school would hurt their chances for future success.

Another of the findings related to the students' home: Parents exert a profound and lasting effect on their children's achievement in school by three things they do:

1. *Deliberately or casually, they communicate specific messages to their children about teachers, schools, and learning.* Their children quickly learn whether school is or isn't important, and whether they should expend much effort there.

2. *Parental behavior sends clear and unmistakable signals about the importance the parents place on schooling.* Disregarding notices from the school, not attending parental functions, refusing to volunteer in school activities, all paint a stark picture for children—"School just isn't that important, no matter what I may say."

3. *Their parenting style encourages, or discourages, engagement in school.* Interestingly, Steinberg found that such parental activities as checking homework or encouraging children to do better in school were not the most significant forms of parental engagement. What seemed to make a real difference was the actual physical presence of the parents at school: attending school programs, participating in teacher conferences, joining in extracurricular events, and so on.

Quite obviously, not all students will be fortunate enough to have cooperative parents, and you'll work with students from different types of families. Families change, and as they do,

The context of a student's learning environment is a major influence in the teaching-learning interaction.

they exercise different effects on a child's development—some significant, others not so (Scarr, 1992). For example, children who remain in an intact family, or who experience the death of a parent, or who go through a parental divorce—even though the experiences are quite different—all undergo changes that must affect development. You can see the need to carefully consider the out-of-school influences of students to better understand their classroom behavior.

THEMES OF THIS BOOK

To help you relate the theories and research that you'll be reading about to the everyday world of teaching and to prepare you for the kinds of decisions that you'll be faced with, we have developed TIPS for each chapter. TIPS stands for **T**eaching **I**nteraction **P**rinciples and **S**trategies and are brief summaries of key teaching principles and related instructional actions. Our TIPS focus on five themes that permeate the lives of teachers: *communication, learning, motivation, time,* and *assessment.* Let's briefly examine each of these themes that we see permeating the lives of teachers and their students of the future.

Communication

This is certainly the broadest of the themes we present, and it may well be the most important when you think about successful teacher–student interactions. The summary of characteristics of effective teaching and learning we examined earlier in this chapter provides strong evidence of the role that communication plays in the establishment of learning and behavior expectations, teacher–student interpersonal relationships, and the delivery of quality instruction, which involves questioning, praising, and individualized feedback.

Learning

Many of our students initially talk about learning as something a student does, but if you read and listen during your journey through this book you will learn that learning is the outcome of an interaction—an interaction between a teacher and a student, two or more students, a student and a computer, a student and a parent, and so on—and is often a social and active enterprise. Given that learning is an interactive enterprise and often takes place in classrooms, it is desirable to create environments where routines are smooth and efficient, instruction facilitates personal connections between what is taught and a person's prior knowledge, students' attention is maintained and they are frequently asked to act and use information, and material is periodically reviewed and retaught because students learn at different rates and in different ways.

Motivation

Theoretical and practical aspects of motivation are presented explicitly in only one chapter (Chapter 9) in this book, yet we see it as a pervasive theme with theoretical roots in both behavioral and cognitive psychology and practical connections to effective learning and behavior management. In our introductory review of the qualities of effective teaching and learning, motivational issues were featured as part of incentives and rewards used to promote excellence and positive personal interactions between teachers and students. Many other aspects of teaching and the classroom environment can influence the motivation of students, which in turn impact achievement and behavior. Therefore, understanding what motivates students to learn will be an ongoing topic of inquiry for every reader of this book.

Time

Perhaps time is the most pervasive theme in all our lives. Did you realize, however, that students spend between 11% and 14% of their lives in school (grades K to 12)? Many people are surprised by this small amount of time allocated to learning, given the expectations that parents and educators have for students. Therefore, more has to be done with time. That is, the proportion of actual learning or engaged time within this small segment of time must be used wisely and ideally increased. This is generally accomplished by being organized (that is, smooth and efficient classroom routines), maintaining a brisk instructional pace where students get opportunities to respond, requiring homework and out-of-class learning activities, and communicating with parents about learning expectations and homework.

Assessment

Although assessment is discussed near the end of this book and primarily occurs after teaching and learning, it plays a central role in planning instruction and documenting the effects of teaching. The role of assessment in teaching is emphasized as frequently monitoring the learning progress of students. How you achieve such progress monitoring depends on the skills and behaviors of interest and who you are trying to communicate with. In most cases, daily work assignments, projects, and teacher-constructed tests are the main tools that will be used to assess and communicate results. In other cases, when schoolwide or even statewide comparisons of learning are deemed important, professionally developed tests will be the best tools to use. Regardless of the assessment method used, effective teachers must have a command of tests and basic measurement concepts. This knowledge of assessment thus enables them to communicate about learning with their students, the students' parents, and other educational stakeholders.

Case Studies of Teachers in Action

To further advance your application of the content of this book, we have designed three case studies featuring teachers and students. Each case study is comprised of five components: a case description located in the opening pages of a section, a case-opening box at the start of each chapter, case notes embedded throughout each chapter, a case reflections section at the end of each chapter, and a teachers case conference located on the closing pages of each section. Specifically, in the opening of Section 1 you will be presented with the case of Marsha Warren, an experienced third-grade teacher who is nearly overwhelmed by her heterogeneous class of students. Then throughout each of the four chapters in this section on the *Development of Students,* readers will find chapter-opening boxes to focus the general case on the specific chapter and case notes where we offer *observations, hypotheses,* and *possible actions* designed to illustrate how the content of each chapter applies to the case of Marsha Warren and her class. In the opening pages of Section 2, you will be invited to work on the case of Mark Siegel, a fourth-grade teacher who is puzzled by the learning problems of one of his students and also challenged by the student's parent to do more to help her child. The four chapters in this section on *Learning Theories and Implications for Practice* afford many perspectives on learning; consequently, the case notes on Mark Siegel illustrate the old adage "that there is nothing more practical than a good theory." Finally in the Section 3 opener, you will meet Melissa Williams, a novice seventh-grade teacher who finds herself in a high-achieving school and feeling pressure from her teaching team members to maintain the superior end-of-year test scores that the previous teacher had accomplished with similar students. The four chapters in this section on *Effective Teaching and the Evaluation of Learning* result in numerous case notes that document ideas for successfully solving the problems confronting Melissa.

We believe you will find these cases to facilitate connections between educational psychology and teaching, and they may even help you develop a passion for teaching and learning. In the words of Fried (1995):

Passionate teachers convey their passion to novice learners—their students—by acting as partners in learning, rather than as "experts in the field." As partners, they invite less experienced learners to search for knowledge and insightful experiences, and they build confidence and competence among students who might otherwise choose to sit back and watch their teacher do and say interesting things. (p. 23)

CHAPTER HIGHLIGHTS

Education Psychology

- Educational psychology is the application of psychology and psychological methods to the study of learning and teaching.
- Educational psychology is a broad discipline that focuses on the interaction of human development, cognitive science, instructional methods, measurement and assessment.

So You Want To Teach

- Teachers have their own unique expectations as they enter the classroom.
- Novice teachers ask several key questions about their beginning days.
- Research on effective teachers has revealed consistent indicators that associate several behaviors or practices with good teaching. These include: lesson clarity, instructional variety, task involvement, careful use of praise, consistent classroom guidelines, and periodic feedback about learning.

What Teachers Need To Know

- Teachers need three types of knowledge: teaching knowledge, subject matter knowledge, and teaching subject matter knowledge.
- Teaching knowledge refers to the principles and strategies of subjects.
- Good teachers are masters of their subjects.
- Teaching subject matter knowledge refers to the best manner of presenting content.
- Good teachers display the characteristics of both artist and scientist.

Important Topics in Educational Psychology Today

- Educational psychology has maintained its vitality by addressing important and practical issues, three of which are constructivism, diversity, and out-of-school influences.
- Constructivism refers to the manner in which students construct their personal views of the world.
- Effective teachers have learned to capitalize on the diversity in their classrooms and to design instructional environments that accommodate a wide range of learners with varying backgrounds and experiences.
- For students to achieve their maximum potential, teachers should be aware of the impact of out-of-school experiences.

Themes for Organizing and Building Knowledge of Educational Psychology

- The five core themes of educational psychology offer practical guidance and help to teachers. These themes focus on communication skills, understanding of the learning process, motivating learners, using time well, and using assessment methods to provide feedback to students and educators.

WHAT DO YOU THINK?

1. If you are thinking about becoming a teacher, you probably have several ideas about teaching and what you hope to accomplish. These ideas are known as teacher expectations. What are they? Compare your expectations with those of your classmates. How similar are they?

2. When you consider the relationship between teaching and learning, are there other characteristics of good teachers that you would mention? Think about a teacher you have had who you really thought was effective. What characteristics made him or her effective for you?

3. After reading about several issues that have captured the interest of educational psychologists, do you agree with their importance in teaching and learning? Why?

The
Development
of
Students

The Case of Marsha Warren

An experienced third-grade teacher is overwhelmed by the problems created by her heterogeneous class, which includes eight students who have unique home and personal situations that are affecting their schooling.

José glared at Tyrone. "Quit looking at me, you jerk!"

"I wasn't lookin' at nothin', creepy," replied Tyrone vehemently.

Marsha Warren looked up sharply at the two boys and made a cutting gesture through the air. "That's enough from both of you. You should both be looking at your books, not each other."

"I was lookin' at my book!" protested Tyrone.

"Just stop!" repeated Marsha. "Please continue reading, Angela."

Angela rolled her eyes at no one in particular and resumed reading aloud in a bored, expressionless tone. Her progress was slow and halting.

Marsha Warren was a third-grade teacher at the Roosevelt Elementary School in Littleton. She was trying to conduct a reading group with the eight slowest readers in her class of twenty-two while the other children worked in workbooks at their seats. But each time an argument erupted among the children in the reading group, most of the children at their desks snapped to attention to watch the sparks fly.

"You can stop there, Angela," interrupted Marsha as Angela came to the end of a paragraph. "Bettie Ann, will you read next?" As she spoke, Marsha also put a hand out to touch another child, Katie, on the shoulder in an attempt to stop her from bouncing in her chair.

Bettie Ann didn't respond. She was gazing out the window at the leafless November landscape, sucking her thumb and twirling her hair with her other hand. "Bettie Ann, I'm talking to you," repeated Marsha.

"Your turn," yelled José as he poked Bettie Ann's shoulder.

"Shut up, José," interjected Sarah. Sarah often tried to mediate between the members of the group, but her argumentative streak pulled her into the fray as often as not.

"That's it!" Marsha exclaimed. She slammed her hand down on the reading-circle table and stood to face the entire class. "Put your heads on your desks, and don't say another word—everyone!" By the time she finished the sentence, Marsha realized she had been shouting, but she didn't care. Her class gazed at her in stunned disbelief. Mrs. Warren had always been so gentle! "Now!"

Marsha quickly turned and walked from the room, not bothering to look back to see if her command had been obeyed. She closed the door to her classroom, managing not to slam it, and tried to control her temper and collect her thoughts. "What in God's name am I going to do with this class?" she asked herself. "I've got to calm down. Here I am in the hallway with twenty-two kids inside who have driven me out—they've absolutely won." Marsha suddenly felt paralyzed.

Academically the class was fairly average, but Marsha did have two instructional challenges: There were three really bright students, whom Marsha tried to encourage with extra instruction and higher expectations, and there were three students (besides the Hispanic children in her slow-reading group) who spoke little or no English. The most remarkable characteristic of the students, though, was their overall immaturity. Each child seemed to feed off the antics of the others, and every issue was taken to its extreme. For example, whenever one child laughed, the entire class would begin to giggle uncontrollably. The students' behavior was simply inappropriate for their age and grade.

The core of Marsha's problem was the lowest-level reading group. This group provided the spark that set off fireworks in the entire class, day after day. The slow readers were rude and disruptive as a group, and they were instigators on their own.

When Marsha thought of each child in the lowest reading group individually, she was usually able to summon some sympathy and understanding. Each of the eight had an emotional or academic problem that probably accounted, at least in part, for his or her behavior.

José, for instance, topped her list of troublemakers. He was a loud, egocentric child. His mother, Marsha thought, probably had surrendered long ago, and his father did not live with them. José had little respect for or recognition of authority; he was boisterous and argumentative; and he was unable to take turns under any condition. When something didn't go his way, he would explode. This low flash point, Marsha felt, was just one of many signs of his immaturity, even though José was repeating the third grade and was actually older than his classmates.

José had a slight learning disability in the area of organizational skills, but Marsha didn't think this justified his behavior. His mother spoke only Spanish, and, although José was fluent in both Spanish and English, when Marsha sent notes home, she would first have to find someone to translate for her. Conferring with José's mother on the telephone was out of the question.

Angela was also repeating the third grade, and Marsha thought the child's anger over this contributed to her terrible attitude in class. The child just refused to learn. She could be a low-average achiever if she would apply herself, but it was clear that Angela's agenda was not school. She was concerned with her hair, her looks, her clothes—preoccupations that Marsha found inappropriate for a third-grader. Angela came from a middle-class black family, and her parents were also angry that she had been held back; consultations with them were not usually fruitful. Angela seemed truly upset if Marsha asked her to do any work, and

Marsha was sure her frustration with the child was occasionally apparent.

Tyrone, on the other hand, was a very low-average learner, but he, at least, worked to his capabilities. He even tried to mediate arguments among members of the group. But Tyrone had a very stubborn streak, which was typical, Marsha thought, of slow learners. If he was on the wrong track, he just would not get off of it. She frequently asked him to redo work and helped him with his errors, but when he presented it to her the next day as though it were different, it would contain the same mistakes.

Sarah, too, knew right from wrong and generally wanted to do her work, but she was easily pulled into the fray. Sarah had appointed herself protector of Bettie Ann, an overweight, emotionally insecure child who had difficulty focusing on the topic at hand. Bettie Ann was the baby of her family, with several near-adult siblings at home. Marsha wondered if Bettie Ann's position in the family was the reason she assumed no responsibility for her own actions and no control over her own fate. Bettie Ann seemed hungry for Marsha's attention, but she exhibited no independence or initiative at all.

Katie was one of the brighter students in the reading group, but her hyperactivity caused her to be easily distracted and argumentative. She could neither sit still physically nor pay attention mentally. Katie had a rich home background, full of books and middle-class aspirations, but Marsha thought she also encountered pressure

at home to perform, perhaps to levels beyond her capability.

Rhea, another child with at least average intelligence, was one of the more heartrending cases. Her mother was an alcoholic who neglected her, and Rhea had to do the housework and care for her older brother, who was in a special education class. She had no time for homework, and there were no books or even conversations at home. Rhea had been held back in the second grade, and while she tried to do her work, the language deficit at home was so severe that she kept falling further behind.

Finally, there was Maria, a petite, immature native of El Salvador. She had average intelligence and a cooperative spirit, but Spanish was spoken in her home and her limited English vocabulary severely limited her progress.

Marsha tried to analyze what it was among these children that fostered such animosity. Not a day passed that they didn't argue, fight, or insult one another. The reading group was not the only arena for these combatants; they fought in the playground, in line, on the bus, and in the cafeteria. They were troublemakers in previous grades, and some of the teachers at Roosevelt called them the "Infidels."

Marsha stood on tiptoe to look through the window of the classroom door. The children were sitting in their places looking at one another uneasily and at the door, clearly wondering what would happen next. With a sigh, Marsha turned the knob.

two

Cognitive and Language Development

You have just read about the trials and tribulations of Marsha Warren, a troubled but conscientious teacher. As you read this chapter, try to think of ways you would react to José's outbursts: Would Piaget's ideas about carefully matching the curriculum to level of cognitive development be useful? Would Vygotsky's explanation of inner speech help Maria with her language difficulties?

The story of cognitive and language development is the relationship between thought and speech. This powerful story can't be told without tracing the theory and research of two titans of psychology: Jean Piaget and Lev Vygotsky. Separated by thousands of miles, one in Geneva, the other in Moscow, and working independently of each other, they wrestled with the secrets of how children think and speak. Piaget's and Vygotsky's ideas are similar in intent and different in interpretation. Their ideas dominate the field of cognitive and language development.

We can use the cognitive map they have drawn to guide us in our search for clues to thought and language. To interpret students' behavior, you must understand the normal path of development that they follow, which will help you to adapt instruction to meet their needs. In this chapter we'll first explore Piaget's work, with its emphasis on logic and science, and then examine Vygotsky's theory, with its emphasis on culture. Next, we'll identify several milestones in the language development of children.

THE MEANING OF DEVELOPMENT

As Figure 2.1 illustrates, assuming a fourteen-year-old student, physical, cognitive, and social development do not occur at the same rate. Students may be the same chronological age, but their growth ages (physical, cognitive, and psychosocial) will vary. Some will be tall for their age, and some will be short; others may be mentally delayed or accelerated.

If you are aware of the processes of development, you can reassure a self-conscious adolescent whose growth in height is slightly delayed but whose weight is normal. You can look for opportunities to reinforce the social skills of a student whose mental growth has outpaced her social growth. Or you may realize that several members of an eighth-grade civics class are floundering because they haven't fully acquired the ability to think abstractly. In these and other ways, familiarity with developmental theory and characteristics will enable you to determine appropriate techniques and content to match individual differences.

Considerable variation exists within these developmental patterns, and this variation affects student performance. For example, some children are reading by the time they enter school; others immediately display unusual mathematical ability; still others seem more socially mature than their classmates. (Marsha Warren's students are a good example of these variations.) Consequently, the more you know about development, the better you can adjust methods and curriculum to the individual needs of students.

Objectives

When you finish reading this chapter, you should be able to

- explain how biopsychosocial elements influence students' learning and achievement

- explain the basics of Piaget's theory

- use Piaget's ideas to describe how students pass through his four cognitive stages

- summarize the key ideas in Vygotsky's theory

- analyze Vygotsky's belief that culture powerfully shapes cognitive development

- identify the major points on which Piaget and Vygotsky disagree

- suggest techniques using Piaget's and Vygotsky's ideas that could improve classroom instruction

- analyze the path of language development

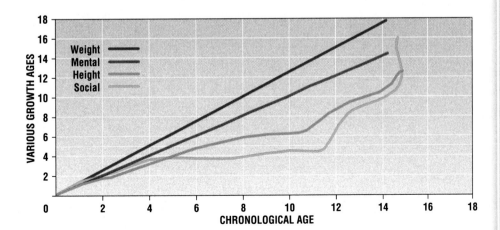

FIGURE 2.1

The Complexity of Development

The Biopsychosocial Model

To understand the variations in students' development, picture development as a continuous series of **biopsychosocial** interactions. If you think of students' development as the product of the interaction of biological, psychological, and social forces, you can better understand and appreciate the complexity of development. Understanding biopsychosocial interactions also provides an opportunity to explore cross-cultural and sociocultural issues that greatly enrich our understanding of human development, as you'll particularly note in Vygotsky's work.

Biological elements range from the role of our genes to adult health issues; psychological elements include all aspects of cognitive and personality development; social elements refer to such influences as family, teachers, school, and peers. We believe the biopsychosocial model illustrates the constant interaction of heredity (nature) and environment (nurture) that explains the complexity of development.

If you examine Table 2.1 carefully, you'll note several characteristics listed for the biological, psychological, and social categories of our model. These elements certainly aren't exhaustive but suggest many developmental features that affect growth. More importantly, however, think about the interactions that occur among the three categories and how these interactions affect development and learning. To give a simple example, children who receive little stimulation in the early years may well develop psychological problems leading to school problems and poor social relationships.

By analyzing children's development with the biopsychosocial model, you'll have a tool that better enables you to understand and remember the need for developmentally appropriate materials and methods. This model also helps to emphasize sociocultural features that so decisively influence development and learning.

Psychologists have accumulated considerable data about child development. The cognitive and language theorists you'll read about offer a wealth of information and suggestions. As you read about their ideas, here are several questions to guide your thinking and help you to form applications.

- *In what way does a specific age group see the world differently from you?* Students entering kindergarten and first grade are still quite egocentric, that is, they tend to think everything relates directly to them. (You certainly won't be surprised to learn that adolescents react in much the same way.)

Table 2.1 EXAMPLES OF BIOPSYCHOSOCIAL CHARACTERISTICS

Bio	Psycho	Social
Genetics	Cognitive development	Attachment
Fertilization	Information processing	Relationships
Pregnancy	Problem solving	Reciprocal interactions
Birth	Perceptual development	School
Physical development	Language development	Peers
Motor development	Moral development	Television
Puberty	Self-image	Stress
Menstruation	Self-esteem	Marriage
Hormonal balance	Personality	Family

> ## CASE NOTES
>
> **Observation**   The interactions among biopsychosocial elements help to explain the behavior of the members of the troublesome reading group in Marsha Warren's class.
>
> **Hypothesis**   The interactions among the personalities, experiences, and classroom demands of the various group members have an explosive impact on relationships among the students.
>
> **Possible Action**   Understanding the biopsychosocial elements can suggest ways to improve the behavior of José and Tyrone.

- *How can you recognize signs of developmental growth in students and use these signs to determine their readiness to acquire new skills?* Educational psychologists like to use the expression "developmentally appropriate methods" to explain this type of teaching. For example, a secondary school teacher who realizes that a student is bright and understands scientific concepts when explained, but who also has a reading problem, can reach this student by using high-interest, low-vocabulary reading material.

- *Do the theorists provide any insights into the relationship between the abilities of students and their classroom performance?* As you read this chapter, try to discover how each theorist's interpretation of development can help to improve teaching. Piaget, for example, has made us more aware that students need a carefully structured sequence of materials and ideas, while Vygotsky has alerted us to the powerful role that culture plays in development and learning.

PIAGET AND COGNITIVE DEVELOPMENT

Probably no one has influenced our thinking about cognitive development more than Jean Piaget. Born in Neuchatel, Switzerland, in 1896, Piaget was trained as a biologist, and his biological training had a major impact on his thinking about cognitive development. Piaget called himself a "genetic epistemologist," a term that reflected his interest in the process of how we acquire knowledge changes as we develop. He was fascinated by the processes that lead children to give incorrect answers on reasoning tests, and he turned his attention to the analysis of children's developing intelligence. Until his death in 1980, Piaget remained active in cognitive development research. Many people believe that he is responsible for the resurgence of interest in cognitive studies.

Piaget's analysis of cognitive development can help teachers match curriculum to the abilities of children. Say, for example, a teacher is working with an 11- or 12-year-old student who seems to be having trouble with comprehension (perhaps both verbal and mathematical). Piaget's ideas suggest that the teacher should provide more concrete examples and more tangible materials, because most preteens are not yet ready to do much abstract thinking.

Jean Piaget (1896–1980), one of the most influential developmental psychologists, has significantly influenced educational theories and practices.

STRUCTURES
Piaget's term for the psychological units of the mind that enable us to think and know.

ADAPTATION
Piaget's term for one of the two psychological mechanisms used to explain cognitive development (organization is the other); refers to the two complementary processes of assimilation and accommodation.

ORGANIZATION
Piaget's term for the connections among cognitive structures.

FUNCTIONAL INVARIANTS
Piaget's term for the cognitive mechanisms adaptation and organization.

Key Concepts in Piaget's Theory

After many years of observing children of all ages, Piaget concluded that cognitive development has four stages, each of which builds on the previous one. Cognitive functioning begins as babies respond to what they can touch, taste, or see. The ability to use symbols and to think abstractly increases with each subsequent stage until adults are able to manipulate abstract concepts and consider hypothetical alternatives. How did Piaget explain these accomplishments?

Functional Invariants

Piaget (1952) stated that we inherit a method of intellectual functioning that enables us to respond to our environment by forming cognitive structures. He also believed that intelligence is essentially a form of organization. By **structures** he meant the organizational properties of intelligence. He suggested that two psychological mechanisms, **adaptation** and **organization,** are responsible for the development of our cognitive structures. Because we use these same two mechanisms constantly throughout our lives, Piaget called them the **functional invariants.**

Adaptation   Piaget believed that adaptation consists of **assimilation** and **accommodation.** When we assimilate something, we incorporate it; that is, we take it in. The process is like eating. We take food into the structures of our mouths and change it to fit the struc-

---

CASE NOTES

Observation   When students find material to be radically different from what they're used to, they may be unable to assimilate it because they don't have the necessary cognitive structures.

Hypothesis   Experiencing difficulty with the classroom language, Maria's work inevitably suffers. She may attempt to memorize subject matter and repeat it on demand with little, if any, comprehension.

Possible Action   Such "learning" will persist only for a brief moment, and Maria won't be able to relate it to other topics; it will not expand or enrich her knowledge. Marsha Warren must find some way, or someone, to help Maria understand the classroom work.

---

tures of our mouths, throats, and digestive tracts. We take objects, concepts, and events into our minds in a similar way; we incorporate them into our mental structures, changing them to fit those structures just as we change food to fit our physical structures.

For example, you are now studying Piaget's views of cognitive development. These ideas are unique and require effort to be understood. You are attempting to comprehend them by using the cognitive structures you now possess. You're assimilating Piaget's ideas; you are mentally taking them in and shaping them to fit your existing cognitive structures.

But we also change as a result of assimilation; that is, we accommodate to what we have taken in. The food we eat produces biochemical changes; likewise, the stimuli we incorporate into our minds produce mental changes. We change what we take in; we are also changed by it. As you read this chapter, not only are you taking in Piaget's ideas, but they are changing your views on intelligence and cognitive development. Your cognitive structures are changing, and if you understand Piaget's concepts, you will never look at children in quite the same way again. The change in your cognitive structures will produce corresponding behavioral changes; this is the process of *accommodation*.

The adaptive process is the heart of Piaget's explanation of learning. We begin by trying to "fit" new material into existing cognitive structures, to assimilate the material in a process called **equilibration.** We try to strike a balance between assimilation and accommodation. We will make mistakes, but by continually interacting with the environment, we correct our mistakes and change our cognitive structures (we have accommodated). But our mental life doesn't consist of random activities; it is organized.

Organization   The cognitive structures that we form enable us to engage in ever more complex thinking. Physical structures can again provide an analogy. To read this text, you are balancing the book, turning the pages, and moving your eyes. All of these physical structures are organized so that you can read. Likewise, for you to understand the material, your appropriate cognitive structures are organized so that they assimilate and accommodate.

Although Piaget was primarily interested in the development of thinking, his work has great value for teachers, providing insight into comprehension, transfer, and problem-solving ability.

Schemes   Organization and adaptation are inseparable. As Piaget stated (1952), they are two complementary processes of a single mechanism. Every intellectual act is related to

ASSIMILATION
Piaget's term to describe how human beings take things into their minds; one part of adaptation.

ACCOMMODATION
Piaget's term that refers to a change in cognitive structures that produces corresponding behavioral changes.

EQUILIBRATION
Piaget's term for the balance between assimilation and accommodation.

FIGURE 2.2

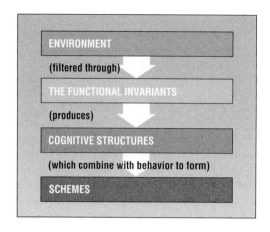

FIGURE 2.2

The Process of Cognitive
Development

SCHEMES

Piaget's term for our organized patterns of thought.

other similar acts, which introduces Piaget's notion of scheme. **Schemes** are organized patterns of thought and action, that is, the cognitive structures *and* behavior that make up an organized unit. Schemes help us to adapt to our environment and may be best thought of as the inner representation of our activities and experiences. A scheme is named by its activity: the grasping scheme, the sucking scheme, the kicking scheme, the throwing scheme.

For an idea of how schemes develop, consider how babies reach out and touch something, such as a blanket. They immediately begin to learn about the material—its heaviness, its size, its texture. In other words, babies form a cognitive structure about the blanket. Piaget called the combination of knowledge about the blanket with the act of reaching for it a *scheme*—in this case, the grasping scheme.

How do these concepts "work" in Piaget's theory? It may help if you think of his theory in this way. Stimuli come from the environment and are filtered through the functional invariants, adaptation and organization. The functional invariants use the stimuli to form new structures or to change existing structures. (For example, you may have had your own idea of what intelligence is but now you change your structures about intelligence because of what you have learned about Piaget's ideas.) Your **content,** or behavior, changes because of the changes in your cognitive structures. This process is shown in Figure 2.2.

CONTENT

Piaget's term for behavior.

One of Piaget's classic experiments illustrates the process. To replicate this experiment, you'll need a 5-year-old child (in Piaget's preoperational stage), a 7-year-old child (in Piaget's concrete operational stage), six black tokens, and six orange tokens. Put the black tokens in a row. If you give the 5-year-old child the orange tokens with instructions to match them with the black tokens, she can easily do it. When the tokens are in a one-to-one position, a 5-year-old can tell that both rows have the same number of tokens.

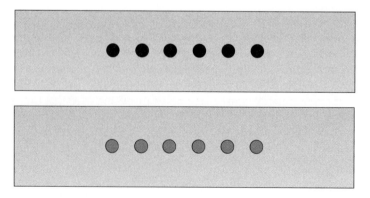

But if you spread out the six black tokens to make a longer row, the 5-year-old most likely will say that the longer row has more tokens!

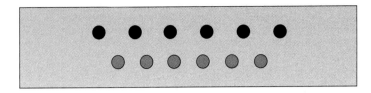

Even when Piaget put the tokens on tracks and let the child move and match them, the younger child still believed the longer row had more tokens. If you present the 7-year-old with the same problem, he'll think it is a trick—both rows obviously still have the same number of tokens.

These and related experiments hold an important lesson for teachers: Cognitive structures change with age. Consequently, subject matter must be presented in a form that matches the cognitive structures of pupils. For example, a kindergarten teacher often has to show students how to hold the paper, grasp the pencil, and print on the line. By the time these children are in third grade, they immediately know how to adjust the paper, hold the pencil, and print on the line.

PIAGET'S FOUR STAGES OF COGNITIVE DEVELOPMENT

For Piaget, cognitive development means passage through four stages or periods: *sensorimotor, preoperational, concrete operational,* and *formal operational.* (See Table 2.2.)

The age at which children reach the four stages varies, but the sequence of the stages never varies. In other words, Piaget's theory is *stage invariant, age variant.* Every child must pass though the sensorimotor stage before the preoperational, the preoperational stage before the concrete operational, and the concrete operational stage before the formal operational.

As you read about Piaget's stages of cognitive development, keep in mind four interacting influences that aid passage through the stages: maturation, experience, social interactions, and equilibration (Piaget & Inhelder, 1969). *Maturation* means just what its name implies: physical development, especially that of the muscular and nervous systems.

Piaget believed that there are two types of *experience.* One involves acting on objects to learn about them: To determine which of two objects is heavier, pick them up and compare their weights. The second type of experience refers to what we learn from simply using objects. For example, whether a child arranges ten pebbles in a row or a circle, there are still ten pebbles.

Social interactions means that children acquire knowledge from others in their culture: Parents read them books; teachers instruct them in subject matter; and children learn from others.

Finally, *equilibration* refers to a process of self-regulation in which there is constant interplay between assimilation and accommodation. For example, students learn something

---

Table 2.2 PIAGET'S COGNITIVE PERIODS AND APPROXIMATE AGES

1. *The Sensorimotor Period*—Birth to 18–24 months

2. *The Preoperational Period*—2 to 7 years

3. *The Concrete Operational Period*—7 to 11 years

4. *The Formal Operational Period*—over 11 years

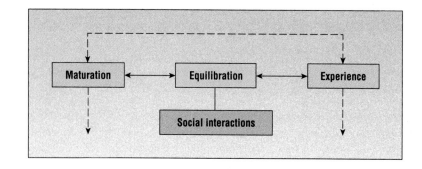

FIGURE 2.3

Influences on Cognitive
Development

new in their science class (they assimilate); after studying it, discussing it, and reading about it, they accommodate. But in the next class, they learn something else, and the equilibration process continues.

Figure 2.3 illustrates these interactive forces.

The Sensorimotor Period

The *sensorimotor* period extends from birth to about 2 years old. The cognitive development of infants and toddlers comes mainly through their use of their bodies and their senses as they explore the environment, hence the label sensorimotor.

Infants "know" in the sense of recognizing or anticipating familiar, recurring objects and happenings, and they "think" in the sense of behaving toward these objects and events with mouth, hand, eye, and other sensory-motor instruments in predictable, organized, and often adaptive ways (Flavell, Miller, & Miller, 1993). A good example can be seen in the way a baby follows her mother with her eyes and in how she will often smile at her mother's face, expecting pleasant consequences.

Features of the Sensorimotor Period

Several characteristics of the sensorimotor period that help to explain how an infant thinks are described next.

A baby's universe is initially *egocentric,* entirely centered on self. Piaget used egocentric in a cognitive sense; that is, egocentric children are simply unaware of any other viewpoint. (Egocentric adults, however, know there are other viewpoints but disregard them.) Very young children lack social orientation. They speak at, rather than to, each other, and two children in conversation will be discussing utterly unrelated topics. Through cognitive development in the sensorimotor period, however, they begin to learn that others exist, that there is a world beyond themselves.

Infants initially don't have a sense of **object permanence.** An object or person removed from their field of vision ceases to exist. Let's say that an infant is playing with a teddy bear. If you move it behind a chair out of the baby's sight, she simply stops searching for it. This explains the pleasure infants show when someone plays peek-a-boo with them. The face no longer exists when it is hidden, since the baby has not yet acquired object permanence.

Gradually, as babies begin to crawl and walk, they realize that there is distance between the objects that they are using to steady themselves. They are developing concepts of space and time. For example, how many times have you seen infants pull themselves up by a chair, drop to the floor, crawl some distance, and then pull themselves up using a table? By moving from object to object, they learn about space and the time it takes to move from object to object.

OBJECT
PERMANENCE

Piaget's term for an infant's ability to realize that an object or person not within sight still exists.

Table 2.3	OUTSTANDING CHARACTERISTICS OF THE SENSORIMOTOR PERIOD
Stage 1	During the first month, children exercise the native (that is, inborn) reflexes, for example, the sucking reflex. Here is the origin of mental development because states of awareness accompany the reflex mechanisms.
Stage 2	Piaget refers to stage 2 (from 1 to 4 months) as the stage of primary circular reactions. Infants repeat some act involving the body, for example, finger sucking. (Primary means first; circular reactions means repeated actions.)
Stage 3	From 4 to 8 months secondary circular reactions appear; that is, children repeat acts outside themselves. For example, infants continue to shake or kick the crib.
Stage 4	From 8 to 12 months, children coordinate secondary schemes. Recall the meaning of schemes: behavior plus mental structure. During stage 4, infants combine several related schemes to achieve some objective. For example, they remove an obstacle blocking a desired object.
Stage 5	From 12 to 18 months, tertiary circular reactions appear. Now children repeat acts, but not only for repetition's sake. For example, children of this age repeatedly drop things. Piaget interprets such behavior as expressing their uncertainty about what will happen to the objects when they release them.
Stage 6	At about 18 months or 2 years, a primitive type of representation appears. For example, one of Piaget's daughters wished to open a door but had grass in her hands. She put the grass on the floor and then moved it back from the door's movement so that it wouldn't blow away.

As children use their growing sensorimotor intelligence, they begin to find order in the universe. They begin to distinguish their own actions as causes, and they begin to discover events that have their causes elsewhere, either in other objects or in various relationships between objects (Piaget & Inhelder, 1969). This concept is known as **causality.** For example, an infant will push a toy and watch it roll, gradually realizing that her own actions caused the truck to roll.

CAUSALITY
Children distinguish their own actions as causes.

Infants pass through six subdivisions of the sensorimotor period (see Table 2.3). As they do, they progress from reliance on reflex actions (such as sucking and grasping) to a basic understanding of the world around them and the beginnings of the ability to represent the world through language.

Educational Implications

Piaget's analysis of infant cognitive development not only is important for day-care staff and others who care for infants (since some day-care centers specialize in the care of infants as young as 6 weeks), but it also has implications for the classroom. What happens during the first two years of life provides the foundation for more formal work. Children's cognitive achievements during the sensorimotor period enable them eventually to go on to the use of symbols (such as those used in language and mathematics).

If you work with infants, remember Piaget's suggestions for furthering cognitive development (1969):

- *Provide multiple objects of various sizes, shapes, and colors for babies to use.* Think about the label sensorimotor for a moment. What meanings do you attach to it? One meaning undoubtedly includes the active use of the senses or body; through bodily use (reaching, touching, creeping), infants learn about their environment. Consequently, parents and day-care centers should furnish toys and objects that are circular, square, soft, hard, stationary, or mobile. (They don't have to be expensive; for example, rubber balls, plastic cups, or pieces of fruit are perfectly satisfactory.) By manipulating these simple objects, babies' physical actions form the cognitive groundwork of their cognitive lives.

TIPS ON LEARNING
The Sensorimotor Period

PRINCIPLE   Babies learn about other human beings from the way they are treated from birth.

STRATEGY   The human face is the most exciting plaything an infant experiences. It smiles, frowns, makes noises, and responds to the baby. Use pictures of faces in magazines, photographs, or even circles with features drawn on them to help babies respond positively to those around them. Use your own face to elicit positive responses from infants.

STRATEGY   Talk *to* infants, not at them. Babies find adult speech, properly used, one of the most stimulating parts of their environment.

PRINCIPLE   Children are active processors of information from birth.

STRATEGY   Since newborns can see to a distance of only about ten inches, place colorful, safe objects such as mobiles and rattles within that range.

STRATEGY   Hang a soft animal or a cloth ball within their range to attract their attention and stimulate movement.

STRATEGY   Watch their responses and use their behavior as clues as to what you should do. Be what developmental psychologists call *sensitively responsive.*

- *If infants are to develop cognitively as fully as their potential permits, they must actively engage with environmental objects.* Babies must touch them, mouth them, push them, pull them, squeeze them, drop them, throw them, and perform any other conceivable actions because infants learn through sensory and motor activity. The ball they push and see roll, the square block that falls and makes different sounds when it falls on the wooden floor or a rug, or the different sounds that come from kicking the rungs of the crib as compared to the solid front and back—interacting with these objects furthers cognitive development. (You can see how a lack of these experiences impedes a baby's cognitive development.)

The Preoperational Period

OPERATIONS

Piaget's term for actions that we perform mentally to gain knowledge.

When Piaget referred to **operations** (as in the term *preoperational*), he meant actions that we perform mentally to gain knowledge (Ginsburg & Opper, 1988). To know an object is to act on it. You mentally compare it, change it, and then return it to its original state. *Knowledge is not just a mental image of an object or event.* It's not enough to look at an object, or to picture an event. You twist it, you turn it (mentally, of course), but the important thing is that you do something to it.

You compare it with other objects, noting similarities and differences; you place it in a particular order in a series; you measure it; you take it apart and then put it back together. Piaget also believed that mental actions are reversible; that is, you can think in opposite directions: You add but you can also subtract; you join things mentally, but you can also separate them. For example, if 2 is added to 2, the result is 4; but if 2 is taken away from 4, the original 2 returns.

Preoperational, then, refers to a child who has begun to use symbols (such as language) but is not yet capable of mentally manipulating them. Children who cannot take something apart and put it together again, who cannot return to the beginning of a thought sequence (that is, who cannot comprehend how to reverse the action of $2 + 2$), who cannot believe that water poured from a short, fat glass into a taller, thinner one retains the same volume—these children are at a level of thinking that precedes operational thought.

Features of Preoperational Thought

Between the ages of 2 and 7, children are starting to recognize that there's a world "out there" that exists independently of them. Recognizing the abilities of young children, as well as their cognitive limitations, we can identify the following features of preoperational thought: realism, animism, artificialism, and transductive reasoning.

Realism refers to the ability to slowly distinguish and accept a real world, thus identifying both an external and internal world. Piaget believed that youngsters initially confuse internal and external; they confuse thought and matter. The confusion disappears at about age 7. For example, a young child who is jealous of a newly born sibling gradually realizes that his parents "can't take it back."

Animism refers to a child's tendency to consider a large number of objects as alive and conscious, objects that adults consider to be inert. For example, a child who sees a necklace wound up and then released explains that the necklace is moving because it "wants to unwind." Children overcome this cognitive limitation as they recognize their own personalities. They then refuse to attribute personality to things. Piaget believed that comparison of one's own thoughts with the thoughts of others—social intercourse—slowly conquers animism as it does egocentrism. Piaget identified four stages of animism:

1. Almost everything is alive and conscious.

2. Only those things that move are alive.

3. Only those things that manifest spontaneous movements are alive.

4. Consciousness is limited to the animal world.

Artificialism refers to the assumption that everything is the product of human creation. For example, when asked how the moon began, some of Piaget's subjects replied, "because we began to be alive." As egocentrism decreases, youngsters become more objective, and they steadily assimilate objective reality to their cognitive structures. They proceed from a purely human or divine explanation to an explanation that is half natural, half artificial; the moon comes from the clouds, but the clouds come from people's houses. Finally, at about 9 years old, children realize that human activity has nothing to do with the origin of the moon. (Realism and artificialism are examples of both the abilities and limitations of preoperational thought. The decline of artificialism parallels the growth of realism.)

Transductive reasoning refers to reasoning that is neither deductive nor inductive. Rather, reasoning moves from particular to particular, which is quite characteristic of preschool children. The following are examples of transductive reasoning:

The sun won't fall down because it's hot.
The sun stops there because it's yellow.

Limitations of the Preoperational Period

What are some obstacles that preoperational children still struggle to overcome? Although symbolic activity steadily develops during the preoperational period, several important limitations exist.

REALISM

Piaget's term for a child's growing ability to distinguish and accept the real world.

ANIMISM

Piaget's term for a child's tendency to attribute life to inert objects.

ARTIFICIALISM

Piaget's term to describe a preoperational child's tendency to assume that everything is the product of human creation.

TRANSDUCTIVE REASONING

Piaget's term for a preoperational child's reasoning technique—from particular to particular in a nonlogical manner.

CENTERING

*Piaget's term to describe a
child's tendency to concentrate
on only part of an object or
activity. Characteristic of
preoperational children.*

EGOCENTRISM

*Piaget's term for children's
tendency to see things as they
want them to be.*

IRREVERSIBILITY

*Piaget's term for children's
inability to reverse their
thinking.*

Centering refers to concentrating on only part of an object or activity. Children ignore the relationships among the various parts. Recall Piaget's experiment with the tokens. When the tokens were spread out, preoperational children could not relate space to number.

Egocentrism is a central characteristic of both the sensorimotor and preoperational periods. For preoperational children, things are what they want them to be; other opinions are meaningless. For example, children may believe that the moon follows *them* around; everything focuses on them.

Irreversibility is the inability to reverse one's thinking. Preschoolers cannot return to the original premise. They may have learned that $2 + 2 = 4$, but they cannot yet grasp that $4 - 2 = 2$.

Educational Implications

To help students, particularly at the kindergarten and first-grade levels, teachers should encourage the manipulation of materials (especially objects and activities that help to provide a foundation in math and science). Also, if you're working with this age group, provide as many hands-on experiences as possible. Activities that preoperational children like and that improve their growing skill to represent things internally (imitating, pretend play, etc.) include the following (Piaget & Inhelder, 1969):

1. *Deferred imitation.* Preoperational children can imitate some object or activity that they have previously witnessed; for example, they might walk like an animal that they saw at the zoo earlier in the day.

2. *Symbolic play.* Children enjoy pretending that they are asleep, or that they are someone or something else.

3. *Drawing.* Children of this age project their mental representations into their drawings. Highly symbolic, their art work reflects the level of their thinking and what they are thinking. Encourage children of this age to talk about their art.

4. *Mental images.* Preoperational children can represent objects and events but they cannot change or anticipate change in their thinking. Recall Piaget's experiment with the 5-year-old who thought there were more tokens in a row when they were spaced farther apart.

5. *Language.* For preoperational children, language becomes a vehicle for thought. Parents, teachers, and others provide ample opportunities for children to talk with adults and with each other.

For teachers working with children of this age, their cognitive accomplishments suggest several kinds of activities. For example, a teacher could cut out pictures from magazines, brochures, or newspapers and have the children tell stories about what they see. This would not only help in assessing their language ability, but also will reveal much about their cognitive development. For example, how egocentric are they (in Piaget's terms)? Is their ability to reason at an appropriate cognitive level? You could group ten circular objects (coins, chips, marbles) in a circle and then put ten in a straight line. Ask them which has more. Watch their reactions. Do they immediately point to the straight line? Do some hesitate? Why? These and similar activities can furnish clues to children's cognitive development as they approach Piaget's next stage, the concrete operational period.

The Concrete Operational Period

Children at the concrete operational stage (which should be the level of Marsha Warren's class) demonstrate striking differences in their thinking as compared with children at the

TIPS ON LEARNING
The Preoperational Period

PRINCIPLE   Preoperational children learn through active explorations and interactions with adults, other children, and materials.

STRATEGY   Help kindergartners to make short story books such as "What's on My Street?" Use vocabulary words that they have already learned, and have them illustrate their stories. Then have the children take their stories home and read them aloud to their parents.

STRATEGY   Toward the end of the preoperational period, when teaching a unit like the solar system to second-graders, have the children play the role of the planets, the satellites, and the sun.

PRINCIPLE   Piaget believed that the great accomplishment of the preoperational period is a growing ability to manipulate things mentally.

STRATEGY   Put a series of circles and lines on the board. Give pupils a few minutes to study the sequence, then erase it. Have them write the circles and lines in the same sequence on their papers.

STRATEGY   Provide opportunities for pupils to tell jokes. They enjoy this, and it promotes socialization, improves memory, and aids pragmatic skills, such as social interactions with their peers.

---

preoperational stage. Between 7 and 11 or 12 years of age, children overcome the limitations of preoperational thinking and accomplish true mental operations. Students can now reverse their thinking and group objects into classes.

Cognitive limitations at the concrete operations stage still exist, however. Children can perform mental operations only on concrete (tangible) objects or events, and not on verbal statements. For example, if they are shown blocks A, B, and C, concrete operational children can tell you that A is larger than B, that B is larger than C, and that, therefore, A is largest of all. But if you tell them that Liz is taller than Ellen who is taller than Jane, they cannot tell you who is tallest of all (especially in the early years of the period). These results explain why Piaget designated the period "concrete operational."

Features of the Concrete Operational Period

Several notable accomplishments mark this period.

Conservation is the realization that the essence of something remains constant, although surface features may change. In Piaget's famous water jar problem, children observe two identical jars filled to the same height. While they watch, the contents of one container are poured into a taller and thinner jar, so that the liquid reaches a higher level. By the age of 7 most children will state that the contents are still equal; they conserved the idea of equal amounts of water by *decentering*, that is, by focusing on more than one aspect of the problem. They can now reverse their thinking; they can mentally pour the water back into the original container.

As Figure 2.4 shows, different types of conservation appear at different times during the concrete operational period.

CONSERVATION

Piaget's term for the realization that the essence of something remains constant although surface features may change.

During the concrete operational period, children grasp the meaning of reversibility.

FIGURE 2.4

Different Kinds of Conservation Appear at Different Ages

(From John F. Travers, *The Growing Child.* Copyright © 1982 HarperCollins College Publishers, Glenview, Illinois. Reprinted by permission.)

Conservation of	Example		Approximate age
1. Number	Which has more?	● ● ● ● ● ● ● ● ● ● ●	6–7 years
2. Liquids	Which has more?		7–8 years
3. Length	Are they the same length?		7–8 years
4. Substance	Are they the same?	● ━	7–8 years
5. Area	Which has more room?		7–8 years
6. Weight	Will they weigh the same?	● ●	9–10 years
7. Volume	Will they displace the same amount of water?		11–12 years

Piaget (1973) believed that youngsters use three arguments to conserve:

1. *The argument of identity.* The concrete operational child says that since no water has been removed or added to either jar, it is still the "same thing." By 8 years of age, children are amused by the problem, not realizing that a year earlier they probably would have given a different answer.

2. *The argument of **reversibility**.* Concrete operational children say that you just have to pour the water back to see that it is the "same thing."

3. *The argument of compensation.* Concrete operational children say that the water is higher in the taller beaker, but it is narrower. That is, these youngsters compensate for the height increase by noting the circumference decrease and realize that there is the same amount of water in both beakers.

Seriation is the ability to arrange objects by increasing or decreasing size. As we noted earlier, concrete operational children can arrange concrete objects, such as blocks. If, however, the operation is in pure language, such as the preceding word problem mentioned comparing the heights of three girls, it becomes more complicated and the concrete operational child cannot solve it.

Classification is the ability to group objects with some similarities within a larger category. If preoperational children are shown a picture of six roses and six tulips, they'll be able to correctly answer questions about the number of tulips and the number of roses, but when asked "Are there more roses or flowers?" they'll answer "Roses." Concrete operational children, however, are able to classify both roses and tulips as flowers.

In a classic experiment illustrating mastery of classification, Piaget showed children at both the preoperational and the concrete operational levels twenty wooden beads, sixteen of which were brown and four white. When he asked, "Are there more brown beads or more wooden beads?" the preoperational children typically answered "brown" while the older children answered correctly.

Number concept is not the same as the ability to count. As Piaget's experiment with the two rows of tokens showed, even though the preoperational child can count, "one" isn't always "one." When the six tokens in one row were spread out, the child was convinced that it contained more than six tokens. Only after children acquire the concepts of seriation and classification will they be able to understand the "oneness of one"—that one boy, one girl, one apple, and one orange are all one of something.

These thought systems of the concrete operational child gradually come into a well-organized equilibrium, which Piaget refers to as *cognitive operations.* When children reach this phase of cognitive development, they are on the threshold of adult thought, or formal operations. Consequently, we can see that middle childhood pupils have experienced an intellectual revolution. Their thinking has become logical and more abstract, their attention improves, and their memory becomes more efficient as they develop new strategies.

Educational Implications

Are youngsters capable of meeting the problems they face in the classroom? Yes and no. They can assimilate and accommodate the material they encounter, but only at their level. Elementary school children up to the age of 10 or 11 are capable of representational thought, but only with the concrete, the tangible. Consequently, we cannot expect them to comprehend fully any abstract subtleties.

A striking example of concrete operational thinking was evident in a science project involving sixth-graders. While discussing the fishing industry off the coast of Massachusetts, the teacher had the students construct topographical ocean zone maps. Each student put many class hours into the project. They cut and positioned as many as twenty-five layers of ocean bottom before completing their map. In the end, each student had sore hands but a thorough understanding of the varying ocean depths that influenced fishing off the coast of Massachusetts.

REVERSIBILITY
Piaget's term for children's ability to use cognitive operations "to take things apart," to reverse their thinking.

SERIATION
Piaget's term for the ability to arrange objects by increasing or decreasing size.

CLASSIFICATION
Piaget's term for the ability to group objects with some similarities within a larger category.

NUMBER CONCEPT
Piaget's term for children's understanding of the meaning of numbers; the oneness of one.

TIPS ON ASSESSMENT
The Concrete Operational Period

PRINCIPLE   Concrete operational students are developing classification skills.

STRATEGY   Have pupils play a classification game by pairing common household objects like a knife and a fork, a towel and a bar of soap, a toothbrush and toothpaste, a brush and comb. Include some pairs that are obvious and some that are less so. Have one pair for each child. Spread all objects on a table. Let each student take a turn choosing two items that belong together. Have students explain why they grouped the objects as they did.

STRATEGY   Celebrate with a "food fest" in social studies. Assign two students to learn about a particular country, perhaps the country from which their families originated. Locate recipes and types of food typical of each country. Enlist the parents' help to cook the food. Make decorations, costumes, and provide music for your celebration.

If you're teaching children of this age-stage, provide opportunities for your students to engage in tasks that will help them at this level. For example, take the common objects in your classroom (pencils and pens) and ask your students to group them. Then ask them why they put certain things together. Have them look at the various types of glass in the classroom (in doors and windows) and ask them to group them by size. Are there more large glass windows than glass windows? Why? Have your students explain their answers.

The Formal Operational Period

According to Piaget, the *formal operational* period, during which the beginnings of logical, abstract thinking appear, commences at about 11 or 12 years of age. During this period, youngsters demonstrate an ability to reason realistically about the future and to consider possibilities that they actually doubt. Adolescents look for relations, they separate the real from the possible, they test their mental solutions to problems, and they feel comfortable with verbal statements. In short, the period's great achievement is a release from the restrictions of the tangible and the concrete (Elkind, 1994).

When younger children were asked to assume that coal is white, they replied that coal had to be black, whereas adolescents accepted the unreal assumption and reasoned from it. In one experiment, children were given a cue stick, a cue ball, and a billiard-type table with several targets on it. The children were asked to hit the target with the cue ball by bouncing it off the side (banking their shots). When asked about what had happened, concrete operational children explain in very tangible terms—"If I hit it this way (demonstrates) it goes that way" (again demonstrates). Formal operational children, on the other hand search for explanatory principles—"The rebound depends on the angle at which I held the cue stick" (Piaget & Inhelder, 1969).

Remember, though, that some students at this age may still be concrete operational, or only into the initial stages of formal operations. Many adolescents have just consolidated their concrete operational thinking and continue to use it consistently. Unless they find themselves in situations that demand formal operational thinking (such as science and math classes), they continue to be concrete operational thinkers. As Elkind noted (1994), learning how to use formal operations takes time and practice. With these pupils you must continue to blend concrete and abstract materials.

CASE NOTES

Observation   Many of Marsha Warren's students seem to experience little success or satisfaction in school.

Hypothesis   Marsha can turn to Piaget's analysis of concrete operations for help in dealing with her students. Piaget's ideas on such topics as conservation, classification, and reversibility will help her understand her students' thinking and help her shape a positive and exciting learning environment.

Possible Action   Marsha Warren can take a major step in improving the classroom atmosphere by ensuring that her students receive praise and success for honest achievement by using developmentally appropriate materials and methods.

Another interesting feature of adolescent thought is what Elkind (1994) referred to as *adolescent egocentric thinking.* He stated that adolescents assume that everyone else thinks as they do and shares their concerns. This is due to the changes occurring in their bodies and their sensitivity to others, which leads to intense concentration on themselves—"But why is everyone looking at me?" They thus create an *imaginary audience.*

Features of the Formal Operational Period

There are several essential features of formal operational thinking:

1. *The adolescent's ability to separate the real from the possible,* which distinguishes the formal operational child from the concrete operational. The adolescent tries to discern all possible relations in any situation or problem and then, by mental experimentation and logical analysis, attempts to discover which are true. Flavell (1963) noted that there is nothing trivial in the adolescent's accomplishment; it is a basic and essential reorganization of thought processes that permits the adolescent to exist in the world of the possible.

2. *The adolescent's thinking is propositional,* which means that she uses not only concrete data, but also statements or propositions that contain the concrete data. Dealing with abstract concepts no longer frustrates her. For example, you could ask a class of adolescents a question like the following and expect that they will be able to respond:

   You've been appointed to a committee that oversees a drug prevention program in your school. What are some new, but realistic, ideas you would suggest?

   Also, their increasing ability to deal with "if this, then that" statements may cause them to argue more vigorously with you on any controversial matter such as drug use, school programs on sexual conduct, or political matters.

3. *Adolescents attack a problem by gathering as much information as possible and then making all the possible combinations of the variables that they can.* They proceed as follows. *First,* they organize data by concrete operational techniques (classification, seriation). *Second,* they use the results of concrete operational techniques to form statements or propositions. *Third,* they combine as many of these propositions as possible. (These are hypotheses, and Piaget often refers to this process as hypothetico-deductive thinking.) *Fourth,* they then test to determine which combinations are true.

Educational Implications

Although most adolescents are comfortable with appropriate materials and activities, teachers should be careful not to exaggerate students' abilities. If you recall Piaget's statement that children construct their own world, then your students must manipulate material as much as possible. Provide as many concrete examples as you think are necessary before asking students to formulate general principles. Try to discover how students sequence materials and activities so that you can match their developmental levels. The activities should challenge students' thinking, but should not be so difficult as to frustrate them and cause failure. Students should concentrate on the activities and not on the teacher, thus providing the teacher more time to observe and to guide.

Let's assume you're teaching a class on World War II. After your students have mastered the basic facts, you walk into your class one day and ask them to write their ideas about what would have happened if Germany had won the war and Hitler had become the most powerful leader in the world. Observe their reactions as they search for ideas. Keep in mind the features of formal operational thought:

- Can students separate the real from the possible? Some students will still have a difficult time.

- Are they comfortable with the propositional thinking needed? Can they take the concrete material they've learned and transform it into abstract, even contradictory, ideas?

- Can they gather as much data as is needed and combine many and varied ideas, forming new propositions?

Students may find it easy, difficult, or impossible to combine propositions and speculate about the future. This ability can't be forced, but students can learn to improve their thinking if teachers ask such questions as: "What's the significance of the great battles?" "What if the outcomes of particular battles had been reversed?" "How would that have affected other nations?" In other words, you should try first to have the student *understand* the facts and the reasons for them and then *guide* students to draw implications from the data.

TIPS ON LEARNING
The Formal Operational Period

PRINCIPLE   Formal operational students can generate many possible solutions to problems.

STRATEGY   Students should be able to discuss how things would be different today if the following imaginary events had occurred:

a. In 1492, Christopher Columbus sailed west into an area known as the Bermuda Triangle and mysteriously disappeared.

b. Martin Luther King was not assassinated in 1968.

c. George Washington proclaimed himself as King of America instead of its first president.

d. Margaret Thatcher had never become prime minister of Great Britain.

Finally, keep in mind that many adolescents and adults never reach the stage of formal operations. Whether this is due to cognitive limitations, neurological difficulties, or restricted environmental opportunities remains an unanswered question. Perhaps, also, many individuals simply refuse to place importance on tests demanding highly abstract reasoning, which may well be a function of their culture.

Piaget and Language Development

Now that we have covered Piaget's four stages of cognitive development, let's look at his ideas on the development of language. Piaget believed that language emerges not from a biological timetable, but rather from existing cognitive structures and in accordance with a child's needs. Piaget's basic work on language, *The Language and Thought of the Child* (1926), begins by asking: What are the needs that a child tends to satisfy when talking? That is, what is the function of language for a child? Piaget answered this question by linking language to cognitive structures. Thus, language function differs at each of the four cognitive levels (see Table 2.4).

Piaget had little to say about language in the sensorimotor period, believing that these first two years were a preparation for the appearance and growth of language during the preoperational years. Recording the speech of two 6-year-old children, Piaget identified two major speech categories of the preoperational child: egocentric speech and socialized speech. Children engage in *egocentric speech* when they do not care to whom they speak, or whether anyone is listening to them (Piaget, 1926, p. 32). There are three types of egocentric speech:

1. *Repetition,* which children use for the sheer pleasure of talking and which is devoid of social character.

2. *Monologue,* in which children talk to themselves as if they were thinking aloud.

3. *Collective monologue,* in which other children are present but not listening to the speaker.

CASE NOTES

Observation   Children engage in *socialized speech* when they exchange views with each other, criticize one another, ask questions, give answers, and even command or threaten. Obviously, José and Tyrone have a limited understanding of each other.

Hypothesis   Piaget estimated that about 50% of a 6-year-old's speech is egocentric and that what is socialized is purely factual. He also warned that although most children begin to communicate thought between 7 and 8 years of age, their understanding of each other is still limited.

Possible Action   Marsha Warren must adopt techniques to help José, such as a combination of positive and negative reinforcement (see Chapter 6). Tyrone needs the individual attention that will lead him to have greater insights into the reasons for his persistent stubbornness.

Table 2.4 PIAGET ON LANGUAGE AND THOUGHT

Period (age in years)	Characteristics	Outstanding Language Equivalent
Sensorimotor (0–2)	1. Egocentrism 2. Organization of reality by sensory and motor abilities	Language absent until final months of period
Preoperational (2–7)	1. Increasing symbolic activity 2. Beginnings of representation	1. Egocentric speech 2. Socialized speech
Concrete Operational (7–11)	1. Reversibility 2. Conservation 3. Seriation 4. Classification	1. Beginnings of verbal understanding 2. Understanding related to concrete objects
Formal Operational (over 11)	1. Development of logico-mathematical structures 2. Hypothetico-deductive reasoning	1. Language freed from the concrete 2. Verbal ability to express the possible

The early childhood years see the slow and steady disappearance of egocentrism, except in verbal thought, where traces of egocentrism remain until children are about 11 or 12 years old. Usage and complexity of language increase dramatically as children pass through the four stages of cognitive development. Piaget insisted that the striking growth of verbal ability does not occur as a separate phenomenon, but reflects the development of cognitive structures.

CRITICISMS OF PIAGET

Although Piaget has left a monumental legacy, his ideas have not been unchallenged. Piaget was a believer in the stage theory of development; that is, he viewed development as a sequence of distinct stages, each of which entails important changes in the way a child thinks, feels, and behaves. However, the acquisition of cognitive structures may be more gradual than Piaget believed. For example, a child may not be completely in the sensorimotor or preoperational stage but may be in a combination of both. A child's level of cognitive development seems to depend more on the nature of the task than on a rigid classification system.

By changing the nature of the task (for example, reducing the number of objects children must manipulate), by allowing children to practice (for example, teaching children conservation tasks), and by using materials familiar to children, researchers have found that children can accomplish specific tasks at earlier ages than Piaget believed (see Gelman & Baillargeon, 1983; Halford, 1989). Such criticisms have led to a more searching examination of the periods during which children acquire certain cognitive abilities.

For example, Piaget believed that infants from 8 to 12 months of age can retrieve an object that is hidden from them. Before this age, if a blanket is thrown over a toy that the baby is looking at, the baby stops reaching for it as if the toy doesn't exist. Tracing the ages at which object permanence appears, Baillargeon (1987) devised an experiment in which infants between 3½ and 4½ months old were seated at a table on which a cardboard screen could be moved back and forth. It could be tilted forward (toward the baby) until it lay flat on the table or backward (away from the baby) until its back touched the table.

Baillargeon then placed a painted wooden block behind the cardboard screen so that the infant could see the block when the screen was in a forward, flat position. But when the screen was tilted backward, it came to rest on the block, removing it from the baby's sight. Occasionally, Baillargeon secretly removed the block so that the screen continued to tip backward until it rested flat on the table. The 4½-month-olds showed surprise at the change by looking at the screen longer; even some of the 3½-month-olds seemed to notice the "impossible" event. These findings suggest that infants may develop the object permanence concept earlier than Piaget originally thought.

In a wide-ranging review of hundreds of studies that have tested Piaget's ideas, Gelman and Baillargeon (1983) also questioned the idea of broad stages of development, although they supported the notion of cognitive structures that assimilate and accommodate the environment. The idea of stages with no overlap seems to lack empirical evidence to support it.

In a typical Piagetian experiment, a doll was placed at different positions around a model of three mountains; children were then asked how the mountains looked to the doll at each position. Children under 6 reported their own views, not the doll's. Yet when Gelman and Baillargeon (1983) showed cards with different pictures on each side to 3-year-old children, the children correctly reported both what they had seen and what the tester would see.

As we end our study of Piaget's analysis of cognitive and language development, what can we conclude? Two major contributions of Piaget come immediately to mind: First, thanks to Piaget we have a *deeper understanding* of children's cognitive development. Second, he has made us more alert to the need for greater comprehension of *how* children think (the processes that they use), and not just what they think (the products of their thinking).

For the Classroom

Knowledge of Piaget's theory can help teachers to assess the level of students' cognitive development. By observing students closely, teachers can link their behavior to their cognitive level and utilize appropriate subject matter. For example, curriculum planners can profit from Piaget's findings by attempting to answer two questions. Are there ideal times for teaching certain subjects? Is there an ideal sequence for a subject that matches Piaget's sequence of cognitive development? The simple answer is "yes."

For example, Piaget's ideas on cognitive development have been used to formulate programs in related fields, such as health and AIDS prevention. Walsh and Bibace (1990) have proposed a developmentally based program that attempts to educate, not merely inform, students about the reality of AIDS. Arguing that schools will inevitably be drawn into the struggle to contain the spread of AIDS, these researchers urge that HIV/AIDS programs be included at every school level. To be most effective, such programs should be developmentally based, since children understand themselves and their world according to their level of cognitive development. With this caution goes another: Program designers should remember that not all students of the same age are at the same level of cognitive development.

Children seem to follow Piaget's sequence of cognitive development in understanding AIDS. For example, Walsh and Bibace (1990) state that young children (about 4 or 5 years old) remain quite egocentric, with a tendency to focus on external events, and don't show much concern for cause and effect. They define AIDS by something with which they are familiar. It's a "bad" sickness, and anyone who is seriously ill can have AIDS.

Current Issues & Perspectives

Should Piaget's Theory of Cognitive Development Drive Public School Curricula?

American schools are varied and diverse. There is no one overarching philosophy or methodology of education in the tens of thousands of schools across our fifty states. While most educators accept, in general, Piaget's stages of cognitive development, teachers and school systems are not required to demonstrate a curriculum sensitive to developmental considerations for learning. Nevertheless, teachers and psychologists believe that teaching methods and the subject matter should demonstrate a developmental approach.

For example, although there may be disagreements about the particulars of Piaget's theory of cognitive development, children's progression through successively sophisticated levels of cognitive development is widely supported. The ways in which students learn, marked by definite clues at different levels of development, give us great insight into how best to present subject matter to maximize a student's learning.

Yet there are those who believe that commitment to any one approach to learning limits opportunities to try something new. All teachers know that students learn in many different ways and at different rates. Even the same learner may be on different cognitive levels in different subjects. In Piaget's theory, students are constructors of their own knowledge through experiential learning, but the reality of the classroom dictates that teachers be free to use whatever style best suits the needs of their students on any given day.

Another issue that causes controversy is the idea that hands-on experience should be the cornerstone of the curriculum. Adherents of this belief argue that through direct experience students come to an understanding of the material. Consequently, comprehension, which is necessary for real learning to take place, is enhanced.

Others, however, argue just as forcefully that while some hands-on experiences help students "see" a concept or make a connection, teachers cannot always provide their learners with this kind of experience. With ten units to get through in social studies, for example, the class does not have time to constantly use hands-on work. Also some students, or entire classrooms, seem unable to settle in or settle down easily. For these learners, any departure from a teacher-directed activity is an invitation to chaos.

Finally, the matter of reporting arises in these discussions of Piaget's ideas. Should a report card evaluate a child's level of cognition and reasoning capabilities, as well as content learning? Proponents of this view believe that letter grades are insufficient, telling us little about where our children are as learners. They most often reflect specific content learning. What does a C− tell us? Is the problem one of reasoning, understanding, or memory? A complete assessment provides an evaluation of the child's level of cognitive development and reasoning capabilities as well as one of content learning.

Others are skeptical, saying that grades have for many years been the accepted and the expected measure of a child's school progress. Having come through this system themselves, today's parents know how to gauge their children's progress using these measures. A developmental evaluation might inform a future teacher of the child but would be of little value to a student or parent.

These issues are current and controversial and you may well find yourself in the middle of the various arguments. What's your opinion on each of them?

Children who are older (about 7 to 11 years) and at a concrete level of cognitive development can differentiate more accurately and interpret AIDS according to specific bodily symptoms. They initially interpret the cause of AIDS in concrete terms: "A bug caused it," or "using someone else's straw caused it." Older children (11 years and older) are capable of more complex thinking and can understand the possibility that many interacting elements may be at work in the disease. For example, they realize that AIDS may be caused by sex and/or dirty needles, but that these behaviors may not always cause AIDS (Walsh & Bibace, 1990).

You can see how Piaget's work provides data for teachers to construct positive learning conditions. For example, during Piaget's first two stages (sensorimotor and preoperational), youngsters should constantly interact physically with their environments. During the concrete operational period, pupils should be able to use as many tangible objects as possible. Finally, adolescents should encounter verbal problems, master learning strategies, and test their solutions.

As we conclude our work on Piaget, here are some general suggestions to keep in mind for your teaching: *Piaget always insisted that his theory stressed the interaction between the individual and the environment.* Students must "operate" on curricular materials. For example, adolescents with reading problems must have materials that are appealing and that actively involve them in skill development and comprehension.

Carefully consider how much direction and guidance each pupil needs. A youngster who has a language problem requires prompt assistance to prevent a persistent speech deficit. But a student who has the necessary formula to solve a math problem should be permitted to make a few mistakes and to discover the correct solution rather than being told the answer.

Be careful about the materials that you use. If you encourage interactive learning, what your pupils "operate on" must be appropriate for them physically (can they physically manipulate the materials?) and cognitively (can they understand what they are supposed to do?).

Use instructional strategies appropriate to students' ethnic and racial backgrounds (Rogoff, 1990). For example, studies of Hispanic students have shown that they tend to be influenced by personal relationships and praise or disapproval from authority figures. Pueblo Indian children from the American Southwest show higher achievement when instruction utilizes their "primary learning" patterns (those that occur outside the classroom). These students respond well when instruction incorporates the concerns and needs of the community. For example, such tasks as measuring the amount of rainfall (in inches) per year and relating it to crop production can be used in math classes.

Vygotsky and Cognitive Development

Another theorist who thought deeply about cognitive development and whose ideas about the role of culture in development have direct classroom application is Lev Vygotsky. Born in Russia in 1896, Vygotsky was educated at Moscow University and quickly turned his attention to educational psychology, developmental psychology, and psychopathology. An appealing figure in the history of psychology, Vygotsky is described by his daughter as follows:

> *[He was] a very lively, emotional person who knew well the entire scale of human emotions. . . . He had a wonderful sense of humor, loved and appreciated a joke, could make jokes himself. . . . Not only would he let me bring in friends from our yard, but sometimes he would insist on it. When kids would drop by, we would start playing right there beside him, while he would sit at his desk, working*

Lev Vygotsky (1896–1934) with his daughter. Vygotsky believed that children's cognitive development is advanced through social interaction with skilled individuals and intertwined within a sociocultural environment.

and from time to time turning around and looking with a smile as we played before immersing himself in his work again. (Vygodskaia, 1995, p. 59)

Although his career was abruptly terminated when he died of tuberculosis in 1934, because of its cultural emphasis his work is more popular now than it was when he died. In contrast to Piaget, Vygotsky relied heavily on social interactions to explain children's cognitive development.

Basic Themes in Vygotsky's Theory

Just as we carefully laid the foundation to help you understand the key concepts in Piaget's theory before reading about his developmental stages, we'll use the same technique here. If you understand Vygotsky's basic ideas, you'll be able to apply his theory to your classroom work. In this way you'll fully appreciate the richness and practicality of his ideas.

Vygotsky believed that he had devised a unique idea of development, one that identified dual paths of cognitive development: (a) elementary processes that are basically biological, and (b) higher psychological processes that are essentially sociocultural (Vygotsky, 1978). Children's behaviors emerge from the intertwining of these two paths. For example, brain development provides the physiological basis for the appearance of external or egocentric speech, which gradually becomes the inner speech children use to guide their behavior.

Three fundamental themes run through Vygotsky's work: the unique manner in which he identified and used the concept of development, the social origin of mind, and the role of speech in cognitive development.

Vygotsky's Concept of Development

Vygotsky's *concept of development* is at the heart of his theory. He thought that elementary biological processes are qualitatively transformed into higher psychological functioning by developmental processes. In other words, speech, thought, and learning are explained by development. Let's concentrate on speech for a moment.

Think of the noises that babies make in their speech development—crying, cooing, babbling—all of which are accompanied by physical movement. Children gradually begin to point at objects, and adults tell them the name—ball, cup, milk. First words come, children start to string words together, talk aloud, and finally restrict speech much the way adults do.

Instead of seeing these behaviors as a series of independent accomplishments, Vygotsky viewed these changes as a *series of transformations brought about by developmental processes.* He thought developmental psychologists focused too often on the *products* of development (babbling, pointing, words, etc.) rather than the *processes* that caused them (Vygotsky, 1978, p. 64). He was the first to admit that we lack definite knowledge about these processes, and they should be the focus of developmental research.

The Social Origin of Mind

Vygotsky believed that to understand cognitive development, we must examine *the social and cultural processes* shaping children (Wertsch & Tulviste, 1992). But how do these processes affect cognitive development? Vygotsky (1978) argued that every function in a child's cultural development appears twice, on two separate planes: first, in an interpsychological category (social exchanges with others), and, second, within the child as an intrapsychological category (using inner speech to guide behavior).

The question now is: What happens to transform external activity to internal activity? For Vygotsky, the answer is to be found in the process of **internalization.** As he stated, the transformation of an interpersonal process (egocentric or external speech) into an intrapersonal process (inner speech) is the result of a long series of developmental events (Vygotsky, 1978, p. 57). He termed this internalization process "the distinguishing feature of human psychology," the barest outline of which is known.

INTERNALIZATION
Transforming interpersonal processes into intrapersonal.

Speech and Development

Although Vygotsky lacked hard data to explain this theory, he believed that *speech* is one of the most powerful tools humans use to progress developmentally:

> [T]he most significant moment in the course of intellectual development, which gives birth to the purely human forms of practical and abstract intelligence, occurs when speech and practical activity, two previously completely independent lines of development, converge. (Vygotsky, 1978, p. 24)

Since Vygotsky viewed speech as a defining moment in cognitive development, let's examine his ideas about speech more closely.

Vygotsky and Language Development

Speech, especially inner speech, plays a critical role in Vygotsky's interpretation of cognitive development. Here, again, we should turn to his basic ideas about language before examining his use of inner speech. In *Thought and Language* (1962), he clearly presented his views about the sequence of language development, which he believed entailed four stages: preintellectual speech, naive psychology, egocentric speech, and inner speech.

Preintellectual Speech

The first stage, which he called **preintellectual speech,** refers to the elementary processes (crying, cooing, babbling, bodily movements), the biological sources that gradually

PREINTELLECTUAL
SPEECH
Elementary processes that develop into speech.

develop into more sophisticated forms of speech and behavior. As human beings we have an inborn ability to develop language, which must then interact with the environment if language development is to fulfill its potential. Michael Cole (1996) employs a garden metaphor to help explain these issues: Think of a seed planted in damp earth in a jar and then placed in a shed for two weeks. The seed sprouts, a stem emerges, and leaves appear. But for further development the plant must now interact with sunlight.

Naive Psychology

NAIVE PSYCHOLOGY

Children explore the concrete objects in their world.

Vygotsky referred to the second stage of language development as **naive psychology,** in which children explore the concrete objects in their world. At this stage, children begin to label the objects around them and acquire the syntax of their speech. They only gradually acquire an understanding of the verbal forms they have been using; that is, they realize that language influences their thinking and shapes their relationships with others.

Egocentric Speech

EGOCENTRIC SPEECH

A form of speech in which children talk, whether anyone is listening or not.

Around the time that children turn 3, **egocentric speech** emerges. This is a form of speech in which children carry on lively conversations, whether or not anyone is present or listening to them. As Vygotsky noted (1962, p. 46), egocentric speech is speech on its way inward but still mostly outward.

Inner Speech

INNER SPEECH

Vygotsky's name for that time in a child's life when speech turns inward and guides behavior.

Finally, speech turns inward (**inner speech**) and serves an important function in guiding and planning behavior.

For example, think of a 5-year-old girl asked to get a book from a library shelf. The book is just out of her reach, and as she tries to reach it, she mutters to herself, "Need a chair." After dragging a chair over, she climbs up and reaches for the book. "Is that the one?" "Just a little more." "OK." Note how speech accompanies her physical movements, guiding her behavior. In two or three years, the same girl, asked to do the same thing, will probably act the same way, with one major exception: She won't be talking aloud. Vygotsky believed she would be talking to herself, using inner speech to guide her behavior, and for difficult tasks she undoubtedly would use inner speech *to plan her behavior.*

In many cases children who aren't permitted these vocalizations *can't accomplish the task!* In fact, the more complex the task, the greater the amount of egocentric speech. Note how Vygotsky and Piaget disagreed about the function of egocentric speech: Piaget believed it simply vanishes, while Vygotsky believed that it's an important transitional stage in the formation of inner speech. But what does all of this mean for your work with children? To answer this question, let's turn to Vygotsky's notion of the *zone of proximal development.*

The Zone of Proximal Development

Commenting on the relationship between learning and development, Vygotsky (1978) noted that learning, in some way, must be matched with a pupil's developmental level, which is too frequently identified by an intelligence test score. Vygotsky believed that we cannot be content with the results of intelligence testing, which only identifies a student's developmental level at the time of testing.

For example, after administering a Stanford-Binet Intelligence test, we find that a pupil's IQ on this test is 110, which would be that student's current level of mental development. We then assume that the pupil can only work at this level. Vygotsky argued, however, that with a little help, pupils might be able to do work that they could not do on their own.

We know that pupils who have the same IQ may be quite different from one another in other respects. Motivation, interest, health, and a host of other conditions produce different achievement levels. For example, our student with an IQ of 110 may be able to deal effectively with materials of various levels of difficulty. That is, when working alone, he might be able to do only addition problems, but with his teacher's help, he can solve subtraction problems as well.

To explain this phenomenon, Vygotsky introduced the **zone of proximal development,** which he defined as the distance between a child's actual developmental level, as determined by independent problem solving, and the higher level of potential development as determined by problem solving under adult guidance or in collaboration with more capable peers (Vygotsky, 1978). It is the difference between what children can do independently and what they can do with help.

Scaffolding

These ideas of Vygotsky lead to the notion of **scaffolding.** Think of scaffolding as a way of helping students move from initial difficulties with a topic to a point where, with help, they come to perform the task independently. Your job is similar to that of workers who build a scaffold around a building they're constructing; they need this support in the early stages, and then it's gradually removed.

Picture a child learning to play tennis. She volleys fairly well but has difficulty serving. Watching her, you notice that when she tosses the ball into the air and starts to swing, her grip slips slightly. You mention this to her and suggest that she change her grip. She tries, and still has difficulty. You remind her of the proper finger placement; she continues to practice; gradually it all comes together, and you fade gracefully into the background.

Scaffolding applies to children's school work as well. Let's assume that a mother approaches you as her son's math teacher. Worried about her son's math, trying to help but feeling uncomfortable with anything mathematical, she accurately concludes she can't fake math skills she doesn't have. So you suggest she show her son how important math is in the consulting work she does, in keeping score in the tennis games she loves, in shopping, and in anything else the mother can think of that makes math relevant. You may also suggest that she get books and software for math games that require problem-solving and logical thinking skills and play them with her son.

While all of this is going on you urge the mother to constantly tell her son, "You're not bad in math; you just need to catch up on a few things." In this case, both you as the teacher, and the mother, while not forcing anything on the child, provide support (a scaffold) that will gradually be withdrawn.

As Vygotsky noted (1978), instruction is effective only when it proceeds ahead of development. That is, teaching awakens those functions that are already maturing and that are in the zone of proximal development. Although teaching and learning are not identical to development, they can act to stimulate developmental processes.

Literary Lunches

Another example of the value of Vygotsky's zone of proximal development can be seen in a phenomenon called *Literary Lunches,* which are becoming quite popular across the United

Helping children move from initial difficulty with a task to a point where, with help, they perform the task independently is an example of scaffolding.

States. Teachers invite several senior citizens to read the same book as middle school students, and then both students and adults meet for lunch to discuss the book. The seniors help the students grasp the more subtle themes in the story, while the students help the seniors realize that most of the students in our schools are good people with ideas of their own. The understanding of both groups is extended and enriched by their interactions.

In one recent class, both groups read the enormously popular *Nothing But The Truth* by Avi, the author of many outstanding books for young people. In this story, the conflict between a student and teacher has community-wide ramifications that hurt everyone involved. Reading this story led to an animated discussion of character development in which the students gained a greater perspective of the forces working on adults, and the seniors acquired a more sympathetic idea of the pressures on students—Vygotsky's zone of proximal development in action.

Language Development

Let's now turn to the specifics of language development. Children quickly acquire their native languages, a task of such scope and intricacy that its secrets have eluded investigators for centuries. As Pinker (1994, p. 276) stated:

> *The three-year-old, then, is a grammatical genius—master of most constructions, obeying rules far more often than flouting them, respecting language universals, erring in sensible, adultlike ways, and avoiding many kinds of error altogether.*

Children proceed from hesitant beginnings to competent usage by the age of 6 or 7 years, and they use language to control their environment. Instead of leaving the table, walking to the refrigerator, and taking out the milk, they may simply ask someone else to do it for them.

Finally, Table 2.5 will help you to identify the most significant differences between Piaget and Vygotsky.

CASE NOTES

Observation   Vygotsky's ideas on cognitive and language development can benefit the students in Marsha Warren's class.

Hypothesis   If she understands the social and cultural processes affecting her students' development, Marsha can more effectively encourage them to internalize their behavior.

Possible Action   Marsha Warren can provide better scaffolding techniques more tightly linked to her students' backgrounds. If she successfully adopts this technique, Vygotsky's notion of the zone of proximal development would come alive with students such as Maria and Sarah. For example, Marsha can search for someone in the community to work with Maria on her language difficulty, and help Sarah realize that she shouldn't let herself be drawn into disputes between other class members.

Table 2.5 KEY DIFFERENCES BETWEEN PIAGET AND VYGOTSKY

	Piaget	Vygotsky
Perspective	Individual child constructs view of world by forming cognitive structures—"the little scientist"	Child's cognitive development progresses by social interactions with others ("social origins of mind")
Basic psychological mechanism	Equilibration—child acts to regain equilibrium between current level of cognitive structures and external stimuli	Social interaction, which encourages development through the guidance of skillful adults
Language	Emerges as cognitive structures develop	Language begins as preintellectual speech and gradually develops into a sophisticated form of inner speech; one of the main forces responsible for cognitive development
Learning	Assimilation and accommodation lead to equilibration	Learning results from the interaction of two processes: biological elementary processes (such as brain development), plus sociocultural interactions
Problem solving	Child independently searches for data needed to change cognitive structures, thus enabling child to reach solution	Two aspects of problem solving: 1. key role of speech to guide "planful" behavior; 2. joint efforts with others

Language Accomplishments

All children, whether they live in a ghetto or in a wealthy suburb, manifest similar patterns of speech development at about the same age. Language seems to be the same experience for all human beings no matter what language they speak, where they live, or how they

Senior citizens and students discuss books and ideas, coming together for lunch and conversation in an activity called Literary Lunches.

interact with their language models (Hulit & Howard, 1997, p. 25). Within a short span of time and with almost no direct instruction, children (from all cultures) completely analyze and acquire their languages at about the same rate (Owens, 1996, p. 233).

Although refinements are made between the ages of 5 and 10, most children have completed the greater part of the process of language acquisition by the age of 4 or 5. Recent findings have also shown that when children acquire the various parts of a given language, they do so in the same order. As Menyuk, Liebergott, and Schultz noted (1995), most children develop words at the same rate and the same ages.

By the time they are ready to enter kindergarten, most children have a vocabulary of about 8,000 words; they can use questions, negative statements, and dependent clauses; and they have learned to use language in a variety of social situations (Berk, 1997a). They have discovered that there are rules for combining sounds into words, and that individual words have specific meanings. They also have come to realize that there are rules for combining words into meaningful sentences and that there are rules for participating in a dialogue.

> By the time a child enters elementary school, he or she is an extremely sophisticated language-user, operating a communicative system which no other creature, or computer, comes close to matching. The speed of acquisition and the fact that it generally occurs, without overt instruction, for all children, regardless of great differences in a range of social and cultural factors, have led to the belief that there is some "innate" predisposition in the human infant to acquire language. (Yule, 1996, p. 175)

Children don't learn to speak by imitating adults nor do most parents reward their children for good grammar (deCuevas, 1990).

Yule goes on to point out that our innate ability isn't, of itself, enough to explain language acquisition. Reflecting Vygotsky's beliefs, Yule stated that our language ability requires interactions with other language users to flourish.

We tend to take language acquisition for granted, but closer inspection of this accomplishment testifies to the enormity of the task. Children seem to be programmed to talk and to use all forms of language to adjust to their environments. The form that the particular language takes—whether English, Arabic, or Cantonese—is incidental. From birth, children tune into the language that they hear around them and feed these sounds into their unique ability to master language.

The Language Components

When linguists examine a language, they identify four major components: **phonology** (or sound), **syntax** (or grammar), **semantics** (or meaning), and **pragmatics** (or usage).

Phonology

Every language possesses certain distinctive, fundamental sounds, which are the **phonemes** of that language. These are the smallest language units. For example, the words *thin* and *shin* sound alike, but the initial sounds differ sufficiently to differentiate the words, thus qualifying the initial sounds (*th, sh*) as phonemes.

The order in which sounds appear isn't that simple. As Pinker (1994) asked, why do we say *fiddle-faddle* or *ping-pong* rather than *faddle-fiddle* or *pong-ping*? The answer is that the vowels where your tongue is high and in the front always come before the vowels where the tongue is low in the back. Try it. Still, this is no real answer; we just don't know why.

The smallest unit of language to have meaning is the **morpheme.** Morphemes may be whole words or parts of words that signify meaning, such as the endings *er, ed,* and *ing.* The word *older* has two morphemes: *old,* signifying age, and er signifying comparison. Morphemes are composed of a series of phonemes (the morpheme *er* consists of two phonemes, while *old* consists of three phonemes).

Syntax

Morphemes are arranged in the grammar, or *syntax,* of a language. The task of any syntax is to arrange morphemes in meaningful sentences. Grammatical studies have repeatedly shown that any speaker can say and any listener can understand an infinite number of sentences. Children learn the syntactic rules of their languages with little adult instruction.

Semantics

As children acquire the basics of their language, they also learn the guidelines that make language such a powerful tool. For example, by the age of 4 or 5, children will have discovered that rules exist for combining sounds into words, that individual words have specific meanings, and that there are rules for combining words into meaningful sentences and for participating in dialogues. These rules help children to detect the meaning of a word with which they are unfamiliar. Called **fast mapping,** this technique enables children to use context for a word's meaning, thus helping them to continue rapid vocabulary development. (Fast mapping is an excellent example of the interlocking relationship between thought and language, as we saw in the work of both Piaget and Vygotsky.)

Grammar seems to be designed to convert ideas into word combinations. The relationship between ideas and words is the source of meaning, or *semantics.* To integrate language elements, children must be able to represent various kinds of knowledge, to combine them, and to evaluate their relevance in context.

PHONOLOGY
The use of sounds to form words.

SYNTAX
The grammar of a language; putting words together to form sentences.

SEMANTICS
The meaning of words, the relationship between ideas and words.

PRAGMATICS
The ability to take part in a conversation, using language in a socially correct manner.

PHONEMES
The distinctive, fundamental sounds of a language.

MORPHEME
The smallest unit of language to have meaning, may be a whole word or part of a word (old, er).

FAST MAPPING
Refers to a child's ability to quickly grasp the meaning of a word from the context in which it appears.

Children use language competently by the time they enter school.

Teachers must be alert to the possibility that students may understand more than they can articulate, which can be an important consideration in assessment of their progress. For example, there seems to be a consistent difference between the rates of comprehension (understanding) and language production (speech). In their excellent series of studies, Menyuk and her colleagues (1995) found that 1-year-old children understand 50 words five months before they can produce them. As these authors stated (1995, p. 175):

> There is a great deal of variation among the children we observed in the rate at which they develop aspects of language. For the most part, these differences in the rate of development did not result in apparent problems in language development. Most of the differences in the rate of development occur in the production of language.

These words could have been written for teachers. Observe students carefully for any signs of a discrepancy between comprehension and production.

Pragmatics

Children must also learn how to *use* their language, which requires the development of *pragmatic* skills. Language is a remarkably sophisticated developmental accomplishment, one part of which is the increasing success children have in making their communication clear.

All children, regardless of their native tongue, manifest similar patterns of language development. The basic sequence of language acquisition is as follows:

- *At about 3 months* children use intonations similar to those of adults.

- *At about 1 year* they begin to use recognizable words.

- *At about 4 years* they have acquired the complicated structure of their native tongue.

- *At about 5 years* children use adultlike language.

- *At about 6 or 7 years* they speak and understand sentences that they have never previously used or heard.

Table 2.6 reviews these developmental changes during the early years.

Table 2.6 THE SEQUENCE OF EARLY LANGUAGE DEVELOPMENT	
Language	**Age**
Crying	From birth
Cooing	2–4 months
Babbling	4–6 months
Single words	12 months
Two-word phrases	18 months
Longer phrases	2 years
Short sentences and questions	2–3 years

LANGUAGE DEVELOPMENT IN INFANCY

Infants tune into the speech they hear and immediately begin to discriminate distinctive features. They also seem to be sensitive to the context of the language they hear; that is, they identify the *affective* nature of speech. The origins of language appear immediately after birth, in infants' gazes and vocal exchanges with people around them. Although these are not specific language behaviors, they are an integral part of the language continuum. During the first year particularly, mothers (also fathers and other adults) use a simplified form of speech (short sentences, high-pitched tone, frequent pauses) called **motherese.** We don't know exactly why adults do this. It certainly isn't an attempt to teach babies language, but it probably indicates a desire to hold their attention and attempt to further understanding. (At any rate, it seems to work; infants clearly like motherese and respond happily.)

Newborns vocalize by crying and fussing, which are forms of communication. At about the sixth to the eighth week, *cooing* appears; these are sounds that resemble vowels and consonants. These precursors of language blend with *babbling,* which then merges into the first words. Language development continues with the appearance of two words, phrases, and sentences. The sequence is as follows.

At about 4 months, children begin to babble, that is, to make sounds that approximate speech. For example, you may hear an "eee" that makes you think that the infant is saying "see." It seems, however, that babbling does not depend on external reinforcement: Deaf as well as hearing children babble. Deaf children, however, continue to babble past the age when hearing children begin to use words. Babbling probably appears initially because of biological maturation.

Late in the babbling period, children use consistent sound patterns to refer to objects and events. These sound patterns are called *vocables* and seem to indicate that children have discovered that meaning is associated with sound. For example, a child may hear the doorbell and say "ell." The use of vocables may be a link between babbling and the first intelligible words. These speechlike sounds increase in frequency until about 1 year of age, when children begin to use single words. At this stage, babbling is still interspersed among the single words.

MOTHERESE
That tendency to talk to infants in short sentences with a high-pitched voice.

Mothers often speak to their infants in a simplified form of speech called motherese.

At about 1 year, the first words appear. (The age can vary markedly, however, depending on how the proud parents or other observers define what qualifies as a word.) Often called *holophrastic* speech, these first words are difficult to analyze. They are usually nouns, adjectives, or self-invented words, and they may even represent multiple meanings. "Ball" may mean not only the ball itself but also "Throw the ball to me." Children's first words show a phonetic similarity to adult words, and children consistently use these words to refer to the same objects or events.

Between the ages of about 12 and 18 months, *children begin to use single words to convey multiple meanings.* At first, "ball" refers to a round, moving object. Gradually, "ball" acquires the meaning of "give me the ball," "throw the ball," or "watch the ball roll." "Ball" now means much more than a round object. When toddlers begin to use their words to convey these more complex ideas, they are getting ready to move to the next stage of language development. The single-word phase flows into the use of multiple words and the development of grammar.

When the *two-word stage appears, at about 18 months,* youngsters initially struggle to devise some means of indicating tense and number, and they typically experience difficulty with grammatical correctness. At first they employ word order to suggest meaning. They do not master inflections (plurals, tenses, possessives) until they begin to form three-word sentences. A youngster's efforts to inject grammatical order into language is a good sign of normal language development.

At about 2 years of age, children's vocabularies expand rapidly and simple sentences, or telegraphic speech, appear. Research indicates that the amount of speech children hear from their caregivers is closely related to a child's vocabulary growth (Huttenlocher, Haight, Bryk, Seltzer, & Lyons, 1991). Although young children use primarily nouns, adjectives, and verbs (rather than adverbs, conjunctions, or prepositions), their sentences demonstrate definite syntactic structure. While the nouns, adjectives, and verbs of children's sentences differ from those of adults, the same organizational principles are present. **Telegraphic speech,** like holophrastic speech, contains considerably more meaning than the sum of its words. For example, "milk gone" means "my milk is all gone."

Once syntactic structure emerges in two-word sentences, inflection soon appears, usually with three-word sentences. The appearance of inflections seems to follow a pattern: first the plural of nouns, then tenses and person in verbs, and then possessives.

Vocabulary constantly expands. As their symbolic activity increases and becomes more abstract, youngsters learn that everything has a name, and their vocabulary expands at an enormous rate (which explains why these months are often called the time of the *language explosion*). Between the ages of 1 and 2 years, a toddler's vocabulary grows by at least 2,500% to as much as 6,000%. The growth rate in the subsequent years of early childhood is less spectacular but still quite remarkable. Estimates of vocabulary are extremely tentative, however, since youngsters know more words than they articulate.

LANGUAGE DEVELOPMENT IN EARLY CHILDHOOD

Children will not speak before they are about 1 year old—this is a biological given and nothing will change it. But once language appears, it is difficult to retard its progress. Usually only some traumatic event such as brain damage or dramatically deprived environmental conditions will hinder development. To give you an example of the staggering rate of language development, let's look at vocabulary growth. As Anglin (1993) noted, the basics of syntax and phonology are acquired during the preschool years, but vocabulary continues to develop constantly throughout the school years.

Anglin estimated vocabulary size by taking a representative sample of words from an unabridged dictionary, testing children on them, and then multiplying the proportion of words the children knew by the total number of words in the dictionary. For example, if a child knew 10% of the words taken from a 250,000-word dictionary, Anglin assumed that the child had a vocabulary of about 25,000 words. Using this technique, he discovered that fifth-grade children knew on the average 39,994 words, which is 29,596 more words than first-grade children, who knew 10,398 words. Consequently, children learn on the average 20.02 words per day from the first grade to the fifth grade.

To encourage language development during the early childhood years, Hendrick (1992) recommended that teachers give students something real to talk about and then listen carefully to what they say. Since young children are beginning to use more socialized speech, try to encourage as much conversation as possible—among teachers and students, among students, and with other adults. (Urge parents to have their children talk about their day during the evening meal, asking the children questions that require more than one-word answers.)

As Owens noted (1996, p. 101), even 5-year-olds use very adultlike language, although they are missing some syntactic structures. Children proceed from hesitant beginnings to almost complete acquisition of their native languages by the time they are about 7 years old. All children manifest similar patterns of speech development; a particular culture has little to do with language emergence, although it has everything to do with the shape that language assumes. Children in France and Kenya, for example, may use different words for the same objects but the appearance of single words, two-word sentences, and other achievements follows the same developmental pattern.

All children likewise begin to realize that they are language users and understand what this means for interacting with their environments. This development is referred to

TELEGRAPHIC SPEECH
The use of two or three words to convey more sophisticated meanings ("milk gone" means "my milk is all gone").

as **metalinguistic awareness;** that is, at about the age of 6, youngsters acquire the ability to "look at language and not through it."

Speech Irregularities

When should a teacher be concerned about the possible existence of a language problem? Youngsters who consistently miss the milestones should be evaluated. Speech/language pathologists, professionals who are trained in speech and language problems, are often available in the schools and should be contacted if there are any questions. (See Chapter 5 for more information on communication disorders.) But don't confuse a serious language problem (such as lack of comprehension) with temporary setbacks or with speech irregularities that are a normal part of development.

As speech emerges, certain irregularities appear that are quite normal and to be expected. For example, *overextensions* mark children's beginning words. A child who has learned the name of the family pet—"doggy"—may temporarily use that label for cats, horses, donkeys, cows, and any other animal with a head, tail, body, and four legs. As children learn about their world, they quickly eliminate overextensions.

Overregularities are a similar fleeting phenomenon. As youngsters begin to use two- and three-word sentences, they struggle to convey more precise meanings by mastering the grammatical rules of their language. For example, many English verbs add *ed* to indicate past tense.

> *I wanted to play ball.*

Some verbs, however, form the past tense by a change in the root.

> *Daddy came home.*

Most children, even after they have mastered the correct forms of such verbs as *come, see,* and *run,* still add *ed* to the original forms. That is, youngsters who know that the past tense of *come* is *came* will still say:

> *Daddy comed home.*

This tendency to overregularize persists only briefly. It is another example of the close link between language and thought. We know that from birth children respond to patterns. For example, infants look longer at the human face than they do at diagrams because the human face is more complex. Once children have learned a pattern such as adding *ed* to signify past tense, they have considerable difficulty in changing the pattern.

The Whole Language Movement

Building on a growing knowledge of language development, many educators, long dissatisfied with the way reading and writing were taught, have adopted a new strategy called **whole language.** A technique by which all language processes (speaking, listening, reading, and writing—including spelling and handwriting) are studied in a more natural context, as a whole and not as a series of facts, whole language has both gathered support and generated controversy.

The whole language movement rests on the basic premise that children learn their language by actually using it and that this should be the acquisition model for reading and writing (Giddings, 1992), especially during the early childhood years. This premise leads to several educational guidelines. For example, oral and written language are best acquired through actual use in meaningful situations. Instruction should be guided by the needs and interests of the learners using real literature as opposed to imaginary and fanciful stories. (Giddings, 1992).

The proponents of whole language believe that it is consistent with Piaget's theory of human development because the individual child's use of language materials matches that child's level of cognitive development. Proponents also claim that it is consistent with Vygotsky's work because of the important role that context plays in a child's attempts to master reading and writing (Tchudi, 1991). Still others believe that the whole language movement is a natural outgrowth of several earlier educational beliefs such as the emphasis on the integrated curriculum and individualized reading (Goodman, 1989).

Explaining the Whole Language Concept

Shifting from dependence on a basal language series to whole language requires teachers to rethink their assumptions about literature and language learning. Many teachers using the whole language technique work with themes, for example, friendship, loyalty, or honesty. First, students will read a story that illustrates the theme. This is known as *experiencing the literature*. Next, the teacher may read a related story or poem; pupils are listening to the literature.

Now the teacher may attempt to *expand* the concepts that the pupils experienced in their literature and simultaneously work on vocabulary using various techniques. Next, students may read the selection cooperatively (taking turns with their partners or reading aloud about a particular character in the story). They then discuss the characters in the story.

Students then *respond* to the literature by completing a story form (finishing sentences with missing words, explaining the beginning and ending, telling how the story's problem was solved). The teacher may ask them to evaluate the characters' actions in the story or give their own opinions about the story. Some pupils may now explore language; that is, if they need help with vocabulary or phonics, or with general reading strategies, they are guided to appropriate activities.

The students then shift from reading to writing. For example, they may write a paragraph explaining a particular part of the story. They apply the words they have learned in their reading to their writing. They can be taught how to proofread and to revise in this phase.

With their reading and writing experiences completed, and if time permits, students may *extend their reading experiences*. That is, if the theme of their work was friendship, they may do independent research that could include examples of friendship in stories, friendship among leaders of nations, or friendship among people of different cultures.

Tchudi (1991) summarized the main features of whole language as follows:

- The *level* of students' language development becomes the starting point.

- Language skills develop *naturally*.

- Instruction capitalizes on the *natural* connection between literature and language.

- *Integration* of all components of the language arts (reading, writing, listening, speaking) is critical.

- Whole language builds on a student's *personal experiences*.

- Language is viewed as a *whole* structure, not discrete units.

Yet many critics of the whole language approach believe that children can miss many necessary fundamentals (such as a thorough grounding in phonics) because of the lack of a structured curriculum. They particularly focus on a child's need for thorough phonics instruction. A controversial topic, the whole language issue needs additional research to provide clear answers to the many questions swirling around the concept at this time.

LANGUAGE DEVELOPMENT IN MIDDLE CHILDHOOD

In middle childhood we find students immersed in a verbal world. By the age of 7, almost all children have learned a great deal about their language. They appear to be quite sophisticated in their knowledge even though considerable development is still to come. During the middle childhood years, children improve their use of language and expand their structural knowledge. By the end of the period, they are similar to adults in their language usage. Children who experience language difficulties, such as those in Marsha Warren's class, find themselves at a serious disadvantage.

Changes in Language Usage

Three types of change in language usage occur during these years (Menyuk, 1982):

1. *Students begin to use language for their own purposes,* to help them remember and plan their actions. They move from talking aloud when doing something, to inner speech. From about age 7 on, children use language to help them recall things. (Remember that Vygotsky thought inner speech guides behavior.)

2. *Language during these years becomes less literal.* Students now use language figuratively. On going to bed, an 11-year-old may say, "Time to hit the sack." Children display this type of language by a process we mentioned earlier, *metalinguistic awareness* (that capacity to think about and talk about language). You can see how this is impossible until children acquire the cognitive abilities discussed in the first part of this chapter.

3. *Students are able to communicate with others more effectively. They understand relationships; they can also express these relationships accurately, using appropriate language.* In a sense, more effective communication is the product of the interaction of many developmental forces: physical growth as seen in the brain's development; cognitive development as seen in the ability to use symbols and to store them; and language development as seen in vocabulary development and usage. Language has now become an effective tool in adapting to the environment, especially the classroom.

Table 2.7 illustrates general language achievements for the middle childhood years.
Table 2.7 is interesting because it encompasses almost all aspects of development for these years. Note the steady progression in motor skills: from acquiring the ability to grasp a pencil and print at about age 7 to writing lengthy essays just three years later. Increasing visual discrimination is apparent in the accurate description of events and the elimination of letter reversals (for example, *b* for *d*). Growth in cognitive ability is seen in the detection of cause and effect, and the appeal of science and mystery stories.

TIPS ON LEARNING
Language in the Classroom

PRINCIPLE   Understanding the spoken word and using a variety of words in their own speech prepares children for meeting words on the printed page.

STRATEGY   Encourage children to make place associations. Tell pupils for the next minute to name everything they can think of that they might find in a grocery store, on a farm, or in a sports shop. Encourage children to use specific names for people and objects.

STRATEGY   Pose problems for children to solve on their own or by acting out the situations with puppets. For example, give pupils the following scenario: Four friends want to go on a picnic, but it starts to rain, and they have to stay inside. What can they do to have fun? Insist that children use complete sentences as they make up their dialogues.

STRATEGY   See how well students listen and understand what they hear by giving them verbal directions for drawing a mystery object on paper. Have a picture of the object ready for them to check their own drawings against.

STRATEGY   Check problem-solving abilities and language skills by giving pupils a story problem and omitting vital information needed to solve it. Ask the children to pinpoint what else they need to know before they can figure out the answer.

Table 2.7   TYPICAL LANGUAGE ACCOMPLISHMENTS

Age (years)	Language Accomplishments
6	Has vocabulary of several thousand words; understands complex sentences; uses language as a tool; possesses some reading ability
7	Is able to print several sentences; begins to tell time; losing tendency to reverse letters (b, d)
8	Can write as well as print; understands that words may have more than one meaning (ball)
9	Describes objects in detail; writes well; uses sentence content to determine word meaning
10	Describes situations by cause and effect; writes fairly lengthy essays; likes mystery and science stories; masters dictionary skills; good sense of grammar

For children between 6 and 10, the relationship of language development (in the sense of mastering a native tongue) to reading is crucial. From signs on buses and streets as they go to school, to an educational curriculum that is overwhelmingly verbal, children must interpret the written word. In our society the functional illiterate faces a daily battle for survival.

(continued)

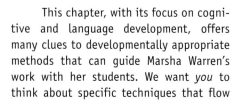

CASE NOTES

Observation   Marsha Warren can use her students' improving communication skills to better their relationships with each other.

Hypothesis   Emphasizing to her students how their language—what's said and how it's said—affects their classmates may help.

Possible Action   Marsha Warren must reach her students who have language difficulties, perhaps through bilingual volunteers, to help them with subject matter and their relationships with other students.

Case Reflections

This chapter, with its focus on cognitive and language development, offers many clues to developmentally appropriate methods that can guide Marsha Warren's work with her students. We want *you* to think about specific techniques that flow from your reading of this chapter. For example, give specific examples of how Piaget's ideas can improve the relationship between Sarah and Bettie Ann, or how you can use Vygotsky's belief in inner speech in the classroom.

CHAPTER HIGHLIGHTS

The Meaning of Development

- The biopsychosocial model helps to illustrate the many forces influencing students' development.
- Knowledge of cognitive development will help with instructional decisions.

Piaget and Cognitive Development

- Piaget's basic ideas help teachers to decide on developmentally appropriate materials and instructions.
- Piaget's theory helps us understand that "children think differently from adults."

Piaget's Four Stages of Cognitive Development

- His stages of cognitive development help us to understand what we can expect cognitively from pupils of different ages.
- Piaget's belief that students must interact with the environment for learning to occur has classroom implications.

Vygotsky and Cognitive Development

- Vygotsky's interpretation of development is at the heart of his theory.
- His use of inner speech and social interactions helps to explain his belief in the relationship between thought and language.
- Vygotsky's concept of a zone of proximal development offers insight into the relationship among learning, development, and social processes.

Language Development

- Like other cognitive processes, language development follows a predictable sequence in children of all cultures.
- Language acquisition offers definite clues to a pupil's developmental progress, which can help you in working with your pupils.

Language Development in Infancy

- Infants immediately begin to distinguish the sounds of their language, and react to the context of their language.

Language Development in Early Childhood

- Vocabulary development proceeds at a rapid rate.
- Whole language is a relatively modern method of teaching language skills.

Language Development in Middle Childhood

- Students become quite skillful in their use of language in settings such as the classroom.

WHAT DO YOU THINK?

1. From your present knowledge of children, do you think Piaget's stages give a realistic picture of a child's cognitive development. Why or why not?

2. Do you think Piaget placed enough emphasis on culture in his explanation of cognitive development? Give specific reasons for your answer.

3. Why do you think Vygotsky has become such a popular figure in psychology? Be specific.

4. How would you use the heredity–environment controversy to explain language development? In other words, do you think language development is mainly biological? Or is it learned? Or is there another explanation?

three

Psychosocial and Moral Development

When Marsha Warren fled from her classroom in despair, she could think of little else to do but slam the door behind her. Standing alone and shaken in the corridor, frustrated as to her next step, she pondered what to do next. Visualizing Jose, Tyrone, Angela—in fact all of the *Infidels*—she thought of something she had noticed just the other day in their reading group. *They all were so immature.* As you read this chapter dealing with psychosocial and moral development, relate their immaturity to this chapter's content to suggest possible avenues for this beleaguered teacher to follow.

In the case study that opened this section, Marsha Warren was constantly challenged by the widely varying maturity levels of her students. When this happens to you, as it will, you'll find yourself seeking insights into the needs of students and searching for appropriate methods and materials to satisfy those needs. A theorist who has dealt with this issue with great perception and sensitivity is Erik Erikson. His explanation of psychosocial development offers many clear guidelines for understanding students' behavior.

A major contributor to the psychosocial health of students is their moral development. During the school years, moral matters permeate students' work: Should I cheat on the next exam? Should I lie about my homework? Should I bring my marks home? In a time when morality has become a national issue, the ideas of Lawrence Kohlberg about the path of moral development deserve our consideration since his work has been directly applied to the classroom.

Consequently, we'll begin this chapter as we did Chapter 2, providing a theoretical basis for analyzing the work to follow. We'll then turn our attention to two critical elements in the psychosocial development of students: the interplay between the forces of socialization and individuation. **Socialization** means the need to establish and maintain relations with others and to regulate behavior according to society's demands. **Individuation** refers to the fullest development of one's self (self-esteem and self-control).

Students will attempt to reconcile the tensions between socialization and individuation by mastering several developmental tasks such as learning to function more independently, recognizing and accepting who they are (that is, coming to grips with their self-concepts in a way that eases the very real struggle between socialization and individuation), developing strategies that lead to self-control and impulse control; beginning to understand and live by moral standards, and knowing what it means to become a member of a society with duties and responsibilities as well as rights.

PSYCHOSOCIAL DEVELOPMENT

We are intensely aware today that children are deeply affected by the social agents (family, school, peers, and the media) that surround them. For example, we know that the rapid brain and cognitive development of infants enables them to take in and interpret information, an ability that continues to improve with age. By linking children's development to the interactions and interrelationships with the critical agents in their environment, Erik Erikson has dramatically called our attention to the significance of social context.

Born in Frankfurt, Germany, in 1902, as a young man Erikson became interested in both education and psychoanalysis. He came to the United States in 1933 and settled in Boston, where he was the first child psychoanalyst in the city. His work with Native Americans and World War II veterans helped Erikson to realize that many emotional problems were due to identity confusion.

Erikson's views on development and the search for identity are widely popular today. He proposed a series of psychosocial stages during which an individual has to establish changing concepts of self and reality. During the "working out" of the psychosocial stages, students will grapple with both positive and negative influences as they strive for self-identity.

ERIKSON'S PSYCHOSOCIAL STAGES

Erikson believed that personality emerges from a series of inner and outer conflicts, which, if resolved, result in a greater sense of self. These crises arise at each of eight stages of life identified by Erikson. Each crisis results in a period of increased vulnerability and heightened potential and can lead to either maladjustment or increased psychic strength. During

Objectives

When you finish reading this chapter, you should be able to

- identify Erikson's stages of psychosocial development

- formulate ways in which the strengths of each of Erikson's stages help students adjust to the crises inevitably awaiting them

- summarize the key ideas in Kohlberg's theory

- suggest techniques that enhance the moral development of your students

- describe the major forces influencing socialization and explain how they affect student achievement

- suggest specific ways to help students acquire a positive and realistic self-esteem

SOCIALIZATION

The need to establish and maintain relations with others and to regulate behavior according to society's demands.

INDIVIDUATION

Refers to the fullest development of one's self (self-esteem and self-control).

Erik Erickson proposed an
influential theory of
psychosocial development.

the adolescent years, for example, teenagers are besieged by self-doubt—about their bodies, their abilities, their popularity—yet with patience and proper guidance, they can acquire a positive self-identity.

In his famous *Childhood and Society* (1950), Erikson stated that *personality develops according to one's ability to interact with the environment.* Society invites this interaction with the environment and encourages and safeguards the successive appearance of the eight stages, the first of which occurs in the first year of life. (The crises, strengths, and major environmental influences that characterize each stage are outlined in Table 3.1.)

The Early Years

The early years of a child's life (birth to 5 years) encompass Erikson's stages of trust and autonomy.

Stage 1. Trust versus Mistrust (birth to one year)

Erikson believed that a healthy personality requires a sense of trust toward oneself and the world, a belief that develops during the first year of life. Infants derive security and comfort from warm relationships with their parents. Cold parental care and rejection cause mistrust and affect all later development. (For a more detailed summary of these studies, see Dacey & Travers, 1999).

As babies develop greater control over their bodies (for example, more accurate grasping of objects), they learn to trust their bodies as well, thus increasing their psychological sense of security. The world becomes a safe and orderly place as children take their first steps toward personal mastery.

Development during this stage has long-term consequences, since research demonstrates that **attachment** (usually to the mother) appears during the last half of the first year (Ainsworth, 1979; Bowlby, 1969). If attachment is not nurtured by the parent or other caregiver, children may not develop the trust necessary to establish lasting relationships with others.

Although relationships with parents are a key element in the development of attachment, other developmental factors also contribute. For example, a child's inborn temperamental tendency to be fearful or relaxed in unfamiliar situations affects that child's behavior. In other words, children are psychologically different from each other from birth, a fact that has been ignored in the attachment studies (Dacey & Travers, 1999).

Children are not born as passive sponges; they immediately seek stimulation from their environment and *instantly interpret and react to how they are being treated,* a process

ATTACHMENT
Behavior intended to keep a child (or adult) in close proximity to a significant other.

Table 3.1 ERIK ERIKSON'S PSYCHOSOCIAL THEORY DEVELOPMENT

Age (Years)	Stage	Psychosocial Crisis	Psychosocial Strength	Environmental Influence
1	Stage 1: Infancy	Trust vs. mistrust	Hope	Maternal
2–3	Stage 2: Early childhood	Autonomy vs. shame, doubt	Willpower	Both parents or adult substitutes
4–5	Stage 3: Preschool, nursery school	Initiative vs. guilt	Purpose	Parents, family, friends
6–11	Stage 4: Middle childhood	Industry vs. inferiority	Competence	School
12–18	Stage 5: Adolescence	Identity vs. identity confusion	Fidelity	Peers
18–35	Stage 6: Young adulthood	Intimacy vs. isolation	Love	Partners: spouse/lover, friends
35–65	Stage 7: Middle age	Generativity vs. stagnation	Care	Family, society
Over 65	Stage 8: Old age	Integrity vs. despair	Wisdom	All humans

From CHILDHOOD AND SOCIETY by Erik H. Erikson. Copyright 1950, ©1963 by W. W. Norton & Company, Inc., renewed © 1978, 1991 by Erik H. Erikson. Reprinted by permission of W. W. Norton & Company, Inc.

called **reciprocal interactions.** Think of it this way: You react to me in a particular manner and I change. As a result of the changes that occurred in me, you change. Back and forth, on and on it goes, constantly changing the relationship.

For example, I tell you a joke and you laugh. Your laughter makes me feel confident. In turn, I feel comfortable with you and want your friendship. You sense these feelings and reciprocate. This same give-and-take occurs in the classroom. Reciprocal interactions are a fact of life and affect all relationships, including those between teachers and students.

Stage 2. Autonomy versus Shame, Doubt (2–3 years)

For Erikson, the theme of the second stage, which usually appears during toilet training, is **autonomy** versus shame and doubt. During this period, personality is shaped by the child's learning the meaning of self-control. These years are decisive for establishing a proper balance between standing on one's own feet and being protected (Erikson, 1950). Parental reactions are crucial, since the objective of this stage is the child's development of self-control with no loss of self-esteem. Loss of self-esteem because of parental overcontrol results in self-doubt and shame; children may feel they can't do anything right on their own.

Although children need to maintain a sense of trust to further their self-confidence, parents, day-care providers, and nursery school teachers must also introduce restraints to help youngsters develop self-control, competence, and maturity. For example, youngsters of this age love to play in a sandbox and love to throw sand. They need to learn to avoid doing things that can hurt other children, even when they want to or when they are provoked. Erikson states:

> Outer control at this stage, therefore, must be firmly reassuring. (1950, p. 252)

Educational Implications—The Early Years

Ideally, youngsters should achieve considerable emotional self-control as well as control of their bodies during these years. If you're working with children of this age, make every effort to protect them from injury and to prevent them from harming others. At the same time,

RECIPROCAL INTERACTIONS

Process in which we respond to those around us and they change; their changed behavior then causes changes in us; emphasizes a student's active involvement in teacher-student interactions, that is, students are not merely passive recipients in any exchange.

AUTONOMY

Erikson's term for a child's growing sense of independence. Attained in stage 2 (autonomy versus shame and doubt).

remember that they need opportunities to exercise and develop their talents, which will help them to acquire sufficient self-mastery to seize the opportunities that life presents.

How you accomplish these objectives will depend on your individual style of interacting with others and the unique personality of each child. From Erikson's perspective, it is important never to humiliate a child, either physically or verbally, when you must impose restrictions. Your use of firm but tactful restraint will help youngsters to recognize and to respect you as an authority figure while retaining their sense of autonomy and initiative.

The Need for Discipline   *Young children require consistent and reasonable discipline.* Since children of this age are so attuned to adult authority, any adult behavior that confuses them can have a lasting impact. As they grow older, children must abide by rules; these years are the time for them to acquire respect for reasonable rules reasonably administered. They won't always obey, of course; when you must reprimand, do so, and then as soon as possible offer a warm response to their acceptable behavior.

The Need for Activities   *Children of this age need opportunities to do things for themselves* such as moving their chairs into a circle, getting out the crayons for an art project, and helping to put the blocks away. Activities that teachers devise will help children gain mastery over themselves and their surroundings, thus contributing to their autonomy.

The Need for Role Models   *Young children also need good role models.* Two- and 3-year-olds love to imitate, so use your behavior to encourage good behavior and to protect them from unwarranted fears. Young children have a limited cognitive capacity as well as an aptitude for fantasy, and they may develop unreasonable anxieties and fears. Unreasonable punishment or, conversely, excessive permissiveness can cause them to become unduly fearful of a parent or a teacher, and that fear may transfer to other adults. Your best reaction to a child's unwarranted fear is to listen, to explain, and to set a positive example.

Try to visualize how the troublesome students in Marsha Warren's class might have been treated during this stage. For example, do you think Angela learned a proper balance between autonomy and self-control?

Stage 3. Initiative versus Guilt (4–5 years)

Children in Erikson's third stage show greater freedom of movement, perfection of language, and expansion of imagination. A sense of **initiative** emerges that will serve as a basis for realistic ambitions and purposes. As Erikson noted, the indispensable contribution of this stage to later identity development is to free the child's initiative and sense of purpose for adult tasks that promise fulfillment of human capacities:

> There is in every child at every stage a new miracle of vigorous unfolding, which constitutes a new hope and a new responsibility for all. Such is the sense and the pervading quality of initiative. (Erikson, 1950, p. 235)

Erikson noted that preschoolers realize who they are, have a lively imagination, are mobile, and have a good grasp of language. Their world challenges them to master new tasks, such as learning to read, adapting to school, and dressing themselves. Their growing symbolic ability, which was discussed in Chapter 2 in the section on Piaget's preoperational stage, enables them to meet the tasks that Erikson identifies for these years. Scoffing at children's ideas and efforts can cause them to develop a sense of guilt.

INITIATIVE

Erikson' term for children's ability to explore the environment and test their world. Attained in stage 3 (initiative versus guilt).

The Role of Play   Parents who encourage children to do things (play, help in the home, etc.) encourage a sense of initiative. Play, this seemingly simple, happy behavior is, nevertheless, difficult to define with any degree of precision. Play is usually thought of as an activity that children engage in because they enjoy it for its own sake. For Erikson, however, play can be just fun, but it can also be an opportunity to further cognitive development, an occasion of social sharing, a means of working out emotional problems (Erikson, 1950). Let's look at each of these.

Play and Cognitive Development   We can say that play allows children to explore their environment on their own terms and to take in any meaningful experiences at their own rate and on their own level (for example, running through a field and stopping to look at rocks or insects). Consequently, play aids cognitive development; cognitive development aids play. Through play, children learn about the objects in their world, what these objects do (balls roll and bounce), what they are made of (toy cars have wheels), and how they work.

Play and Social Development   Play also helps social development during this period because the involvement of others demands a give-and-take that teaches early childhood youngsters the basics of forming relationships. Why are some 5- and 6-year-olds more popular with their classmates than others? Watching closely, you can discover the reasons: decreasing egocentrism, recognition of the rights of others, and a willingness to share. These social skills do not simply appear; they are learned, and much of the learning comes through play.

Play and Emotional Development   Finally, play provides an emotional release for youngsters. There are not the right or wrong, life-and-death feelings that accompany interactions with adults. Children can be creative without worrying about failure. They can also work out their emotional tensions through play, which should provide some funny moments. (Table 3.2 presents several types of play and the ages at which they occur.)

    Another interesting development during this stage is the emerging *role of conscience*. Children now have the ability to cope with the environment, but they are also encountering yes and no reactions from their parents. Consequently, they experience guilt feelings when they know they have done something their parents or teachers disapprove. If children face too many restrictions, they can acquire emotional problems early in life, which may diminish the excitement of initiative. They may become fearful of expressing themselves and thus not be able to fulfill their potential.

Table 3.2 TYPES OF PLAY

Play Type	Age	Definition	Examples
Functional play	1–2 years	Simple, repetitive motor movements with or without objects	Running around, rolling a toy car back and forth
Constructive play	3–6 years	Creating or constructing something	Making a house out of toy blocks, drawing a picture, putting a puzzle together
Make-believe play	3–7 years	Acting out roles	Playing house, school or doctor; acting as television character
Games with rules	6–11 years	Understanding and following rules in games	Playing board games, cards, baseball, etc.

Based on Berk, 1997.

TIPS ON LEARNING

Erikson's Early Stages

PRINCIPLE   A healthy personality requires a sense of trust toward oneself and the world.

STRATEGY   If you find yourself working with infants in a day-care setting, have as much physical contact with the infants as possible. For infants, physical contact helps to establish a sense of security and trust.

STRATEGY   Once separation anxiety appears, be careful of the way that you leave infants. Although you can't be with each child every minute, you can contribute to their psychological comfort and trust by doing such simple things as putting a familiar toy with a child before you leave.

PRINCIPLE   For healthy development, children must acquire not only control over their bodies but also self-control.

STRATEGY   Help students who tend to lose their tempers easily to change. Talk to them and remind them of any times when they maintained control—"Do you remember last week when Jimmy pushed you; you didn't scream? You acted very grown-up. You told him to stop or you would tell me."

STRATEGY   Encourage self-control in students by asking "How would you feel if somebody picked on you?," thus helping them to understand someone else's feelings.

Educational Implications—The Preschool Years

The characteristics of preschool children have led to a concern for *developmentally appropriate curricula*. Consequently, teachers of these children have the responsibility of preparing a developmentally appropriate environment to ensure that children have the right toys or objects to match muscular development and coordination. Children at the beginning of this period, for example, need to use large crayons when drawing. The best advice for dealing with children of this age is to meet them *on their level*, but still challenge them. (Think of Vygotsky's zone of proximal development.)

Youngsters who acquire a sense of initiative will bring to the classroom a healthy desire to face challenges. These are the students who will try to read a sentence, who will attempt a new activity, who are undaunted by facing the computer. Young children have much to learn about the world, and a well-structured environment—including age-appropriate objects in a wide variety of colors, plants, animals—helps them to label and order their world, thus extending cognitive, language, and psychosocial development. Schooling at this level must capitalize on a child's spontaneous learning, thus aiding the development of competence and security, two of the great objectives of this period.

The Middle Years

The middle years (about 6 to 11) find children experiencing the constantly widening horizons provided by school and peers.

Stage 4. Industry versus Inferiority (6–11 years)

Children now possess a sense of being able to do things well; they want to win recognition by producing things, which is the meaning of **industry**. Youngsters in elementary school

INDUSTRY

Erikson's term to describe a child's sense of being able to do things well and to win recognition in this way. Attained in stage 4 (industry versus inferiority).

Calvin and Hobbes   **by Bill Watterson**

are coming into their own; they sense their growing competence, both physical and mental, and if challenges match their abilities, they feel fulfilled. Horizons widen as children encounter a wide variety of people, tasks, and events.

As Erikson noted (1950, p. 227), children

> learn to win recognition by producing things.... They develop industry—that is, they adjust themselves to the inorganic laws of the tool world. They can become eager and absorbed units of a productive situation.

During these years the school becomes a proving ground. Can children establish positive relationships with their teachers? Can they do well in subjects? Are they able to form friendships? Some degree of success contributes to both personal adjustment and social acceptance. Conversely, children who despair of their skills and their status with their peers can easily acquire a sense of inadequacy.

Erikson's ideas of industry and inferiority are particularly relevant for students of diverse backgrounds. Pupils who enter a classroom in which language and customs seem strange may feel overwhelmed by self-doubt. Teachers who encourage these students to bring elements of their cultures into the classroom help to enhance their self-esteem by accepting their identity as members of particular groups. Adults' behavior will set an example for students and motivates those students from different cultures to participate more fully in classroom activities. Teachers can then use students' strength as competent members of their cultures as a bridge to successful classroom work in this new environment with its challenging tasks (Tiedt & Tiedt, 1990).

Educational Implications—The Middle Years

Erikson aptly described the elementary school years in this way—"I am what I learn." For youngsters at this stage, learning occurs from almost everything they do. They learn through play, from their peers, in sports and other activities, and, of course, in school.

Elementary school youngsters understandably are eager to use the abilities that they developed during their first six or seven years. This eagerness means they will inevitably encounter failure as well as success, especially in their schoolwork. The balance between these two outcomes will decisively affect a child's self-esteem. The teacher's task is to channel a child's energy and talent in positive directions.

Teachers help pupils gain a sense of mastery over the environment by matching content with ability (or level of cognitive development, as emphasized by Piaget) so that they achieve at their own levels. Predicting what pupils will do from their behavior (recall Piaget's use of *content*), from tests, and from their classroom work, adults can direct children to tasks that are challenging but within their range of ability. Children can gain a feeling of competence, a sense of being capable, if their performance attains tangible goals.

CASE NOTES

Observation   Achievement and acceptance go hand in hand in this socially significant stage.

Hypothesis   Youngsters of this age who do well in spelling bees, who become team leaders in subject matter areas, and who read well usually are popular.

Possible Action   Marsha Warren's efforts to match content with cognitive level—*for all pupils*—have intellectual, emotional, and social consequences. For example, the *Infidels* seem to be students who need individual attention so that they may achieve greater success, which would improve their sense of self-esteem. What would you suggest to Marsha Warren?

TIPS ON LEARNING

Erikson's Middle Years

PRINCIPLE   Elementary school children acquire knowledge about the world beyond their families.

STRATEGY   Ask children to participate in a global project to track down the origins of foreign products. Have students check their clothing labels to find manufacturing locations. Locate these places on a world map and encourage children to speculate about how the items arrived in your area. Next, ask pupils to look through their kitchen cupboards at home. Are any of the food products from out of the country? Mark these spots on your map, too. And finally, investigate the origins of toys, appliances, even cars. Help children develop a growing awareness of how they are "connected" to the rest of the world.

STRATEGY   Explore local history. Visit historical houses; discuss how children lived in earlier days as compared with today.

STRATEGY   Develop ways pupils can keep in touch with the community: take field trips to manufacturing plants, museums, hospitals, community centers, nursing homes, and so on.

Social Interactions and Educational Technology

Given Erikson's concerns with the relationship between development and social interactions, you may well wonder how computer usage affects psychosocial development. With the growing popularity of educational computer programs and of computer networks, educational technology has become increasingly widespread in classrooms. When computers first appeared in classrooms, many educators worried that students' social development would suffer and that classroom interactions would be adversely affected. However, a review of computer usage by young children (preschool through elementary age) indicated that, contrary to these fears, students working on computers often showed a higher amount of social interaction than students working on noncomputer activities such as art projects or reading (Clements & Nastasi, 1992).

For example, some students showed increases in turn-taking, and others showed increases in providing explanations to other students. The reason for these results isn't clear. Perhaps the nature of computer activities plays a role because some computer activities such as programming large-scale projects are difficult to accomplish alone.

Proponents of networking argue that involvement in networked research projects encourages students' social development. In such projects, students collaborate with others in different locations, sometimes even different countries, using computers connected to the Internet. These projects can be particularly helpful in improving students' knowledge and acceptance of different cultures. Consequently, computer technology, combined with effective social interactions, can produce more, and perhaps better, learning and problem solving, an outcome that Erikson would welcome.

The Adolescent Years

The adolescent years, from about 12 to 18, have come to be identified with Erikson's colorful description of them as the time of "identity versus identity confusion."

Stage 5. Identity versus Identity Confusion (12–18 years)

Erikson's fifth stage sees the end of childhood and the beginning of adulthood. Youngsters become concerned with what others think of them, and peer opinion plays a large part in how they think of themselves. If uncertainty at this time results in *identity confusion*, a bewildered youth may withdraw, run away, or turn to drugs. Youngsters faced with the question "Who am I?" may be unable to answer. The challenges are new; the tasks are difficult; the alternatives are bewildering. Needless to say, adults must have patience and understanding.

Minority children may be particularly susceptible to identity concerns. To help them cope with their search for identity, be sure that everything possible is done to keep these teens in school; attempt to make them more health conscious; identify potential social support systems; develop a sense of group pride; and, finally, sensitize teachers to the needs of these students (Spencer & Markstrom-Adams, 1990).

Erikson believed that the young in our society are searching for something, someone to be true to. They yearn for stability in an age of change, and their search may lead to extremes. But the search is a time for testing both self and the world.

The Search for Identity

Adolescence is the period Erikson is most often associated with, mainly because of his speculations about the adolescent **identity crisis.** Faced with a combination of physical, sexual, and cognitive changes joined with heightened adult expectations and peer pressure, adolescents understandably feel insecure about themselves—who they are and where they're going. By the end of adolescence, those who have resolved their personal crises have achieved a sense of identity. They know who they are. Those who remain locked in doubt and insecurity experience what Erikson calls **identity confusion.** Erikson's views on identity have generated considerable speculation, theorizing, and research.

For example, Marcia (1966, 1980) concluded from a series of studies that adolescents seem to respond to the need to make choices about their identity (particularly regarding career, religion, or politics) in one of four ways:

1. **Identity diffusion,** or the inability to commit oneself; the lack of a sense of direction.
2. **Identity foreclosure,** or making a commitment only because someone else has prescribed a particular choice; being "outer-directed."
3. **Identity moratorium,** or the desire to make a choice at some time in the future but being unable to do so.
4. **Identity achievement,** or the ability to commit oneself to choices about identity and maintaining that commitment under all conditions.

IDENTITY CRISIS
Erikson's term for those situations, usually in adolescence, that cause us to make major decisions about our identity.

IDENTITY CONFUSION
Those who experience doubt and uncertainty about who they are.

IDENTITY DIFFUSION
An inability to commit oneself to choices—the lack of a sense of direction.

IDENTITY FORECLOSURE
Making a commitment under pressure, not as the result of the resolution of a crisis.

IDENTITY MORATORIUM
Desiring to make a choice but lacking the ability to do so.

IDENTITY ACHIEVEMENT
Committing oneself to choices about identity and maintaining that commitment.

> # TIPS ON COMMUNICATIONS
> ## *Erikson's Adolescent Years*
>
> **PRINCIPLE**   During the adolescent years, teenagers engage in excruciating self-scrutiny.
>
> **STRATEGY**   Consider giving teenage students "free time." Have an interesting classroom full of learning aids, interest areas (books, microscopes, educational games, etc.) easily accessible to students. Let students use the items at their discretion, after establishing a few rules for "free time" (ordinary rules of conduct are to be followed: only a certain number are allowed in any one area at a time; when the teacher says time is up, each student must clean up the area in which he or she is working). As the students work independently, you walk around, talking, explaining when asked, but mainly listening. You demonstrate your trust in them. They may also reveal personal problems as well as topics that interest them.
>
> **STRATEGY**   Have each student write a journal entry and submit it to you. Tell students they can write about anything they wish. Many will write about personal problems. After all the papers are submitted, write back answering their questions and commenting on the information in the entries.
>
> **STRATEGY**   Develop communication strategies like rap sessions and pep talks. If students are bothered by something, get them to ask: Is this really worth getting upset about? Present hypothetical situations that relate to their experiences and have the students judge whether the matter is worth their consideration. If students feel that it is, ask why. Help them to discover if there are other solutions to the situation.

The growing and developing youths, faced with a physiological revolution within them, and with tangible adult tasks ahead of them are now primarily concerned with what they appear to be in the eyes of others as compared with what they feel they are, and with the question of how to connect the roles and skills cultivated earlier with the occupational prototypes of the day. (Erikson, 1950, p. 261)

Educational Implications–The Adolescent Years

If you're working with adolescents, try to help your students integrate the physical, sexual, and cognitive changes of adolescence. By urging them to focus on clearly defined goals that are realistic, you'll help them in their search for identity. You'll find that you can help your adolescent students acquire psychosocial maturity by doing the following:

- *Treating them as almost adult;* that is, providing them with independence, freedom, and respect. For example, give them the chance to discuss, argue, and present their own views but always within the framework of classroom control.

- *Challenging them with realistic goals* that coordinate classroom activities with college and career choices. For example, have them research ways in which the math or science that they are studying in class relates to job skills.

- *Using materials that challenge, not defeat,* and that are both biologically and psychologically appropriate. For example, if a student has difficulty reading at the secondary level, try to find reading material that is interesting but not too difficult; that is, high interest, low vocabulary.

- *Constantly addressing the issue of identity versus identity diffusion.* For example, help students to discover their strengths and weaknesses through their classroom work. Suggest they read stories in which the characters work out a personal problem and in so doing find out about themselves.

The Later Years

These years, which extend from young adulthood to old age, although not directly related to your teaching, offer many rich insights into the strengths and problems that all of us face as human beings.

Stage 6. Intimacy versus Isolation (18–35 years)

Erikson's sixth stage, intimacy versus isolation, encompasses the years of young adulthood (ages 18 to 35). He believed that a sense of **intimacy** goes beyond being sexual and involves the capacity to develop a true and mutual psychosocial intimacy with friends, the ability to care for others without fearing a loss of self-identity. Young people of this age continue to develop their identity by close relationships with others. If the young adult fails to acquire a sense of intimacy with others, a sense of isolation may appear. Relationships are avoided and there is a refusal to commit to others.

Stage 7. Generativity versus Stagnation (35–65 years)

During middle age, individuals think about the future of both society and their own children. Care for others is an outstanding characteristic of this period, which implies an obligation to guide the next generation by passing on desirable social values. If a sense of **generativity** (which is similar to productivity and creativity) is lacking, individuals may stagnate, suffering from morbid self-concern. Basic to a sense of generativity is care; that is, individuals assume responsibility for the well-being of the next generation.

Stage 8. Integrity versus Despair (over 65 years)

As Erikson (1950) stated, those individuals who have taken care of things and people over the years and have adapted to the triumphs and disappointments of life are the people who reap the harvest of the first seven stages. The person who can view his or her life with satisfaction and accept its ups and downs has achieved a sense of **integrity,** which implies that one looks back and sees meaning in life. No despair over age, failure, and missed opportunities clouds this outlook. Basic to a sense of integrity is wisdom, a detached yet active concern with life and its meaning.

FOR THE CLASSROOM

In a thoughtful commentary on the role of schools, Erikson (1968) stated that children require systematic instruction. He believed that good teachers, those who are trusted and respected by the community, know how to alternate play with work, games with study. They also know how to work well with students to whom school is just not important right now, something to endure rather than enjoy.

Effective teachers know how to pace their instruction to maximize learning. (This topic is discussed in greater detail in Chapter 13.) If we link the importance of pacing to Erikson's comments, we can see that optimal scheduling and time on task demands a good knowledge of students: their cognitive level, attention span, interests, and motivation.

INTIMACY

Erikson's term for the ability to be involved with another without fearing a loss of self-identity. Attained in stage 6 (intimacy versus isolation).

GENERATIVITY

Erikson's term for productive and creative responsibility for the next generation. Attained in stage 7 (generativity versus stagnation).

INTEGRITY

Erikson's term for the ability to look back and see meaning in life. Attained in stage 8 (integrity versus despair).

Table 3.3 PSYCHOSOCIAL STRENGTHS AND TEACHING STRATEGIES

Strength	Strategy
Hope	Arrange a nurturing environment; provide appropriate, but stimulating, objects.
Willpower	Establish a stable and secure environment that encourages children to exercise their developing skills.
Purpose	Guide activities in a way calculated to enhance students' feelings of mastery.
Competence	Devise methods that teach children to interact effectively with their environment under all circumstances.
Fidelity	Help adolescents know and understand themselves by providing a positive learning atmosphere in which the classroom give-and-take leads to personal insight and realistic self-esteem.

Regardless of the level at which an individual teaches, students will be on the move. Elementary school students may move from room to room for special projects, assignments, special classes (reading, music, art, science, and physical education, among others). At the secondary level, students move from class to class and to various locations for study periods, lunch periods, and free periods.

Teachers quickly become aware of the classroom implications of these activities and build their techniques around them. For example, pupils coming into the classroom from recess need a few minutes to settle down. Adolescents returning from a lunch period usually are not ready to immerse themselves instantly in a subject; they must be led into it through questions, announcements, or other activities that set the tone for instruction.

Remember that student attitudes toward school itself will affect pacing. In the early grades, pupils tend to be swept up in the academic life of the school. It is why they are there. At the secondary level, however, school adds a new dimension; learning must compete with friendships, peer pressure, and rivalries. Accept these facts of school life and build them into planning.

If you encourage students to express their opinions about psychosocial issues and if you model high levels of moral behavior, you will help to advance students' insights into matters of right and wrong. In his biography of Erikson, the noted child psychiatrist Robert Coles has provided us with a pertinent introduction into the processes by which students develop a sense of right and wrong with the help of parents and teachers:

> We learn to trust because we learn about another person. Each of us learns to know a mother, to recognize her in a particular way—which is encouraged and sanctioned and given ritual form by a society and its traditions. Similarly, we learn about right and wrong, what is and is not ours, what we can and what we dare not initiate—all through the experience of approval and disapproval, through the meeting up with the applause or discouragement in more or less ritualized ways. (Coles, 1970, p. 288)

Table 3.3 illustrates how you can use the psychosocial strengths of children (identified by Erikson) to improve teaching.

With these ideas in mind, let's turn to a major concern in the psychosocial world of children, that of moral development.

MORAL DEVELOPMENT

What is meant by the term *moral?* The very use of the word can cause heated debate. Consequently, educators approach the topic cautiously, if at all. However, in a time of terrorism, racism, assassinations, nuclear arms, war, and a burgeoning drug culture, moral education deserves consideration.

> ### CASE NOTES
>
> **Observation** Marsha Warren made several efforts to introduce innovative and motivational elements into her classroom but seemed to stop short of the type of effort to understand her students that Erikson urged.
>
> **Hypothesis** Erikson's message to teachers and students is clear: Make every effort possible to understand students, and the teacher-learner interaction can be both productive and enjoyable for teachers and their students.
>
> **Possible Action** Analyze the descriptions of Marsha Warren's students in the case study. Try to discover any of Erikson's psychosocial strengths in each of these students, and use them to suggest ways of improving their behavior.

What is the school's role in moral education? Some believe that moral issues do not belong in the classroom; others state that moral education goes on in every classroom every day: Students learn about and discuss revolution in history; they detect honesty or deceit in leaders; they wrestle with environmental issues; in other words, moral issues abound. Given these realities, many schools have felt the necessity to address the role of moral development through education.

In the classroom you'll be faced with an unavoidable fact: You make moral decisions every day on real issues such as stealing, lying, and cheating. For example, interviewing thousands of adolescents from 1969 to 1989, Schab (1991) found that the students themselves were pessimistic about the increase in cheating.

Yet you want your students to be good, truthful, kind, wise, just, courageous, and virtuous. You also want them to behave, *in all circumstances,* according to an internalized code of conduct that reflects these desirable characteristics, a tall order indeed! As Mark Twain once said, "Always do right. This will gratify some people, and astonish the rest." To help you evaluate the theories and research dealing with moral development, we would like you to keep these questions in mind:

- How do children *think* about moral development? Do the theories and the research shed light on this question? Do the theories have practical application?

- How do children *feel* about moral matters? The role of emotions in morality deserves our attention because of the manner in which emotions interact with how students think and behave in moral situations. To make this more meaningful, think of yourself for a moment. How do you "feel" when you know you hurt someone else by something you said, even if you didn't mean to? The answer is that you feel awful. So do most students when they do the same thing.

- How do students *behave* in moral situations? Do their thoughts and emotions dictate how they act morally? An intriguing question, one that both fascinates and frustrates psychologists, and one that challenges our ingenuity to answer.

As we begin our analysis of children's moral progress, we would like you to keep in mind that moral behavior is a complex mixture of *cognition* (thinking about what to do), *emotion* (feelings about what to do or what was done), and *behavior* (what is actually done).

The Pattern of Moral Growth

As you read the theories and research in this chapter, try to fit them into a general scheme of moral growth that makes sense to *you*. To help you do this, here is a brief summary of the overall pattern of moral development.

The Initial Stages

As students develop, their thinking, feeling, and behavior interact to produce a general pattern of moral growth. Initially, young children (birth to about 2 or 3 years) begin to learn about right and wrong from their parents. During these early years, modeling is especially effective. Lacking cognitive sophistication, young children who have a good relationship with their parents usually are enormously impressed by what they see their parents doing. So parents who talk to their children, model desirable moral behavior, reinforce their children's good behavior, and use mild punishment if necessary, usually start their children off on a positive moral direction.

The Early Childhood Stage

The next phase (about 2 to 6 years) reflects children's growing cognitive maturity and their developing ability to decide what's right or wrong. They now begin to interact with a variety of authority figures other than their parents—teachers, counselors, spiritual advisers, coaches, directors—who make reasonable demands on them. These individuals assume great importance in children' lives, and by their directions, explanations, expectations, and indicating the consequences of behavior for others, they provide welcome support to a teacher's own efforts.

The Middle Childhood Stage

As children move into the next phase (about 6 to 11 years), they are also interacting with their siblings, with their schoolmates in classroom experiences, and with their friends in games and other social activities. Here they again encounter the reality of rules, rules not established by parental edict. As a result, they learn about making and following regulations *as well as deriving insights into those children who don't*. In this way, children act as both participants in games and activities when they must obey the rules and authority figures when they occasionally make the rules. (Think about the troublesome students described in the case study and how they react to rules.)

The Adolescent Stage

With growing maturity (about 12 or 13 years—the beginning of adolescence is difficult to identify, see Dacey and Travers, 1999), children learn to tame those impulsive actions that clash with the rules and regulations of their society. Adults now become firmer in dealing with older children; they judge them according to their adherence to a set of moral rules. Try to create situations for older students that strengthen their moral judgments and values.

Up to now, for the most part, adults have generally told children what's right and what's wrong. Within the peer group, however, the time has come for students to make decisions on their own. They have to evaluate the values of their friends and decide, on their own, if this is the right path for them. What influences their decisions at such times?

Think of what you know about students' development: Their experiences at home, their relationships with parents and teachers (and other adults), coupled with their grow-

Children quickly become involved in making moral decisions as they weigh their own interests against the claims of others.

ing cognitive ability and unique personality needs, combine to shape their decisions. But you can never forget the enormous pressure of the peer group, which may actually support or conflict with what an adolescent has learned at home.

KOHLBERG'S THEORY OF MORAL DEVELOPMENT

Can students be moral philosophers? Lawrence Kohlberg obviously thought so. Fascinated with the study of a child's moral development during his doctoral work at the University of Chicago, Lawrence Kohlberg (1927–1987) attempted to apply Piaget's cognitive rationale to moral development. His doctoral dissertation forced a rethinking of the traditional ideas on moral development. After teaching at the University of Chicago for six years, Kohlberg accepted an invitation to join the Harvard faculty where he continued his longitudinal studies of moral development until his death.

The Moral Dilemma

Kohlberg believed that moral stages emerge from a child's active thought about moral issues and decisions (Colby, Kohlberg, Gibbs, & Lieberman, 1983; Kohlberg, 1975). He developed his ideas by presenting children with a series of **moral dilemmas** and then asking them *what* they would do and *why* they would do it. The dilemmas were real or imaginary conflicts that forced children to make decisions based on their moral reasoning. Here's a summary of his *Heinz Dilemma*, one of the most famous:

MORAL DILEMMA
Conflicts causing subjects to justify the morality of their choices.

Lawrence Kohlberg
(1927–1987)

A woman was near death from cancer and needed a miracle drug to save her life. A druggist in the town had discovered a drug that worked on this particular form of cancer but was charging an outrageous price for it–ten times what it cost. The woman's husband, Heinz, didn't have the necessary money and could borrow only about half of it. He returned to the druggist to give him the money he had collected and promised to pay the rest later. The druggist refused. Later that night, a desperate Heinz broke into the drug store and stole the drug.

Should he have broken the law? Why? Why not?

Interviewing children after they had given their answers, Kohlberg probed their replies, trying to get at their reasoning. For example, here are some of his questions.

If Heinz didn't really love his wife, should he still steal and break the law? Why? Why not?

Should you do everything you can to save another person's life? Why? Why not?

Heinz stole and we know that's against the law. Is that morally wrong, even in trying to save someone's life? Why? Why not?

Using these and similar questions, Kohlberg was probing ever more deeply to discover how children's thinking affected their ideas about moral issues and how these ideas changed with age. He found that children begin to think about moral issues at about 4 years of age as they begin their passage through the first of six stages of moral development. The six stages are grouped into three levels: *preconventional* (4 to 10 years), *conventional* (10 to 13 years), and *postconventional* (13 years and over). Kohlberg's six stages of moral development are illustrated in Table 3.4.

When students make a moral judgment, they weigh the claims of others against their own self-interest. Children who still believe that the world centers on them can't recognize the legitimate claims of others; they're too wrapped up in themselves. Consequently, some children don't progress too far in Kohlberg's hierarchy; they're like children

Table 3.4 KOHLBERG'S STAGES OF MORAL DEVELOPMENT

Level I. Preconventional (about 4 to 10 years)

During these years children respond mainly to cultural control to avoid punishment and attain satisfaction. There are two stages:

Stage 1. Punishment and obedience. Children obey rules and orders to avoid punishment; there is no concern about moral rectitude.

Stage 2. Naive instrumental behaviorism. Children obey rules but only for pure self-interest; they are vaguely aware of fairness to others but obey rules only for their own satisfaction. Kohlberg introduces the notion of reciprocity here: "You scratch my back, I'll scratch yours."

Level II. Conventional (about 10 to 13 years)

During these years children desire approval, both from individuals and society. They not only conform, but actively support society's standards. There are two stages:

Stage 3. Children seek the approval of others, the "good boy–good girl" mentality. They begin to judge behavior by intention: "She meant to do well."

Stage 4. Law-and-order mentality. Children are concerned with authority and maintaining the social order. Correct behavior is "doing one's duty."

Level III. Postconventional (13 years and over)

If true morality (an internal moral code) is to develop, it appears during these years. The individual does not appeal to other people for moral decisions; these decisions are made by an "enlightened conscience." There are two stages:

Stage 5. An individual makes moral decisions legalistically or contractually; that is, the best values are those supported by law because they have been accepted by the whole society. If there is conflict between human need and the law, individuals should work to change the law.

Stage 6. An informed conscience defines what is right. People act, not from fear, approval, or law, but from their own internalized standards of right or wrong.

From *Moral Development and Behavior: Theory, Research, and Social Issues* edited by Thomas Lickona. Copyright © 1976. Reprinted by permission of Thomas Lickona.

getting on an elevator. Some get off at the first floor; others get off at the second; a few make it to the top. It's the same with moral development: For one or many reasons, many children (and adults) become fixated at one of the lower levels.

Even those children who progress to the third level as adults may not always act in a moral manner. In other words, knowing the right answers to the moral dilemmas doesn't guarantee moral behavior. How many times have you read about greedy and corrupt executives, gruesome murderers, and rapists who are absolutely brilliant? They know all the right answers but are morally destitute.

Take a few moments and study the meaning of the levels and stages and the examples of each. Think about your own students. Do they "fit" any of Kohlberg's levels and stages?

The Early Years

During these years children respond mainly to control; they do the right thing to avoid punishment and obtain personal satisfaction. Children of this age simply don't have the cognitive maturity to weigh the moral worth of two competing arguments; they are at Kohlberg's level I, **Preconventional thinking** (4 to 10 years). Examples of children's moral thinking at the two stages of level I are as follows:

> *Stage 1. You'll be in big trouble if you let your wife die.*
>
> *When you steal, the police put you in jail.*

PRECONVENTIONAL THINKING

Kohlberg's first level of moral development when children respond mainly to reward and punishment (about 4 to 10 years of age).

TIPS ON ASSESSMENT
Moral Development–The Early Years

PRINCIPLE   Moral development occurs because of a child's active thought about moral issues and decisions and interactions with others about these matters.

STRATEGY   Pose a situation for your class in which each class member pretends to be the teacher. The teacher in the story is upset because he knows that someone in his class is breaking bottles on the playground. But no one will admit it. The teacher must decide if he should punish the whole class or ask class members if they know who did it. Have your pupils write down what they would do if they were the teacher. After they have done this, use their answers for class discussions.

STRATEGY   Ask your pupils what they would do in this situation. You have just seen your best friend cheat on an important test that will decide who receives the class prize. Should you tell the teacher? Should you pretend you didn't see it? What will you say to your friend later? If you were the teacher and discovered it, what would you do? Why?

PRINCIPLE   Moral judgments necessitate weighing the claims of others against self-interest.

STRATEGY   It may happen that two of your students constantly are "at each other." The tension between them may even flow into your classroom. Have a discussion with them in which you act as moderator. Try to get each of them to see the other's point of view and work out a plan so that when one irritates the other, they won't start to fight immediately.

Stage 2. You can ride my bike if you let me play with your baseball cards.

Heinz knows that he could wind up in jail if he steals but he can still do what he wants.

The Later Years

Your students in the preteen years are looking for approval because they do the "right thing." Urge them, when you can, to move beyond this level of moral reasoning by helping them to be more sensitive to the feelings of others. When they hurt a sibling or friend, talk about it with them and help them understand what happened. Appeal to your expectations for them, rather than have them concentrate on winning someone's approval. Children of these years are at Kohlberg's level II, **Conventional thinking** (10 to 13 years). Examples of level II thinking (stages 3 and 4) are as follows:

Stage 3. Heinz couldn't look at himself in the mirror if he didn't try to help his wife.

Stage 4. Of course Heinz wants to save his wife's life, but stealing is wrong for everybody; he should find some other way of getting the drug.

If true morality (an internal moral code) is to develop, it appears at about 13 years of age, the **postconventional thinking** level (level III). Laws and the approval of others are not the basis for moral decisions. Moral behavior is determined by an individual's "enlightened

CONVENTIONAL
THINKING
Kohlberg's second level of moral development when children desire approval both from others and society (from about 10 to 13 years of age).

POSTCONVEN-
TIONAL
THINKING
Kohlberg's third level of moral development when individuals act according to an enlightened conscience.

CASE NOTES

Observation   The interactions among the members of Marsha Warren's reading group cause both tension and turmoil in the classroom.

Hypothesis   Thinking about these students leads to the conclusion that Kohlberg's ideas could help her improve the atmosphere in her classroom.

Possible Action   If she encourages them to think at a higher moral level by using any or all of the *Strategies* previously mentioned, she may be able to make them more aware of the needs of other class members.

TIPS ON COMMUNICATIONS
Moral Development–The Later Years

PRINCIPLE   The developmental changes of the teenage years explain many of the conflicts that seem to buffet Level III youth. Frequently, in critical self-examination, they dislike what they see; they become desperate to be popular and retreat into 'everybody's doing it' excuses.

STRATEGY   Balance independence and control. Your task will be to have students accept your control. Fairness in dealing with your students, when accompanied by appropriate opportunities for their independent actions, helps to establish a harmonious, healthy classroom climate. Remember: You are dealing with "almost adults."

PRINCIPLE   Students are impressed by the moral behavior of their teachers.

STRATEGY   Be consistent in your own behavior, don't just talk about fairness and justice to all, but demonstrate these traits when you interact with all of your students, regardless of race, gender, and beliefs.

STRATEGY   Treat all students in the same manner; what's wrong for one should be wrong for all.

conscience." That is, people decide to act on what *they* think is right for everyone, regardless of law or any kind of social agreement. Not many people make it to this stage because it demands a high level of complex and abstract thought. Here are examples of postconventional thinking:

Stage 5. Sure, there's a law against stealing, but saving someone's life is more important. Either change the law for situations like this, or be certain judges interpret it humanely.

Stage 6. Heinz doesn't have any choice. Saving someone's life is more important than a profit on a drug it's more important than any property.

USING KOHLBERG'S WORK
IN THE CLASSROOM

Many teachers are now using moral dilemmas as a teaching tool in their classrooms. As you have seen, these are thought-provoking dialogues that probe the moral bases for people's thinking. They are real or imaginary conflicts involving competing claims, for which there is no clear, morally correct solution.

Some Specific Suggestions

For example, with younger students, you might try something like this: Set the scenario of a classroom with a newly arrived foreign student. Yasmin has just arrived from Lebanon, and she is being mocked by some classmates because of differences in language and customs. Ask your students what they would do if their friends would no longer play with them if they were friendly with Yasmin. Would they risk their friendships by being nice to the new girl?

Since most younger students have had little experience in resolving moral dilemmas, at first you should act as a guide during the discussion and only later introduce more complex issues that require resolution at the stage above students' present moral level. Certain strategies will help make classroom discussions of moral dilemmas most effective.

Ask "Why"

This helps students identify the dilemma and discover their level of moral reasoning. For example, after discussing Hong Kong's reunion with China with older students, why not ask them what people should do if, while working on a Hong Kong newspaper, they were forbidden to write a story critical of the Chinese government. Their family's lifestyle and security could be at stake. Yet the writer feels strongly about freedom of the press. (Ask students why theirs is a good solution.)

Complicate the Circumstances

This adds a new dimension to the problem. Pose this problem to teenage students: Imagine an official in the Cuban government with family in the United States. He is torn between trying to retain power in Cuba and moving to the United States and rejoining his family. Begin by discussing loyalty, then gradually introduce complications, such as civil conflict, family ties, regional or national commitment, and then ask, "What would you have done?"

Use School Examples

Present examples based on incidents at school, such as the pupil who surreptitiously sets off an alarm that disrupts the entire school. Should the teacher punish the whole class unless the offender confesses? His friend knows who did it. When the offender doesn't admit his guilt, what should his friend do, let the innocent class be punished or tell on his friend?

Effective discussions of moral dilemmas also require an atmosphere, conducive to moral instruction, which can be encouraged by the teacher's attention to the following four points:

1. *Create an atmosphere of trust and fairness in which students are willing to reveal their feelings and ideas about the moral dilemma with which the group is wrestling.* In the lower grades, teachers can avoid becoming the authority when resolution of an issue remains elusive; in the upper grades, teachers must work to bring older students to the point where they will share their beliefs with others.

2. *Such an atmosphere results from respecting students and valuing their opinions.* Teachers who are decent and fair in their relations with their students and who respect their pupils can do much to create a positive atmosphere for moral instruction.

3. *An atmosphere of trust does not appear overnight.* Students need time to evaluate teachers, to judge how teachers react to them as individuals. They also need time to decide how teachers will handle sensitive discussions and to feel secure that a teacher will not ridicule or humiliate them.

4. *Be sensitive to what students are experiencing.* Teachers must especially be alert to students who find the discussion painful, for whatever reason. Make every effort to provide a forum—within the group or in private conversation—for them to express their feelings on their terms.

CRITICISMS OF KOHLBERG'S THEORY

As you probably would anticipate, many questions have been raised about applying Kohlberg's work to all individuals in all cultures. For example, parenting practices make a major difference in a child's moral development. Parents who listen to their children and discuss moral matters with them have children who proceed to higher levels of moral development than do children who have parents who yell at and threaten their children (Walker & Taylor, 1991).

Years of schooling also seem to make a difference, with individuals who have higher levels of education demonstrating greater moral maturity. Individuals in industrialized societies move through Kohlberg's stages more quickly and to higher levels than those from less-developed societies. Is this, however, a purely cultural phenomenon? Does Kohlberg's work apply mainly to Western societies? (For an excellent discussion of these issues, see Berk, 1997a, 1997b.)

In a Different Voice

Several commentators have also expressed concern about Kohlberg's use of an all-male group. Most notably, Carol Gilligan (1977, 1982; Gilligan, Ward, & Taylor, 1988) has questioned the validity of Kohlberg's theory for women. Gilligan believes the qualities the theory associates with the mature adult (autonomous thinking, clear decision making, and responsible action) are qualities that have been traditionally associated with "masculinity" rather than "femininity." The characteristics that define the traditional "good woman" (gentleness, tact, concern for the feelings of others, display of feelings) all contribute to a different concept of morality.

As a result, Gilligan and colleagues (1988, p. 7) argued that different images of self lead to different interpretations of moral behavior. Girls, raised with the belief that attachment is desirable, fuse the experience of attachment with the process of identity formation (Gilligan, 1982, p. 8). Boys, however, raised with the belief that separation is desirable, develop along a path of independence. Yet dependence, commonly associated with attachment, is part of the human condition, male as well as female. It implies helping and caring, and the ability to have an effect on others (Gilligan et al., 1988, p. 16).

Current Issues & Perspectives

Schools and Character Development

Addressing the issue of a troubled society and the role of our schools in that society, Lickona (1991, 1993) argued that schools cannot be ethical bystanders. With the realization that our young people are experiencing difficult times, schools are beginning to become concerned once more with the issue of character development. As educators cautiously commence work on this topic, they are attempting to avoid the controversies that surrounded the early values clarification movement, whose programs were intended to help children clarify their own values. Today's efforts are directed at identifying and building into programs such universal values as honesty, kindness, responsibility, and respect, all concepts that teachers have traditionally introduced into their work (Brooks & Kann, 1993).

As Lickona (1993) noted, character development in the classroom takes many forms: a teacher treats students with love and respect; makes sure that students treat each other with care and concern; involves students in a democratic classroom (helping them to accept responsibility); and encourages students to extend these ideas beyond the classroom. In a similar manner, Brooks and Kann (1993) urged teachers to be sure their students understand the meaning of the concepts they are trying to instill. For example, do students really know what "courage," "responsibility," and "respect" mean?

Because there is no way to really know what another person is thinking, we can identify good character only by watching and listening to our students (Wynne, 1988). Therefore it makes sense for schools to encourage and reward the good conduct of their students. For example, the *For Character* program, developed in the Chicago area, publicly acknowledges the good conduct and academic efforts of its students, including such character-building activities as tutoring peers or students in other grades, serving as crossing guards, acting as student aides, acting as class monitors, and joining school or community projects.

The program also provides public recognition to motivate students through awards and ribbons presented at school assemblies and through mention over the school's public address system, and in school bulletins. Such recognition is given to individual pupils, groups of students, and entire classes.

Do you think schools should make a more conscious effort to become involved in matters of character education? Why?

Consequently, since women's moral decisions are based on an *ethics of caring* rather than a *morality of justice,* Gilligan argues for a different sequence for the moral development of women. For males, *separation from mothers* is essential to the development of masculinity, whereas for females, femininity is defined by *attachment to mothers*. Male gender identity is threatened by attachment, whereas female gender identity is threatened by separation. Women define themselves through a context of human relationships and judge themselves by their ability to care (Gilligan, 1982, p. 17).

Gilligan does not argue for the superiority of either the male or the female sequence but urges that we recognize the difference between the two. As she notes, by recognizing two different modes, we can accept a more complex account of human experience, which acknowledges the importance of separation and attachment in the lives of men and women, and we can discover how these events appear in different modes of language and thought.

Carol Gilligan

SOCIALIZATION AND DEVELOPMENT

Using the work of Erikson and Kohlberg as a basis for interpretation, we now turn to the interplay of two powerful influences that shape a student's psychosocial development: socialization and individuation. As we mentioned in the chapter opening, socialization refers to those forces that help your students establish and maintain satisfactory relationships with others and regulate their behavior to meet society's demands. As you can well imagine, the role of the family is critical in the socialization process. Individuation, on the other hand, refers to the processes that help students achieve their personal potential, especially the means by which your students acquire a sense of self-esteem.

First, let's turn to the socialization process and focus on the role of the family.

The Changing Family

The family has long been recognized as *the* great socializing agent in children's lives. Remember that all families are dynamic, not static. Families change, and as they do, they exercise different effects on a child's development—some significant, others not so (Scarr, 1992).

For example, children who remain in an intact family, or who experience the death of a parent, or who go through a parental divorce have unique experiences that must affect both development and learning. We need not be so dramatic, however. All families sustain normal change in the course of the lives of their members.

The fastest-growing group of single parents is that of the nonadolescent, nonmarried woman.

As a result of these changes, the very idea of what constitutes parenting has been drastically altered for both men and women. Mothers often work outside of the home (whether by choice or necessity), which means that their children may require some form of day care. Many fathers take an active, nurturing role with their children as the traditional family roles are changing. As more women enter the workforce, attachment research has raised new questions: How much separation from its mother can a child tolerate? How far can the fibers of attachment be stretched before they break? How does a child's development change because of a father's more active involvement? If there's one thing we've learned about the relationships between parents and their children, it's this: What's right means what works for parents and their children in their culture.

Children of different ages, with different problems, and from different cultures need different types of parenting. We're quite sure now that parents and children actually *construct* their relationships; no one model fits all children and parents. Parents do many things—select clothes, limit television time, impose rules—but they themselves can't determine the nature of the relationship with their children. Parents and children are in it together, for better or worse, which is why children inevitably feel the tensions of divorce.

Children of Divorce

The United States has a larger number of single parents than any other developed country. About 25% of our children live with one parent. Who are these single parents? Although you probably answered that most of them are divorced—and you'd be right, about 65% of single parents are divorced—single parents represent a remarkably diverse group. They may be divorced, widowed, unmarried (about 2.5 million women have elected to have children outside of marriage), female, male (about 12% of all single parents are fathers, almost all of whom are divorced), adolescents or in their 30s, natural parents or adopting parents (Weinraub & Gringlas, 1995). Another distressing fact children must face is that the divorce rate following a remarriage is higher than that in first marriages, thus children can experience the effects of divorce, then a period of several years in a single-parent home, then the changed circumstances of a remarriage, and then another divorce (Hetherington & Stanley-Hagan, 1995).

We can only guess at the effects of those angry, tense times before separation and divorce, and also the difficult days following the divorce. Divorce affects children in complex ways we don't yet fully understand (Fagot, 1995). Not only is their physical way of life changed (perhaps a new home or reduced standard of living), but psychologically children are immersed in an emotionally charged home environment and in a world of deteriorating relationships, conditions that may reach into the classroom and affect achievement.

When families experience difficulties such as divorce, learning is usually affected. Following a divorce, research has disclosed that children are absent from school more frequently and often are more disruptive in the classroom than they previously were. Peer relationships may suffer when parental divorce occurs during the middle childhood years, and, in general, their social behavior seems to deteriorate. That is, girls become more dependent, and boys become more aggressive. Academic competence also declines (Collins, Harris, & Susman, 1995). Yet there is a positive side to school attendance: Teachers and fellow students may offer needed support during a child's time of distress. (Marsha Warren doesn't have much to say about the families of her students. What she does mention reveals that most of her contact with family members was negative. Think about this.)

Day Care

Another consequence of changes in the American family is the rapid increase in the number of children in **day care.** Almost two-thirds of women with children under age 14, and more than one-half of mothers with children under age 1, are in the labor force. In fact, the single largest category of working mothers is those with children under age 3 (Zigler & Lang, 1991). Estimates are that by the year 2000, about 70% of mothers with children under 6 years will be employed outside of the home (Clarke-Stewart et al., 1995). What happens to children while their parents are at work? Obviously someone must be taking care of these youngsters, and it is precisely here that questions are raised about day care. How competent are the individuals who offer these services? Is the day-care center healthy and stimulating? Is it safe? What are the long-term developmental consequences of day-care placement?

Facts about Day Care   Reliable facts about day care are hard to come by, chiefly because of the lack of any national policy that would provide hard data. About 35,000 to 40,000 "places" provide day-care services (that is, principal income is from offering child care). "Places" is perhaps the best way to describe these facilities because of the wide variety of circumstances that exist: Zigler and Lang (1991) refer to them as a "patchwork of arrangements." For example, one mother may charge another mother several dollars to take care of her child. A relative may care for several family children. Churches, businesses, and charities may run large operations. Some may be sponsored by local or state government as an aid to the less affluent. Others are run on a pay-as-you-go basis. Almost everyone agrees that the best centers are staffed by teachers who specialize in day-care services (about 25% of day-care personnel).

Developmental Outcomes of Day Care   Regardless of what you may have heard or read, no definite conclusions have been reached concerning the long-term developmental consequences of day care. One reason is that careful follow-up of children from day care is not yet available (Clarke-Stewart, 1993). Conclusions about the developmental outcomes of day care often conflict and reveal the uncertainty of our present knowledge. Consequently, we must exercise caution about either positive or negative statements concerning the effects of day care.

DAY CARE
A place where a child spends part of a day outside of his or her own home in the care of others.

Almost two-thirds of women with children under age 14, and more than one-half of mothers with children age 1, are in the labor force.

Several general findings about day-care placement are possible, however (Clarke-Stewart et al., 1995):

- *Physical development.* Children typically maintain their normal course of physical development during their time in day care. Disadvantaged children gain height and weight rapidly and advance their motor skills in a day-care setting;

- *Cognitive development.* Children with experience in day care during the early childhood years manifest more-advanced cognitive and language development than those who remain at home. Since most studies have been of good centers, questions arise about centers of poorer quality. Also, do individual differences in the children affect the results?

- *Social development.* Children in day care seem to be more assertive, independent, and self-confident. These children have also been found to be less pleasant, polite, and compliant with adults' requests.

As you read these conclusions, you see how difficult it is to obtain reliable data because the findings are still shaky.

Homelessness

Traditional definitions of *homelessness* focused on the lack of a permanent place to live. Researchers now, however, tend to be more specific and concentrate on those who rely on shelters for their residence, or who live on the streets or in parks. The homeless today represent a different population from the days when they were seen as alcoholic men clustered together on skid rows. The so-called new homeless population is younger and much more mixed: more single women, more families, and more minorities.

Families with young children may be the fastest-growing segment of today's homeless population. On any given night, 100,000 children in this country will be homeless (Walsh, 1992). They are also characterized by few social contacts, poor health, and a high level of contact with the criminal justice system. Although the paths to homelessness are many, we cannot avoid discussing the role that poverty plays in this growing phenomenon.

The homeless in today's society include more single women and families than before.

The Impact of Homelessness on Development   Homeless children are particularly vulnerable to health problems, hunger and poor nutrition, developmental delays, psychological problems, and educational underachievement (Rafferty & Shinn, 1991). Homelessness seems to be a composite of several conditions and events: poverty, changes in residence, schools, and services, loss of possessions, disrupted social lives, and exposure to extreme hardship (Molnar & Rubin, 1991). Any one of these conditions, or any combination, may produce different effects on children such as the following:

- *Health problems.* Homeless children have much higher rates of acute and chronic health problems, which may have their roots in the prenatal period (Reed-Victor & Stronge, 1997). For example, homeless women have significantly more low-birth-weight babies and experience greater levels of infant mortality. Their children are more susceptible to asthma, ear infections, diarrhea, and anemia. As you might expect, these children are also subject to immunization delays.

- *Hunger and poor nutrition.* A homeless family often struggles to maintain an adequate and nutritionally balanced diet while living in a hotel: no refrigerator, no stove, poor food, and lack of food. Homeless children and their families often depend on emergency food assistance. But many times those facilities are themselves suffering from a lack of resources, such as a lack of playing areas, with the result that the children, and their families, go hungry (Bartlett, 1997).

- *Developmental delays.* Homeless children experience, to a significantly higher degree than typical children, coordination difficulties, language delays, cognitive delays, social inadequacies, and a lack of personal skills. For example, they don't know how to eat at a table. The instability of their lives, the disruptions in child care, an erratic pattern of schooling, and how parents adapt to these conditions also impede development (Molnar & Rubin, 1991).

- *Psychological problems.* Homeless children seem to suffer more than typical children from depression, anxiety, and behavioral problems. Again, remember the composites of homelessness discussed earlier that may contribute to these psychological problems. Data are simply lacking that enable us to identify the particular aspect of homelessness that causes a child's anxiety or depression. We must also consider that parental depression affects children and that children's problems may reflect the parents' feelings of helplessness.

- Parental stress often translates into poor parenting practices (depression, irritability, abuse), which can lead to behavioral and emotional problems and academic difficulty. Finally, as we are aware from the daily news, these children often witness, and are the targets of, violence such as physical assault, rape, and shootings. The danger in all of this, of course, is that poverty becomes a self-perpetuating cycle (Huston, McLoyd, & Garcia Coll, 1994).

- *Educational underachievement.* As we have seen, little research has been done on this issue other than to show that homeless children do poorly on reading and mathematics tests (Reed-Victor & Stronge, 1997). This finding should come as no surprise, given that these children have difficulty in finding and maintaining free public education for substantial periods. Missing educational opportunities is bad enough, but with the frequent moves their families make, these children also miss the remedial work they so urgently need. As Rafferty and Shinn (1991) note, school is especially critical for homeless children because it often produces a sense of stability that is otherwise lacking.

In her interviews with homeless children, Walsh (1992) noted that children, because of their status and lack of power, cannot directly solve the problem of homelessness. Instead they concentrate on coping with the emotions that arise from becoming homeless, perhaps by restructuring the circumstances surrounding their homelessness. Younger children, for example, may unrealistically attribute their problems to some external event that is unrelated to them or their parents. Older children may try to explain away the cause, especially if it pertains to a parent. For example, rather than blame a parent's alcoholism or drug use, a youngster may say that the parent is sick or has problems.

CASE NOTES

Observation   Socialization, that process producing satisfactory relationships with others, has faltered for some students in Marsha Warren's classroom.

Hypothesis   Her efforts to improve relationships have failed, and she still has unruly students upsetting the rest of the class and hindering learning.

Possible Action   Marsha Warren's attempts to involve the students' parents seem to have been minimal, and she should try to establish closer contact with the families of these students, including home visits.

Homelessness and poverty have robbed these children of a good part of their childhood. They have been forced to worry about the things that most children take for granted—food, safety, and a roof over their heads. Some become "little adults" in their efforts to help themselves and their families to survive. And yet, as their stories remind us, they are children. They cherish their toys, they play at the hint of any opportunity, they rush to get lost in the world of fantasy. They think in the magical and concrete ways of children, constructing their world with the logic of childhood. And they make clear in their stories that they would like to be treated as children—to be less burdened by worry and more able to depend on adults for the basics of survival. (Walsh, 1992, p. 178)

Individuation and Development

While family, school, and friends are forces designed to help children adjust to the rules and regulations that encourage them to maintain satisfactory relationships with others and to function smoothly in society, individuation refers to those processes that inspire children to become the best they can possibly be. To help you understand these phenomena, we'll trace the development of self-identity and self-esteem as examples of individuation.

The Emerging Self

Imagine for a moment you're looking in a mirror. What do you see? Don't laugh; *you* see *you*. But what exactly do you see? When you look in the mirror, you see yourself, of course. But there are two sides to this vision of yourself. The first is referred to as the "I" self, that part of you that is doing the actual looking. The second part of what you see is the "Me" self; that is, the "Me" is the person being seen (Harter, 1993).

We have the great American psychologist, William James, to thank for this division of the self into two distinct parts. James believed that the "I" part of the self was the knower that thinks, makes judgments, recognizes it's separate from everything it sees, and controls the surrounding world. The "Me," on the other hand, is the object of all of the "I's" thinking, judging, and so on. Think of the "Me" as your self-image, which helps you to understand how the "I" develops feelings of self-esteem: As a result of the "I" evaluating the "Me's" activities, the self is judged good or bad, competent or incompetent, masterful or fumbling. As another great American psychologist, Jerry Seinfeld, once said, "I can't marry her. She's too much like myself. I hate myself."

When I and Me Are We

As a practical example of the relationship between I and Me, consider the case of Julia Ming Gale. Born in Taiwan of Chinese parents, adopted by American Caucasian parents, product of an American upbringing, Julia Ming Gale often looks in the mirror and asks herself, "Who am I?" In her mind she sees a young woman with curly red hair, green eyes, and freckles, an image that causes her considerable sadness. Adopted by parents with two children of their own, the Gales had lived in Taiwan for three years, studied the Chinese language, had many Chinese friends, and kept Chinese items in their American home—books, scrolls, and furniture.

But Ming's world was Caucasian and she couldn't recall a time when she didn't feel Caucasian, even though every time she looked in the mirror she faced an inescapable reality: the face looking back at her was Chinese. Periodic reminders of her Chinese heritage plagued her. Once doing the dishes, her younger brother came in with a friend. Telling his friend she was the maid and didn't speak any English, her brother was joking, but Ming still remembers the hurt. Bewildered, she began to fantasize that her birth mother was some famous Asian woman.

Nevertheless, her inner self didn't want to be any more Chinese than she had to be, and she resisted any efforts her parents made to encourage the flourishing of her Chinese roots. She just wanted to be treated as another Caucasian. By the time she was 12, she learned she had been born in Taiwan, not in China, which only increased her sense of cultural rootlessness. She was bothered that she couldn't claim the culture she grew up in. She even tried to force herself to "go Chinese," but it didn't work. Wanting to be Caucasian, she couldn't bridge the gap between the two cultures.

As her parents gradually realized what she was going through, they tried to help her reconcile her conflicts. Ming, at 24 years of age, has slowly started to explore her Chinese background through language lessons, courses in Chinese history, and readings that show her interest in both China and adoption. The career she has chosen reflects her own background: helping Chinese adoptees discover their identities, to help them live with the duality that caused her so much pain.

In Ming's case two selves existed in conflict and she spent more than two decades trying to reconcile the differences between them. A novelist couldn't create a better example illustrating how knowing who you are shapes a child's development, furnishing the poise and assurance to undertake challenges they may otherwise shun. Too often children feel a conflict between the self they want to be and what they actually see themselves as, two different versions of the same self, *when "I" and "Me" are "We."*

The Development of Self

How do your students construct a sense of **self,** this sense of who they are and what makes them different from everyone else? In a famous and ingenious study of self development, psychologists Michael Lewis and Jean Brooks-Gunn (1979) devised different strategies for uncovering how children discover they are distinct from their surroundings.

- Working with infants between 5 and 8 months old, the investigators placed them before a mirror. The children looked at themselves intently, smiled at their images, and even waved at the mirror, but gave no indication that they knew they were looking at themselves.

- Next, infants between 9 and 12 months reached out to the mirror to touch their bodies and turned toward other people or objects reflected in the mirror.

- The researchers then dabbed red rouge on the noses of infants between 15 and 18 months. When they saw themselves in the mirror, they pointed to their noses (on their own faces, not in the mirror) and tried to rub off the rouge.

- Finally, between 21 and 24 months, infants used their names and correctly applied personal pronouns. When placed with other same-sex infants in front of the mirror, they accurately identified themselves.

We're safe in saying, then, that children will usually have acquired a sense of self by 18 months of age.

After infants take this initial step on the path to self development and understanding, the next phase centers on the early childhood years. Children's growing—even astonishing—ability to understand things provides them with ever-deepening insights into themselves. When asked to tell who she was, a 4-year-old replied as follows:

I go to preschool. I like it. I play with my brother a lot. I have dark brown hair. I like to talk.

Here are the comments of a 6-year-old girl when asked to describe herself:

I'm the youngest in my family. I'm happy most of the time. I like riding my bike. I eat a lot and I like different kinds of food. I have brown eyes. I have lots of freckles. I like almost everybody and I have lots of friends. Sometimes I get a little scared. When I'm a little older, I want to be a babysitter and I'll protect people. When I grow I'm going to be a librarian.

Her reactions are fairly sophisticated for a 6-year-old. Note the more abstract ideas of happiness, friendship, and protecting others, concepts that usually appear at later ages. Most children of her age focus on the physical—hair color, color of eyes, and so on—or on tangible objects such as food, toys, even freckles.

As children grow, their sense of self isn't limited to their reflections in a mirror; they have acquired language and are able to tell us what they think of themselves. Note how children change from identifying themselves by physical characteristics (hair or eye color) to more social and emotional characteristics (feeling good or bad about themselves). As they get older, they usually begin to compare themselves with others. Here are the remarks of a 9-year-old girl when she described herself:

I'm going to be a hippie for Halloween. I'm good at rollerblading. I like going to the movies and playing basketball. I wear a ponytail. I've got a lot friends who like me because I'm a good friend. When I'm through school, I'm going to be a pastry chef. Now I've got a brain drain.

Culture also contributes to self development. Here is an adolescent Mexican American boy speaking:

As I moved to junior high, the issue of my ethnicity became a problem. I remember thinking I would be a great deal more popular if only I had Bobby's face and body and brains. I would look in the mirror and imagine what I would look like. (The mythical Bobby was, of course, always white and popular with girls.) (Schoem, 1991)

As you can see, many elements contribute to the sense of self. Physical, cognitive, and psychological influences all are active forces in self development. Table 3.5 lists several of the factors contributing to a sense of self.

The Changing Self

We'll now demonstrate the tight link between your students' realistic self-esteem and their attainment of competence. What do we mean by **self-esteem?** A good way to think of it is as a feeling of confidence and self-satisfaction with one's self. Self-esteem seems to be composed of several elements that contribute to a child's sense of worth:

SELF-ESTEEM
A feeling of confidence and self-satisfaction with one's self.

- *A sense of physical safety.* Children who feel physically secure aren't afraid of being harmed, which helps to develop feelings of confidence.

Table 3.5 FACTORS CONTRIBUTING TO A SENSE OF SELF

Physical	Cognitive	Language	Psychosocial	Gender
Health	Representation	Speech	Attachment	Identity
Coordination	Evaluation	Referents	Separation	Role
Appearance	Problem solving	Labeling	Relationships	Stereotypes

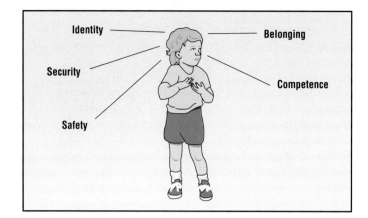

FIGURE 3.1

Elements contributing to self-esteem

- *A sense of emotional security.* Children who aren't humiliated or subjected to sarcasm feel safe emotionally, which translates into a willingness to trust others.

- *A sense of identity.* Children who know "who they are" have achieved a degree of self-knowledge that enables them to take responsibility for their actions and relate well with others.

- *A sense of belonging.* Children who are accepted by others are comfortable in seeking out new relationships and begin to develop feelings of independence and interdependence.

- *A sense of competence.* Children who are confident in their ability to do certain things are willing to try to learn to do new things and persevere until they achieve mastery (Youngs, 1991). Figure 3.1 illustrates these influences.

Concern with competence appears at about 7 or 8 years of age and suggests that developmental changes occur in self-esteem. Interestingly, before entering school, children coming from a supportive home typically feel very good about themselves, very self-important. As they begin to measure themselves against their classmates, however, confidence in their own abilities becomes more realistic. By the second grade, what they think about their self-esteem comes close to the opinions of those around them. In other words, children's evaluations of their abilities match teacher ratings, test scores, and direct observations (Berk, 1997b).

Self-Esteem and Competence

Beware the pop books discussing self-esteem; most of them have detailed suggestions for improving a child's self-something (self-concept, self-esteem, self-efficacy, etc.) without any clear idea of what they're talking about. Susan Harter, a developmental psychologist at the University of Denver, has been a longtime student of the self, self-development, self-concept, and self-esteem, and her research has been a beacon of light in an otherwise murky field (Harter, 1993).

Studying children 8 to 13 years of age, Harter identified five types of competence that seem to be central to a child's level of self-esteem: scholastic competence, athletic competence, social acceptance, behavioral conduct, and physical appearance. Trying to determine what produces a child's sense of self-esteem, Harter posed a basic question:

How do children's evaluations of their competency affect the level of their self-esteem?

Many factors contribute to a sense of self and also affect feelings of self-esteem.

Devising a questionnaire that tapped children's perception of their competence, the researchers used items such as the following:

Some kids have trouble figuring out the answers in school.

but

Other kids can almost always figure out the answers.

Children would then indicate which of the answers best described them, thus creating a profile of their feelings of competence. The results were fascinating. Children don't feel they do equally as well in all five types of competence Harter identified. Most children show a "sawtooth" profile, indicating that they feel good about themselves in some activities but not so good in others. Not only that but some children who have noticeably different profiles have quite similar levels of self-esteem. Other children, with similar profiles, have vastly different levels of self-esteem. Table 3.6 shows the profiles of two children. (Note the difference in level of self-esteem for these two children.)

You can see from the data in Table 3.6 that each child has a similar profile but a much different level of self-esteem. Self-esteem was affected only by the things they viewed as important (social acceptance, looks, etc.). The first child did not see school or athletics as important; therefore, not doing well academically or athletically doesn't matter. The other child, however, valued sports and studies and feels inadequate with an accompanying loss of self-esteem.

In the second phase of her study, Harter probed to discover how what others think about children affects their self-esteem. She used questions similar to the following:

Some kids have classmates that like the kind of person they are.

but

Other kids have classmates who do not like the kind of person they are.

The results were as you probably anticipated. Children who receive considerable support from the important people in their environment had a high regard for themselves. Those who obtain little, if any, support from their significant others showed the lowest self-esteem. Taken together, these findings provide you with penetrating insights into how children acquire their sense of self-esteem.

Examining the data, Harter proposed several troublesome questions about the information she and her colleagues uncovered. For example, in all of her studies there was a

Table 3.6 SIMILAR PROFILES—DIFFERENT LEVELS OF SELF-ESTEEM

Child 1

	Scholastic Competence	Athletic Competence	Social Acceptance	Behavioral Conduct	Physical Appearance	Self-Esteem
High					•	•
Medium			•	•		
Low	•	•				

Child 2

	Scholastic Competence	Athletic Competence	Social Acceptance	Behavioral Conduct	Physical Appearance	Self-Esteem
High					•	
Medium			•	•		
Low	•	•				•

CASE NOTES

Observation   One possible explanation for the behavior of the *Infidels* may be their lack of self-esteem.

Hypothesis   Children and young adolescents for whom personal appearance and the opinion of others determine their sense of self have lower levels of self-esteem. Those who believe that their sense of self and their competency caused others to think highly of them have higher levels of self-esteem.

Possible Action   This lesson should be clear for Marsha Warren: To help children enhance their self-esteem, she should encourage her students to examine their sense of worth carefully, but not to look through the glass darkly. Make some specific suggestions that she could use for each of the *Infidels*.

strong link between what children thought of their physical appearance and their level of self-esteem. In fact, what children think of their looks is the leading predictor of their self-esteem. As Harter wondered, is self-esteem only skin deep?

Harter asked the young adolescents in her study whether they felt that their appearance determined their self-esteem or did their sense of worth lead them to favorably evaluate their looks. She discovered that those who believed their looks determined their self-esteem felt worse about their appearance, had lower self-esteem, and were more subject to bouts of depression.

Teachers (and students' parents) must walk a thin line between providing the necessary support and encouragement for students to face "the great battle of life" on the one hand and the equal necessity of keeping their feet securely planted in reality on the other. We again want to emphasize the need to praise and recognize children's *honest* achievements.

But if an adult's reactions are an island of praise in a sea of neutral, even negative, evaluations, eventually children will ignore the praise. Children shouldn't be subjected to a salvo of criticisms, but reactions to their efforts can't be transparently false. You can't fool your students; they cut right through any sham, especially if something is meaningful to them. It's better to be honest. "You didn't do that well this time, but I know if you study (practice, rehearse, whatever the activity) hard, you'll do better next time." Honest evaluation, coupled with support and encouragement, go a long way toward deserved self-esteem.

There is, however, a flip side to this positive look we've taken at the self. For their own good, and the good of those around them, students must develop self-control.

The Self in Self-Control

For children to be successful in any of their endeavors and enjoy pleasant relationships with others, they must exercise restraint in deciding what to do, how to do it, what to say, and how to say it. In other words, controlling their impulses becomes an increasingly important feature in their lives.

Psychologists have found the study of impulsivity alluring, much as standing at a window and peering into the depths of a child's personality. And what they see is not only revealing but has serious long-term developmental implications. (You may also have seen impulsivity referred to as a child's lack of ability to delay gratification or, of course, self-control.) Children who are reflective as opposed to impulsive seem destined to achieve at higher levels, attain greater emotional maturity, and gain appreciable personal popularity (Mischel & Mischel, 1983; Yuochi, Mischel, & Peake, 1993).

What do we know about impulsivity and the developmental path it follows? Like the tributaries of a river joining to form the major body, the streams of research into impulsivity converge on delay of gratification studies. Picture this setting: Children are placed in a position in which they are presented with something they enjoy—candies, toys—and told if they don't eat the candy or play with the toy until the researcher returns, they can have two pieces of candy or an even bigger toy. The researcher then leaves the room and observes the children through one-way mirrors. The results were as you would expect: Some children ate the candy immediately or played with the toy; others resisted by trying to distract themselves.

The truly amazing part of this work, however, was the follow-up research. The same children who displayed impulsivity at 4 years of age were the more troubled adolescents; they had fewer friends; they experienced more psychological difficulties including lower self-esteem; they were more irritable and aggressive, and less able to cope with frustration. The 4-year-olds who delayed their gratification could better handle frustration, were more focused and calm when challenged by any obstacle, and were more self-reliant and popular as adolescents. The behavior of the 4-year-olds on delay of gratification tests predicted success in both elementary and secondary schools, and even turned out to be a powerful predictor of how they would do on their SATs (Mischel & Mischel, 1983).

Impulsivity and the Classroom

If you're teaching or plan to teach preschool children, you can help them to develop self-control by urging them to think of other things, that is, to distract themselves. As they grow a little older, perhaps by first grade, a phenomenon called *transformation* appears; that is, children learn to think about what they shouldn't do in different terms. If they're instructed not to eat marshmallows, for example, they may think of the marshmallows as white clouds (something they don't eat). From this time on, students do well at devising their own strategies as they become more competent with their growing cognitive abilities. In fact, children exercise greater self-control when using strategies they themselves have devised than using those suggested by adults.

You can see how important the studies of impulsivity are for teachers in the classroom, especially for any decisions they may have to make about disruptive students. In their study of fifth-grade antisocial boys, Walker and Sylvester (1991) found that by the seventh grade 21 of the 40 most antisocial boys had been arrested 68 times for criminal behavior. These authors suggested that three simple measures taken when the boys were in the fifth grade would have predicted the later problems:

1. Teachers' ratings of social skills

2. Negative playground behavior of the boys and their playmates

3. Disciplinary contacts with the principal's office.

Teachers *should* play a critical role in obtaining early help for troubled students. By the time they are identified and placed in programs in the late middle and adolescent years, they're well on the way to serious trouble, which has increased the interest in early childhood programs. These students are part of a system of social institutions (family, school, community), and well-designed programs can help parents to interact with these institutions and secure needed help such as health care, improved child-rearing practices, and counseling (Burke, 1991).

Adolescents and Individuation

For teachers, especially those working with adolescent students, helping them to integrate the physical, sexual, and cognitive changes of adolescence and focus on clearly defined goals becomes a crucial task, one whose successful attainment helps students to develop self-control and to acquire healthy feelings of identity. Teachers play a key role in this process because of their daily contact with students. In fact, teachers may be the first to observe changes in behavior such as mood changes, outbursts of anger, drop in school achievement, truancy, feelings of fatigue, and new friends that may signal oncoming problems.

Although the transition from childhood may be difficult, most teens escape the scourge of such major problems as teen pregnancy, drug dependency, and suicide. As Dacey and Kenny (1997, p. 31) noted:

> *History suggests that from ancient times parents have feared that their adolescent children were more unruly and less reasonable than they were in their youth. In line with this traditional view, some researchers suggest that it is normal for adolescents to be in a state of turmoil much of the time. Many others, however, find the majority of teenagers to be well-balanced, reasonably happy, and pleasant to work with.*

Nevertheless, in a society in which adolescents are constantly seduced by advertising that urges them to become part of the smart set by smoking, drinking, and acting provocatively, some teenagers do succumb. In a survey conducted by the University of Michigan Institute for Social Research (1994), 15% of eighth-graders, 24% of tenth-graders, and 28% of twelfth-graders reported drinking five or more consecutive alcoholic drinks during the preceding two weeks. Interestingly, the use of marijuana is reported to have declined to 10.6% of the adolescent population, down from 17.4% in 1988 (U.S. Bureau of the Census, 1994).

Finally, if you find yourself involved with disruptive students, encourage, support, and participate in pertinent intervention programs. Several core elements occur in worthwhile intervention programs. These include the *school's leadership role in establishing the program* as soon as students' antisocial behavior begins to appear, the earlier the better. The program should include instruction in critical personal, academic, and social skills that these at-risk students need for school success; a vital part of this instruction would be the interest and help of peer and teacher mentors. *A brief training program* for parents that emphasizes awareness of their children's activities and the parents' appropriate involvement in their children's lives plus the skillful use of praise and rewards is needed (stressing the positive) coupled with fair discipline (Walker & Sylvester, 1991).

Case Reflections

One of the major features of this chapter was the application of impulsivity research to classroom achievement. Consider how immaturity and impulsivity contribute to the problems in Marsha Warren's reading group.

Also try to capitalize on the strengths of Erikson's and Kohlberg's work by suggesting techniques that would further the psychosocial and moral development of these students.

CHAPTER HIGHLIGHTS

Psychosocial Development
- Erik Erikson's eight stages of psychosocial development provide a structure for analyzing the crises and strengths in students' lives.
- Understanding the meaning of these stages in your pupils' lives can only help to enhance and enrich teacher-learner interactions.

Moral Development
- Children begin to understand the moral consequences of their actions.
- To explain moral development Kohlberg has formulated a cognitive interpretation that incorporates Piagetian thinking.
- Using the technique of moral dilemmas and analyzing an individual's reasoning, Kohlberg has traced progress through stages of moral development.
- Kohlberg's ideas have been challenged, especially by Carol Gilligan, who proposes a different path for girls' and women's moral development.
- Many educators believe that the concepts of moral development can be translated into classroom practice.

Socialization and Development
- Changes in the family have caused changes in parenting practices.
- The number of divorces remains high, causing children to adapt to transitions in their living conditions.
- The number of children in day care has risen steadily as family styles have become more diverse.
- Firm conclusions are still elusive with regard to the developmental outcomes of day care.

Key Terms

Attachment 72
Autonomy 73
Conventional thinking 88
Day care 95
Generativity 81
Identity achievement 79
Identity confusion 79
Identity crisis 79
Identity diffusion 79
Identity foreclosure 79
Identity moratorium 79
Individuation 71
Industry 76
Initiative 74
Integrity 81
Intimacy 81
Moral dilemma 85
Preconventional thinking 87
Postconventional thinking 88
Reciprocal interactions 73
Self 100
Self-esteem 101
Socialization 71

Individuation and Development

- Children usually acquire a sense of self by the age of 18 months.
- Children's sense of self changes noticeably with age.
- The emergence of self-control is a critical feature of psychosocial growth as children develop their ideas of right and wrong.

WHAT DO YOU THINK?

1. Controversy continues to surround the consequences of day care. Do you think there are both positive and negative outcomes, or are you firmly on one side or the other? Consider such variables as age of placement and the personalities of children in your answer.

2. Assume that you are a middle-school teacher and have just discovered one of your pupils flagrantly cheating. You have heard that this student has a history of cheating, but because of parental pressure and influence, little has been done. What would you do?

3. Divorce causes an emotional upheaval in the lives of children. If the parents of one of your students were in the midst of a divorce, what would you do? Remember: Some students may not want to discuss it at all. Would you still try to offer emotional support?

4. In this chapter, you read about the conditions that contribute to high self-esteem. What do think you can do in your classroom to further your students' self-esteem in a realistic manner?

four

Diversity in the Classroom: Culture, Class, and Gender

The bubbling cauldron of emotions that is Marsha Warren's classroom reflects many of the issues that face our society today. Members of different groups who mistrust each other mainly because of a lack of understanding find it difficult, if not impossible, to interact without tension and turmoil. Social class problems seem to defy solution. Gender discrimination still abounds. And yet, the diversity among us has the potential to be our greatest strength. Children of different cultures, classes, and genders come together to learn in our classrooms, and how we interact with our students has far-reaching implications for how they view themselves and each other.

Objectives

When you finish reading
this chapter, you should
be able to

- apply your
  knowledge of cultural
  differences to the
  methods and
  materials you
  introduce into your
  classroom

- identify potential
  sources of bias in
  classroom
  interactions,
  curriculum, and
  materials

- analyze the ways in
  which social class
  differences can affect
  a student's behavior
  and achievement

- detect any gender
  biases that influence
  participation,
  classroom success,
  and testing results

- evaluate the
  relationships in a
  classroom on the
  basis of culture, class,
  and gender

If we stay for a moment with Marsha Warren's classroom, we quickly note the impact of diversity on teaching and learning in today's schools. How many of her problems are due to a lack of understanding her students' backgrounds? Cultural and language differences, and home-school communication testify to the wisdom of Vygotsky's belief that social and cultural processes are major forces in shaping development. As Jerome Bruner, a long-time proponent of applying psychological theory and research to education, has stated (1996, p. 4):

> *Culture, then, though itself man-made, both forms and makes possible the workings of a distinctively human mind. On this view, learning and thinking are always situated in a cultural setting and always dependent upon the utilization of cultural resources. Even individual variation in the nature and use of mind can be attributed to the varied opportunities that different cultural settings provide, though these are not the only source of variation in mental functioning.*

Marsha Warren would have been more successful if she understood and capitalized on the rich traditions of her students. We urge you to study, understand, and apply the strengths inherent in students' backgrounds.

To help you achieve these goals, we'll first discuss the significance of cultural differences in students' lives. We will stress the need to avoid misunderstandings and misconceptions, and the importance of learning from different cultural experiences. We'll then turn our attention to the role that culture plays in the classroom, focusing on the function of multicultural education for a rapidly growing and diverse school population.

But culture isn't the only external influence on classroom performance. Studies have repeatedly shown that social class also powerfully affects students' achievement. Consequently, we'll identify the inroads that class differences make on education, from the physical condition of the schools themselves to the availability and quality of classroom materials and to learning opportunities for all students. Finally, we'll turn our attention to the kind of education that girls and boys receive. It may be in the same building with the same teacher, but is it really equal? (Another rich source of diversity in the classroom—children with developmental challenges—is discussed in Chapter 5.) Your work in this chapter should alert you to how culture, class, and gender interact to influence academic achievement.

DIFFERENT CULTURES, DIFFICULT ADJUSTMENTS

Census figures reveal the rapid and sharp shift in the backgrounds of students in the United States. Table 4.1 presents U.S. Bureau of Census (1996) figures showing the percentages of different groups in the United States in 1996, as compared with the estimated percentages in the year 2050.

These figures graphically illustrate our reasons for urging you to recognize and appreciate the cultural diversity in classrooms.

Consequently, in this opening section, we want to discuss in general terms several important issues relating to a growing and changing population. Americans pride themselves on living in a culturally diverse nation that encourages newcomers to share their way of life, yet, even under the best of conditions, the path can be difficult for many students.

Misconceptions and Misjudgments

Before focusing on students and the classroom, we'd like you to consider a revealing report that highlights the need to recognize and capitalize on the backgrounds of students. Several American psychologists traveled to Rwanda to help with the massive psychological problems, particularly painful for children, caused by the heartrending violence of the

Table 4.1 ORIGINS OF THE U.S. POPULATION: 1996–2050		
	1996 (%)	2050 (%)
White Americans	72	52
Hispanic Americans	11	25
African Americans	13	14
Asian Americans	3	8
Native Americans	1	1

past few years (Seppa, 1996). The psychologists soon found that traditional Western therapeutic methods, such as individualized therapy, were useless. Successful programs in Africa demand programs that help restore social supports and relationships.

They also discovered that urging patients to "talk it out" simply did not work. Using native songs, dances, and storytelling, which their patients found natural and comforting, proved to be much more effective. Here is a telling example of the value of understanding the attitudes, customs, behaviors—in other words, the culture—of individuals if we are to interact positively with them.

Understanding Cultures

What does it mean to be Hispanic in this country? Today Hispanics are thought to be those who trace their roots to the Spanish-speaking countries of Latin America or Spain (Marin, 1994). Although there are wide variations among Hispanics, as with any other group, Hispanics possess a unique set of cultural beliefs that distinguish them from Asian Americans or African Americans. For example, Hispanics value personal interdependence, which makes them cherish interpersonal relationships and makes them especially sensitive to the feelings of others.

Consequently, many Hispanics prefer people in authority, such as teachers, to be understanding and nurturing. They carry these ideas into the school and function more effectively (good relationships with others, satisfactory academic work) when they find a similar classroom atmosphere. These characteristics help to explain a Hispanic student's perspective on relationships: warm, caring, and thoughtful. A more authoritarian teacher, unaware of these characteristics, may inadvertently affect a Hispanic student's achievement by a brusque response or abrupt manner. (Could this be part of Marsha Warren's difficulties—a failure to understand the backgrounds of her students?)

Teachers will want to be aware of the *learning styles* of students. (Although learning styles research leaves many questions unanswered, we'll turn to observable characteristics that should provide useful clues to guide instruction.) For example, Hispanic students usually don't like to be singled out; they function more effectively when working in groups. Relationships are extremely important to them, so their interactions with teachers become critical for their success (Marin, 1994). "Get tough" policies seem to alienate rather than help Hispanic students. Consequently, encouragement, group work, and establishing a sense of belongingness help to create a positive learning experience for these students.

The same rationale applies to other groups. For example, summarizing research into the learning styles of African American students, Manning and Baruth (1996, p. 98) concluded:

- *African American students tend to respond to the whole picture rather than parts.*

- *African American students tend to approximate space, numbers, and time.*

Today's children are experiencing great diversity in their relationships with friends and in the classroom.

- *African American students are proficient in nonverbal communication.*

- *African American students prefer to focus on people rather than things.*

Teachers who appeal to this type of learning style should expect maximum achievement from and good relationships with their students.

Shaping classroom techniques to the cultural needs of students is nothing new. Good teachers have been doing it for years, but with a growing and diverse population, the need has become more acute. For example, among our Asian American students, we have heard the same story so frequently that it bears retelling. A young Korean girl, let's call her Lee, was adopted by a white, middle-class American couple and raised in a culture reflecting their values: suburban schools, regular church attendance, a busy schedule of after-school activities, parties, and the agonies and ecstasies of a typical adolescence. Thinking of herself as an American adolescent, she was jolted when an acquaintance asked her how long she had been in America. On another occasion, a fellow student said, "Ask Lee, she's Japanese."

Analyzing the learning styles of Asian American students provides revealing insights into the link between learning and culture. These students are often reluctant to express their opinions, sometimes remaining silent when they know the answer to a teacher's question. They may do less well in group discussion as compared with their independent work. They seem to prefer a well-structured, orderly environment where their work is recognized and reinforced on its own merits; that is, they don't have to call attention to it.

Situations similar to that of Lee arise more often than you would imagine and suggest a subtle (and sometimes not so subtle) form of racism that often is inadvertent and not intended to hurt, but racist nevertheless. A tendency to evaluate others by surface characteristics can affect other groups including African Americans. Here's a quote from an African American psychologist that speaks for itself (Jones, 1994):

> *When I read the literature in social psychology, I felt it was inadequate to address the problem of race in the United States. It focused too much on prejudiced individuals, bigots, and usually southerners. In my view as a black man who grew up in northern Ohio, I knew that bigotry was not limited to the South, and that institutional practices maintained the status quo of limited racial*

CASE NOTES

Observation   Remember that students will use standards from their own cultural backgrounds to form opinions about others.

Hypothesis   Helping them understand *why* people from other groups behave as they do should lead students to be less inclined to conclude that "different is deficient."

Possible Action   When meeting children from another culture, children initially see only differences in behavior, speech, clothing, and food. If these differences aren't too sharp, they accept the other children; otherwise they may judge them unfavorably *unless teachers encourage them to look beyond superficial differences*. Don't underestimate your ability to play a major role in smoothing students' relationships with others. As role models, teachers can actively encourage the idea that we are all human beings; we share many more similarities than differences, and what differences there are can help us learn about the world around us.

---

contact, and lower opportunities for blacks. We could set pins at the bowling alley, but we couldn't bowl there. We could caddie at the country club, but we couldn't join it. We could skate at the roller rink but only on Thursday nights when blacks came from all over northern Ohio for black night at the rink. The interesting thing, though, is that growing up in a racist society had its problems, but it also demanded a certain amount of ingenuity, resilience, determination, and hard work.

At this point we'd like to make several general suggestions. First, it's important to remember that the experiences of culturally diverse students will enrich everyone they encounter. For example, inner city students have long been welcomed in the suburban schools of Lexington, Massachusetts. In the course of the year, the parents of the inner city students visit Lexington on sightseeing excursions. Recently, Lexington parents visited the homes and neighborhoods of the inner city parents and students, touring churches, playgrounds, and recreation centers, a trip that the Lexington parents found richly rewarding. (The value of obtaining greater parental cooperation seems to have escaped Marsha Warren.)

Second, if you know that you will be having students from other cultures in your classroom, take the time to become familiar with the characteristics that make these children unique.

Third, be honest with yourself; try to recognize any of your own preconceived notions and ideas.

Objectively answering the following questions may help you attain insights into your own beliefs and feelings:

- Do I have any prejudices toward this group?

- What stereotypes do I associate with Asian Americans, African Americans, and so on?

- What do I know about different cultures?

- Is there any conflict between my values and those of my students?

Although many Americans still choose to live with their own ethnic or racial groups, strong majorities of all colors profess tolerance of other races and ethnic groups. And most seem to agree with historian John Hope Franklin, chairman of the presidential task force on race relations, that a continued push for racial integration is "in the long run the only way you can bring about any kind of peaceful, diverse society" (Yemma, 1997).

Culture and the Schools

If you think of **culture** as the customs, values, and traditions inherent in one's environment (Sue & Sue, 1990), you'll recognize that different cultures have different educational and developmental expectations for their children. *Asian* children, for example, are encouraged to avoid emotional displays, a characteristic that does not necessarily apply to *Asian American* children. Appreciating students' behavior demands an understanding of their cultures, which seems to occur at three levels:

1. You understand at a *superficial* level; that is, you know the facts that make up a student's cultural history.

2. You understand at an *intermediate* level; that is, you understand the central behaviors that are at the core of a student's psychosocial life. Language usage is a good example here. Does a student's culture tolerate, even encourage, calling out in the classroom, which could be a major problem for teachers not familiar with the acceptable behaviors of this student's culture?

3. You understand at a *significant* level; that is, you grasp the values, beliefs, and norms that structure a student's view of the world and how to behave in that world. In other words, you change psychologically as you acquire information about and interact with a different culture (Casas & Pytluk, 1995).

We hope that by the time you finish reading this chapter and this book, you will have developed a rich and deep understanding of the significant role culture plays in students' education.

Merging Cultures

You can now more readily appreciate how members of one group—Irish American, Italian American, African American—can use standards from their own cultural backgrounds to form opinions about those from other cultures. If we understand why people from other groups behave as they do, there is less of an inclination to conclude that "different is deficient." Understanding can humanize others. If these differences aren't too sharp, we accept people; otherwise we judge them unfavorably. Remember, however, if you were a member of the "other" group, you would probably behave just as they do (Triandis, 1990).

If we take the time and make the effort to understand these differences, our relationships with people from different groups can move to a level of mutual understanding. Consider, for example, how many minority children have had to make major adjustments to the dominant culture in the classroom (Spring, 1997). If teachers are aware of the differences between students' home cultures and that of the school, they'll do much to ease these adjustments and ensure that all their students succeed academically and personally to the extent of their potential. And children from the dominant culture will be enriched by knowing and learning from students with different backgrounds, strengths, and experiences.

A good example of teachers being sensitive to their students' backgrounds can be seen in Kim's (1990) description of Hawaiian children's school experiences. Many Hawaiian children achieve at the lowest academic level and are labeled as lazy and disruptive by some teachers. Yet these same children are remarkably responsible at home—cooking, cleaning, taking care of their brothers and sisters. In the home setting, they demonstrate considerable initiative and a high performance level. When something needs to be done, they get together and make a group effort to do whatever is necessary. When they find themselves in an individualistic, competitive classroom, however, their performance suffers. In a series of experiments, teachers were encouraged to model desired behaviors and not assign specific tasks to students. Kim reported that by the end of the academic year, third-grade students would begin the day by examining the schedules of their learning centers and then divide themselves into groups that assigned tasks to individual members, obtained materials, and used worksheets. Their achievement scores improved significantly. However, once the students were returned to regular classrooms for the fourth grade, a familiar pattern of problems appeared.

Our Shrinking World

The classroom is not the only place where cultures merge. In government, professions, and business, people of various cultures work side by side. Also, women and minorities—African Americans, Asian Americans, Hispanic Americans, Native Americans—have assumed leadership positions in which members of the dominant culture report to them. As companies become more global and as the number of international markets increases steadily, the workplace is beginning to resemble the classroom as a meeting place of cultures (Brislin, 1990).

Our goal in urging you to adopt a multicultural perspective in your classroom is to help you develop a greater understanding and appreciation of students who seem "different." If you adopt this perspective, you will come to realize that different people have different worldviews that decisively influence their thinking (Shweder, 1991). In this way, you can work, play, or study more congenially with others, thus becoming part of the movement to establish better relationships throughout our society. When you genuinely display understanding and appreciation of people from other cultures, students will be encouraged to imitate your behavior, enriching your own and your students' lives.

Cultural Compatibility in Our Changing Classrooms

Children from different cultures are increasingly interacting with one another, thus presenting parents and educators with unique opportunities for further understanding across cultures. Given these circumstances, is it any wonder that our classrooms have become the focus of efforts to achieve such understanding? The old cliche that the school reaches all the children of all the people is as true today as it ever was. Helping children of all cultures to achieve as fully as possible, while simultaneously adapting to one another, demands innovative strategies on the part of parents, teachers, and administrators.

Rogoff (1990) offered an excellent example of the need for cultural understanding and adaptation in teaching when she examined the behavior used to define intelligence in various cultures. She found that definitions of intelligence may range from an ability to remember facts (Chinese) to a slow, careful approach to a problem (Ugandan). In a similar manner, the way in which problems are attacked varies according to culture. With some groups, problem solving is seen as demanding a collective effort. With others, using a companion is seen as cheating. Teachers must be alert to these differences to promote cultural harmony in the classroom. They should remember also that children may be socialized to think and behave one way at home and another at school.

Don't think of a student in the classroom as just Asian American, but also as male and middle class. Thus a student who is a member of an oppressed minority may also be a member of a dominant gender and social class group. This student's view of the world is probably quite different from that of a middle-class Asian American girl or a lower-class Asian American boy (Grant & Sleeter, 1993, p. 51).

Forces for Compatibility

In a wide-ranging and pertinent essay, Tharp (1989) identified several psychocultural variables that link cultural compatibility to teaching and learning. Beginning with the inescapable fact that students from some cultural groups (Chinese, Japanese) have done better in North American schools than those from other groups (Native American, Hispanic American,

CULTURAL COMPATIBILITY
Compatibility of instruction with the cultural patterns of students.

African American), Tharp traced the changes that have recently come about in attitudes toward those students experiencing school difficulty. Today's focus, which recognizes the strengths of many cultures, has moved from a *cultural deficit* belief to an appreciation of *cultural differences*. In this way, changed expectations are leading to better student achievement. *When instruction is compatible with cultural patterns, learning improves* (Nieto, 1996).

Tharp (1989) then identified four variables that seem to produce greater compatibility between students' classroom experiences and their cultural background: social organization, cognition, motivation, and sociolinguistics.

Social Organization   As far as *social organization* is concerned, one of the keys to successful educational design is to make teaching, learning, performance, and assessment compatible with the social organization of students. In a typical classroom, as we have just seen, Hawaiian children may show low attention to teachers and a high level of attention seeking from their peers. When the social structure of the classroom was changed to include more student collaboration and cooperation, achievement scores and motivation increased noticeably.

When these ideas (collaboration and cooperation) were introduced into Navajo classrooms, the results were positive, even though the Navajo children were more independent, neither seeking nor giving assistance, which is not surprising given their tradition. While the Hawaiian children worked better with others in mixed-sex groups, Navajo children, when working in groups, accomplished more in same-sex groups.

Another example of cultural influences on classroom dynamics was the behavior of African American children, whose peer interactions were intense and sensitive. Their physical expressiveness and behavior caused some teachers to label them as disruptive. Other teachers, however, capitalized on these behaviors, by having the students give performances in front of the class that were related to the subject under discussion, while their "audience" watched intently to detect mistakes and thus be able to take their place. These and similar culture-compatible techniques heighten motivation and lead to higher achievement.

Cognition   We'll be spending considerable time on Tharp's second variable—*cognition* (see Chapter 7)—so we'll only discuss it briefly here. Children whose patterns of cognitive functioning are compatible with the school's are usually successful; children whose cognitive patterns do not match the school's usually do poorly. A good example can be seen in the work of Stevenson et al. (1990). Studying 1,440 Chinese and Japanese first- and fifth-grade students in the public schools of Minneapolis, Stevenson and his colleagues tested the children on reading and mathematics, interviewed the mothers, interviewed the principals, and administered a questionnaire to the teachers.

The interviews with the mothers revealed that the Chinese and Japanese mothers paid greater attention to their children's academic abilities than did American mothers. The Chinese and Japanese mothers also viewed academic achievement as the most important part of their children's lives. American mothers were less interested in academic achievement than in their children's general cognitive growth. American mothers also tended to overestimate their children's academic abilities, whereas the Chinese and Japanese mothers held higher academic standards for their children. In this example, you can see that the Chinese and Japanese mothers surpassed their American counterparts in their adherence to the traditional school model, which helps to explain the continued academic success of their children.

Motivation   Tharp's third variable, *motivation*, underlies all successful teaching. We know that one of the major contributions teachers can make to the successful integration and accomplishments of multicultural students is to provide an understanding, supportive environment. For example, in attempting to heighten the motivation of African American boys to succeed, teachers should publicly recognize the successful academic experiences of young African American men, thus helping students to grow in self-concept, self-esteem, and academic confidence.

To illustrate strategies that help to meet the needs of multicultural students, Gary and Booker (1992) suggested several techniques to empower African American students to achieve academic success. These students should be helped to establish goals early in life. Adults who recognize and foster children's early interests help children engage in long-term thinking and also help them avoid seeking immediate gratification. It is useful also to remember that many African American students learn best in an environment that encourages human interaction and verbal dialogue. In reading Marsha Warren's reactions to her students, it's interesting to note that she didn't mention anything about her students' interests.

Sociolinguistics   Tharp's final variable, *sociolinguistics* refers to conversational practices that reflect students' backgrounds. Imagine that you've just entered your first classroom to meet your students. Much to your surprise, several students whom you will be teaching this year do not speak or write English as their primary language. Today there are more than 30 million Americans for whom English is not their primary language, and of them about 6 million have "limited English proficiency" (LEP).

What happens to students who do not speak the language of the school? Unfortunately, many will achieve below their potential and drop out of school. In an effort to combat this problem, *The Bilingual Education Act of 1988* stipulated that students with LEP receive **bilingual education** until they can use English to succeed in school.

Bilingual Children

As research begins to accumulate about bilingual education programs, we're learning more about the students themselves. For example, the better that children speak both languages, the better their level of cognitive attainment. This makes sense when you realize that when children retain their native language, they maintain comfortable relationships within their families and community.

Research also suggests that the native language does not interfere with second language development (Hakuta, 1986). Since the acquisition of languages is a natural part of our cognitive system, both first and second language acquisition seem to be guided by similar principles. In fact, the rate of acquisition of the second language seems to be related to the level of proficiency of the first. With these ideas in mind, what programs have been devised to help LEP students?

Bilingual Education Programs

As you read these words, about 40% of public school students are from ethnically diverse backgrounds, and these students may be at risk because of an English language deficit. Here are two approaches to help these LEP students:

1. The *English as a Second Language (ESL)* program usually has students removed from class and given special English instruction. The intent is to have these students acquire enough English to allow them to learn in their regular classes that are taught in English.

2. With the *bilingual* technique, students are taught partly in English and partly in their native language. The objective here is to help students learn English by subject matter instruction in their own language and in English. Thus, they acquire subject matter knowledge simultaneously with English.

BILINGUAL
EDUCATION
Programs designed to help students who have problems with the language of the school.

Large numbers of children participate in bilingual education programs.

In today's schools, the bilingual technique has become the program of choice, although as this book is being written, controversy over bilingual education continues to rage. Bilingual education is a major commitment because academic fluency takes about seven years.

Proponents of bilingual education believe that students in such programs are not penalized because of a language deficit. They are able to stay current with their studies because subjects are taught in their native languages, which helps to maintain students' self-esteem while they gain proficiency in English.

Opponents argue that bilingual education is not very helpful to these children. Students who eventually succeed in the marketplace are proficient in English. Bilingual education wastes valuable time reinforcing students' native languages instead of teaching them English. English as a Second Language (ESL) is a good alternative. Since English is the official language of government and commerce in the United States, classroom instruction in public school classrooms should be in English. After all, ESL proponents argue, one of the goals of public school education is fluency in spoken and written English. If students are in an environment where only English is spoken, they will learn the language more quickly. These students may have initial difficulty, but once they have acquired English proficiency, they typically catch up. ESL is a desirable program because most of a student's coursework is in English, with separate time allotted for specific English language instruction. Students are grouped according to grade level, and the ESL teacher uses the student's classroom curriculum.

Proponents of bilingual education state that ESL does not give students support in their native languages. In spite of English language training, these students fall behind. Older students in particular have difficulty with this technique. Non-English-speaking students are often put in classes with younger students while they gain English proficiency. Or if they are put in with their peers, they suffer because they cannot keep up with the coursework. Both of these conditions result in a loss of self-esteem, which can then affect total academic performance and may cause students to drop out of school altogether.

One reason for the controversy surrounding these programs is that research has yet to grapple with many of the important variables. For example

- What should be evaluated, English proficiency or subject matter success?

- How can the quality of the program be assessed?

- How alike are the children in any program (ability, socioeconomic status, proficiency in their native languages, the level of English on entering the program)?

Since the use of two languages in classroom instruction actually defines bilingual education, several other important questions arise:

- What is an acceptable level of English that signals the end of a student's participation in a bilingual program?

- What subjects should be taught in each language?

- How can each language be used most effectively? (That is, how much of each language is to be used to help a student's progress with school subjects?)

- Should English be gradually phased in, or should students be totally immersed in the second language (which, for most of the students we are discussing, would be English)?

Dialects   You'll also notice that some children speak with decided dialects. Think of a **dialect** as a variety of a language distinguished by vocabulary, grammar, and pronunciation that differs from the standard language. In the United States, for example, those from the Boston area are distinguished from those living in the South or the Midwest. You should remember that specific dialects such as Black English, although sounding different, are every bit as logical and rule governed as Standard English.

Pinker (1994) gives several examples of the systematic use of rules in Black English (BE) and Standard American English (SAE):

There's really a God. (SAE)	*Don't nobody know? (BE)*
It's really a God. (BE)	*If you're bad (SAE)*
Doesn't anybody know? (SAE)	*If you bad (BE)*

These linguistic facts raise interesting questions, particularly for teachers. What should teachers do with students who bring their dialect to the classroom? Here we have a clear illustration of what's meant by the distinction between cultural deficits and cultural differences. The children speaking Black English are using an undeniably logical system. Yet, at the same time, their speech may work against them in a nation that bestows achievement, occupational success, and status on those skillful in Standard American English.

A consensus seems to have gathered around techniques that show no disrespect to a student's language (which would be an insult to that student's culture, identity, and, undoubtedly, self-esteem). As noted, schools that are effective with culturally diverse populations are sufficiently flexible to accommodate a range of dialects learners bring to school. For example, teachers are urged to allow dialects in social and recreational settings and encourage these same students to use Standard English in school settings (Manning & Baruth, 1996).

Although these issues continue to spark controversy, bilingual programs allow students to retain their cultural identities while simultaneously progressing in their school subjects. Carefully planned programs also offer the opportunity for students to become truly bilingual, especially if programs begin early:

Educational programs that do not attempt to maintain the child's first language deprive many children of economic opportunities they would otherwise have as bilinguals. This is especially true of

DIALECT

A variety of a language distinguished by vocabulary, grammar, and pronunciation that differs from a standard language.

children who speak world languages used for international communication such as Spanish,
Japanese, Chinese, and the like. If these children's first languages are not maintained, one of this
country's most valuable resources will be wasted. (McLaughlin, 1990, p. 74)

Interactions in the Classroom

For some children, the path to understanding and self-esteem can be difficult. As Billingsley (1992) noted, many African American families are caught between conflicting tensions: the economic, physical, social, psychological, and spiritual demands of their members on the one hand, and the demands of a dominant society on the other. That is, the
struggle for better housing and schools, higher incomes, and more satisfying occupations
requires adjustment to a different lifestyle.

If a child's single most important psychological necessity is self-esteem, then it's clear
that rejection can only frustrate the development of a positive self-regard (Garbarino &
Benn, 1992). The notion of rejection as an obstacle to the development of healthy self-
esteem is not confined to rejection by individuals, that is, a parent's rejection of his or her
child. Rejection because the child is a member of a particular group can work in exactly
the same way.

When children interact with individuals from other cultures, these experiences
help them to accept and learn from people with different customs, languages, and ideas.
Although this may sound idealistic, helping youngsters to achieve this objective is the social goal of multicultural education. Children are encouraged to form positive cultural,
racial, and class identities for themselves and for others; this in turn leads to high self-
esteem and the ability and willingness to interact with different people.

Cultural Differences and Testing Practices

A child's ability to take tests often powerfully influences the results of a test (see Chapters
11 and 12). This is especially true of intelligence tests. Tests can frighten students or cause
them anxiety. Whatever the reason for test anxiety—parental pressure, students' own concerns, or the testing atmosphere—merely taking a test can affect performance, which is especially true for pupils with different cultural experiences from the majority. Language,
reading, expectations, and behavior may be different for these students and may influence
test performance (Stigler, Shweder, & Herdt, 1990).

Equity in Testing

In an effort to ensure equity in testing, a new national system of *authentic assessment* has
been proposed (Madaus, 1994). These tests supposedly engage students in real-world tasks
rather than multiple-choice tests (Darling-Hammond, 1994). For example, President Clin-
ton's Goals 2000 Educate America Act rests on the assumption that the federal government
can help state and local communities in their striving for educational reform by specifying
goals, providing financial support to attain these goals, and establishing a voluntary assessment mechanism for accountability (Pullin, 1994). The intent is to ensure that *all* students
will be competent in the core academic subjects (reading, writing, arithmetic); this can occur only if all disadvantaged groups have effective and complete opportunities to learn.

The goals are clear; the task itself is difficult. As Madaus noted (1994, p. 79), since social and cultural groups differ in the extent to which they share the values that underlie
testing and the values that testing promotes, any national testing system raises questions
of equity. The values of the test makers and the test takers don't necessarily match. For example, various cultural groups may have specific intellectual traditions that tests (of
whatever design) may not measure.

TIPS ON COMMUNICATION
Improving Interactions with Students

By pausing for a moment and considering the implications of the types of interactions you have with your pupils, you can better understand how a particular relationship has developed. For example, you work with either a group or with an individual. You provide correction and feedback. You answer questions. We could create a lengthy list of your activities; in all of these, you are interacting with students. Do you ever step back to analyze the interactions you engage in with your students? By doing so, you could improve both relationships and achievement.

Occasionally during the year, once your rules are in place and your class knows what is expected, why not try something like this? Ask your students to complete a checklist about you, perhaps like the one that follows. Make it as easy as possible for students to fill out.

DIRECTIONS   Put a check on the line where you think your teacher {name} belongs.

	HIGH	LOW
1. Fair		
2. Plays favorites		
3. Firm		
4. Easy		
5. Helpful		
6. Ignores pupils		
7. Friendly		
8. Aloof		
9. Concerned		
10. Disinterested		

Obviously you can include other items to obtain an appraisal of your relationships with your pupils. Whether you decide to use this checklist technique or another, it's a good idea to evaluate yourself; if a negative profile emerges, you have a chance to assess what is wrong and fix it.

That children of different cultures want to succeed is reflected in interviews with many of them: Almost 50% were spending one to two hours on homework every night. (Of the Southeast Asian students, 25% reported spending more than three hours each night.) Here is an instance in which sensitivity to the needs of multicultural children (in this case, recognition of previous hardships) can only aid their adjustment and achievement in school.

Reducing Anxiety in Test Taking

When children feel comfortable, they perform better. This is particularly true for test taking. Children need information about why the test is being given, when it is being given, what material will be tested, and what kinds of test items will be used. These are just a few topics to consider. Language should not be a barrier to a child's test performance. For example, students need to understand the terms in the directions of a test: what *analyze* means, what they should do when asked to *compare,* what *discuss* means.

Helping students in this way takes extra time and effort for teachers. But it is teaching, just as teaching English or history is teaching. As more and more multicultural students become users of classroom tests, they must not be allowed to do poorly simply because they don't understand the mechanics of or the language of the tests.

Multicultural Education

Considering the issues we've just discussed, it seems logical to conclude that there is a real need for multicultural education. But for multicultural programs to be successful, it's necessary to incorporate social, historical, and political contexts (Nieto, 1996). With this in mind, such programs should do the following:

- Teach children to recognize, accept, and appreciate cultural, ethnic, social class, religious, and gender differences

- Instill in learners during these crucial developmental years a sense of responsibility and a commitment to work toward the democratic ideals of justice, equality, and democracy (Manning & Baruth, 1996, p. 3)

Successful multicultural programs require more than facts. A variety of students necessitates a variety of appropriate curricular materials that contribute not only to students' academic achievement but also to the development of their self-concepts and that vital motivation needed to sustain their academic progress.

But materials and methods must do more than engender "feel good" reactions, which can only shortchange students. Educational efforts should further students' fundamental skills and provide opportunities for them to exercise these skills in practical situations that demand critical thinking and problem-solving abilities. One means of achieving this goal is through the use of educational technology.

Multicultural Education and Educational Technology

Educational technology is a boon to successful multicultural education in several ways. For example, networking and other forms of Web-based instruction—instruction in which students learn from materials presented over the World Wide Web and interact with other students and teachers via the Web—help students to communicate and work

A wealth of information about other cultures is available on the Internet.

TIPS ON COMMUNICATION
Building Positive Attitudes

The goals we're discussing should be implemented in an atmosphere conducive to positive attitudes toward one's own cultural background and understanding and respecting those of others. What we're urging here is a concept of multicultural education for all students across all grades.

Are you ready for this? Why not test yourself and find out.

The Culture Quiz: Multicultural Education

Directions: Mark the following as True or False.

_____ 1. Multicultural education should be an integral part of the elementary but not the secondary curriculum and should focus on academic matters.

_____ 2. Multicultural education programs are only necessary in schools that have considerable cultural diversity among learners.

_____ 3. Multicultural education programs should emphasize to all learners the importance of assimilating toward majority culture expectations.

_____ 4. Multicultural education programs should use a unit or thematic teaching approach, rather than being incorporated into all areas of the curriculum.

_____ 5. Multicultural education programs should address as many culturally diverse groups as possible.

_____ 6. Multicultural education programs are a political tool that forces cultural diversity on European Americans.

_____ 7. Multicultural education programs do not interfere with the academic areas of learning.

_____ 8. Multicultural education is a popular trend in education and will likely lose its impetus as its popularity wanes.

_____ 9. Multicultural education should focus on cultural and ethnic diversity, as well as on racism, sexism, classism, and the acceptance of handicapped conditions.

_____ 10. Multicultural education can have a significant and positive impact on the education reform currently occurring in the United States.

1. F		6. F	
2. F		7. T	
3. F		8. F	
4. F		9. T	
5. T		10. T	

From Manning, M. L. and Baruth, L. *Multicultural Education of Children and Adolescents*, 2/e. Copyright © 1996 by Allyn & Bacon. Reprinted by permission.

cooperatively with others from sites all over the world. Pen pal programs (across state or country) are an informal, relatively unstructured way of exposing students to different cultures and backgrounds.

Through technology, a more diverse store of information and expertise becomes available to students than would otherwise be possible. For example, CD-ROM databases, and the World Wide Web provide access both to national and international databases and to top-level experts. These materials allow students to view and learn interactively about events that are central to different cultures and nations, providing a better understanding of the culture's characteristics, social environment, and psychological concerns.

Exposure of students to multicultural diversity has a host of positive effects. Cooperative projects over the World Wide Web can lead to a greater appreciation that cultures vary in how they approach problems and in what solutions are considered to be adequate and acceptable. Students learn to reflect on and modify their own ways of identifying, understanding, and solving problems. They come to realize that a person's views are always shaped in some way by culture, and thus alternative views are usually possible.

We also know that technology is useful in helping classroom teachers deal with students who differ in not only their ethnic, racial, and cultural backgrounds but also in their levels of knowledge, interest, motivation, and learning styles. For example, computer-based instruction and intelligent tutoring systems have as one of their goals appropriate individualized instruction.

Different learning preferences are also taken into account when using multimedia-based instruction, which usually include visual, verbal, and auditory components. Some CD-ROMs allow elementary students to view text, hear it being read by one voice, hear it being "acted" by multiple actors, see and/or hear it in more than one language (for example, English and Spanish), or any combination of these. Students who prefer "nonlinear" explorations in learning can take advantage of CD-ROMs as well, since (like the World Wide Web) many of these systems have branching capabilities that allow students to pursue topics in whatever order they prefer.

These technological capabilities require intelligent utilization and planning by teachers. Instructional technology must consciously consider and include diversity in its design (Branch, 1997; Sheffield, 1997). Branch (1997) noted that incorporating diversity and culture are vital at every step of instructional design, and Sheffield (1997) emphasized that teachers must understand the learning characteristics of each student and design instruction to best fit each learner.

The issues discussed in the preceding also apply to economically deprived students who arrive at school with, perhaps, a different sense of values from those of their middle-class teachers.

CASE NOTES

Observation   A lack of compatibility was spreading throughout Marsha Warren's class, affecting all class members.

Hypothesis   She may have greater success if she groups those children who benefit from certain techniques (working in small groups, cooperative learning, etc.).

Possible Action   Perhaps, when Marsha changes her reading groups, and if she pays more attention to the backgrounds of the students in the new groups, she may have greater success.

SOCIAL CLASS AND ACADEMIC ACHIEVEMENT

Before discussing the relationship between social class and academic achievement, it would be well to examine briefly the conditions under which some children in the United States live. First, however, we would like to emphasize that although we have separated this chapter into the topics of culture, class, and gender for discussion purposes, remember that these three topics are almost impossible to separate in the real world. For example, African Americans, Hispanics, other immigrants, and women are overly represented at the poverty level. Since almost any discussion of class differences leads into the effects of poverty, let's turn our attention to this phenomenon.

The Culture of Poverty

In a penetrating essay, Weissbourd (1996) urged a comprehensive view of poverty, suggesting that poverty hurts children in a range of subtle ways. Noting the tendency to equate poverty with disadvantage, Weissbourd argued that most vulnerable children are *not* poor, and all the poor are *not* alike. For example, the African American youth living in an urban ghetto experiences a quite different set of problems than a malnourished, chronically diseased white child in Appalachia.

Although about 8% of American children are poor for more than six years, more than 30% of our children experience poverty at some time in their lives.

> *In the last three decades, huge numbers of skilled workers were laid off because of farm and factory closings, divorced middle-class mothers, and ousted professionals have suffered downward mobility, a sudden and severe loss of income, creating unfamiliar physical and emotional burdens for their children. (Weissbourd, 1996, p. 10)*

The children of poverty experience more health problems, usually due to a lack of medical care. More of these children die in the neonatal and infancy periods. They also suffer more accidents than more economically fortunate children and are exposed to greater stress: occupational, financial, housing, and neighborhood. We know that parental stress can often translate into poor parenting practices (depression, irritability, and abuse), which can lead to behavioral and emotional problems and academic difficulty for the children. As we also know from the daily news, these children often witness and are the targets of violence, such as physical assault, rape, and shootings.

The number of children living in poverty remains distressingly high. For example, more than *15 million children under age 18* live in poverty, which is about 21% of the total child population (U.S. Bureau of the Census, 1996). Figure 4.1 illustrates that more children than adults live in poverty.

The danger in all of this, of course, is that poverty becomes a self-perpetuating cycle. The conditions we have described here put children at an immediate disadvantage: They are subject to school difficulties (perhaps culminating in their dropping out), low self-esteem, troublesome behavior, limited occupational opportunities, and encounters with the law. Erratic employment contributes to poverty, and the cycle commences again.

The Poverty Level

To give you an idea of the numbers involved, Table 4.2 summarizes the number of individuals, including children, who fall below the current **poverty level** of $16,036 for a family of four.

POVERTY LEVEL
Government-determined level of poor who need assistance ($16,036 for a family of four).

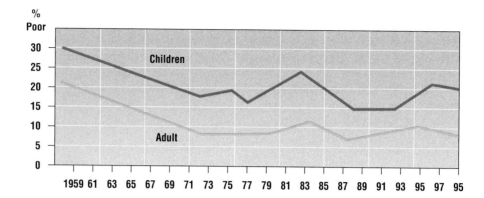

FIGURE 4.1

Child and Adult Poverty
Rates, 1959 to 1995.

(From U.S. Bureau of the
Census, September, 1996.)

Table 4.2 NUMBER OF CHILDREN EXPERIENCING POVERTY

	Number	Percentage
Total Poor	36,425,000	13.8
Related Children	13,999,000	20.2
Total White Poor	24,423,000	11.2
Related Children	8,474,000	15.5
Total Black Poor	9,872,000	29.3
Related Children	4,644,000	41.5

Source: Bureau of the Census, U.S. Department of Commerce, 1996.

It's an interesting table. You see immediately that children of all types are overrepresented in poverty, and, then, breaking the figures down by black and white, you note the large numbers of black children living in poverty.

Analyses of the children of poverty typically focus on income, education, occupation, and social status, yet other, potentially more powerful, psychological forces are also at work. For example, can children living in poverty avoid feelings of powerlessness? It doesn't take them long to perceive that in comparison to their more economically advantaged classmates, they have little influence in their society, have access to fewer societal opportunities, and are more likely to have their lives directed by others.

How do these facts translate into meaningful differences in the classroom? One example relates to scores on standardized intelligence tests. Although our interpretation and use of intelligence tests has changed dramatically (see Chapter 12), these tests remain an indicator of achievement. Today children at a lower socioeconomic level score 10 to 15 IQ points below middle-class children. These differences not only are *present by the first grade* but persist throughout the school years. When profiles of lower-class children were drawn, they showed the children to be like the middle-class children, but they scored lower on all abilities; that is, class differences, not native ability, led to differences in test scores (Hetherington & Parke, 1993).

For example, in a study of eighth-graders, low-socioeconomic status (SES) white children were as likely as low-SES African American and low-SES Hispanic American students to have poor grades. In this same study, low-SES Asian American students did not

Tremendous variation exists in the quality of the schools available to children.

achieve much better than other low-SES students (Weiss, Farrar, & Petrie, 1989). These and similar results testify to the conclusion that SES, more than any other variable, predicts educational outcome.

But remember, social class is thought to be a carrier variable (Ceci, 1996), that is, social class consists of many components such as family income, parental education, occupational prestige, neighborhood demographics, and housing cost.

Social Class and Education

As the importance of education in our society has increased, the need for every American child to receive a high school education has become widely accepted. Consequently, our schools' high dropout rate has become a matter of national concern, especially in those schools serving the poor and minorities. In some school districts, particularly in urban and rural communities, the dropout rate ranges from 20% to 40%. What this says about the future of these students is evident. For example, salaries for dropouts who are between 18 and 24 years old average no more than $6,000 per year (Hayes, 1992). Since one in five children is poor, if our concerns about the relationship between poverty and education are correct, the chances of these children for productive employment in a technological society are starkly limited.

Escaping Poverty

In her thoughtful commentary, Renyi (1993) noted that Americans have been firm believers that schools in poverty areas are the means for students to turn their lives around. But too many poor and minority students continue to attend schools that don't address their needs and in which they learn little. The idea that all students should graduate from high school, however, has radically altered current views of teaching and learning.

Attempting to identify the causes behind high school dropout rates, failure, and low achievement, Renyi (1993, p. 14) discovered that the differential success rate for white and black populations is closely related to the economic success of the population as a whole in a particular school building. As she stated, the critical difference for any child was whether that child attended a school with others who were affluent. For example, a poor black child in a white middle-class school had a better chance of academic success than a rich white child in a school in which the majority of the children were poor.

Given the goal of a high school education for all, not every student can adjust to the role of white middle-class America, where everyone goes to school but the schools remain dedicated to white middle-class goals. The constant calls for school reform have ignored the nature of the *total* school population, which helps to explain why about 15% of our students continue to drop out. Our schools are not reaching this group.

Renyi (1993) analyzed this 15% group, composed of the poor and minority students of today, compared it with similar groups in previous generations, and concluded that in the past, children of the poor were not expected to complete high school. They were expected to leave school before graduation and get a job offering a living wage. But now members of this same group are expected to finish high school and eventually assume the status of the middle-class citizen—a task easier to talk about than to accomplish. Children who come to school hungry and listless, often carrying memories of violence, are not overly concerned with academic achievement.

In high-poverty school districts, the schools themselves tell a similar story: not enough texts for all the students; limited, perhaps nonexistent, materials; metal detectors at school entrances. One of the authors, early in his career, shifted from teaching secondary school biology in the suburbs to teaching in the upper grades of an urban elementary school. Materials were so limited in the urban school that the teachers used their own money to buy paper, crayons, and workbooks. This concern of teachers for their students will never be forgotten; such generosity is a quality we hear about too infrequently. How does this type of educational environment affect the classroom performance of both teachers and students?

Teaching, Learning, and Social Class

In his biting commentary on current conditions in America's schools, Kozol (1991) drew some vivid comparisons. In schools populated with children of the poor, students are crowded into small, squalid spaces, and in some cities overcrowding is so bad that some schools function in abandoned factories. In one school, students eat their lunches in what was once the building's boiler room; reading classes are taught in what used to be a bathroom; there are no microscopes for science classes; and one counselor serves 3,600 students in the elementary grades. In the high school of the same district, there is a single physics section for 2,200 students; two classes are being taught simultaneously in one classroom.

For more details of these students' lives, here are Kozol's words:

> The city was so poor there had been no garbage pickup for four years. . . . On the edge of the city is a large chemical plant. There is also a very large toxic waste incinerator, as well as a huge sewage treatment plant. . . . The city has one of the highest rates of infant mortality in Illinois, the highest rate of fetal death, and also a very high rate of childhood asthma.

> The schools, not surprisingly, are impoverished. . . . The entire school system had been shut down after being flooded with sewage from the city's antique sewage system. I did meet several wonderful teachers in the school, and I thought the principal of the school was excellent. The superintendent is also a very impressive person. (Kozol, 1991, p. 5)

A high school in a more affluent district in the same state presents a different picture. There is a greenhouse for students interested in horticulture; the physical sciences department offers fourteen courses; there are eighteen biology electives. The school's orchestra has traveled to the former Soviet Union. Beautifully carpeted hallways encourage students to sit and study; computers are everywhere. The ratio of counselors to students is 1 to 150. Parents of these students recently raised money to send the school choral group to Vienna.

Economic differences among school systems is also reflected in access to educational technology. Implementation of simple, basic uses of technology, such as teaching students how to use various software packages, requires a substantial investment for acquiring machines and software. Some schools, due to fiscal restraints, may find it necessary to cut supplies and expense budgets, resulting in fewer and less-sophisticated machines and software available to their students. The resulting "technology gap" (the gulf between schools that can afford basic or more elaborate equipment and supplies and those that cannot) may well widen the already existing gap between quality of schooling for those students in poorer versus wealthier areas.

Family Attitudes

A family's attitude toward the education of their children makes a significant difference in the classroom achievements of these students. As Garbarino and Benn noted (1992), parents may not be present in the classroom, but they have a profound influence on the ways their children view school and learning. The extent to which the parents support the school's objectives directly affects their children's academic performance. Too often, low parental expectations for their children reflect the parents' own educational experiences. If parents themselves encountered difficulties in school, they may exercise a negative impact on their children's attitudes, expectations, and performance. The reverse also holds true.

Comer Schools

You may well ask at this point: Is it possible to improve teaching and learning when the inroads of poverty are clutching at students? A successful attempt to improve education under trying economic conditions was proposed by James Comer (1988). Working with two beleaguered schools in New Haven, Connecticut, Comer formed a school-based management of principal, parents, and teachers who jointly ran the school. He also put together a mental health team, consisting of a social worker, a psychologist, a special education teacher, and a school counselor. These two teams, working smoothly together, foresaw, and forestalled, many problems that otherwise would have developed into full-blown crises. The key to success, of course, is the meshing of the two teams. With the right blend of personalities, experience, and willingness to experiment, they achieved a level of flexibility that encouraged considerable innovation.

After examining the **Comer schools,** and several others, Weissbourd (1996) concluded that several principles led to effective education for vulnerable children. Among them are the following:

- An emphasis on academic achievement

- A capacity to react swiftly to the social and emotional needs of the students

- A safe and orderly, but not restrictive, school atmosphere

- An open and encouraging attitude toward active parental participation in the running of the school

- A true partnership between school administrators and all staff personnel

- A close relationship with the community, which furthers the achievements of students

Attempts to improve education for needy students have also been made at the national level.

COMER SCHOOLS
Strategy advocated by James Comer by which a school-based management team runs the school.

```
┌─────────────────────────────────────────────────────────────────────┐
│                                                                   C   │
│  CASE  NOTES                                                          │
│                                                                       │
│  Observation   Marsha Warren's contacts with the parents of her students seem limited, │
│  given the extent of her problems.                                    │
│                                                                       │
│  Hypothesis    Positive models and sources that cross cultural gaps could lead to │
│  improvements in behavior and achievement.                            │
│                                                                       │
│  Possible Action   This teacher should familiarize herself with the community and then │
│  reach out for help with her specific problems.                       │
│                                                                       │
└─────────────────────────────────────────────────────────────────────┘
```

Head Start

HEAD START

Intervention program intended to provide educational and developmental services to preschool children from low-income families.

Conceived as part of President Lyndon Johnson's War on Poverty, **Head Start** was originally headed in 1964 by Sargent Shriver, who had been shocked at the extent of poverty in the United States. Data indicated that about one-half of the nation's 30 million poor were children and most of these were under 12 years of age. Shriver's main objective became the preparation of poor children for entrance into the first grade.

As Hauser-Cram, Pierson, Klein Walker, and Tivnan (1991) noted, Head Start was intended to provide educational and developmental services to preschool children from low-income families. Improving children's health became a primary goal: Children received pediatric and neurological assessments, plus two nutritious meals a day (Zigler & Muenchow, 1992).

Head Start programs had six components: preschool education, health screening and referral, mental health services, nutrition education and hot meals, social services for the child and family, and parental involvement (Zigler & Styfco, 1994). Since its beginning more than 13 million children have been served by Head Start.

Long-term Gains   Unfortunately, some of the early claims about the gains to be realized from Head Start programs revolved around changes in IQ; some proponents stated that as a result of participation in Head Start, a child's IQ would increase by one IQ point a month. In the mid-1960s, critical evaluations of intelligence tests had not reached today's level of sophistication. Edward Zigler, a member of the Head Start planning committee, deplored reliance on increases in IQ scores as the means of evaluating Head Start.

His fears were quickly justified, as follow-up studies of Head Start children showed a "fadeout effect." That is, although graduates of these preschool programs showed immediate gains in intelligence and achievement test scores, after several months in the public schools, the Head Start children seemed to lose these cognitive benefits (their test scores went down) (Zigler & Styfco, 1994, p. 128). Nevertheless, even if Head Start graduates do not maintain *academic* gains, they have improved their readiness for school and the advantages of Head Start extend to other parts of their lives.

More recent follow-up studies confirm these conclusions. Studies of cognitive (Barnett, 1995) and social outcomes (Yoshikawa, 1995) continue to demonstrate that these programs contribute to short-term IQ gains, but they also indicate important long-term positive effects on school achievement, grade retention, and needed placement in special education classes. The social adjustment of students enrolled in these programs showed marked improvement and considerable promise in combating violent, antisocial behavior. (For a detailed analysis of the long-term consequences of early childhood education programs such as Head Start, see Barnett, 1995.)

Today, with the stunning rise of children living in poverty, the need for early intervention programs to aid these children seems more compelling than ever. In her summary of the need for greater support of preschool programs, Kassebaum (1994) pointed out that 21% of all American children live in poverty, 25% of all children live with a single parent, 25% of all babies are born to unmarried mothers, and every night at least 100,000 children are homeless.

These statistics cry out for attention because the children they represent not only suffer educational disadvantages but also face other developmental difficulties. For example, as we have seen, children of these families are more frequently born premature, their families suffer devastating and widespread deprivation, and the children themselves are more subject to physical illness and lowered cognitive performance. As more of these children enter the public schools, is it any wonder they are unable to meet the ordinary demands of the classroom (Hauser-Cram et al., 1991)? By meeting some of the many needs of these children we see the value of programs such as Head Start, with its hope of bringing these children successfully into the mainstream of school life and the wider community. If we are to succeed, we must identify the skills, both academic and social, that our students need.

Resilient Children

All of us should be particularly careful about such labels as "poor" or "underclass," because it's deceptively simple to assume that these children don't have a chance, that they'll never make it. The reality is far from it, as the research and literature analyzing **resilient children** clearly show.

RESILIENT CHILDREN
Children who, in spite of daunting hardships, manage to thrive.

Who are these resilient children who grow up in the most chaotic and adverse conditions, yet manage to thrive? Clues may be found in a remarkable long-term study, entitled *Overcoming the Odds,* conducted by Emmy Werner and Ruth Smith (1992). They studied all the children (837) born on the island of Kauai in the year 1955. (Kauai is an island in the Hawaiian chain.) What's unusual about this study is that the authors studied 505 of these children from their prenatal days until they were 3 ½ years of age. (The drop in numbers from the original 837 was due to some of the participants dying, and others moving away.)

Of the 505 individuals followed over the thirty-plus year span, one in three was born with the odds stacked dramatically against them. They either grew up in poverty, experienced birth problems, or were members of dysfunctional families (desertion, divorce, alcoholism, mental illness). Two children out of three in this particularly vulnerable group encountered four or more risk factors before they were 2 years old and developed serious learning and/or behavior problems.

Nevertheless, one out of three of these high-risk children developed into a competent, confident young adult by the age of 18. How can we explain this phenomenon? What protective factors were at work in these children that let them overcome daunting adversity? To be perfectly honest, nobody can tell you that if you do this or that or if you encourage certain characteristics in students, they'll be protected for life against the ravages of stress.

As the authors noted (Werner and Smith, 1992, p. 209):

The life stories of the resilient youngsters now grown into adulthood teach us that competence, confidence, and caring can flourish, even under adverse conditions, if children encounter persons who provide them with the secure basis for the development of trust, autonomy, and initiative. From odds successfully overcome springs hope—a gift each of us can share with a child—at home, in the classroom, on the playground, or in the neighborhood.

Teachers of these children should be encouraged by such findings and do all they can to capitalize on the strengths of these children. With amazing frequency, these students mention teachers who offered them support and guidance. For example, some of these children may have a special talent you can appeal to, such as a facility with numbers, or a love of reading, or artistic or musical ability. Encourage their problem-solving skills as much as possible so they can make the best of things around them (see Chapter 8) and do well in school.

We turn now to the final subject in our analysis of diversity and the classroom: the role that gender plays in academic achievement.

GENDER, DEVELOPMENT, AND THE CLASSROOM

"Manhood" needs to be redefined in a way that allows women equality and men pride. Our culture desperately needs new ways to teach boys to be men. Via the media and advertising, we are teaching our sons all the wrong lessons. Boys need a model of manhood that is caring and bold, adventurous and gentle. They need ways to be men that don't involve violence, misogyny, and the objectification of women. (Pipher, 1994, p. 290)

Let's work for a culture in which there is a place for every human gift, in which children are safe and protected, women are respected and men and women can love each other as whole human beings. Let's work for a culture in which the incisive intellect, the willing hands and the happy heart are beloved. Then our daughters will have a place where all their talents will be appreciated and they can flourish like green trees under the sun and the stars (Pipher, 1994, p. 293).

These words, taken from the remarkably popular *Reviving Ophelia*, pose one of the major difficulties in any discussion of how students acquire their gender identity in a way that they themselves and their society find acceptable. "Acceptable" means many things to many people, and gender roles for boys and girls/men and women are only slowly, even grudgingly, changing. And yet, understanding how girls and boys acquire their gender identity, the appropriate behavior accompanying their gender roles, and identifying what influences the process, will help you to assess the relationship between gender and classroom achievement.

You may well ask if an understanding of gender issues is that critical for effective teaching and learning. We'll answer that question by asking two others: Are females receiving the support they need, particularly in the classroom, to fulfill their potential? Or is their development being frustrated by a form of discrimination so subtle and sophisticated that it has become part of our daily lives? Once classroom achievement is pictured in a boy–girl frame, you can see the implications.

Before beginning our analysis of the relationship between gender and classroom achievement, we should first examine several pertinent and related topics.

Gender Equity

Let's begin by defining terms that we should use in a consistent manner. For several years psychologists, responding to Unger's plea (1979; Unger & Crawford, 1996), have urged that we use the terms *sex* and *gender* more carefully. In this new context, sex would refer to *biological* maleness or femaleness (for example, the sex chromosomes), and gender would suggest *psychosocial* aspects of maleness and femaleness (for example, changing gender roles). Although no absolute distinction is possible—we can't completely separate our ideas

Gender equity in the classroom means equally recognizing and rewarding the achievements of *both* girls and boys.

about gender from a person's body—this distinction can help us to focus on the major forces contributing to the acquisition of gender identity. Within this framework, we can now distinguish among gender identity, gender stereotypes, and gender roles.

- **Gender identity** is a conviction that one belongs to the sex of birth.

- **Gender stereotypes** reflects those beliefs about the characteristics associated with being male or female.

- **Gender role** refers to culturally acceptable sexual behavior.

The Danger of Stereotyping

Gender stereotyping refers to the beliefs that we have about the characteristics and behavior associated with males and females. From an early age we form ideas of what males and females should be, begin to accumulate characteristics about male and female, and assign labels to those categories.

As concern about gender equity has received more publicity, stereotypes about females and males are slowly eroding. However, many people are still treated according to stereotypical characteristics, severely limiting their potential. Lest you think we exaggerate, look carefully at Table 4.3, which speaks for itself. These figures are, in a sense, a microcosm of the entire chapter. Note the discrepancies due to sex and race, which translate into social class distinctions. The issues we're discussing in this chapter are deep-rooted, far-reaching (into classrooms), and long-lasting. (For an excellent summary of the place of women in education, see Sadker & Sadker, 1994, pp. 15–41.)

Although gender stereotyping is only one part of gender development, it illustrates the importance of the relationship between gender, schooling, and development. At an early age, children construct social categories from the world around them, attach certain characteristics to these categories, and then label the categories. This process may be positive because it helps children to organize their world. It may also be negative if the characteristics associated with a particular category are limiting: "Girls just can't do math" (Serbin, Powlishta, & Gulko, 1993).

GENDER
IDENTITY
The conviction that one belongs to the sex of birth.

GENDER
STEREOTYPES
Beliefs about the characteristics associated with males or females.

GENDER ROLE
Culturally acceptable sexual behavior.

Table 4.3 AVERAGE ANNUAL EARNINGS BY EDUCATION, SEX, AND RACE

	Total	No H.S.	H.S. Grad	Some College	Bachelor's Degree	Advanced Degree
Male	32,087	16,633	25,038	27,636	46,278	67,032
Female	18,684	9,189	14,995	16,928	26,483	39,905
Hispanic	18,568	13,733	17,323	21,041	29,165	51,898
White	26,696	13,941	20,911	22,648	37,996	56,475
Black	19,772	12,705	16,446	19,631	30,938	48,653

Source: Bureau of Census, U.S. Dept. of Commerce, 1995.

TIPS ON LEARNING AND MOTIVATION
Avoiding Gender Stereotyping

PRINCIPLE Girls and boys should have equal opportunities in the classroom.

STRATEGY Be aware that the characteristics associated with a particular gender can have a negative image. "Oh, girls can't do math; boys shouldn't cry." The attitudes behind such comments contain pitfalls, especially for teachers. Watch your behavior to be certain that you call on girls or give them the same attention you do boys in science and math classes.

STRATEGY Recall Vygotsky's zone of proximal development and apply this concept to any of the girls in your class that you believe may have lost confidence because of an assumption that "girls can't do. . . ." Give them as much time and help as possible to bring them to the upper level of their potential.

PRINCIPLE Interactions with all students in all subjects should be as equal and positive as possible.

STRATEGY Call on girls as frequently as boys in questioning sessions. Use these exchanges to bolster confidence and encourage participation by the girls in your class.

STRATEGY Reinforce the responses of girls to the same extent and in the same manner as you do boys. Attention, opportunity, and reinforcement will go a long way in undoing previous damage.

One of the first categories children form is sex related; there is a neat division in their minds between male and female. Children then move from the observable physical differences between the sexes and begin to acquire gender knowledge about the behavior expected of males and females. Although its content varies according to the source of this knowledge, gender role stereotyping has commenced, and attitudes toward gender are being shaped. As Serbin and her colleagues (1993) noted, despite the societal changes we have seen in acceptable gender roles, gender role stereotypes have remained relatively stable. What do we know about the acquisition of gender identity?

Becoming Boys and Girls

We may find clues to identifying and understanding the current status of females in our schools by examining the processes by which boys and girls acquire their sense of gender identity. Both biology and the environment contribute to this in a complex, interactive manner. Most psychologists today believe in a reciprocal interaction model of development to explain behavior. That is, we respond to those around us, and they change; they respond to us, and we change; it's an ongoing process. (Remember Piaget's ideas of assimilation and accommodation.) Clearly, then, the reaction of others to ideas of gender, particularly if they are stereotypical, can influence children's gender identity.

Does the Environment Count?

Boys may be born boys, and girls may be born girls, but it doesn't take them long to discover which behavior "fits" boys and which "fits" girls (Fagot, Leinbach, & O'Boyle, 1992). Children have the cognitive competency to acquire their own gender identity by 2 to 3 years of age, so you can understand their rapid assignment of appropriate behavior to either male or female. Lott (1989) reported that by preschool age, most children are well aware of their own gender, of which parent they are most like, and of the gender of family members and peers (Martin, Wood, & Little, 1990).

How soon do children begin to make decisions about appropriate behavior based on sex? Lott (1989) reported the result of a study that required children from 2 to 7 years of age to assign various occupations to either a male or a female doll. As early as 2 years of age, they assigned traditionally male occupations to male dolls. For example, 67% 2- and 3-year-olds chose the male doll to be a doctor.

In an attempt to explain these and similar findings, Martin and colleagues (1990) found a developmental sequence to the appearance of gender stereotypes. In the initial phases, children learn what kinds of things are associated with each sex, for example, a football for boys, a doll for girls. From the ages 4 to 6 years, children move to the second stage, where they begin to learn the more complex associations for their own sex, such as the different kinds of activities associated with a toy: A boy realizes you just don't throw a football, you can also pick it up and run with it, or try to tackle someone else. By roughly 6 to 8 years, children make the same types of associations for the opposite sex. Where do these ideas come from? Among the most influential of the socialization agents are family, peers, and the media.

Family Evidence clearly suggests that parents treat boy and girl babies differently from birth. Adults tend to engage in rougher play with boys, give them stereotypical toys (cars and trucks), and speak differently to them. By the end of the second year, parents respond favorably to what they consider gender appropriate (that is, stereotypical) behavior and negatively to cross-sex play (girls engaging in typically boys' play and vice versa). For example, Fagot (1985; Fagot & Hagan, 1991), who observed toddlers and their parents at home, discovered that both mothers and fathers differentially reinforced their children's behavior. That is, they reinforced girls for playing with dolls and boys for playing with blocks, girls for helping their mothers around the house and boys for running and jumping.

Lips (1993) believes that parents are unaware of the extent to which they engage in this type of reinforcement. In a famous study (Will, Self, & Data, 1976), eleven mothers were observed interacting with a 6-month-old infant. Five of the mothers played with the infant when it was dressed in blue pants and called "Adam." Six mothers later they played with the same infant when it wore a pink dress and was called "Beth." The mothers offered

"Oh, it's just more white-male stuff."

a doll to Beth and a toy train to Adam. They also smiled more at Beth and held her more closely. The baby was actually a boy. Interviewed later, all the mothers said that boys and girls were alike at this age and *should be treated identically.*

Siblings also influence gender development. Brothers and sisters differ markedly in personality, intelligence, and psychopathology in spite of shared genetic roots. Since about 80% of children have siblings and spend considerable time with one another, these relationships exercise a considerable and complex influence (Berk, 1997b). An older brother showing a younger brother how to hold a bat (or the older brother showing his sister how to hold a bat), a younger sister or brother watching an older sister play with dolls, quarrelling among siblings—each of these examples illustrates the impact that sibling relationships have on gender development. We also know that parents react differently to brothers and sisters. Consequently, males and females grow up in quite different learning environments, with important psychological implications for development. Peers are another important part of these different learning environments.

Peers   Admit it; you still smile when you recall certain childhood friends, or grimace at the thought of others. Think back for a moment. When you started to make friends and played with them, weren't most of your friends the same sex? And didn't your games and activities foster and maintain the gender stereotypes of your day?

Studies show that by the age of 3, children reinforce each other for gender-typed play; by age 4, children play with same-sex playmates three times as much as they do with other-sex friends; and by age 6, the ratio has climbed to 11 to 1 (Berk, 1997b). When they engage in "gender-inappropriate" play (boys with dolls, girls with a football), their peers immediately criticize them and tend to isolate them. This tendency increases with age, until most adolescents react with intense demands for conformity to stereotypical gender roles.

Here, again, we see the influence of imitation and reinforcement. During development, youngsters of the same sex tend to play together, a custom called **sex cleavage** which is encouraged by parents and teachers. Even in adolescence, despite dating and opposite sex attraction, both males and females want to live up to the most rigid interpretations of what their group thinks is ideally male or female. Imitation, reinforcement and cognitive development all come together to establish firmly what a boy thinks is masculine and what a girl thinks is feminine (Berk, 1997b).

The Media   Another influence on gender development, one that carries important messages about what is desirable for males and females and one that reaches into the home, is the media, especially television (Unger & Crawford, 1996). Television has assumed such a powerful place in the socialization of children that it is safe to say that it is almost as significant as family and peers. What is particularly bothersome is the stereotypical behavior that it presents as both positive and desirable. As Lips (1993) stated flatly, television teaches gender stereotypes. The more television children watch, the more stereotypical is their behavior.

Framing the Picture   A telling example of television's ability to grip the mind and form stereotypes is seen in the words of a powerful network executive in television's early days:

> We were learning how to serve it up, how to make it more dramatic, more exciting. We were dealing with something called the attention span; my job was to capture and hold the attention of the American public by putting on the best show, like putting a frame around a picture. (White, 1975, p. 39.)

When the picture is gender, how it's framed shapes the meaning of that picture, and if the frame casts a shadow of gender stereotypes, the impact on developing minds is insidious, powerful, and long-lasting.

Programs such as *Murphy Brown* and *Dr. Quinn, Medicine Woman* are the exception. The rule is that the central characters of shows are much more likely to be male than female, themes will be action-oriented for males, and the characters typically engage in stereotypical behavior (men are the executives and leaders, women are the housewives and secretaries). Much the same holds true for television commercials. There is little doubt that children notice the different ways television portrays males and females and it affects their views of gender. In one study, when asked to rate the behavior of males and females, children aged 8 to 13 responded in a rigidly stereotypical manner: Males were brave, adventurous, and intelligent and made good decisions. Females, on the other hand, cried easily and needed to be protected (Lips, 1993).

These distinctions apply to other, much more subtle, features of television programming. To understand a television program, children must know something about story form: how stories are constructed and presented. They must use their general knowledge of the world and situations and events to grasp television's content; this prior understanding often reinforces what they are watching. They must also have knowledge of television's forms and conventions to help them understand what is happening on the screen. Music and visual techniques, even camera angles, all convey information (Liebert, Sprafkin, & Davidson 1988).

In other words, children learn more than the contents of a program from television. Among other things, they learn the many cues that signal "male" or "female": Loud music, rapid scene changes, multiple sound effects, and frequent cuts mean just one thing: a male-oriented show. Shows designed for females have soft background music, gentle cuts, and soothing sound effects. Children as young as 6 years can use these cues to identify which shows are intended for males and which for females (Lips, 1993). Children understand

Sex Cleavage
The tendency of children of the same sex to play together.

television programs according to their development, and their level of development is affected by their television viewing, with all that implies for gender development. We now turn our attention to several theories that attempt to explain gender development.

Theories of Gender Development

Several theories of gender development have generated most of the research during the past ten years: social learning theory, cognitive developmental theory, and gender schema theory. Proponents of *social learning theory* believe that parents (as the distributors of reinforcement) reinforce appropriate gender role behaviors. By their choice of toys, by urging "boy" or "girl" behavior, and by reinforcing this behavior, parents encourage their children to engage in gender-appropriate behavior (Bandura, 1997, pp. 430–436). If the parents have good relationships with their children, they become models for their children to imitate, encouraging them to acquire additional gender-related behavior. Thus children are reinforced or punished for different kinds of behavior. They also learn appropriate gender behavior from other male and female models (such as those in television shows and in their classroom—their teachers!).

A second explanation, quite popular today, is found in *cognitive developmental theory.* We know from Piaget's work that children engage in symbolic thinking by about 2 years of age. Using this ability, children, by assimilation and accommodation, acquire their ideas about gender, apply these ideas to themselves, and then begin the process of acquiring gender-appropriate behavior.

A third theory, **gender schema theory**, is a newer, and different, cognitive explanation (Bem, 1992, 1993). As discussed earlier, a schema is a mental blueprint for organizing information, and children develop a schema for gender. This schema helps a child to develop gender identity and formulate an appropriate gender role. Consequently, children develop an integrated schema or picture of what gender is and should be.

This brief examination has shown that both biological and environmental forces contribute to gender, and that several theories attempt to explain the process. But are males and females actually that different?

Gender Similarities and Differences

As knowledge about gender behavior increases, there is a growing consensus that the differences between the sexes are not as great as they were once thought to be. In a benchmark study of gender differences published in 1974, Maccoby and Jacklin concluded that males were superior in mathematical and visual-spatial skills, whereas females had better verbal skills. Recent studies identified gender similarities and differences. (For a summary of this research, see Berk, 1997b.) We can capsulize this research by stating that there are many similarities between males and females and that any differences that do exist aren't necessarily caused by biological forces.

The recent work of Pinker (1994) helps to give a balanced perspective on differences between any human beings. Pinker noted that anthropologists frequently stress differences between peoples (the "strange behaviors" of others) and often understate the many similarities among all humans. Pinker specified universal human characteristics such as humor, insults, fear, anger, storytelling, laws, dreams, words for common objects, binary distinctions, measures, common facial expressions (happy, sad, angry, fearful), crying, and displays of affection, among others. Pinker identified these attributes as complex interactions between a universal human nature and the conditions of living in a human body on this planet (Pinker, 1994, p. 415). Obviously, the point of this discussion is that humans are quite similar, regardless of any male-female distinctions.

GENDER SCHEMA
THEORY

A mental blueprint for organizing information about gender.

Shared classroom experiences help to further relationships between boys and girls and also help to dispel any lingering gender stereotypes.

Nevertheless, some differences do exist, as seen in Table 4.4. As studies of the environment become more sophisticated, however, it's important to point out that these differences are not fixed. That is, changes in our understanding occur as more-sophisticated research techniques produce new data. One example of this is the realization that differences in mathematical abilities are not as great as they were once thought to be.

With these ideas in mind, we turn to how gender impacts classroom performance.

Gender and Classroom Achievement

Many young women are less whole and androgynous than they were at age ten. They are more appearance-conscious and sex-conscious. They are quieter, more fearful of holding strong opinions, more careful of what they say and are less honest. They're more likely to second-guess themselves and to be self-critical. They are bigger worriers and effective people pleasers. They are less likely to play sports, love math and science and plan on being president. They hide their intelligence. Many must fight for years to regain all the territory that they lost. (Pipher, 1994, p. 264)

These words, heard over and over again, must be a red flag for teachers. The relationship of gender to classroom performance has inspired considerable research that has taken a definite direction. Teacher–student and student–student interaction patterns, curricular content, and testing have all been scrutinized in an effort to detect gender bias. Achieving gender equity in the classroom means equally recognizing and rewarding the achievements of both boys and girls. Let's begin by looking at interaction patterns.

Interaction Patterns

Before examining how gender may possibly affect teacher–student interactions, we should pause to consider the importance of **interactions.** As we mentioned earlier in the chapter, a relationship develops from a pattern of intermittent interactions over an extended period of time. Do any clues exist as to why the quality of interactions with teachers can vary so widely from student to student?

INTERACTIONS
Exchanges between individuals.

Table 4.4 OBSERVED GENDER DIFFERENCES

Characteristic	Gender Difference
Physical Differences	Although almost all girls mature more rapidly than boys, by adolescence, boys have surpassed girls in size and strength.
Verbal Ability	Girls do better on verbal tasks beginning in the early years, a superiority that is retained. Boys also exhibit more language problems than girls.
Spatial Skill	Boys do better on spatial tasks, which continues throughout schooling.
Mathematical Ability	There is little, if any, difference in the early years; boys begin to do better during the high school years.
Science	Gender differences seem to be increasing; females are falling behind while the performance of males is increasing.
Achievement Motivation	Differences here seem to be linked to task and situation. Boys do better in stereotypically "masculine" tasks (math, science), and girls in "feminine" tasks (art, music). In direct competition between males and females, beginning around adolescence, girls need for achievement seems to drop.
Aggression	Boys appear to be innately more aggressive than girls, a difference that appears early and is remarkably consistent.

As we have indicated, many teachers treat boys and girls differently. The elementary school has frequently been characterized as a feminine domain, more conducive to the needs and interests of girls than to those of boys. But several interesting issues arise upon examining the data more carefully. Although girls, in general, do better than boys in the elementary grades, girls lose this achievement edge in secondary school, especially in such subjects as science and mathematics. Why? One reason may be an extension into the classroom of stereotypic attitudes toward gender: Boys are reinforced for intellectual pursuits, girls for nurturing activities. Teachers more frequently attribute failure in boys to lack of motivation, while girls more frequently are seen as lacking ability.

How teachers interact with their students has long intrigued researchers. One finding has been consistent: Regardless of the level of schooling, teachers pay more attention to boys than to girls. Frequently, boys simply demand more attention than girls. These findings are particularly applicable to math and science classes. Teachers reported to researchers that they had similar expectations for boys and girls; yet, when the same teachers were observed in class, they questioned the boys as much as 80% more than the girls. Also, in science classes, it was much more common to have the experiments demonstrated by a boy (Bailey, 1993).

The Sadkers (1994) reported that although teachers believed they held all of their students accountable to classroom rules (for example, raising their hands when they want to speak), their observed behavior was quite different. In the give-and-take of the classroom, boys quickly dominated any discussion; they called out eight times more often than girls (Sadker & Sadker, 1994, p. 43). An interesting finding associated with this research is that even when the boys' called-out comments were irrelevant, teachers still responded to them. When girls, on the other hand, called out, teachers frequently reminded them of the calling-out rules, a clear sign of differential treatment.

Gender differences also appear in the nature of teacher–student interactions, that is, the types of comments teachers use when they are interacting with boys as compared with

---

CASE NOTES

Observation   An examination of the way teachers interact with different types of students may yield additional insights into classroom relationships.

Hypothesis   We no longer believe in the model that active teachers do something to passive students. As we now know, changes in one member of the relationship produce changes in the other. Teachers change as the result of changes in their pupils.

Possible Action   Marsha Warren must initially be sure that she herself has no negative feelings about any group members and constantly be alert to the cultural, class, and gender nuances in her classroom.

---

girls. Identifying four types of teacher comments (praise, acceptance, remediation, and criticism), the Sadkers (1994) found that males received more of *all* types of comments but particularly more praise, criticism, and remediation, which are more useful kinds of comments. In other words, boys received more precise teacher feedback. As you might imagine, these findings were particularly applicable to math and science classes.

In reading the motivation literature, you will come across terms such as *learned helplessness* and *attribution*. Do girls acquire a sense of academic helplessness and lose their scholarly initiative as a result of differential treatment? Do they attribute feelings of powerlessness in the classroom to their perceived lack of ability? These are difficult questions to answer, yet ones that research must continue to address (American Association of University Women [AAUW], 1992). Similar issues appear in any examination of the relationship between gender and the curriculum. A good example can be seen in students' attitudes toward computers.

Gender and Educational Technology

In most studies assessing gender differences, girls tend to show less favorable attitudes to the use of technology than boys (Krendl & Broihier, 1992; Martin, Heller, & Mahmoud, 1992; Todman & Dick, 1993), a finding that spans ages—elementary, middle, and high school students—as well as national boundaries—the United States, Britain, Canada, China, and the former Soviet Union. These differences become significant when you consider the increasingly central role computers play in schools, careers, and everyday life.

How do we explain these differences? Is it that girls tend to have less experience with computers and technology in general than boys, and so show more negative attitudes toward them (Martin et al., 1992)? Or could it be that both girls and boys see computers as a more male-appropriate domain than female-appropriate (Wilder, Mackie, & Cooper, 1985)? You can see, then, the need for continued research to pinpoint the reasons for these observable differences.

Although gender differences consistently appear, the news is not all bad. Evidence exists that the gap between males and females may actually be narrowing. For example, Parasuraman and Igbaria (1990) found no gender differences in computer attitudes when the study participants consisted of highly educated adults whose jobs depended on the use of computer technology. Although Ayersman (1996) found that male college students rated themselves as having significantly greater general computer knowledge than females rated themselves, he found no gender differences in computer anxiety.

Girls and boys alike need to be encouraged from an early age to view computers as an integral and natural part of their lives. Teachers and parents can help by modeling positive attitudes and reinforcing both genders for their interest in and work on computers and other forms of technology.

Gender and the Curriculum

If you were to select one document that illustrates a classroom's, school's, district's, or state's views on a particular issue, you would do well to look at its curriculum. The message that it contains reveals a particular position on matters of culture, class, and gender. At a cursory glance, a curriculum might seem to address only academic subjects. But a closer look would disclose some important underlying assumptions. For example, certain attitudes toward women are reflected in a course in American history in which there is little, if any, mention of outstanding American women of the particular period being studied.

Most state curriculum guides identify the philosophies that undergird specific curriculum content. A state curriculum should also give suggestions for adapting content to special groups, helping teachers to highlight, for example, the role of American women in education, medicine, business, and the armed forces.

A school system uses state guidelines and applies them to the local population (Borich, 1992). Then the instructor takes the state and school district suggestions, examining them for specific resources that address a particular issue (such as gender and achievement). Do these materials offer help in determining definite units of study and daily lesson plans? Are there illustrations of the tangible accomplishments of outstanding women, for example, Nadine Gordimer, the South African woman who won the Nobel Prize for Literature in 1991, or the psychologist Eleanor Gibson, who won a National Medal of Science in 1992? Illustrations such as these are easily woven into a curriculum and can only produce positive results.

An educator who wants to teach specific contributions of women in history can collect stories, books, videotapes, and films that illustrate and support this objective as well as the larger goal of increasing regard for the role of women in general. The teacher can also ask leading women of the community to come to the classroom to explain the nature of their work. This is a sure and simple way to raise the self-esteem of the girls in the class.

Banks (1993a) offered a helpful framework for including gender material (as well as cultural and class content) in a curriculum. He has identified four levels of integration, the first of which is the *contributions approach*. This typically is the initial step used by teachers and school systems and involves using heroic figures as curricular illustrations (for example, Rosa Parks, whose refusal to move to the back of the bus triggered the overt activities of the American civil rights movement). The curriculum remains the same except for the inclusion of the heroic figures.

The second level is the *additive approach*. Here various themes and perspectives are added to the curriculum without changing its overall structure. Something new is brought to the curriculum, such as material about pioneer women or a book such as *The Color Purple*. The third level of integration is the *transformational approach* in which the goals, structure, and perspectives of the curriculum are changed. Banks (1993a, p. 203) gave the example of studying the American Revolution: The perspectives of the revolutionaries, the loyalists, women, African Americans, Native Americans, and the British all need to be considered.

At the fourth and final level, *the social action approach*, students make decisions and take actions that incorporate the changes of the transformational level. The goal is to encourage students to undertake social criticism and social change by teaching them decision-making skills. At this level, questions similar to the following can guide your efforts to introduce positive gender concepts in the classroom: Why are women discriminated against? What causes this discrimination? Does it occur in the classroom? What can be done about it? At this point we should also consider the possibility of test bias.

Current Issues & Perspectives

Equal Education for All: Does That Include Girls?

The introduction to a report commissioned by the American Association of University Women, *How Schools Shortchange Girls* (1992), begins:

> *There is clear evidence that the educational system is not meeting girls' needs. Girls and boys enter school roughly equal in measured ability. On some measures of school readiness, such as fine motor control, girls are ahead of boys. Twelve years later, girls have fallen behind their male classmates in key areas such as higher level mathematics and measures of self-esteem. Today's students are tomorrow's citizens, parents and workers. It is they who will bear the responsibility for maintaining a vital and creative society. To leave girls on the sidelines in discussions of educational reform is to deprive ourselves of the full potential of half of our work force, half of our citizenry and half of the parents of the next generation.*

Many educators attribute the drop in girls' self-esteem to the negative message the curriculum delivers over and over to girls: Men's lives count for more. To counter any such opinions, ask yourself if females are being adequately represented and justly portrayed in the material you're using. Is the reading list for the year authored mostly by men? Are the stories about boys' adventures? Are the masterpieces for discussion all, or mostly all, works by males? Are the scientists and mathematicians cited all male?

Others disagree with this point of view and argue that if women are included in the curriculum that's well and good, but teachers cannot dismiss the scope of a curriculum based on any one issue. You have barely enough time as it is to do your work and can't be expected to spend all the hours it would take to revamp a curriculum and to supplement the students' lessons with additional information.

Interactions within the classroom itself are as important as the curriculum for contributing to lowered self-images for girls. Studies have repeatedly shown that boys receive more precise teacher comments than do girls, for both scholarship and conduct. Teachers should be trained in classroom interaction strategies to establish more equitable classroom environments. But teachers are not always aware of the way they interact with their students, thus inservice training sessions would benefit teachers and all of their students.

Those who disagree with this reasoning believe that teachers have to be able to respond to the needs of the classroom quickly. When you ask a question or comment on a behavior, you don't always have the time or presence of mind to reflect and consider whether it is a boy or a girl. Consequently, teachers cannot be expected to keep mental tallies in their minds of how many times they have responded to boys versus how many times they have responded to girls. Most teachers try to make sure they are responding to the individual needs of their students, regardless of gender.

Several strategies have been identified as promoting a more equitable gender learning environment. Thus you should experiment with different groupings within your classroom, keeping the gender issue constantly in mind. Since you rearrange your students for different subjects, it's easy for you to add the gender dimension to your groups.

Yet opponents of this viewpoint state that teachers cannot always form ideal groups. In the lower grades, the socialization that takes place within the classroom is as important as academic work. What kind of message would the teacher be sending to encourage children to sit only with other boys or only with other girls? We must teach our students to work together.

What do you think? What's your opinion on these issues?

Test Bias

An important aspect of the relationship between curriculum and gender is evaluation. Do the same issues apply to testing that we have seen with regard to other school activities? To put it simply: Is gender bias evident in school testing? The intent here is not to analyze the strengths and weaknesses of various types of tests; that will be done in Chapters 11 and 12. In this section we want to call your attention to the inherently powerful role that testing plays in determining the future of your students.

In a statement concerning the place of assessment in helping to attain equity, Madaus (1994, p. 77) identified one role of assessment as a large-scale, high-stakes policy tool, used to drive reform of schools and curricula and to make important decisions about individuals. It is in the "important decisions about individuals" that the possibility of bias exists. Pullin (1994, p. 46) argued that the potential for gender differences resides in almost any testing or assessment program, especially if the testing involves mathematical skills. For example, examining the scores on the Scholastic Achievement Test (SAT) reveals that performance is consistently higher for males than for females.

If gender bias in testing exists, it must be addressed. As Pullin (1994) noted, any allegation of gender bias in assessment could be subject to legal challenge, given the provisions of Title IX, which bars any form of sex discrimination in all educational programs and activities conducted by recipients of federal financial aid. These safeguards are intended to ensure access to equal educational opportunity, both in schools and the workplace. The rationale behind this directive is that assessment programs should be used to survey the possibilities for student growth, and not just to designate students as ready or not ready to profit from standard instruction.

Is there any basis for these concerns? To answer this question, we turn once again to the notion of equal access to opportunity. One example was offered by Rosser (1989), who pointed out that girls are more likely than boys to go to college but that scholarships based on test scores are twice as likely to go to boys. Another example of possible bias is the use of SAT scores to predict college success. SAT scores underpredict women's success and overpredict men's (AAUW, 1992). When researchers examined the SAT scores of men and women who received the same grades in the same college courses, they discovered that the women's SAT scores were 35 points below the men's. Finally, the National Commission on Testing and Public Policy (1990) reported that women averaged 56 points lower than men on the SAT. (Incidentally, relative to whites, African Americans averaged 92 points lower, Puerto Ricans 90 points lower, Mexican Americans 63 points lower, and Asian Americans 37 points lower.)

What can you as a teacher do to help reverse the discrepancy between male and female scores? Just being aware of the differences that appear in math and science scores, for example, suggests certain techniques. Make sure your questions and comments are evenly distributed to boys and girls; involve girls in math and science cooperative learning activities. If you are particularly concerned about gender differences in performance, provide a setting in which girls (and any boys experiencing problems) can study math and science topics with guidance before they are covered in class. These and similar practices can help girls feel more at ease with science and mathematics and gradually help them to improve their test scores and to give them equal access to opportunity.

Teacher–Student Relationships: A Summary

Finally, remember that regardless of a student's actual ability, teachers, using a number of variables (including cultural, social, and gender), form certain expectations for their students. They then, subtly or otherwise, communicate these feelings to individual students who quickly grasp the messages and react accordingly. Students begin to see themselves as bright or slow, as individuals of whom much is expected or those of whom little is expected.

TIPS ON COMMUNICATION
Valuing Relationships

PRINCIPLE Interactions with students determine the value of the relationship.

STRATEGY Fairness is a teacher characteristic that students cherish and one that powerfully affects the teacher–student relationship. Check your behavior often in this regard. Keep these questions in mind: Am I fair to all of my pupils, regardless of culture, social class, or gender? Do I treat them all in the same way?

STRATEGY Remember to treat *all* of your students with dignity and respect. If you treat them courteously, the majority of students will respond in kind. In any survey of desirable teacher characteristics, students always say something like this: "The teacher always acted nice toward us; you feel good as a person." Dignity, respect, and courtesy are remarkably strong forces in creating a positive relationship.

STRATEGY Use occasional humor in your interactions with your students. Don't attempt to be a stand-up comic, but remember that students appreciate it when you react humorously to some lighthearted incident in the classroom or when you joke about an innocent mistake in class.

Here you can observe the telling impact of reciprocal interactions. You as a teacher behave toward a student in a certain way; the student reacts to your behavior; you react in turn. The norms are set and the student performs in a manner consistent with the interactions that have shaped the relationship between the two of you. In this chapter, we have stressed that teacher and students each bring givens with them—their culture, their social class, and their gender—and that the resulting interactions of the distinct personalities affect the classroom atmosphere and are the basis of teacher–student relationships.

If you think about your role and how you visualize your instruction, you should become more sensitive to the reasons for your reactions to specific pupils. As you do, try to assess your interactions with particular pupils: good, positive, too negative, too infrequent. If you decide that a change in a particular relationship is necessary, focus on the specific interactions with that student and attempt to determine why you (and this student) are acting as you do. Are you reacting to a stereotype? Have you formed prior expectations? In this way, you'll improve your relationships with your students, thus improving your teaching and your students' learning.

Case Reflections

This chapter, with its focus on classroom diversity, reflects many of the problems Marsha Warren faces each day. As you read this chapter and thought about her classroom, what were your immediate reactions? Obviously, the teacher realized she wasn't reaching several of her students, and the resultant clashes she had with them were affecting the rest of the class. Were there clues in her students' behavior that she was missing? Do you think she was overlooking possible sources of help? With your classmates, suggest some new avenues for Marsha to explore.

CHAPTER HIGHLIGHTS

Different Cultures, Difficult Adjustments

- Awareness of cultural differences helps teachers to avoid misjudgments in working with a diverse group of students.

Culture and the Schools

- Cultural differences imply the transmission of ideas from generation to generation by significant members of older generations. Differences are not deficits, nor do differences imply something "wrong" or "bad."

- The cultural compatibility hypothesis suggests that when instruction is compatible with cultural patterns of problem solving, learning improves.

- Four variables that have been manipulated to bring about greater compatibility with different cultures are (1) social organization, (2) cognition, (3) motivation, and (4) sociolinguistics.

- The growing diversity in the nation's classrooms highlights the need for a greater emphasis on multicultural education.

- In an effort to help students with limited language proficiency to succeed in schools, the number of bilingual education programs has grown rapidly.

Social Class and Academic Achievement

- Socioeconomic status (SES) is a reliable predictor of school achievement and suggests that students from the same social class will perform in a similar manner.

- Parents can have a profound influence on their children's view of school and learning.

Gender, Development, and the Classroom

- Gender refers to psychosocial aspects of maleness and femaleness, whereas sex refers to biological maleness and femaleness.

- Gender identity is a conviction that one belongs to the sex of birth.

- Gender stereotypes reflect those beliefs about the characteristics associated with being male or female.

- Gender role refers to culturally acceptable sexual behavior.

- Researchers have consistently reported that teachers pay more attention to boys than girls. Boys simply demand more attention than girls. These findings are particularly applicable to math and science classes.

- The quality of the relationships between teachers and students will influence the success of instruction, classroom management, and students' learning.

WHAT DO YOU THINK?

1. The expression "different is not deficit" has received wide acceptance. When you think of your friends who have cultural backgrounds that differ from yours, do you understand why this concept needs to be emphasized? Explain your answer.

2. Some individuals have stated that cultural compatibility is just another fad. Students will learn, regardless of their culture. How do you respond to this?

3. Do you agree with the statement that since all students are expected to graduate from high school, schools must adapt to their changing population to lower the dropout rate? Why?

4. From your own classroom experiences, would you agree that there is a difference in how boys and girls are treated?

Exceptional Students

Chapter Outline

Marsha Warren is a third-grade teacher who is experiencing a challenging class. The class includes eight students who are experiencing problems in the school and/or home that are influencing their academic progress. In this chapter we will focus on some issues that will help you understand students with exceptional education needs.

Objectives

When you finish reading this chapter, you should be able to

- identify the various types of exceptionalities
- appraise the progress of mainstreamed students in your class
- discriminate the range of individual differences among your students
- contrast educational programs for specific exceptionalities
- formulate appropriate classroom techniques for students to address their specific exceptionalities
- apply what you have learned to the case of Marsha Warren

EXCEPTIONAL

A term that refers to one or more kinds of special needs or characteristics in children.

AT RISK

A term used to describe those children who have a high probability of developing a disability.

In Chapters 2 and 3, we described the typical course of development for most students, tracing the manner in which they learn and best respond to instruction. Although all students exhibit individual differences, some have been identified as *students who are exceptional.* (Note: **Exceptional** is a general term referring to one or more kinds of exceptionality.) This chapter is devoted to an analysis of exceptional students and their classroom activities. There is a wide range of disabilities from those students who have learning problems to those that have multiple physical disabilities to those who are gifted and talented. This chapter will help you understand the wide range of exceptional students teachers encounter in the classroom. The chapter will also help you understand some of the educational and psychological services that can be provided to these students.

EXCEPTIONAL CHILDREN IN THE CLASSROOM

Individual differences fascinate and challenge the instructional skills of every teacher. There are countless individual differences among students who have been identified as exceptional learners with exceptional needs. As we attempt to meet all these needs, the students' developmental characteristics can guide us to choose appropriate curriculum materials and foster a supportive classroom atmosphere. Instruction in any subject must be adapted to students who differ in a wide range of abilities. To understand students who are exceptional, let's start our discussion with students who are considered at risk for developing serious problems. We also describe how students with varying abilities are grouped for instructional purposes.

Children at Risk

Although this chapter focuses on students who already have been identified as exceptional, there is another group of students who are considered **at risk.** These children are not currently identified with disabilities, but they are considered to have a high probability of becoming disabled (Heward & Orlansky, 1988). Many children who fall into the at-risk group are preschoolers. Another way of characterizing these students is that they are in danger of failing to complete their education with adequate levels of academic skills (Slavin & Madden, 1989). In fact, a number of variables lead us to predict that such students are at risk for dropping out of school. These risk factors include low academic achievement, grade retention, low socioeconomic status, social behavior problems, and poor school attendance (Slavin, 1989).

As you can imagine, a large number of programs have been designed for children at risk. In a comprehensive review of programs designed to help these children succeed in school, Slavin and Madden (1989) provided the following research synthesis for what works (and what does not work) with students at risk. Do these challenge any of your beliefs?

- First-grade prevention programs that include intensive resources, tutors, and small-group instruction increase students' reading achievement.

- Cooperative learning programs and continuous-progress models accelerate the achievement of students at risk.

- Frequent assessment of student progress that results in a restructuring of instructional content characterizes effective programs.

- Effective programs are comprehensive and include teachers' manuals, curriculum guides, lesson plans, and many other supportive materials.

You can expect to find a wide range of individual differences in schools.

■ Ineffective strategies include retention, which negatively affects achievement, and special pullout programs, which only keep students in the early grades from falling farther behind their regular education peers.

Many of the instructional and behavior management procedures that have been found to be effective with students at risk can and should also be used with students with exceptional needs. Keep these points in mind as you continue to read this chapter.

CHILDREN IN NEED OF SPECIAL EDUCATION

Teachers will encounter many students who are in need of special education services. These students will have one or more disabilities, and there is a great deal of diversity that characterizes students with disabilities.

Special-needs children have certain rights based on federal legislation. In 1975, Congress passed the Education for All Handicapped Children Act (PL94-142), which ensured that every child had some form of public education. In 1990, the Individuals with Disabilities Education Act (IDEA) amended PL41-142, and in 1997, PL105-17 was passed to further extend PL94-142. Some highlights of the legislation include the following (see Haring & McCormick, 1986):

1. *All children must be provided with a free, appropriate public education, regardless of the severity of their handicap.* The rationale for this requirement lies in our national commitment to education for all. PL105-17 extends "child find" (that is, locating children in need of services) to children in private schools. One important feature of this stipulation addresses the financial responsibility of government at all levels—not only an exceptional child's program but also any specialized service deemed vital must be supported.

2. *Children with disabilities must be included in general state and districtwide assessments and with appropriate accommodations.* In the past, many schools (and states) excluded children from general testing because of their disability. Many students can participate in traditional achievements and performance assessments given that an appropriate accommodation is made for their disability.

3. *All children who are potentially disabled must be fairly and accurately evaluated.* Historically, these children have suffered unnecessary burdens because of poor

---

TIPS ON LEARNING
The Importance of Individual Differences

PRINCIPLE Students with exceptional educational needs increase the range and scope of individual differences in the classroom.

STRATEGY To help understand student differences in the classroom, consider variations in physical, behavioral, and cognitive dimensions.

STRATEGY Conduct frequent curriculum-based assessment to help understand students in the classroom.

STRATEGY Meet with parents to help understand the contribution the home environment makes to individual differences.

---

evaluation procedures that led to faulty labeling and improper program placement. One outcome of these practices was that minority students, often experiencing language difficulties and cultural bewilderment, were placed in classes for children with mental retardation.

4. *The education of children who are exceptional must "match" individual capacities and needs.* One of the main features of the legislation is that each exceptional child receives an *individualized educational plan (IEP).* The IEP, based on the student's needs, is prepared annually by a committee that includes at least one regular education teacher if the child is in a regular education environment, at least one special education teacher, a school representative, an individual who can interpret evaluation results, and the child's parents. The IEP must incorporate a statement about the student's present level of functioning, long-term goals, short-term objectives, special services needed, and any other pertinent information. Figure 5.1 illustrates a typical IEP and the description of services to be provided to the child.

5. *Children who are exceptional must be educated in the least restrictive, most normal educational environment possible.* In addition to guiding classroom placement, PL105-17 also mandates the task of ensuring that those students who need separate placement be brought together with nondisabled students for physical education (where appropriate), assemblies, and lunch periods.

6. *Students' and parents' rights must be protected throughout all stages of evaluation, referral, and placement.* Parental involvement and consent have become an integral part of the entire process. To give you an idea of the role envisioned for parents in the process, consider several measures relating to need assessment and parental involvement.

Parents must receive a written notice in their native language about any change in identification, evaluation, or placement of their child. If parents remain dissatisfied with placement and education, they may initiate a due process hearing, which is conducted by someone not presently responsible for the child's education.

The legislation, sweeping in its scope, illustrates why some observers believe that it has produced and will continue to produce radical changes in education. Of importance here is the teacher's role in the process. Somewhere in the identification, evaluation, and placement procedure, teachers will be asked to comment on the child's classroom performance. (Some states have the teacher play a key role in presenting current and past educational information.)

Samuel A. Kirk

CASE NOTES

Observation   Students in Marsha Warren's class exhibited poor academic performance, attention problems, hyperactivity, language difficulties, and aggression.

Hypothesis   It is quite likely that several students in Marsha's class would meet criteria for exceptional educational needs.

Possible Action   How can Marsha learn more about students and their characteristics? She can record specific behaviors of concern. She can keep a close check on dates to determine the time between incidents. For example: What was the time of day?, Was it the same time each time the incident occurred?, What was the subject matter when the incident occurred? With these and other simple techniques, teachers can keep a close check on the progress of students who are exceptional.

Since the legislation also requires each state to develop and implement a comprehensive system of personnel development, teachers will experience changes in preservice education and in-service training. Sooner or later they will encounter the ramifications of PL94–142 and PL105-17.

According to regulations in IDEA, students are eligible for special education services based on two primary criteria. The first is that a student must meet criteria for one or more of the thirteen disability categories (described in the next section). Second, the student must require special education services to receive an appropriate education.

As we noted above, federal law also mandates that these students be placed in the **least restrictive environment** in which they can achieve success. *Least restrictive* means that students are to be removed from the regular classroom, home, and family as infrequently as possible. Their lives should be as "normal" as possible, and intervention should be consistent with individual needs and not interfere with individual freedom any more than is

LEAST RESTRICTIVE ENVIRONMENT

A learning environment or classroom situation that provides necessary support for a disabled student's continuing educational progress while also minimizing the time the student is removed from a normalized educational environment. In many ways, it has the same philosophical base as the practice of mainstreaming.

INDIVIDUALIZED EDUCATION PROGRAM   *9/11/98*
                                                                   Date

Student: _____ **Last Name** _____ **First** _____ **Middle** _____

_____ *5.3* _____ *8-4-85*
School of Attendance ___ **Home School** ___ **Grade Level** ___ **Birthdate/Age**

School Address _____ **School Telephone Number** _____

                                                    LD Teacher
Child Study Team Members _____ **Case Manager** _____

            Homeroom   *Parents*
Name _____ **Title** _____ **Name** _____ **Title** _____

            Facilitator
Name _____ **Title** _____ **Name** _____ **Title** _____

            Speech
Name _____ **Title** _____ **Name** _____ **Title** _____

Summary of Assessment Results
IDENTIFIED STUDENT NEEDS: *Reading from last half of*
_____ *DISTAR II—present performance level* _____

_____

_____

_____

LONG-TERM GOALS: *To improve reading achievement level by at*
_____ *least one year's gain. To improve math achievement to*
_____ *grade level. To improve language skills by one year's gain.*

_____

_____

SHORT-TERM GOALS: *Master Level 4 vocabulary and reading skills.*
_____ *Master math skills in basic curriculum. Master spelling*
_____ *words from Level 3 list. Complete Units 1-9 from*
_____ *Level 3 curriculum.*

_____

_____

        White copy–Cumulative folder   **Goldenrod–Case manager**
        Pink copy–Special teacher   **Yellow copy–Parent**

FIGURE 5.1   An individualized education program and the description of services to be provided.

(James Ysseldyke and Robert Algozzine, *Introduction to Special Education*, 2nd ed. Copyright © 1990 by Houghton Mifflin Company. Reprinted (or adapted) with permission.)

DESCRIPTION OF SERVICES TO BE PROVIDED

Type of Service	Teacher	Starting Date	Amt. of time per day	OBJECTIVES AND CRITERIA FOR ATTAINMENT
SLD Level III	LD Teacher	9-11-98	2 1/2 hrs.	Reading: will know all vocabulary through the "Honeycomb" level. Will master skills as presented through DISTAR II. Will know 123 sound-symbols presented in "Sound Way to Reading." Math: will pass all tests at basic 4 level. Spelling: 5 words each week from Level 3 list. Language: will complete Units 1-9 of the grade 4 language program. Will also complete supplemental units from "Language Step by Step."

Regular Education Classes	Teacher	Amt. of time per day	OBJECTIVES AND CRITERIA FOR ATTAINMENT
		3 1/2 hrs.	Out-of-seat behavior: sit attentively and listen during mainstream class discussions. A simple management plan will be implemented if he does not meet this expectation. Mainsteam modifications of Social Studies: will keep a folder in which he expresses through drawing the topics his class will cover. Modified district social studies curriculum. No formal testing will be made. An oral reader will read text to him, and oral questions will be asked.

The following equipment, and other changes in personnel, transportation, curriculum, methods, and educational services will be made:

DISTAR II Reading Program, Spelling Level 3, "Sound Way to Reading" Program, vocabulary tapes

Substantiation of least restrictive alternatives:
The planning team has determined the student's academic needs are best met with direct SLD support in reading, math, language, and spelling.

ANTICIPATED LENGTH OF PLAN _1 yr._ **The next periodic review will be held:** _May 1999_
DATE/TIME/PLACE

☒ I do approve this program placement and the above IEP
☐ I do not approve this program placement and/or the above IEP   PARENT/GUARDIAN
☐ I request a conciliation conference

Principal or Designee

Table 5.1 IMPLEMENTING LEAST RESTRICTIVE ENVIRONMENT PLACEMENTS

---

1. Not all disabled children benefit from being placed in the "mainstream." So-called restrictive environments such as residential institutions, resource centers, and self-contained special education classrooms in many cases offer a child developmental opportunities that would be impossible to achieve in a "less restrictive" setting.

2. Placement of disabled children should be decided on an individual basis, based on the readiness of the special student and the preparedness of the receiving classroom to meet individual children's special needs.

3. Placement decisions should take into consideration a child's social and emotional developmental opportunities, as well as intellectual and physical development.

4. Teachers should be involved in placement decisions to ensure acceptance of the exceptional child in the classroom and to evaluate the capability of the classroom to accommodate the individual child's special needs. Regular teachers should be informed of special placements in their classes.

5. Transitional periods are often necessary to prepare both disabled and nondisabled students to adjust to new situations.

6. Staff development programs to prepare teachers to work with exceptional children in their classes must be available prior to such placements, and continuous support and training are necessary to meet problems as they arise. Special education teachers specialize in certain areas and may require in-service training when assigned children with disabilities in which they have little or no expertise. In-service training also is needed for paraprofessionals and other support personnel.

7. Class sizes must be kept low in special education, whether in a "restrictive" environment or in the regular classroom, to ensure the necessary individualization of instruction.

8. Certified special education teachers must be retained to continue to meet the needs of children in special classes and to work with regular teachers in developing appropriate instructional programs for exceptional children.

9. Counselors, psychologists, psychiatrists, and other auxiliary personnel must be readily available to special and regular teachers and parents.

10. Teachers should have regularly scheduled release time for consultations with support personnel.

11. Instructional materials, equipment, and facilities must be adapted to the needs of exceptional children in the regular classroom and throughout the school.

12. Scheduling of the educational program and buses should conform to the needs of exceptional children rather than vice versa.

13. Safeguards should exist to see that funds designated in special education follow the child, even if in a less restrictive environment, including the regular classroom.

From M. Rauth, "What Can Be Expected of the Regular Teacher? Ideals and Realities" in *Exceptional Education Quarterly*, Vol. No. 2, pp. 27–36. Copyright © 1981 by PRO-ED, Inc. Reprinted by permission.

absolutely necessary. For example, children should not be placed in special classes if they can be served adequately by resource teachers, and they should not be placed in institutions if special classes will serve their needs just as well (Hallahan & Kauffman, 1988). Given the importance of serving disabled students in the least restrictive environment, we offer Table 5.1 as a concise summary of guidelines for implementing least restrictive services.

Two other laws pertain to children with exceptionalities. These include the Americans with Disabilities Act of 1990 (ADA) and Section 504 of the Rehabilitation Act of 1973 (called 504). ADA is a civil rights law that protects individuals from discrimination solely on the basis of disability in employment, public services, and accommodations. Under

---

TIPS ON MOTIVATION
The Importance of Individualizing

PRINCIPLE   Students with exceptional educational needs may respond to the motivational tactics that can be used for any student.

STRATEGY   Provide positive reinforcement and feedback for good student performance.

STRATEGY   Provide students with good models of what final performance on an academic task would be.

STRATEGY   Provide interesting tasks for students to learn.

ADA, an individual with a disability is defined as a person who has a physical or mental impairment that substantially limits one or more life activities, has a record of such an impairment, and is regarded as having such an impairment. Children between the ages of 3 and 21 who are identified by the multidisciplinary team in a public school are eligible for protection under ADA if they fall into one or more of the thirteen categories of disability. Section 504 is a civil rights law that prohibits discrimination on the basis of disability in programs and activities, public and private, that receive any financial assistance. An individual who has a physical or mental impairment that substantially limits one or more major life activities, has a record of such an impairment, or is regarded as having such an impairment is protected under this law. A major difference between ADA and Section 504 is ADA's presumption that there may be systematic and widespread workplace discrimination against disabled individuals. Section 504 was designed to eliminate discrimination in the workplace and provide its standards for a judgment if an individual is a victim of discrimination.

IDEA provides a list of conditions that make a child eligible to receive special education services. Specifically, the condition must affect the student's education and typically results in the need for special education. In contrast, Section 504 is broader in that there is no categorical listing of disabling conditions. Technically, it is possible for someone to be eligible for special services under Section 504 but not under IDEA. Nevertheless, if a child is eligible for special education under IDEA, he or she will also be protected under Section 504. A number of potential disabilities are covered under Section 504, however, that may not be covered under IDEA, such as communicable diseases, temporary handicapping conditions, attention deficit disorder, behavior disorders, chronic asthma and severe allergies, physical handicaps, and diabetes. However, these conditions may adversely affect the child's education and thus qualify the child for special education under IDEA.

Let us now consider how these students are identified as exceptional.

AREAS OF EXCEPTIONALITY

To give you an idea of the diversity of students who may be in a typical classroom, the federal IDEA has identified the following thirteen categories of exceptionality: autism, deaf-blindness, deafness, hearing impairment, mental retardation, multiple disabilities, orthopedic impairment, other health impairment, serious emotional disturbance, specific learning disability, speech or language impairment, traumatic brain injury, and visual impairment. Specific criteria for the classification of these disabilities are provided for only the learning disabilities category. Table 5.2 provides a definition of the thirteen categories based on the federal regulation in IDEA.

Table 5.2 CATEGORIES OF DISABILITY ACCORDING TO IDEA

Disability	Definition
Autism	A developmental disability significantly affecting verbal and nonverbal communication and social interaction, generally evident before age 3, that adversely affects educational performance. Characteristics often associated with autism are engagement in repetitive activities and stereotyped movements, resistance to environmental change or change in daily routines, and unusual responses to sensory experiences. The term does not apply if a child's educational performance is adversely affected primarily because the child has a serious emotional disturbance.
Deaf-Blind	Concomitant hearing and visual impairments, the combination of which causes such severe communication and other developmental and educational problems that they cannot be accommodated in special education programs solely for children with deafness or children with blindness.
Deaf	A hearing impairment that is so severe that the child is impaired in processing linguistic information through hearing, with or without amplification, that adversely affects a child's educational performance.
Hearing Impairment	An impairment in hearing, whether permanent or fluctuating, that adversely affects a child's educational performance but that is not included under the definition of deafness in this section.
Multiple Disabilities	Concomitant (such as mental retardation-blindness, mental retardation-orthopedic impairment, etc.), the combination of which causes such severe educational problems that they cannot be accommodated in special education programs solely for one of the impairments. The term does not include deaf-blindness.
Orthopedic Impairment	A severe orthopedic impairment that adversely affects a child's educational performance. The term includes impairments caused by congenital anomaly (for example, clubfoot, absence of some member, etc.), impairments caused by disease (for example, poliomyelitis, bone tuberculosis, etc.), and impairments from other causes (for example, cerebral palsy, amputations, and fractures or burns that cause contractions).
Other Health Impairments	Having limited strength, vitality, or alertness due to chronic or acute health problems such as a heart condition, tuberculosis, rheumatic fever, nephritis, asthma, sickle cell anemia, hemophilia, epilepsy, lead poisoning, leukemia, or diabetes that adversely affect a child's educational performance.
Serious Emotional Disturbance	The term means a condition exhibiting one or more of the following characteristics over a long period of time and to a marked degree that adversely affects a child's educational performance: a. An inability to learn that cannot be explained by intellectual, sensory, or health factors; b. An inability to build or maintain satisfactory interpersonal relationships with peers and teachers; c. Inappropriate types of behavior or feelings under normal circumstances; d. A general pervasive mood of unhappiness or depression; or e. A tendency to develop physical symptoms or fears associated with personal or school problems.

(continue)

Table 5.2 (CONTINUED)

Disability	Definition
	The term includes schizophrenia. The term does not apply to children who are socially maladjusted, unless it is determined that they have a serious emotional disturbance.
Specific Learning Disability	A disorder in one or more of the basic psychological processes involved in understanding or in using language, spoken or written, that may manifest itself in an imperfect ability to listen, think, speak, read, write, spell, or to do mathematical calculations. The term includes such conditions as perceptual disabilities, brain injury, minimal brain dysfunction, dyslexia, and developmental aphasia. The term does not apply to children who have learning problems that are primarily the result of visual, hearing, or motor disabilities of mental retardation, of emotional disturbance, or of environmental, cultural, or economic disadvantage.
Speech or Language Impairment	A communication disorder such as stuttering, impaired articulation, a language impairment, or a voice impairment that adversely affects a child's educational performance.
Traumatic Brain Injury	An acquired injury to the brain caused by an external physical force, resulting in total or partial functional disability or psychosocial impairment, or both, that adversely affects a child's educational performance. The term applies to open or closed head injuries resulting in impairments in one or more areas, such as cognition; language; memory; attention; reasoning; abstract thinking; judgment; problem solving; sensory; perceptual and motor abilities; psychosocial behavior; physical functions; information processing; and speech. The term does not apply to brain injuries that are congenital or degenerative, or brain injuries induced by birth trauma.
Visual Impairment Including Blindness	An impairment in vision that, even with correction, adversely affects a child's educational performance. The term includes both partial sight and blindness.

Teachers might wonder what types of exceptional students they will encounter in schools. Researchers have reported the incidence and prevalence of various categories of exceptionality to give us some idea about this issue. The terms *incidence* and *prevalence* are sometimes used interchangeably in discussions of exceptional children; however, they should be differentiated from each other (Hallahan & Kauffman, 1988). Incidence refers to the number of new cases of exceptionality during a given period, such as one year. In contrast, prevalence refers to the total number of existing cases (new and old) in the population at a particular time.

When discussing students with exceptional needs, it is useful to consider prevalence by three broad divisions. First, there are *high-prevalence* categories, which typically include students with learning disabilities, gifted and talented abilities, and those with speech and language problems. In the *moderate-prevalence* categories are students with cognitive disabilities and emotional disturbances. A number of categories of exceptionality are considered *low-prevalence,* for example, students with hearing and visual problems, health and orthopedic handicaps, and multiple handicaps.

The range of exceptional abilities and needs varies widely, and any particular difficulty will affect performance in some academic subjects more than in others. A student confined to a wheelchair, for example, may do quite well in academic areas but be prevented from full participation in certain motor activities. Visual problems, depending on their severity, can cause major problems in adaptive behavior, or can be accommodated quite simply by eyeglasses. Note also that we have included the gifted and talented among the categories, since these children are unquestionably exceptional.

The Gifted/Talented

GIFTED

A term describing those with abilities that give evidence of high performance capabilities.

What to do with **gifted** and/or talented students has perplexed educators for as long as these children have been recognized as exceptional. Even defining the term *gifted* has caused considerable controversy. Initially, the results of IQ tests were used, with some arbitrary score such as 120 or 140 used as the cutoff point. This definition, however, was considered too restrictive; youngsters who have exceptional talent in painting or music, or who seem unusually creative, can also be considered gifted (Reis, 1989). The *Gifted and Talented Children's Education Act* of 1978 defined these students as follows:

> *The term gifted refers to children and (whenever applicable) youth who are identified at the preschool, elementary, or secondary level as possessing demonstrated or potential abilities that give evidence of high performance capabilities in specific areas (which could be intellectual, creative, specifically academic, related to leadership, or related to the performing and visual arts), and who, by reason thereof, require services or activities not ordinarily provided by the school.*

Recent U.S. government reports reflect interest in the gifted, stating that the gifted are a minority who need special attention. They are a minority, characterized by their exceptional ability, who come from all levels of society, all races, and all national origins, and who represent both sexes equally (Sternberg & Davidson, 1986).

If these children are so talented, why do they require special attention? For every Einstein who is identified and flourishes, there are probably dozens of others whose gifts are obscured. Thomas Edison's mother withdrew him from first grade because he was having so much trouble; Gregor Mendel, the founder of scientific genetics, failed his teacher's test four times; Isaac Newton was considered a poor student in grammar school; Winston Churchill had a terrible academic record; Charles Darwin left medical school.

"But isn't it more important to learn how to be a decent human being?"

H. Schwadron in Phi Delta Kappan.

In spite of a concentrated effort to ensure multicultural equality in our schools, minority students remain woefully underrepresented in programs for the gifted (Frasier, 1989). Many explanations have been offered for this phenomenon, among them low IQ test scores (not low IQ) and the lack of stimulating socioeconomic backgrounds. Some writers have speculated that problems in identifying minority gifted adolescents are the major cause of underrepresentation of these groups (Genshaft, 1991).

We are now seeing a reconsideration of the role of a student's home life in intellectual development. Research has shown that the environments of those homes that foster intellectual achievement are quite similar, regardless of income level (Frasier, 1989). R. Brown (1988), examining model youth, pointed out the considerable support for intellectual development in the African American community.

In an interesting analysis, Sue and Okazaki (1990), arguing against either heredity or environment as the explanation of high levels of achievement, turned to the concept of *relative functionalism*. They suggested that the behavior (including achievement) patterns of Asian Americans, for example, result from a combination of cultural values and status in society. That is, education provides an opportunity for upward mobility; it becomes increasingly functional when other avenues are blocked.

Positive models in the home environment can foster high academic achievement at school.

Frasier (1989) suggested that we change the screening procedures that have inherent limitations built into them for multicultural students. Why not use behavioral characteristics indicating giftedness, such as the use of language rather than a test question *about* language? Parents of multicultural students could help educators reword items on rating scales. Vignettes describing successful multicultural students could be used for motivational purposes.

These and similar techniques broaden the concept of giftedness in multicultural populations. Different concepts of intelligence (such as Sternberg's triarchic model or Gardner's multiple intelligences—see Chapter 8) can enrich the use of intelligence as a criterion for a gifted program. Other attempts to identify potential for a gifted program could include:

- Seeking nominations from knowledgeable professionals and nonprofessionals in the community

- Using behavioral indicators to identify those students who show giftedness in their cultural traditions

- Collecting data from multiple sources

- Delaying decision making until all pertinent data can be collected in a case study

Remember: The gifted in our schools are a diverse group.

How have the schools treated gifted students once they have been identified? Usually one of three different techniques has been adopted: acceleration, enrichment, or some form of special grouping (Eby & Smutny, 1990).

Acceleration means some modification in the regular school program that permits a gifted student to complete the program in less time or at an earlier age than usual. Acceleration can take many forms: school admission based on mental rather than chronological age, skipping of grades, combining of two years' work into one, elimination of more basic courses, and early admission to high school and college. For example, gifted and talented elementary, middle, and high school students in the Minneapolis public schools are able to take classes at the University of Minnesota (Ysseldyke & Algozzine, 1995). To say that reactions to acceleration are mixed would be an understatement. Recent reactions, however, have turned more positive.

Enrichment is a term designating different learning experiences in the regular classroom. Enrichment techniques usually follow one or more of these procedures:

- Attempt to challenge gifted students by assigning extra readings and assignments, and permit them to participate in related extracurricular activities. For example, if parents could arrange the time, they could take their scientifically advanced daughter to special classes at an institution such as the New England Aquarium.

- Group a school's gifted students so that they are together occasionally, enabling interested teachers to challenge students' abilities through group discussions and independent research.

- Provide special offerings, such as classes in a foreign language or in advanced mathematics.

- Employ for each school system a special teacher who could move from school to school, identify the gifted, aid regular teachers, and actually work with the gifted in seminars or group discussions.

Enrichment has advantages and disadvantages. The chief advantage of enrichment is that it can provide challenging, meaningful work for gifted youngsters while they remain with their peers. If teachers can satisfactorily adjust their instruction, enrichment can engage gifted youngsters in academic work. The major disadvantage is the tendency to

ACCELERATION

A change in the regular school program that permits a gifted student to complete a program in less time or at an earlier age than usual.

ENRICHMENT

A method of instruction for gifted students in which they are furnished with additional, challenging experiences.

CASE NOTES

Observation   Marsha Warren has three really bright students in her class.

Hypothesis   It is possible that she has students who are gifted.

Possible Actions   These students may profit from an acceleration program. One option for Marsha Warren is to contact the teachers from upper grades and work with them on special work assignments for her three students. Another option for her is to use the enrichment strategies we discuss in this chapter.

TIPS ON COMMUNICATION
Working with the Gifted and Talented

PRINCIPLE   The gifted are often excellent readers, enjoy working with abstract materials and complex relationships, and are initially curious.

STRATEGY   Encourage the gifted to go on field trips with parents and other classes, and combine this activity with written and oral communication of the experience.

STRATEGY   Provide situations in which the gifted child can work with other gifted students on some complex project you have devised. Encourage them to communicate support for their beliefs and yet be challenged by equally inquiring minds.

STRATEGY   Provide opportunities for the gifted child to fill their free time with activities that are enjoyable but educationally profitable.

---

provide the gifted with busywork and call it enrichment. More of the same is not enrichment. Another disadvantage is that extra work, discussions, or classes may not match the talent and interests of the particular gifted child.

Special grouping implies self-contained special classes, or even special schools, not merely the temporary groupings mentioned in our discussion of enrichment. Considerable controversy swirls around self-contained units for the gifted, some of which relates to the Jeffersonian versus the Jacksonian concepts of equality. Should a democracy encourage and establish an intellectual elite? Aside from this philosophical issue, no evidence exists indicating a clear superiority of special grouping over other techniques. Research is inconclusive, and experts remain uncertain as to the social desirability of grouping or its effect on achievement.

SPECIAL
GROUPING
A term that implies self-contained special classes or schools for the gifted.

Sensory Handicaps

Increasing numbers of students with sensory handicaps are being educated in the regular classroom. Typically these students will have visual and/or hearing impairments. In the following sections you will learn about how these students can be served in schools.

Visual Impairment

Some students will enter your classroom with visual problems, but educational and psychological assessments will have shown that they are at or above grade level in cognitive (for example, intellectual), general psychomotor (for example, physical), and auditory (for example, hearing) skills. Consequently, these students will spend most, if not all, of the day in the regular classroom (depending on the severity of the impairments). The following definitions of visual impairment (Livingston, 1986) are widely used today:

- **Visually impaired.** Individuals with any type of reduction in vision are described by this general classification. When a child has a problem seeing even with correction (for example, prescription lenses or surgery), which adversely affects his/her educational performance, a visual impairment has been defined (Ysseldyke & Algozzine, 1995).

- **Visually limited.** When students have difficulty seeing under average conditions but have the condition corrected by adaptation (glasses), they are considered to be visually limited, and they are classified as sighted for educational purposes.

- **Legally blind.** You probably recall from any eye examinations you may have had that normal vision is 20/20. The numerator of this fraction indicates the distance at which you can read figures on a chart (usually the Snellen). The denominator indicates the distance at which a person with normal vision could read those same letters. If for example, your vision is 20/60, that means you can read at 20 feet what the person with average vision can read at 60 feet. Legal blindness refers to those individuals with vision of 20/200 or less in the better eye (after correction).

The National Society for the Prevention of Blindness recommends that children be referred for an eye examination if their attempts to read lines on the Snellen chart have the following results:

- 3-year-olds: 20/50 or less

- 4-year-olds through third grade: 20/40 or less

- fourth grade and above: 20/30 or less

An accurate count of visually impaired children remains elusive, because data collection varies from state to state. In recent years, approximately 24,000 students with visual impairments received special education services (about .04% of school-age youth and about .5% of students with disabilities; Ysseldyke & Algozzine, 1995). Ysseldyke and Algozzine (1995) presented a "top ten" list of potential signs of visual impairments (see Table 5.3).

Myths about the Visually Impaired   We should dispel some of the myths surrounding persons who are visually impaired. They are not born with greater auditory acuity (better hearing), tactile sense (sense of touch), or musical talent. However, exceptions can always be noted. Superior performance may result from more constant use of a particular sense. On the other hand, visual problems do not adversely affect cognitive, language, motor, and social abilities. Such views represent the stereotypes of society.

For example, though concept development may initially be delayed, visually impaired students demonstrate normal performance during the elementary school years. Language development may also be delayed, but again, most youngsters progress to normal levels during the school years. Any social problems that may arise seem to be more the result of the attitudes of others than of the impairment itself. Perhaps the best way to summarize the developmental characteristics of visually impaired children is to note that they are like other children in many more ways than they are different from them.

If your classroom is the least restrictive environment for a visually impaired student, then that student belongs there and should be taught the same sequence of topics as stu-

---

Table 5.3 TOP TEN LIST OF POTENTIAL SIGNS OF VISUAL IMPAIRMENTS

1. Student frequently experiences watery eyes.
2. Student frequently experiences red or inflamed eyes.
3. Student's eye movements are jumpy or not synchronized.
4. Student experiences difficulty moving around the classroom.
5. Student experiences difficulty reading small print.
6. Student experiences difficulty identifying small details in pictures or illustrations.
7. Student frequently complains of dizziness after reading a passage or completing an assignment involving vision.
8. Student tilts head or squints eyes to achieve better focus.
9. Student uses one eye more than the other for reading or completing other assignments.
10. Student frequently complains of headaches or eye infections.

Ysseldyke, J.E., & Algozzine, B. (1995). *Special education: A practical approach for teachers* (3rd ed.) Boston: Houghton Mifflin. (p. 379). Reprinted with permission.

TIPS ON ASSESSMENT
Working with the Visually Impaired

PRINCIPLE   Teachers should help identify students with visual problems in the classroom.

STRATEGY   Teachers can observe students in their classroom and look for such symptoms as clumsiness, adopting an awkward head position to see, asking others to tell them what is written at a distance, and constant squinting and rubbing of the eyes.

STRATEGY   Contact the student's parents and describe the symptoms; ask the parents for verification of the problems observed in the classroom.

STRATEGY   Contact the school nurse or school psychologist and ask for their assistance in the identification and assessment of the visual problems the student is

---

dents with normal vision. Students with visual impairment should be monitored carefully so that they acquire appropriate nonacademic skills as well, enabling them to interact with and be accepted by their peers.

Hearing Impairment

Hearing is the sense that children use to learn those language and speech skills necessary for social interaction and academic success. Hearing-impaired students possess the same potential for acquiring language as other children, but they lack linguistic input, the raw material of language acquisition (Lowenbraun & Thompson, 1986).

The following definitions are widely used today (Marschark, 1993): **Hearing impairment** refers to any type of hearing loss, ranging in severity from mild to profound. There are two subdivisions of hearing impairment:

HEARING IMPAIRMENT
A term referring to any type of hearing loss, from mild to profound.

(1) *Deafness:* Individuals who are **deaf** possess a hearing disability so acute that they are prevented from processing linguistic information through audition, with or without a hearing aid.

(2) *Hardness of hearing:* Individuals who are **hard of hearing** have sufficient hearing potential that with the use of hearing aids, they can process linguistic information through audition.

There is a clear distinction between *deafness* and *hardness of hearing,* because deafness implies a hearing loss so severe that normal activity is impossible.

Estimates are that about 8% of Americans, or more than 17 million people, experience some form of hearing difficulty. Within this group, approximately 100,000 preschool youngsters, 600,000 elementary and junior high students, and almost 1,000,000 high school and college students have some degree of hearing loss, but only about 60,000 of these young people have been educated through special services (U.S. Department of Education, 1993). These numbers mean that not all youth who may need services are receiving them.

Since most classrooms rely heavily on both spoken and written language, students with any type of hearing impairment remain at a distinct disadvantage in their learning. One of the most common dangers these students face is being labeled mentally handicapped. If initially we lacked hard evidence of a hearing problem, we could too easily label a student as slow or difficult, with all the attendant problems that accompany such categorizing.

For the hearing impaired, controversy surrounds the meaning of the term least restrictive environment (Lowenbraun & Thompson, 1986). If interaction with typically developing peers is deemed vital, a regular classroom would seem most suitable, but it is also fraught with potential communication pitfalls. Most experts agree, however, that a regular classroom is most beneficial if specialized support is available. For example, interpreters may be asked to assist in the regular classroom.

Try to detect students with hearing impairments as early as possible. Table 5.4 lists the top ten potential signs of hearing impairments. Students with mild hearing loss (and even some with more severe loss) often adapt sufficiently to go for several years in school without being identified. They compensate in ways that cause teachers to miss the problem. But these students suffer because they cannot work to their full potential, and they frequently become frustrated and anxious.

Table 5.4 TOP TEN LIST OF POTENTIAL SIGNS OF HEARING IMPAIRMENTS

1. Student experiences difficulties following oral presentation and directions.

2. Student watches lips of teachers or other speakers very closely.

3. Student turns head and leans toward speaker.

4. Student uses limited vocabulary.

5. Student uses speech sounds poorly.

6. Student shows delayed language development.

7. Student often does not respond when called from behind.

8. Student is generally inattentive during oral presentations.

9. Student constantly turns volume up on radio or television.

10. Student complains of earaches, has frequent colds or ear infections, or has ear discharge.

Ysseldyke, J.E., & Algozzine, B. (1995). *Special education: A practical approach for teachers* (3rd ed.) Boston: Houghton Mifflin. (p. 391). Reprinted with permission.

Communication Disorders

Speech and language problems are high-prevalence categories of exceptionality with about one million children served in special education (U.S. Department of Education, 1993). Some students have speech and language problems that are unrelated to sensory handicaps or cognitive difficulty. These students are delayed in demonstrating language or have difficulty expressing themselves. *Speech or language impairment* is defined as a communication disorder such as stuttering, impaired articulation, language impairment, or voice impairment, that affects educational performance.

Students with problems in any or all of the three aspects of language (sound, meaning, and grammar) will experience communication disorders, which may be divided into two categories: (1) *speech disorders,* such as *misarticulation* (which refers to difficulty with phonemes—the fundamental, distinctive sounds of a language), *apraxia* (which refers to difficulty with commands to the muscles controlling speech), *voice disorders* (which are deviations of pitch, loudness, or quality), and *fluency disorders* (which usually take the form of stuttering; and (2) *language disorders,* which usually refer to difficulty in learning the native language with respect to content, form, and usage or function, and possibly are present in those students with delayed language development).

What are possible causes of communication disorders? They may range from neuropsychological elements (such as brain damage) that interfere with cognitive development and information-processing strategies to structural and physiological elements (such as the hearing problems just discussed), and environmental causes (such as deprived sociocultural conditions). These elements rarely act in isolation. For example, hearing impairments may adversely affect peer interactions, causing a student to engage in fewer attempts at communication with peers and adults.

Here are some signs of communication disorders you should watch for:

1. Is there any kind of articulation delay or disorder?

2. Is there anything unusual about a student's voice (loudness, uneven pitch)?

3. Is there a smooth flow of speech?

4. Does a student use the same type of speech (similar words to describe actions, people, objects) with the same meanings as typical students do?

5. Does a student use speech to achieve goals in the same manner as other students?

To aid students with communication disorders, teachers can structure classroom small-group activities to maximize interactions among students with communication disorders and peers, provide supports (such as written materials, clear expectations, individual help) that allow all students to be successful, and work with the speech and language therapist to assist students with communication disorders in acquiring social communication skills. Encourage nondisabled classmates to talk to these students as much as possible and reinforce them for doing so. Also urge their peers to play with them frequently, thus increasing all forms of interaction. Be a clear and positive model to students with communication problems as you have them use increasingly more complex speech patterns.

Medical, Physical, and Multiple Disabilities

Students with *medical disabilities* are included under "orthopedic impairment" and "other health impairments" in the federal guidelines for students with special learning needs. Orthopedic impairments, including congenital disorders, disease, and impairments from other causes, may influence the students' ability to learn. Students with other health impairments include those with heart conditions, tuberculosis, rheumatic fever, nephritis, asthma, sickle cell anemia, hemophilia, epilepsy, lead poisoning, leukemia, or diabetes. We (the authors) do not include students with attention deficit/hyperactivity disorder under the health-impaired category, although these students are eligible for services within this category under the federal definition. (See the section "Attention-Deficit/Hyperactivity Disorders," later in this chapter.) Teachers are also likely to experience increasing numbers of children who have acquired immune deficiency syndrome (AIDS) caused by the human immunodeficiency virus (HIV). Increasingly schools have provided guidelines for teachers to deal with children with AIDS, under the health impaired category.

Children with *physical disabilities* experience conditions that have been affected by the central nervous system or other body systems. Children with orthopedic impairments have conditions that involve muscular, skeletal, or central nervous system features and affect their ability to move around and participate in academic and social activities in the classroom.

Children with medical, physical, and multiple disabilities present unique challenges in the classroom. Teachers should learn about the special disabilities that the student may have so that instructional and evaluation accommodations can be made. For example, a child with AIDS may need special medications to function in school. There may also be a need for the teacher and other school professionals to educate other students about the condition and the accommodations that are necessary to function in the regular classroom.

Traumatic Brain Injury

Traumatic brain injury (TBI) is defined as follows:

> *Acquired injury to the brain caused by an external physical force, resulting in total or partial functional disability or psycho-social impairment, or both, that adversely affects the child's educational performance. The term applies to open or closed head injuries resulting in impairments in one or more areas, such as cognition; language; memory; attention; reasoning; abstract thinking; judgment; problem solving; sensory; perceptual, and motor abilities; psycho-social behavior; physical function; information processing; and speech. (Individuals with Disabilities Act, 1990)*

As you can see from this definition, in school systems, TBI refers to injuries caused by external forces only. This definition is used to differentiate TBI from disorders resulting from internal causes such as strokes, tumors, or toxins. However, in many cases the concerns, limitations, and interventions related to internal and external injuries can be similar.

Traumatic brain injuries can range from mild to severe in nature. The severity of an injury is usually determined by the length of the child's loss of consciousness following injury. Injuries resulting in a loss of consciousness of less than one hour are considered mild. Injuries resulting in loss of consciousness of one to twenty-four hours are considered moderate; loss of consciousness of longer than twenty-four hours is associated with severe brain injury.

Students with TBI can exhibit significant limitations that affect classroom functioning, and they may experience cognitive, physical, behavioral, and emotional difficulties that interfere with educational performance. Of particular concern are problems with memory, learning new information, attention, and challenging behaviors. Sometimes following a TBI, a student will appear on the surface to be recovering well; however, investigation of the student's performance may reveal that the student has recovered formerly mastered skills but is having difficulty mastering new skills. Also, students with TBI often experience difficulty with "executive functions," the skills that allow us to set a goal (such as planning a social activity with friends) and work toward carrying it out. Traumatic brain injury in young children can be especially serious, since younger children have mastered fewer skills prior to the injury; often the extent of injury to the young developing brain does not become apparent until the child grows older and expected higher level skills fail to develop.

Autism

Many teachers are likely to have in their classes children who are diagnosed with autism. The federal definition of autism is as follows:

> *Autism means a developmental disability significantly affecting verbal and non-verbal communication and social interaction, generally evident before age three, that adversely affects a child's educational performance. Other characteristics often associated with autism are engagement and repetitive activities in stereotype movements, resistance to environmental change or change in daily routines, and unusual responses to sensory experiences. The term does not apply if a child's educational performance is adversely affected primarily because the child has an emotional disturbance. (Individuals with Disabilities Act, 1990)*

Children with autistic disorder may be encountered in your classroom. Although this is a relatively rare disorder (for example, it has been reported to occur in four to five cases per 10,000 persons), it is a disorder that many individuals, including special education teachers, find challenging. Autism is considered a pervasive developmental disorder (PDD), which is characterized by impairment in several areas including social and communication skills (especially reciprocal interaction), abnormal language development, and a very restricted range of behavioral skills and interests (Klinger & Dawson, 1996). Although IDEA includes a definition of autistic disorder, you can find more developed criteria for diagnosing this childhood problem in the *Diagnostic and Statistical Manual of Mental Disorders* (APA, 1994) (see Table 5.5). Research has indicated that autism occurs more frequently in males (that is, three or four males for every female). The exact cause of autism is unknown, but there is evidence that genetic factors play a role in this PDD.

Great progress has been made in early diagnosis and intervention with autism. Early intervention procedures have been developed and include teaching attention, compliance, motor imitation, communication, and a variety of social skills. Typically these children need highly structured teaching environments and specific strategies to generalize the skills that they acquire. Most environments for these children are quite structured so as to make them predictable and routine. Many special education programs have been developed for these children to help them make the transition from preschool to community settings. Most intervention programs that have been successful have involved the family (see Klinger & Dawson, 1996 for a review of these issues).

Multiple Disabilities

Children with *multiple disabilities* are likely to present special challenges to regular and special educators. Students with multiple disabilities include those who have more than one disability and those with a primary disability and with secondary conditions (Ysseldyke & Algozzine, 1995). Teachers who experience children with medical, physical, and multiple disabilities will need specific education from their colleagues and continuing education to identify and serve children who present major unique challenges in these categories.

Increasingly, schools are offering a full range of medical, mental health, and social services, a trend called "full-service" schools (Reeder, Maccow, Shaw, Swerdlik, Horton, & Foster, 1997). Thus, comprehensive services for these children are becoming more and more available. Once your initial anxiety is over, you will be concerned mainly with ensuring that these students are able to share fully in class activities without lowering your expectations for them. The classroom teacher needs to work with the special student to design educational supports and accommodations to allow the child to succeed in school.

Table 5.5 DSM-IV DIAGNOSTIC CRITERIA FOR AUTISTIC DISORDER

A. A total of six (or more) items from (1), (2), and (3), with at least two from (1), and one each from (2) and (3):

  (1) qualitative impairment in social interaction, as manifested by at least two of the following:

    (a) marked impairment in the use of multiple nonverbal behaviors such as eye-to-eye gaze, facial expression, body postures, and gestures to regulate social interaction
    (b) failure to develop peer relationships appropriate to developmental level
    (c) a lack of spontaneous seeking to share enjoyment, interests, or achievements with other people (for example, by a lack of showing, bringing, or pointing out objects of interest)
    (d) lack of social or emotional reciprocity

  (2) qualitative impairments in communication as manifested by at least one of the following:

    (a) delay in, or total lack of, the development of spoken language (not accompanied by an attempt to compensate through alternative modes of communication such as gesture or mime)
    (b) in individuals with adequate speech, marked impairment in the ability to initiate or sustain a conversation with others
    (c) stereotyped and repetitive use of language or idiosyncratic language
    (d) lack of varied, spontaneous make-believe play or social imitative play appropriate to developmental level

  (3) restricted repetitive and stereotyped patterns of behavior, interests, and activities, as manifested by a least one of the following:

    (a) encompassing preoccupation with one or more stereotyped and restricted patterns of interest that is abnormal in either intensity or focus
    (b) apparently inflexible adherence to specific, nonfunctional routines or rituals
    (c) stereotyped and repetitive motor mannerisms (for example, hand or finger flappng or twisting, or complex whole-body movements)
    (d) persistent preoccupation with parts of objects

B. Delays or abnormal functioning in at least one of the following areas, with onset prior to age 3 years: (1) social interaction, (2) language as used in social communication, (3) symbolic or imaginative play.

C. The disturbance is not better accounted for by Rett's Disorder or Childhood Disintegrative Disorder.

Note. From American Psychiatric Association (1994, pp. 70–71). Copyright 1994 by the American Psychiatric Association. Reprinted by permission.

Emotional Disturbances

Here we encounter a particularly baffling cluster of problems whose exact definition and prevalence have continually frustrated investigators. Some students in this category are unusually restless and active, to the point of continually disrupting a classroom; others seem to explode into tantrums at the slightest provocation; still others may be terrified of the most simple situations (such as the student who will not enter a classroom unless the lights are on). These few examples should give you a sense of the wide range of problems encompassed by the label *emotional disturbance* (the term emotional disturbance is now used in PL105-17 and was changed from "serious emotional disturbances" in 1997).

Characteristics

Emotional Disturbance includes any conditions in which one or more of the following characteristics are exhibited over a long period of time and to a marked degree, adversely affecting educational performance:

- *An inability to learn* that cannot be explained by intellectual, sensory, or health factors

- *An inability to build or maintain satisfactory interpersonal relationships* with peers or teachers

- *Inappropriate types of behavior or feelings* under normal circumstances

- *A general pervasive mood of unhappiness or depression*

- *A tendency to develop physical symptoms or fears* associated with personal or school problems. (Individuals with Disabilities Act, 1990)

As you can well imagine, determining the causes of many disorders can be difficult, with assessments incorporating biological and environmental elements. Some of these youngsters can be difficult to work with; some teachers may hope that students with **behavior disorders** will be removed from regular classrooms. However, often students with emotional disturbance can be successfully served in a structured, supportive regular classroom. Working with the special education support staff, regular education teachers can implement strategies to help these students attain their potential. Before rendering judgment, teachers should keep firmly in mind the interactive nature of the factors involved.

BEHAVIOR DISORDERS

Any conditions in which environmental conflicts and personal disturbance persist and negatively affect academic performance.

Attention-Deficit/Hyperactivity Disorder

One of the more challenging problems that teachers may experience in a school setting is teaching a student diagnosed with **attention-deficit/hyperactivity disorder (ADHD)**. Some scholars include ADHD as a childhood behavior disorder or even a problem that can be classified as an emotional disorder. We discuss it as a separate problem while realizing there are problems classifying it. Research shows that ADHD occurs in approximately 3% to 5% of U.S. elementary school students and is three times more common in boys than in girls (Braswell & Bloomquist, 1991). Although there is considerable controversy over the diagnosis of this problem (some authors discuss it as primarily a language disorder—see Lovinger, Brandell, & Seestedt-Stanford, 1991), most researchers rely on the diagnostic criteria presented by the American Psychiatric Association in its *Diagnostic and Statistical Manual of Mental Disorders (DSM-IV)* (APA, 1994). The two core symptoms of ADHD are (1) inattention and (2) hyperactive-impulsive behavior (or what is called disinhibition) (Barkley, 1996). Table 5.6 presents the diagnostic criteria for ADHD from the *DSM-IV*. Note

ATTENTION-DEFICIT/HYPER-ACTIVITY DISORDER (ADHD)

A disorder usually appearing in childhood that is characterized by various symptoms of inattention and/or hyperactivity-impulsivity.

Some children who have high activity levels will require a high level of teacher intervention and management.

Table 5.6 ATTENTION-DEFICIT/HYPERACTIVITY DISORDER

A. Either (1) or (2):

1. Six (or more) of the following symptoms of inattention have persisted for at least 6 months to a degree that is maladaptive and inconsistent with developmental level:

   Inattention

   a. often fails to give close attention to details or makes careless mistakes in schoolwork, work, or other activities
   b. often has difficulty sustaining attention in tasks or play activities
   c. often does not seem to listen when spoken to directly
   d. often does not follow through on instructions and fails to finish schoolwork, chores, or duties in the workplace (not due to oppositional behavior or failure to understand instructions)
   e. often has difficulty organizing tasks and activities
   f. often avoids, dislikes, or is reluctant to engage in tasks that require sustained mental effort (such as schoolwork or homework)
   g. often loses things necessary for tasks or activities (for example, toys, school assignments, pencils, books, or tools)
   h. is often easily distracted by extraneous stimuli
   i. is often forgetful in daily activities

2. Six (or more) of the following symptoms of hyperactivity-impulsivity have persisted for at least 6 months to a degree that is maladaptive and inconsistent with developmental level:

   Hyperactivity

   a. often fidgets with hands or feet or squirms in seat
   b. often leaves seat in classroom or in other situations in which remaining seated is expected
   c. often runs about or climbs excessively in situations in which it is inappropriate (in adolescents or adults, may be limited to subjective feelings of restlessness)
   d. often has difficulty playing or engaging in leisure activities quietly
   e. is often "on the go" or often acts as if "driven by a motor"
   f. often talks excessively

   Impulsivity

   g. often blurts out answers before questions have been completed
   h. often has difficulty awaiting turn
   i. often interrupts or intrudes on others (for example, butts into conversations or games)

B. Some hyperactive-impulsive or inattentive symptoms that caused impairment were present before age 7 years.

C. Some impairment from the symptoms is present in two or more settings (for example, at school [or work] and at home).

D. There must be clear evidence of clinically significant impairment in social, academic, or occupational functioning.

E. The symptoms do not occur exclusively during the course of a Pervasive Developmental Disorder, Schizophrenia, or other Psychotic Disorder and are not better accounted for by another mental disorder (for example, Mood Disorder, Anxiety Disorder, Dissociative Disorder, or a Personality Disorder).

Code based on type:

314.01 Attention-Deficit/Hyperactivity Disorder, Combined Type:
If both Criteria A1 and A2 are met for the past 6 months
314.00 Attention-Deficit/Hyperactivity Disorder, Predominantly Inattentive Type:
If Criterion A1 is met but Criterion A2 is not met for the past 6 months
314.01 Attention-Deficit/Hyperactivity Disorder, Predominantly Hyperactive-Impulsive Type:
If Criterion A2 is met but Criterion A1 is not met for the past 6 months
Coding note: For individuals (especially adolescents and adults) who currently have symptoms that no longer meet full criteria, "In Partial Remission" should be specified.

Reprinted with permission from the *Diagnostic and Statistical Manual of Mental Disorders,* Fourth Edition. Copyright 1994 American Psychiatric Association.

that some children may display primarily inattention while others display hyperactivity-impulsivity, or these behaviors can occur together as a combined disorder.

ADHD (sometimes simply called hyperactivity) seems to be caused by a variety of factors—neurological, emotional, dietary, and/or environmental—and can encompass a range of behaviors (DuPaul & Stoner, 1994; Greene, 1987). For example, some students may exhibit only mild and infrequent episodes, whereas others are chronically disruptive. Among the methods used with these students are medication, behavior modification, skills training, and special family support.

School can become a problem for these children, because it may be the first place where they are required to demonstrate self-control and adjustment to a structured environment. In fact, parents may not realize until the time of school entrance that their child experiences ADHD. Previously they may have dismissed such behavior as just "part of growing up." These students may shout things out in class, demand a teacher's immediate attention, and not wait their turn. If this behavior is accompanied by emotional outbursts, those around such children may begin to suspect that they are behaviorally disordered.

Medication is commonly used to treat children who experience ADHD. If a child in the classroom has been diagnosed with ADHD, there is a good chance that he or she is on one of several medications commonly used for this problem. The major issue surrounding drug therapy is that the drug must be carefully prescribed and monitored (DuPaul & Barkley, 1998, p. 140). Reflect on the following questions:

1. Has the child had an adequate physical and psychological evaluation?

2. How old is the child?

3. What has been the success of other therapies?

4. How severe is the child's current behavior?

5. Can the family afford the medication and associated costs (for example, follow-up visits)?

6. Are the parents sufficiently intelligent to adequately supervise the use of the medication and guard against its abuse?

7. What are the parents' attitudes toward pharmacotherapy?

8. Is there a delinquent sibling or drug-abusing parent in the household?

9. Does the child have any history of tics, psychosis, or thought disorder?

10. Is the child highly anxious, fearful, or more likely to complain of psychosomatic disturbances?

11. Does the physician have time to monitor medication effects properly?

12. How does the child feel about medication and its alternatives?

What can you do to help these students? Here are a few suggestions you may find helpful (Ingersoll, 1988):

■ Keep your own emotions under control. Though this may be easier said than done given the demands that these students may make upon you, it's nevertheless true that you only add to the problem if you respond in anger. Remember: It's not the student who so aggravates you; it's the disorder.

■ Provide structure and feedback. Because these students sometimes cannot organize their own world, you have to assist them. These students should know exactly where they should be at all times and where things should go. Perhaps most important of all, they must receive clear, precise instructions from you.

- Use feedback to improve their behavior. Positive feedback can be a major force in helping to improve this behavior. Reinforce often, reinforce small steps, and vary the reinforcers.

- Help these students with their peer problems. Reinforce peers for including ADHD students in their activities. Also try to plan activities that require mutual cooperation for success.

Most students develop normally, that is, with a minimum of difficulties. Even those who experience some emotional and behavioral problems usually do not experience serious psychiatric illness. The roots of their conditions may be traced to many sources—the student, family, school, society. This situation dramatically illustrates the importance of an interactive analysis.

It is deceptively simple to classify a student's problem along a single dimension: a disturbed personality, parental separation, or the school. But a student's behavior represents the interaction of many factors. There is no avoiding the biological (physical), psychological (emotional), and social (behavioral) consequences of a problem. For example, it is possible to classify many of the disorders discussed in this section as emotional. To do so is a disservice to the student who is experiencing the problem. There may well be a physical cause behind an apparent emotional problem, such as anxiety; any physical difficulty, such as asthma, can have definite, even serious emotional consequences.

Working with students who display behavior disorders requires both knowledge and patience, characteristics not always in plentiful supply. Although most educators believe that mainstreaming these students is positive, good guidelines for the best way to handle them in the regular classroom are still lacking. Figure 5.2 illustrates several behavior patterns that students might display in the classroom. Some of these are teacher-related; others are peer-related. Students who demonstrate externalizing (acting-out) patterns typically have more difficulty in their adjustment to the expectations of teachers. In contrast, internalizing students may not have as much difficulty with teachers but will likely have considerable difficulty with peers, who may neglect or reject them.

FIGURE 5.2

Interrelationships of bipolar behavior patterns and school adjustment types.

(From "Behavior Disorders and the Social Context of Regular Class Integration: A Conceptual Dilemma?" by H. M. Walker and M. Bullis, p. 82, in J. W. Lloyd, N. N. Singh, and A. C. Repp, eds., *The Regular Education Initiative: Alternative Perspectives on Concepts, Issues, and Models.* Copyright © 1991 by Sycamore Publishing Co. Reprinted by permission of Brooks/Cole Publishing Company, a division of Thomson Publishing, Inc.)

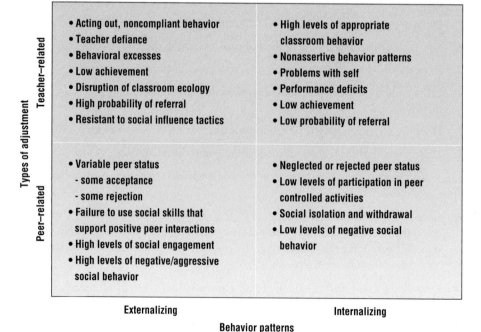

Types of adjustment

Teacher-related

- Acting out, noncompliant behavior
- Teacher defiance
- Behavioral excesses
- Low achievement
- Disruption of classroom ecology
- High probability of referral
- Resistant to social influence tactics

- High levels of appropriate classroom behavior
- Nonassertive behavior patterns
- Problems with self
- Performance deficits
- Low achievement
- Low probability of referral

Peer-related

- Variable peer status
  - some acceptance
  - some rejection
- Failure to use social skills that support positive peer interactions
- High levels of social engagement
- High levels of negative/aggressive social behavior

- Neglected or rejected peer status
- Low levels of participation in peer controlled activities
- Social isolation and withdrawal
- Low levels of negative social behavior

Externalizing   Internalizing

Behavior patterns

> ## CASE NOTES
>
> **Observation**   Katie is exhibiting hyperactivity in Marsha Warren's class. She cannot sit still or pay attention.
>
> **Hypothesis**   Katie may be experiencing a disorder called attention deficit/hyperactivity disorder (ADHD).
>
> **Possible Actions**   Marsha needs to become more familiar with ADHD and the characteristics that children exhibit. In addition to the strategies mentioned in the text (see p. 171), she could review a video by Barkley (1994) entitled *ADHD in the Classroom: Strategies for Teachers.*

Learning Disabilities

Of all the categories of exceptionality we have discussed, perhaps none has caused as much difficulty in definition as **learning disabilities** (LD), or learning disorders. Prior to 1965, special education textbooks contained no reference to the term *learning disabilities* (Myers & Hammill, 1990). Hammill (1990) reviewed twenty-eight textbooks that included definitions of learning disabilities. There were eleven different definitions of learning disabilities, and in some cases, there was little agreement among the different definitions. Dissatisfaction with existing definitions (including the one offered by the U.S. Department of Education in 1977) caused representatives of several organizations to meet and propose a new definition that has become more widely accepted. Hammill (1990) suggested that there is a growing consensus around one definition.

In 1981, the National Joint Committee for Learning Disabilities (NJCLD) proposed the following definition of learning disabilities:

> *Learning disabilities is a generic term that refers to a heterogeneous group of disorders manifested by significant difficulties in the acquisition and use of reading, writing, reasoning, or mathematical abilities. These disorders are intrinsic to the individual and presumed to be due to central nervous system dysfunction. Even though a learning disability may occur concomitantly with other handicapping conditions (for example, sensory impairment, mental retardation, social and emotional disturbance) or environmental influences (for example, cultural differences, insufficient-inappropriate instruction, psychogenic factors), it is not the direct result of the conditions or influences. (Hammill, Leigh, McNutt, & Larsen, 1981, p. 336)*

A special study group of the National Institute of Health expanded this definition to encompass social skills and the relationship between learning disabilities and attention-deficit disorder. Though controversy may swirl around definitions, professionals working with students with learning disabilities are in general agreement about the following aspects of the problem (Morsink, 1985):

- *Discrepancy.* There is a difference between what these students should be able to do and what they are actually doing.

- *Deficit.* There are some tasks others can do that a child with LD can't do (such as listen, read, or do arithmetic).

- *Focus.* The child's problem is centered on one or more of the basic psychological processes involved in using or understanding language.

LEARNING
DISABILITIES

A term referring to a handicapping condition characterized by a discrepancy between ability and achievement, most commonly manifested in reading, writing, reasoning, and/or mathematics.

■ *Exclusions.* Learning disabilities are not the direct result of poor vision or hearing, disadvantage, or cognitive disabilities, but these students still aren't learning.

Development and Learning Disabilities

An *exclusion component* is now used to identify as accurately as possible students with learning disabilities. This component means that the problems are not a result of mental retardation, visual or hearing impairment, motor handicaps, or environmental disadvantage. You have probably concluded that learning disabilities occur widely among school-age children; they are difficult to detect in young children. Reading, mathematics, and language are the vulnerable subjects, with research focusing on the psychological processes that may cause the problem. To help you separate myth from fact, Table 5.7 presents and addresses several misconceptions about learning disabilities.

The Role of Previous Knowledge in Learning Disabilities

Studies of students with learning disabilities have underscored the key role of specific knowledge and skills in learning (Brown & Campione, 1986). As psychological theory has shifted to a greater cognitive emphasis, the role of previous knowledge (the knowledge that a student already has) is critical. It is essential to determine the extent to which a student can function effectively with the knowledge needed to perform a specific academic task. Rather than seeking underlying mental problems, teachers can help these students to acquire the necessary prerequisite knowledge and skills. Can this student move on to fractions? Does that student understand the logic behind the experiment?

Instruction, then, should focus on where the student is now, and the use of appropriate methods to match a particular level of competence. If possible, have students with learning disabilities work with expert peers who guide their efforts and carefully structure the environment for them. This strategy may help these students to adopt regulatory and structuring activities of their own. If it is successful, you will have provided considerable social support for students with learning disabilities.

Mental Retardation

Much of the dramatic change in our thinking about exceptionality can be traced to the relatively recent surge of interest in **mental retardation.** After decades of neglect, the public has willingly supported programs designed to educate, rehabilitate, and care for exceptional children, a large number who have mental retardation.

The topic of mental retardation has been of great interest to scientists and practitioners for many years. It is also an area of exceptionality where there has been considerable controversy in definition. The main complication in defining mental retardation has been the fact that two professional groups have produced differing definitions and classification manuals. The American Psychiatric Association (APA, 1994) classifies mental retardation as a developmental disorder. The American Association on Mental Retardation (AAMR, 1992) has produced a definition that has been quite controversial in the field of psychology and education. Definitions of mental retardation consider both the intellectual potential of the individual as well as the adaptive behavior dimensions.

Hodapp and Dykens (1996) provide an overview of the main definitions of mental retardation. We have also added the definition recently produced by Division 33 of the American Psychological Association and reviewed in detail by Jacobson and Murlick (1996). A lot of controversy surrounds the 1992 AAMR definition, especially the over-representation of individuals with mental retardation with this definition (see Gre-

Table 5.7 MYTHS AND FACTS ABOUT LEARNING DISABILITIES

Myth	Fact
All LD students are brain damaged.	Learning problems occur without brain damage.
All LD students have perceptual problems.	Many students with learning disabilities show no such evidence.
Perceptual training will lead to academic gains.	Perceptual training improves perceptual skills, which may lead to academic gain.
Hyperactivity is easily controlled by drugs.	The effective use of drugs is complicated and requires the cooperation of students, teachers, parents, and physicians.
LD students do not have math problems.	Two out of three students with learning disabilities receive special instruction in math.
A student's learning disability is the result of brain injury.	Such a diagnosis is of little help to a teacher (it may help staff or medical personnel).

Adapted from Hallahan and Kauffman (1988), *Exceptional Children: Introduction to Special Education,* Englewood Cliffs, NJ: Prentice-Hall.

TIPS ON TIME
Working with Children with Learning Disabilities

PRINCIPLE   Students with learning disabilities often require additional time to complete classroom assignments.

STRATEGY   Give students who are experiencing learning problems shorter assignments to allow more time for completion of work.

STRATEGY   Ask students to monitor or record the amount of time they are engaged in academic activity.

STRATEGY   Provide additional lead time for students with learning disabilities when making assignments or beginning new activities.

sham, MacMillan, & Siperstein, 1995). We therefore recommend the definition provided by Division 33 of the American Psychological Association. In this context, mental retardation refers to "a) significant limitations in general intellectual functioning, b) significant limitations in adaptive functioning, which exist concurrently and c) onset of intellectual and adaptive limitations before the age of 22 years" (Jacobson & Murlick, 1996, p. 37). In this context, mental retardation is typically assessed by individual measures of intelligence and by individual assessment of adaptive behavior. There is growing consensus that a diagnosis based solely on intellectual functioning and age of onset is an inappropriate criterion. Typically within school settings, the classification of mental retardation is conducted by a psychologist or other professional who has specific training in various psychometric instruments that allow a reliable and valid assessment of this disorder.

With instructional accommodation, children with cognitive disabilities can participate in many activities in a classroom.

Thus, the current definitions of mental retardation consist of a multidimensional approach that is designed to broaden the traditional ideas of mental retardation, to reduce or avoid the sole reliance on the use of IQ scores to assign a disability, and to include an individual's level of support (how much support a person needs to live in their environment). Figure 5.3 provides a summary of the process used in diagnosis, classification, and evaluation of support systems.

The evaluation of support is designed to focus on the level of needed services. The level of support needed by an individual is typically determined by a multidisciplinary team (for example, school psychologist, school nurse, special education teacher). Table 5.8 provides an illustration of how the concept of support intensities might be used.

Common Problems of Students with Cognitive Disabilities

Mental retardation can result from many causes: genetic, prenatal, perinatal, postnatal, and cultural. These general categories encompass specific causes such as PKU (phenylketonuria), rubella, oxygen deprivation at birth, brain injury, drugs, and economic deprivation. You should remember that in spite of having limitations in reasoning and problem solving, students with mental retardation have the same basic needs as typically developing peers and demonstrate considerable individual differences.

Mentally retarded children will have difficulties at specific levels of learning. Among the more common problems are the following:

- Attention, which may be both limited and nonselective

- Cognitive processing, especially with regard to organization, classification, and strategies

STEP 1. Diagnosis of mental retardation *determines eligibility for supports*

Mental retardation is diagnosed if:
1. The individual's intellectual functioning is approximately 70 to 75 or below.
2. There are significant disabilities in two or more adaptive skill areas.
3. The age of onset is below 18.

Dimension I:
Intellectual functioning
and adaptive skills

STEP 2. Classification and description *identifies strengths and weaknesses and the need for supports*

1. Describe the individual's strengths and weaknesses in reference to psychological/emotional considerations.
2. Describe the individual's overall physical health and indicate the condition's etiology.
3. Describe the individual's current environmental placement and the optimal environment that would facilitate his/her continued growth and development.

Dimension II:
Psychological/emotional
considerations
Dimension III:
Physical/health/etiology
considerations
Dimension IV:
Environmental
considerations

STEP 3. Profile and intensities of needed supports *identifies needed supports*

Identify the kind and intensities of supports needed for each of the four dimensions
1. Dimension I: Intellectual functioning and adaptive skills
2. Dimension II: Psychological/emotional considerations
3. Dimension III: Physical health/etiology considerations
4. Dimension IV: Environmental considerations

FIGURE 5.3 The three-step process: diagnosis, classification, and systems of support.

(From *Mental Retardation: Definition, Classification, and Systems of Support*, 9th ed. Copyright © 1992 American Association on Mental Retardation, Washington, DC. Reprinted with permission.)

Table 5.8 DEFINITION AND EXAMPLES OF INTENSITIES OF SUPPORTS

Type of Support	Definition and Examples
Intermittent	Supports on an "as needed" basis. Characterized by episodic nature, person not always needing the support(s), or short-term supports needed during life-span transitions (for example, job loss or an acute medical crisis). Intermittent supports may be high or low in intensity when provided.
Limited	An intensity of supports characterized by consistency over time, being time-limited but not of an intermittent nature, perhaps requiring fewer staff members and less cost than more intense levels of support (for example, time-limited employment training or transitional supports during the school-to-adult-provided period).
Extensive	Supports that are characterized by regular involvement (for example, daily) in at least some environments (such as work or home) and not time-limited (for example, long-term support and long-term home living support).
Pervasive	Supports characterized by their constancy and high intensity; provided across environments; and of a potentially life-sustaining nature. Pervasive supports typically involve more staff members and intrusiveness than do extensive or time-limited supports.

From *Mental Retardation: Definition, Classification, and Systems of Support*, 9th ed. Copyright © 1992 American Association on Mental Retardation, Washington, DC. Reprinted by permission.

- Memory, which may be poor for short-term retention

- Transfer to new tasks, which may be a particularly difficult activity

- Distractability, which results in excessive attention to incidental information

Exceptionality in Infancy and Toddlerhood

Many readers of this book will be interested in working with infants, toddlers, and pre-school children. Some of you may already have had these experiences, and you may have a variety of questions pertaining to the development of very young children and, specifically, the development of exceptional patterns of behavior. In recent years psychologists and educators have become more concerned with disorders and risk in infancy and toddlerhood and how these problems might be identified in educational and community settings.

Lyons-Ruth, Yeanah, and Benoit (1996) discuss two quite different mental health traditions characterizing the development of special children. The first approach views babies within a risk/protection dynamic, the interaction of which may predict the child's outcome. Risk factors can be due to biological or social factors, or to a combination of both. For example, growing up in a very poor family can be a risk factor leading to problems in preschool and early elementary grades. However, growing up in an intact family, even though very poor, might protect a child from the risks. It is a balancing act.

The second tradition is that young children, even during infancy, can be characterized as experiencing various disorders. For example, *DSM-IV* (APA, 1994) includes a number of psychiatric disorders that could emerge during the first three years of life (see Table 5.9). In addition, the National Center for Clinical Infant Programs (1994) has proposed a diagnostic classification for children ages 0 to 3 (see Table 5.10). And a 0–3 casebook for assessment and treatment planning has also been developed (Lieberman, Wieder, & Fenichel, 1997). In this

---

Table 5.9 PSYCHIATRIC DISORDERS OF THE FIRST 3 YEARS: DSM-IV

Axis I: Primary Diagnosis

Feeding and Eating Disorders of Infancy or Early Childhood

        Pica
        Rumination Disorder
        Feeding Disorder

Reactive Attachment Disorder of Infancy or Early Childhood

Pervasive Developmental Disorders

        Autistic Disorder
        Rett's Disorder
        Childhood Disintegrative Disorder (after age 2)

Problems Related to Abuse or Neglect

        Physical Abuse to Child
        Sexual Abuse to Child
        Neglect of Child

Relational Problems

        Parent-Child Relational Problem

Note: Axis I diagnostic categories particularly relevant to infants and toddlers appearing in American Psychiatric Association (1994).

view of childhood, individual children who demonstrate specific characteristics that meet the diagnostic criteria will be formally diagnosed as having one of the various disorders that are featured in the *DSM* or *0–3 Casebook*.

In recent years, educators have begun to reexamine patterns of behavior in early childhood and pay more attention to these children. Many school districts now conduct systematic child screening activities at the preschool level. However, some educators believe that this is not early enough. Lyons-Ruth et al. (1996) suggest that mental health experts and educators need to take a developmental view of childhood deviance and exceptionality. In fact, many early risk factors do predict the development of problems. Second, they note the importance of the family. Increasingly, mental health experts and educators have stressed the importance of family involvement in community activities and the education of the child. Schools can often promote positive academic and social relationships through involvement with positive parent programming. Important in this work is the development of positive relationships between parent and child. Finally, these authors note that although the traditional diagnostic systems noted in this chapter might be useful at the descriptive level, it is important for early child educators to understand the development of children, risk factors, protective factors, and the important role that families play in development of childhood difficulties.

Table 5.10 PROPOSED DIAGNOSTIC CLASSIFICATION: 0–3

Axis I: Primary Diagnosis

  Disorders of Relating and Communicating

       Multisystem Developmental Disorder

  Regulatory Disorders

  Eating Behavior Disorder

  Sleep Behavior Disorder

  Traumatic Stress Disorder

  Disorders of Affect

      Anxiety Disorders
      Mood Disorders
      Mixed Disorder of Emotional Expressiveness
      Gender Identity Disorder
      Reactive Attachment Disorder

  Adjustment Disorder

Axis II: Relationship Disorder Classification

  Perturbation

  Disturbance

  Disorder

Axis III: Other Medical and Developmental Conditions

Axis IV: Psychosocial Stressors

Axis V: Functional Emotional Developmental Level

Note: Diagnostic system proposed in Zero to Three/National Center for Clinical Infant Programs (1994).

THE ASSESSMENT AND CLASSIFICATION OF CHILDREN

Assessment is an information-gathering process central to decision making about exceptional children. It can be a complex process and is given detailed consideration in Chapters 11 and 12. The discussion of assessment in this chapter focuses on children who are exceptional. Before you start evaluating a student, several issues require attention (Rutter, 1975):

1. *The awareness that children are developing organisms.* Any evaluation must consider the student's developmental level, since one of the major criteria in judging the abnormality of behavior is its age appropriateness. Since students behave differently at different ages, it is important to know what behavior is typical of a given age. Students are vulnerable to different stresses at different ages. At some ages they may be particularly susceptible to an interruption of physical development whose consequences are both physical and psychological (anorexia nervosa in adolescents, for example, may disrupt development). At an earlier age, interference with psychological development may have physical and psychological consequences (separation from the mother during the first months of life, for example).

2. *Epidemiological considerations.* Since any information concerning the nature and dimensions of a problem will help evaluating that problem (How often does it occur? When? In the classroom or the schoolyard?), studies that examine the distribution of the problem in the general population are usually helpful. These studies show that from 5% to 15% of all children experience sufficiently severe disorders to handicap them in daily living. Though the precise number may vary, it is clear that except for a minority of cases, students with these disorders are not qualitatively different from their classmates.

3. *The abnormality and severity of the handicap.* Several criteria are used in assessing abnormality, the first of which is the age- and gender-appropriateness of the behavior. Certain behavior is normal at one age but not at another. For example, bedwetting is common for a child of 4 or 5 years of age, but uncommon by the time a child reaches 10 years of age. Persistence of a problem is another criterion; a reluctance to leave home and attend school is normal in the early years, but abnormal in the later grades. Other criteria that cluster and indicate a problem are the extent of the disturbance and the intensity of the symptoms under different circumstances.

   The severity of a problem can be judged by four criteria:

1. The degree of personal suffering that a student experiences (can the student function in the classroom?).

2. The social restriction involved (does the problem prevent a student from doing what is desired, such as actively participating in the classroom?).

3. Whether there is any interference with development (does dependency on the parents become so intense that a student finds it impossible to form normal peer relationships?).

4. Whether there is an effect on others (has a student's behavior become so maladaptive that interpersonal relationships in the classroom deteriorate?).

Guidelines for Diagnosis/Classification

Use these four criteria to determine if an assessment is needed, and if the answer is yes, we next face the issue of classification. Remember: Most problems are too intricate to be explained by one cause and are unraveled only in a search for multiple causes. The diagnostic process is both complex and controversial, given the unreliability of the diagnostic and classification systems now available. For example, the widely used *DSM-IV* of the American Psychiatric Association (1994) has been criticized for yielding unreliable results in the classification of children and youth. The categories of exceptionality used in education are even more unreliable, and the labels used to classify students may not convey accurate information (McDonnell, McLaughton, & Morison, 1997).

For example, use of the term *minimal brain damage* can be misleading, even dangerous. There are several brain-damage syndromes, not one, and the form they take is often indistinguishable from the behavior of students without brain damage. Furthermore, brain damage does not directly lead to psychiatric disorder, although it may increase a student's vulnerability to environmental stress. For example, parental pressure to excel may precipitate a problem.

Potential Problems with Labeling Students

The term *exceptional* includes both persons who are talented and those who have disabilities. These students have characteristics—physical, mental, behavioral, or social—that require special attention for them to achieve to their potentials. Awareness of the characteristics and needs of exceptional students points to an important conclusion: A student may be considered disabled in one situation, and not in another. A student who appears at the classroom door in a wheelchair may be an outstanding scholar; a physical disability does not imply cognitive difficulties. Avoid the pitfall of stereotyping students who are exceptional. Labeling also assumes that there is a knowledge base to teach children with disabilities in unique ways, yet for some disorders like mild retardation or learning disabilities there is no separate knowledge base (Wang, Reynolds, & Walberg, 1994/1995).

It has been estimated that approximately 250 million standardized tests are administered to children in American schools each year (Ysseldyke, Algozzine, & Thurlow, 1992). Most of the testing that is conducted is designed to make classification decisions related to special education services. Children who are labeled as learning disabled or emotionally disturbed, for example, obtain access to special services through the labeling process. Consider the following issues and the pros and cons of labeling:

Labeling is the most effective way to get students access to special education services in our public schools.

Pro—When done correctly by a qualified professional, the labeling process is a good strategy to ensure that children who need special resources have access to these resources. Such resources should change situations in which children are not learning to the best of their ability.

Con—Labeling does not necessarily lead to improved educational services for children. Just being labeled does not mean that a child has improved educational services.

Pro—Labeling serves as a method to organize the field of special education and therefore can guide research on a variety of childhood problems. Detailed understanding of a particular problem through research can lead to better treatment for children experiencing a certain type of problem.

Con—Labels can actually produce negative effects on students, especially if those students are members of certain minority groups. Such labeling of minority students can limit their access to opportunities that occur in the regular classroom setting.

Pro—The labeling process as linked to special education services is a remarkable success story for special-needs children. Labeling has allowed millions of children access to services that have improved the quality of their lives and the lives of their families. Moreover, the labeling of children has provided documentation needed for special legislation and funding of special services.

Con—There are many noncategorical methods of determining student needs, and these needs can often be met in the regular classroom. Documentation of student needs can be accomplished without using a labeling system that is useless in designing intervention programs and also harmful to students.

Where do you stand on labeling? Think about it from a teacher's perspective, a parent's perspective, and a student's perspective.

Although labels sometimes may be necessary for identifying exceptional students and making available appropriate services, problems result from a rigid classification system. These pitfalls range from indiscriminate exclusion from a regular classroom to the very real danger that the label itself could become a self-fulfilling prophecy. Ysseldyke and colleagues (1992) noted that labeling should be examined from the perspectives of the impact of the label on the person being labeled and the impact of the label on those who interact with the labeled person. Sensitive to these problems, today's educators emphasize the skills that an exceptional child possesses (rather than what that child lacks), and they attempt to improve inadequate skills.

MAINSTREAMING AND INCLUSION

MAINSTREAMING
Integrating physically, mentally, and behaviorally disabled students into regular classes.

REGULAR EDUCATION INITIATIVE (REI)
A movement to include more of the mildly disabled in regular classrooms.

Your classroom could be the least restrictive environment for some youngsters with exceptional needs. We want to introduce you to some concepts such as **mainstreaming,** inclusion, and the **regular education initiative (REI).** During the 1980s mainstreaming was a hot topic, and during the late 1980s and early 1990s, so was REI. Today the issue of inclusion is at the forefront, and there has been debate over all these concepts (see Fuchs & Fuchs, 1994). Mainstreaming's admirers praise it as the single greatest educational change since school integration. Critics question it as a headlong plunge into chaos in the classroom. As usual, reality lies somewhere between these two extremes.

What Is Mainstreaming and Inclusion?

Mainstreaming can be defined as

> the process of developing a special education instructional program for academic or social purposes (or both) designed to accommodate a handicapped youngster in a regular education classroom for some part of the school day. We distinguish between mainstreaming and integration, which we consider to be synonymous with placement of handicapped children in classes with non-handicapped peers, without a defined instructional program accompanying the placement. There can be no mainstreaming without integration; there can certainly be integration without mainstreaming (Lloyd, Singh, & Repp, 1991, p. 97).

Mainstreaming means integrating children with disabilities and children who are gifted and talented into regular classes. In the past (before the enactment of PL94-142), the vast majority of these students were educated apart from their peers for a majority of the time (especially in the case of students with disabilities) or received no public education at all.

The practice of mainstreaming was supported by the REI movement. Proponents of REI argued that the practice of serving special education students in a combination of special and regular classes created a dual system of education that was basically "dysfunctional, ineffective, and excessively costly" (Hocutt, Martin, & McKinney, 1991, p. 17), so the goal of REI was to include all exceptional students within the regular education classroom. For further discussion of REI, see the Current Issues and Perspectives box later in this chapter.

The term *inclusion* or *inclusive school movement* is more difficult to define. As Fuchs and Fuchs (1994) note, the meaning ranges from the earlier concepts associated with the REI to new education agendas including decentralization of power and the empowerment of teachers; reorganization of teaching methods; and most radically, the elimination of special education.

Including all children within regular education, however, may be a mixed blessing for some exceptional children. Insensitive classmates can make life miserable for individuals with learning disabilities. Teachers' organizations generally favor mainstreaming with reservations, but some individual teachers are not sure how to provide services for students with disabilities. Regular education teachers need additional training to teach exceptional students, and this training may not always be provided. In addition, administrators must designate funds to install ramps, elevators, and other special equipment; otherwise, school life could become excessively difficult for a child with a physical disability.

The favorable but cautious attitude toward inclusion reflects an awareness of the dangers of pendulum swings in education—for example, from enthusiasm for special classes to a rush away from them. Some educators believe that the current zeal for inclusion, resulting from excessive expectations for special classes, may in turn lead to excessive expectations for inclusion. Others believe that full inclusion has been oversold and underfunded. We must meet the range of needs displayed by children through a range of educational opportunities. We need both quality special education and appropriate integration of exceptional children into regular classes.

Regular Classroom Support for Exceptional Students

Mainstreaming, or the inclusion of exceptional children into regular classrooms, means that children with disabilities—of all categories—may require additional classroom support. Special education teachers will function as resource personnel, helping regular teachers to plan a student's schooling. The plan for a student might include adaptation of classroom activities and tasks to remain consistent with the student's IEP goals.

The scope of the federal and state special education legislation has caused educators to realize that almost 50% of school children experience problems, some of which require special help. Unless teachers possess both competence and understanding, inclusion simply will

CASE NOTES

Observation   Several students in Marsha Warren's class (for example, José, Angela, Tyrone, Sarah) appear to have exceptional education needs.

Hypothesis   Marsha Warren has students in her class who might benefit from special education support.

Possible Actions   To determine how best to meet the needs of the students, Marsha Warren should contact the school psychologist and discuss several possible intervention strategies.

What are some of the most important issues in the special education of the handicapped?

not achieve its desired objectives. Ultimately, then, much of the responsibility rests with teachers. Faced with this assignment, teachers have many questions, such as the following:

- How can I help all students become part of a classroom community?

- Exactly what are my obligations under inclusion?

- How many students who are disabled will be in my class?

- Will I receive help in planning programs?

- What is the responsibility of resource personnel?

- How can I spare the time?

- How can I learn more about special needs?

- How can I best help students with special needs achieve their goals?

Though most teacher-preparation institutions have incorporated planning for exceptional children into their courses, you may find several professional activities helpful. These include:

- *Classroom visitation.* Observation and demonstration by others can be invaluable. Having a skilled expert observe you, make constructive suggestions, and actively demonstrate techniques for you can substantially enhance your own expertise.

- *Teacher demonstrations.* Administrators and supervisors can schedule visits for you to see other schools and classrooms where master teachers offer demonstration lessons. Learning theorists have amply demonstrated the persuasiveness of observational learning.

- *Meetings, institutes, and conferences.* These assemblies can be helpful if they are planned to discuss pertinent problems and permit meaningful participation.

- *Professional libraries.* Since the vast special education literature and the rapidly accumulating database often provide profitable suggestions, sample as many bibliographies, articles, books, and government pamphlets as possible. You will find the following journals particularly helpful: *Journal of Learning Disabilities, American Journal of Orthopsychiatry, Teaching Exceptional Children, Educational Leadership, Exceptional Children, Behavioral Disorders, Mental Retardation, Journal of Special Education,* and *Remedial and Special Education.* Many resources are also available on the Internet.

- *Curriculum and research.* Thoughtful school officials may encourage teachers to publish bulletins, to prepare curriculum alterations, and to cooperate in writing course objectives. Scholarships may be available. Universities may offer course vouchers as a courtesy for student teacher placement. Some teachers may conduct research with their classes. All of these activities promote professional growth and furnish information that may produce more efficient teaching and learning.

Traditionally, when a teacher was concerned about a student who was experiencing an academic or behavioral problem, the first step was to refer that student for a special education evaluation. Marsha Warren's experience with her students, especially José, Angela, Bettie Ann, and Rhea might lead to a referral for special services. This process has changed dramatically in recent years. Due to the increasing emphasis on mainstreaming exceptional students and the concept of least restrictive environment, more and more students are being maintained in the regular classroom through prereferral intervention. Marsha does have the option to get professional help with her students and keep them in her classroom or refer them for an evaluation.

What is Marsha's role both prior to and after the referral? The role of the regular education teacher in this decision-making process is in providing services to the exceptional student at the prereferral stage. In this phase, teachers have the consultation support of various school professionals in developing the prereferral intervention program. Where does she start? Figure 5.4 provides an overview of the prereferral consultation process. Table 5.11 provides some information on the teacher's role during the decision-making process.

Does the prereferral intervention process help students and teachers? There is modest support for prereferral interventions (Nelson, Smith, Taylor, Dodd, & Reavis, 1991; Sindelar, Griffin, Smith, & Watanabe, 1992). Nelson et al. (1991) found that various prereferral intervention approaches can have a positive impact on special education service delivery practices and increase the abilities of teachers to work with students as well as improve their attitudes toward special-needs students. The authors also noted that student performance improved as a function of the various interventions used.

Sindelar and his associates (1992) note that more research is needed to support the outcomes of various prereferral interventions. They highlight various models of intervention ranging from collaborative teams of teachers to single teacher consultation models that involve a problem-solving framework (for example, Bergan & Kratochwill, 1990). Increasingly, parents are also being brought into the problem-solving models (for example, Sheridan, Kratochwill, & Bergan, 1996).

Some Results of Inclusion

In the years that have passed since PL94–142 took effect, the reactions of educators and the results of a wide variety of studies have been used to evaluate the effects of inclusion on learning (Baker, Wang, & Walberg, 1994). Three studies have summarized the research on inclusion through a methodology called meta-analysis (see the appendix at the end of this

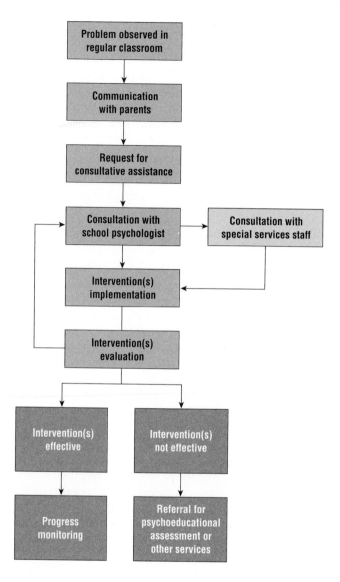

FIGURE 5.4

Flowchart for prereferral
consultation process.

book) (Baker, 1994; Carlberg & Kavale, 1980; Wang & Baker, 1985/1986). Baker et al. (1994)
interprets these results as demonstrating "... a small-to-moderate beneficial effect of inclusive education on the academic and social outcomes of special-needs children" (p. 33).
Baker et al. (1994) note that the segregation of students into separate classrooms is not desirable and that special students generally perform better in the regular classroom.

    We must be cautious, however, in interpreting the results of studies investigating
differences between special-needs students included in the regular classroom and those in
self-contained special education classes, particularly with regard to these factors:

■ *The nature of the disability.* Students with emotional disturbance may find greater
    difficulty in adjustment and peer acceptance in regular classes than do those
    students with other disabilities, such as children experiencing vision and hearing
    difficulties.

■ *Parental warmth, acceptance, and cooperation.* These factors have a powerful
    impact on a student's self-efficacy of control and achievement.

Table 5.11	HOW THE REGULAR CLASSROOM TEACHER PARTICIPATES IN SPECIAL EDUCATION DECISION MAKING
Stage	**Description**
Prereferral Stage	
Regular Education Process	The teacher notices that a student is performing differently from most of the other students in the class.
	The teacher checks with other teachers to verify his or her observations, then checks with the student's parents to eliminate special circumstances at home that might explain the exceptional performance.
	The teacher tries different methods of instruction (prereferral interventions) to identify the nature of the problem and gathers information about the student's performance in other areas.
	The teacher decides the prereferral intervention was effective and continues to use instructional modifications to provide special education in the regular classroom.
	Or the teacher decides the student's performance is sufficiently different to warrant special services and refers the student to the school's special education support team.
Postreferral Stage	
Special Education Process	The teacher reviews the results of individual psychological and educational testing, then consults with other team members and compares the student's performance to established criteria for eligibility for special education.
	The teacher offers an opinion about the appropriate placement for the student.
	The teacher cooperates with other team members in providing special services and evaluating their effectiveness.

James Ysseldyke and Robert Algozzine, *Introduction to Special Education*, Second Edition. Copyright © 1990 by Houghton Mifflin Company. Reprinted (or adapted) with permission.

- *Uncontrolled, multiple variables.* Some of these variables are sibling reaction, self-esteem, and teacher behavior.

Consequently, care must be taken before interpreting these conflicting results; the final verdict on inclusion has yet to be rendered. Perhaps the safest route is for our schools to follow these general inclusion guidelines:

- Students should be capable of doing some work at grade level.

- Students should be capable of doing some work without requiring special materials, adaptive equipment, or extensive assistance from the regular classroom teacher.

- Students should be capable of "staying on task" in the regular classroom without as much help and attention as they would receive in the special classroom or resource room.

- Students should be capable of fitting into the routine of the regular classroom.

- Students should be able to function socially in the regular classroom and profit from the modeling and appropriate behavior of their classmates.

Current Issues & Perspectives

The Regular Education Initiative

An important movement among many special educators has raised questions about the extent to which the original intent of PL94-142 was fully realized. Called the regular education initiative (REI), its thrust has been to call into question the exclusion of students who are mildly disabled (identified as the learning disabled, the emotionally disturbed, and the educable mentally retarded). Supporters of REI argue that most of these students can and should receive all of their education in the regular classroom.

Descriptions of REI contain many statements with which few educators could or would disagree, such as the following:

· Better integration and coordination of services for students with handicaps is needed.
· Effective and economical methods of educating these students should be a priority.
· Students should be identified as needing special services only when necessary.
· Special education should be reserved for those students needing the most specialized help.
· Some students are labeled because of the inadequacies of regular classroom teachers (Kauffman, Gerber, & Semmel, 1988).

Some evidence suggests that there is a small-to-moderate beneficial effect of inclusive education on both academic and social outcome of students with special needs (Baker et al., 1994). Some evidence indicates that inclusion of students with disabilities with nondisabled peers does not harm the latter and may indeed benefit them. However, research in this area is limited.

As the implications of REI spread throughout the educational community, it received a more searching examination, and several important issues were identified:

1. Can regular classroom teachers distribute instructional resources for all students?
2. Does REI distinguish sufficiently between elementary and secondary levels?
3. Research does not support the belief that all students with handicaps should be in regular classrooms.
4. Although there are problems with identifying (labeling) such students, the disabilities nevertheless exist.

In an *Educational Leadership* article, Fuchs and Fuchs (1995) argued that sometimes separate is better. Specifically, they noted "when children are not benefitting from instruction in a regular class, a compromise must be struck between legitimate social needs and equally valid educational needs" (p. 23). You can see, then, that REI is a hotly debated topic that cuts to the core of the controversy surrounding the effectiveness of special education services.

Services across the categories of exceptionality do not always provide students with the individualized instructional strategies that they need. Frequently, the same instructional tasks are used with nondisabled students and with different types of disabled students, which ignores the need to individualize instruction for all students (Ysseldyke, Christenson, Thurlow, & Bakewell, 1989).

The issues have been defined; the lines have been drawn; the implications are far-reaching. You should be alert to the direction this controversy takes, since it can affect all classrooms. Several books are devoted to these issues (see Goodlad & Lovitt, 1993; Jennings, 1997; Lloyd, Singh, & Repp, 1991).

- The physical setting of the classroom should not interfere with the student's functioning (or the environment should be adapted to their needs).

- It should be possible to work out scheduling to accommodate the students' various classes, and the schedules should be kept flexible and be easy to change as students progress.

- The classroom teacher should have adequate support to serve the needs of all children placed in the classroom.

MULTICULTURAL STUDENTS AND SPECIAL EDUCATION

Of growing concern to U.S. educators is the large number of multicultural students in special education classes. Faced with both standardized tests in a language that may cause them difficulty and adjustment to a new culture, many of these students experience achievement problems. Too often they are assigned to special education classes.

Difficulty in identifying students in need of services remains the culprit. Is the child's problem a limited ability in English? Is it the assessment strategies used by professionals? Is it uneasiness with a new culture? Is it sheer unfamiliarity with American schools? Or is it actually some handicapping condition? If you examine these questions objectively, you probably will agree that there is a real risk that some multicultural students will be inappropriately placed in special education classes.

Students from different ethnic groups reflect their distribution in the general population most closely in the learning disability, emotional disturbances, and speech impaired categories, although Asian students are underrepresented in each of these categories. White and Asian students are underrepresented in the mental retardation category, where African Americans are overrepresented. Asian students are overrepresented in gifted and talented programs, while African American, Hispanic, and Native American students are underrepresented (Ysseldyke & Algozzine, 1995).

Frequently, a physical problem is at the root of a student's difficulties, particularly since many of these students may have undetected health problems (for example, a chronic allergy). Occasionally, emotional problems follow the traumatic experiences of some of these students (for example, development of severe fears). Some school systems, wishing to avoid unwarranted special education placement, evaluate multicultural students when they first enter their school system.

Few linguistically and culturally appropriate assessment instruments exist for the students who speak languages other than English or Spanish, and there seems to be a limited understanding of many of the different cultures from which students come. Consequently, educators hesitate to place a newly arrived immigrant student who does not present a physical handicap into special education (First & Carrera, 1988). Nevertheless, many of these students seem to be candidates for special education. As a teacher or potential teacher of such students, try to determine just what is the source of any problem, so that your judgment is based as much on your knowledge of a student's knowledge as on immediate behavior.

Once a child has been identified as having special needs, a plan that is acceptable to the family, school, and specialists is implemented, and the student begins the specified program. The process does not end here but provides continuous evaluation to determine the program's effectiveness, and, if necessary, to devise a new plan. As we have emphasized

CASE NOTES

Observation   Marsha Warren may be teaching a student with limited English proficiency (LEP).

Hypothesis   Remember that José's mother speaks only Spanish, and although José speaks Spanish and English, it is unknown if his English skills are at his grade level of performance. It is possible that like Maria (where only Spanish is spoken in the home), José has LEP and needs further services to function in Marsha's third-grade classroom.

Possible Actions   What are the choices for these students? Remember that there are options that might be matched to a child's language abilities and skills, rather than to special education programs. For example, it is possible that José could profit from a "maintenance" program (which would allow him to remain in the language program even after he has developed English proficiency), whereas Maria might benefit from a "transition" program (to encourage the rapid development of English so that she can come back to Marsha's classroom as soon as possible). These options could be explored. Marsha could contact the speech and language professional in her school and discuss options for these students.

throughout this chapter, you should prepare for involvement at two key points: helping to identify a student's needs by reporting on educational status, and working with the student and specialized personnel to implement the educational plan.

TECHNOLOGY AND EXCEPTIONAL STUDENTS

Every category of exceptionality discussed in this chapter has been affected in some way by educational technology. In fact, a new field of study has emerged, known as *special education technology,* that is dedicated to the understanding, development, and application of technology to the education of exceptional students. The same federal legislation that mandated appropriate, least restrictive education for students with disabilities also addressed the use of technology for special education. The amendments to federal law which resulted in the IDEA legislation include "assistive technology device" and "assistive technology services." An *assistive technology device* is defined as "any item, piece of equipment, or product system, whether acquired commercially off the shelf, modified, or customized, that is used to increase, maintain, or improve functional capabilities of individuals with disabilities." An *assistive technology service* is "any service that directly assists an individual with a disability in the selection, acquisition, or use of an assistive technology device." An example of an assistive technology device is a pencil with an adaptive grip or an electronic book. These devices might be used by a person with a physical disability.

Further policy statements specified that the use of assistive technology devices and services must be done on a case-by-case basis and should be considered during the development of each student's IEP. Any device or service deemed necessary for that student's appropriate education must be provided by the school district at no cost to the student's family.

With assistive technology, children can meaningfully participate in educational activities.

Advantages of Assistive Technology

Simply put, technology often allows a child with exceptional needs to do things in a class-room that were impossible before. For example, a student with severe cerebral palsy might be able to communicate meaningfully with peers, write original stories, produce music, and create artwork via a specially designed computer that can be activated by puffing air into a special input device. Without such technological interventions, the student could communicate in only rudimentary ways. Rena Lewis discusses the benefits of technology for students with disabilities as an ABC model: technology can be used to "Augment abil-ities, and Bypass or Compensate for disabilities" (1993, p. 7).

Lewis (1993) notes several benefits of technology for students with disabilities, in-cluding improvement of academic performance, increasing motivation for academic tasks, improving behavior, allowing accomplishment of tasks previously considered impossible, increasing feelings of self-worth, and producing more positive perceptions by peers and family. The notion that students become more empowered and are able to accomplish at new levels, and that such changes can produce positive changes in how students with dis-abilities are viewed by others in their lives, are quite important for students' self-concepts and their motivation to try new and harder things in the future.

Limitations of Assistive Technology

Several factors can limit the effectiveness of technology with exceptional students. The first concerns the approach to using assistive technology. Whether used to overcome challenging conditions or to accelerate the pace of learning, technology must be seen as an educational tool rather than a cure-all. Technology, as with any other educational tool, is most effective when used as part of an integrated and thoughtful educational pro-gram. Second, it is important to keep in mind that assistive technologies can be quite ex-pensive. While the benefits may outweigh the costs, the costs can be high. Finally, curious as it may seem, the major limiting factor is sometimes the student. In describing student reactions to attempts to integrate technology with one group of students with severe motor disabilities, Holmstrom (1988) noted that the students were very resistant to the changes and did not want to give up their familiar ways of communicating. As with any other educational method, students must be willing and motivated to use it before it can be effective.

Assistive Technology for Each Category of Exceptionality

As we noted before, gifted and talented students also can be a challenge for classroom teachers because they are often far ahead of their classmates in both skill levels and interest, at least in some subject areas. Technology is quite useful for helping these students move at their own pace and in directions of personal interest. For example, well-programmed educational software will allow students to operate at varying levels of knowledge and skill, with students who are ready to move ahead of their peers easily allowed to do so. Problem-solving software and computer simulation programs allow students to test their knowledge and skills at more-sophisticated levels and in settings that would not be possible in the real world. The Internet enables gifted students to connect with others (databases, other students, adult mentors, or university faculty) for work on specific projects or topics. (Dale, 1993, provides a review of a number of different programs and possibilities for using computers effectively with gifted and talented students.)

Students with visual and/or hearing difficulties, as well as those with communication disorders, can benefit from modified computer systems. For example, enhanced screens with large print are easily available for those with limited vision. Keyboards and output devices are also available in Braille. Systems can be modified to be less reliant on sound cues for those with impaired hearing. Speech synthesizers that can read aloud text a student has typed into the computer can help students with speech disorders (for example, misarticulation, apraxia, voice disorders, and fluency disorders) communicate their ideas to others. Software programs can also provide guided practice with feedback for those students who have difficulty using language effectively. Different programs focus on different aspects of language learning, such as clear expression of ideas or grammar and linguistic form.

Assistive technology is extremely helpful to students who have physical disabilities. Speech synthesizers allow those with impaired speech ability to hear their ideas expressed fluently. And a variety of clever input devices enable students to accomplish tasks previously thought to be impossible. Those with some degree of control over their hands and fingers can use touch screens to input information, while those with little muscle control can use switches or light pens to control computer keyboards. Consider the following description of Scott:

> Scott suffers from cerebral palsy and has been severely physically disabled since birth. Scott's mind was filled with ideas, stories, and jokes, but, like many people with this handicapping condition, his lack of motor control made it almost impossible to communicate. Scott could neither speak nor write. … Scott was provided with a computerized communication system that attached to his wheelchair. … As Scott became more adept at using the new technology, his teachers and fellow students were surprised to discover his high level of cognition. Scott graduated magna cum laude from his high school and went on to study accounting at the local university. (Maddus, Johnson, & Willis, 1997, p. 261)

For students with behavior disorders, technology is sometimes useful as a motivational tool. If the student enjoys working on the computer, it can serve as a very effective reinforcer for appropriate classroom behavior. Software can be useful for those with specific learning disabilities by providing practice in number and letter recognition. Utility programs like spell-checkers in word processing packages can help these students by signaling and helping correct spelling errors. Instructional software programs can be useful for students with certain kinds of cognitive disabilities, depending on the severity of the disability. Some students benefit from being allowed more time to practice basic word and number skills. Software that allows students as many repetitions and as much learning time as necessary to master these basics can be especially useful.

Resources for Assistive Technology

Assistive technology changes rapidly. Several resources are available to help beginning teachers learn more about this area. Closing the Gap is an organization that publishes information on assistive technology, hardware, software, and other relevant topics. Apple and IBM both offer information concerning assistive possibilities with their machines. The Internet is an instantaneous and up-to-date source for information, discussion, and support for many aspects of assistive technology.

Case Reflections

Students who are exceptional and who spend time in a typical classroom often display behaviors that challenge their teachers. Students in Marsha Warren's class exhibit poor academic performance, attention problems, hyperactivity, language difficulties, and aggression. Marsha Warren clearly has students in her class who have exceptional educational needs. In particular, José and Maria exhibit difficulties in language development and English as a second language. They were referred to the speech and language teacher for evaluation. Bettie Ann appears to have some emotional problems that required referral to the school psychologist to help her overcome her weight problem and emotional insecurity. Katie eventually met the criteria for ADHD and received special services and medication to function in the regular classroom. Marsha was able to monitor these students in her classroom to assist the school psychologist to facilitate prereferral interventions for each of the kids. However, eventually they needed additional resources to function effectively in her classroom setting.

Marsha participated in a process called *prereferral intervention* in which she identified characteristics of the students who needed some assistance. In her third-grade classroom she worked with the school psychologist to get services for Angela, Tyrone, Sarah, and Rhea without a formal referral for special education. She checked with other teachers to verify her observation, and she tried several other methods of instruction to identify the problems and gather information on these students. She continued interventions to help further understand the nature of these children's problems. In this way, the students were able to continue to be mainstreamed.

Eventually, José was able to receive services through a maintenance program for LEP. Maria participated in a transitional LEP program that facilitated her English language development. Each of these students who were exceptional profited from Marsha Warren's ability to monitor them and to learn more about their individual differences and exceptional needs. However, she was not alone in this process and worked with other professionals in the school to solve some of her problems.

Traditionally, when a teacher was concerned about a student who was experiencing an academic or behavioral problem, the first step was to refer that student for a special education evaluation. Marsha Warren's experience with her students, especially José, Angela, Bettie Ann, and Rhea, might have led to a referral for special services. This process, however, has changed dramatically in recent years. Due to the increasing emphasis on mainstreaming exceptional students and the concept of least restrictive environment, more and more students are being maintained in the regular classroom through prereferral intervention, rather than being separated into special education classrooms. Marsha does have the option to get professional help with her students.

What is Marsha's role both prior to and after the referral? The role of the regular education teacher in this decision-making process is in providing services to the exceptional student at the prereferral stage. In this phase, teachers have the consultation support of various school professionals in developing the prereferral intervention program.

CHAPTER HIGHLIGHTS

Exceptional Children in the Classroom

- You can expect to find a wide range of individual differences in your classroom: physical, cognitive, and behavioral.

- Federal law requires that students with handicaps be placed in the environment that is "least restrictive" for them.

Areas of Exceptionality

- Students who are gifted and/or talented have often been overlooked in our classrooms. Today we realize they deserve special attention to further their abilities in a manner calculated to provide normal social and emotional development.

- Students with sensory impairments (visual and hearing) require early detection to prevent lingering problems that may affect performance. The cognitive ability of many of these students will be in a normal range. Teachers should understand each child's strengths and limitations and be familiar with the student's IEP goals.

- Students with communication disorders may experience a developmental delay in language acquisition or find difficulty in expressing themselves. Knowledge of language development should help teachers to identify these students.

- Students with medical, physical, and multiple disabilities need help in physically adjusting to the classroom and participating in all class activities.

- Students with behavior disorders present a range of problems that are caused by some interaction of personal, environmental, and even physical factors. Teachers will need considerable sensitivity in working with these students to help them achieve as fully as possible.

- Students with learning disabilities are now identified by applying an exclusion component; that is, the difficulty is not attributed to some other cause, such as mental retardation or a physical problem. In working with these students, teachers must be careful that some other surface difficulty does not mask the learning disability.

- Students with cognitive disabilities will be in the class; they require a carefully sequenced program consistent with individual abilities and goals.

- Several support systems, ranging from a student's family to professional staff, operate to help adapt classrooms and instruction to the student's needs.

The Assessment and Classification of Children

- Assessment plays a critical role in placement decisions about students.

- Any classification system of students with handicaps must avoid the dangers of labeling.

Mainstreaming and Inclusion

- Mainstreaming or inclusion is a policy of placing students with handicaps into regular classrooms whenever possible.
- Teachers will undoubtedly be involved at some point in educational decisions about these students: their identification, evaluation, and placement.
- Informed input requires knowledge from reading, classroom visits, and workshops (among other sources).

Multicultural Students and Special Education

- Considerable sensitivity is needed in making decisions about multicultural students, since many factors may affect their performance.

Technology and Exceptional Students

- Technology often allows students with exceptional needs to do things that were previously impossible.

WHAT DO YOU THINK?

1. What are the guidelines for implementing least restrictive environment (LRE) placements? Consider a child in your classroom who is experiencing a severe behavior problem. Apply the criteria of LRE to this case.

2. Monitor mainstreamed students carefully when they are in class. To do so, you can try something like this (Bos & Vaughn, 1988):

   Student Helped (Name) _____

   Date   Time   Comments
   _____

   Carefully mark the date and time and use appropriate comments, such as these:
   - difficulty with long and short vowels
   - trouble with two-place multiplication

   Use this technique with behavioral problems as well. Keep a close check on dates to determine if the time between incidents is improving.
   - What is the time of day?
   - Is it the same time each time the incident occurs?
   - What is the subject matter when the incident occurs?

   With these and other simple techniques, you can keep a close check on the progress of your students who are exceptional.

3. Suppose you are presenting an in-service program to novice teachers on gifted and talented students. What suggestions would you offer to teachers working with such students in their classes?

4. Outline guidelines that you would use for working with students who are visually and hearing impaired and students who are physically or health impaired.

5. What can you do to help a student with attention-deficit/hyperactivity disorder?

6. Name myths and facts about learning disabilities. Discuss a child whom you know who may have a learning disability.

7. Identify types of mental retardation and describe characteristics of school-age children with each type. How would these characteristics influence your teaching strategies?

Teachers' Case

This section focused on the "Development of Students" and featured a case concerning Marsha Warren, an experienced third-grade teacher who has a very heterogeneous class of students in terms of ability and maturity. Consequently, Ms. Warren felt challenged almost daily by several of her students. Over the course of Chapters 2 through 5, we have provided you some insights into this case via Case Notes and Case Reflections. Now it is time to examine some additional perspectives on this case. We asked two experienced teachers, Jodine Hideg and Hilda Ramirez-Powell, to share their reactions to Marsha Warren's classroom.

Jodine Hideg

First-Grade Teacher
Lockport, Illinois

While Marsha Warren's task is difficult, it is not insurmountable. While, at first glance, it may seem that Ms. Warren's reaction to her class has made this difficult situation worse, it may, rather, have provided her with the opportunity to reflect on her own behavior and give her the occasion to make beneficial changes. She obviously has taken a positive first step by looking into the "why" of her students' behavior.

One strategy that may prove advantageous in Ms. Warren's classroom would be cooperative learning sessions. When students are working together toward a common goal, they form a bond that, hopefully, will carry over into other situations. Partnering students who exhibit those behaviors considered appropriate with students whose behavior is socially unacceptable may prove worthwhile to both groups. Not only would the "infidels" have greater exposure to appropriate behavior, but those students exhibiting socially acceptable behavior may gain greater understanding and, perhaps even more importantly, compassion toward their peers.

Ms. Warren also needs to quit avoiding parent contact. Teaching is a three-way partnership—parent, student, teacher. Instead of finding excuses to dodge interactions with parents, she needs to find ways that she can effectively communicate with those parents. Perhaps finding an interpreter for those non-English-speaking parents.

Planning lessons that involve parents in the academic setting would help bring parents into the classroom—"parent readers," "parent tutors" (being certain to have tutors for those students considered "academically advanced" as well as those considered "academically deficient"), and even "parent helpers" who come in to help with clerical tasks will make parents feel a more integral part of the school climate.

For those parents who are unable to come in during the school day, some events could be planned for evenings—perhaps a play, poetry recital, Mother's Day Tea, the list could go on and on. While these approaches require more time and effort on the part of the teacher, the benefits to the classroom atmosphere can prove immeasurable!

Finally, expectations must be held high for all students, not only those considered "academically superior." Students are able to "read" teachers' feelings about them and respond accordingly.

Conference

Hilda Ramirez-Powell

Elementary School Teacher
Giddings, Texas

It is clearly apparent that Marsha Warren, a third grade teacher, has multiple issues to be concerned about. Anyone in her situation would not find teaching fun. As a point of reference, the following five concerns summarize the overall atmosphere of her classroom: (1) Lack of overall control and discipline, (2) Lack of respect from the students to Ms. Warren as well as their peers, (3) Explosive environment, tension, and short tempers, (4) Continuous shouting, and (5) Wasting of valuable time refocusing and redirecting the students.

Ms. Warren has eleven years of teaching experience. With that, she brings several strategies to the forefront. However, taking what Ms. Warren has already tried and utilizing some of those techniques, there are additional ideas and resources that she might consider. For example, the most important element in any successful classroom/program is control as well as management skills. Ms. Warren should focus on the rules of the classroom, but this time involve the students in recreating the rules and positive/negative consequences. When the students see their input implemented, it is more likely that the rules will be followed. The hope is that the "good students" will remind the "problematic students" about their behavior and that they will not tolerate it any more, once again, empowering students to reinforce positive behaviors and ignore negative behaviors.

Ms. Warren also can utilize available resources such as:

- Peer/Tutoring: pairing her academically stronger students with weaker ones. This would allow for positive peer interaction and would free her time to follow through on other issues or present lessons.
- Ask the school counselor or school psychologist to come in and observe the behavior of the students. There may be a need to refer some of the more problematic students for counseling, which should help with the overall attitude of the classroom.

Finally, Ms. Warren can implement cooperative learning—change the makeup of the reading groups. The eight slowest readers should not be in one reading group. Through cooperative learning, all students would benefit and develop learning strategies that they could build on.

Marsha Warren works in a culturally rich and stimulating environment. If she focuses on class management, more of the positives from her and her students will emerge.

We trust you found the insights of these two experienced educators concerning the case of Marsha Warren interesting and empowering. These comments coupled with the numerous Case Notes and Case Reflections provide you with many ideals about tactics you might use when confronted with your own classroom of diverse learners.

Learning Theories *and* Implications *for* Practice

The Case of Mark Siegel*

A fourth-grade teacher is challenged by a parent who visits him regularly, demanding more effective teaching for her son. The boy is seemingly uninterested in learning and is a bit of a social outcast in the classroom. The teacher believes that he has tried everything and that the problem rests with the child and the demanding parent.

Mark Siegel shifted uncomfortably in his chair. This latest conference with Kyesha Peterson was going no better than the earlier ones. Realizing he had stopped listening to her, Mark tuned back in and heard her say, "Karim isn't learning enough in your class. It's November, and he still isn't catching up. What are you going to do for him?"

"Mrs. Peterson, we've had this conversation before. I'm continually trying to help Karim, but he also has to want to help himself."

"We certainly have had this conversation before. And I don't see any evidence that you've made things better for Karim in your class."

"You're right. Karim has not made any great breakthroughs since our last meeting. He isn't responding to any of the strategies I used in my classroom. He simply shows no interest in participating in class activities."

Mrs. Peterson continued to look out the window. "Well, it seems to me that it's your job to make school interesting for the students."

Mark gritted his teeth. He was feeling hounded by Mrs. Peterson but decided to keep his cool. "I too am frustrated by Karim's lack of progress. I have tried several instructional tactics that have been effective with other students, but they have not worked with Karim. I will, however, keep trying as long as you will!"

By four o'clock, Mrs. Peterson had said her piece and allowed Mark to escort her to the front of the school. The conference ended with Mark assuring her that he would give Karim more attention and make further efforts so that school would become more compelling for the boy.

Walking back to his classroom, Mark thought about Karim Peterson. A part of Mark felt sorry for the boy because, in addition to the child's academic problems, he seemed like such a social outcast in his class of mostly middle-class Caucasian students. When the difficulties with Mrs. Peterson first began, Mark went to see Paula Fowler, Karim's third-grade teacher the year before. She told Mark quite a bit about Karim's background. Paula indicated that Karim came from a stable family in which he was the youngest of three children. African culture and heritage were emphasized strongly in their home. The mother seemed to be the dominant family figure with regard to education and discipline. Karim's father was a bus driver for the city transportation system, and his mother worked in the Littleton Public Library. Paula had indicated that education and career opportunities were extremely important to the family. She noted that Karim was not allowed to come to the class Christmas party because his family didn't recognize it as a holiday. She also indicated that the family seemed very conscious of racial issues and that Karim had wondered why there were no black children in the highest reading group in his class.

Reflecting on the current year, Mark decided to review his observations of Karim. He had been having difficulty socializing with his classmates; he could be verbally abusive to other students and consequently was seen as a loner. Some students teased him for talking "like a baby." Also when Karim was nervous, he had a habit of sniffing his fingers, and the same students often made fun of him then, too. During the two months that Karim had been in Mark's class, it had become obvious that the other children did not like to be grouped with him. When Mark asked his students to choose and work with partners, Karim had to be assigned a partner. Most of the time he was reluctant to participate in activities that involved peer interaction. When the class had free time, Karim usually sat by himself. His classmates did not include him in their activities, and he did not express any interest in joining them.

Despite his seemingly antisocial behavior, Karim was a reasonably verbal, bright child. His standardized test scores were very high and suggested that he should easily be doing grade-level work. Mark understood why Mrs. Peterson expected better school per-

formance from Karim, given his verbal skills and test scores. Although the boy was working only about half a year behind grade level, his oral reading was slow and labored enough to concern his mother. Mark thought that Karim's inability to focus on his work and maintain his attention contributed to his problems. Karim's short attention span and difficulty with reading meant that he worked very slowly, and he often was unable to finish in-class assignments.

Since Karim's mother began demanding that her son receive special attention Mark had used all the strategies he'd learned in his nine years of teaching fourth- and fifth-graders at Roosevelt Elementary School. His goal had been to improve Karim's reading skills and bring them up to at least grade level. At first, he thought that if he could spark more interest, Karim would respond with increased attention. Mark tried some reading materials that he thought would be of high interest—topics like sports, music, and extraterrestrials—based on his knowl-

edge of other fourth-grade boys. None captured Karim's attention; he did not seem to share many of the interests of his peers. Mark also tried a reward system, offering Karim free time for completing work within an assigned time. Karim didn't respond. Mark then sat down with him and tried to find out what would act as a reinforcer, but he found Karim uncooperative. The boy seemed unwilling to discuss his interests with Mark or to tell Mark what rewards he would be willing to work for.

While Mark was frustrated by Karim, his frustration was exacerbated by Karim's mother, whose demands for after-school conferences were increasing. Since Mark was unable to report any successes with Karim, these meetings were starting to make Mark feel anxious. He had experienced little success in reaching Karim, improving his reading, or getting him to respond positively to his classmates. Mark was beginning to believe that Karim might be one of the kids he couldn't "reach" or teach.

*This case was adapted from the case of Mark Siegel written by Silverman, Welty, and Lyon (1996).

C H A P T E R

Behavioral Psychology and Learning

Mark Siegel is a fourth-grade teacher who is challenged by Karim Peterson and the boy's mother. The mother is a frequent visitor to Mark's class. She demands better teaching for her son who is having academic and social problems in the classroom. Mark is frustrated with the visits and feels that he has done everything to help the child. Look for information on this case throughout the chapter.

Chapter Outline

Classical Conditioning

Thorndike's
    Connectionism

Operant Conditioning

Social Cognitive
    Learning

Behavioral Theories and
    Teaching

Behaviorism and the
    Future

Case Reflections

Chapter Highlights

What Do You Think?

Key Terms

In this chapter, the primary focus is on behavior. Work in behavioral psychology is guided by a philosophy of science called *behaviorism*. Traditionally, individuals who embrace a behavior orientation believe that studies of ideas, percepts, or concepts (such as those cognitive theorists propose) are not highly useful to change behavior; instead we must work directly with behavior itself. (Certain behaviorists, such as Albert Bandura, who are frequently called *neobehaviorists*, do consider cognitive processes such as motivation and intention. Some scholars would now consider Bandura a cognitive theorist, even though his early work embraced a more traditional focus on behavior.) Many of the classroom applications of behavioral psychology have been developed in the field called *applied behavior analysis*. As the name implies, applied behavior analysis is "the science in which procedures derived from the principles of behavior are systematically applied to improve socially significant behavior to a meaningful degree and to demonstrate experimentally that the procedures employed were responsible for the improvement in behavior" (Cooper, Heron, & Heward, 1987, p. 15).

To help you understand the differences among the outstanding behaviorists, we'll first examine Ivan Pavlov's *classical conditioning* and Edward Lee Thorndike's *connectionism*. Next we'll analyze B. F. Skinner's *operant conditioning* and point out key differences between Pavlov and Skinner. Bandura's *neobehaviorism* deserves our attention because of its importance for learning and development. Finally, we'll turn to behaviorism's impact on the classroom, concentrating on applied behavior-analysis management techniques. These theories have continuing and direct relevance for classroom teachers.

CLASSICAL CONDITIONING

Much of the affective behavior (feelings and emotions) that students demonstrate in class can be explained by the work of the Russian physiologist, Ivan Pavlov (1849–1936). Children's fears, anxieties, and joys can be traced to conditions within the classroom, frequently without the awareness of their teachers.

Pavlov's Work

Many years after his death, Pavlov's best-known writings, *Conditioned Reflexes* (1927) and *Lectures on Conditioned Reflexes* (1928), remain highly influential. His studies of digestion in animals led to an important psychological discovery: that of the **conditioned reflex.** In Pavlov's classic experiment, the anticipation of food caused the flow of saliva in dogs.

Saliva flowed at each dog's sight of the food dish or of the attendant, perhaps even at a sound the attendant usually made during feeding. We would expect the sight and smell of food to cause the flow of saliva, but other sights and sounds (such as the attendant or a bell) don't usually cause saliva to flow. Somehow, Pavlov's dogs had "learned" that these sights and sounds signaled the appearance of food, as described in Figure 6.1.

Pavlov called the signal (the sight or sound) that produced saliva the **conditioned stimulus.** He next turned his attention to how conditioned reflexes are established. You may be familiar with the model he used. Food (labeled the *unconditioned stimulus*) was paired with a metronome (first a neutral *stimulus*). At the beginning of the conditioning experiment, the salivary reflex (labeled the *unconditioned response*) was elicited only in the presence of the food; in other words, the dogs salivated only when there was food. Pavlov repeatedly paired the food with the metronome and found that, in time, the metronome itself, (now the conditioned stimulus) independent of the food, elicited salivation (labeled a *conditioned response*). The sequence in **classical conditioning** is as follows:

1. US (unconditioned stimulus) produces UR (unconditioned response)
   food→saliva

Objectives

When you finish reading this chapter, you should be able to

- distinguish between classical and operant conditioning

- recognize how students may acquire fears through classical conditioning

- explain how a theory such as Thorndike's connectionism had widespread classroom application

- identify the major elements of operant conditioning

- understand how the principles of reinforcement and punishment can be used in the classroom

- apply the principles of social cognitive theory (such as imitation and modeling) to your instructional techniques

- apply the principles of behavior psychology to the case of Mark Siegel

CONDITIONED REFLEX
A response that is elicited by a conditioned stimulus when the unconditioned stimulus is not present.

CONDITIONED STIMULUS
A previously neutral stimulus that has acquired the power to elicit a response.

CLASSICAL CONDITIONING
Pavlov's explanation of conditioning in which a neutral (conditioned) stimulus gradually gains the ability to elicit a response because of its pairing with a natural (unconditioned) stimulus.

Ivan Pavlov (1849–1936) in his laboratory flanked by his assistants and one of his dogs.

FIGURE 6. 1

Pavlov's Research Apparatus. In studying the digestive process, Ivan Pavlov would present a dog with meat powder and collect saliva through a tube inserted into one of the dog's salivary glands. The amount of salivation was recorded by a stylus writing on a rotating drum. Pavlov found that dogs salivated to stimuli associated with the presentation of food, such as the mere sight of the laboratory assistant who brought the food.

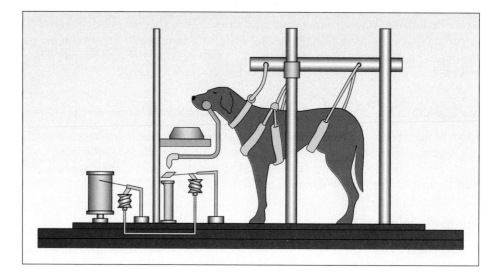

2. NS (neutral stimulus) produces no response
       metronome alone→no response

3. NS + US (neutral + unconditioned stimulus) produces UR (unconditioned response)
       metronome plus food→saliva

4. CS (conditioned stimulus) produces CR (conditioned response)
       metronome alone→saliva

The conditioned stimulus (the sound of the metronome) acquired some of the response-producing potential of the unconditioned stimulus (the food). Note that the conditioned stimulus has been conditioned to the unconditioned stimulus.

Features of Classical Conditioning

Before discussing the classroom implications of Pavlov's work, we should review several principles of classical conditioning that Pavlov discovered (Kalish, 1981). These include stimulus generalization, discrimination, and extinction.

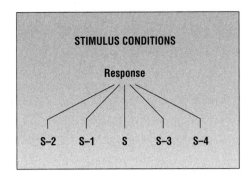

FIGURE 6.2

Stimulus Generalization. S is some stimulus. The response—stopping—is made to S1, red traffic light; S2, red light over door; S3, red stop sign; and S4, red flag.

Stimulus generalization refers to the process by which the conditioned response transfers to other stimuli that are similar to the original conditioned stimulus. For example, once we learn that the color red means "stop," we tend to stop or hesitate at red lights, signs, and flashing red bulbs. In Figure 6.2, think of the various stimuli as different forms of the red condition meaning "stop."

Stimulus generalization is a process that lies at the heart of transfer of learning in the classroom. We want our students to be able to use the material they learn in class in a variety of circumstances. Teenagers who have learned to avoid drug usage in school, through the use of written and visual materials, will, we hope, avoid drugs if they actually are offered to them on the street. Remember, though, that the less closely the stimulus resembles the conditioned stimulus, the weaker the response will be. Reading about a drug transaction is far different from being approached by someone who is offering drugs.

Generalization appears to explain the transfer of a response from one situation to another. A first-grade youngster terrified by a stern teacher may transfer that fear or anxiety to anything about school: teachers, books, the school building itself. Two facts about generalization are worth noting:

1. Once conditioning to any stimulus occurs, its effectiveness is not restricted to that stimulus.

2. As a stimulus becomes less similar to the one originally used, its ability to produce a response lessens accordingly (Hulse, Egeth, & Deese, 1980).

Discrimination refers to the process by which we learn *not* to respond to similar stimuli in the same way. You would probably not yell at a uniformed police officer as you would at a uniformed opposing football player. *Discrimination* is just the opposite of generalization. Whereas *generalization* means responding in the same way to two different stimuli, discrimination means responding differently to two similar stimuli.

For example, your car absolutely refuses to start in the morning (nothing happens when you put the key in the ignition). You can be fairly sure that this problem is electrical. It might be the battery; it might be the starter. If, however, you hear a clicking sound, chances are good that the starter is faulty. Based on prior experiences, you have discriminated the starter as the problem. We respond differently to different stimuli because of our previous experiences in which certain of our responses were successful in the presence of certain stimuli.

Again, we can draw important classroom implications. Youngsters learning to read might have big problems if they cannot tell the difference between circles and curved lines, or horizontal from vertical lines. They could not (or at least not consistently) discriminate the letters *v* from *u* or *b* from *d*, which could lead to reading problems. Similar

STIMULUS GENERALIZATION
Transfer of a trained response to situations or stimulus conditions other than those in which training has taken place. The behavior generalizes to other situations. Contrast with response generalization.

DISCRIMINATION
The process by which we learn not to respond to similar stimuli in an identical manner.

(margin note) classroom implication for generalization

(margin note) classroom implication - for discrimination

CASE NOTES   C

Observation   Karim's classmates have been excluding him from various activities.

Hypothesis   Karim's classmates have been conditioned to respond to Karim with avoidance and isolation.

Possible Action   Establish new and positive social activities that Karim can participate in and where the interactions will create positive feelings in the group.

---

discrimination challenges exist for young learners confronted with pairs of numbers such as 21 and 12, or 75 and 57. Learning to make discriminations of form and, later in life, of substance is a critical component of successful learning.

EXTINCTION

Refers to the process by which conditioned responses are lost.

classroom implication

    Extinction refers to the process by which conditioned responses are lost. In his experiments, Pavlov found that by presenting the sound of the metronome alone, eventually he could eliminate the conditioned response. In other words, if over time there is no food accompanying the metronome, the dog will stop salivating at the presence of the metronome only. The brother who warned his younger sister about that "terrible Mrs. Smith" who would be her next year's teacher could easily cause the girl to be anxious around Mrs. Smith. After several nervous weeks at the beginning of school, however, the girl's discovery that Mrs. Smith is a pleasant person gradually extinguishes the anxiety.

    Behaviorists who have followed Pavlov are interested in the consequences of the responses that students make and in deliberately shaping behavior. This issue leads us to the work of Thorndike.

THORNDIKE'S CONNECTIONISM

CONNECTIONISM

Thorndike's explanation of learning (by selecting and connecting).

Edward Lee Thorndike (1874–1949) believed that all learning is explained by connections (or bonds) that are formed between stimuli and responses. These connections occur mainly through trial and error, a process Thorndike later designated as **connectionism,** or learning by selecting and connecting. Thorndike formulated laws of learning, which are not inflexible laws, but rules that learning seems to obey. His three major laws of learning (*readiness, exercise,* and *effect*) have direct application to education.

The Law of Readiness

When organisms, both human and animal, are ready to form connections, to do so is satisfying and not to do so is annoying. Thorndike believed that readiness is an important condition of learning, because satisfaction or frustration depends on an individual's state of readiness. He stated (1913, p. 133) that readiness is like an army sending scouts ahead of a train whose arrival at one station sends signals ahead to open or close switches. Schools can't force students to learn if they aren't biologically and psychologically prepared. They can only learn when they are ready.

The Law of Exercise

The law of exercise states that any connection is strengthened in proportion to the number of times it occurs and in proportion to the average vigor and duration of the connection. Conversely, when a connection is not made between a stimulus and response for

Edward Thorndike
(1874–1949)

some time, the connection's strength decreases. However, continued experimentation and criticism forced Thorndike to revise the original law of exercise after 1930. He realized that practice alone was not enough for improvement. There must also be a strengthening of the bond by reinforcement; that is, the law of effect must also operate. When students practice, they should be aware of the consequences of what they are doing. Otherwise, practice becomes ineffective—even harmful—if error creeps in.

The Law of Effect

Probably the most important of Thorndike's laws, the law of effect states that responses accompanied by satisfaction are more firmly connected with a situation; responses accompanied by discomfort have their connections weakened. The greater the satisfaction or discomfort, the greater is the strengthening or weakening of the bond. In 1932, Thorndike revised the law to stress that the strengthening effect of reward is much greater than the weakening effect of punishment. Pupils tend to learn more effectively (and easily), and to retain that learning longer, if it has pleasant consequences.

For many years, Thorndike had a powerful influence on educational practice because of his insistence on a scientific basis for education. For example, his explanation of the transfer of learning is still meaningful. Called *identical elements,* the theory states that learning can be applied to new situations only when there are identical elements in both situations (for example, similar learning materials).

Hergenhahn (1988) stated that Thorndike believed good teaching begins with knowing what you want to teach: the stimuli. You must also identify the responses you want to connect to the stimuli and the timing of appropriate satisfiers. Thorndike would say this:

- Consider the pupil's environment.

- Consider the response you want to connect with it.

- Form the connection (with satisfaction).

Thorndike's remarkable energy and drive led to an astounding number of publications, and he provided education with the scientific emphasis it so desired. His work with the law of effect was an early statement of the importance of positive reinforcement, a concept B. F. Skinner greatly expanded.

OPERANT CONDITIONING

B. F. Skinner (1904–1990) received his doctorate from Harvard, and after teaching for several years at the universities of Minnesota and Indiana, he returned to Harvard. It was there that he continued to refine the differences between classical and operant conditioning and applied his ideas to a wide range of human endeavors.

Convinced of the importance of reinforcement, Skinner developed an explanation of learning that stresses the consequences of behavior: What happens after we do something is all-important. Reinforcement has proven to be a powerful tool in the shaping and control of behavior, both in and out of the classroom.

Skinner's Views

B. F. Skinner was in the forefront of psychological and educational endeavors for several decades. Innovative, practical, witty, and ahead of his time, Skinner's work has had a lasting impact. In several major publications—*The Behavior of Organisms* (1938), *Science and Human Behavior* (1953), *Verbal Behavior* (1957), *The Technology of Teaching* (1968), *Beyond Freedom and Dignity* (1971), and *About Behaviorism* (1974)—and in a steady flow of articles, Skinner reported his experiments and developed and clarified his theory. He welcomed the challenge of applying his findings to practical affairs. Education, religion, psychotherapy, and other fields have all felt the force of Skinner's thought.

Although Skinner initially made his impact during the 1930s when the classical conditioning of Pavlov was popular and influential, he demonstrated that the environment had a much greater influence on learning and behavior than Pavlov realized. In his explanation of **operant conditioning,** Skinner argued that the environment (that is, parents, teachers, peers) reacts to our behavior and either reinforces or eliminates that behavior. *The environment holds the key to understanding behavior* (Bales, 1990).

For Skinner, behavior is a causal chain of three links: (1) an operation performed on the organism from without—a girl comes to school without breakfast; (2) some inner condition—she gets hungry; and (3) a kind of behavior—she exhibits listless behavior in the classroom.

Lacking information about inner conditions, teachers should not indulge in speculation. For example, the child just mentioned is listless and disinterested during class. Skinner would scoff at those who would say the girl is unmotivated. Skinner would ask, "What does this mean?" "How can you explain it behaviorally?" The teacher or counselor searching for causes has mistakenly stopped at the second link: some inner condition (the girl is hungry). The answer lies in the first link: something done to the student (her lack of breakfast). Physical difficulty or trouble with parents would be similar operations.

Until his death in 1990, Skinner emphasized the important effect of consequences on behavior and cautioned us about the limitations of a cognitive-oriented psychology:

> So far as I'm concerned, cognitive science is the creationism of psychology. It is an effort to reinstate that inner initiating-originating-creative self or mind which, in a scientific analysis, simply does not exist. I think it is time for psychology as a profession and as a science in such fields as psychotherapy, education, developmental psychology and all the rest, to realize that the science which will be most helpful is not cognitive science searching for the inner mind or self, but selection by consequences represented by behavior analysis.
>
> Looking back on my life—sixty-two years as a psychologist—I would say that what I have tried to do, that what I have been doing, is to make that point clearer; to show how selection by consequences in

OPERANT CONDITIONING

Skinner's explanation of learning, which emphasizes the consequences of behavior.

B. F. Skinner working in his lab.

the individual can be demonstrated in the laboratory with animals and with human subjects and to show the implications of that for the world at large—in not only the profession of psychology, but in consideration of what is going to happen in the world unless some very vital changes are made. Any evidence that I've been successful in that is what I should like to be remembered by. (Skinner, 1990)

Skinner and Reinforcement

Throughout our analysis of Skinner's system, we will constantly encounter the term *reinforcement*, which Skinner considers a key element to explain how and why learning has occurred. Reinforcement is typically used as follows:

- A **reinforcer** is a *stimulus event* that, if it occurs in the proper temporal relation with a response, tends to maintain or increase the strength of a response, a stimulus-response connection, or a stimulus-stimulus connection (Hulse et al., 1980, p. 23). In our discussion of Skinner's work, it is important to distinguish between the basic principles of behavior and various behavior change procedures. Reinforcement is a *principle of behavior,* in that it describes a functional relationship between behavior and controlling variables. In contrast, a *behavior change procedure* is a method used to put the principle into practice. Praise, for example, is a procedure that may be a powerful reinforcer. If you praise a student's correct responses immediately and the student increases correct responses, praise can be identified as a behavior change procedure that functions as a reinforcer.

- The term *principle of reinforcement* refers to an increase in the frequency of a response when certain consequences immediately follow it. The consequence that follows behavior must be contingent upon the behavior. A contingent event that increases the frequency of behavior is referred to as a reinforcer (Kazdin, 1989, p. 105). Once you praise a student's correct response, you increase the probability that the student will exhibit the response in future, similar situations.

REINFORCER

A consequential stimulus that occurs contingent on a behavior and increases the behavior.

3 classroom application

CASE NOTES

Observation   One attempt by Mark Siegel to use a reward system with Karim Peterson to increase his work completion rate was reportedly unsuccessful.

Hypothesis   Given that external reinforcement methods have been found to be quite effective at increasing desired behaviors, (such as work completion), it seems likely that the teacher may not have identified a reinforcer (for example, free time) for Karim or the implementation of the reward system was poor—possibly too delayed or too infrequent.

Possible Action   Discuss the use of external reinforcement methods with Mark Siegel and provide a detailed implementation and evaluation plan for using reinforcement with Karim to increase his work completion rate.

- *Reinforcement* is not synonymous with *reward*. Parents may buy a child an ice cream cone as a reward for "being good"; a basketball coach may take the squad out for pizza as a reward for a "good game." These are broad statements, in which no specific behavior is identified. Psychologists, however, view reinforcement quite specifically. They believe that reinforcement becomes effective when applied to specific behaviors: A student receives a teacher's praise for the solution to a problem or the correct answer to a question.

The Skinnerian model attempts to link reinforcement to response as follows:

antecedents—response—reinforcement

The antecedents represent the range of environmental stimuli, the unknown antecedents acting on an organism at a given time. If we focus on what is observable (the response) and reinforce it, control of behavior passes to the environment (that is, teachers, parents). For example, when a teacher praises a student, an environmental change occurs in the student's behavior) and we experience change in behavior. (Note that Pavlov concentrated on conditioned *stimuli,* which is why his theory is called *Type S conditioning.* Skinner focused on *responses,* and thus his theory is called *Type R conditioning.*)

[margin handwritten note: Type S conditioning - Pavlov vs Type R conditioning - Skinner]

The Nature of Reinforcement

In his analysis, Skinner (1953) concentrated on behavior that affects the surrounding world because the consequences of that behavior feed back into the organism (the student), thus increasing the organism's tendency to reproduce that behavior under similar circumstances. Once Skinner reached that conclusion, he had at his disposal a powerful tool for analyzing behavior.

Using Reinforcement

Imagine that you are a 10-year-old with a sweet tooth. Your father has prodded you all summer to mow the lawn: "Do it today"; "Do it before I get home, or else." But your mother, with a shrewd understanding of human behavior, discovers that the local variety store carries a new brand of ice cream bars that you like—but they're expensive. She promises you a package each week after mowing the lawn. By the end of the summer you are cutting the grass on a regular basis, with no threats, coercion, or scolding.

This simple illustration contains all the elements that made fervent believers of many of Skinner's readers. It also demonstrates why Skinner was dissatisfied with the Pavlovian model as a technique for explaining our behavior. Skinner was determined that he would work only with the observable in order to build a scientific structure of learning and behavior.

In our example, no one can identify the stimulus that caused you to mow the lawn during August. The only tangibles that we have to work with are your behavior (the fact that you mowed the lawn) and the reinforcer (the ice cream). (Remember: Your father told you to do it, and you avoided the task.) Skinner began his analysis with pigeons and rats in exactly the same way, and he quickly recognized that the consequences of behavior—the reinforcers—were powerful controlling forces. Perhaps we could summarize his thinking by saying this: *Control the reinforcers, control the behavior.* (Control the ice cream, control the mowing.)

So far we have discussed **positive reinforcers,** or events that are presented after a response has been performed and that increase the behavior or activity they follow. There are also **negative reinforcers,** which are stimulus events *removed* after a response has been performed, whose removal also increases the behavior or activity they follow (Kazdin, 1989). Skinner (1953) noted that an event is a negative reinforcer only when its removal increases performance of a response. For example, if you are talking on the phone and you close the door to reduce some noise blasting from your brother's CD player, the stimulus (noise) is removed contingent upon a response (closing the door). There is an increased probability that in the future, you will perform the same behavior (closing the door) again. In Skinner's analysis (1974, p. 46), "A negative reinforcer strengthens any behavior that reduces or terminates it." Both positive and negative reinforcement functionally *increase* behavior. Negative reinforcement should not be confused with punishment, however, which decreases behavior (as we shall see later in the chapter).

Negative reinforcement operates in many situations. It is necessary for some aversive event to be present for the principle to operate. Since you want to avoid establishing aversive events in the classroom, this procedure should be used infrequently in educational programs. Nevertheless, it is important to understand the concept and its potentially strong impact on behavior.

> **POSITIVE REINFORCERS**
> *Those stimuli whose presentations increase the rates of responses.*
>
> **NEGATIVE REINFORCERS**
> *Stimuli whose withdrawal strengthens behavior.*

Types of Reinforcers

As Skinner continued to study behavior from this viewpoint, he examined reinforcers more carefully and categorized them according to their power:

1. *Primary reinforcers* are those that affect behavior without the necessity of learning: food, water, sex. In this sense, they are natural reinforcers.

2. *Secondary reinforcers* are those that acquire reinforcing power because they have been associated with primary reinforcers. For example, if one of Skinner's pigeons pecked a disk, a green light would go on, followed a second later by the arrival of a piece of corn. The green light remained on and, after repeated trials, gradually acquired reinforcing potential of its own.

3. *Generalized reinforcers,* a form of secondary reinforcers, are those that acquire reinforcing power because they have accompanied several primary reinforcers. Money belongs in this category because it leads to the possession of food, liquids, and other positive things; it then becomes a generalized reinforcer for a multitude of behaviors. Table 6.1 illustrates the various types of reinforcers.

Table 6.1   CATEGORIES OF REINFORCERS

Category	Types	Usage
Primary	1. Biological (natural) a. food, liquids, sensory pleasures	Giving candy, ice cream, soft music (used with young or exceptional students)

Secondary	1. Social
	   a. facial expression
	   b. proximity
	   c. words
	   d. privileges
		
		Frowning, smiling
		Changing seats
		Praise
		Appointment to leadership role

	2. Activity a. pleasant or "high-frequency" behavior	Playing a game following completion of class assignment

	3. Generalized
	   a. tokens
	   b. points
	   c. anything that can be used to obtain pleasure
		Allowing student who compiles 25 points to select pleasant activity, such as free reading, playing a game, building models

Schedules of Reinforcement

INTERVAL REINFORCEMENT

Scheduled reinforcement, in which the reinforcement occurs at definite established time intervals.

RATIO REINFORCEMENT

Reinforcement occurring after a certain number of responses.

INTERMITTENT REINFORCEMENT

Reinforcement in which reinforcers occasionally are implemented.

FIXED RATIO

Term describing a schedule in which reinforcement depends on a definite number of responses.

VARIABLE RATIO

Term describing a schedule in which the number of responses needed for reinforcement varies from one reinforcement to the next.

Skinner identified two kinds of intermittent reinforcement: interval and ratio reinforcement. **Interval reinforcement** is scheduled reinforcement, or that which occurs at definite established time intervals; for example, you may decide to praise a student who talks out only if that student remains quiet for five minutes. Following the praise, no additional reinforcement is given until another five minutes pass.

Ratio reinforcement is reinforcement that occurs after a certain number of responses. For example, you may insist that one of your students complete four math problems before playing a game. If the ratio is slowly altered, an amazing number of responses may result from a very low number of reinforcements. Skinner also developed variable schedules for both interval and ratio reinforcement, whereby reinforcement can appear after any time interval or number of responses (Ferster & Skinner, 1957).

The importance of reinforcement and the identification of classes of reinforcers led Skinner to consider what happens to behavior that escapes constant reinforcement for some reason. You don't reinforce your students for every desired response they exhibit. Students receive periodic grades, and workers receive weekly or monthly checks, but both students and workers continue to behave appropriately.

The answer lies in the effectiveness of **intermittent reinforcement** (that is, when only some occurrences of a response are reinforced), especially the use of schedules of reinforcement. Studies of four classes of schedules (see Table 6.2) have produced consistent findings, as follows:

1. **Fixed ratio,** where reinforcement depends on a definite number of responses. If you require students to complete thirty workbook problems before they can do something else, perhaps more exciting, you have put them on a fixed ratio schedule.

2. **Variable ratio,** where the number of responses needed for reinforcement varies from one reinforcement to the next. The number of required responses may vary, and students never know which response will be reinforced. For example, some

Table 6.2 SCHEDULES OF REINFORCEMENT

Type	Meaning	Outcome
Fixed ratio (FR)	Reinforcement depends on a definite number of responses—for example, every tenth response.	Activity slows after reinforcement and then picks up.
Variable ratio (VR)	Number of responses needed for reinforcement varies—ten responses, reinforcement; five responses, reinforcement.	Greatest activity of all schedules results.
Fixed interval (FI)	Reinforcement depends on a fixed time—for example, every thirty seconds.	Activity increases as deadline nears (for example, students must finish paper by a certain date).
Variable interval (VI)	Time between reinforcements varies.	Steady activity results.

teachers don't want to see only completed projects. They ask to see them during various stages of progress, and mark what has been done.

3. **Fixed interval,** where a response results in reinforcement after a specific length of time. The sequence is as follows: reinforcement—twenty seconds—reinforcement; reinforcement—twenty seconds—reinforcement. Note that responses made during the twenty-five-second interval are not reinforced. Teachers occasionally fall into a pattern in which they have students work independently, and then ask for responses perhaps ten or fifteen minutes into the work period. Students learn this pattern and start to work just before the teacher is due to call on them.

FIXED INTERVAL
Term describing a schedule in which a response results in reinforcement only after a definite length of time.

4. **Variable interval,** where reinforcement again depends on time and a response, but the time between reinforcements varies. Rather than waiting for a standard ten or fifteen minutes, teachers ask for responses at different times: immediately, later, and in the middle of the class.

VARIABLE INTERVAL
Term describing a schedule in which the time between reinforcements varies.

What can we conclude from Skinner's analysis of reinforcement schedules?

First, continuous reinforcement (when a response is reinforced each time it occurs) produces a high level of response only as long as reinforcement persists. The lesson for teachers is not to constantly reinforce students because they will come to expect it.

class implication

Second, intermittent reinforcement takes longer to work but is more likely to continue.

Third, ratio schedules can be used to generate a high level of responding, but fatigue may hinder student performance. Fixed ratios are common in education; we reinforce our students for papers, projects, and examinations. However, after students respond and receive reinforcement, behavior drops off sharply and learning efficiency declines (Skinner, 1953).

Fourth, interval schedules produce the most stable behavior. Skinner (1968, p. 159) summarized the meaning of these schedules for education as follows:

The student will be less dependent on immediate and consistent reinforcement if he is brought under the control of intermittent reinforcement. If the proportion of responses reinforced (on a fixed or variable ratio schedule) is steadily reduced, a stage may be reached at which behavior is maintained indefinitely by an astonishingly small number of reinforcements.

intermittent reinforcement — most useful in classroom

TIPS ON LEARNING
Using Operant Techniques in the Classroom

PRINCIPLE   Learning occurs when new academic behaviors are reinforced.

STRATEGY   Watch for opportunities to find students engaged in academic behaviors (for example, reading, attending to task). Reinforce the behavior with social attention such as praise.

STRATEGY   Find academic tasks that the students will find interesting. Make learning tasks fun by placing students in groups that involve cooperative learning opportunities. Once students engage in a task, reinforce the behaviors that involve academic attending and production.

STRATEGY   Use intermittent reinforcement to maintain performance of academic skill such as spelling. Start by reinforcing often when the student spells words correctly. Thereafter, be less frequent in reinforcement of good spelling performance.

CASE NOTES

Observations   Karim appears uncooperative in providing information on what rewards he may be willing to work for. He has not responded to typical fourth-grade rewards.

Hypothesis   Mark Siegel, while focusing on rewards, has not found functionally effective reinforcers.

Possible Action   Mark Siegel could discuss possible reinforcers with Mrs. Peterson. He could try several strategies to determine if they really function as reinforcers. Remember, rewards and reinforcement are not the same.

Skinner and Punishment

So far we have stressed the key role of reinforcement (both positive and negative) in controlling behavior: *positive reinforcers* are those stimuli whose presentation strengthens behavior, and *negative reinforcers* are those stimuli whose withdrawal strengthens behavior. But what happens when a teacher or parent withdraws a positive reinforcer (for example, says that a child cannot go to the movies) or introduces something unpleasant (for example, scolding)? Skinner believed that these two types of actions constitute **punishment.**

Kazdin (1989) defined punishment more formally as "the presentation of an aversive event or the removal of a positive event following a response that decreases the frequency of that response" (p. 144). Note that Kazdin mentioned two aspects of punishment:

1. *Something aversive (unpleasant) appears after a response.* This is called an *aversive stimulus.* For example, a parent may slap a child who yells at the parent; teachers may reprimand students who are talking in class. In each case, something unpleasant follows behavior.

2. *Something positive (pleasant) disappears after a response.* A child who kicks another youngster while playing may be sent indoors. A teenager who violates her curfew

[margin handwritten note:] Punishment as per Skinner + as per Kazdin

PUNISHMENT
Refers to the presentation of an aversive stimulus or removal of a positive stimulus contingent upon a response that decreases the probability of the response.

may lose use of the car for the next weekend. In both instances, something unpleasant follows undesirable behavior.

Categories of Punishment

In behavioral programs, *punishment* refers to the presentation or removal of some event that results in a reduction in the frequency of a behavior. There are three general categories of punishment: the presentation of aversive events, the withdrawal of positive consequences, and consequences based on activity (Kazdin, 1989).

The most commonly recognized form of punishment involves presenting something aversive following the performance or response of an individual. If the event presented reduces the frequency of the behavior, it is functionally defined as punishment. Note that certain aversive events (such as shouting) may actually increase some behavior, and therefore would be defined as reinforcers, even if the intention of the person doing the yelling is to decrease the offending behavior. Verbal statements such as reprimands commonly function as punishment, but they may lose their effectiveness if done over and over. Other aversive events, such as physical intervention (corporal punishment), have been identified as having functional punishing effects, but they should not be used except in extraordinary circumstances, and even then, their use remains quite controversial.

Withdrawal of positive consequences can also serve to reduce the frequency of some behavior and may serve as punishment. The two major forms of withdrawal of positive consequences are **time out** from reinforcement and **response cost.**

Time out from reinforcement has a long history of use in educational settings. You may have heard of or seen instances in which students were involved in "time out" or "time away" by being placed in a chair in the hall or sent to the principal's office. Many of these procedures did not qualify as punishment and may actually have led to greater misbehavior.

Time out from positive reinforcement refers to the removal of all positive reinforcers for a specified period of time. Time out is often not effective, because not all sources of reinforcement are removed. For example, a student sent to the hallway for a time-out period may actually receive considerable attention from peers who happen to be walking by. Brief time out has been found to be effective but has some disadvantages in educational settings. First, teachers and others tend to use time out as the sole method of discipline. During these periods, the child is often excluded from learning activities. There also is the danger that teachers might revert to longer and longer time-out periods with no real benefit to the student.

Response cost involves a loss of a positive reinforcer and, unlike time out, does not involve a period during which positive events are unavailable. Response cost most often involves a fine or penalty of some sort. For example, students given access to some reinforcer may have that time taken away for inappropriate behavior. Like time out, response cost should be used with positive procedures. Indeed, response cost depends on positive events being present to work effectively.

A relatively new class of punishment techniques is based on *aversiveness following some response.* For example, requiring a person to do something that involves effort or work may reduce the response and therefore serve as punishment. **Overcorrection** is a procedure that is included in this category; it involves a penalty that includes two components. First, restitution is involved, since the person corrects the effects of some negative action. For example, a student who breaks another student's pencil would be required to replace it. Second, positive practice is included; this procedure consists of repeatedly practicing an appropriate behavior. For example, the same student may be required to demonstrate the correct use of a pencil, by writing, for example. Of course, not all behaviors that a teacher is trying to reduce would be handled with both components of overcorrection.

TIME OUT

A form of punishment in which a student loses something desirable for a period of time.

RESPONSE COST

A form of punishment involving the loss of a positive reinforcer (for example, after misbehavior, a student may no longer be a classroom monitor).

OVERCORRECTION

A form of classroom management involving both restitution and positive practice.

"First, she tells us how much fun reading is. Then, she assigns me three extra chapters as punishment when I snicker."

Robert Hageman. Courtesy of Phi Delta Kappan.

How Punishment Works

Studying the psychological mechanisms underlying punishment, researchers have identified several key elements that influence its effectiveness (Kazdin, 1989):

1. *Schedule of punishment.* Generally, punishment is more effective when it is delivered every time, rather than intermittently. However, if you discontinue punishment, start-up of the response that was originally punished is greater when there had been continuous punishment than when punishment didn't occur every time. A teacher who reprimands a student for some rule infraction would be advised to use the reprimand each time the problem behavior occurs. Nevertheless, once a behavior has been suppressed, the punishment procedure should be used intermittently to keep it from reappearing.

2. *Intensity of punishment.* It was once believed that increasing the intensity of punishment increases its effectiveness. However, this is not the case. If punishment is to be considered, you should use mild forms.

3. *Source of reinforcement.* Punishment is usually enhanced when other sources of reinforcement that maintain the behavior are removed. It is important to recognize that behavior (both positive and negative) is maintained by various reinforcement contingencies. Therefore, punishment will be more effective when a certain behavior is not reinforced at the same time that punishment is involved. For example, when a teacher tries to use punishment in the classroom, it is common for a student's peers to reinforce the child's inappropriate behavior through laughing or clapping. Punishment would be expected to be less effective when peers reinforce the child.

4. *Timing of reinforcement.* Most student behavior consists of a series of actions that make up a response class, or group of behaviors. Punishment is usually more effective when it is delivered early in a sequence of behaviors that form a response group. Consider the student who throws spit wads in the classroom. The act of throwing spit wads is actually made up of a series of actions that lead to the final act of throwing. The child usually takes out a piece of paper, rolls it into a ball, puts the magic solution on the ball, and proceeds to toss it across the room. Punishment early in the sequence leading to the act of throwing will be more effective in breaking up the chain of problematic behaviors.

5. *Delay of punishment.* The longer the interval between behavior and punishment, the less effective is the punishment. The consequences of behavior, pleasant or painful, are most effective when they immediately follow that behavior. The explanation for the effectiveness (or not) of punishment lies in the interval between behavior and punishment: If it is lengthy, the unwanted behavior may be reinforced by something or someone else in the environment. By the time you get around to disciplining a student, he or she may have received the attention of peers, who may laugh or give the "thumbs up" signal or some other form of support that encourages additional misbehavior.

   Also, punishment becomes more effective (in a positive sense) if students know exactly why you're punishing them. Punishing an entire class for something a few may have done can produce only bad feelings and tension. Make sure students understand the what and why of punishment, and be consistent: If you punish something once, you must punish the behavior each time it appears, regardless of the offender. Otherwise, students are confused and continue to exhibit the behavior.

6. *Variation of punishment.* Kazdin (1989) noted that although punishment usually consists of a contingency applied after some behavior, varying the punishment that follows a behavior can actually enhance the effects of the punishment. It is possible that some type of adaptation to (getting used to) the repeated effects of the same punishment occurs (for example, always reprimanding a child will be less effective if done over and over). Kazdin, however, was careful to point out that variation does not imply combination. Combining several aversive events would be objectionable on ethical and practical grounds.

7. *Reinforcement of alternative behaviors.* Kazdin made two important points that must be considered in any use of punishment techniques. First, aversive events of relatively weak intensity (mild punishment) can effectively suppress behavior if reinforcement also is provided for an alternative positive response. Second, punishment usually trains a person in what not to do, rather than in what to do. Thus, it is important that you follow up with positive reinforcement when punishment is used, because it will increase the effectiveness of punishment as a procedure, focus your attention on teaching positive behaviors to replace the negative ones you are trying to reduce, and reduce the negative side effects of using aversive strategies.

v. important –
punishment (even weak)
w/ reinforcement for
an alternative - positive
behavior

At this point you should consider two generalizations about punishment: (1) regardless of what you may personally think of punishment as a means of controlling behavior, punishment is highly effective when properly used; (2) there is little doubt that the side effects of punishment, most of which are undesirable, accompany punishment that is routinely, even thoughtlessly, applied.

For the Classroom

B. F. Skinner was a constant and critical observer of current educational practices. Using the teaching of arithmetic as an example, Skinner noted that students must learn special verbal responses—words, figures, signs—that refer to arithmetic functioning. Consequently, teachers must help their students to bring this behavior under stimulus control.

Students must learn to count, add, subtract, multiply, and divide before they can solve problems. Teaching these procedures entails the proper use of positive reinforcement, which should be immediate and frequent (particularly in the first stages of instruction). For example, Skinner estimated that during the first four school years, teachers can arrange only a few thousand behavior-reinforcement contingencies, but that efficient mathematical behavior requires at least *twenty-five thousand contingencies* during these years (Skinner, 1968). How might positive contingencies be increased?

Skinner believed that schools should search for positive reinforcers that they now have at their disposal, such as paper, paints, puzzles, and activities that students enjoy. The next step is to make their use contingent upon desired behavior. One way of combining both of these features would be the use of *teaching machines* (today, we have computers), which divide materials to be learned into small units and reinforce successful behaviors. These devices are mechanical (which students usually like) and they provide positive reinforcement (which everybody likes). They also eliminate aversive stimuli.

behavior - reinforcement
contingencies to
reinforce learning

There are several advantages in the use of teaching machines:

- Reinforcement for the right answer is immediate; just using these machines can be reinforcing.

- Machines make possible the presentation of carefully controlled material in which one problem can depend on the answer to the preceding problem, eventually leading to the development of complex behaviors.

■ If the material lacks sufficient inherent reinforcing characteristics, other reinforcers (such as those just mentioned) can be made contingent upon completion of the program (Skinner, 1986).

Tracing the history of teaching machines, Skinner (1986) noted that teaching machines are a great asset for motivation, attention, and appreciation. Motivation is enhanced because good programs "maximize the effects of success" by having students take small steps and helping them to do so successfully (Skinner, 1986, p. 108). Attention increases because students (like all of us) attend to those things that reinforce us. Appreciation of art, music, or a discipline is enhanced by a carefully arranged series of reinforcements.

Having students proceed, successfully, at their own rate means that some students will master many fields quickly, while those who move more slowly will, nevertheless, survive as successful students. Education can become more efficient if it utilizes the existing technology of teaching machines and moves away from those ideas that have proven fruitless for the past several decades. Today's more-sophisticated teaching machines include desktop models with earphones and voice feedback, and microcomputers designed for programmed instruction. We discuss the use of technology and behavior psychology at the end of the chapter.

Finally, Skinner's work has definite implications for teachers:

■ *Reinforcement remains such a powerful tool in controlling behavior* that teachers should constantly be aware of the consequences they provide.

■ *The well-known* **Premack principle** *has valuable classroom implications.* David Premack (1965) stated that all organisms engage in some activities more than in others. After noting a student's preferred activities, you can then use these as positive reinforcers. For example, noting that several boys who avoid anything mathematical enjoy playing ball, a shrewd teacher could promise them free time to play ball after completing their math work.

■ *Aversive stimulation (punishment) may cause more problems than it solves.* Use punishment sparingly and carefully, realizing that there may be occasions when nothing else works. If you must punish, try to get the offending student to do something that you can positively reinforce—and do so as soon as possible.

■ *Teachers should be alert to the timing of reinforcements.* Though it may be impossible to reinforce all desirable behaviors, when you decide that a certain behavior is critical, reinforce it immediately. Do not let time elapse.

■ *Teachers should determine precisely what they want their students to learn,* and then arrange the material so that they make as few mistakes as possible.

A study of disruptive behavior in secondary school classes illustrates these ideas (McNamara, Evans, & Hill, 1986). The classes were in remedial math; one consisted of seventeen pupils aged 12 to 13 years; the other had fifteen pupils aged 13 to 14. Both groups were noisy and disruptive at the beginning of class; they pushed their tables together and talked loudly, making it impossible to begin the lesson.

The teacher, a 23-year-old woman, had one year of experience teaching in the school and felt she related well to the students individually but lacked group control. Several procedures were suggested to make up the intervention technique:

1. The tables were set in rows with two students at each table. (Here the teacher was attempting to structure the classroom environment to aid in her use of behavior techniques.)

PREMACK PRINCIPLE

The theory that states that access to high-frequency behaviors acts as a reinforcer for the performance of low-frequency behaviors.

2. Rules of the classroom were displayed on a large chart placed at the front of the classroom. The rules also were printed on sheets of paper and distributed to the class. The rules were these: Arrive on time, work quietly, bring necessary materials, do not shout, don't bother others. (The rules identified acceptable behavior.)

3. The teacher was asked to make evaluative statements about conduct (to tell the students how they did) at the end of the lesson. (Here assessment measures were introduced.)

4. If the evaluation was positive, the class could spend the final ten minutes of the lesson doing puzzles. (Recall the Premack principle.)

5. Self-assessment consisted of the students' checking off the rules that they had followed on the sheets that had been distributed. (Here the teacher was striving for student self-control.)

The results showed a substantial improvement in student on-task behavior and a notable increase in positive teacher behavior. (We shall return to Skinner's ideas on behavior modification in greater detail in Chapter 12.)

SOCIAL COGNITIVE LEARNING

Albert Bandura received his doctorate in 1952 from the University of Iowa, where he was influenced by the learning research tradition. Applying these principles to human behavior, Bandura initiated a sweeping program of theory and research that led to the development of social learning theory. Although some scholars now consider Bandura and those who embrace his theory to be cognitive theorists, we discuss his work in this section because it has strong behavioral foundations (Kazdin, 1994). His theory, however, does have many cognitive features. Considerable evidence exists that learning occurs through observing others, even when the observer does not reproduce the model's responses during acquisition and therefore receives no direct reinforcement (Bandura, Ross, & Ross 1963). For Bandura, **social cognitive learning** means that the information we process from observing other people, things, and events influences the way we act.

SOCIAL COGNITIVE LEARNING
According to Bandura's theory, the process whereby the information we glean from observing others influences our behavior.

Albert Bandura

Children in all cultures learn and develop by observing experienced people engaged in culturally important activities. In this way, teachers and parents help students to adapt to new situations, aid them in their problem-solving attempts, and guide them to accept responsibility for their behavior (Rogoff, 1990).

Observational learning has particular classroom relevance, because children do not do just what adults tell them to do, but rather what they see adults do. If Bandura's assumptions are correct, teachers can be a potent force in shaping the behavior of their students with the teaching behavior they demonstrate in class. The importance of models is seen in Bandura's interpretation of what happens as a result of observing others:

- The observer may acquire new responses.

- Observation of models may strengthen or weaken existing responses.

- Observation of models may cause the reappearance of responses that were apparently forgotten.

If students witness undesirable behavior that either is reinforced or goes unpunished, undesirable student behavior may result; the reverse also is true. Classroom implications are apparent: Positive, consistent teacher behavior contributes to a healthy classroom atmosphere.

In a classic study, Bandura and colleagues (1963) studied the effects of live models, filmed human aggression, and filmed cartoon aggression on preschool children's aggressive behavior. The filmed human aggression portrayed adult models displaying aggression toward an inflated doll. The filmed cartoon aggression portrayed a cartoon character displaying the same behavior as the humans. The live models displayed aggression identical to that in the films. Later, all the children exhibited significantly more aggression than youngsters in a control group. Also, filmed models were as effective as live models in transmitting aggression. Research suggests that prestigious, powerful, competent models are more readily imitated than models who lack these qualities (Bandura et al., 1963). Based on the pretense influence of modeling in the teaching process, some programs make heavy use of video

Bandura's study of imitation and children's aggressive behavior. Children reproduced the aggressive behavior of the female model they had observed on film.

modeling. For example, Webster-Stratton (1996) developed a parent training program for treatment of children with conduct problems that uses a video modeling tape series.

An Explanation of Modeling

Modeling behavior may be described as one person's observation of another's behavior and acquiring of that behavior in representational form, without simultaneously performing the responses (Bandura, 1977, 1986). Four important processes seem to be involved in observational learning:

1. *Attention.* Mere exposure to a model does not ensure acquisition of behavior. An observer must attend to (pay attention to) and recognize the distinctive features of the model's response. The modeling conditions also must incorporate the features previously mentioned, such as attractiveness of the model (for example, gender) and reinforcement of the model's behavior (for example, praise). Students who recognize these characteristics in their teachers will attend to the important features of their instructors' presentation. That our students are attracted to the compelling features of desirable models can be seen in their imitation of the clothing, hairstyles, and mannerisms of today's rock stars, athletes, and actors.

2. *Retention.* Reproduction of the desired behavior implies that a student symbolically retains the observed behavior. Bandura believes that "symbolic coding" helps to explain lengthy retention of observed behavior. For example, a student codes, classifies, and reorganizes the model's responses into personally meaningful units, thus aiding retention. What does this mean? As your students observe you, they must also form some type of image or mental schema that corresponds to what you are actually doing. (Note: They cannot form this mental picture unless they attend.) Your task is to urge them, either covertly or overtly (or both), to form this image while you are demonstrating.

3. *Motor reproduction processes.* Bandura noted that symbolic coding produces internal models of the environment that guide the observer's future behavior. The cognitive guidance of behavior is crucial for Bandura, because it explains how modeled activities are acquired without performance. But cognitive activity is not autonomous; stimulus and reinforcement control its nature and occurrence. Again, what does this mean? After observation and after urging your students to form an image of the task's solution, have them demonstrate the solution as soon

---

CASE NOTES

Observation   Karim has strong models to imitate at home but does not appear to have a person or persons at school to model.

Hypothesis   Karim would show more interest in learning and would be more likely to form a meaningful personal relationship if he had a salient model, either another student or teacher, to imitate.

Possible Action   Discuss possible peer models for Karim with Mrs. Peterson and Mark Siegel. Consider a slightly older student from another classroom in the school who would be willing to be a peer tutor or study buddy for Karim.

as possible. Can they do it? You can then reinforce correct behavior and alter any incorrect responses. Don't be satisfied with "show and tell" on your part; have them reproduce the necessary behavior so that all of learning's mechanisms are used: stimulus–cognition–response–reinforcement.

4. *Motivational processes.* Although a child acquires and retains the ability to perform modeled behavior, that behavior or task will not be performed unless conditions are favorable. For example, if reinforcement previously accompanied similar behavior, the individual tends to repeat it. But vicarious reinforcement (observing a model being reinforced) and self-reinforcement (satisfaction with one's own behavior) are also powerful human reinforcers.

Bandura introduces a subtle distinction here that helps to distinguish social learning theory from Skinner's operant conditioning. Reinforcement acts on our students' *motivation* to behave, and not on the behavior itself. In this way, Bandura notes the resulting learning is stronger and longer-lasting than that produced by reinforcing behavior alone.

Self-Efficacy

As we have seen (and we'll discuss in Chapter 7), social cognitive learning results from the interactions among behavior, environmental variables, cognitive processing, and personal factors (Schunk, 1989). These factors, especially the environment (in the form of modeling or the feedback we get from others), influence our feelings of competency on a particular task or skill. Such feelings of competency, called **self-efficacy,** develop from information conveyed by four sources (Bandura, 1981, 1986, 1997):

1. *Enactive mastery experiences.* We acquire personal and effective information from what we do; we learn from firsthand experience how successful we are in mastering our environments.

2. *Vicarious experiences.* Watching "similar others" perform, we persuade ourselves that we can probably do that action. The reverse is also true.

SELF-EFFICACY
Individuals' beliefs in their abilities to exert control over their lives; feelings of competency.

Self-efficacy develops from performance accomplishments, vicarious experience, verbal persuasion, and emotional arousal.

3. *Verbal persuasion.* Persuasion can lead our students into believing that they can overcome their difficulties and improve their performance.

4. *Physiological and affective states.* Stressful situations constitute a source of personal information. If we project an image of ourselves as inept and fearful in certain situations, then we enhance the possibility of just that behavior. But if an admired model demonstrates "coolness under fire," that behavior reduces our tendency toward debilitating emotional behavior.

Receiving data from these sources enables us to judge the extent of our self-efficacy; that is, success raises our sense of self-efficacy, whereas failure diminishes it. You can see how your feedback to your students can have a powerful effect on their feelings of competency. As a respected model, your evaluations carry significant weight. When you say, "Of course you can do it, Kelly," you are providing strong verbal persuasion. You should then follow through on this encouragement by ensuring that the student's performance accomplishment meets your (and the student's) expectations.

Your instructional techniques also are important. Research has consistently shown that when students are taught how to go about a task—that is, when they are given strategy training—their performance improves (Paris, Cross, & Lipson, 1984). This in turn influences their self-efficacy: Belief that they know what they are doing improves their control over a situation.

Using models also can be effective in improving self-efficacy. Working with elementary school children who were experiencing difficulty in mathematics, Schunk, Hanson, and Cox (1987) had the students observe videotapes of other students under a variety of learning conditions:

- Some of the students observed a teacher helping students solve problems.

- Others observed peer models who solved the problems easily and then made positive statements reflecting self-efficacy.

- Still others observed coping models in which the students had difficulty and made mistakes but also uttered coping statements ("I'll have to work hard on this"). The students were then seen to become more skillful.

Observation of the coping models seemed to produce the most beneficial results.

Thus far we have indicated that social cognitive learning offers pertinent suggestions for understanding our students' behavior, particularly by making us aware of the modeling power of our behavior and the importance of self-efficacy to our students' learning. How can we apply these principles to the classroom?

CASE NOTES

Observation   Karim's mother, Mrs. Peterson, wants Mark Siegel to take full responsibility for Karim's learning and lack of achievement.

Hypothesis   Establishing a learning program that will involve Mrs. Peterson in delivery of reinforcement at home for good learning and class behavior may be a powerful procedure for Karim.

Possible Action   Discuss a home-based reinforcement program for Karim to promote better learning and classroom behavior.

Multicultural Models

Our discussion of modeling provides an excellent opportunity to stress the benefits of presenting models from various cultures. Different cultures have different values, beliefs, and motives that appear in the behavior of members of those cultures. If teachers can introduce into their classroom outstanding representatives of a particular culture, they can then reinforce the characteristics, abilities, and behaviors that members of that culture hold in esteem.

The visit of Nelson Mandela to the United States is a good example. His trials and ultimate triumph have been a source of inspiration to black youth. Study of such an individual not only engenders pride in black students, but also reminds other students of the respect and honor that a model like Mandela commands. By inviting such outstanding figures into the classroom or initiating study projects about them, teachers also have the chance to promote intercultural understanding. Individuals who are honored by their cultures because they further interpersonal relations teach students an important lesson.

With regard to inviting models, consider these questions that can help selection:

- Do they have status? Models should possess those features that lead to status; they should be knowledgeable, educated, and admired.

- Are they competent? Probably so, or they would not have achieved status.

- Are they respected? Though we may quibble over the definition of "respect," outstanding individuals eventually must behave in a manner that elicits the respect of others.

TIPS ON LEARNING
Using Social Cognitive Theory in the Classroom

PRINCIPLE Learning occurs from observing others even when the observer doesn't practice the observed behavior.

STRATEGY Film or video while groups of your students make social studies presentations (using maps, transparencies, models, etc.). As they watch the video, let them criticize the quality of their presentations, their methods, how they gained (or did not gain) the interest of the class, and how they would improve their presentations.

STRATEGY Show a filmstrip or a video of a favorite story. Set up groups in the class to critique the filmstrip and compare it with the story. Is it true to the book? Are the characters depicted the way they imagined they would be? What did they learn from observing the way that the characters acted?

STRATEGY Discuss the subject of "heroes" with your students. Who are they? What makes them heroes? Are they all particularly courageous? Did they take risks and overcome obstacles to achieve outstanding goals? Did they contribute something of lasting value to society? Do you believe that a person has to give up his or her life to become a hero? Under what circumstances? What is the difference between an idol and a hero? Do popular culture heroes fit the criteria of a true hero? Your class may want to make a Hall of Fame and nominate their heroes for membership.

Children from different cultures, like all of us, try to make sense of their world by developing explanatory models. By reinforcing the values and attitudes that express the best in their cultures, you help to instill pride in these students and contribute to greater intercultural understanding.

For the Classroom

Bandura's ideas have particular relevance for the classroom, especially since they give us information about the characteristics of desirable models and the personal features of students, notably their self-efficacy. Certain characteristics of models seem to relate positively to observational learning: Those who have high status, competence, and power are more effective in prompting others to behave similarly than are models of lower standing (Bandura, 1977, p. 88).

The behavior of those who have achieved status and distinction undoubtedly has produced successful consequences, thus suggesting a high functional value for observers. In other words, students may want the same success as the guest in the classroom, so the students may model the behavior that has led to that success. The model's behavior, then, also furnishes information about the probable consequences of similar behavior by the observer. Thus, model characteristics attract observers not only because the models themselves have achieved status, even adulation (as in the example of rock stars), but also because their behavior has resulted in tangible rewards, such as money and power.

As for students, Bandura (1981) expressed concern about the development of self-knowledge, particularly the notion of self-efficacy, which he states "is concerned with judgments about how well one can organize and execute courses of action required to deal with prospective situations that contain many ambiguous, unpredictable, and often stressful, elements" (1981, p. 201). Schunk and Zimmerman (1997) reviewed research on the social origins of self-regulation. They noted that the effects of models on observers (for example, students in classrooms) depends on perceptions of self-efficacy. Building self-efficacy in students should be a major goal of teachers.

Estimates of self-efficacy affect choices of activities and situations: We avoid situations that we fear will exceed our abilities, but confidently perform activities that we think we can handle. Self-efficacy estimates also affect the quality of our behavior and our persistence in difficult tasks.

Schools offer an excellent opportunity for the development of self-efficacy; consequently, educational practices should reflect this reality (Bandura, 1997). That is, materials and methods should be evaluated not only for academic skills and knowledge, but also for what they can accomplish in enhancing students' perceptions of themselves and social relationships. Patrick (1997) noted that social cognitive research has identified many of the same social cognitive factors important in regulation of academic work to be important for social relationships.

Finally, to translate social learning theory into meaningful classroom practice, remember:

1. What exactly do you wish to present to students (the specific behaviors to be modeled)?

2. Is this worth their doing? (What are the kinds of reinforcements available for the correct response?)

3. How are you going to tell them, show them, and urge them to visualize the desired behaviors?

4. Does the lesson possess qualities that will improve students' self-efficacy?

BEHAVIORAL THEORIES AND TEACHING

Our objective thus far in this chapter has been to explain the theory and research that comprise behaviorism, while offering general applications. With this information as a basis, we can now turn to specific illustrations of how the theory "works" in the classroom. Our discussion will include techniques for increasing, decreasing, and maintaining behavior. Also, since the use of behavioral principles has not been without criticism, we will conclude this section by considering certain ethical issues.

Techniques to Increase Behavior

In our earlier discussion of reinforcement, we emphasized that only those events that strengthen or increase behavior can be called reinforcement. Positive reinforcement is any event following behavior that increases the future rate and probability of increasing that behavior. Negative reinforcement also involves the probability of increasing a behavior following the removal of an aversive event after the behavior is performed.

As we have seen, consequences must be contingent upon the appropriate behavior. The sequence in positive reinforcement is as follows:

1. The teacher has made it quite clear to a student that the math seatwork must be finished before the student plays with a puzzle or game.

2. The student completes an assignment.

3. The student starts to play with the game.

4. There is increased probability that this student will complete seatwork in the future.

   Figure 6.3 illustrates the process.

Effective Reinforcers

It is not always easy to identify positive reinforcers because what one student reacts to well may antagonize another. Attention is a good example. Adolescents particularly can show considerable variation in their reactions to teacher attention. For a few, it is something they wish to escape from or avoid, depending on their reinforcement history. Occasionally, when reinforcement does not seem to produce the desired result, it is not that reinforcement principles are faulty, but rather that inappropriate reinforcers have been chosen for a particular student.

FIGURE 6.3

Contingency of
Reinforcement.

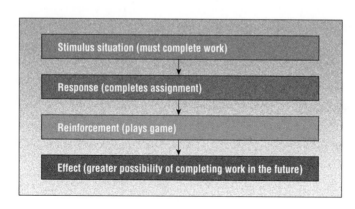

If you wish to use positive reinforcers (and we all do, deliberately or otherwise), then be aware of how you apply them. One way to select appropriate reinforcers is to consult Chapter 9, which covers the topic of motivation. You may want to use the following list as a guide in selecting reinforcers:

- Consider the ages, interests, and needs of students. Pieces of candy are not too motivating for adolescents, but they must be great for first-graders.

- Know precisely the behavior you wish to strengthen and make your reinforcer sufficiently desirable.

- List potential reinforcers that you think would be desirable. A reinforcer menu could be valuable here.

- Don't forget the demonstrated effectiveness of the Premack principle.

- Vary your reinforcers.

- Keep a record of the effectiveness of various reinforcers on individual students.

Secondary Reinforcers

Earlier in this chapter we discussed the difference between primary and secondary reinforcers. (Primary reinforcers are those that have biological importance; secondary reinforcers are those that acquire their power through association with primary and/or other secondary reinforcers.) Most teachers will use secondary reinforcers frequently. These can be grouped into three major categories (Alberto & Troutman, 1986):

1. *Social reinforcers,* which typically include attention, can be verbal or nonverbal. For example, the expression on your face can carry an unmistakable message to a student. Usually, however, social reinforcers are verbal, either accompanying some other form of reinforcement ("John, you can act as class monitor because of the way you behaved in gym") or taking the form of words of praise that signal your pleasure about a specific behavior. Social reinforcers may include expression, contact, proximity, privileges, and words.

2. *Activity reinforcers,* which we mentioned in discussion of the Premack principle, are high-frequency behaviors. As reinforcers, **activity reinforcers** are used following low-frequency behaviors. For example, the chance to work on a ship model as a class project may appeal to a student and can be used to reinforce the behavior of turning in an assignment when due. Again, however, be sure you know what individual students like.

3. *Generalized reinforcers* are those associated with a variety of other reinforcers. A smile at a student, for example, has a history of being associated with a variety of pleasant experiences. Generalized reinforcers may also be things—money or tokens—that may be exchanged for other things of value.

ACTIVITY REINFORCERS
High-frequency behaviors used to reinforce low-frequency behaviors.

Suggestions for Use

Positive reinforcement is a powerful principle and can be applied to great advantage in the classroom. All of us who teach, from the preschool to the doctoral level, use positive reinforcement. We must avoid, however, making students too dependent on the reinforcement we provide, particularly if we have initiated structured programs for students. *We want them to work for those reinforcers that are natural to them.*

Thinning is the process of reducing dependence on reinforcers like points or tokens or any other artificial reinforcers, by providing reinforcement less frequently. Greater amounts of appropriate behavior must occur before reinforcement occurs. You should realize the following benefits from thinning:

- A more constant rate of responding with appropriate behavior (students consistently follow classroom rules)

- A lessened anticipation of reinforcement (students learn not to rely on outside reinforcement)

- Shift of control to typical classroom procedures, such as occasional praise (students gradually acquire a sense of satisfaction from their own classroom successes)

- Maintenance of appropriate behavior over longer periods of time (students no longer need constant reinforcement to successfully complete a task)

Remember: The correct use of positive reinforcement demands that the teacher present the reinforcing stimulus (praise, candy, tokens, points) as soon as the appropriate behavior appears.

Techniques to Decrease Behavior

The use of positive procedures should be the teacher's goal as often as possible. Sometimes, however, when the goal is to reduce or eliminate misbehavior, teachers consider using punishment (aversive procedures). A word of warning: Don't fall into the trap of relying on punishment. It's easy; it frequently works for a short time (although not as well with secondary school students); and it gives you a feeling of having established control, which is fine unless you rely exclusively on punishment as a means of maintaining order. But punishment also can destroy your rapport with students if excessively used, it produces a ripple effect that touches all students and affects your own teaching, and it may have side effects of which you are unaware.

Where do you stand on the use of punishment as a behavior change procedure? How often do you think that punishment is used in educational settings? Also, how often is punishment in a behavioral theory context confused with the use of aversive techniques that have no functional role in behavior change?

TIPS ON MOTIVATION
Don't Rely on Punishment

PRINCIPLE   Use of punishment often results in negative interactions with students and, sometimes, undesirable side effects occur; therefore, alternatives to punishment should be sought.

STRATEGY   Reinforce positive behaviors rather than punish negative behaviors of students in the classroom.

STRATEGY   Reinforce behaviors that are incompatible with the negative behaviors that would otherwise be punished.

STRATEGY   Arrange the physical environment (for example, furniture, curriculum materials) to maximize the chances that positive behaviors will occur in student–teacher interactions.

Analyzing punishment and its alternatives, Alberto and Troutman (1986) offered a sequential hierarchy with four levels as a means of reducing inappropriate behavior. This hierarchy begins at level I with the least restrictive and least aversive methods, and gradually progresses to level IV methods that are more restrictive and aversive. The best professional practice dictates beginning with level I and moving to a higher level only when a student's behavior does not improve in a reasonable time period.

Level I Strategies

These procedures are designated as the preferred option, because in using them, teachers use positive techniques. They are based on the idea of *differential reinforcement;* that is, they rely on reinforcement to decrease or completely eliminate some behavior. Differential reinforcement of low rates of behavior is a technique designed to prevent that same behavior from becoming disruptive. For example, it would motivate students to contribute to but not dominate group discussion. In another example, you may wish to eliminate a student's talking-out behavior. Using differential reinforcement of low rates of behavior, you would select a period of time, perhaps ten minutes; when the student had remained silent, you would offer praise and time to work on a model plane. You would then gradually stretch the time period for remaining silent.

Differential reinforcement of incompatible behavior means that you reinforce some behavior that is totally incompatible with the behavior you want to eliminate. For example, you may decide to reinforce silent reading; a student cannot read silently while talking out.

Level II Strategies

The strategies of this category are intended to reduce misbehavior by *withholding reinforcement.* As Alberto and Troutman (1986) noted, teachers discontinue attention to reduce behavior that is being maintained by their attention. (Again, note the need to know what reinforces students.) Extinction is best used in conjunction with the positive reinforcement of appropriate behavior.

Don't be discouraged if the effects of extinction are not immediate, because students will be demonstrating a phenomenon called *resistance to extinction.* Teachers may even encounter an increased rate of misbehavior before the effects of extinction become noticeable. Even after the misbehavior disappears, it may occasionally surface once again, a phenomenon called *spontaneous recovery.* (Once this happens, however, ignoring behavior causes it to disappear rapidly.)

Teachers must be careful that other students don't pick up the misbehavior when they see the teacher ignoring it in one of their classmates. If teachers are successful at identifying the source of the misbehavior (perhaps peer attention), they can usually manipulate other reinforcers to bring about a combination of extinction and positive reinforcement.

Level III Strategies

Note that level III strategies involve the use of punishment techniques, ranging from less to more severe. In the first of the suggested strategies, *response cost,* the teacher attempts to reduce behavior by removal of a reinforcer (Alberto & Troutman, 1986, p. 246). Once the targeted misbehavior occurs, specific reinforcers are withdrawn.

For example, telephone companies, at different times in different localities, have addressed the problem of excessive requests for information about telephone numbers. They typically provide this service free of charge, certainly a positive reinforcer for callers. When companies begin to charge for this service, the number of requests drops dramatically. Withdrawal of reinforcement (free service) acts as punishment.

Current Issues & Perspectives

Alternatives to Punishment

In recent years, there has been considerable discussion about the use of aversive techniques (see Kazdin, 1994, and Repp & Singh, 1990, for a review of various perspectives). The use of punishment may even be associated with some myths (Donnellan & LaVigna, 1990).

ISSUE

Should we use punishment in schools?

Pro: Punishment is necessary. It is an effective behavior change technique and often results in immediate change in behavior.

Con: Positive reinforcement can be used as an alternative in almost all cases. Reinforcement is effective and more likely to lead to generalization than is punishment.

Pro: Punishment is more effective than other control techniques. There is strong evidence that as a technique it can control a large range of even severe behavior problems.

Con: The evidence for the effectiveness of punishment is not really any stronger than that for the effectiveness of reinforcement. Moreover, the side effects of punishment may be greater.

Pro: Punishment is easier to implement than are many other behavioral techniques.

Con: Some punishment techniques may be easier to implement than reinforcement. However, the ease with which punishment is applied may lead to its frequent use when other procedures are available.

In a perceptive analysis, Skinner questioned the reasons for teaching failure and settled upon the excessive reliance upon punishment; Skinner's expression for this was aversive stimuli. Although corporal punishment, legal in some states, is used infrequently today, other forms of punishment that are perhaps even more damaging psychologically, such as ridicule and sarcasm, have grown more common. With these forms of aversive control, we can force students to read books, listen to lectures, and take tests; but if these activities are disliked, they are usually accompanied by unwanted by-products. In fact, some behaviorists argue that behavior problems can be solved with nonaversive strategies under virtually all conditions (LaVigna & Donnellan, 1986).

Students are ingenious in their methods of avoiding and escaping from aversive stimuli: They come late; they become truant; they develop school phobia; they feign illness; they simply "turn off" to the teacher and anything educational. They may even become abusive and destructive, turning to vandalism.

Note: There is a difference between escape and avoidance behavior:

1. Escape behavior occurs when a response eliminates an aversive event. Keeping a student from joining classmates in a pleasant activity until a task is completed illustrates the escape technique: When the appropriate responses are made, the aversive stimulus or punishment (in this case, isolation) is removed.
2. Avoidance behavior allows a student to prevent or postpone contact with something aversive. Feigning illness in the morning to stay home so as to avoid a teacher's punishment is a good example of avoidance behavior.

Attractive settings, multisensory materials, and insultingly easy material provide few, if any, answers. Students will not learn unless positive reinforcement prevails. Students remember what happened in school and transfer that learning to new situations because of the

(continued on next page)

consequences of their behavior in the classroom. If we present material mechanically and don't offer students the opportunity to respond in order that we may reinforce those responses, school becomes difficult for students.

Teaching will become more pleasant, teachers more successful, and teacher–student relationships more positive when teachers abandon aversive techniques in favor of designing personally satisfying schedules of reinforcement for students (Skinner, 1968).

Teachers can adopt similar practices in their classroom. A technique proven to be effective combines a token reinforcement system with response cost. Students can not only earn tokens toward something desirable but also lose tokens by misbehavior. A talking-out student acquires tokens by periods of silence but also loses tokens by inappropriate talking.

Consider these suggestions for productive use of the response cost technique (Alberto & Troutman, 1986):

- Be sure that you actually withdraw the reinforcers when needed. It is probably best to avoid using physical action. If you move to take away candy with younger students, they may put as much as possible in their mouths and eat it. Taking tokens away from a six-foot-four football player would be considerably more difficult. Try positive reinforcement initially.

- Know what reinforces individual students.

- Be sure that students understand clearly what constitutes misbehavior and its cost.

- Don't trap yourself; be certain that you can indeed withdraw a reinforcer.

- Combine response cost with positive reinforcement for behavior.

The second of the level III strategies entails the use of *time-out procedures,* in which students are denied reinforcement for a specific period. Again, teachers must be sure that they know exactly what reinforces their individual students.

There are two basic time-out procedures:

1. *Nonseclusionary time out:* The student remains in the classroom but is barred from normal reinforcement. Use of the directive "Put your head on your desk for the next five minutes" prevents the student from receiving reinforcement from either the teacher or classmates. Any type of procedure that prevents reinforcement while keeping the student in the classroom belongs in this category.

2. *Seclusionary time out:* The student is removed from an activity or from the classroom itself. You may resort to this technique by seating a student alone in a remote corner of the room for some specified period. Putting a student in a separate room is a technique usually reserved for special situations and must be used with sensitivity and caution.

Level IV Strategies

This level involves the use of aversive stimuli and is what is most frequently regarded as punishment. For example, an individual might present aversive stimuli (for example, loud noise) following a response. If the noise reduces the frequency of behavior, it serves as punishment. These procedures should seldom, if ever, be used in schools. Since we have discussed the pros and cons of punishment in considerable detail earlier in this chapter, we can conclude by stressing that regardless of the procedure used to reduce or eliminate behavior, you should remember to combine these techniques with positive reinforcement.

Techniques to Maintain Behavior

Once a student's behavior has changed, you want that student to maintain the desirable behavior over time and without programmed reinforcement. You also want students to demonstrate appropriate behavior in other classes. For example, after you have successfully reduced talking-out behavior in your history class, you also want students to talk out less in English class. In other words, teachers strive for generalization.

Strategies for Facilitating Generalization

Teachers hope that what they teach students in the classroom will transfer to other settings and be remembered over time. Behavioral researchers have developed a technology that teachers can use in classrooms to help students generalize their knowledge and behavior. Building on some of the classic work of Stokes and Baer (1977), White and his associates (1988) presented a review of the strategies for facilitating generalization that is of special value to teachers. They described the following twelve strategies:

1. *Teach and hope.* In this traditional strategy, the teacher provides regular instruction and hopes that the child's behavior will generalize. For example, the teacher introduces some new vocabulary words in class, emphasizing their meaning. Some children may remember, but most likely some will not. You hope that most will remember. "Teach and hope" is actually the absence of any special techniques to facilitate generalization and is common in many classrooms.

2. *Teach in the natural setting.* Teaching is conducted directly in at least one setting in which the skill or knowledge will actually be used. Generalization is then assessed in other, nonteaching settings. For example, the teacher might ask parents to teach new vocabulary words at home after they are taught in the classroom. Effective teachers use this tactic quite often.

3. *Teach sequentially.* This strategy is an extension of strategy 2, in which teaching is conducted in one setting and generalization is assessed in other settings. If necessary, teaching is conducted sequentially in more and more settings, until generalization to all the desired settings is observed. For example, a teacher interested in teaching social skills might schedule the teaching of the skill in school, at home, and on the playground.

4. *Introduce students to natural maintaining contingencies.* In this strategy, the teacher ensures that the student experiences the natural consequences of a new skill, by (a) teaching a functional skill that is likely to be reinforced outside of the instructional setting; (b) teaching to a level of proficiency that makes the skill truly useful; (c) making sure that the learner actually experiences the natural consequences; and (d) teaching the learner to seek reinforcement outside of the instruction. You may consider using academic content that will be useful to students outside the classroom, such as teaching words that they will likely use when interacting with peers and adults.

5. *Use indiscriminable contingencies.* Sometimes natural consequences cannot be expected to facilitate and maintain generalization. In such cases it may be necessary to use artificial consequences. It is best that the learner cannot

determine precisely when those consequences will be available. Teaching social skills to preschoolers, a teacher might praise the children after progressively greater delays rather than after each skill is demonstrated, as would be the strategy during initial teaching.

6. *Train students to generalize.* With this strategy, the student is reinforced only for performing some generalized instance of a new skill. Performance of a previously reinforced version of the skill is no longer reinforced. For example, students could be taught the names of various shapes. Reinforcement then would be provided when students named shapes that had not been taught previously in the classroom.

7. *Program common stimuli.* The teacher can select a salient, but not necessarily task-related, stimulus from the situation to which generalization is desired and include that stimulus in the teaching program. For example, students might be taught skills in the presence of their peers. These skills would then be expected to be available in other settings when the peers were present (that is, when the stimuli were present).

8. *Use sufficient exemplars.* This strategy entails the sequential addition of stimuli to the teaching program until generalization to all related stimuli occurs. Different skills may require a different number of examples to ensure generalization, and you should make this determination based on a student's performance. For example, when teaching, the spelling rule "*i* before *e* except after *c*" should provide many illustrations across spelling challenges.

9. *Use multiple exemplars.* Using this technique means that you will teach, at the same time, several examples of the stimulus class to which generalization is desired. The teacher who uses multiple examples of a concept or skill will increase the chances that a student will use the skill in a nonteaching setting.

10. *Conduct general case programming.* To use this strategy, the teacher must conduct a careful analysis of both the skill and the environment to which generalization is desired. Thereafter, the teacher selects and teaches stimuli in the presence of which the skill should be used, stimuli in the presence of which the skill should not be used, and stimuli that should not affect skill use but could inappropriately do so. For example, in teaching high school students to use a stick shift in a driver education class, it would be useful to analyze the range of stick shift options found in most cars and trucks and teach this universe of options. One could then anticipate that good generalization to most cars in the community would occur.

11. *Teach loosely.* By "teaching loosely," we do not mean that you should become an incompetent teacher. What we mean is that you should teach in a variety of ways, so as to avoid a ritualized, highly structured, invariate program that inhibits generalization. Teaching that involves a variety of settings, materials, and reinforcers will help facilitate generalization.

12. *Mediate generalization.* This tactic involves teaching a strategy or other procedure to help the student remember when to generalize, or at least reduce the differences between the teaching and generalization settings. Students can be taught to monitor their own behavior across settings.

Each of the twelve strategies to facilitate generalization will be helpful to teachers. It is important to remember that the strategies can be used in combination to increase the chances that students will transfer their knowledge and skills. Remember that according to behavioral educators, teaching is not enough. You must do more than teach and hope: Use those strategies that facilitate generalization. Research has also indicated that reward

TIPS ON COMMUNICATION
Communicate to Help Generalize Behavior

PRINCIPLE   Generalization can be facilitated through helping students to remember when to generalize.

STRATEGY   To generalize learning, communicate to the student a strategy or procedure to help him/her remember to use a behavior in a new setting.

STRATEGY   Reduce the differences between the teaching situation and the setting where you want to generalize the behavior.

STRATEGY   Teach students to monitor their own behavior across settings (see TIPS on Time, page 235).

for creative performance can be used to generalize creativity (Eisenberger & Cameron, 1996). That is, if teachers reward students for high creativity on one task, they are likely to be creative on a new task.

Techniques of Self-Control

Since you cannot monitor a student constantly, a major objective in working with students is to have them accept responsibility for their own behavior, that is, exercise self-control. Kazdin (1994, p. 269) offered a good definition: "Self-control usually refers to those behaviors that a person deliberately undertakes to achieve self-selected outcomes."

In aiding students to acquire this ability, be sure that they know precisely what behavior produced reinforcement in a given instance. Encourage them to talk about why they were or were not reinforced, thus helping them to understand their behavior. Remember: It is the students' self-control; therefore, they must be active in the process.

Once you have made them aware of the inappropriateness of some behavior and they are willing to cooperate, have them note, with your help at first, the frequency of their positive behaviors—a kind of self-recording device. For example, have them record the number of times that they were helpful to one of their fellow students.

Next, involve them in the management of reinforcement: let them help decide what reinforcers should be used, when they should be given, what constitutes misbehavior, and how much each instance of misbehavior should cost them. In this way, responsibility slowly shifts from you to the student. For example, ask them to select some social activity that they would like to participate in and the criteria for the reinforcement.

Teaching Students Self-Control

Some children learn to regulate their own behavior during their early years within the family. Many children, however, can benefit from learning some strategies to help them control their own behavior in social and learning settings. In recent years, psychologists have developed programs that teachers and other professionals can use to help children in their psychosocial development (Esveldt-Dawson & Kazdin, 1982; Workman, 1982). There are three components of self-control that can be used to teach students self-control: (1) self-assessment, or self-analysis; (2) self-monitoring; and (3) self-reinforcement.

TIPS ON TIME
Student-Managed Learning

PRINCIPLE   Students who learn self-control techniques can take responsibility for their own learning.

STRATEGY   Inform students what behaviors they should take responsibility for in learning.

STRATEGY   Teach students to self-assess or self-monitor their own behavior. This tactic helps students to understand their behavior in relation to the instructional environment (see TIPS on Assessment, page 237).

STRATEGY   Shift reinforcement from you to student self-reinforcement strategies. Tell the student to select reinforcers and self-administer reinforcement for the target behavior (for example, work completion, good behavior).

Self-assessment requires that students examine their own behavior or thinking and determine whether they have performed some behavior or thought process. To foster this assessment, a teacher might ask one of her students if the child has been completing math assignments, for example. It is important that children have some idea or standard that they can use in self-assessment, a standard that often comes from the performance of significant adults and peers. Remember that all students do not routinely set self-standards, and that it is therefore helpful to teach these skills.

Self-monitoring is a procedure in which students record their performance or keep a record of what they are doing. Interestingly, the very act of recording some action has been shown to change performance. For example, if you encourage kind or positive statements from students when they interact with peers, self-monitoring of this social interaction is likely to increase. Researchers have shown that self-monitoring can increase academic performance, but may not be sufficient in itself to sustain any improvement (for example, Piersel & Kratochwill, 1979).

Self-reinforcement refers to students' giving themselves a reward following successful completion of the activity being monitored. Self-reinforcement can be a very potent strategy for increasing the occurrence of a student's performance. Students can be taught to praise themselves or arrange some pleasant activity as a self-reward, which then acts to sustain performance.

Workman (1982) identified several advantages of using self-control strategies:

- Self-control strategies allow students to manage their own behavior in the absence of the teacher or other adults.

- Self-control strategies can help students develop responsibility for their own behavior.

- Self-control can help improve the chances that a student's behavior will transfer to other settings with other individuals.

Although some students appear to regulate their behavior quite well without formal attempts to teach this skill, others may need additional assistance to regulate their behavior. Teaching self-control strategies to these students can increase both their sense of self-efficacy and their sense of responsibility.

CASE NOTES

Observation   Karim does not appear to want to help himself or to take responsibility for his own learning.

Hypothesis   Mark Siegel has relied almost exclusively on external management of Karim's learning behaviors in the classroom.

Possible Action   Mark Siegel could develop a self-control plan to help Karim take responsibility for his own behavior and learning.

BEHAVIORISM AND THE FUTURE

Behaviorism, which has remained remarkably stable in its basic orientation, has recently shown signs of change. Faced with the challenge of a renewed, dynamic cognitive psychology, behaviorists have reacted by adopting several strategies. They have attempted to do the following:

- Strengthen and refine their methodology

- Incorporate, on behavioral terms, cognitive concepts within their frameworks

Behaviorists have made significant contributions to education. For example, behavioral studies have demonstrated that almost all students, regardless of preparedness, disabilities, or deprivation, can learn. Behaviorism also has helped to remove blocks to student learning (Sulzer-Azaroff & Mayer, 1991).

Applying Behavior Analysis to Schooling

In this chapter, we have noted that many of the behavioral procedures urged by Skinner have been successfully applied to educational problems. As Skinner stated (1984), the survival of humankind depends on how well we educate. Education, however, has not widely adopted many of his suggestions. Critics of behavioral techniques (such as Brophy, 1983) have noted that behavioral procedures are often ignored because they apply to circumscribed or isolated problems in the schools.

To increase the use of behavioral procedures in the schools, Greer and his associates at Columbia University Teachers College have developed a model called the Comprehensive Application of Behavior Analysis to Schooling (CABAS) (Greer, 1996; Selinske, Greer, & Lodhi, 1991). The model is designed to apply behavior analysis to the school roles of students, teachers, and supervisors. It also includes such behavioral components as direct instruction, a personalized system of instruction, programmed instruction, and an organizational behavior management component for supervision and administration. Following is a description of each of the components:

- *Application to students.* This section consists of collecting data for all teaching. Scripted curricula specifying the antecedent stimuli, responses, and consequences for all teaching are used. The following is an example of a one-trial teaching sequence for handicapped children:

   The student was presented with a three-dimensional object (for example, a cube); the student felt the object and the teacher asked, "What shape?" The student had a 5-second period (for example) to

---

TIPS ON ASSESSMENT
Recording Student Behavior

PRINCIPLE   Recording student target behaviors is an essential feature of understanding the relationship between student behavior and the environment.

STRATEGY   Try to use permanent product recording because it is typically part of the teacher's regular classroom information base (for example, worksheets completed, spelling words correct).

STRATEGY   Ask the student to self-record or self-monitor his/her own behavior. This strategy might even result in student improvement if conducted on positive behaviors.

STRATEGY   Ask a friend or other staff member to help assess student behavior. You can always return the favor.

---

produce the correct signed or vocal response. An incorrect response resulted in a correction procedure (that is, "This is a cube"). A correct response resulted in praise and the presentation of an edible reinforcer, a token, or a brief activity period with a toy. The teacher recorded a minus for the lack of a response or an incorrect response or a plus for a correct response, and then proceeded to the next trial. (Greer, 1996, pp. 109–110)

- *Application to teachers.* This section involved instructing the teachers to use the skills and terminology of behavior analysis with on-the-job training and out-of-class instruction through a personalized system of instruction. The teachers then applied the behavioral principles to their work with the students.

- *Application to supervisors.* Supervisors were involved in the training of the teachers. Specifically, they designed the teacher modules and tutored the teachers to the point of mastery. The supervisors also maintained logs of their own activities, and they themselves had to meet criteria for job performance.

The CABAS has been subjected to some program evaluation. For example, Greer and his associates (Selinske et al., 1991) evaluated the CABAS program in a school that served blind and multiple handicapped students. The program produced educationally significant increases in trials taught and correct trials; also, it identified student objectives. Teachers also evaluated the program positively. Support for the program has been modest, however, because of its limited application in a small school that serves handicapped students. Though a better test would be set in a regular public school, the program does indicate that a combination of behavioral principles has merit in teaching academic skills.

Skinner's Suggestions

As you might expect, Skinner (1984) pronounced on the state of American education and found it wanting, mainly because it neglects many behavioral principles. Skinner believed that the resurgence of humanistic and cognitive psychology has proven a major obstacle to any progress in our schools (progress, by the way, that he believes began with his work on programmed instruction).

To solve our educational dilemma, Skinner (1984) recommended a return to the principles and objectives of behaviorism:

1. *Be clear about what is to be taught.* This implies that teachers should concentrate on what is to be learned. For example, we don't teach "spelling"; we teach students how to spell words.

2. *Teach first things first.* Teachers should avoid any attempt to reach the final product too quickly, since any subject and its subdivisions contain a series of steps that students must master before reaching the final stage.

3. *Teach to individual differences.* Here is one of Skinner's favorite themes: Students can progress only at their own rates. To respond to this truism, Skinner long ago advocated teaching machines, programmed instruction, and computers.

4. *Program subject matter.* Unlike typical texts, individual programs induce students to do or say the things that they are supposed to do or say. Skinner called this "priming" the behavior and stipulated that the prompts that are built into the program must be gradually eliminated until the behavior appears without help. At that point, the reinforcing consequences of *being right* become highly effective in sustaining behavior. Referring to concerns about education, Skinner stated:

> *There is a better way: give students and teachers better reasons for learning and teaching. That is where the behavioral sciences can make a contribution. They can develop instructional practices so effective and so attractive in other ways that no one–student, teacher, and administrator–will need to be coerced into using them. (Skinner, 1984, p. 952)*

Among the accomplishments behaviorists claim are the following:

1. Although behaviorism has proven its worth in the successful education of disabled youngsters, its range of achievements also incorporates the other end of the spectrum; its carefully controlled techniques likewise have been shown to help students to learn at *advanced levels.*

2. Though behaviorism is usually thought to be effective in teaching simple topics, evidence exists that *complex behaviors* are equally as teachable. Complex procedures such as shaping, differential reinforcement, and fading have all become tools of educators.

3. Behaviorism has made clear that the key to teaching complex skills is to distinguish, clearly and precisely, the *critical features* of the task—exactly what behavior is to change under what conditions. Closely allied to the careful identification of objectives is the use of effective and natural reinforcers.

4. Behaviorism has attacked the problem of individual differences in the classroom in a unique manner. If any of your students fail to achieve objectives, it may well be that *they lack the basic prerequisite skills.* Your task, then, is to divide the learning task into its component parts, including those subskills that lead to complexity. For example, you cannot expect students to solve division problems until they can add, subtract, and multiply.

If behaviorism is to continue to progress, certain barriers must be overcome:

- Many educators simply lack information about the value of behavioral strategies.

- Even those who appreciate the benefits of behavioral techniques may lack the skills to implement them.

- Current societal contingencies (for example, the reward system or lack there of in education) impede the implementation of behavioral techniques.

By working to overcome these challenges, most behaviorists feel confident about the future of their theory, both its viability and its application.

Technology and Behaviorism

Many educators took up Skinner's call to program instruction. Though Skinner was not referring to computerized programming of instruction, the advent of the microcomputer has led many educators to do just that. Computer-assisted instruction (CAI) uses the computer to present material to students and then assist them in mastering it. Earlier versions of CAI were based in behaviorist theory. They emphasized progressive shaping of behavior toward a final goal via small steps and frequent use of positive reinforcement. (More recent programs are based in cognitive theory and will be discussed in Chapter 13.)

Programmed Instruction

In general, programmed instruction consists of a set of instructional materials that students can use to teach themselves about a particular topic, skill, or content area. As you read earlier in this chapter, Skinner was one of the earliest proponents of this approach (Skinner, 1968). He argued that teachers depend too heavily on punishment while neglecting their use of positive reinforcement. Instruction should be designed to progress in small steps toward a well-defined final goal and sequenced so that students can give correct responses the majority of the time. This tactic would allow teachers to use positive reinforcement more frequently. Earlier versions of programmed instruction were often either not computerized or were presented on "teaching machines." Programmed instruction has evolved into a variety of types of computer-assisted instruction, all of which are computer-based, but which incorporate the underlying principles Skinner developed.

Many children develop a sense of self-efficacy when participating in self-instructional programs on the computer.

Skinner argued that programming instruction would result in students learning "twice as much in half the time" (Skinner, 1984, p. 948). He cited a study in which eighth-grade students were taught algebra via instruction programmed on "crude teaching machines"—machines nowhere near the power of those available today. The students went through the entire eighth- and ninth-grade curricula in one semester. Tests of comprehension and use of the information indicated that these students not only remembered the information up to one year later, their performance on problem-solving tests at the end of the one-semester program was on a par with students finishing ninth grade. Many critical details are left out of Skinner's account of the algebra study (for example, Was this a typical, run-of-the-mill class of students, or were they specially selected for their interest, aptitude, or motivation in some way? What was the teacher like? What was the comparison group like?), but Skinner's description does point out that programmed instruction can be very effective even when implemented on quite simple machines.

Skinner outlined several principles that are important to consider in programmed instruction, whether it is computerized or not. These should look very familiar to you after having read the earlier part of this chapter:

- Clearly define the final goal, or terminal behavior, stating it in objective and concrete terms.

- Solve the problem of the first instance, that is, get the student to show some part or form of the desired behavior so that positive reinforcement can be provided. Initial responses must be ones that the student is capable of making.

- Instruction must be carefully and thoughtfully sequenced, with careful definition of the subgoals that the student should progress through on the way to achieving the final desired behavior. This sequence is critically important for complex behaviors, like those in most school subjects. In essence, the program will be reinforcing progress toward the final goal, or shaping the student's behavior.

- As much as possible, prevent incorrect responses so that punishment can be avoided and positive reinforcement used.

- Provide immediate, nonthreatening, but clear feedback in responding to correct and incorrect answers.

There are several types of programmed instruction. As noted earlier, a more traditional type is called linear programmed instruction. Students are presented with an exercise or problem and required to respond. If the response is correct, the student is told so and the next problem in the sequence is presented. If the answer is wrong, the student is simply told that the answer was not correct and is given the correct answer; then the next problem in the sequence is presented. The sequence of problems is the same regardless of whether the answers are correct, and no instruction is given to explain why the answer the student provided was wrong. It may seem odd that incorrect responses are not explored, but the reasoning behind this type of programming is that time spent exploring or explaining incorrect responses in essence reinforces those incorrect responses. Students need to be corrected and told the right answer, but no more time and attention than necessary should be paid to wrong answers to avoid reinforcing mistakes.

A second, more recent type of programmed instruction is a branching program. In this type, the student receives an example or problem and a response is required. If the answer is correct, the student is positively reinforced and the next problem in the sequence is presented. If the answer is incorrect, however, the student is "branched," or sent, to a different part of the program to receive instruction as to why the response was incorrect, additional instruction in the correct answer, and/or additional problems or examples dealing with the same concept. This type of programmed instruction incorporates aspects of a cognitive approach to instruction in that it involves helping the student explore their current understanding of the concept, though it retains many aspects of behaviorism in its emphasis on sequencing for correct answers and positive reinforcement. We'll consider cognitive approaches in detail in Chapter 7.

Drill and Practice

Another kind of CAI is the drill and practice program. As the name implies, the goal of these programs is to help students master the basic elements in mathematics, reading, spelling, and any other subject in which they must acquire fundamental facts. The computer presents a stimulus, elicits a response, and provides reinforcement. Whereas programmed instruction is intended to provide the initial introduction to and instruction in skills and knowledge, drill and practice programs are intended to help students practice and master the skills after they have already received initial instruction in them. For example, many drill and practice programs are available to help master and automatize (that is, be able to quickly recall) basic math facts, or to help students master spelling of vocabulary words.

Among teachers who use computers, particularly in elementary schools, drill and practice programs are quite common. There are many drill and practice programs readily available, and they can easily be incorporated into many teachers' existing styles of teaching. Students can be initially introduced to the material in whatever way the teacher is used to, then do short amounts of individual practice (for example, fifteen to twenty minutes) with the program during spare moments. These programs can certainly be used in cooperative groups as well, however. Surprisingly, in a study of 200 primary schools involving more than 600 teachers in which computers were used for drill and practice, the students (5 to 11 years) showed an increase in cooperative behavior when they worked in small groups (Jackson, Fletcher, & Messer, 1988).

Lockard, Abrams, and Many (1994) describe several levels of drill and practice programs. At the basic level, a program may offer students a fixed number of problems to solve. All students face the same tasks, and only after successful completion can they move on to a higher level. They spend as much time as needed to work to mastery. Next is the program that has an arbitrary mastery criterion—six successive successful completions may be required. Note that some students may well meet this criterion on their initial effort, while others might need several attempts. A more adaptive program could require students to reach mastery after relatively few responses, or increase the difficulty of the materials, or even force students to switch the operations needed—for example, from multiplication to division. For a student experiencing difficulty, the program would then branch to a less difficult context or return the user to a lower level. As Lockard et al. (1994) note, such constant adjustments are intended to develop mastery without causing either boredom or frustration.

Opponents of using computers for drill present the following arguments:

- Programs are boring.

- All students receive the same content, regardless of ability.

- Programs may provide undesirable feedback.

- Some teachers use computers for primary instruction, rather than as a tool to practice and automatize material to which students have already been introduced. Although using the computer for primary instruction is generally viewed by experts in the field as a good use of technology, these particular types of programs are not designed for this task. There are other programs that do a much better job of instruction.

- Using computers for drill is an expensive waste of money.

- Drill and practice results in memorized knowledge but does nothing to help students understand the meaning behind the knowledge or how and why it is important to learn.

One the other hand, supporters argue the following:

- Extra practice is provided where it is needed most.

- Attention can be maintained during practice sessions.

- Where problems exist, they are usually the result of poorly designed programs.

- Unexpected bonuses, such as a student's fascination with the computer itself or interest in programming, can often result.

The effectiveness of CAI in general has been examined in many studies. Two summaries of this work examined almost 300 studies and included students ranging from kindergarten age to adults (Kulik & Kulik, 1991; Ryan, 1991). Compared with students who did not use CAI, students using CAI showed achievement gains equivalent to about three months in a school year (Ryan, 1991) or increasing from the fiftieth to the sixty-second percentile (Kulik & Kulik, 1991). Interestingly, the CAI in the Kulik and Kulik analysis was very effective when used for four weeks or less. When continued for several months or longer, the effects were less robust, raising the possibility of a novelty effect (that is, the effect was because the CAI was new to the students, and not because it was a better teaching method).

Ryan's (1991) analysis also pointed to an important factor in achievement gains from using CAI: teacher training. The amount of training provided to teachers was significantly related to academic achievement of students in the CAI groups. Short-term training (less than ten hours) was actually counterproductive, with students whose teachers had one to ten hours training showing smaller effect sizes than students whose teachers had no training. This is a critical point for successful use of CAI in classrooms, and it underscores the need for strong and continuing administrative support.

So what can we conclude about using CAI in the classroom? First, be aware that the results will only be as good as the quality of the program used. CAI programs are readily available, but their quality varies tremendously. Teachers must carefully examine any software to make sure it is well programmed and will meet students' needs. Second, it appears that using CAI can help students master basic skills, particularly automatic recall of basic facts (for example, arithmetic facts, spelling vocabulary). Third, keep in mind the possible novelty effect. It may be that students are simply enamored with this new activity. Of course, you can take advantage of the novelty—after all, if students are increasing their attention and learning then that's the ultimate objective—but you may see decreases in all these outcomes after students get used to the programs. Finally, teachers and administrators alike must keep in mind the need for continuing support and training for teachers using CAI in their classrooms. Too little training not only appears to not help, but may actually be harmful.

Case Reflections

Our chapter on behavioral psychology provided a number of new knowledge areas for consideration in the case of Mark Siegel. Remember that Mark was a fourth-grade teacher who was challenged by a mother who visited him on a regular basis and demanded more effective teaching for her son, Karim. Although Karim appeared uninterested in learning and had some social interaction problems with youngsters in his classroom, the teacher was interested in trying a variety of techniques to help the child. Behavioral psychology provides a number of potential strategies and tactics that teachers might use in dealing with challenging cases like those that Mark Siegel experienced.

We found that Karim's classmates had been excluding him from various activities and hypothesized that his classmates may have been conditioned to respond to Karim with avoidance and isolation. We also observed that Karim was uncooperative in providing information on rewards that he would be willing to work for in the classroom. Our hypothesis was that Mark Siegel had not found any functional reinforcers to be effective with Karim. In addition, we observed that Karim did not have any strong models in the school site and that given the development of a salient model (for example, a student or teacher), he would be able to imitate their learning activities. It was also important to note that Karim's mother, Mrs. Peterson, felt that Mark Siegel was responsible for solving Karim's learning difficulties. Efforts to involve Mrs. Peterson in a home-based reinforcement program could be considered in this regard. Finally, we also observed that Karim does not appear to take responsibility for his learning activities in the classroom and that Mark has relied very heavily on external management for Karim's learning and behavior.

To deal with these issues we proposed a number of possible actions that could be used by Mark Siegel to help Karim to deal with his situation. We proposed, for example, that establishing new and positive social interactions could create positive feelings among his peer group. Such a strategy would also likely facilitate the development of positive social models. Mark Siegel could discuss possible reinforcers that Mrs. Peterson could use in a recommended home program as well as generate ideas to facilitate more effective functional reinforcers within the classroom setting. Such a strategy would help facilitate both home-based and classroom-based positive academic and social responses. Finally, we thought that to shift the burden of responsibility, Mark Siegel could investigate the possibility of setting up a self-control program for Karim. This last option may also circumvent some of the need for external management strategies that could be helpful but might take considerable time and effort to implement by Mrs. Peterson and, in the classroom, by Mark Siegel.

Key Terms

Activity reinforcers 227

Classical conditioning 203

Conditioned reflex 203

Conditioned stimulus 203

Connectionism 206

Discrimination 205

Extinction 206

Fixed interval 213

Fixed ratio 212

Intermittent
   reinforcement 212

Interval
   reinforcement 212

Negative reinforcers 211

Operant conditioning 208

Overcorrection 215

Positive reinforcers 211

Premack principle 218

Punishment 214

Ratio reinforcement 212

Reinforcer 209

Response cost 215

Self-efficacy 222

Social cognitive
   learning 219

Stimulus
   generalization 205

Time out 215

Variable interval 213

Variable ratio 212

CHAPTER HIGHLIGHTS

Classical Conditioning

- Ivan Pavlov's work has educational implications, especially with regard to generalization, discrimination, and extinction of behavior.
- Conditioning principles should make teachers aware of a need to use classroom stimuli sensitively.

Thorndike's Connectionism

- Edward Lee Thorndike was a powerful force in American psychology, and his ideas remain influential today, especially the law of effect.

- The law of effect influenced Skinner, and Thorndike's views of exercise and transfer are still applicable.

Operant Conditioning

- B. F. Skinner's interpretation of conditioning has become the most accepted and widely used form of behaviorism today. Its impact is felt in education, psychology, and business.
- Skinner's ideas on reinforcement have led to broad acceptance of programmed instruction and computers as effective teaching tools.
- His views of punishment have clarified its meaning and use.

Social Cognitive Learning

- Albert Bandura's stress on the impact of modeling has shown the potency and far-reaching effects of this type of learning.
- Observational learning attempts to include the influence of cognitive processes within a behavioral framework.
- The principles of observational learning emphasize the need for multicultural models that meet the needs of a variety of students.

Behavioral Theories and Teaching

- The principles of behaviorism are widely used in today's classrooms.
- Techniques for shaping behavior can be effectively used in the classroom, if thoroughly understood and carefully applied.

Behaviorism and the Future

- The future success of behaviorism demands clear adherence to its basic principles, while introducing compatible changes from related disciplines.
- Programmed instruction consists of a set of instructional materials that students can use to teach themselves about a particular topic, skills, or content area.

W H A T   D O   Y O U   T H I N K ?

1. Develop an example of classical conditioning in the classroom. Identify the sequence in classical conditioning, including naming the US, UR, CS, and CR.

2. Provide an example of a primary, a secondary, and a generalized reinforcer. Apply use of the three types of reinforcers to a student who is learning math.

3. Describe how schedules of reinforcement affect the rate and strength of responses for a child who is disruptive in your classroom.

4. How could the Premack principle be implemented with a child who is not paying attention in your class?

5. What processes are involved in observational learning? Develop a teaching strategy that uses these programs.

Cognitive Psychology and the Construction of Knowledge

This chapter has many ideas to offer

Mark Siegel in his quest to understand

Karim Peterson as a learner. As you

recall, Karim was experiencing some

difficulties with reading

comprehension and had difficulties

with attending to school work. As you

read through this chapter, think about

ways of applying some of the theories

and findings from cognitive

psychology research to the education

of Karim.

Objectives

When you finish reading this chapter, you should be able to

- define cognitive psychology and identify typical topics researched by cognitive psychologists

- understand the key role that representation plays in learning

- help students construct meaning from classroom material

- put forth a model of information processing

- recognize elements of instruction that affect student memory

- understand that how material is framed or structured will influence students' thinking and decision making

- identify activities and teaching methods that can facilitate students' construction of knowledge.

Teachers must be knowledgeable about students' cognitive competence, their capacity to engage in abstract thought, and their mnemonic strategies. In this chapter, we introduce you to cognitive psychology and explore the relationship between cognitive psychology and the construction of knowledge (learning). If you have read our earlier chapters on cognitive and language development, you have already met two theorists, Jean Piaget and Lev Vygotsky, who have stimulated much of the work in modern cognitive psychology. So this chapter is a continuation of these theorists' work with emphasis on the application of cognitive psychology in the classroom.

The field of cognitive psychology has experienced rapid change during the past two decades and as the field has sharpened its focus on information processing, its contribution to teaching and learning has grown noticeably. In this chapter, we examine major themes within modern cognitive psychology and indicate pertinent classroom applications of these topics. Also, we examine the significance of mental representations and the human brain in cognitive studies. Current interpretations of perception, recent studies, and speculation concerning classification, how the human memory might work, and the influence of culture on cognitions will also be presented. Because so much work in psychology concerns how we learn, Chapter 8 continues this examination of the applications of cognitive theory to learning by discussing mnemonics, problem-solving strategies, and other related topics.

THE MEANING OF COGNITIVE PSYCHOLOGY

What is cognitive psychology? Cognitive scientists are in general agreement that their work encompasses the study of memory, attention, perception, language, reasoning, problem solving, and creativity. That is, cognitive psychology is the study of the structures and components for processing information (Phye & Andre, 1986). Gardner (1985) identified five features of cognitive science: representations; computers; deemphasis on affect, context, culture, and history; belief in interdisciplinary studies; and being rooted in classical philosophical problems. Each of these key features is presented in Table 7.1. Gardner (1985) considers representations and computers to be "core assumptions," and the latter two features listed to be strategic features. With this in mind, let us discuss the first two issues in greater detail.

Central to cognitive psychology is a belief in **mental representations,** or the coding of external events so that they become retrievable in internal forms (Glass, Holyoak, & Santa, 1987). These internal forms are not direct copies of the external stimuli but can be significantly altered and affected by prior knowledge, beliefs, and experiences. As you can see, this orientation is a departure from early writings on behaviorism, which we discussed in Chapter 6.

Stored in memory, mental representations have become a legitimate focus of speculation and research. Cognitive psychologists believe that the stimulus situation (the external event, or what happens) does not directly determine human behavior. For example, the way that students think about a teacher, their classroom, and their school influences their learning (not only what their teacher does). Interposed between an external stimulus and a person's response is cognitive activity. Thus, according to cognitive psychologists, thought processes are not an accumulation of stimulus-response connections, as theorized by behaviorists; cognition intervenes and distinctly colors human reactions.

Most cognitive scientists have been strongly influenced by the computer (Gardner, 1985). Because computers carry out tasks that we often regard as "thinking" (for example, transforming information, storing things in memory), they have become a

MENTAL REPRESENTATIONS
The coding of external events so they are retrievable in an internal form.

Table 7.1	FIVE KEY FEATURES OF COGNITIVE SCIENCE	
Key Feature	Definition/Characteristics	Example
Representations	Human cognitive activity is explained by representing cognition through internal entities.	The student has an idea or image of some event or person.
Computers	The computer serves as a model of human information processing or human thought.	The computer can be programmed to store large amounts of information in memory.
Deemphasis on affect, context, culture, and history	These concepts are not considered of primary importance in understanding mental processes.	The context that surrounds a student's thinking does not really influence the basic thinking process.
Interdisciplinary studies	There is an emphasis in cognitive psychology on interdisciplinary study to develop the field.	Researchers from psychology and neuroscience work together.
Classical philosophical problems	Traditional philosophical problems have served as a springboard for issues studied in the cognitive psychology field.	Can thinking be represented in the chemistry of the brain?

Source: H. Gardner, *The Mind's New Science.* Copyright © 1985 Basic Books, New York.

model of human thinking. In other words, humans, like computers, can be viewed as "symbol manipulation devices" that code external information into internal representations, manipulate or store these internal representations in some way, and then produce some output (or response). Also, as Gardner noted, the computer is often used in research on information processing and, therefore, is a valuable tool in cognitive science work. Indeed, the computer has often been used as a model to describe thinking from the cognitive perspective, and it provides one way of conceptualizing information processing (Ellis & Hunt, 1993). Figure 7.1 provides the sequence of information processing that divides cognition into three components: input processing, storage, and output. Although there are many arguments against the computer model of the mind, it provides a useful introduction to understanding the main ideas thought to be involved in cognitive functioning.

Today, cognitive psychology enjoys great appeal and, as noted in the chapter opening, has become a potent force in the classroom (Brooks & Brooks, 1993; Siegler, 1998). One source of cognitive psychology's appeal is its perspective on human beings. Students organize information into goals and subgoals in a fraction of a second and achieve remarkable results: They remember, they decide, they solve problems, they learn (Siegler, 1998). If you can aid students in organizing and processing information, you will help them to become more competent and to improve their learning both in and out of the classroom (Glaser, 1991).

Cognitive conceptions of learning have entered the classroom with far-reaching effects. For example, psychologists and teachers are extremely aware of the important effects of students' prior knowledge and memory strategies on learning (Shuell, 1986; Siegler, 1998). But human beings also face cognitive limitations: We can simultaneously manipulate only a certain number of symbols at a time, with limits on the speed at which we can manipulate them (Kinsbourne, 1986). Consequently, students are taught or must invent strategies to help them overcome these obstacles: They organize material to help them remember; they rehearse information over and over; they devise schemes to help them solve problems. The use, or lack of use, of strategies to overcome speed-to-capacity limits has been a major focus of cognitive research and has important implications for educators.

FIGURE 7.1

Sequence of information processing.

(From H. C. Ellis and R. R. Hunt, *Fundamentals of Cognitive Psychology,* 5th ed. Copyright © 1993 Wm. C. Brown Communications, Inc. Dubuque, IA. All Rights Reserved. Reprinted by permission of Times Mirror Higher Education Group, Inc., Dubuque, IA.

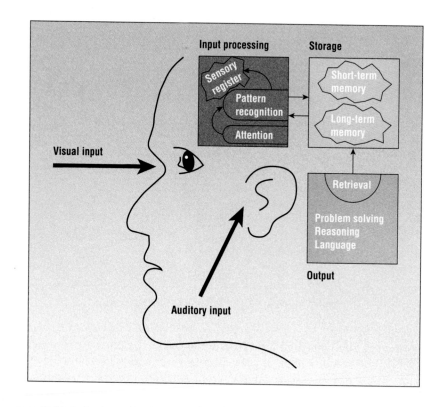

Computers provide many learners with an opportunity to acquire and construct new knowledge.

THE EMERGENCE OF COGNITIVE PSYCHOLOGY

The history of cognitive psychology, like that of any science, is rooted in many fields. Today's cognitive psychology has been influenced significantly by the conceptual framework of Gestalt psychology, especially from its emphasis on perception, an emphasis that strongly shaped the thinking of modern cognitivists such as Jerome Bruner.

The early Gestaltists Max Wertheimer, Wolfgang Köhler, and Kurt Koffka were convinced that behaviorism could not account for the full range of human behavior. Consequently, they launched a determined and effective attack against early behaviorism.

Current Issues & Perspectives

Does a Computer Provide a Reasonable Model of Human Cognition?

The computer has served a central role in the development of the cognitive science field. Several authors (for example, Ellis & Hunt, 1993; Gardner, 1985) have outlined a number of controversial issues that pervade the cognitive psychology field, including the use of computers in cognitive science research. An important point of controversy is whether the computer should serve as a model of human thought. Some cognitive scientists believe that the computer model of thinking is central to progress in the field. Critics in cognitive psychology suggest that the computer model will never replace the human brain. See, for example, *What Computers Can't Do* (Dreyfus, 1979).

ISSUE

The computer should serve as a model of human thought.

Pro: The computer is our best model for how the human brain operates. The computer can store vast amounts of information, code this information, and sort it into categories, among other information-processing functions. In this regard, the computer serves as a good model for human thought.

Con: The computer, like a lot of other machines, has served as a useful tool in cognitive science research, but it will never serve as a model of the human brain. The human brain is far too complex to be represented in a computer model, such as those used in studying artificial intelligence.

Pro: The computer is particularly useful in helping us understand the workings of the human mind, especially in promoting research on mental representations in cognitive psychology. Much of our understanding of thinking has come from the development and programming of the computer.

Con: The computer can never serve as a good model for human thinking or information processing because a computer removes the study of these psychological processes from the context people use to process information and store it in memory. People perform in a social and cultural context, and the computer cannot consider these variables in the study of cognition.

What do you think? Do you believe that the computer is a reasonable model for the study of human cognition? Revisit the question and your answer to it after you read this chapter and learn about the complex cognitive processes that a human brain can perform.

Wertheimer, the founder of the movement, discovered that if two lights were turned off and on at a definite rate, a human reported the impression that a single light was moving back and forth. This finding, which Wertheimer called the *phi phenomenon*, could not be effectively explained by the behaviorists' stimulus-response model; when processing these stimuli, people added something to the incoming sensory data to form their perception of movement.

From their academic base in Germany, the Gestaltists earned rapid acceptance by their European colleagues, but it was not until Wertheimer, Koffka, and Köhler were forced to flee Nazi Germany that Gestalt psychology was recognized as a viable psychological force in the United States. Given the preeminence of behaviorism in American psychology, the Gestaltists were attempting no small feat.

With their views on perception and perceptual learning finding acceptance in many quarters, the Gestaltists widened their efforts to bring a cognitive interpretation to human development, intelligence, and especially problem solving. One of the lasting legacies of Gestalt theory has been its principles of perceptual organization, which we discuss in more detail later in this chapter.

Bartlett and Schema

Unhappy with existing methods used to study memory, Bartlett (1932) presented exotic stories to his research participants and then asked them to recall the stories at different times. One of his most famous stories, "The War of the Ghosts," follows:

> One night two young men from Egulac went down to the river to hunt seals, and while they were there it became foggy and calm. Then they heard war cries, and they thought: "Maybe this is a war party." They escaped to the shore, and hid behind a log. Now canoes came up, and they heard the noise of paddles, and saw one canoe coming up to them. There were five men in the canoe, and they said: "What do you think? We wish to take you along. We are going up the river to make war on the people."
>
> One of the young men said: "I have no arrows."
>
> "Arrows are in the canoe," they said.
>
> "I will not go along. I might be killed. My relatives do not know where I have gone. But you," he said, turning to the other, "may go with them."
>
> So one of the young men went, but the other returned home.
>
> And the warriors went on up the river to a town on the other side of Kalama. The people came down to the water, and they began to fight, and many were killed. But presently the young man heard one of the warriors say: "Quick, let us go home: that Indian has been hit." Now he thought: "Oh, they are ghosts." He did not feel sick, but they said he had been shot.
>
> So the canoes went back to Egulac, and the young man went ashore to his house, and made a fire. And he told everybody and said: "Behold I accompanied the ghosts, and we went to fight. Many of our fellows were killed, and many of those who attacked us were killed. They said I was hit, and I did not feel sick."
>
> He told it all, and then he became quiet. When the sun rose he fell down. Something black came out of his mouth. His face became contorted. The people jumped up and cried.
>
> He was dead.

Bartlett, "War of Ghosts" From F. C. Bartlett and Walter Kintsch, *Remembering : A Study in Experimental and Social Psychology.* Copyright © 1954. Reprinted by permission of Cambridge University Press.

Without looking back at Bartlett's story, try to rewrite the story as you recall it. This might take a few minutes, but give it a good try.

Now check your story against the original. How different is it? Did you add to or subtract from the original? Is it essentially the same story? When asked to recall the story, most readers imposed an order and organization on it that are missing from the original. With increasing time, study participants made the story even more meaningful, more logical, and more consistent with their own personal experiences. Thus, **schemata** (plural of **schema**) of events are mental frameworks that modify incoming data so that they "fit" a person's experiences and perceptions (Phye & Andre, 1986).

When presenting new material, teachers quickly learn to expect a familiar refrain. One of the students will undoubtedly say, "That's like Mrs. Anderson said last year." The student is trying to fit something new into an existing cognitive framework, or schema.

In 1967, Pompi and Lachman conducted an experiment in which individuals read stories that lacked words ordinarily associated with the themes of the stories. For example, one

SCHEMATA (PL. OF SCHEMA)

Hypothetical mental frameworks that modify incoming information so it fits a person's experiences and perceptions.

story concerned a surgical operation, but words such as *doctor, nurse, scalpel,* and *operation* were left out. After reading the story, the participants were then given a list of words that included *doctor, nurse, scalpel,* and *operation* and were asked if these words had appeared in the story. The participants invariably stated that these words had appeared in the story.

The investigators believed that people grasp a story theme, compare it with the test words, and then match on the basis of familiarity. The stimulus for the participants' responses must have been mental; that is, they used their knowledge of medicine and surgery in their replies, even though no such specific cues appeared in the story.

To explain this tendency toward logic and the familiar, cognitive psychologists turned to the schema, a term that refers to some form of abstract cognitive structure. These schemata are the basis of memory and result from our previous experiences, which we organize in an individual manner. The organization of information is at the heart of the concept of schema. Organization of one's knowledge is a central ingredient of learning. Consequently, organization is important at three levels: (1) organization that already exists in one's long-term memory; (2) organization that can be perceived or generated within the material to be learned; and (3) organization that links the first two levels, thus allowing new material to be integrated with one's existing knowledge (Baddeley, 1990).

For example, after listening to a reading of "The War of the Ghosts," you would use your own schemata to interpret and recall the story's theme. You may have some familiarity with canoes; you may have had previous encounters with ghost stories or Indian adventure stories. If these matched corresponding parts of the story, you may recall these themes quite accurately. If, however, your schemata varied widely from the story's themes, you would probably add to "The War of the Ghosts" from your own schemata, introduce a more acceptable (to you) story theme, and distort the theme even further on additional recalls. Thus, memory is not a passive retelling of past events; rather, activity and even creativity characterize most learner's recall. That is, memory is believed to be more of a reconstruction of past events than a literal recalling of them.

The Role of Schema in Contemporary Cognitive Psychology

Schema has remained a viable concept in cognitive psychology (Phye & Andre, 1986). Think of a schema as a unit of organized knowledge about events, situations, or objects, one that guides informational input and retrieval (Leahey & Harris, 1985). A schema may be quite specific, such as the technique used to add a column of numbers, or quite general, such as an interpretation of intelligence. In other words, the material that students must learn will not in itself explain exactly what they do learn. The material contains potential information; that is, it possesses cues and directions that should guide students to use their own knowledge, thus obtaining the fullest possible information that they can.

The rationale for accepting the notion of schema has been a growing realization that human beings do not approach any topic totally devoid of knowledge; we have both prior knowledge and present expectations. We possess schemata that shape how we encode incoming material, and indeed, even affect how we "feel" about such material.

Consider the following experiment as an example of the way the latest theories and results from research into cognitive psychology are finding their way into the classroom. Rahman and Bisanz (1986) were interested in examining how students use a schema of stories to aid recall and in discovering how a schema affected strong reconstruction. Working on the assumption that inadequate knowledge of a story's structure could cause difficulty for poor readers, the authors were directly reflecting the most recent thinking about schema theory.

Rahman and Bisanz (1986) attempted to answer four questions:

1. Do both good and poor readers typically utilize a story schema?

2. Can both groups ignore the standard sequence of the story and retrieve information from a jumbled format?

3. Can both groups use a story schema when cued to do so?

4. Do poor readers improve when the task is repeated?

They studied forty-eight good readers (mean age 11.5 years) and forty-eight poor readers (mean age 11.8 years) from the sixth grade. The students heard a story in either standard or scrambled form. They were then told to recall and reconstruct the order of the story as they had heard it, or as it should be. The same procedure was repeated in a second phase, with one change: Before hearing the story, the children were told about the story's format and given possible ways to rearrange it if the story's sequence were askew.

The authors were able to draw several conclusions concerning schema use. First, both poor and good readers could recall and reconstruct a story presented in standard form, although poor readers' stories were not well developed. Second, good readers consistently used a strong schema when cued to do so on any task (both standard and scrambled), but poor readers could demonstrate a story schema only with a standard format. And finally, in the second phase of the experiment, poor readers improved only on the standard format. The authors concluded that comprehension research is vital in studies of poor readers; in so doing, they emphasized the growing importance of cognitive research for the classroom. Their findings point to the need to provide poor readers with a clear structure of what they are reading. If their comprehension is to improve, then techniques such as outlining, sequencing, and finding main features must be incorporated into their programs. A given student's learning style will largely determine which techniques to use with that student. The goal is to find the best way that students represent material.

Schema and Problem Solving in the Classroom

One way of improving teachers' relationships with students is to help students decrease their feelings of frustration when faced with a challenging situation. As an example of how mental representations affect classroom performance, even at higher levels, consider an experiment described by de Jong and Ferguson-Hassler (1986). Using evidence indicating that possession of knowledge does not necessarily lead to effective problem solving, the authors wished to investigate the problem schemata that their students used. (By "problem schemata" they meant knowledge students have that is related to and relevant for solving a problem, such as types of information likely to be needed; questions likely to be asked; and relevant facts, formulas, and underlying principles.)

Experts use more adequate and complete problem schemata; that is, they attack problems according to underlying principles, whereas novices focus on surface characteristics of problems. Expert problem solvers tend to use the correct data and appropriate procedures.

Studying forty-seven first-year university physics students, the authors presented them with twelve problems that involved sixty-five elements. (The subject matter was electricity and magnetism.) The sixty-five elements were then printed on cards, and the students were asked to sort them into coherent piles: A card in any one pile was to be more closely connected to the other cards in that pile than to the cards in other piles.

The authors found that the good problem solvers organized their knowledge in a much more problem-type-centered fashion than did the poor problem solvers; the former had well-developed problem schemata that allowed them to organize their information into coherent problem types in a way that showed some underlying principles. Interestingly, a high correlation was discovered between course examination scores and problem-centered scores.

Utilization of problem schemata thus appears to be an extremely efficient way both to solve problems and to do well on examinations. To encourage this ability in students, the authors urged teachers to help their students organize memory by the underlying (rather than surface-level) characteristics of a problem situation, the necessary data, and the correct procedural knowledge.

To use this information in the classroom, try to have students feel comfortable with the basic types of problems in a given subject, make sure they master the fundamental data, and ensure that they are familiar with the necessary steps to solve a problem (such as changing signs when an amount is moved from one side of an equation to another). If teachers work at this technique, they will help students form more positive attitudes toward a subject, reduce the chances of unhappiness and discipline problems, and increase learning (Foster, 1986).

MAJOR APPROACHES TO LEARNING WITH A COGNITIVE PSYCHOLOGY ORIENTATION

Meaningful Learning

In his analysis of learning, David Ausubel (1968, 1977; Ausubel et al., 1978) made two basic distinctions: one between reception and discovery learning and the other between rote and meaningful learning. He suggested that the first distinction is significant because most of students' learning, both in and out of school, is presented to them; that is, it is **reception learning.** Reception learning can be quite meaningful for students as long as it is not based on *rote,* or the memorization of material without an effort to comprehended it's meaning.

Reception learning and discovery learning pose two different tasks for students. In reception learning, the potentially meaningful material becomes meaningful as students internalize it. In **discovery learning,** however, students must discover what is to be learned and then rearrange it to integrate the material with existing cognitive structures.

Ausubel has long been an outspoken advocate of **meaningful learning,** which he defines as the acquisition of new meanings. Note that two important ideas are contained in his definition. Meaningful learning implies that the material to be learned is potentially meaningful (is appropriate for the student). The acquisition of new meanings refers to the process by which students turn potentially meaningful material into actual meaningfulness.

Ausubel noted that meaningful learning occurs when the material to be learned is related to what students already know. If, for example, an English teacher is teaching Hemingway's *For Whom the Bell Tolls* in her Modern Literature course, she could help her students' attempts to transfer potentially meaningful themes (such as belief in a cause or loyalty to others) into actual meaning by relating those themes to her students' schemata, such as their willingness to help one of their friends or their joining a student club dedicated to fighting the use of drugs. She would then have utilized the important ideas in Ausubel's definition of new meanings.

One of Ausubel's most important ideas for teachers is that of **advance organizers,** which he described as a form of expository teaching, that is, explaining what is to come (Williams, 1986). Ausubel (1960, 1980) defined an advance organizer as an abstract, general overview of new information to be learned that occurs in advance of the actual reading. Continuing our example of teaching *For Whom the Bell Tolls,* a teacher could summarize the major features of the novel before her students read the book. She could then lead a discussion of important concepts such as loyalty and steadfastness in terms that her students understand.

RECEPTION LEARNING

One part of meaningful learning that refers to using information in the form in which it was received without imposing a new order or meaning.

DISCOVERY LEARNING

Bruner's term for learning that involves the rearrangement and transformation of material that leads to insight. This is a major aspect of meaningful learning.

MEANINGFUL LEARNING

Ausubel's term to describe the acquisition of new meanings.

ADVANCE ORGANIZERS

Ausubel's term for an abstract, general overview of new information before the actual learning is expected.

CASE NOTES

Observation   Karim Peterson's slow rate of reading is causing him to have some comprehension difficulties and has resulted in below grade level performances in several subjects.

Hypothesis   His reading comprehension suffers because he must allocate most of his attention to identifying words correctly and because he is not using cognitive schema to effectively organize and recall what he is reading.

Possible Actions   Mr. Siegel and Mrs. Peterson could both spend time working directly with Karim to improve his reading comprehension skills by teaching him techniques such as outlining, summarizing, and labeling of main ideas. The use of brief advanced organizers may also be useful to facilitate Karim's development of a schema to interpret what he reads.

This introductory material is intended to help students ready their cognitive structures (that is, their minds) to incorporate (that is, learn) potentially meaningful material. Advance organizers are presented before introducing the new material and at a slightly higher level of abstraction, because meaningful material is better learned and retained if it can be subsumed under already existing relevant ideas. Students already have their own ideas about loyalty to friends.

To help students acquire meaning, follow Ausubel's advice: Identify relevant anchoring ideas that students already possess (in their cognitive structures). You want to relate new, potentially meaningful material to some topic with which students are already familiar. In Chapter 2, you read about Piaget's initiating this process when he described assimilation and accommodation.

 Advance organizers are effective when they utilize the anchoring ideas already present in the students' cognitive structures, thus helping to reduce the students' dependence on rote memorization. Ausubel summarized the principal function of advance organizers as bridging the gap between what students already know (their ideas of loyalty to their friends, for example) and what they need to know before they can successfully learn new material (the abstract notion of loyalty inherent in the novel). In this way, learners receive an overview of the material before they actually encounter it and are provided with organizing elements that are the core of the new material.

Ausubel's ideas, however, must be used with caution. Advance organizers have not always produced more efficient learning, although the results of research indicate that advance organizers have a consistent, moderate, and positive effect on learning (Corkill, Glover, Bruning, & Krug, 1989). Such learning variables as a student's cognitive structures and general state of developmental readiness must be taken into consideration. In other words, potentially meaningful material must be biologically and psychologically appropriate. Introducing a preschooler's story by referring to concepts such as loyalty without giving appropriate examples frustrates the entire process of meaningful learning. But by talking about the relationship between a child and a dog, a teacher could introduce the concept at the proper psychological level and then gradually help the students apply a label to it.

Although Ausubel emphasized meaningful reception learning, another leading cognitive psychologist, Jerome Bruner, concentrated his efforts on discovery learning. Bruner's work has also been in the forefront of the development and acceptance of cognitive psychology.

TIPS ON LEARNING
Using Schema to Enhance Student's Comprehension and Memory

PRINCIPLE   Learning involves the acquisition and modification of schemata. Meaningful learning occurs when students incorporate new information into an existing schema or when they can create new schemata by way of analogy to old schemata.

STRATEGY   To help students form schemata, teachers should present multiple instances of something, such as a word problem, and have students identify and discuss the common features of the instances.

STRATEGY   When a topic is new, teachers can evoke appropriate schemata before presenting a topic in lecture or before students read about the topic by using advanced organizers and trying to connect the new information with their prior experiences or knowledge.

Discovery Learning

The ideas that flourished during the early years of cognitive science had a strong influence on the creative mind of a young psychologist named Jerome Bruner. In 1956, with colleagues Jacqueline Goodnow and George Austin, Bruner, published an ingenious and important account of categorization called *A Study of Thinking*. In it, they analyzed categorizing and expressed their belief that it explains why humans are not overwhelmed by environmental complexity. Bruner, Goodnow, and Austin effectively showed that their research participants actively participated in the classification process. As you can imagine, the great value of Bruner's work in the 1950s and 1960s lay in the energy it supplied to the renewed cognitive movement. Gardner (1985) noted that Bruner's study participants were treated as active, constructive problem solvers, rather than as passive reactors to whatever stimuli were presented to them. The active construction of solutions to problems implies that students turn to their cultural environment for clues to aid them in their task.

According to Bruner and his associates, three types of concepts exist: conjunctive, disjunctive, and relational. *Conjunctive concepts* rely on the joint presence of several attributes. These attributes are abstracted from many individual experiences with an object, thing, or event. So there are categories, such as *boy, car, book,* and *orange. Disjunctive concepts* are composed of concepts, any one of whose attributes may be used in classification. That is, one or another of its attributes enable an object to be placed in a particular category. A good example of the disjunctive category is the strike in baseball. A strike may be a ball thrown by the pitcher that is over the plate and between a batter's shoulders and knees, or a ball at which the batter swings and misses, or a ball that the batter hits as a foul (outside the playing limits of the diamond). Any one of these attributes enables the observer to classify it as a strike. *Relational concepts* are formed by the relationship that exists among defining attributes. The authors illustrate this category by using income brackets. There are many income levels or classes, all of which exist because of the relationship among income, eligible expenses, and number of dependents. The combination of these properties determines an individual's income class. These are relational categories.

Bruner, Goodnow, and Austin concluded that categorizing implies more than merely recognizing instances. Rules are learned and then applied to new situations. Students learn that a sentence—subject, object, predicate—is the basic unit in writing, in history class as well as in English class. The various categories (conjunctive, disjunctive, relational) are really rules for grouping attributes to define the positive instances of any concept. Bruner's work on discovery learning, along with that of Piaget and Vygotsky, led to constructivism, the current prevailing approach to the study and application of cognitive psychology.

Constructivism

For years, one of us (JLC) and her sister had a running argument over an orange sweater. JLC would come home from college, find the sweater in her sister's closet, and take it. After all, it belonged to JLC, who had only loaned it to her sister, not given it to her to keep. JLC distinctly remembered buying the sweater, including the store where she found it and how pleased she was with how well it fit. Her sister was simply wrong when she said that the sweater was hers, that she remembered buying it and that JLC only happened to be with her when she picked it out. This argument went on until JLC very generously decided to just let her sister have the sweater (it didn't fit anymore and orange was "out" anyway).

Who was right in the famous sweater argument? Have you ever had an experience where you were absolutely certain of yourself and your facts, and the person you were disagreeing with was equally as certain? A recent theory of learning and cognition helps explain such incidents. Cognitive **constructivism** holds that people actively construct their own knowledge, and that reality is determined by the experiences of the knower, rather than existing as an objective truth distinct from the individual (Jonassen, 1991). In other words, humans cannot know an objective, "true" reality apart from their own interpretation of it because all knowledge is filtered through and interpreted in light of past experiences and what is already known. The orange sweater was JLC's in the sense that is how she remembered and interpreted the events. But in her sister's construction of the events, the sister owned it. Who was really "right"? Does it even matter in terms of how it affects later behavior? According to cognitive constructivism, truth, like beauty, is in the eyes (or minds) of the beholder!

CONSTRUCTIVISM

An approach to learning that holds that people actively construct or make their own knowledge and that reality is determined by the experiences of the knower.

Extracting both textual and graphic information requires advanced cognitive processes.

At first glance, the cognitive constructivist perspective may seem a rather radical change in theorizing about human thinking and learning. But the main ideas of this approach have been around for some time. If you've ever studied philosophy, you'll recognize the rudiments of constructivism in the thinking of philosophers like Socrates and Kant. However, the roots of the current cognitive constructivist view of human cognition are usually attributed to Jean Piaget, Lev Vygotsky, and contemporary work on human knowledge representation by Jerome Bruner, Howard Gardner, and Nelson Goodman, to name but a few.

Like most theories, constructivism is not one single perspective, but all the variations share some defining characteristics. Let's first summarize the main ideas of the cognitive constructivist position, then discuss how this theory about learning affects teaching. The first three of the following six points describe the cognitive constructivist view of what knowledge is, and the last three address how learning occurs, or that is, how knowledge is constructed.

1. *We cannot know an objective reality.* Rather, we construct our own subjective understanding of our experiences, interpreting everything in light of what has already been experienced and learned. "The key idea that sets constructivism apart from other theories of cognition was launched about 60 years ago by Jean Piaget. It was the idea that what we call knowledge does not and cannot have the purpose of producing representations of an independent reality, but instead has an adaptive function" (von Glaserfeld, 1996, p. 3). Our cognitive representations of all aspects of our environment (physical, social, and cultural) serve to help us adapt to those environments and survive in them. Our personal representations may reflect some external reality to the extent that such a thing is necessary to survive and thrive in it, but this accuracy is certainly not a given.

2. *Knowledge is subjective.* No two people have the same experiences, physiologies, or environments; therefore, no two people will construct the same knowledge.

3. *The knowledge of two people can be said to be "taken-as-shared" to the extent that their constructions seem to function in the same way in given situations* (Cobb, 1991). This cannot be taken as evidence that their knowledge constructions are the same, only that they are compatible enough to allow common understanding, expectations, and behavior. As an example, think about the last time you and a close friend both viewed the same event, then simply looked at one another and began laughing. No words were needed. Your cognitive constructions of the event, its implications and meaning were so similar that it wasn't necessary to explain to one another why the event was funny—you both simply knew. Many of the unspoken cultural rules that govern social interactions are "taken-as-shared" knowledge, which can really cause headaches for someone new to the culture!

These first three ideas, though simple, are sometimes surprisingly hard to grasp, and they can be particularly hard to keep in mind as one interacts with others. For example, think about research on eyewitness testimony (Loftus & Palmer, 1974). This work has shown that two people can view the same set of events, an automobile collision, for example, yet come up with very different reports of the events. What the witnesses perceive and store depends on their subjective physical environments (for example, subtle differences in lighting, different positions from which the accident was viewed), physical capabilities (for example, acuity of eyesight, hearing), how well they were attending to the event (daydreaming, watching the cars involved closely because they looked like those of a good friend), and prior experiences (one observer had previously been seriously injured in a car accident, while another has never even had a dinged door), as well as factors such

Constructing knowledge for novices is best done by following a model or blueprint.

as how questions are phrased. The witnesses honestly report what they saw, but their cognitive constructions of the supposedly same events can be radically different.

4. *Knowledge is constructed through the process of adapting to the events and ideas one experiences* (Fosnot, 1996; von Glaserfeld, 1996). A major influence on the cognitive constructions we build is experiencing conflict. As Piaget described, cognitive conflict leads to cognitive disequilibrium. Humans seek to resolve the conflicts, and in doing so engage in reflective abstraction about the conflict. In other words, they think about things they don't understand. As a result, existing knowledge structures are reorganized (that is, reconstructed) and new knowledge structures are constructed. And since no two people have exactly the same experiences, no two cognitive constructions are the same (though they may be similar enough to be taken-as-shared for a specific situation).

   Not all cognitive constructivists will use such strongly Piagetian terms to describe how knowledge is constructed, but the basic ideas are similar. There is some existing understanding (construction) that encounters something that doesn't fit, or some event that isn't understandable, with the current understanding. Some sense of confusion or curiosity results, and the person must do something to deal with it. If the person decides that the conflict is trivial (that is, it will have little or no impact on his/her ability to adequately exist in this environment), then there won't be any change in the person's cognitive construction. If, however, the person thinks that this conflict is important enough or interesting in some way, then the new information or event is considered, an attempt is made to understand it, and the existing cognitive construction changes at least a little.

   As most veteran teachers know, one of the best ways to create cognitive conflict is to engage students in discussions. *Discourse,* as cognitive constructivists call it, serves two important functions in knowledge construction. First, it can create the conflict that signals to a person that their current knowledge construction may not be sufficient. This can set in motion the events just described for changes in understanding. Second, discourse can have a significant influence on how the cognitive conflict is resolved. In other words, discourse can affect the new knowledge that gets constructed by directing attention to things the person didn't notice before or thought were unimportant, adding new information for the person's consideration, or by helping the person see new or different relationships among the various aspects of the topic being considered. The particular "community of discourse" one regularly engages with (that is, the group of people one has regular contact with) also influences what kinds of cognitive constructions are seen as acceptable within that group, in essence allowing some kinds of constructions while discouraging (sometimes not even tolerating) others.

5. *The construction of knowledge is significantly influenced by one's environment and by the symbols and materials one uses or has ready access to* (Fosnot, 1996). Environment refers to not only the physical surroundings but also the immediate social contacts one has as well as one's larger cultural environment. Clearly the environment influences the resources one has available for survival—if there isn't enough food or water, then one cannot continue to develop cognitive constructions at all. But the influence that cognitive constructivists are referring to is that the environment makes certain substances, materials, and symbol systems more readily available, useful, and acceptable. These symbols and materials become the "tools to think with" and affect how one perceives, interprets, and functions in their environment.

For example, children who grow up in some cultures learn to use a metric system for measuring objects, while others use a decimal system. Children use their respective systems to think about and solve measurement problems and often encounter difficulty using the other system if they are ever in a situation that requires it. Some Pacific Island societies must navigate long sea distances without landmasses to guide them. These cultures use stellar constellations as "landmarks" to guide them as they sail. This particular symbol system is available to other societies, but it is not encouraged and therefore is not used as frequently. The particular symbol systems one uses affects the kind of knowledge constructions one develops—Pacific Islanders are more likely to think of directions and distances in terms of successive changes in the appearance of stars and constellations; Europeans and Americans think in terms of kilometers and miles.

Similarly, the physical surroundings and culture influence the materials that will be available and encouraged for use. Early pioneers on the plains were used to building their homes from wood when they lived in the heavily forested areas of the eastern United States. They resisted the idea of using sod as a building material because their culture did not encourage it, even thought it was strange. The physical surroundings made using wood very difficult though, and they began using the easily available sod from the plains. Once transportation made lumber more easily available, they went back to using wood because wood houses, in the opinion of their culture, were "better."

Different materials give rise to different interpretations and thus to different cognitive constructions of the things one experiences (Fosnot, 1996). For example, have you ever tried representing information from this text using different media and materials? You probably read the information, take notes on it, and use forms to represent it verbally. But have you tried drawing a picture of it? Making a diagram? Making a sculpture to represent the relations among the different schools of thought? Writing and producing a play to represent the different theories at work in a classroom? Each tactic uses different materials, highlights different aspects of the information, and results in different cognitive constructions. Research on use of different media within art indicates that the specific media used (Styrofoam versus clay; clay versus paper and pencil) results in representation of different kinds of details, perspectives, and objects (Sherman, 1978; Golomb, 1974).

So one's culture influences the materials one prefers (as we saw with the Plains settlers), and the materials used influence what gets represented in one's cognitive constructions. But the influence of culture goes even further, affecting what you actually perceive from the physical surroundings (Segall, 1994). For example, there is a famous optical illusion called the *Müller-Lyer Illusion* (see Figure 7.2). If this drawing is shown to people from a Western culture like the United States, they typically say that the line with the short segments pointing outward (the top drawing) is longer than the one that looks like an arrow (the bottom drawing). They have great difficulty believing that the lines are of equal length, even after they measure the lines. But people from other cultures have less difficulty seeing the equivalence of the lines. The difference seems to be that some cultures have a great deal of experience with intersection of straight lines, and they thus learn to interpret visual information in their environment in terms of the angles formed as straight lines cross one another. People in these cultures quickly learn to infer measurement of length, distance, and even speed of movement on the basis of these angles, and their cognitive constructions and subsequent behavior are significantly influenced by this information. People from other cultures, in contrast, have much less experience with intersection of straight lines. Their experience consists more of rounded, rather than straight, visual elements, so they have no difficulty separating the angle and direction of the line's intersection with the line's length. The point here is that culture influences the symbol systems used (for example, metric versus decimal versus stellar constellations), preferences for certain materials over others (for example, wood versus sod), and even the way one sees the surrounding physical world (for example, in terms of intersecting lines or rounded shapes). All these things influence what and how information is put together in one's cognitive constructions, which in turn govern behavior, expectations, and ways of thinking.

The groups with whom you regularly interact are another important influence on cognitive constructions. These discourse groups affect the kinds of constructions and solutions developed, and they even affect the kinds of problems that are seen as socially acceptable to think about. These groups also provide a vocabulary with which to think. For example, among psychologists, the term *degrees of freedom* is a way of talking about how much room for maneuvering one has or how many paths of action are open in a particular situation. It has a basis in the statistics that all psychologists learn, but this term is also used as a kind of shorthand for communication. Most professions have such professional "jargon" that almost seems designed to keep novices from ever understanding the field.

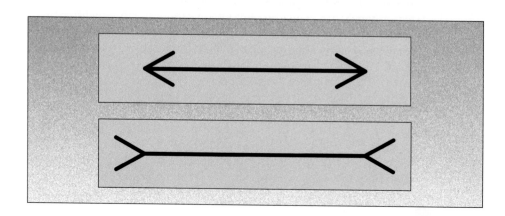

FIGURE 7.2

Müller–Lyer Illusion

(Think about computer jargon—bits, bytes, RAM, ROM, CPU, baud rate, bandwidth, and so on—and you'll know exactly what we mean!) But in fact, professional jargon usually serves the purpose of helping the members of that particular group quickly and efficiently understand one another. So the immediate social environment affects both the content and form of one's cognitive constructions.

6. *"Readiness to learn" has a different meaning for cognitive constructivists.* The concept of readiness to learn is important in most theories of learning but is conceptualized quite differently in the different approaches. For cognitive constructivists, individuals are ready to learn about a concept when their cognitive constructions are able to incorporate some aspect of that concept. The knowledge of the concept that is constructed may not be "correct" according to an outsider's criterion, but that does not mean that nothing was learned about the concept or that the existing knowledge was not altered in some way. Encountering a given experience may trigger a radical restructuring for one student while leading to only a minor change for another. Both have learned about the concept, but the change in the first student's knowledge was much greater. Vygotsky's idea of the zone of proximal development is relevant here because it captures the idea that different students may both be "ready" to learn about a given concept, and they may learn different things about the concept from the same experience. Vygotsky also recognized that different students may require different levels of assistance from others to be able to complete a task. The amount and type of assistance needed gives an indication of the kind of cognitive construction the student has.

The existing cognitive constructions that students bring to an experience will lead each student to focus on and learn about different aspects of the same materials. As a result, each student will understand and use the materials and ideas differently. For example, one of us (JLC) has three children who all love to play the "Memory Game." This is a standard children's game with about fifty small cards containing pictures of common objects and animals. Each card has an exact match, for twenty-five pairs. Will likes to play the game as it was intended, putting all the cards out face down, turning over two at a time, and trying to remember where the different items are so he can get a "match." Rachel loves the game too, but her way of understanding and playing this game is quite different. She picks up each card and attempts to identify the object, complete with any distinctive sounds ("RRRRRRR" for a car), facial expressions (face scrunched up, sniffing for a flower), or body movements (hopping around for a rabbit). Lily has yet another cognitive construction of this game. She likes to try to eat the cards. (She doesn't get to play too often!) Each child is "ready" to play the game and learns something from it, thus affecting the cognitive construction that is built. But the kind of information represented in the construction, and the actions taken on the basis of it, are quite different.

These six central tenets describe the general idea of cognitive constructivism. But keep in mind that there are different emphases within this theoretical camp. One of the biggest dimensions of difference among constructivists concerns how much emphasis is placed on the role of culture and other contexts versus the role of the individual in the development of cognitive constructions. For example, a perspective referred to as *situated learning* emphasizes the context of development as having a tremendous influence on what knowledge is constructed. Others (such as Piaget) talk about this influence but focus more on the individual's reflective abstraction of conflicts.

Applying Cognitive Constructivism in the Classroom

The idea that each of us constructs our own knowledge has important implications for teachers and students. There are important differences between a teaching approach based on cognitive constructivism and a more traditional teaching approach. Table 7.2 summarizes some of the main differences.

In general, a teacher using a constructivist approach acts as a facilitator of knowledge and skill acquisition, as a guide or resource person whose purpose is to structure the learning environment to help each student come to his or her own understanding of the information. Learning is very individualized and personalized for each student, taking into account each student's prior knowledge, interests, cognitive level and skills. The teacher relinquishes at least some degree of control over what and how students learn, since the most appropriate ways to explore information and develop understanding differ substantially from one student to another. As a result, teachers cannot prepare a single lecture or set of learning exercises for an entire class, but must respond to each student's individual needs. The teacher is very often a fellow student in that the teacher is exploring and learning along with the students, facing real problems and challenges for which the teacher does not have a ready answer. Students play a much more active and self-directive role, taking on much of the responsibility for their own learning and making choices as to how, and sometimes what, they are learning. Assessment of learning is different as well, often taking place more often and in less formal ways. Teachers more often assess the products, projects, and/or presentations students produce rather than emphasizing results from on-demand tests.

Table 7.2 SOME DIFFERENCES BETWEEN TRADITIONAL AND CONSTRUCTIVIST CLASSROOMS

Traditional Approach	Constructivist Approach
The primary emphasis is on developing basic skills and building understanding from the "bottom up."	The primary emphasis is on the "big ideas" and developing understanding from the "top down."
Classroom activities are usually based on textbooks and workbooks.	Classroom activities are usually based on primary data sources and manipulation of materials.
Students are viewed as passive recipients of information supplied by the teacher-expert.	Students are viewed as active knowledge seekers, creating their own personal understandings of information.
Teachers are viewed as experts, providing information to students on predetermined topics.	Teachers are viewed as guides for learning, assisting as students develop and answer their own questions on topics and/or activities of interest to the student.
A limited number of correct answers exist and are accepted .	Students' hypotheses, questions, and views are accepted and used to guide further learning.
Students often work individually on teacher-developed assignments.	Students often work collaboratively on projects of their own design.
Assessment is usually done separately from instruction, often taking the form of objective tests.	Assessment is usually incorporated into the learning process, often taking the form of teacher observations, student performances or exhibitions of projects, and/or student self-assessments.

Source: Adapted from J. G. Brooks & M. G. Brooks, 1993.

How do you use a constructivist approach in your classroom? The following five guidelines were developed by Brooks and Brooks (1993) and are useful in thinking about how to adopt a constructivist framework:

1. *Pose problems of emerging relevance to students.* It would be wonderful, and wonderfully easy for teachers, if all students came to every class with a question of burning interest, relevant to the topics that particular course was to cover, which they couldn't wait to address. Unfortunately, this is not the case. A cognitive constructivist approach to teaching does not mean that a teacher can only plan to pursue topics and activities that a student shows initial interest in. If this were the case, a teacher would never be able to do advance planning! Instead, interest and relevance can be created and students drawn in if teachers are adept at creatively setting up and mediating interesting problems for students to ponder.

   So how does a teacher set up such conditions? Take advantage of the power of cognitive conflict for encouraging change. Create cognitive conflict by presenting students with an interesting problem, one that students can make testable predictions about, discuss among themselves, elaborate upon to develop further knowledge, and see as relevant in some way (Brooks & Brooks, 1993; Greenberg, 1990). The problem must be sufficiently complex so that students have to genuinely think hard about its solution(s): "Complexity often serves to generate relevance and, therefore, interest. It is oversimplification that students find confusing" (Brooks & Brooks, 1993, p. 39).

   Students must also be allowed plenty of time to grapple with the problem and come to a deeper level understanding of the concepts involved. This differs from the way most curricula are currently structured, with set limits on the time allocated for each discrete piece of a given topic. "If the conceptions presently held by students are not explicitly addressed, new information is filtered through a lens that may cloud, rather than clarify, that information" (Brooks & Brooks, 1993, p. 40).

   A teacher from the constructivist perspective must be continually on the watch for each student's understanding of the relevant concepts. If the teacher observes a student not recognizing or giving adequate thought to some relevant aspect of the concept, the teacher must find some way to guide the student to a

---

CASE NOTES

Observation   Karim Peterson shows little interest in much of the subject matter discussed in Mark Siegel's class and he is rarely actively engaged in conversations with classmates.

Hypothesis   If Karim were presented with some dilemmas or controversial topics, he might find debating possible solutions with classmates exciting and interesting. Remember verbal skills are a relative strength of his that could be used more.

Possible Actions   Consider using a constructivist approach to instruction by setting up some cognitive conflict situations several times a week where groups of students can debate an issue or topic. Topics that Karim might find interesting might include: What is the best way to motivate somebody? What is the best way to build a house? Why should students do homework? If you were lost in the woods, how would you go about getting help?

One's thinking often is refined with feedback from others.

clearer recognition of the aspect. This is best done by providing an activity that will highlight the aspect's importance as the student attempts the activity and reflects on it (again, experiencing and reflecting on cognitive conflict), rather than simply telling the student to consider the aspect. The particular aspects and activities will be different for different students, adding to the complexity (but also to the interest!) of the teacher's job.

For example, think about the case studies presented in this textbook. They can serve as the "problem" that students are initially presented with and the framework around which instruction in educational psychology can be built. The situation presented in each case offers opportunities to think about classroom instruction and specific problems that arise, as well as the opportunity to discuss possible solutions to them. These cases are complex and give students relevant issues to deal with. Depending on the issues a given student focuses on initially, a teacher can use the cases along with other examples and materials to help guide the student to a recognition of other issues that may be relevant in that case. This can lead to a richer understanding of this particular slice of classroom life.

2. *Structure learning around primary concepts.* In other words, teachers should identify the "big ideas" that are important for the students to come to understand and structure teaching around them. As students work to understand and elaborate on these main concepts of a discipline, the details will be added because they are necessary for a more complete understanding. But having the main idea in mind from the beginning serves to guide students' exploration through the details,

giving them a focal point, an organizational structure that can be used to organize and interpret all the details. This is often referred to as a "top-down" approach.

As an example, this text is built around five themes that we think are centrally important to educational psychology: *learning, communication, motivation, assessment,* and *time.* Throughout the text, we have tried to tie concepts to these themes, offering TIPS boxes and discussions about how the content is relevant for and can be useful to understanding these themes. We hope that when you have completed the course, your understanding of educational psychology will not be in the form of a collection of unrelated facts, but organized around these central themes and seen as useful tools for solving classroom problems and improving teaching skills. And if you reorganize these themes, adding others and modifying as you gain experience, so much the better! The main point is to keep in mind and build on the themes, concepts, or ideas that are central to your discipline, rather than building knowledge piecemeal from the bottom up.

3. *Seek and value students' points of view.* Teachers talk a lot; constructivists encourage them to listen carefully as well. "Students' points of view are windows into their reasoning. Each student's point of view is an instructional entry point that sits at the gateway of personalized education" (Brooks & Brooks, 1993, p. 60). Listening to students explain the reasons for their answers gives invaluable information as to how they understand concepts and gives guidance to teachers as to what kinds of instructional materials and activities might be most useful to help that particular student modify the current understanding.

Unfortunately for many students, the minute a teacher asks "Why?" in response to an answer, the student assumes the answer is wrong and begins the process of trying to guess the right answer. This guessing process is usually accompanied by an emotional reaction, feeling insecure, and sometimes downright unintelligent. Consistently asking students to explain their answers, and valuing the responses by building on current knowledge, will help students see that the reasoning process and underlying understanding are the topics of interests, rather than simply a right or wrong answer. This does not mean that anything a student says or thinks is simply accepted as is. But the message that is communicated to the student is that is it important for both the teacher and student to understand how one is currently thinking about a concept in order to know how to further develop the knowledge.

4. *Adapt curriculum to address students' current understandings.* If the curriculum doesn't fit the student, change the curriculum. Adapt it to best fit the student's current understanding as well as to best guide the student's further knowledge development. The observation of students and adaptation of the curricula are continual, taking place before as well as during classroom activities, seizing opportunities to foster knowledge construction whenever they occur. Different adaptations, and thus different activities, will be needed for different students.

Of the five guidelines offered, this may be the most difficult for teachers to implement. Most teachers face a great deal of pressure to cover certain amounts of material in a limited amount of time, and to produce students who will perform at a satisfactory level on an objective assessment of their knowledge. The constructivist approach says that this pressure to cover the material works against good student understanding of concepts, and in fact encourages students to focus on quickly acquiring surface level knowledge. It also works against teachers investing time and energy into understanding students' current knowledge and adapting the preexisting curriculum to individual student's needs. The goal in such a system, they argue, is not to really understand the material and develop usable, detailed knowledge of it. The goal is to pass the test.

5. *Assess student learning in the context of teaching.* This guideline encourages teachers to move beyond an emphasis on simple right or wrong answers as well as to continually assess students' learning, using the information to adjust the instruction offered. Try to understand how answers, correct and incorrect, were arrived at. Did the student perhaps interpret the question differently than it was intended? Does the student's response indicate a partial understanding of the concept, one that could be built upon and elaborated? Asking students to explain their answers and really listening to their explanations are the only ways teachers can get such information. In some cases, it is more useful to know what a student can do with assistance from someone else than what they can do on their own. As Vygotsky pointed out with his zone of proximal development, it is the emerging understandings that provide the most fruitful focus for a teacher's efforts. Such assessments are most helpful if they take place within the context of teaching. The results can be used literally on a minute-to-minute basis to alter the kinds of activities, questions, comments, and suggestions offered to students while they are in the midst of struggling to resolve some cognitive conflict.

    One interesting and important aspect of assessment within the context of teaching is the idea of nonjudgmental feedback. Providing such feedback is difficult for most teachers because we are all so used to being told our answers are right or wrong. Nonjudgmental feedback techniques try to use tactics such as questions, plausible contradictions, and requests for examples to help students evaluate their own work. Teachers not only gain more information about the student's understanding than they would by simply marking answers as right or wrong, but also students begin to learn self-assessment skills. They take more responsibility for evaluating their own work, learning to assess the quality and clarity of their thinking, knowledge base, and way of expressing themselves. Nonjudgmental feedback in the context of teaching also offers another important advantage—it can help circumvent the negative emotional reactions that many students quickly develop to being evaluated. If it is clear that the teacher is seeking to better understand what a student is thinking, rather than trying to figure out what the student doesn't know, the emotional climate of the interaction becomes more positive. Students, in turn, may be more willing to express their understandings and confusions, offering a clearer picture of their current knowledge for both of them.

Up to this point in this chapter we have examined cognition and cognitive theories about thinking and the human mind with little consideration to actual brain anatomy or functioning. It is time now to examine the human brain and its relationship to learning behaviors and cognitions.

THE BRAIN AND THINKING

We begin by asking a fundamental question: Can there be learning, developing, and thinking without a biological base? Although no one would argue against this premise, considerable controversy arises when we speculate about the relationship between brain and mind, that is, thinking and cognition. For an overview of basic brain anatomy, examine Figure 7.3, noting the brain areas and their various specialized functions.

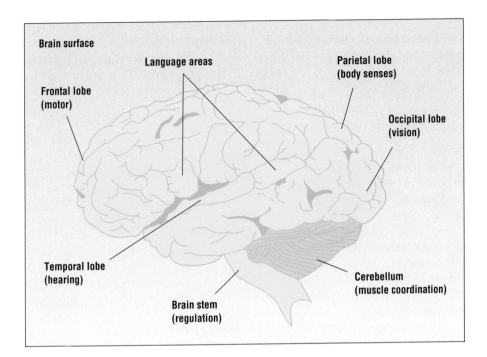

FIGURE 7.3

The brain and its functions.

The Relationship of Brain and Mind

Until recently, extreme positions have been the rule when it comes to discussing the brain–mind relationship. Philosophical advocates virtually have ignored the existence of the brain, and more currently physiologists and biologists have insisted that the mind is nothing more than a system of connecting neurons. Rose (1987) raised this question: How are data transformed as they pass in a series of electrical signals along particular nerves to central brain regions, where they interact with one another, thus producing certain kinds of responses? One attempt to answer this question was made by Alexander Luria, a Russian neuropsychologist. Luria (1980) proposed a less extreme, but still a distinct neurological view.

According to Luria, intellectual activity begins with analyzing the conditions of the task and then identifying its most important elements. In an example, he traced the thinking process through four stages. In the first stage, thinking begins only when a person is motivated to solve a problem for which there is no ready solution. When students recognize problems and realize that they have the tools to solve them, their motivation remains high. The second stage is not an attempt to solve the problem immediately. Rather, it entails the restraint of impulsive responses. The individual must carefully investigate any possible solutions. We have commented previously on the need to identify a problem's basic elements. In the third stage, the person selects what seems to be the most satisfactory alternative and creates a general plan. Students must be taught to pause, use the critical elements they have identified, and take the time to plan for a solution. Finally, the individual must put into action the methods and operations of the proposed solution, asking these questions: Does it work? Have I reached a satisfactory solution?

Neuropsychological deficits differentiate specific aspects of the brain–mind relationship. Noting that lesions in different parts of the brain cause different types of intellectual disturbances, Luria described the impact of frontal zone lesions on the ability to formulate plans. He noted that people suffering from these lesions are unable to form a preliminary basic plan of action. Any system of connections that arises will be random, having lost its goal-directed and selective character.

This information on the relationship between brain and mind shows why it is important to include information about brain functioning in our discussions of cognitive thinking skills. We'll now examine brain characteristics that appear particularly suited to expand our views of cognition, such as lateralization, pattern matching, and biological basis of learning.

Lateralization

Which hand do you use for writing? If you were to kick a football, would you use the leg on the same side of your body as the hand you use for writing? Pick up a pencil or ruler and pretend it is a telescope. Which eye do you use? Are you using the same side of the body that you would use for writing and kicking? Your answers to these questions should give you some idea of the meaning of **cerebral lateralization.**

CEREBRAL
LATERALIZATION
The extent to which a function is predominately controlled by one cerebral hemisphere.

We tend to think of the brain as a single unit, but actually it consists of two halves: the cerebral hemispheres. The two halves are connected by a bundle of nerve fibers (the corpus callosum), and the left hemisphere controls the right side of the body while the right hemisphere controls the left side of the body. Although the hemispheres seem to be almost identical, your answers to the preceding few questions provide clues about important differences between the two.

These differences, called *functional asymmetry,* offer insight into your brain's organization. If you are right-handed, for example, your left cerebral hemisphere is lateralized for handedness and also for control of your speech. You are "left lateralized." There is general agreement today that although there may be some rationale for the distinction between left and right hemispheric dominance, both hemispheres are involved in all activities (Caine & Caine, 1990).

Much of our knowledge of cerebral lateralization has resulted from the study of individuals with brain damage. Patients with left hemisphere damage, for example, typically encounter speech difficulties; damage to the right hemisphere frequently causes perceptual and attentional disorders. The right hemisphere often has been relegated to a "minor" position because as humans we rely so heavily on language that the left hemisphere came to be thought of as the dominant or "major" hemisphere. Today, however, psychologists place much importance in the right hemisphere's control of visual and spatial activities.

As interesting as these data are, our concern must focus mainly on developmental and educational implications. Data clearly suggest functional asymmetry in hemisphere use at various ages and between the two sexes (Rourke, Bakker, Fisk, & Strang, 1983). Can we draw implications from the lateralization literature with regard to education? Answering this question requires two significant considerations:

1. Are there gender differences that are definitely related to lateralization? Without reviewing here the enormous body of literature addressing this question, we can safely state that gender differences exist in certain abilities, such as verbal and spatial skills. Females generally seem superior in anything relating to language, whereas males excel in spatial tasks. But these differences tell us nothing about why they exist. They may result from either biological or cultural factors, or both. The differences are too tenuous and too subject to a variety of interpretations (Caine & Caine, 1990). Our interest, however, focuses on one question: Should these demonstrated differences dictate different instructional practices for males and females? Though these research results should be considered, we believe they should not be the basis for curriculum construction or different instructional techniques. For one thing, males and females are much more alike in brain functioning than they are different.

2. To what extent, then, should educators recognize these differences? Since the results of lateralization studies have become known, criticism has been directed at the schools for "teaching to the left hemisphere." Reading, writing, and mathematics all favor logical, sequential processing: left hemisphere functions. Should we teach to the right hemisphere? Although the temptation to teach for right hemispheric involvement is great, research to date remains vague as to how much involvement of either hemisphere is present in the activities of the other, in other words, how much one interferes with the other. Perhaps we can best conclude that acceptance of current findings means accepting the reality of greater or lesser hemispheric activity in any particular activity, but also being aware that human activity, especially learning, entails the commitment of both hemispheres.

One way of integrating current knowledge of lateralization into the curriculum is to become aware of your reliance on verbal directions (Grady, 1984). Most teachers depend heavily on linear tasks, such as having students respond to specific questions or following directions. Try also to present material graphically, in visual form, and encourage students to express their understanding of a topic in a creative manner.

Pattern Matching

Pattern detection and pattern matching seem to be inherent functions of the brain. In fact, some authors (Caine & Caine, 1997) believe that the brain resists having meaningless patterns imposed on it, so it tries to make sense of the stimuli presented to it by seeking patterns!

Hubel (1979), discussing how the brain organizes information (by patterns), noted that at the input end, the brain is primarily preoccupied with extracting from the outside world information that is biologically interesting. At the output end, nerve impulses stimulate behavioral responses. What happens between input and output remains vague, and as Hubel stated, understanding the neural mechanisms that explain perception (pattern matching) remains a major goal.

Commenting on the brain's tendency to match patterns, Hart (1983) stated that the brain detects, constructs, and elaborates patterns as a basic, built-in, natural function. He believes there is no concept, no fact in education that is more important than the brain's pattern-matching function, because it is at the heart of all learning. Caine and Caine (1997) agree with this assertion and have written a book about brain-based learning and how educators can design curricula to take advantage of the brain's proclivity to seek and use patterns to learn.

Hart (1983, p. 67) summarized his thinking about the brain's pattern-matching ability as follows:

- The brain is naturally a pattern matcher, even in infants.

- Pattern matching utilizes both specific elements and relationships and is aided by the effective use of clues.

- Negative clues play an important role, since they instantly alert the brain that "something is wrong."

- The brain uses clues in a probabilistic manner; that is, we use a minimum number of clues to reach a correct decision or solution.

- Pattern matching depends on the experience an individual brings to any situation; the more clues the person recognizes, the quicker is the match.

- Patterns are continually changing to meet the demands of new experiences.

Since the human brain seems predisposed to search for patterns, teachers can help students to improve their classroom performance by using what we know of pattern matching. One technique is to have them develop chronological pattern guides. For example, after students have read a story (or page or paragraph), give them a mixed series of statements and ask them to arrange these statements in the order in which they appeared in the story. Students react well to such exercises, because they are predisposed to identify patterns. Teaching that attempts to present information in a way that helps their brains to extract patterns—as is found in an integrated curriculum, thematic teaching, and the current use of whole language—helps students to make sense of what they are learning (Caine & Caine, 1997).

Biological Basis of Learning

Regardless of hemispheric lateralization and our efforts to capitalize on current findings, we can safely state that classroom learning finds its biological base in the cerebral cortex. For the successful functioning of such complex mental processes as perception, cognition, and decision making, perfectly tuned and smoothly operating synapses are essential.

PLASTICITY

Resiliency or flexibility shown by humans.

Human beings show amazing resiliency or flexibility (which is the meaning of **plasticity**); recovery from injury has been a well-documented fact of biological and psychological research. Yet there are limits to plasticity, and thus we are faced with a puzzle: Under what conditions will children and adults recover from damage? As you can well imagine, the research and literature that have addressed this problem are enormous.

What seems to distinguish the human brain is the variety of specialized activities it is capable of learning. The difficulty still facing investigators lies in the unexplored gap between the psychological reality of learning and knowledge about the structure, biochemistry, and physiology of the brain. One possible approach to bridging this gap is to determine whether brain cells undergo change because of learning.

Hyden (1985) discovered that, in animals, both brain cells and their synapses show an increase in protein production during and after learning. Hyden believed that a "wave of protein synthesis" pervades the brain at learning; that is, system changes occur in brain cell protein during learning. He then hypothesized that when learning begins, inner and outer stimuli cause electrical changes in the nervous system that induce the production of specific proteins in the brain. Calcium production also increases.

What also should interest us are the developmental changes that occur in brain structures and size, the number of connections, and changes in such brain support systems as the glial cells. The growth of intellectual capacity in our students strongly appears to match the brain's anatomical and biochemical changes. Although this match still lacks biological proof, the fact that the brain's role in learning and cognition seems well established testifies to the need for a comprehensive theory of thinking to acknowledge a brain basis.

For example, teachers know that some students prefer to learn with noise surrounding them, or while they move around, talk to others, or just fidget. They don't act in this manner to irritate a teacher. They are, however, responding to signals from their central nervous systems (Garger, 1990). Frequently, a student's approach to learning (for example, wanting to listen to music while studying) is a neurophysiological response.

INFORMATION PROCESSING AND THE ACQUISITION OF KNOWLEDGE

INFORMATION PROCESSING

A process of information gathering that encompasses such topics as attention, perception, thinking, memory, and problem-solving strategies.

As we begin to examine specific aspects of cognition, the significance of information processing for both teachers and students becomes more apparent. Think of **information processing** as encompassing such topics as attention, perception, thinking, memory, and problem-solving strategies. Representation lies at the very heart of information processing.

Perceiving and translating the world around them are advanced cognitive skills that many people do automatically.

Its importance for teachers becomes apparent from observing student behavior. How many times, when you have observed a fellow student answer a teacher's question, have you said to yourself, "I wonder what he's thinking?" or asked yourself, "Now, how could she have arrived at that answer?"

Cognitive psychologists are attempting to discover techniques that will allow us to analyze students' thinking, which, if successful, could have positive and far-reaching implications for both understanding learning and improving instruction. It seems reasonable to assume that students have ideas and use symbols; however, translating these simple statements into testable situations demands that researchers explore the domain of representation: symbols, schemata, images, ideas, and their interactions.

The Meaning of Representation

The manner in which information is recorded or expressed is a representation of that information (Glass et al., 1987). The simple word *car* is a representation, because it represents a certain idea; the idea conveyed can also be represented in different ways: *auto, automobile,* or *motor car.* In each example, however, the information represented remains the same. This common represented information is called the content of the representation; the different ways that the information can be expressed are called the representational codes.

The way students represent the material they encounter in the classroom raises important issues for both curriculum and instruction. We appear to use two types of codes for representing information: mental imagery and verbal processing (Foster, 1986).

Stop for a moment and think about the last time you went to the beach. Were there waves? Was the beach crowded? What color was the water? Answering these questions takes you into the world of mental imagery, a world that has long intrigued philosophers and psychologists. You undoubtedly formed a "picture in your mind" to answer each of the questions. Your **mental image** represented or resembled the waves, the people at the beach, the color of the water. If you think about your answers, you will sooner or later question the accuracy of your image. Just how precise is it? Was the water exactly that blue-green color you recall? Though almost all of us use mental imagery, today's psychologists are concerned with the reliability of our reports.

MENTAL IMAGE

A conscious representation of previous perceptions in any sense modality, less vivid and not finely detailed as a picture.

Paivio (1974), a researcher of mental imagery, asked his study participants to imagine two clocks whose times were 12:05 and 9:15. Then he asked them on which clock the hands formed the larger angle. You think about this question for a moment. How did you answer the question? Didn't you form an image of each clock similar to the following? Paivio's participants reported that they had formed pictures of the clocks; they also needed more time to answer if the angles were similar, as in a comparison of 12:05 and 1:10.

Another example of mental images can be found in the work of Kosslyn (1980), who attempted to have readers get an intuitive feeling for the topic by trying to answer the following questions: What shape are a German shepherd's ears? Is a tennis ball larger than a pear? Does a bee have a dark head? Is a Christmas tree darker green than a frozen pea? Most people report that they mentally picture the named objects in the course of trying to answer these questions.

Any discussion of imagery must reckon with the widespread conviction that a visual image is a picture in our memory, much as a snapshot is stored in a photo album (Kosslyn, 1980). Yet an image is not like a picture stored in memory, waiting to be retrieved. Imagine a tiger. How many stripes does it have? You may have difficulty with this notion; it is difficult to "pull" a tiger picture from memory and count its stripes. Images are abstract, while pictures are linked to the visual properties of actual objects.

Our general knowledge can distort our images (Anderson, 1985). In one study, participants were told that a drawing of two circles connected by a straight line was a dumbbell; others were told that it was eyeglasses. When asked to draw the object from memory, the individuals who had been given the label "eyeglasses" often bent the connecting line. Those persons who were given the label "dumbbell" strengthened or doubled the connecting line. Anderson interpreted these results to indicate that the participants' general knowledge distorted their memories of the physical properties of the objects. Reproducing an actual picture would not result in such distortions.

Thus, though image may be difficult to define, Anderson (1985) specified several properties of images:

- Images represent continuously varying information.

- Images possess the capability of responding to certain mental operations (for example, we can "rotate" them: imagine a cat's face, now its tail).

- Images are not linked to a "picture" of the object but are part of our representational system.

- Images often change because of the knowledge that we possess (recall the dumbbell experiment).

Unlike mental imagery, **verbal processing** does not resemble in any way what it represents. Language is a good example: In no way does the word *car* resemble an actual automobile. The distinction between mental imagery and verbal processing has classroom significance. Consider that although most people use both codes, individuals typically prefer one over the other. If teachers can determine which code each of their students prefer, then teachers can use instructional methods that match preferred codes whenever possible. For example, several methods described in the next chapter are designed to help students with their memories. Some of these methods, such as *rehearsal,* emphasize verbal processes; others, such as *method of loci* or *paired associations,* emphasize mental imagery.

The Role of Perception in Learning

Our ability to recognize the familiar and to realize what we do not know is **perception.** Perceiving something means that you can recall past experiences with this person, object, or event; you experience meaning; and you have certain expectations about the person, object, or event. Consequently, perception seems to entail more than just the ability to react to something; considerable processing is necessary to integrate multiple sources of information into a single representation.

PERCEPTION

The process or act of perceiving information and making sense of it.

Human beings do not respond to elements in our environments on an item-by-item basis. In this regard, cognitive psychologists have learned much from the early Gestaltists. For example, examine the following figure.

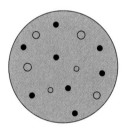

What do you see? Undoubtedly your reply would be something like, "I see a circle with dots and smaller circles inside it." You would not say, "I see one dot, and another dot, and another dot, and a small circle, and another small circle, and a big circle." You grouped the stimuli and expressed your answer in some related manner. You used your past experience by combining it with this present experience.

When someone asks you what time it is, do you carefully observe all of the minute markings on your watch? No. Your past experience enables you to ignore the irrelevant and concentrate on the section where the hands and numbers are.

Human beings organize the relevant stimuli, and ignore the irrelevant, moving them into the background, thus creating a figure-ground relationship. The more prominent qualities of the stimulus pattern emerge more clearly (as a figure), and the less prominent qualities recede (into the background). In the example of telling time, the hands resting on the minute markings representing the time form the figure while the remainder of the face of the watch is the ground.

Perception is the giving of meaning to the discrete, meaningless stimuli that initially arouse awareness. The meaning that an individual gives to any stimulus depends upon the manner in which that person patterns it. For example, a young boy hears a sound. From his past experiences he realizes that it is a whistle. As he continues to relate this stimulus to his experience, perceptual meaning becomes richer. He notes the time element; the whistle always blows at seven o'clock, morning and evening. Passing through town one evening at seven o'clock, he hears the whistle from the fire station. He has located its source. When he hears it from now on, he will identify it as the seven o'clock whistle coming from the firehouse.

The way stimuli are structured determines the quality of the perception and, ultimately, the concept. The strong reaction against history as the memorization of dates, and against geography as the memorization of places, is negative proof of the importance of perceptual meaning. When a subject is presented as a mass of sheer facts, students are unable to form patterns and establish meaningful relations among the stimuli, or to link them with their own past experiences. The result is a distorted concept of all aspects of history and geography, and a distressing tendency to avoid these subjects later in life.

Teachers should use materials that form meaningful patterns for youngsters. Only then can we hope to encourage students to see the value of a particular subject and help them to make its topics more meaningful. This in itself is no easy chore; it requires a thorough knowledge of individual students. But the effort is richly rewarded when students acquire awareness and begin to discern meaning in their schoolwork.

We have emphasized that perception is a crucial element in learning. The sensory experiences that students have are not just mechanically registered and then filed away. Incoming information merges with past information, and with similar experiences; these all combine with present physiological and psychological states to produce a particular perception (Speth & Brown, 1988). Perception, then, depends on both learning and maturation.

Almost from birth, children react to patterns of stimuli as they perceive them at the moment. Learning, maturation, emotions, needs, and values are all intertwined in perception. In one classic study (Bruner & Goodman, 1947), several 10-year-old children from poor families and a like number from upper-income families were asked to estimate the size of coins. The experimenters first showed the youngsters coins ranging in value from a penny to a half dollar and then asked them to duplicate the coin sizes by adjusting a knob that projected circles onto a screen. The circle on the screen could be made larger or smaller. Interestingly, the poor children greatly overestimated the sizes of the coins; the value they placed on them affected their perceptions. The youngsters from upper-income families only slightly overestimated the coin sizes.

How does a student proceed from a gross reaction to a discriminated response? In Figure 7.4 a gradually more detailed pattern of a face is given. Older individuals often identify it as a face as soon as they see the second figure, while some students of even third- or fourth-grade age are unable to identify it until the last line is drawn. Why? What delays the recognition? The older students, because of their experiences, added the necessary details themselves. (The ability to perform these closure tasks is a good predictor of reading readiness.)

Fantz (1961, 1963) indicated that newborn infants not only see but also have preference for certain patterns. He studied eighteen infants under five days old by placing them in the bottom of a test chamber. At the top of the chamber was an illuminated slot into which cards could be placed, and a peephole next to the slot that en-

FIGURE 7.4

Gradual differentiation of a face.

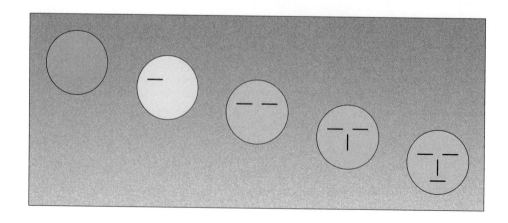

abled the investigator to observe the infant's eyes. When the image was established in the eye, the length of time the infant focused on a particular color, pattern, or form was recorded. The infant was given a range of choices: a schematic face; a patch of newsprint; a bull's-eye; and a red, a white, and a yellow circle. The infants looked longest at facial patterns, then at the newsprint, and then at the bull's-eye. None looked longest at the circles.

What can we conclude from these results? We cannot conclude that there is any instinctive reaction to the human face. But the experiment seems to suggest that there are definite properties in the visual world of the infant, because visual attention focuses earlier on patterns than on color differences. If this is so (and all evidence supports this conclusion), then perceptual training should commence much earlier in life, since children show an early readiness for perception.

For classroom purposes, it is especially significant that developmental changes occur in the attainment of perceptual acuity. Your answers to the four questions in Figure 7.5 will demonstrate the perceptual phenomena involved in these developmental changes.

In examining these illustrations, you probably answered as follows:

- Three figures of XO. (You grouped them.)

- You probably identified B as the larger. (Objective measurement reveals that they are identical; the surrounding elements affected your perception of the middle circle.)

- You probably saw an O in the first illustration and an X in the second. (The difference between the central figure and its surrounding elements is so striking that you focused on the central figure.)

- Your first reaction was probably to say line b was longer. (Measurement shows that they are the same length.)

The main point that we wish to emphasize is that perceptual learning allows students to make finer and finer discriminations, so that they can make more and more fine-grained analysis of stimuli. Younger students are more easily confused (they may,

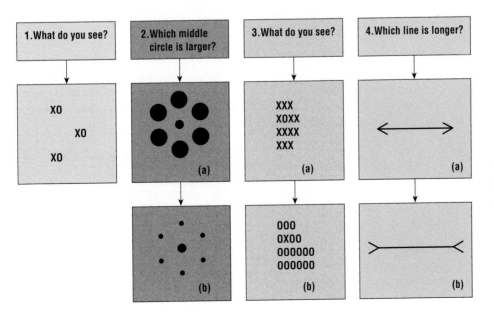

FIGURE 7.5

Perceptual learning involves making discriminations.

for example, confuse b with d), but they gradually get better at interpreting complex stimulus patterns. The task then becomes one of aiding them to acquire perceptual acuity as early as possible, since this is a capacity they possess almost from birth (Foster, 1986). For example, many of the skills that a child must master in school (such as reading) require accurate discriminations and competence in detecting the unchanging nature of stimulus patterns (like letters) in spite of possible surface changes (words). A teacher's knowledge of the perceptual process would aid in both the construction of suitable curriculum materials and the nature of instruction.

Teachers can capitalize on their students' tendency to group; that is, students want to organize and structure, and you can help them by recalling certain principles:

1. People tend to group by familiar objects. What do you see in the following figure? Most people report seeing two groups of circles, not ten isolated figures.

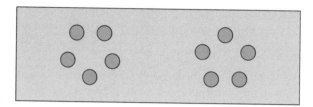

2. Objects that are similar form natural groups. What do you see in the following figure? Most people report seeing a group of crosses and two circles because they grouped similar things.

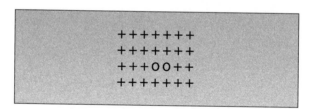

These basic perceptual principles aid in meaningful learning because through them, students can organize material. We cannot overemphasize the importance of meaning and structure to students. Human beings often experience difficulty in thinking and problem solving because "facts" are buried by their surroundings—they are "camouflaged." Can you find the digit 4 in the following diagram?

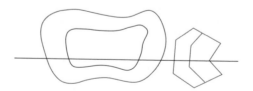

It is buried within unfamiliar shapes, so you may have a little trouble finding it. If you do have trouble, see the following diagram.

Students often have similar trouble discovering and finding meaning within unfamiliar subjects. Students' past experiences should be used to form cognitive schemata in their efforts to master new materials, solve problems, and look at subjects more creatively.

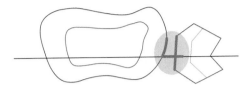

Categorizing Information to Better Understand It

Students interact successfully with their environments according to their ability to organize information. Placing objects into categories and then inventing a name for the category is one of the fundamental organizing activities in which all students engage. The words *book, pupil, teacher, car, doll,* and *water* are examples of the human tendency to categorize. With this skill, you avoid the necessity of responding separately to each and every object in your environment. For example, when you hear the word *book,* you need not seek an actual book to ascertain its characteristics. If you have a concept of book, you have placed this recent utterance in a category with other similar objects that are made of bound sheets and have pages with words and illustrations. Upon hearing "book," you recall the concept that includes the common properties of that category.

Bruner, Goodnow, and Austin (1956) summarized the importance of categorizing information; their insights, although dated, have stood the test of time and are worth repeating today:

1. *Categorizing reduces the complexity of the environment.* Abstraction enables students to group objects, and then students gradually respond to classes of objects rather than responding to each and every thing they encounter.

2. *Categorizing permits us to identify the objects of the world.* We identify objects by placing them in a class, and when similar objects are met, we can say, "Ah, there is another one of those little redheaded Venusians."

3. *Categorizing allows humans to reduce their need of constant learning.* Each time we experience an object, we are not forced to form a new category; we merely categorize with no additional learning. This object has attributes X, Y, Z; therefore, it belongs to the category entitled car.

4. *Categorizing provides direction for instrumental activity.* When we see a road sign that reads Danger Ahead, we alter our driving to meet the anticipated conditions. We become more alert, proceed more cautiously, and drive more slowly.

5. *Categorizing encourages the ordering and relating of classes.* Since we react to systems and patterns, once we place an object in a category, we vastly increase the possibilities of establishing relationships for that particular object. For example, once students decide on the characteristics of the "good" president, they can then match any president to this category.

"I don't get it! They make us learn reading, writing, and arithmetic to prepare us for a world of videotapes, computer terminals, and calculators!"

H. Schwadron in Phi Delta Kappan.

This classic view of how we organize information (to form categories or concepts) has come under considerable revision, so that today a new interpretation is widely accepted. The impetus for this development began with research into how we name colors.

If you think about it, there is no clear rationale for the color names that we have designated, since color is actually on a continuum. We arbitrarily divide color as we see fit. A question that intrigued cognitive psychologists was: Does the manner in which we label things structure the way that we classify them? Brown and Lenneberg (1954), showed English-speaking study participants twenty-four colors and asked them to label the colors. Those colors readily named were called codable. Another group of participants was shown a small set of colors and then a large set, and asked to specify which ones they had seen in the small set. Individuals readily recognized those colors that the researchers had identified as codable.

The matter rested there until 1973, when Rosch, studying a Stone Age tribe in New Guinea that had only two color terms (one for bright, one for dark), discovered that although her research participants had difficulty identifying by name the intermediate colors, they showed the same recognition characteristics as had the English-speaking participants (that is, they remembered what colors they had seen in the small early set when viewing the later larger set). Thus, differences in naming between the two cultures did not reflect differences in memory storage: Cognitive processing determined the color categories they formed. Upon her return to the United States and with continued experimentation, Rosch (Mervis & Rosch, 1981) concluded that her discoveries concerning color categories extended throughout the classification process to explain how we form all categories. The classic theory of classification described at the beginning of this section holds that a category consists of certain definite criteria. If an object possesses these criteria, it belongs to that category; if it lacks the defining criteria, it must be a member of another category. But Rosch's work leads us to believe that it is not the objects themselves that create objective categories, but active human cognitive processing that creates these categories.

Not all categories, however, possess neat, defining sets of criteria. Gardner (1985, p. 345) noted that some categories are better identified by the actions that they signify. For example, a "drinking vessel" is defined by its potential for being held and drunk from. These and similar difficulties caused Rosch to propose an explanation that cuts across many natural categories. The explanatory concept she proposed is called a *prototype*, which contains not clearly defined critical attributes, but a common standard form (Glass, Holyoak, & Santa, 1987, pp. 343–345). For example, though technically both chickens and robins are birds, most people would state that the robin is a more typical example of a bird; it is more natural; it is a prototype for a bird.

What does this change in thinking about categorizing or classification mean for teachers? It probably reinforces what teachers have been doing intuitively for years. When teaching an idea, or concept, good teachers never have their students memorize long lists of attributes that best describe it. Rather, they consistently give examples, and they compare the concept to other categories that do not include it. Good teachers generally appeal to information in a child's natural world and do not depend solely on artificial criteria.

Concepts are vital to thinking, reasoning, and perceiving relationships. The quality of a student's concepts is the best measure of probable success in learning, because meaning is basic to learning. Also, concepts determine what we know, believe, and do. Concepts, then, are vital to all phases of life. They order the environment, add depth to perceptual relationships, clarify thinking, and, particularly, facilitate the entire learning process. Meaningful concepts are also a great aid to memory.

Memory at Work

Acquiring concepts in itself is not enough; we want our students to remember what they acquire. In the late 1960s and 1970s, the study of memory attracted considerable attention among cognitive psychologists. An analysis of memory that cognitive psychologists widely accepted was the distinction made between episodic and semantic memory (Tulving, 1972).

TIPS ON COMMUNICATION
Teaching New Concepts and Making Connections among Ideas

PRINCIPLE A concept is a fundamental element of knowledge and facilitates mental representations of ideas. Concepts function as building blocks of knowledge and communication of knowledge to others. Remember that concepts are only as valuable as the meanings they convey. Be careful that you do not accept the symbol alone as evidence that students have attained a concept. You should continually probe to guarantee that meaning is associated with the symbol. For example, students probably can define the concept, but can they describe it, give examples, and explain the various types (Wilson, 1987)?

STRATEGY Provide varied experiences for the learner. Students should encounter the concept under different conditions. Where possible they should see and feel and talk about it, connecting the object with as many senses as possible. Learners should occasionally encounter negative examples of the concept. That is, some negative examples are effective, if mixed with many positive, clear instances.

STRATEGY Utilize assorted methods of presenting the concept. Different techniques of presentation are most efficient. Teachers cannot be satisfied with one method, whether it is telling, discovery, or reading. A combination of methods is definitely indicated.

STRATEGY Encourage students to apply the concept. Once students have partially attained the concept, they should begin to use it. They should read it and explain it; they should furnish it as a missing word; they should use it to solve problems. Above all, if they are to use it outside the classroom, teachers should supply experiences that are not routinely educational. Students must realize that they can use it at home, work, or play; that is exactly what is meant by the maxim that concepts aid in the economical adjustment to the environment.

STRATEGY Relate the concept or category to your students' prior knowledge in a systematic manner. Encourage students to think about how they organize their knowledge about a particular set of concepts or categories. For example, if they are studying about metals such as silver and gold, have them relate this content to existing information they may have about minerals. Depending on the students' prior knowledge and schemata about metals, they may find the hierarchical organization (like that illustrated in Figure 7.6) similar to their own organized schemata. If not, such a graphic organizer should facilitate further inquiries and learning. In some cases in which hierarchical organization of information is not known or readily apparent, encourage students to create their own subjective representations of information (Baddeley, 1990).

Episodic memory is recall of personal experiences within a specific context or period of time. Think of it as autobiographical; episodic memory provides an individual with a personal history. Here are some examples:

- John and I watched the Red Sox play the Yankees last Friday night.

- I saw Harrison Ford play Indiana Jones in "The Temple of Doom" when it first opened in San Francisco.

EPISODIC MEMORY
The recall of personal experiences within a specific context or period of time.

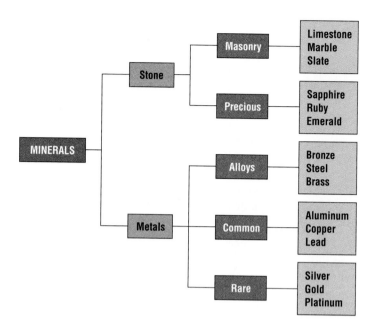

FIGURE 7.6

A conceptual hierarchy for the concept of minerals.

SEMANTIC
MEMORY

Memory necessary for the use of language.

Semantic memory is the memory necessary for the use of language, a kind of dictionary without reference to our personal experiences that represents our general knowledge. It is the organized knowledge that a person possesses about words and other verbal symbols. Here are examples:

- I know Madison is the capital of Wisconsin.

- I know *friend* is an acceptable English word.

Note that we can verify the accuracy of semantic memory. Written testimony (geography books, state and federal listings) attest to the truthfulness of the statement that Madison is the capital of Wisconsin. No such tests exist for episodic memory.

In a particularly influential model of episodic memory, Atkinson and Shiffrin (1968) proposed a three-store system: the sensory register, the short-term store, and the long-term store. These three stores are structurally distinct because they hold information differently, for varying times, and for different purposes. The authors also stated that the three stores lose information differently. Figure 7.7 illustrates a multistore model.

SENSORY
REGISTER

The ability, which is highly selective, to hold information in memory for a brief period.

The **sensory register** holds input in almost the same form as the sensory image; that is, cognitive processes do not begin to alter data until after they pass through the sensory register. Information is lost from the register in less than a second, either through spontaneous decay or through the entry of new data. The sensory register momentarily preserves information so that it can be selectively transmitted into the memory system. The selective character of the sensory register prevents us from being overwhelmed by sensory input. For example, what attracts the attention of some students does not do so with others.

SHORT-TERM
STORE

The working memory; consciousness is involved.

The **short-term store** is the working memory, which entails conscious processes. Input to the short-term store comes from both the sensory register and the long-term store, both of which feed data to the short-term store for conscious manipulation. Information can be held indefinitely here if attention remains constant; otherwise, decay commences and data are lost in fifteen to thirty seconds. The critical nature of the short-term store lies

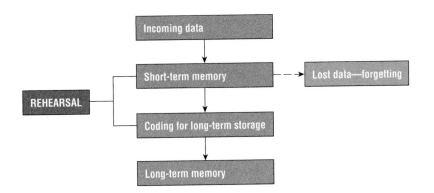

FIGURE 7.7

An early multistore model.

in its conscious content; neither the sensory register nor the long-term store entails consciousness. The longer information remains in the short-term store, the greater is the chance that it will be transmitted to the long-term store.

The **long-term store** holds both conscious and unconscious data. For example, you can recall how the clams tasted at a beach cookout when you were a child. You probably still talk about the smell of the kitchen when an apple pie was baking. Although information may be stored indefinitely, data may be lost (through interference, lack of retrieval cues, perhaps even sheer decay). The significance of long-term memory lies in its survival and adaptation value; humans require an enormous amount of information to survive in modern society.

Consequently, the more meaningful teachers can make material for their students, the better students will relate it to their own experiences. The more successful teachers are in motivating their students, the greater the level of understanding, since students will select their information from the sensory register, keep it active in the short-term store, and transfer it to the long-term store.

Although multistore models of memory have a neatness and elegance that many find appealing, the interests of most cognitive scientists are shifting away from this view (Baddeley, 1990). Several cognitivists have advocated a **levels of processing** analysis (Craik & Lockhart, 1972), which focuses on the depth of processing. Information is not transformed by moving through a series of stores. Data are processed by various operations called perceptual-conceptual analysis.

The perceptual-conceptual analysis reflects an individual's attention. If you deem incoming material worthy of long-term recall, you will analyze it differently from material you judge as relatively unimportant. Whether the stimulus is processed at a shallow level or at a deeper level depends on the nature of the stimulus; the time available for processing; and the person's own motivation, goals, and knowledge base. Thus, the operations performed during input determine the fate of the incoming information.

Consequently, the initial processing of a word will determine the length of time students remember it and which aspects are remembered. For example, if you are interested only in the color of a word's printed letters, you will not remember that word as you would if you had examined the word for its meaning (Sherry & Schachter, 1987).

Recognition, Recall, and Forgetting

Basic questions about memory remain to be answered: Why do we forget? Do all individuals experience the same types of problems with memory? Are there specific types of memory problems? Are they related? How exactly do we memorize? How can we become skillful at remembering (Neisser, 1982)? As a result of decades of research, speculation, and common-sense reasoning, certain generalizations are possible. Among them are the following:

LONG-TERM STORE

The aspect of memory that holds both conscious and unconscious data for long periods of time; related to meaningfulness of material.

LEVELS OF PROCESSING

Describes analysis of memory focusing on the depth at which humans process information.

- Similarity of material can cause interference.

- Personally meaningful material aids recall.

- Time on task helps students to remember.

- Rehearsal (going over something repeatedly) is an important memory strategy.

- Mnemonic strategies can help students remember.

Before proceeding further, we should pause to make some basic distinctions that will help to clarify this potentially complex topic.

In the study of memory, it is important that you distinguish between **storage** and **retrieval.** Storage implies "putting information into" memory, which occurs as a result of attending, encoding, and the use of memory strategies. Retrieval, on the other hand, implies recognizing, recalling, and reconstructing what has previously been "put in."

For example, students may have memorized the names of the major battles of the Civil War on Monday, but on Wednesday some of the class can't recall them. The teacher then furnishes a cue. "Henry, how would you describe the tip of your pencil?" "It's sharp, Miss Smith. Oh, I get it. Sharpesville is the name." This student knew the name but couldn't retrieve it without help. Two other topics that have special relevance for the classroom are recognition and recall.

If you think for a moment, you will quickly realize the importance of these concepts for the classroom. In teaching, teachers constantly appeal to students' basic knowledge; teachers are asking students to recognize something familiar in a new work that they are teaching. In testing, teachers want students to recognize familiar cues in the questions. Academic success or failure is closely tied to both recognition and recall.

Recognition is the act of comparing a present, incoming representation with a representation already stored in memory. Is the number of your apartment 29? You have just performed a recognition task; note that you were not asked to recall the number of your apartment, but to compare it to 29.

Three major elements are involved in recognition: similarity, prior experience, and expectation and context. The need for similarity seems obvious: We probably will not recognize something we have never encountered before, or something familiar in a radically altered form—for example, a friend at a costume party. But as essential as it seems, the notion of *similarity* can lead to difficulty in the classroom. If you use multiple-choice questions, the alternate answers you select, if too similar to the correct one, can hinder recognition. *Prior experience* refers to the frequency and recency of encounters with the object, event, or person. Repeated exposures exercise a strong impact on recognition. The term *expectation and context* refers to the expectation of meeting certain things or people in certain circumstances. For example, youngsters in the early grades are almost always surprised to meet their teachers in the supermarket. They do not expect to see them in these circumstances. The expectations that arise from context, of course, are not limited to elementary school youngsters. A continuing frustration for teachers is the inability, almost refusal, of some students to recognize and apply mathematical principles anywhere but in math classes. Different context; different expectations.

What are the names of the Great Lakes? Who won the 1986 World Series? Who was the president of the United States before Lyndon Johnson? These questions force you to recall information. Recall goes beyond recognition, because you are not given a "copy" of the representation. Any retrieval cue is minimal; consequently, students must generate their own cues in their search for the necessary information. For a search to be effective, the information sought must have been stored in a reasonably organized manner; otherwise, the target information remains elusive and recall usually falters. Again we note the importance of a schema or organizational property for understanding cognitive processes.

STORAGE

The act of putting information into memory.

RETRIEVAL

The act of recognizing, recalling, and reconstructing what we have previously stored in memory.

RECOGNITION

The act of comparing an incoming representation with a representation already in memory.

Forgetting, unfortunately, is a normal process and here does not refer to an abnormal loss of memory occasioned by aging, shock, or brain injury. Under normal daily conditions, what causes your students to forget previously acquired material? Theorists have proposed several explanations (Sherry & Schachter, 1987):

- Forgetting as disuse or fading. Once they have learned it, students will forget an item unless they use it. This explanation of forgetting has been referred to as the *trace decay hypothesis* (Ebbinghaus, 1885). Deterioration of the information develops and learning slowly fades. Though this is still a popular belief, today psychologists question it. For example, if individuals memorize a list of words to errorless recall, and then wait for various lengths of time before testing, they experience loss as illustrated by the retention curve in Figure 7.8.

The exact details of the curve may vary depending on the nature of the material, the degree of overlearning, and other material studied between the time of learning and the time of recall. But note two aspects that have important implications for teaching:

- The rapid decline of information recalled after initial learning.
- The stability of the portion of retained materials with increasing time.

Other possible interpretations of the forgetting (or retention) curve exist. Certain skills, such as riding a bicycle, swimming, and ice skating, show remarkable endurance. Even some verbal material is not quickly forgotten. You probably recall several lines from an elementary school play or show while forgetting something you learned last semester; decay over time does not explain this. Other variables, such as motivation, also must influence retention. Still, time exacts its toll, and you should consider this when teaching by conducting periodic, meaningful reviews with students. Thus, some of the other explanations for forgetting can be summarized as:

- Motivated forgetting, or repressed forgetting. Unquestionably, you have had experiences that you try to forget because of the unpleasantness, fear, or anxiety

FORGETTING
The loss of previously acquired material from memory.

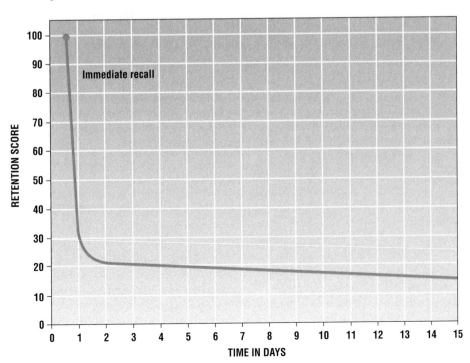

FIGURE 7.8

The curve of retention.

associated with them. If experiences are sufficiently severe, amnesia (partial or total loss of memory) results. The extent of repression as a cause of normal forgetting remains unestablished because of the lack of experimental control that can be introduced.

- Forgetting because of interference. Psychologists agree that most forgetting happens because new learning interferes with past learning. Interference can be either retroactive (the interference is produced by learning that occurs after the memory event) or proactive (it is produced by learning that occurred prior to the memory event) (Ellis & Hunt, 1993).

- Forgetting because of extinction and reorganization. Because of disuse and a lack of reinforcement, students forget a response. When forced to recall it, they apply newly acquired experiences and undoubtedly reshape the original response, so that it may or may not suit the original stimulus. We have seen an example of this situation in the exercise using "The War of the Ghosts," earlier in this chapter.

Given the present understanding of the forgetting and retention phenomenon, what are some specific measures teachers can adopt to aid students' storage and retrieval? First, repeatedly urge students to remember. This suggestion refers not to obvious exhortation, but to student self-activity, whereby material acquires both meaning and personal significance—it is organized and stored. For example, overlearning aids memory because it more sharply distinguishes the item to be stored and facilitates coding, which lowers the possibility of **negative transfer** (when something a person learns at one time hinders his or her learning or performance at a later time) and increases the possibility of **positive transfer** (when something a person learns in one situation helps him or her learn or perform in another situation). Another suggestion to diminish forgetting is to encourage comprehension, not mere mastery of facts. Such understanding depends on the kind of material presented and how you present it. Words are remembered better than nonsense syllables, and solutions of problems are better remembered than isolated facts. Try to guide students to perceive and use relationships within the material and between the topics and their own backgrounds.

Given that much of what students must remember is based on material they read, there are several strategies for increasing comprehension of written material. These include the following (Pressley & Harris, 1990): (a) summarization, or creating a representation of the central idea; (b) imagery, or constructing an internal visual representation of text content; (c) story grammar, or identifying the setting, problem, goal, action, and outcome in a story; (d) prior knowledge activation, or having students relate what they already know to the content of the text; (e) self-questioning, or devising questions that help to integrate the content being read; and (f) question-answer, or teaching students to analyze questions carefully as a way of helping them to respond.

Another critical aspect to minimizing forgetting is providing distributed practice rather than mass practice and ensuring that overlearning occurs. It is better to teach ten foreign language words a day for five days than to force memorization of all fifty words in a single period. The periodic review of lecture notes is more effective than cramming.

Forgetting also is reduced when one conducts periodic reviews. Review soon after learning and at short intervals, gradually widening the lengths of time between reviews. Reviews need not consist of dogmatic, formal sessions. Quizzes, assignments, and use of material are effective review techniques. Periodic reviews are especially significant considering the retention curve, which dramatically illustrated the initial loss of learning. Meaningful reviews are an excellent tool to overcome this loss.

NEGATIVE
TRANSFER

When something a person learns at one time hinders their learning or performance at a later time.

POSITIVE
TRANSFER

When something a person learns in one situation helps them learn or perform in another situation.

Finally, reduce interference in learning situations. Recall that some things you learned previously can interfere with new learning (proactive) and some things you learn after new material can interfere with recall of the new material (retroactive). This is referred to the proactive-retroactive inhibition paradigm. Teachers, and especially administrators, should try to schedule subjects that reinforce and not interfere with each other. After a history class involving complicated names, dates, and places, you would probably not want to move into a discussion of Henry V in an English class, if you can help it.

For teachers, the customary method of recall is to ask students to retrieve information in its original form. If teachers present cues (questions) different from the form in which the information was originally stored, students experience much greater difficulty. Consequently, teachers should use questions carefully, so that they may help students to acquire a method of problem solving or to think creatively. To demand recall in the original form is to promote convergent thinking (often but not always a needed and desired technique) at the expense of divergent or creative thinking. Try to encourage both types of thinking—convergent at the introduction of a topic, when mastery of facts is required, and divergent once facts have been acquired and problem solving and creativity can be encouraged.

If students rapidly learn a large amount of nonmeaningful material, they will forget it just as quickly. The rate of loss slows when most of the material has been forgotten. But occasionally a surprising phenomenon seems to occur: After a rest period, there may be an actual gain in retention. For example, after thirty minutes of studying twenty spelling words, students may be able to spell fifteen of them correctly. Yet, the next morning, they may spell seventeen correctly. This **reminiscence** is hard to explain. Is it true learning, or is it the product of faulty experimentation? There are two possible causes of reminiscence:

REMINISCENCE
The phenomenon that after rest, memory seems to improve.

1. Fatigue developed during the original learning and affected retention, which then improved after rest.

2. The experiment was faulty because the initial test of retention was actually another learning experience that aided performance in the next test of retention.

Another important feature of memory relates to the position of items to be memorized. Students learn items at the beginning and end of any memory task much more easily than they do the middle elements. Undoubtedly this is a function of interference; isolated items in these lists are learned more readily and retained longer. What can teachers do to help students with those difficult middle sections? One technique is to furnish some organization or structure to which they can relate them. For example, ask students to select two or three words in a middle section that have particular meaning for them and have them use these words as clues, or have them imagine a picture related to the section, or use some words to form pictures. This procedure helps to reduce interference, which may produce the phenomenon seen in Table 7.3. Procedure A is the control; there is no interference. Procedure B is retroactive inhibition; that is, new material (Task 2) interferes with previously learned material (Task 1). Procedure C is proactive inhibition; that is, previously learned material interferes with the recall of new material. For example, studying the same historical period in English and history could lead to either proactive or retroactive interference, unless students have formulated a clear structure of the topic in both subjects.

Help to eliminate interference by ensuring that the material to be learned is meaningful and organized. Learning meaningful material to mastery lessens students' susceptibility to interference. If students comprehend the meaning inherent in any content, they learn it more rapidly and retain it longer. The meaningfulness in material depends on either some pattern that the learner recognizes (such as 1, 7, 13, 19, 25, 31) or the familiarity of the material (such as previously learned details).

Table 7.3 THE PROBLEM OF INTERFERENCE

Tasks	Retention
A. Task 1	Test Task 1
B. Task 1 Task 2	Test Task 1
C. Task 1 Task 2	Test Task 2

Students differ in their abilities to remember. Psychologists have become interested in the reasons for these differences and have attempted to discover whether students can learn to improve their performance. These efforts have led to the phenomenon of metacognition, the ability to examine and influence one's own cognitive processes.

Metacognition

Although interest in **metacognition** is relatively recent, its content has always been with us. For example, our thoughts about a decision we have made or about how we are doing on a project all entail metacognitive processes. When we discussed Piaget's stage of formal operations in Chapter 2, we were exploring metacognitive thinking about hypotheses and possibilities.

Metacognitive skills seem to be involved in many classroom cognitive activities: comprehension, evaluation, reading, writing, and problem solving, among others. Discussing metacognition, Flavell (1985) analyzed it as including two domains: metacognitive knowledge and metacognitive experiences. **Metacognitive knowledge** refers to an individual's knowledge and beliefs about cognitive matters, gained from experience and stored in long-term memory (Flavell, 1985, p. 105). Humans acquire metacognitive knowledge about people, tasks, and strategies. In a classroom, metacognitive knowledge of tasks operates when the nature of a task forces us to think about how we'll manage. If it's a difficult task, perhaps we decide to allocate more time, or perhaps to prepare an outline.

METACOGNITIVE
KNOWLEDGE
An individual's knowledge and beliefs about cognitive matters, gained from experiences and stored in long-term memory.

When we discuss memory or learning strategies, cognitive psychologists make a distinction between cognitive strategies (used to achieve goals) and metacognitive strategies (monitoring one's progress toward a goal; monitoring the effectiveness of the cognition strategies being used; monitoring one's level of understanding). Over time, we have all learned much about which strategies are best suited for success on particular tasks. For example, you have a strategy for recalling what you have read in this chapter. This strategy may be simple (repeatedly going over the material) or complex (imagining that you place certain topics in different parts of your house). Since learning strategies can be taught, teachers can help students appreciate the value of a strategy by having them concentrate on just what they do when they must learn.

Derry (1989), in her research on learning strategies, provides us an example of the importance of such strategies. Imagine that you are a student who has arrived at school and discovered that your first period teacher is giving a test on Chapter 5. You mistakenly studied Chapter 4. You have fifteen minutes before the class. How would you most wisely use the time? Derry actually assigned a reading, allowed fifteen minutes, and then tested her students. At the end of the quiz she asked them to describe in detail what they did when they studied. Not many had done well on the quiz. One student who had stated that she initially read the chapter summary and then skimmed the chapter, concentrating on the chapter headings, looking for organization. With the remaining time, she read

To be effective problem solvers, we often must learn to use tools that support our mental processing of information.

the topic sentences in as many paragraphs as possible. Another student, who had done poorly, said he felt panic and started to read through the chapter as fast as he could, but didn't get too far.

Here is a striking example of the difference between successful and unsuccessful learning strategies, or plans used for attaining a goal. By teaching students how to attack a problem, you can do much to improve their achievement.

Metacognitive experiences are either cognitive or affective experiences that relate to cognitive activities. For example, while you are reading this chapter you may feel a little uncertain or doubtful about one of the topics, or you may be quite concerned that you didn't understand it. As Flavell (1985) noted, metacognitive experiences are most likely to occur when careful, conscious monitoring of your cognitive efforts is required. The uncertainty or confidence that you may feel about a topic is tied to relevant metacognitive knowledge.

You can see, then, how valuable these metacognitive experiences can be. If you are puzzled by one of these topics, then your sense of uncertainty will cause you to read the section again, discuss it with other students, or bring up questions in class. By making students aware that they can "think about their thinking," teachers will also help them to improve those cognitive behaviors that can result in better classroom performance.

METACOGNITIVE EXPERIENCES
Cognitive or affective experiences that relate to cognitive activities.

Cognition across Cultures

In their classic analysis *Culture and Thought* (1974), Cole and Scribner provided interesting observations into the cognitive differences among various cultures. Noting that perceptual variations are common among different peoples, Cole and Scribner believed that our modes of responding to stimuli are not "experience-free." Rather, our reactions depend on our past histories of dealing with similar stimuli. Stating that what children "see" in geometric patterns may be related to the actions they are asked to perform (recognize the pattern, copy it, or reconstruct it), Cole and Scribner (1974) believed that different actions require different perceptual information. Consequently, children master their perceptual worlds as they master new activities. An example of this issue can be seen in the authors' work in Liberia. They asked some individuals to sort cards and others to describe the cards. The two groups showed different preferences for stimuli, depending on whether they were asked actually to sort (preference: form) or to describe verbally (preference: color).

With regard to such conceptual processes as classifying, the authors found similar differences. The characteristic used for classifying reflected the nature of the task: how familiar it was; the source of the task (for example, animal or plant); and the form in which it was presented.

CASE NOTES

Observation   Karim and his family value the African American culture. Other students in the class generally are not as aware of their cultural background as Karim.

Hypothesis   Currently Karim's interest in his own culture seems to have created distance between him and his classmates. Yet, this interest and respect for one's culture may be a useful avenue for communicating with Karim and his classmates.

Possible Actions   Encourage all students in the class to identify their families' cultural roots and to discover (a) something unique about their culture and (b) something that is common about their culture and all other cultures. Students should be encouraged to share this information with peers in small-group discussions and in a short paper that focuses on what they are proudest of about their culture. Students could also invite a parent or grandparent to come to class to discuss what role their culture has in their lives.

Classifying processes seem to change with experience. In the Cole and Scribner study (1974), when people moved from an isolated village to a city or town or were exposed to a Western-type education, class membership seemed more important for grouping items. Schooling also contributes in a similar manner to the way in which people describe and explain their own mental operations.

Culture influences how people think, relate, and learn. Consequently, we can too frequently misperceive and misunderstand our students' behavior when we interpret it solely from our own cultural perspective. Cognitive activities occur in cultural situations (such as the classroom) that involve interpretations and values by both teachers and students.

Students who come from racial, ethnic, or socioeconomic backgrounds different from those of their teachers and the school administrators may have values, goals, and interests that are highly acceptable to their families and communities, but not to the school community. Consequently, educators may not be able to accept behavior that the students and their parents find completely appropriate (H. Grossman, 1990, p. 339).

A good example of this difference can be found in the school's expectations and assumptions. Most schools and teachers expect that their students will function cognitively in a verbal and analytic manner (Tharp, 1989). Students who conform to these expectations, such as Japanese American and Chinese American students, are more likely to succeed than students who do not. Their patterns of cognitive functioning "fit" school expectations. Native Americans, on the other hand, perform better on performance and spatial tasks than on verbal ones. Consequently, their achievement may decline in traditional school settings.

To offset these disadvantages, the concept of **contextualized instruction** has been introduced; in this approach, a student's personal experiences in a particular culture are used to introduce new material (Tharp, 1989). Materials that reflect the student's cultural community are utilized to provide a basis for developing school skills. These various levels of contextualization—personal, community, and cultural—seem to result in improved academic performance. For example, Navajos reject the idea that "toughness" is at one extreme of the spectrum of appropriate behavior and "niceness" is at the other. Educators who are

CONTEXTUALIZED
INSTRUCTION

An approach to instruction that uses a student's personal experiences in a particular culture to introduce new material.

unaware of these beliefs can be ineffective in their methods of instruction. The Navajos resist open displays of affection but respect their children's individuality and independence. Thus, certain efforts to control behavior by punishment or obvious rewards violate cultural values and are doomed to failure. Consequently, when teachers embed cultural values in classroom practices, they see greater student participation and higher levels of achievement (Tharp, 1989).

These ideas reflect the tendency to view mental life as consisting of two quite different methods of functioning: logical, abstract, scientific thinking; and narrative thinking, a much more personal kind of thinking that concentrates on people and the causes of their behavior (Bruner, 1986). Thus, stories of their particular cultures greatly influence children, and they make up stories about their own lives; that is, they interpret their lives as stories or narratives (Howard, 1991).

HELPING YOU REMEMBER: AN INTEGRATED SUMMARY

This chapter introduced you to a cognitive perspective on human learning. It stressed that mental representations of information are predicated on an interaction between a learner and the type of stimuli perceived by the learner. Cognitive psychologists today have been influenced by a wide array of theorists, starting with the Gestaltist, who were concerned with how individuals perceived information, to developmentalists like Piaget and Vygotsky, and then to computer scientists, whose work has influenced psychologists' models of information processing.

Constructivism, perhaps the most popular orientation to cognitive psychology today, has many implications for teaching and learning. The basic tenet of constructivism is that learners construct knowledge through the process of adapting to events and ideas they experience. Thus, a learner's environment—teachers, parents, materials, tasks, peers, and physical objects—all influence what and how a person learns. Of course, one's culture influences many of the elements in one's environment, and consequently influences what a learner represents cognitively.

The way learners handle information is referred to as information processing and has been conceptualized in one of two ways. Originally, many cognitive psychologists used a multistore, computerlike model to explain how information passed from a sensory register to short-term and then long-term memory. More recently, a levels of processing model has been used to characterize the processing and memory of information. This general model assumes that the more an individual works with material, that is, the more they attend to it and interact with it in meaningful ways, the more they remember and learn.

Of course, nobody remembers everything, but there are ways to enhance what one remembers. We began investigating aspects of memory and how instructional and study methods can diminish forgetting. We also learned that as students develop, they begin to think about their memory ability, which is referred to as metacognition. Learners who are metacognitive are seen as being strategic, engaged learners.

Finally, we noted that cognition is influenced by the cultural context in which it occurs. This is in effect just a further elaboration on that key concept in this chapter. All learners are seen as interacting with their environment and are motivated to make sense of the information they confront by relating it to what they already know and have experienced. Learners are constructors of knowledge, and their construction sites—cultures, classrooms, and homes—influence how they build their knowledge.

Case Reflections

In this chapter we continued to think about ways Mark Siegel could successfully work with Karim Peterson and Mrs. Peterson. We noted that the work of schema theorists and constructivists seemed very relevant to the reading and motivation to learn deficits exhibited by Karim. In particular, it was hypothesized that Karim's reading comprehension would improve if he had a better mental framework or schema for what he was reading. This might be accomplished if Mark Siegel would do more summarizing, outlining, and labeling of the main ideas of the material he reads. In addition, it was hypothesized that Karim would be more likely to get involved in class if some of the discussion stimulated more cognitive controversy. Given his strong verbal skills, it was suggested that he be encouraged to share his ideas and opinions about topics of interest to him and other students. This activity should cause him to construct an argument from his existing knowledge base and also compare some information generated by others to his knowledge. Finally, in keeping with the belief that culture influences cognitions and the construction of knowledge, it was suggested that Karim and other students be encouraged to explore their cultures and share unique and common aspects of them. This action was hypothesized to be motivating for Karim and also would provide opportunities, via discussions, for social interaction with classmates.

CHAPTER HIGHLIGHTS

The Meaning of Cognitive Psychology

- The concept of representation is basic to an understanding of cognitive psychology. We attend, perceive, and reason, and these cognitive activities affect our behavior.

The Emergence of Cognitive Psychology

- Cognitive psychology has a long and rich tradition, with its roots in many disciplines. Among modern cognitive psychologists, Jerome Bruner has been particularly influential. Bruner's studies on perception and thought have been landmarks in modern cognitive psychology.

Approaches to Learning with a Cognitive Psychology Orientation

- Cognitive constructivism holds that people actively construct their own knowledge. Such knowledge is constructed through the process of adapting to the events and ideas one experiences.

- The construction of knowledge is significantly influenced by one's environment and the symbols and materials one uses.

- Teachers who use a constructivist approach act as facilitators of knowledge and skill acquisition, as a guide or resource person whose purpose is to structure the learning environment. Thus learning can be very individualized and personalized for each student, taking into account one's prior knowledge, interests, and cognitive level and skills.

The Brain and Thinking

- Cognitive psychologists have been interested in mind–brain relationships and the functioning of the brain.

- Pattern detection and pattern matching is an inherent function of the human brain. Knowledge of pattern matching is relevant to some instructional methods and has been part of a development movement referred to as brain-based learning.

Information Processing and the Acquisition of Knowledge

- Representation, which is at the heart of information processing, is the manner in which information is recorded or expressed.

- No matter how data are represented, the information remains the same; this is called the content of representation.

- The different ways that information can be expressed are called the representational codes; these codes may be either mental or verbal.

- Perceiving is an active process demanding our involvement with the objects, events, and people in our environment.

- The active process of perception helps us to receive information from our environment.

- Helping students structure, or organize, their environments aids their perceptual processes, thus furthering learning.

- The better students categorize (form classes and put information in these categories), the more efficient learners they become.

- Studies of memory have long fascinated cognitive psychologists because of memory's critical role in thought and decision making.

Cognition across Cultures

- Researchers have noted there are cognitive differences across cultures. One area in particular where differences have been noted is in the process of classifying information or objects.

- Because culture is perceived to make a difference in how some students learn, the concept of contextualized instruction emerged among cognitive psychologists. In this approach, a student's personal experiences in a particular culture are used to introduce new material.

WHAT DO YOU THINK?

1. Now that you have read about behavioral theories of learning and cognitive theories of learning, which one do you think best explains classroom learning? Which aspects of these different perspectives of learning really makes them different?

2. If you want to teach somebody a new concept, what do you think are the most important steps in the instructional process? List at least three things you would do to increase the likelihood that a student would learn the concept.

3. Think about how you learn best. Does a constructivist approach to learning characterize your activities as a learner? If not, why not?

4. Think about how your memory works. This is part of metamemory. Do you often intentionally think about how you are going to remember something? Does it help you to plan ways to remember information? How can you get students to think about their memory abilities?

eight

Thinking Skills and Problem-Solving Strategies

The topics in this chapter should help to improve Mark Siegel's relationship with Karim Peterson. Thinking skills and problem-solving strategies, when tied tightly to the critical issues in students' lives, can have remarkable motivational qualities.

For example, Karim was having difficulty with thinking skills, which worked against everything he did, especially his classroom achievement. If Mark Siegel could help Karim master thinking & problem-solving skills, he could pose realistic problems for him and guide him in searching for solutions. In this way, he would be not only helping him with a problem, but also aiding him in developing generalized strategies for attacking problems, which would also facilitate a maturing sense of self.

A wonderful book about the theater (and one you would enjoy reading) is Moss Hart's *Act One.* In it, Hart tells of writing his first play in collaboration with the famous and irascible George Kaufman. The play was called *Once in a Lifetime* and in it Hart takes us through the agony of spending an incredible amount of time writing, changing scenes, and rewriting until finally the play was ready for its pre-Broadway debut.

For the first two acts everything went smoothly—people laughed in the right places, enjoying their night out. But suddenly, in act three, they stopped laughing. Something terrible had happened! The play was dying in front of their eyes. Hart and Kaufman tried every rewriting trick they could think of; nothing seemed to help. And two weeks away their Broadway opening beckoned!

And then fate strikes. Dining with a friend, Hart bemoaned the failure of the third act, when his friend, rather casually spoke. "I wish, kid," he sighed, "that this weren't such a noisy play." It was as if a light went on in a dark room. Hart realized that just too much was happening in the third act. He and Kaufman rewrote it; the play was a dazzling success, and Hart took the first step on what was to become a brilliant career.

What does *Act One* have to do with educational psychology? The simple answer is, everything. This brief account of a fascinating book highlights the topics we'll be discussing in this chapter: thinking, problem solving, creativity, and transfer. We selected this example to illustrate the practical nature of thinking, intelligence, and problem solving. Not only are the topics themselves refreshingly practical, but we'll be asking you to participate in hands-on exercises designed to inform you of your own thinking and problem-solving skills. We hope you find the exercises not only enjoyable and personally informative but also lasting reminders of what students face every day.

One of the authors, when proofreading this chapter, laughed and recounted the story of his daughter when she was in the second grade. When she came home from school and was asked about her day, she replied, "Daddy, I can't think about it any more. My head hurts." She was right; thinking and problem solving are hard work, but they're also the signs of competent behavior. If you are contemplating a future as a teacher, you should be encouraged to know that students, with your help, can improve both their thinking and problem-solving skills.

After a general discussion of thinking, we'll turn our attention to the nature of problem solving and urge you to teach students to use a problem-solving model when faced with difficult tasks. Finally, we'll offer specific suggestions that will help in teaching students to be good problem solvers.

THINKING

Our work in this chapter is guided by a basic principle: *Thinking skills and problem-solving strategies produce competence,* which is, after all, a highly desirable and sought-after quality. If students have difficulty because of poor thinking skills or problem-solving strategies, everything—from achievement to self-esteem—suffers.

Consider the daily demands made on students. From the moment they decide what to eat for breakfast, select their route to school, concentrate on their classroom assignments, and pick a television show to watch after their homework is done, their day's activities demand thinking, decision making, and problem solving.

You probably agree that thinking is hard work, but it's also a sign of intelligent behavior. However you define intelligence, you would probably agree that students demonstrate intelligence by acquiring knowledge, thinking about knowledge, and using knowledge. As Ann Brown (1990), a prominent psychologist, noted, thinking means knowing

- when you know.

- what you know.

Objectives

When you finish reading this chapter, you should be able to

- identify strategies that help students acquire fundamental facts and skills

- apply strategies that will help students with their thinking and problem solving

- suggest strategies that will help students search for insights into their learning

- help students identify the nature of a problem

- improve students' willingness to undertake problem solving

- teach students the basics of a problem-solving model that they can apply both in and out of school

- identify the weaknesses in students' problem-solving skills

Students have their personal preferences for studying and learning, which are called learning or cognitive styles.

- what you need to know.

- when to acquire new knowledge.

THINKING
SKILLS
Skills and strategies that enable students to adapt to constant change.

When your students master these **thinking skills,** they're obviously demonstrating intelligent behavior. You should also be encouraged by realizing that students, with help, can improve *both* their thinking skills and their problem-solving strategies, thus also improving their classroom performance.

Cognitive Style

STYLE
A strategy used consistently across a wide variety of tasks.

COGNITIVE
STYLES
Strategies involved in thinking and problem solving.

LEARNING
STYLES
Preferences in learning and studying.

One of the major tasks teachers will face in helping students with their thinking skills and problem-solving strategies will be to make them aware of *how* they prefer to go about it. What strategies are they comfortable with? They can't answer this question unless they know certain things about themselves, which takes us into the world of cognitive and learning styles.

Think of **style** as a strategy used consistently across a wide variety of tasks (Snow, Corno, & Jackson, 1996). You probably have heard of cognitive styles and learning styles. **Cognitive styles** are involved in thinking and problem solving, while **learning styles** point to preferences in learning and studying, which really are two sides of the same coin (Messick, 1994). We'll use these labels interchangeably since no sharp distinction exists between them (Snow et al., 1996). Your learning style, for example, includes your preferences in learning and studying (concentrating on one part of an assignment, or attempting to grasp the meaning of the entire material from the beginning), as well as the cognitive activities you use in these tasks (memorizing, decision making), which helps to explain why it's so difficult to distinguish between the two.

You can see, then, how style is linked to a range of preferences, from particular cognitive strategies to specific environmental conditions. For example, how do you prefer to prepare for a test? Do you like it perfectly quiet, or do you prefer music playing in the background? Do you like it warm or cool, bright or medium light? Do you study better in the morning or evening? Your answers to these and many other questions reflect your learning style.

Classroom Implications

Why should you be concerned by your style and that of students? As Robert Sternberg noted (1997), cognitive style has important classroom implications. For example, in their recent research, Harvey Silver, Richard Strong, and Matthew Perini, 1997) have identified the following four types of leaning style:

1. The *mastery style learner* absorbs information concretely, processes it sequentially, and judges its value by its clarity and practicality.

2. The *understanding style learner* focuses on ideas and abstractions and learns by a process of questioning and reasoning.

3. The *self-expressive style learner* depends more on feelings and emotions to form new ideas and products, and judges the value of learning products by their originality and aesthetics.

4. The *interpersonal style learner,* more social by nature, tends to learn better in groups and judges learning by its potential use in helping others.

These four styles give teachers a practical means of identifying students' style, thus improving the ability to match students' preferences with the teachers' methods. It seems reasonable that this and similar techniques will accomplish more than if a mismatch occurs. (Psychologists refer to this attempted match as *goodness of fit.*)

Sternberg (1997) also raised an interesting question: Will teachers reward students whose learning styles are similar to their own, thus confounding style with achievement? As interest in learning styles grows, Sternberg's warning is timely. Remember: Don't confuse style with ability, otherwise you're apt to teach and assess students in ways that benefit those with certain styles of thinking and learning, but may put other students at a distinct disadvantage (Sternberg, 1994). Once you recognize the importance of identifying and using knowledge about cognitive styles in the classroom, you can expand your teaching techniques to accommodate a variety of student styles. (Here we would ask you to review the work on impulsivity in Chapter 3 and recall its impact on behavior and achievement.)

Analyzing Your Personal Learning Style

First, however, you should develop familiarity with your own style. One way of doing this is to answer the following questions (Lewis & Greene, 1982, pp. 149–150):

1. When studying an unfamiliar subject, do you

   a. prefer to gather information from many topic areas?
   b. prefer to stay fairly close to the central topic?

CASE NOTES

Observation   Mark Siegel, the fourth-grade teacher you read about in the case study at the beginning of this section, cannot motivate one of his students, Karim Peterson.

Hypothesis   Both teacher and student seem to have cognitive styles that, if not in conflict, have little in common.

Possible Action   Devise a plan that would be compatible with Karim's learning style, and try to capitalize on his interest and expertise in African culture.

---

2. Would you prefer to

   a. know a little about a great many subjects?
   b. become an expert on just one subject?

3. When studying from a textbook, do you

   a. skip ahead and read chapters of special interest out of sequence?
   b. work systematically from one chapter to the next, not moving on until you have understood earlier material?

4. When asking other people for information, do you

   a. tend to ask broad questions that call for general answers?
   b. tend to ask narrow questions that demand specific answers?

5. When browsing in a library or bookstore, do you

   a. look at books on many different subjects?
   b. stay in one section, concentrating on one or two subjects?

6. Are you best at remembering

   a. general principles?
   b. specific facts?

7. When performing some task, do you

   a. like to have background information not strictly related to the work?
   b. prefer to concentrate on strictly relevant information?

8. Do you think that educators should

   a. give students exposure to a wide variety of subjects in college?
   b. ensure that students mainly acquire extensive knowledge related to their specialties?

9. When on vacation, would you sooner

   a. spend a short amount of time in several different places?
   b. stay in just one place the whole time and really get to know it?

10. When learning something, would you rather

    a. follow general guidelines?
    b. work to a detailed plan of action?

Now add up your a's and b's; if you scored six or more a's you're holist, or to use Pask's terminology, a **grouper;** if you scored six or more b's, you're a **stringer.** The higher you score in either of the categories, the more closely your learning style approximates the following descriptions.

If you're a *grouper,* you probably prefer as wide a grasp of a subject as possible. You like to learn general principles and attempt to relate the topic under consideration to as many related subjects as possible. You usually learn better in unstructured situations, tending to resist detailed classes and instructional methods. You begin by studying general concepts and the total situation or problem before commencing more detailed analysis. For example, in studying the workings of a particular computer, you probably would start by acquiring knowledge about the history of computers, something about the general technology, and perhaps several examples of computer usage in our society. Then you can set the more systematic study of a particular computer within this broad framework. Occasionally you ignore essential details that could impair problem solution.

If you're a *stringer,* you probably opt for a systematic, methodical analysis leading to mastery of details. You're comfortable with this strategy, and it's only after you have acquired specifics that you turn to more general concepts. You acquire knowledge sequentially and gradually, and it must be information that is directly related to the task. Be careful not to overlook equally essential broad concepts.

Reflecting on your personal style leads to improvement in your own thinking skills and problem-solving strategies. This, in turn, helps you make students aware of their cognitive styles, leading to a goodness of fit that results in both better achievement and adjustment.

Thinking Skills: An Analysis

Accumulating knowledge, however, isn't all you want students to do in the classroom. You want them to plan what to do with the material, like a carpenter who has secured a desirable piece of wood and now has to decide how to shape it. You want students to shape their facts so that they squeeze as much value from them as possible. It's not enough for students just to obtain knowledge; you want them to apply what they have learned, to integrate it with other facts, and then to stand back and ask themselves if they could do any better. All of this leads to helping them *use thinking skills in everything they do.*

To help you devise strategies for improving your students' thinking skills, we'll consider two widely accepted and practical systems: Benjamin Bloom's *Taxonomy of Educational Objectives* and Arthur Costa's *Model of Critical Thinking Skills.* Each of these systems offers a solid basis for the skills it proposes: Bloom's in educational objectives, and Costa's in curriculum goals.

The Bloom Taxonomy

In 1956, Benjamin Bloom and his colleagues published an enduring classification of educational goals entitled *Taxonomy of Educational Objectives, Handbook 1: Cognitive Domain.* (Think of "taxonomy" as a classification system.) Bloom's taxonomy has enjoyed widespread acceptance and today forms the core of many thinking skills programs. The main purpose of the taxonomy is to provide a classification of the goals of our educational system (Bloom, 1956, p. 1). The taxonomy consists of three major sections covering the cognitive, the affective, and the psychomotor domains. Our concern here is with the cognitive taxonomy, which is divided into the following six major classes:

1. *Knowledge*—recalling specific facts

2. *Comprehension*—understanding what is communicated

3. *Application*—generalizing and using abstract information in concrete situations

4. *Analysis*—breaking a problem into subparts and detecting relationships among the parts

GROUPER

Groupers prefer as wide a grasp of a subject as possible.

STRINGER

Stringers prefer a systematic, methodical analysis leading to mastery of details.

Benjamin Bloom

5. *Synthesis*—putting together parts to form a whole

6. *Evaluation*—using criteria to make judgments

Table 8.1 provides an example of Bloom's ideas, plus a sample of the kinds of questions teachers can ask students to sharpen their thinking skills. (We used the American Civil War as an example.)

Many educators believe that the elegant simplicity of Bloom's logic and the detailed presentation of the various categories of the taxonomy have not been fully utilized. With today's interest in teaching thinking skills, many concerned teachers and administrators have again turned to Bloom's categories of analysis, synthesis, and evaluation as the best means available for organizing the teaching of higher-order thinking skills.

When you're helping students improve their thinking skills, be sure you remember the important role played by questions. *We urge you not to focus merely on questions about facts; rather, stretch students' thinking abilities by asking questions that require application, analysis, synthesis, and evaluation.*

Using Questions to Improve Thinking Skills

Even before Socrates, questioning was one of teaching's most common and effective techniques. Some teachers ask hundreds of questions, especially when teaching science, geography, history, or literature. Using questions is a specific example of how teachers can help students to improve their thinking skills. Questioning, if used properly, is an effective technique that helps to produce a positive, interactive classroom. Good questions cause students to pay *attention,* to *process* information, to *organize* their ideas, and to *compose* an answer, a neat summary of thinking and problem solving (Cruickshank, Bainer, & Metcalf, 1995).

Three issues are critical to your efforts to frame thoughtful questions (Cruickshank et al., 1995): Knowing how to ask questions, knowing how to obtain good answers, and knowing how to follow up responses.

How to Ask Questions   Be sure to phrase your questions clearly and concisely. You could well follow Michael Gelb's advice (1996) to use a reporter's classic questions: *What?, Where?, When?, Who?, How?, and Why?* Let's assume you, like all of us, have some problem in your personal or professional life.

Table 8.1 USING BLOOM'S TAXONOMY

Level of Thinking	Sample Questions
Knowledge—recalling specific facts	When did the Civil War begin? When was the Civil War completed? Who was president of the Confederacy during the Civil War?
Comprehension—understanding what is communicated	Why would Americans want to fight against each other? Can you give me a brief summary of the Civil War in your own words?
Application—generalizing and using abstract information	Why did the North want to keep a large army around Washington? Where would you put the Southern cities on this map?
Analysis—dividing a problem into subparts	Can you think of several causes of the Civil War? What were the main features of the Battle of Gettysburg?
Synthesis—putting together parts to form a whole	Why do you think Lee surrendered at Appomatox? Could you write a few sentences describing Lee's personality?
Evaluation—using criteria to make judgments	Many people criticize Grant for losing so many men. Do you think Lincoln made the right decision in putting him in charge of the Union armies? Do you think Lincoln made a mistake in leaving McClellan as head of the Army of the Potomac for so long?

CASE NOTES

Observation   Although reading and attention seem to be weak spots, Karim Peterson's test scores are high.

Hypothesis   Given his obvious intelligence, it would seem that the notion of an appropriate cognitive style might provide insights into his strengths and interests.

Possible Action   Arrange activities that would help to identify particular intellectual strengths, keeping in mind the specific objectives you think Karim should achieve.

What

   is the problem?

   are the basic issues?

   will happen if I ignore it?

Where

   did it begin?

   did it happen?

   else has it happened?

When

   did it start?

   does it happen?

   doesn't it happen?

Who

   cares about it?

   is affected by it?

   can help me?

How

   does it happen?

   can it be changed?

   will I know when it's solved?

Why

   did it start?

   is it important?

   does it continue?

Whatever your questions, be sure that your language is appropriate for students and focuses their attention on your objectives. In other words, don't muddy the waters by introducing unnecessary words or expressions. Also, avoid questions that merely require a yes or no answer. Effective questions will cause students to *think about* what the teacher is asking and to compose an answer. Finally, be sure you ask only one question at a time. Too often teachers think about another aspect of the material they're using and piggyback one or more questions on to the original.

Give careful attention to the level of thought your question is demanding. Table 8.2 illustrates the use of Bloom's taxonomy to organize your questions.

You can see how lower-order questions elicit responses at the knowledge, comprehension, and application levels, while higher-order question require analysis, synthesis, and evaluation.

Questions may also be **convergent questions** (requiring specific material, that is, the right answer) or **divergent questions** (requiring students to expand, explore, be creative). Probably the best advice we can give you is to use a variety of questions depending on your objectives and the cognitive level of students.

CONVERGENT
QUESTIONS
Questions that require specific material, that is, the right answer.

DIVERGENT
QUESTIONS
Questions that require students to expand, explore, be creative.

Table 8.2 USING BLOOM'S TAXONOMY TO FRAME QUESTIONS

Level of Thinking	Examples of Questions
Knowledge	Who did ___? When was ___ completed? Identify the ___ in the list. What does 2 + 6 equal?
Comprehension	Provide a good title for the story you read. In your own words, what was the main theme of the story?
Application	Use the word correctly in a sentence. Design a model that illustrates your understanding of the concept.
Analysis	Categorize all of the elements of the problem. What is the function of ___? How is A related to B?
Synthesis	Identify the common pattern resulting from all of the pictures. Summarize the various points that were made by stating a rule. Integrate the various pieces of information to create a profile of the person.
Evaluation	Judge the best method for testing the hypothesis. Rank order the projects, using stated criteria, from best to worst. Decide which problems were solved correctly.

Obtaining Good Answers   One of the best ways to encourage your students to give their best responses is to *give them enough time to answer*. Research has shown that a wait time of about three to five seconds results in the best answers (Cruickshank et al., 1995).

Also be sure that all students have an equal chance to respond. Don't always depend on volunteers to answer; that's too much like "rounding up the usual suspects." Reach out to those who are reluctant to volunteer. Try this: Ask a question; give everyone enough time to think about it and compose an answer; select a student to respond. Vary the pattern occasionally; go back to a student who has previously answered and whose attention may now be wandering. Remember: You want to maintain a productive pace, not too slow, not too fast, but brisk and lively.

Following Up Student Responses   Once a student has responded, you must react. Try to avoid saying, "OK," and then moving on. You should clarify, expand, and synthesize when you can. Once a student has responded correctly, move on. Never let an incorrect answer stand. Be careful of what you reinforce; that is, you may want to reinforce a student's effort, but be sure the student understands it was an incorrect answer. (We urge you to refer to the discussion of reinforcement in Chapter 6.) You can provide the correct answer and then move on or use additional questions to lead the student to the correct answer, depending on time and circumstances. Table 8.3 illustrates the do's and don'ts of effective questioning.

Use of these strategies is an excellent example of building Bloom's ideas into the teaching of thinking skills. Let's now examine a second approach to teaching critical thinking skills.

Table 8.3 THE DO'S AND DON'TS OF EFFECTIVE QUESTIONING

Do	Don't
1. Match questions to objectives. Use a variety of question levels and types.	1. Emphasize only lower-order or convergent questions.
2. Ask many questions throughout the lesson.	2. Use questions mainly to review at the end of the lesson.
3. Ask a question, pause, and then call on a student by name to respond.	3. Allow callouts or fail to include pauses after your questions.
4. Ensure that all students get equal opportunities to successfully answer questions.	4. Rely on volunteers.
5. Follow up lower-order, inaccurate, and incomplete answers.	5. Overlook or allow to go uncorrected inappropriate or incomplete answers.
6. Write questions, especially critical questions, into your lesson plan.	6. Rely solely on your ability to generate spontaneous questions during interaction.
7. Keep questions clear, brief, and to the point.	7. Use long questions or ask multiple questions simultaneously.
8. Ask questions to keep students engaged.	8. Ask questions as a punitive, disciplinary tool.
9. Write the objectives and summary of the lesson as questions.	9. Use questions only on major points.
10. Match nonverbal behavior with the questions you ask.	10. Show disinterest in asking questions or in students' responses.

From D. Cruickshank, D. Bainer, & Bainer, & K. Metcalf, *The act of teaching.* Copyright © 1995. Reproduced with permission of The McGraw-Hill Companies.

Costa and Thinking Skills

Arthur Costa's (1985) rationale for his discussion of thinking skills is as simple as it is far-reaching: Thinking is hard work, but with proper instruction, human thought processes can be more broadly applied, more spontaneously generated, more precisely focused, more intricately complex, more metaphorically abstract, and more insightfully divergent. With this statement, Costa took a firm stand in favor of *direct instruction* of thinking skills.

Levels of Thinking Skills

Costa suggested a four-level hierarchy of thinking skills that should be helpful in teaching, curriculum construction, and development of instructional materials. The four levels are as follows:

Level I: The Discrete Level of Thinking, which involves individual skills prerequisite to more complex thinking. For example, you'll want to be sure that a lesson's demands match student's abilities. Can students understand the material?

Level II: Strategies of Thinking, which involves a combination of individual, discrete skills to formulate strategies. For example, you'll want to determine that students understand the ideas presented and are able to combine them in a way that leads to problem solving.

Level III: Creative Thinking, which requires the use of strategies to create new thought patterns and innovative solutions. For example, can students apply what they have learned about America's original break with England to the recent changes in Eastern Europe?

Level IV: The Cognitive Spirit, which requires students to display a willingness, disposition, inclination, and commitment to think. For example, you'll want students to be sufficiently motivated to see problems as a challenge rather than as an insurmountable obstacle.

What can you do to foster thinking skills? Costa identified certain teacher behaviors that are quite effective in their impact on thinking skills. Four categories of teaching behavior seem particularly relevant: *questioning, structuring, responding,* and *modeling*—all of which should occur within a discussion format Costa (1985, p. 126).

Questioning   Students derive their cues for expected behavior almost totally from teacher questions and statements. If we assume a relationship between the level of thinking in a teacher's statements and questions and the level of student thinking, then questions containing higher-order thinking will require students to use higher-order thinking skills to answer them.

Questions can activate each part of Costa's model of intellectual functioning. For example, to aid input, questions that require students to name, describe, define, and observe are effective tools. To help students process data, questions that require students to search for relationships, synthesize, analyze, compare, and contrast are appropriate. Questions that force students to apply data in a novel manner should have them evaluate, judge, imagine, and predict.

Structuring   Structure refers to how teachers control the classroom environment. We have long known that teaching success is tightly linked to a well-managed classroom. Note: Well-managed does not imply rigid and unbending rules and discipline; rather, the term applies to a situation in which both teachers and students know what the structure is (firm, tight, relaxed, friendly), and in which the structure remains consistent.

Structuring a classroom to improve students' thinking skills demands clear objectives they can understand. Costa stated that such structure emerges from three instructional goals: (a) instructional clarity, (b) structuring time and energy, and (c) carefully organizing interactions with students.

Responding   In attempting to create a climate conducive to developing student thinking skills, Costa focused on the nature of teacher responses. Teacher responses, which are extremely influential in shaping student behavior, fall into two major categories: closed responses and open responses. *Closed responses* include criticism and praise. Critical responses (in the sense of "put-downs") aren't much help to students' attempts to acquire thinking skills. Remember, however, praise should be used judiciously; otherwise it is relatively ineffective. If used carefully with students experiencing difficulty and if matched with clear standards of achievement for all students, the use of praise can be positive.

Open responses include silence, accepting, clarifying, and facilitating. We can summarize this category by stating that teachers should give students time to answer questions, be nonjudgmental, clearly indicate when they do not understand an answer, and provide feedback.

> **CASE NOTES**
>
> **Observation**　In reading the case study at the beginning of the section, you can't help but notice Mark Siegel's frustration about his inability to reach Karim Peterson.
>
> **Hypothesis**　Because of the disparity in their cognitive styles, the teacher's questions are meaningless to Karim.
>
> **Possible Action**　Formulate a series of questions based on what you know about Karim Peterson, questions designed both to tap his background and discover his interests.

Modeling　Avoid any inconsistencies between what you say and what you do. Students are remarkably perceptive and will quickly discern any discrepancies. If you want students to improve their thinking skills, you must show them that you place a high value on these behaviors. If you truly appreciate innovative solutions, careful inferences, and well-planned predictions, demonstrate your enthusiasm by your own behavior. Look for challenges and welcome obstacles. What you say and do greatly influences students; show how much you value thinking skills.

Thinking Skills Programs

Given the significance of thinking skills in our lives, it's little wonder that several programs have been designed to help students improve their abilities. We'll discuss two well-documented, carefully researched programs: Robert Sternberg and Howard Gardner's *Practical Intelligence for School*, and Edward de Bono's *CoRT Thinking Program*.

The Practical Intelligence for School Program

In the Practical Intelligence for School program students must learn to use their *practical intelligence* effectively in school, because that is where so much of their lives take place. Yet, according to Sternberg and his colleagues, many teachers don't make clear their expectations or share the tacit knowledge that is necessary for success, both inside and outside school (Sternberg, Okagaki, & Jackson, 1990). Since 1987 Sternberg and his team of researchers have worked in cooperation with Howard Gardner's research team to develop a theory-based curriculum called Practical Intelligence for School (PIFS). The PIFS program is an outgrowth of the combination of Sternberg's **triarchic model of intelligence** and Gardner's **multiple intelligences model.** Table 8.4. illustrates how these models of intelligence are combined in the PIFS program. Note that Gardner's theory expresses the domains in which intelligence manifests itself (linguistic, logical-mathematical, musical, etc.), whereas Sternberg's componential subtheory identifies the mental processes involved in these domains. The authors believe that teaching practical intelligence skills like those in the PIFS curriculum can foster success in all students.

The CoRT Thinking Program

As our final example of a thinking skills program, we turn to Edward de Bono's work on **Cognitive Research Trust (CoRT),** which concentrates on the means of acquiring thinking skills and improving problem-solving ability. Linking his theory of thinking skills to a neurological and information-processing base, de Bono (1985) argued for the direct teaching of thinking skills to students. The CoRT program has several objectives.

TRIARCHIC
MODEL OF
INTELLIGENCE

Sternberg's view of intelligence as consisting of three elements: componential, experiential, and contextual.

MULTIPLE
INTELLIGENCES

Gardner's eight relatively autonomous intelligences. These include linguistic, musical, logical-mathematical, spatial, bodily-kinesthetic, interpersonal, intrapersonal, and naturalistic intelligences.

COGNITIVE
RESEARCH TRUST
(CoRT)

de Bono's program that is intended to help students acquire thinking skills.

Table 8.4 THINKING SKILLS AND INTELLIGENCE—THE PIFS PROGRAM

Intellectual Domains	Componental	Contextual Experiential	
	Mental Processes	Application	Transfer
Linguistic	Selecting the steps needed to solve a problem	How to organize your thoughts in order to write a book report	Writing a history report. Writing a letter. Giving directions to someone
Logical-mathematical	Ordering the components of problem solving	How to complete a math worksheet accurately	Figuring out the steps for balancing a budget
Musical	Selecting relevant information	How to pick out the melody from the harmony	Recognizing the main theme in a musical work
Spatial	Selecting a mental representation for information	How to make pictures in your mind to help you remember what you read	Using a schematic to assemble a piece of electronic equipment
Bodily-kinesthetic	Allocating your resources	How to pace yourself throughout a long-distance run	Adjusting your physical exertion during a basketball game or ballet performance
Interpersonal	Solution monitoring	How to understand your teacher's comments on your history report	Restating what someone is telling you to be sure you understand him or her
Intrapersonal	Identifying a problem	Figuring out that something bothers you in school	Figuring out that you are getting annoyed by your brother's teasing

TIPS ON LEARNING
Helping Students With Their Thinking Skills

PRINCIPLE   Teaching thinking skills is a means of improving both thinking and problem solving.

STRATEGY   Don't be satisfied with questions and assignments that are restricted to data collection. Pose themes or problems that require students to make judgments, hypothesize, and react creatively.

STRATEGY   Ask students to predict what the community they're living in will be like in twenty years. Have them hypothesize, collect data, and then justify their predictions.

STRATEGY   Pick a sport students like, for example, baseball. Divide them into teams and have each member of each team write a question about the subject(s) they're studying. You then assign a value to each question: single, double, triple, home run. Each team member takes a turn as the pitcher and "throws" a question at the opposition. You can act as scorekeeper. The students work together collecting data for their questions, writing the questions, and reviewing material for their answers.

The program should be *simple and practical.* A successful program must be teachable for instructors and understandable for students. Expensive materials and special audiovisual materials are unnecessary. It should also *apply to a wide range of ages,* since de Bono believes that thinking processes are fundamental. The thinking skills taught should be *those required in real life;* for this reason the program emphasizes "projective" thinking:

gathering information, inferring from it, and acting on it. Finally, the program should be *independent of any detailed knowledge base,* thus permitting students to *transfer the thinking skills* they acquire to all of life's situations. By the mixture of items in the CoRT program, de Bono believes that students' attention can be directed at necessary thinking processes.

PROBLEM SOLVING

We know a great deal about problem-solving strategies today, and this knowledge can be of great value to students. For example, simply reassuring them that there's nothing to be afraid of when they face a problem and urging them to look for the facts that are given in a problem greatly improves their problem-solving abilities. If students feel confident in analyzing and attacking problems, they're well on their way to functioning effectively in all situations.

Are your students good problem solvers? Are *you* a good problem solver? Should your students be better? Can you help them to improve? We think so, given what we know about the characteristics of good problem solvers. For example, *good problem solvers have a positive attitude toward problems,* believing they can solve them by careful, persistent analysis. *They're concerned with accuracy,* which is a wonderful attitude to foster in children, one that carries over to all aspects of their lives. *They learn to take a problem apart,* to break it down into its smallest, manageable parts, and then integrate the parts into a manageable whole that leads to a solution. Finally, *they learn not to guess and jump at answers,* a valuable tool to remember whenever they are challenged by a problem, in or out of school. (Recall the delay of gratification studies that we discussed in Chapter 3.)

METACOGNITION
The ability to think about thinking.

In a sense, the remainder of this chapter is about **metacognition,** or the ability we develop to "think about thinking." We not only know something, but we also begin to think about what we can do with this knowledge. We will discuss the nature of problem solving, the reasons some of us avoid problems, and the typical kinds of strategies we use when we attempt problem solving. Then we'll examine the details of the DUPE model, which presents a formula for determining the dimensions of a problem, understanding its nature, planning for its solution, and finally, evaluating the success of the solution. We'll also present several interesting problems to help you learn about your own problem-solving ability and to help you understand the techniques that students must master to become good problem solvers.

What Is a Problem?

Have you ever sat baffled while you read an arithmetic word problem? Have you ever been assigned a term paper and not known where to start? In both of these instances, you had a problem; you could not get where you wanted to go. There was a void that you had to cross to solve your problem. When dealing with students' learning or behavior problems, *we like to think of a problem as a significant discrepancy between the actual behavior and the desired behavior.*

One of the authors of this text recently was asked to give a talk to a group of parents on thinking skills and problem-solving strategies for children. To begin, he presented the following problem:

> *Two motorcyclists are 100 miles apart. At exactly the same moment they begin to drive toward each other for a meeting. Just as they leave, a bird flies from the front of the first cyclist to the front of the second cyclist. When it reaches the second cyclist, it turns around and flies back to the first. The bird continues flying in this manner until the cyclists meet. The cyclists both travel at the rate of 50 miles per hour, while the bird maintains a constant speed of 75 miles per hour. How many miles will the bird have flown when the cyclists meet?*

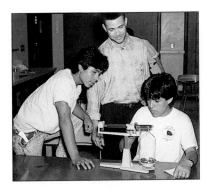

Teachers are concerned about how they can help their students improve their problem-solving strategies in school and have them transfer these strategies to problems outside the classroom.

Examining this problem, you may immediately begin to calculate distance, miles per hour, and constancy of speed. Actually, this is not a mathematical problem; it's a word problem. Carefully look at it again. Both riders will travel for one hour before they meet; the bird flies at 75 miles per hour; therefore, the bird will have flown 75 miles. No formula or calculations are needed, just a close examination of what is given.

The talk to the parents was in the evening. They were tired, and not too attentive. Then they became downright mad at themselves for not getting the correct answer. Now he had their attention, and the parents were determined not to be tricked again. He next asked them to think of something that had frustrated them recently—in other words, a problem—and how they had felt if they couldn't reach a solution.

Finally, he reminded the parents that their children have similar feelings when they are baffled by an arithmetic word problem or bewildered about how to start a term paper. For both teachers and students, a problem exists when they can't get where they want to go; a gap stretches before them. To solve the problem, teachers must construct some way of bridging the gap, which is our task in the remainder of the chapter.

In your own problem solving, you primarily use one of two techniques to bridge the gap. You may try to solve it "in your head" (a form of *internal representation*). Or you may turn to paper and pencil and sketch out a proposed solution (a form of *external representation*). We honestly can't tell you that internal representation is better than external representation, or vice versa. *Whatever works for you is right,* that is, it matches your learning style. Students will react in exactly the same way, some preferring external techniques, others preferring internal techniques. The important point here is that you discover which form students prefer, and then encourage them to use it whenever possible. (Note again the critical role of cognitive or learning style.)

As we shall see later when we examine the nature of a problem in more detail, problem solving requires that we understand the meaning of the gap or discrepancy (that is, we try to represent it in some manner), and then construct ways of bridging the gap.

Improving Problem-Solving Skills

Regardless of how you react to problems, it's possible to improve your ability to solve them, and if it's true for you, it's also true for students. What an encouraging thought! Regardless of students' intelligence or socioeconomic level (or any other characteristic), they can improve their learning skills.

Make no mistake, individual differences in problem-solving ability exist for many reasons. Some of us are simply better at solving problems than others; you may have had previous experience in solving problems; some, with more enriching educations, bring

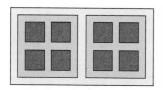  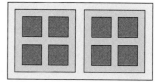

FIGURE 8.1

The integration of Intellectual Components.

more knowledge to a problem; still others are more motivated to solve problems. But this really isn't the issue. What matters most is that students can improve their skills by attending more closely to the nature of each problem that faces them, by better understanding their own thinking processes, and by using the mistakes they make to improve their skills.

A good example of how you—and your students—can improve your skills is that you'll do better with the problems to come in the remainder of this chapter simply because you'll be more cautious and attentive after trying to solve the problem of the bird and the motorcyclists. Try this, and see Figure 8.1.

> *There are three separate, equally sized boxes, and inside each box there are two separate small boxes, and inside each of the small boxes there are four even smaller boxes. How many boxes are there altogether?*

Your attempt to solve this problem is another excellent example of individual differences in problem solving, especially those differences that relate to problem-solving style. Though many readers will try to solve it "in their heads" (with some form of internal representation), others will immediately turn to paper and pencil and draw the various stages (using external representation). Our guess would be that more readers solved the second problem than the first. You attended to it more carefully and considered as many alternatives as possible. (The answer is 33: 3 large boxes + 6 small boxes + 24 smaller boxes.)

When you directly teach learning strategies and tactics to your students, it is reasonable to expect that their ability to solve problems, both in and out of the classroom, will improve. Although efforts to incorporate problem-solving activities and content within the curriculum are increasing, this is still, for the most part, a solitary effort by individual teachers. Rarely are students taught to think; typically the focus is on what to learn, which is unfortunate, since most teachers are good problem solvers. We hope your work in this chapter will help you to improve your students' thinking and problem-solving skills.

What Kinds of Mistakes Do Your Students Make?

Most errors are made not because people lack information about the problems, but mainly because they don't attend to the problem or fully employ their reasoning processes. For example, try this problem:

> *In a different language* liro cas *means "red tomato,"* dum cas dan *means "big red barn," and* xer dan *means "big horse." What is the word for "barn" in this language? (a)* dum *(b)* liro *(c)* cas *(d)* dan *(e)* xer

Here we have a fairly simple problem, but one demanding a systematic comparison of phrases and a careful matching of words. Poor problem solvers often jump at the first clue, with the result that they choose b, c, d, or e.

Among the most common sources of error are the following:

- *Failure to observe and use all the relevant facts of a problem.* Did you account for each word in the language problem?

- *Failure to adopt systematic, step-by-step procedures.* The problem solver may skip steps, ignore vital information, and leap to a faulty conclusion. Did you make a check, or some other mark, against each word?

- *Failure to perceive vital relationships in the problem.* Did you discover the pattern that led to *dum* as the correct answer?

- *Frequent use of sloppy techniques in acquiring and applying vital information.* Did you guess at the meanings of any of the words? Did you try to eliminate the irrelevant words?

Retreating from Problems

Let's be honest: None of us enjoys facing difficult situations. It's much easier to ignore or avoid problems that demand considerable effort to solve. If motivated individuals feel this way, imagine how much more difficult it must be for those students who constantly experience frustration in school and who are more accustomed to failure than to success. These students can react only negatively to any problems that they encounter in the classroom, and as we shall see, they transfer this attitude to other problems they meet.

For example, students often feel frustrated by anything mathematical, and they may too easily develop a fear of failure. For whatever reason—poor instruction, poor materials, lack of motivation at a critical time—these students either avoid or simply refuse to attempt to solve math problems (a habit they may carry into adulthood). As an example of this reaction, try to solve the following problem:

> *Group these numbers in such a way that when you total the groups, they add up to the sum of 1,000.*
>
> 88888888

(We hate to tell you this, but some elementary school youngsters will find the solution almost immediately.) Some of you will never solve it; some of you simply ignore the problem and continue your reading; others will routinely read the problem while their thoughts are on something totally different. Still others react in an almost reflexive manner by saying, "Math—that's not for me."

In case you are still searching for the answer, try this line of reasoning. How many groups are required to produce a zero in the units column when you add them? This is the key to solving the problem, since five is the first number that will result in zero: $5 \times 8 = 40$. Try working with five groups.

> *(Solution: $888 + 88 + 8 + 8 + 8$.)*

Excuses, Excuses, Excuses

What can we say about students who will not attempt to search for solutions? They just give up or decide immediately that they will be unsuccessful. If you listen carefully to their reasons, they seem to fall into a few general categories:

- *I just wasn't born smart.* This popular excuse shifts responsibility for failure from the individual to some mysterious genetic blueprint. You may also hear this excuse as, "I hate to read," "I just can't do math," "I'm not going to be a biologist anyway." We can almost guarantee that if you improve students' problem-solving strategies, you'll improve their school achievement and self-esteem, giving them a valuable skill that will stay with them throughout their lives.

- *I have a terrible memory.* If you listen to students carefully, you'll find that this excuse usually applies to those situations or subjects in which they're having difficulty. Watch them closely when they're working on a subject that troubles them and you'll find they undoubtedly fall into one of the common traps previously mentioned: not attending to detail, not using a systematic approach, or missing relationships.

- *I was never any good at that.* Unfortunately, your students may be right when they appeal to this excuse. Let's assume for the moment that they have at least normal intelligence, do fairly well in school, and betray no alarming symptoms other than difficulty in a particular subject. Any reasonable teacher may wonder what's happening. The scenario may be something like this: First exposed to the subject, students experience difficulty, receive low marks, lose their motivation, and don't understand what's happening to them. No wonder they feel helpless. By teaching them the simple strategies in this chapter, teachers can help students improve their achievement and restore their self-confidence.

Here is an example of the simplicity and clarity of these strategies. One of the most basic techniques that children find useful, once they are aware of it, is working backward. Try this:

What day follows the day before yesterday if three days from now it will be Monday?

Good problem solvers analyze details with considerable care and usually break a problem into sections. They might proceed as follows:

- If three days from now it will be Monday, today must be Friday.

- If today is Friday, yesterday was Thursday.

- The day before yesterday was Wednesday.

- The following day is Thursday.

However you do it, impress upon your students that *attending must be the initial step* because identifying the details and what is required determines the kind of strategy to be used.

Here's another example of the value of simple strategies offered by John Bransford and Barry Stein (1993). Working a problem backward often leads to a quick solution. If you have a 9:00 A.M. examination and you can't be late, one technique would be to decide that you want to arrive at 8:45 A.M. Since it takes thirty minutes for the trip; you want to allow fifteen minutes for potential traffic slowdowns. Therefore, you should leave at 8:00 A.M. Working backward is especially helpful whenever the goal is clear and the initial state of the problem is vague (Bransford & Stein, 1993, p. 31).

Regardless of the reasons people have for retreating from problems, it's a difficult task to help anyone, adult or child, break away from customary attitudes and beliefs. Creative thinking (searching for alternatives to solve problems) is concerned with breaking away from old ideas. This leads to changes in both attitudes and approach: We look differently at situations. If an approach is new, many of us feel uncomfortable trying it. It is much easier

> ## CASE NOTES
>
> **Observation**   Karim Peterson's attitude and lack of interest have created a problem for Mark Siegel.
>
> **Hypothesis**   Given both the mother's and son's attitudes, the teacher is ready to retreat from the problem.
>
> **Possible Action**   Think about ways that Mr. Siegel can restructure his problem, thus viewing his relationship with Karim from a different perspective.

to do the same thing, to follow the same path, even if it has previously led to failure. If, however, you can teach students to use the strategies discussed in this chapter, chances are they will experience greater success, which will in turn encourage them to try again.

We propose now to offer several strategies to help students, regardless of their experiences, to master effective problem-solving techniques.

THE DUPE MODEL

Many models have been proposed to help people solve a wide variety of problems. Often they use a series of steps in the form of an acronym (an acronym is a letter combination like SAC—Strategic Air Command; NATO—North Atlantic Treaty Organization; HOMES—The names of the Great Lakes: Huron, Ontario, Michigan, Erie, Superior; MEGO—My Eyes Glaze Over). We'll use an acronym that you can pass on to students, one that they should be able to remember easily and that they can transfer to any problems. The acronym is **DUPE.** In its full form, its intent is to convey the message, *Don't let yourself be deceived.* Figure 8.2 illustrates the meaning of each letter.

The model you are about to analyze offers several metacognitive strategies that you can pass on to your students. The first step in the DUPE model is to determine the nature of the problem.

Defining the Nature of a Problem

Students are often baffled when confronted by a problem; they have no idea of how to begin, since they're unable to identify the nature of the problem. They have a vague sense that they "just can't do something." In the classroom they're usually told about the problem or read about it, and yet even these clues may offer little tangible help because the nature of the problem still eludes them.

They're not alone in their bewilderment. How would you go about solving this problem presented by Bransford and Stein (1993)?

> *There is a super psychic who can predict the score of any game before it is played. Explain how this is possible.*

This problem poses a challenge to most of us because it's difficult to generate a reasonable explanation. If you are having difficulty, it is probably because you have made a faulty assumption about the nature of the problem. You were not asked about the final score of the game; the score of any game before it is played is 0 to 0. We deliberately presented a tricky problem here to stress that you must attend to details.

DUPE

An acronym for a problem-solving model: **D***etermine just what the problem is;* **U***nderstand its nature;* **P***lan for its solution;* **E***valuate your plan.*

FIGURE 8.2

The DUPE Model.

> **D —** *Define* the nature of the problem.
> **U —** *Understand* the nature of the problem.
> **P —** *Plan* your solution. Select appropriate strategies.
> **E —** *Evaluate* your plan for its suitability and success.

Recognizing a Problem

Before your students can determine the nature of a problem, however, they must realize a problem exists. You can't solve a problem unless you know that you have one. Don't laugh; many students fail to recognize a problem even when you clearly identify it. Imagine the difficulty these same students have when they're faced with problems outside of school, problems that aren't numbered or don't have obvious question marks after them. Teach your students that when things aren't working as well as they should, or a technique that worked on previous occasions doesn't work now, they have a problem. In other words, when things seem wrong, they probably are.

Occasionally students will recognize a problem but not know how to attack it. Teach them to look carefully at the problem itself. Is there anything in the problem that tells them what to do? What are the facts that are given (often simply called *the givens*)? In other words, is the problem telling them to add or subtract, to get certain facts, or to take certain steps? Here's a simple example:

> *If 3 oranges cost 99¢, how much does each orange cost?*

The facts are clearly stated; what is needed are the steps.

1. 3 cost 99¢

2. To find the cost of one, divide 99 by 3

3. Answer: 33

This is a neat, well-defined problem. An ill-defined problem, however, is one in which things are much more vague and the steps to solution more elusive. Such problems require one or two insights into their nature, insights that usually are difficult to achieve. Once they are achieved, however, the problem is quickly resolved (Sternberg, 1996).

The problems presented earlier in this chapter are examples of this type. If you had difficulty with the eight 8s, you could not solve the problem until you achieved the insight that there must be five groups. In the problem with the motorcycles and the bird, once you realized that the solution depended on the bird's speed per hour (since the cyclists traveled for one hour), the answer came quickly.

> *Successfully intelligent people don't wait for problems to hit them over the head. They recognize their existence before they get out of hand and begin the process of solving them. (Sternberg, 1996, p. 158)*

Defining the Problem

How many times have you realized that a problem exists—you may not be doing too well with a particular student, for example—but you can't put your finger on exactly what's causing the difficulty? Let's assume that one of your students is having trouble with homework, not only turning it in late but not completing it. You take the student aside and go over precisely what's needed and how long she should spend on it. Your student agrees, but her work still doesn't improve, and friction starts to build between the two of you. You're unhappy with the quality of her work, and she's unhappy with the amount of time she's spending on it. What should you do now? Well, you could complain to her parents and demand that she spend more time on her work. But, in a real sense, this would be misdefining the problem and only be an added irritant. What seems to be the issue here is your student's time on task. She may well be spending the time with her assignments, but is she focused on them? How much time is spent daydreaming, staring into space, thinking about the weekend? If you've defined this as the problem, you'd be better off to work with the parents. For example, with your guidance, they could develop a plan similar to the following that would help her to stay on task:

What is required? (Attend to detail)

What am I asked to do? (Understand the nature of the problem)

What are the givens? (Decide if additional information is needed)

As Sternberg noted (1996, p. 159), brighter problem solvers spend relatively more time up front figuring out what to do and less time doing it; less-bright problem solvers spent relatively less time figuring out what to do and relatively more time doing it because they really haven't defined the problem.

> *Good definition of a problem paid off for Johnson & Johnson. When someone spiked bottles of Extra-Strength Tylenol with cyanide, the company immediately called together a crisis team, which recommended that all Extra-Strength Tylenol be recalled. Eventually, other Tylenol products were recalled as well. There were those who shook their heads in disbelief, arguing that the recalls would kill the Tylenol brand label. They were wrong. Within a short time, Tylenol had regained the position of market leadership. (Sternberg, 1996, p. 159)*

After students realize that a problem exists and they have defined its basic dimensions, turn to the second stage of the DUPE model, which takes us more deeply into the nature of problems.

Understanding the Nature of a Problem

Understanding the nature of a problem implies that you can both define and represent it, an assumption that has several significant implications. As we have seen, before you define a problem you must have a sufficient amount of knowledge to recognize what's given. To represent it, you must have adequate problem-solving skills. If students lack problem-solving strategies, then their task is next to impossible, which is one of the major reasons why there is growing pressure for schools to teach problem-solving skills.

As an example of the value of teaching problem-solving strategies, consider the following:

> *Tom either walks to work and rides his bicycle home or rides his bicycle to work and walks home. The round trip takes one hour. If he were to ride both ways, it would take 30 minutes. If Tom walked both ways, how long would a round trip take?*

Here you can see the value of dividing what's given in the problem into subgoals. Think for a moment: What are the givens? How long would it take to ride one way? (15 minutes.) How long is a round trip? (One hour.) How long does it take to walk one way? (45 minutes.) How long is the round trip if Tom walked both ways? (45 + 45 = 90 minutes.)

Acquiring information and attending to detail are important characteristics of good problem solvers.

The Knowledge Base

Compare the givens of the preceding problem with the example John Hayes (1989) used to stress the importance of prior knowledge:

> *Liquid water at 212F and 1 atm has an internal energy (on an arbitrary basis) of 180.02 BTU/lb. The specific volume of liquid water at these conditions is 0.01672 ft/lb. What is the enthalpy?*

For anyone with a knowledge of thermodynamics, this is not a particularly difficult problem. If you lack the necessary prior knowledge, however, you are defeated before you start. If you are missing relevant knowledge, an easy problem may appear difficult, if not impossible. *Remember: Much that passes for cleverness or innate quickness of mind actually depends on specialized knowledge* (Hayes, 1989). This helps to explain the current interest in the role of prior knowledge in problem solving. But the acquisition of knowledge in itself is not enough; what also is critical is the availability of knowledge when it's needed. (Retrieval from memory, which we will discuss later in this chapter, is an example of getting at and using information that we have previously stored.)

Problem Representation

The first and most basic step in problem solving is to represent the information in either *symbolic* (words, letters, or numbers), or *diagrammatic* (a collection of lines, dots, or angles) form. In other words, you try to put the problem in a personally meaningful form, that is, to represent it. Representation may be either internal or external.

E X T E R N A L
R E P R E S E N T A T I O N

A method of problem solving in which a person uses symbols or some other observable type of representation.

External Representation Some of us with almost all problems and all of us with complex problems turn to **external representation** (drawing parts; expressing the givens as symbols). Here's an example to test yourself (Lewis & Greene, 1982, p. 204).

As principal of a school with 1,000 students, you have the task of ordering textbooks for each course. Students can elect to study either a language or a science, and this semester you learn from the language department that 400 students have elected to take Spanish and 300 will take French. One hundred and fifty of the language students want to take both languages How many science books must you order to be sure that each student not electing language will have one?

Once again we have a problem that incorporates much of what we have discussed. It is well structured, but the givens require careful attention. Although some readers will derive the solution in their heads, others will immediately reach for paper and pencil. A quick reading of the problem might lead you to conclude that 300 science books should be ordered. But note that 150 students are taking both French and Spanish.

Representing the givens externally, you could proceed as follows:

Total number of students	1,000	
Taking Spanish		400
Taking French	300	
Taking both		150

The total number taking French and Spanish is 700, but 150 of these are the same students; thus, 550 students will take language, leaving 450 students needing science books.

Here we have an excellent example of how external representation can help in problem solving. You can see how writing down a problem's givens helps to focus your attention on the most important concepts. You then begin to see relationships among the givens. Also, if the problem is complex, representing the intermediate steps aids memory since some givens, such as tables or graphs, are quite difficult to visualize in detail.

Internal Representation   In no way is the emphasis on external representation intended to diminish the vital role of **internal representation,** which is the basis of all symbolic and diagrammatic forms. Don't make the mistake of thinking internal representation is an internal copy of an external situation, because internal representation entails adding details to and eliminating details from (fine-tuning) the original interpretation of information (Hayes, 1989).

As a simple example of Hayes's intent, close your eyes for a moment and picture some location in which you typically relax and enjoy yourself, such as a particular beach. You probably added details that are not part of the beach: people, boats, parasols. You undoubtedly omitted some details that usually are present, such as seaweed. Finally, you probably experienced pleasant feelings as you thought about the beach; that is, you interpreted the data.

The manner in which we represent a problem determines the ease or difficulty with which we solve it. A good example of the importance of representation is seen in the classic nine dots problem, as shown in Figure 8.3.

Difficulty arises for those who attempt the solution shown in Figure 8.4.

This strategy has variations, but they always reach the same conclusion: one dot remains untouched. *You will never solve the nine dots problem until you change your representation,* which you can do if you attend to the givens in the instructions. Nowhere were you told to remain within the confines of a square. (We too often impose limits on ourselves when we face problems!) Once you change your representation, the solution follows easily, as shown in Figure 8.5.

Representation, then, is basic for planning an accurate solution: You should remember, and encourage your students to remember, this advice. If you are having difficulty in solving a problem, *change your representation.*

INTERNAL
REPRESENTATION
A mental model of how to solve a problem.

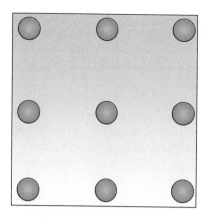

FIGURE 8.3

Nine dots problem. Without taking your pencil from the paper, connect each of the dots by using four straight lines. Each dot must be touched.

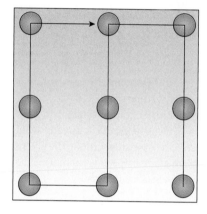

FIGURE 8.4

An incorrect solution to the nine dots problem.

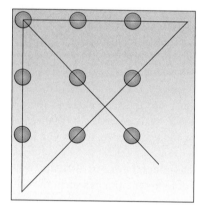

FIGURE 8.5

The nine dots problem solution.

Planning the Solution

Once you have a workable representation of the problem, you must devise a plan for its solution, which involves two critical aspects. *First, students need to be familiar with the core concepts required for solution.* If the problem demands basic arithmetic facts, then students must be able to do the addition or division that is required. For any students lacking the necessary basic knowledge in a field, the problem remains insoluble, like the preceding thermodynamics problem is insoluble for most of us.

Second, students must apply those strategies that are appropriate for the problem. Some strategies, such as *working backward,* can be helpful if the goal and givens are stated clearly. *Means-end analysis* is another general strategy that aids solution when the goal is obvious: Assume that your house needs painting and you decide to do it yourself. The goal is clear, but the means to achieve it requires additional planning. If the old paint is peeling, then the house first must be scraped and roughed up with a wire brush. You must then decide if these spots need priming. Is there hardware you should remove? What kind of paint is best suited to the weather conditions in your area: latex or oil? How you answer this question dictates the kind of paintbrush you should use. Though these steps seem simple, if you omit one, such as scraping, the solution is faulty.

Helping You Plan

Now that you have done the basic preparation for attacking the problem, you can select an array of learning strategies that will help you to formulate a plan for solution. Here are several learning strategies that reflect much of the work we have discussed thus far in this chapter, especially the role of memory (Hayes, 1989).

The Structuring Strategy The strategy of **structuring** is intended to have you search for relations within the learning material; it is a method for discovering structures. What is the relationship among the eight 8s that will enable you to solve the problem? The use of graphic representations is an illustration of a structuring strategy.

STRUCTURING
The strategy of searching for relations in learning materials.

The Context Strategy In the **context** strategy, you are again urged to search for relations in the material to be learned. But this differs from the structuring strategy in that the relations may be between the learning material and what you already know. You know that $8 \times 5 = 40$; therefore, you realize that five groups are needed; analyzing the problem in your new powerful computer is much easier if you have learned how simpler computers work.

CONTEXT
For Hayes, the strategy of searching for relationships between new material and material that is already known.

Instantiation **Instantiation** means to furnish an example. Are there problems similar to the one I am attempting to solve? We may also try to create examples for ourselves or others. If you were trying to explain a foul in baseball, your listeners might find it helpful if you told them that if the baseball stayed outside the white lines before it reached either first or third bases, the hit would be called a foul.

INSTANTIATION
The strategy of furnishing an example.

Multiple Coding Can we represent the information (the givens in our problem) in more than one way: verbally or through mental imagery? Such a process is called **multiple coding.** As you attempted to solve the problem of the cyclists and the bird, you may have made the givens more meaningful by using them in a story or by forming mental pictures of the cyclists moving toward each other and the bird racing between them.

MULTIPLE CODING
The process of representing information in more than one way.

It's time now to move to the final stage of the DUPE model—evaluation.

Evaluating the Solution

If all has gone well, you have formulated a plan that incorporates careful attention to the givens, either an internal or an external representation of the problem (or both), and a plan that you can effectively use. Evaluation now plays an important role in your search for a solution.

Examining Your Plan and Solution

Two aspects of evaluation seem especially pertinent. First is the necessity to stop here and evaluate the plan before you put it into action. Does it include all of the vital givens? Does your representation account for the givens in a way that reflects the essence of the problem? Does your plan use both the vital facts and your representation of the problem so that it is calculated to reach the required solution?

If your answers to these questions are affirmative, then the first evaluation is complete, and you should activate your plan. After you have worked through the plan, the second evaluative phase allows you to decide if you have found a solution or if you are totally satisfied with the solution that you have achieved.

What happens if your answer to the evaluative questions just posed is, "No, I haven't reached the correct solution?" You must continue the search process and not let frustration halt your progress—not an easy task. How can teachers help students reach the level of creativity that helps them to overcome that frustration and continue to search for new and different answers? One answer lies in our current knowledge of the creative process.

The Creative Student

There's an old saying about creativity (true, as are most old sayings): Creativity is a messy business. How could creativity possibly be messy? When you read the definition that most psychologist agree on, you'll understand: *Creativity means generating novel and appropriate ideas.*

Here's an example we'd like you to try: Describe the basic necessities that would be needed in a colony on Mars. Think about it for a moment. You must generate ideas you have not thought about before—that's the novel part—and these ideas must have some basis in reality—that's the appropriate part. If you really stretch your thinking, you undoubtedly would find that your thoughts don't march along in a nice, neat straight line.

For example, you may think about transportation when suddenly your mind flashes to means of food storage. That's just what happens—that's the messy part—and you may find it difficult to tolerate this seemingly chaotic procedure. Yet, if you stop and think about it, isn't this how we deal with life's "messiness"? Your students come to school and suddenly they're faced with a bewildering variety of personalities. Imagine how they must feel. *How do I deal with Tom? I can't do the same thing with Juan. Ms. Smith isn't at all like my teacher last year.* Consequently, they constantly adapt and adjust their relationships. They make connections, see things and people in new ways, recognize patterns, and take risks that their ideas will work out just fine. But is this really what we mean by creativity?

Does It Take a Genius?

Can *you* be creative? Can your students? Or does the spark of creativity only exist in a select few? A growing number of psychologists view creativity as an essential element in human nature. For example, have you ever done something completely novel, at least for you—managed to get something mechanical to work by using a part from a totally different device, or wrote a story with a truly ingenious ending?

All of us seem to engage in two types of thinking: *convergent* and *divergent.* Convergent thinking is directed at finding correct solutions, such as the answers to the following questions:

- How much is 2 plus 2? (Since you'll be doing quite a bit of creative thinking in this chapter, we want you to start slowly!)

- Who first walked on the moon?

- Name two leaders of the feminist movement in the United States.

For creativity to flourish, supportive environments such as the classroom should offer material, encouragement, and acceptance of different ideas and expressions.

Divergent thinking—creativity—searches for novel ideas and products. What would you do when faced with these directions and questions?

- How many words can you make from these letters?

- Look at this picture. How many titles for it can you think of? Which do you think is the best?

- Can you make up a story from these twenty words?

- Here is a book. What are all the things you can do with it?

Efforts to understand the inner workings of creativity continue unabated, so let's turn our attention to what characterizes creative children.

Characteristics of Creative Children

Pick a number, any number—10, 20, 30, 40, 50—and you have a good idea of the sheer range of characteristics assigned to creativity. We've gone through these lists and compiled the following several categories of characteristics that most creative people exhibit (Dacey, 1989a, 1989b, 1989c; Gardner, 1993; Gleick, 1992; Shekerjian, 1990; Sternberg & Lubart, 1995; Wright, 1992):

- *Creative people learn the strategies needed to solve the problems they inevitably encounter.* While working on this chapter a news story appeared about a 6-year-old boy who had been visiting his grandmother when she suffered a heart attack and lapsed into unconsciousness. The little boy, deeply upset, nevertheless dialed 911 and was responsible for saving his grandmother's life. When interviewed, he said that his parents taught him that when something serious happened—and they had used sickness as an example—he was to dial 911 if no one was there to help, a telling lesson for us all. These parents, through direct instruction and modeling, taught their child to face up to life's problems.

- *Creative people don't quit when the going gets tough; they persevere.* Perseverance is a major contributing characteristic of creative students. Once committed to a task, they may continue with it for years until they're satisfied. Howard Gardner (in Shekerjian, 1990, p. 144) has nicely summarized the need for perseverance:

    I think if you're going to write something about creativity for the public, one of the main points is to disabuse them of the nonsense you see advertised: "Come for a weekend, learn to brainstorm, learn to free-associate, we'll make you a creative individual." I mean, that just doesn't work. It's a serious business for serious people. Creative work requires, I think, being a certain kind of person, which includes being able to work on things for years, a drive not likely to come to people who paid five hundred dollars for a weekend under a tent.

Sooner or later all creative people encounter blocks to the expression of their creativity (Sternberg & Lubart, 1995). Obstacles may be either external (a teacher or parent may interfere) or internal (lagging motivation, rigidity in seeking a solution to a problem), but they'll inevitably appear. These researchers stressed that the difference between people who succeed in being creative over long periods of time and those who don't comes down to their ability to persevere.

- *Creative people are sensitive to problems.* Let's assume two of your students looked at a newspaper and read about a plane that crashed on takeoff. The article reported that the wind was blowing from the southwest and that the plane taxied down the runway toward the ocean. Fine; one of them read it and thought nothing of it. The second student read it and said, "Wait a minute; there's something wrong here. A plane wouldn't take off with a tail wind; it needs a head wind to get enough lift." One noticed the discrepancy; the other didn't. Why?

- *Creative people are more fluent than most other people,* that is, they generate a large number of ideas, which is called "ideational fluency." For example, how many round objects can you name in the next thirty seconds? How many other titles can you think of for *The Sound of Music?* How many uses can you think of for this book? Here's John Lloyd Wright speaking of his father, Frank Lloyd Wright (1992, pp. 120–121).

Just say "house" to Dad, if that's what you want. With one eye, he will look you over from head to foot—with the other your building site. Then he will start to dream, but not about the functions as you see them. He will hear the birds sing, he will see them nesting in the protective limbs of the trees round about. He will hear the tinkle of the waterfall as it plays its way over and around the rocks, giving life to nature's many forms of plant growth. Ah! He spies a colossal boulder, half buried in the slope toward the mountain stream. You don't know it but that boulder is already sheared flat by some strong stonecutter to become the hearth for that great stone fireplace, marrying the house to the ground. In his mind, the building grows in and out of the friendly earth, over the water, under the sun.

- *Creative people propose novel ideas that are also useful.* You could use this book as a doorstop, as a brace, as a support, as a prop, as a screen—dozing off while holding it in front of your face. (Not recommended.)

- *Creative people demonstrate considerable flexibility of mind.* If one solution doesn't work, creative individuals immediately look for new combinations or new ways of attacking the problem. For example, in visiting a school recently, one of us watched a first-grade boy trying to separate two Legos stuck together. Tugging away at them, he muttered, "I'm going to let my fingernails grow." Why? "Because," he said, "then I can push my skinny fingernail between the two blocks and move them. I can't do that with my finger."

- *Creative people reorganize the elements.* Did you ever watch closely as young children do a jigsaw puzzle? They have absolutely no hesitation in pulling pieces out, trying them elsewhere, or inserting them in another section. In another way, though with much more intensity, this is how Pablo Picasso approached the beginnings of his cubism period. The novelist Norman Mailer (1995, p. 21) described Picasso at this time of his life:

Picasso's eye could recall objects and paintings as if they were still sitting before him. He had the equivalent of a literary memory that will continue to see a text as it appeared on the printed page when first read. Add to such a faculty the vibration of images that came to him, and one begins to appreciate the delights and torture of the shifting imagery with which he could live by closing his eyes. It would have been difficult not to think of himself as possessed of superhuman powers—or, as he might also wonder, of Satanic gifts.

Table 8.5 summarizes the most frequently mentioned characteristics of creativity. Does your own list of characteristics match those of the experts? We hope you think of some that they missed, which would be an excellent sign of your creativity.

The Role of Memory

Finally, as we saw in Chapter 7, one of the most powerful strategies in solving problems is the efficient use of memory. All memory strategies, however, are not equally effective. Appropriate strategies depend on the level of material involved and the conditions under which the information must be remembered. Try this memory problem:

The following list contains twenty-five words. Take ninety seconds to study the following words.

Table 8.5 COMMON CHARACTERISTICS OF CREATIVITY

Tolerance of ambiguity	Insightful	Intuitive
Flexible	Visualize	Self-critical
Original	Fluent	Risk-taker
Intelligent	Sensitive	Knowledgeable
Independent	Imaginative	Analytical
Synthesize	Connected	Curious
Perseverance	Resilient	Focused

TIPS ON LEARNING AND MOTIVATION
Helping in the Search for Creativity

PRINCIPLE   Creativity by its very nature requires fertile ground in which to flourish. Perhaps the most important fertile ground is the classroom.

STRATEGY   Be sure that the material used to encourage creativity in the classroom matches the developmental level of students.

STRATEGY   Give students experience in deriving as many different responses to a problem as possible. Select an item such as a book and ask students to think of as many uses for it as possible. List them on the board and then ask them for more uses.

STRATEGY   Ask students to imagine, to go beyond the data. For example, assume that the class is studying the opening of the American West. They could write essays that incorporate the basic facts but go far beyond them. A popular book takes the life of General Custer, presents the facts, and then asks the reader to assume that Custer, critically wounded, survived Little Big Horn and had to stand trial for his role in the massacre. *The Trial of George Armstrong Custer is a lesson in creativity.*

STRATEGY   Encourage your students to search for relationships. Creativity tests often ask you to name one word that can be linked with others. Devise lists that are appropriate for students and that require similar thinking.

When time runs out, write as many of the words as you can without looking at the list.

book	light	leaf	pear	tire
page	net	basket	truck	minutes
wheel	orange	referee	clock	court
ball	branch	word	wrench	brake
apple	sneaker	mirror	tree	column

How did you do? Or more importantly from our perspective, *how did you do it?* Were these among the strategies you used?

- Rehearse (repeat) each word until you were sure you had memorized it: tire, tire, tire; book, book, book; branch, branch, branch.

- Rehearse several words: ball, apple, referee; ball, apple, referee.

- Organize the words by category. Note that several words related to cars; others could be grouped as fruit; still others could be categorized as relating to books.

- Construct a story to relate as many of the words as possible.

- Form images of words or groups of words.

You may have tried one or a combination of these strategies, but note that you were not told to memorize them in any particular manner. If you had received specific instructions, each of these strategies would not have been equally as effective. When we are asked to remember a particular telephone number, our tendency is to rehearse it for as long as we need to in order to recall it. But if you attempted to memorize these twenty-five words by straight rehearsal, not by grouping or any other technique, then you undoubtedly could recall only from five to nine words; the average memory span for familiar words is 5.86. If you had been directed to memorize the words in a certain order (the way that they were presented), grouping items by categories would not have been efficient; thinking of a story to link them in the correct order would have been much better.

Retrieval Aids

Because our understanding of ourselves is so dependent on what we can remember of the past, it is troubling to realize that successful recall depends heavily on the availability of appropriate retrieval cues. Such dependence implies that we may be oblivious to parts of our pasts because we fail to encounter hints or cues that trigger dormant memories. This may be one reason why encountering acquaintances we have not seen for years is often such an affecting experience: Our old friends provide us with cues and reminders that are difficult to generate on our own, and allow us to recollect incidents we would ordinarily fail to remember. (Schacter, 1996, p. 63)

A major issue for most of us is what psychologists call **storing** and **retrieving.** Much too frequently we have something in memory (we have stored it), but we can't get at it (we can't retrieve it). We know what the answer is, but just can't recall it. "It's on the tip of my tongue" is a common expression for a familiar experience.

Think for a moment about the list of words you were asked to memorize. A few of them were probably on the "tip of your tongue." If an instructor were to ask you, "Who is Michael Jordan?" you may hesitate. Then the instructor adds, "Chicago." It's as if the teacher had opened a door: Jordan, Chicago, Chicago Bulls, basketball, most valuable player.

There are several techniques that can help us to trigger our memory. Among the most effective retrieval aids are the following.

Cues   Although you were supplied with the cue (Chicago) in the preceding example (Michael Jordan), the most effective **cues** are those that we generate ourselves. Try this memory problem.

Read each of the following sentences once, spending about (no more than) three seconds on each. As soon as you are finished, put the list out of sight and write as many of the sentences as you can recall.

Thomas Jefferson was a Virginian.

The tide was high at 10:45 A.M.

STORING
The ability to hold information in memory.

RETRIEVING
Ability to access information in stored memory.

CUES
Techniques to help us recall; particularly effective if we generate them ourselves.

Evergreens are not deciduous.

Our new car is a turbo diesel.

The lawnmower has a rotary construction.

Light travels at the rate of 186 million miles/second.

John F. Kennedy was born in Brookline, Massachusetts.

Richard Feynman won the Nobel Prize for physics in 1965.

In the colder climates, lobsters usually shed their shells in July.

The new generation of printers is based on laser principles.

Most readers will recall six or seven of these ten sentences.

Our interest is in what happened to the other three or four. Did you fail to encode them? Did you lose them almost immediately? Use these words as retrieval cues for the sentences you cannot recall:

laser	rotary
Virginian	deciduous
tide	lobsters
Brookline	light
turbo	Nobel

This time you probably remembered most, if not all, the sentences that you initially failed to retrieve. With instruction and guidance, students can easily master this technique and will improve not only their problem-solving skills but also their memory in all subjects. Initially, the teacher can teach students how to utilize this technique by providing them with tangible cues for the material the teacher is presenting. The ultimate objective is to help students devise their own cues for any subject they encounter.

A particularly effective cue is the use of *acronyms* and *acrostics*. As mentioned earlier, an acronym is a word consisting of the initial letters in a series of words (for example, DUPE). There is a twofold value to acronyms: (a) the compression of several facts into a smaller number, and (b) the cues they provide for remembering large amounts of data (DUPE acts as a trigger, releasing the facts incorporated under each letter).

A second strategy is to devise a sentence or phrase with words whose first letters are the cues for certain information. Most of us who are nonmusicians have relied on an acrostic to recall the lines in the treble clef: **E**very **G**ood **B**oy **D**oes **F**ine. Using an acrostic is an effective strategy, as long as the material is not too complicated or unique. The strategy should never be more difficult than the task; the goal is to simplify!

Imagery   Some students—as well as readers—tend to visualize objects or events; they function more efficiently in this mode, rather than relying on verbal processes that are less dependent on concreteness. Teachers can encourage the use of **imagery** in all students, and they will find it helpful.

Urge them to form a picture that links the items that they are to remember. For example, if students must remember that John Adams was the second president of the United States, ask them to picture Adams standing to have his portrait painted and holding a large card with the number 2 on it. For those students who function best in this mode, and even for those who are more verbal, the use of imagery can aid retention and recall.

Sometimes you just have to see it:

Imagery
The ability to visualize objects or events.

*When I start describing the magnetic field moving through space, I speak of the **E-** and **B-** fields and wave my arms and you may imagine that I can see them. I'll tell you what I see. I see some kind of vague, shadowy, wiggling lines .... and perhaps some of the lines have arrows on them—an arrow here or there which disappears when I look too closely. (Gleick, 1992, p. 245)*

What's going on here? Well, for one thing, the Nobel Prize–winning physicist, Richard Feynman, is explaining how he endowed abstract symbols with physical meaning. He believed that physicists need imagery, that is, an ability to see and feel things that then translate into thinking. Feynman named this ability "physical intuition" and believed that when Einstein lost it and devoted himself to manipulating equations, he lost his spark of creativity.

Nudging your students into a willingness to attempt different things, to explore different options, to develop an ability to search for different patterns demands your sensitivity, persistence, and understanding. Why? Because your students are no different than the rest of us. It's so easy, so very easy, to do the same thing we've always done, even when it doesn't work! How many times have you seen people faced with a problem follow the same procedures or use the same equation that failed them previously? The danger here is that these attitudes become a way of life, leading to tunnel vision, a vision that can carry over to any difficult task.

The Method of Loci   The preceding techniques are excellent, provided that the retrieval cues are appropriate. Lacking appropriate stimuli, however, you still can devise personal cues to help you remember and recall unrelated items. The **method of loci** (using familiar locations) was originally used by the Greeks and Romans to recall items in a fixed sequence. By utilizing a series of familiar visual images and linking each image to an object to be retained, you will have formulated your personal retrieval cues.

Since the rooms in your house are firmly locked in your memory, they are suitable "locations" in which to place the items to be remembered. First, form an image of the object that you must recall; second, place it somewhere in one of the rooms. Use each location only once; if you placed the term *educational psychology* on the couch in the living room, do not use that specific location again. Try using the method of loci.

Map out a path that you would take in your home, arranging the rooms along the path in the most economical manner possible. Now "picture" each of the following words and place it somewhere on your route:

assimilation	attribution
concrete operations	value
learning	strategy
locus of control	iconic
cognitive	accommodation

Elaboration   To elaborate is to add information to what you're trying to learn so that the material becomes more personally meaningful. It involves using what we already know to help make sense of what we are trying to learn. **Elaboration** strategies that improve students' recall of material are effective because they produce an increased depth of processing (more involvement with material). Elaboration also facilitates storage of new information with related information that is well known to the learner (Weinstein & Mayer, 1986).

The effective use of elaboration strategies depends on students' relating what they are trying to learn to what they already know. The way learners use this strategy can involve a number of specific tactics, such as creating analogies, paraphrasing, summarizing in their own

METHOD OF LOCI
The use of familiar locations to help one visually store things in memory and retrieve them more easily.

ELABORATION
The adding of information to what one is trying to learn so the material becomes more personally meaningful.

Current Issues & Perspectives

Thinking, Problem Solving, and Technology

As this chapter has shown, teaching students about improving their thinking and problem-solving skills is an important, but not easily achievable goal. Can technology help? A number of researchers think so. For example, Seymour Papert (1993) argued that programming requires the programmer to think about her own thinking, clarify it, examine it for flaws in logic, and be extremely precise in expressing the goal and steps needed. Papert and his colleagues at Massachusetts Institute of Technology developed the programming language *Logo*, a language designed so that even preschool children can quickly begin to program, producing simple drawings on the computer screen almost immediately.

Logo is usually introduced by having children create drawings using its cleverly designed graphics capabilities. Children write sets of directions (the program) for a turtle (an icon on the computer screen), telling the turtle what steps it must take to produce a given drawing. The directions can be easily combined to produce a wide variety of interesting, complicated designs. Logo has become quite popular, and elementary schools across the country now routinely introduce it to their students.

Very interesting, but how does Logo enhance students' thinking skills? First, programming forces children to think carefully about their own thinking. They can't write a slipshod, vague program; the program simply won't run. Second, proponents argue that programming requires the consistent use of a number of important problem-solving skills. For example, the most efficient way to program in Logo (as in most programming languages) is to use subprocedures, which require that students define new words (that is, procedures) for the various subparts of a desired product, then tell the turtle how to put these procedures together.

A third aspect of programming that contributes to improved problem-solving skills is the need to "debug," or notice the existence of, identify the nature of, and correct errors. Debugging is clearly an important skill to learn, and Papert and others argue that Logo is a very good vehicle for enhancing such skills in children.

Fourth, programming is a "problem-rich" environment, that is, meaningful and complex problems occur frequently in the course of writing a program, so there is no need to manufacture problems for students to solve. These naturally occurring problems are motivating and interesting because they arise from and block progress toward a goal students are seeking.

How could you use Logo to enhance problem-solving skills? First, you'll need a certain degree of structure in the learning environment. Simply teaching children the basics of the language, then letting them play with it in a free discovery manner doesn't work. You'll find yourself helping students choose certain tasks that are within the students' zone of proximal development (remember Vygotsky's work in Chapter 2), then providing "scaffolding" as students attempt the tasks.

A daily practitioner of these ideas has summarized his attempts to use technology as a gateway to meaningful learning, thinking, and problem solving as follows:

> *Now our students are writing stories with word processors, illustrating diagrams with paint utilities, creating interactive reports with hypermedia, and graphing data they have gathered. (Muir, 1994, p. 30)*

words, transforming information into other forms, such as charts or diagrams, using comparison and contrast methods, and trying to teach what they are learning to someone else.

These are the most prominent techniques designed to improve retention and recall. They can be extremely helpful if you remember two warnings: (1) Be sure that the strategy itself is not so complex and cumbersome that it requires more effort to remember than the content does; and (2) be sure that students adopt techniques that are best suited to them.

Remember: Teachers can help students improve their memory by knowing as much as possible about the different techniques we've mentioned and using the techniques that seem to work particularly well for them. Finally, have students practice, practice, practice.

Strategies, both traditional and creative, that cut across situations and that are not confined to classroom subjects are those that will concern us in the next section.

TRANSFERRING STRATEGIES AND SKILLS

Influences on Transfer

Certain conditions influence what and how much learning will be transferred (Ellis & Hunt, 1989). For example, *task similarity exercises a strong influence on **transfer of learning.*** Imagine changing the color of the traffic lights that govern our driving. Instead of stopping at a red light, we must now stop at the orange signal. Would this bother us? Not too much, because orange is similar to red, and it would be relatively easy to transfer the stopping habit. Learning to make the same response to new but similar stimuli usually produces positive transfer.

Now let's change the conditions. Instead of stopping at red, we must stop at green and go on red. The pattern will be completely reversed. What will happen? Drivers, making new and opposite responses to red and green, will undoubtedly get into more accidents. Here we see an instance of negative transfer: What was previously learned interferes with the new learning. Is it any wonder that students can have difficulty with some English sounds? How will you sound *ou* as it is pronounced in *though,* in *tough,* or in *ouch?* Teachers must be alert to the impact that similarity can have on transfer.

Another important element in transfer is *the degree of original learning.* More practice and greater familiarity with the original material produces more positive transfer. If students are thoroughly familiar with multiplication, for example, they have little trouble determining how much eight apples at 9¢ each will cost them while shopping.

Finally, *personal variables such as intelligence, motivation, and past experiences are important and difficult-to-control influences on transfer.* Personal knowledge of students will help to ensure transfer, since teachers will know something about the extent of their past

TRANSFER OF LEARNING

Learning one topic may influence later learning.

Teachers want their students to use what they learn in the classroom in a variety of situations; that is, to transfer their learning in order to foster new learning and to solve their problems.

learning. Teachers can usually relate some aspect of students' experiences to new material, thus facilitating transfer. For example, knowing places that students have visited can make a social studies lesson more meaningful for an entire class.

Teaching for Transfer

For transfer to occur, students must see similar elements in both situations and must have a good grasp of the original material. Courses in driver education should produce students who obtain their driving licenses and have good safety records. If algebra is intended to be used in physics and chemistry classes, then students should demonstrate this transfer in their science classes. Here are some general suggestions that should help students appreciate the value of transfer:

- *Teach to overlearning.* The more experience students have with the material to be transferred, the more successful will be the transfer. A good idea is to give verbal examples of how material can be transferred and then provide circumstances that encourage students to use the material. In class discussions, assignments, and quizzes, urge students to search for transfer.

- *Be certain that the material taught is well organized.* Meaningful material is more easily transferred. We have previously mentioned how important it is for students to recognize the organization and structure of material. If teachers can bring them to this realization, students will discover principles and generalizations that they can use in many situations. For example, if students thoroughly grasp the reasons for Lincoln's desire not to punish the Southern states, they will transfer this knowledge to modern times and appreciate why presidents tolerate dissent for the sake of national unity.

- *Use advance organizers if possible.* When a teacher is about to teach abstract material, it may be useful to furnish students with *advance organizers* (see Chapter 7 for more information). These general principles will help students to see that the abstract material they are encountering possesses more structure than it would if they met it unprepared. Teachers must know both students and the subject to formulate effective advance organizers: Introductory work reflects what the teacher thinks is important, and it must match students' ability level.

- *Emphasize the similarity between classroom work and the transfer situation.* If you are concerned with transfer, you must attempt to make the classroom condition (source) similar to the transfer situation (target). For example, most algebra tests involve word problems; consequently, as soon as possible teachers should have students work with word problems, perhaps incorporating terms from chemistry and physics. When teaching reading, teachers must be sure that the letters and words they teach have the same forms that the youngsters will see in their readers. If possible, students should receive practice under conditions similar to those in the working or transfer environment.

- *Specify what's important in the task.* Identifying the important features of a task helps students to transfer these elements or to guard against potential difficulties. For example, children frequently confuse *b* with *d,* so teachers should stress the distinction and give them considerable experience with words containing these letters. In algebra, students consistently forget to change signs $(+, -)$ when moving terms from one side of an equation to the other. Constantly call students' attention to the required change of sign, while providing numerous instances that require transposition.

■ *Try to understand how students perceive the possibility of transfer.* Make every effort to help students understand the meaning and importance of transfer. Is it meaningful to them? Do they see how they can use the material in different circumstances? If teachers attempt to see their teaching and the subject from the students' viewpoint, they may present it quite differently, capitalizing more on students' backgrounds and offering more practical possibilities of transfer. This is more easily said than done, but once you try it, you'll be more conscious of the need for emphasizing strategies, meaning, organization, and structure.

Case Reflections

A chapter on thinking and problem solving should offer many different ideas regarding the daily problems teachers will face in the classroom. In this case, a teacher simply is unable to reach one of his students and, to aggravate the situation, he is plagued by a demanding mother. It's obvious from reading the case that Mark Siegel feels overwhelmed by his difficulties.

With what we know today about thinking, problem solving, and creativity, it's possible for this teacher (and you, too, if the occasion arises) to step back and begin to use several of the strategies described in this chapter. For example, given the disparate cognitive styles of teacher and student, Mark Siegel would be well advised to study Karim's learning preferences and attempt to link them to classroom work.

Identifying learning preferences would help this teacher to capitalize on Karim's intellectual likes and dislikes. That is, does Karim seem to function better in situations that demand a verbal response, not just reading, but

listening to stories, telling stories, and so on? Or does he prefer something requiring a physical response, perhaps drawing or painting? Does he show any interest in music?

Finally, has this teacher given up too quickly? We don't ask this question lightly. As experienced teachers, we know how frustrating a Karim Peterson can be, but has Mark Siegel looked at himself here? Is he too ready to retreat? When he thinks about the problem, should he see himself as part of the problem as well as part of the solution?

For example, why hasn't he turned to Karim's interest in African culture and used that to stimulate new efforts? We suggest that Mr. Siegel adopt the characteristics of creative thinkers to solve his problem: Use the strategies discussed in this chapter, search for novel approaches (perhaps initiate an African American literature club), reorganize the elements in his problem (rethink his relationship with Karim's mother, adopt cooperative learning techniques), and, last, persevere, persevere, persevere!

CHAPTER HIGHLIGHTS

Thinking

- The need for thinking and problem-solving skills dominates our lives.
- Cognitive or learning style refers to preferences in learning and studying.
- Knowing your cognitive style and that of your students improves both teaching and learning.

Thinking Skills: An Analysis

- Bloom's Taxonomy of Educational Objectives is intended to specify desirable cognitive objectives in behavioral terms, to suggest means of evaluating the attainment of these goals, and to aid in curriculum construction.

- Costa's Thinking Skills program is based on knowledge of how the brain works, humans' awareness of their own thinking, and the acquiring of knowledge. He urged that an information-processing model should be the basis for teaching, learning, and curriculum construction.
- Several thinking skills programs have been designed to help students.

Problem Solving

- Good problem solvers have identifiable characteristics.
- Though some students are probably better than others at solving problems, the problem-solving ability of all students can be improved.
- Difficulty in solving problems can come from simple mistakes, such as failing to use all of the clues present in the problem.
- Some students are reluctant, for a variety of reasons, to attack problems.

The DUPE Model

- **D**   Determining the nature of a problem helps you to identify the "givens" of a problem and then to decide what actions can be performed on them, that is, "to bridge the gap between where one is and where one wants to go."
- **U**   Understanding the nature of a problem means identifying the nature of the problem and also representing it.
- **P**   Planning means to represent a problem and cast its information in either symbolic (internal) or graphic (external) form.
- **E**   Evaluation of a problem-solving plan can occur at two stages: after the plan is devised (is it adequate?) and after the solution is proposed (did it work?).
- When a solution proves elusive, a new and creative approach is often called for.
- Memory plays a crucial role in problem solving.

Transferring Strategies and Skills

- Transfer refers to the ability to use past experiences to help understand new challenging situations.
- Several factors influence transfer.
- A major goal of instruction should be to teach for transfer.

WHAT DO YOU THINK?

1. How important is it for teachers to recognize the learning styles of their students? Why?
2. What are some of the common sources of error you experience when trying to solve a problem?
3. How would you go about helping students acquire the characteristics of a "good problem solver"?
4. How would you foster creative behavior in a young student?

Motivation and Student Learning

This chapter on motivation focuses on one of the central issues confronting Mark Siegel in his efforts to improve the academic performances of Karim Peterson. As you recall from the case synopsis at the beginning of this section, Karim seems quite uninterested in learning and is somewhat of a social loner or outcast. As you read about motivation theories and research in this chapter, ask yourself how these ideas can apply to Karim and possibly explain his behavior. How can you use a theory of motivation to guide a plan to increase Karim's motivation to learn?

Over the course of students' K–12 educational experience, they will have hundreds of interactions with teachers and many opportunities to learn new information. These early learning interactions, of course, play a major role in what students know, but perhaps even more important, they influence the development of students' motivation to learn, as well as their curiosity and sense of efficacy or competence. In the long run, these characteristics lead to the development of learners who assume control over what they learn and do so with a strong desire toward understanding what they learn. How does a person develop into a motivated learner? What role does schooling play in this development? What theories can explain the development of motivation and self-directed learning? Before delving into the answers to these questions, let's first examine a couple of classroom situations that focus on motivation and students' roles in directing their own learning.

When parents and teachers ask about motivation, they often want to know what causes one student to act highly motivated and another in the same class to be totally unmotivated. Recall Karim Peterson, the student case featured in this section's opening pages, and how his mother and his teacher, Mark Siegel, were both puzzled and frustrated about his lack of achievement. When you finish this chapter, you should have several insights into motivational aspects of Karim's behavior, as well as most other students, and also be able to answer questions about classroom practices that enhance motivation and self-directed learning.

MOTIVATION: MEANING AND MYTHS

Motivation has been a central construct in both educational and psychological research for the past sixty years and plays a significant role in several theories of human development and learning (Weiner, 1990a). *Motivation is defined as an internal state that arouses us to action, pushes us in particular directions, and keeps us engaged in certain activities.* Learning and motivation are equally essential for performance: Learning enables us to acquire new knowledge and skills, and motivation provides the impetus for showing what we have learned. In general, more-motivated people achieve at higher levels.

Motivation is an important psychological construct that affects learning and performance in at least four ways:

1. Motivation increases an individual's energy and activity level (Pintrich, Marx, & Boyle, 1993). It influences the extent to which an individual is likely to engage in a certain activity intensively or half-heartedly.

2. Motivation directs an individual toward certain goals (Eccles & Wigfield, 1985). Motivation affects choices people make and the results they find rewarding.

3. Motivation promotes initiation of certain activities and persistence in those activities (Stipek, 1998). It increases the likelihood that people will begin something on their own, persist in the face of difficulty, and resume a task after a temporary interruption.

4. Motivation affects the learning strategies and cognitive processes an individual employs (Dweck & Elliott, 1983). It increases the likelihood that people will pay attention to something, study and practice it, and try to learn it in a meaningful fashion. It also increases the likelihood that they will seek help when they encounter difficulty.

The concept of motivation has been subject to myths that can lead to inappropriate educational practices. For example: *Failure is a good motivator.* Experience may be a valuable teacher and we all can learn something from our mistakes, if we listen to feedback. But chronic failure often leads to more of the same, unless a better way is substituted. Success, even a small success, is a more potent motivator for most students. Another example of a myth is: *Teachers motivate students.* Realistically, the best teachers can do is make conditions for learning as attractive and stimulating as possible and by matching tasks to student ability. By doing so, one can encourage students' self-motivation. A third common myth is: *Threats increase motivation.* By using the threat of low grades, retention, and parental notification, some teachers believe that they motivate students. Although such stern measures may result in some short-term improvements, in most cases they have been shown to be counterproductive.

Another aspect of motivation often discussed when educational practices are of concern is the relative importance of **intrinsic** and **extrinsic motivation.** Intrinsic or internally oriented motivation means that students themselves demonstrate the desire to learn without the need for external inducements. Obviously, this is an ideal state that can result in considerable learning and a minimum of discipline problems. This ideal state of intrinsic motivation, however, can be elusive for some students. Consequently, marks, prizes, and other tangible rewards have been used to influence some students' behavior. If students respond to these externally controlled inducements, they are said to be extrinsically motivated. In reality, the intrinsic-extrinsic dichotomy is a false one. It is more accurate to say that students are primarily intrinsically or primarily extrinsically motivated to learn. There are always consequences extrinsic to students that may have influenced their efforts. The long-term desired goal of most parents and educators is to see students develop into intrinsically motivated learners. That is, they want to see students who are self-directed, who initiate and maintain interest in what they are learning, and are genuinely pleased when they finish their work.

If you were asked to provide a list of highly motivated individuals, the chances are that your list would include the names of some great athletes. These gifted people did not arrive at their present lofty position by ability alone. Talent plus dedicated determination helped them to achieve their "world-class" accomplishments. Psychologists are convinced that today's great athletes have not yet reached their physiological limitations and that any restraints on performance are psychological. In their efforts to help athletes to overcome these restraints, sports psychologists have devised techniques that can help not only athletes but also classroom teachers. For example, runners are urged to imagine the noise of the crowd, the sound of their own breathing, their position at the starting line, the starter's gun, their first steps, the encouragement of their teammates, and the feeling of the track under their spikes. They are likewise directed to see themselves crossing the finish line first and receiving a victory medal.

INTRINSIC
MOTIVATION
The desire of students themselves to learn, without the need for external inducements.

EXTRINSIC
MOTIVATION
Those rewards and inducements external to students.

CASE NOTES

Observation   Karim Peterson seems very uninterested in class and disconnected from his classmates, yet there are data to indicate he is academically capable.

Hypothesis   Given the differences in his cultural background from the rest of his classmates and his family's strong emphasis on African heritage, it may seem like school and his teacher, Mr. Siegel, are very different and have little to offer Karim.

Possible Action   Think of some ways to bring Karim's knowledge of African American culture into his classroom work.

Listening to students shows you care. Caring and attention are powerful motivators for many students.

The goal of a sports psychologist is to produce in the athletes a feeling of their own competence, which is a strong motivating force. That is, not only *can* they do it, but they *want* to do it. Similar techniques can be effective in the classroom. It is entirely possible that if you match a task with a student's ability, having that student imagine successful performance will produce more effective behavior, which then will aid motivation for the next task. For example, urge students to picture themselves studying. Then have them visualize understanding the material. Finally, have them see themselves in the classroom, relaxed and ready for a test.

Will students learn even if they are poorly motivated? They will learn something, but will they learn what we want them to learn? Everything that we know about learning indicates that if motivation is faulty, learning will suffer: Attention is limited; behavior is not directed at objectives; discipline may become a problem; learning has gone awry.

Although it is relatively easy to describe motivated individuals, it is difficult to specify just what motivation is. When you are motivated, or when you see motivated students, you usually can discover what conditions caused the behavior. Something acted on you, or the students, to produce a certain kind of behavior, which was maintained at a certain level of intensity and was directed at a definite goal. *Thus, motivation arouses, sustains, directs, and integrates a person's behavior.* For example, a student may have been promised a ticket to a rock concert for passing an algebra course, and she did. Or you want to get a good grade in your educational psychology course so that your transcript will be attractive to a future employer, and you do. In both examples, a certain type of behavior was aroused and maintained long enough to achieve a specific goal.

Theories of Motivation: Explanations of Motivated Students

Since motivated students are obviously the most desirable to teach, it is well worth the time and effort for teachers (and future teachers or parents) to learn as much as possible about motivation. One way of coming to grips with the nature and meaning of motivation is to examine several motivational theories. Motivational theories have their roots in the work of developmentalists like Piaget, Erikson, Maslow, and Bruner and learning theorists like Bandura and Skinner. Motivation has always been tied to learning activities and often has been inferred from the outcomes of learning. Early motivation theorists in the 1940s (such as Hull and Spence) focused on hunger and thirst drives or sexual stimulation (Freud). Efforts to apply the results of motivational research to education produced a greater emphasis on the cognitive aspects of motivation. Thus, today, a cognitive emphasis with a focus on the self-system dominates motivational theory and research. For example, causal attributions, self-efficacy, learned helplessness, test anxiety, locus of control, competitive versus cooperative activities, and intrinsic versus extrinsic rewards are all used to explain human motivation (Schunk, 1990) and are examined in this chapter. Although there are numerous theoretical explanations of motivation—biological, learning, cognitive—we shall focus primarily on theories that have direct classroom application. If you grasp the meaning of these motivational theories and related key concepts, you will be in a much better position to understand motivation, or its lack, in individual students. A good place to begin to understand students' motivation and objectives is to examine the needs hierarchy of Abraham Maslow.

Maslow's Needs Hierarchy and Its Application in the Classroom

One of Abraham Maslow's (1987) most famous concepts is that of **self-actualization,** which means that we use our abilities to the limit of our potentialities. If we can convince students that they should—and can—fulfill their promise, they are then on the path to self-actualization. *Self-actualization is a growth concept;* students move toward this goal as they satisfy their basic needs. It is movement toward physical and psychological health. Growth toward self-actualization requires the satisfaction of a **hierarchy of needs.** There are five basic needs in Maslow's theory: *physiological, safety, love and belonging, esteem,* and *self-actualization.* Figure 9.1 illustrates the hierarchy of needs, with those needs at the base of the hierarchy assumed to be more basic relative to the needs above them in the hierarchy.

1. *Physiological needs.* Physiological needs, such as hunger and sleep, are dominant and are the basis of motivation. Unless they are satisfied, everything else recedes. For example, students who frequently do not eat breakfast or suffer from poor nutrition generally become lethargic and noninteracting; their learning potential is severely lowered. Note: This is particularly true of adolescents who can be extremely sensitive to their weight.

2. *Safety needs.* These needs represent the importance of security, protection, stability, freedom from fear and anxiety, and the need for structure and limits. Students who are afraid of school, of peers, of a teacher, or of a parent have their safety needs threatened, and these fears can affect classroom performance.

3. *Love and belongingness needs.* This category refers to our need for family and friends. Healthy, motivated people wish to avoid feelings of loneliness and isolation. Students

SELF-ACTUALIZATION
The full development or use of one's talents and potentialities.

HIERARCHY OF NEEDS
A theoretical model of five needs that Maslow believed every human being had; the needs range from basic physiological and safety needs, to love and belongingness needs, to esteem, and finally at the top of the hierarchy the need for self-actualization.

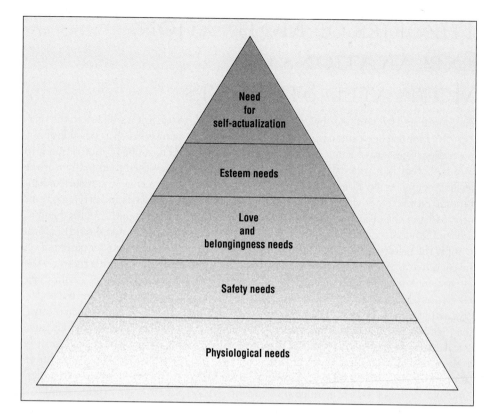

FIGURE 9.1

Maslow's hierarchy of needs.

(Data for diagram based on Hierarchy of Needs from *Motivation and Personality,* Third Edition, by Abraham H. Maslow, Revised by Robert Frager, et al., Harper & Row, Inc. 1954, 1987.)

who feel alone, not part of the group, or who lack any sense of belongingness usually have poor relationships with others, which can then affect classroom learning.

4. *Esteem needs.* These needs encompass the reactions of others to us as individuals and our opinion of ourselves. We want a favorable judgment from others, which should be based on honest achievement. Our own sense of competence combines with the reactions of others to produce our sense of self-esteem. Teachers should be sure to provide opportunities for students to satisfy this need: Help students to achieve and receive deserved reinforcement.

5. *Need for self-actualization.* Here Maslow was referring to that tendency (in spite of the satisfaction of lower needs) to feel restless unless we are being all that we can be. Encourage students to recognize their potential and guide them into activities that will enable them to feel both competent and fulfilled.

Examining Maslow's hierarchy, you can see how a deficit in any one need category will affect student performance. Hungry students, for example, usually are not scholars; their hunger overwhelms all other concerns. Similarly, fearful students (for whatever reason) may find it difficult to concentrate on their studies. Those students who feel rejected and isolated may refuse to participate fully in your class activities.

Students—and all of us—need to feel that we are worthy of respect, both from ourselves and others, a respect that is based on actual achievement. Finally, unless students believe that they are doing all that they could be doing, they will be plagued by feelings of restlessness and even discontent. As you can see, Maslow's remarkably perceptive analysis of human needs furnishes us with rich general insights into human behavior. His work has many aspects in common with the social-emotional developmental framework of Erikson (1950), whose work we examined in Chapter 3.

Support from an adult after a difficult situation can have a positive effect on motivation to succeed.

CASE NOTES

Observation Karim Peterson's physiological and safety needs seem satisfied, but his belongingness and esteem needs are currently unmet.

Hypothesis His poor relationships with classmates is a key aspect to improving his interest in class and subsequent academic achievement.

Possible Action Consider designing an intervention focusing on relationship building skills using a small group approach; also consider identifying a study buddy for Karim.

Bruner and Discovery Learning

In his now classic book, *The Process of Education* (1960), Jerome Bruner stated that any attempt to improve education inevitably begins with the motives for learning. He asked: What results from emphasis on examinations, grades, and promotion? Does it intensify motivation? How intense should motivation be? Bruner believed that there is some ideal level of arousal between apathy and wild excitement, since passivity causes boredom while intense activity leaves little time for reflection and generalization.

One possible solution is Bruner's notion of **discovery learning,** which has captured many educators' imagination with its insights into classroom motivation. Arguing that discovery is rearranging or transforming evidence so that one goes beyond the evidence to form new insights, Bruner stated that discovery proceeds from the well-prepared mind. Encouraging discovery causes students not only to organize material to determine regularities and relationships but also to avoid the passivity that blinds them to the use of the information learned. The result is that students learn to manipulate their environment more actively and achieve considerable gratification from personally coping with problems. We know that students like tasks that permit them to respond actively by interacting with teachers or with each other (Brophy, 1987a).

DISCOVERY
LEARNING
Bruner's term for learning that involves the rearrangement and transformation of material by a learner in a way that leads to insight.

TIPS ON LEARNING
Making Learning Activities Enjoyable for Students

PRINCIPLE   Students enjoy activities or tasks that either satisfy a basic need or fulfill a sense of personal accomplishment.

STRATEGY   Design activities or tasks that can be completed or finished within a reasonable time and have clear goals to pursue.

STRATEGY   Provide students immediate feedback in how well or poorly they are doing on the task and allow opportunities for them to use the feedback to make adjustments in efforts.

STRATEGY   Select activities or tasks that stretch the students' skills and capacities but are viewed as fair by students.

Bruner emphasized that the goal of discovery learning is to have students use their information in solving problems in many different circumstances. One of Bruner's basic assumptions underlying discovery learning is that individuals behave according to their perceptions of their environment. That is, students see meaning in knowledge, skills, and attitudes when they themselves discover it. This is similar to some of Vygotsky's notions about language learning and Piaget's emphasis on active learners.

As we have emphasized in preceding chapters, the challenge for a teacher is to arrange classroom materials and activities so that students learn with a maximum of personal involvement and a minimum of teacher intervention. Try to make the material you're presenting as personal, concrete, and familiar as possible. Relate the material to students' personal experiences, use anecdotes, and show how the material applies to their lives.

Students will always have mixed motives for learning. They must please parents, impress peers, and acquire mastery. But how can teachers help students appreciate the world of ideas for their own sake? One recommendation is to increase students' inherent interest by ensuring that teachers present ideas at the students' level so that they achieve a sense of discovery. If teachers succeed, they not only teach a subject but also instill attitudes and values about intellectual activity in students.

Finally, Bruner noted that knowledge of results (feedback, reinforcement) is valuable if it comes when learners compare their results with what they attempt to achieve. Even then, learners use feedback according to their internal state, that is, their interests, attitudes, anxieties, and the like. Information is least useful when learners are highly anxious or focus on only one aspect of a problem too closely. For Bruner, information is most helpful when it is at the learner's level and encourages self-activity and intrinsic motivation.

Weiner and Attributions about Success or Failure

Even with a need to achieve, students will either succeed or fail. As they do, they search for reasons for their success or failure—they attribute their performance to a specific cause: The test was difficult; the teacher dislikes me; I'm not good in this subject. Students' attributions then serve as a guide to their expectations for future success or failure in that subject. We are all similar in this respect. If, when you are with a certain person, you consistently have an enjoyable time, then your expectation is that you will continue to have a good time in the future. Students who consistently do poorly in a subject expect to continue to do poorly. But before a teacher can hope to have success in changing a student's performance, the teacher must know to what that student attributes subpar performance.

CASE NOTES

Observation   There seems to be limited opportunities in Mark Siegel's classroom for students to engage in discovery learning and to maximize personal perspective in a task or assignment.

Hypothesis   Karim Peterson has interests outside of school that do not presently match up with those typically focused on in the classroom. If he can work on tasks that allow his interests to be utilized, he will demonstrate improved learning.

Possible Action   Discuss with Mark Siegel the possibility of some discovery-oriented tasks that focus on students' personal interests and backgrounds.

Attribution theory rests on three basic assumptions (Petri, 1991). First, people want to know the causes of their own behavior and of others, particularly behavior that is important to them. Second, attribution theory assumes that we do not randomly assign causes to our behavior. There is a logical explanation for the causes to which we attribute our behavior. Third, the causes that we assign to our behavior influence subsequent behavior. If we attribute our failure to a particular person, we may come to dislike that person. The student who believes that "no matter what I do, Mr. Smith won't give me a good grade" will come to dislike Mr. Smith.

Attribution theory also relates well to the need for achievement. Bernard Weiner (1990b) believes that when achievement is aroused, we tend to attribute our performance to one of four elements: ability, effort, task difficulty, or luck. Each of these elements is characterized in Figure 9.2 and described next:

- *Ability:* These attributions of success and failure have important implications for teaching since students' assumptions about their abilities are usually based on past experiences. It is precisely here that we find explanations for math phobia, reading problems, or dislike of science. When students have a history of failure, they often make the rather devastating assumption that they lack ability. This tendency is particularly true if others do well at the task. Once students question their abilities, this doubt spreads to other subjects and other tasks. Soon there is a generalized feeling of incompetence that paralyzes initiative and activates an expectation of failure. Schunk (1989), studying the relationship between self-efficacy (that is, personal judgments of performance capabilities on any task) and learning, reported that students enter a classroom with aptitudes and experiences that affect their self-efficacy for initial learning. When successful, students' sense of self-efficacy increases, and in turn, enhances motivation.

  Students who consistently question their own abilities pose a serious challenge for educators, because the students' history of failure and feelings of incompetence undercut motivation and learning. An initial assumption about these students should be that there must be something that they can do well. Consequently, search for tasks that they can perform with competence and publicly reward them for their success. Remember: Avoid the danger of attributing their initial failure to a lack of ability before searching for alternate causes.

- *Effort:* Weiner (1990b) also made the interesting discovery that students usually have no idea how hard they try to succeed. Students (and all of us) judge their efforts by how well they did on a particular task. Even in tasks involving pure

ATTRIBUTION
THEORY

*A motivational theory that
assumes people want to know
the causes of their behavior.*

FIGURE 9.2

Conditions and characteristics that often influence students' attributions about successes or failures.

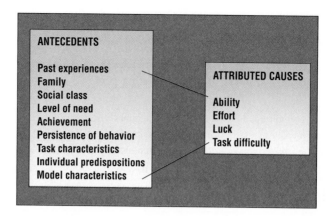

chance, successful students believed that they tried harder than those who were unsuccessful. An important cycle is thus established: Success increases effort; effort produces more success. The educational implications are real and significant. If a skill is to be mastered and the teaching is consistent for an entire group, then student performance will vary because of motivation. Here again we note the importance of ensuring success as a means of encouraging further effort.

- *Luck:* Finally, if there is no tangible link between behavior and goal attainment, the tendency is to attribute success to luck. Those students who have little faith in their abilities attribute their success on almost any task to luck, thus short-circuiting the motivational network just described. Success in this case will not increase effort; lack of effort does nothing to bolster a belief in one's ability, and tasks remain an overwhelming obstacle.

- *Task Difficulty:* Task difficulty usually is judged by the performance of others on the task. If many succeed, the task is perceived as easy, and vice versa. An interesting phenomenon can develop here. If a student consistently succeeds on a task at which others fail, that student will attribute success to ability. But if individual success is matched by the success of others, then the source of the success is seen in the task. Weiner's findings emphasize once again the importance of matching a task with a student's ability, thus enhancing ability and increasing effort.

Applying the Model

In applying his interpretation of attribution theory to the classroom, Weiner (1990b) stated that there is a relationship among a student's attributions (ability, effort, luck, task difficulty), the stability of the attribution, its resistance to extinction, and expectancy of future goal attainment. Consequently, in achievement-related situations, students experience both cognitive and emotional reactions. For example, John just failed his history exam. He is experiencing feelings of frustration and is upset, such as the following:

1. "I failed because I didn't try hard enough," followed by feelings of shame and guilt.

2. "I just don't have the right stuff," followed by feelings of low self-esteem, lack of worth, and hopelessness.

It is a complicated mixture, one to which a teacher should be alert. When attempting to help students, teachers must be aware of their own causal attributions. It is quite easy to be deceived by a student's apparent high level of effort and assign higher ability to

---

CASE NOTES

Observation   Karim Peterson puts forth limited effort and doesn't like to discuss his work.

Hypothesis   He may be intentionally putting forth limited effort to mask what he believes is poor ability.

Possible Action   A closer assessment of Karim is needed to determine whether it is more of a performance problem or an ability problem. Information from Mrs. Peterson about Karim's efforts on homework assignments should be collected.

---

that student than warranted. Students may also deliberately minimize effort to avoid the suggestion they lack ability because teachers first are likely to focus on students' poor effort rather than detect their limited ability.

Examining the subtleties of motivation leads to the conclusion that certain motivational aspects involve learning. Some motivation is learned: We learn to want definite objects; we learn to expect certain outcomes; we learn to fear certain things. But the relationship between learning and motivation is bidirectional—new learning depends on motivation. Motivation is heightened for many students when interesting, new learning opportunities are presented.

As we shall see in the next section, learning theorists have widely different views, and their explanations of motivation reflect their beliefs about learning. Among the most prominent of the learning theorists is B. F. Skinner, whose approach to behavior is usually referred to as *operant* or *instrumental conditioning.*

Skinner and the Use of Reinforcers to Increase Motivation

B. F. Skinner (1971) stated that if you ask people why they go to the theater and they reply that they feel like going, you are usually satisfied. It would be more revealing, however, if you knew what had happened when they previously attended the theater, what they had read about the current play, and what else induced them to go. According to Skinner, behavior is shaped and maintained by its consequences. Thus, the consequences of previous behavior influence students. There is no major internal or intrinsic motivational component in the process. According to Skinner, motivated behavior results from the consequences of similar previous behavior. If students obtain **reinforcement** for certain behavior, they tend to repeat it with vigor. If they don't, students (like all of us) tend to lose interest, and their performance suffers.

Students should not study merely to avoid the consequences of not studying, which may be something aversive such as punishment. Under aversive conditions, students will engage in truancy, vandalism, disruptive behavior, or apathy. How can teachers improve control over their classroom and not abandon it? Skinner believes that the answer lies in the appropriate use of *positive reinforcement.* Students are immediately rewarded upon giving correct responses and are not punished for giving incorrect responses. These students become free and happy in the classroom and outside school because they have established behavioral patterns that produce success, pleasant relations with others, and a deserved sense of accomplishment. These behaviors have developed because students learning to read have been reinforced when their spoken responses to verbal stimuli are correct. You are reinforced during a lecture when the words you hear or see correspond to the responses that you anticipated. If you have been fortunate enough to have received such positive reinforcement, you can understand what Skinner means by self-motivation.

REINFORCEMENT

The use of a consequence to increase the frequency of a response.

Friends and charts can both be effective ways to monitor and reinforce progress.

Finally, in analyzing the relationship between positive reinforcers and motivation, Skinner stated that telling students they don't know something is not highly motivating. Rather, he suggested covering small amounts of material that you can immediately and positively reinforce.

Use of reinforcement in the classroom has drawn a number of criticisms, some of which are legitimate, whereas others indicate a misunderstanding of behavior modification techniques. The most common complaint about reinforcement, and one that is central to discussions of extrinsic motivation, is that reinforcement is bribery. Bribery, however, implies that the behavior being reinforced is somehow illegal or unethical. To the contrary, the appropriate use of reinforcement in schools is designed to facilitate attainment of desired educational objectives, such as work completion, reading, and getting along with other students. A second common complaint about reinforcement is that it develops dependence on concrete, external rewards for appropriate behavior. This complaint is most often leveled by individuals who are strong advocates for intrinsic motivation. This complaint can be countered in two ways: (1) behavior modification does not necessarily involve material reinforcers; social reinforcers, activities, feedback, and intrinsic reinforcers (for example, feelings of accomplishment) are also effective in changing behavior, and (2) reinforcement is often used only after more traditional methods of changing behavior have failed to increase the desired behaviors. It is, however, legitimate to be concerned when a teacher or parent uses extrinsic reinforcement to change a behavior that is already motivated by intrinsic reinforcement. Such actions may undermine the intrinsically reinforcing value of that behavior (Spaulding, 1992).

In summary, reinforcement methods are probably best used with students who exhibit high anxiety about learning, poor motivation, or a history of academic failures. Don't assume that young learners will need extrinsic forms of reinforcement and older students will only need intrinsic reinforcements. Age is not the best indicator of who will benefit from extrinsic reinforcements; rather, success in achieving the desired behaviors is the best indicator. So expect young and older students who are struggling to learn to benefit more from extrinsic reinforcers to facilitate their levels of motivation.

Bandura and the Development of Self-Efficacy

The final theorist whom we shall consider is Albert Bandura (1977, 1986, 1997), who has combined both cognitive and behavioral elements in his explanation of motivation. Bandura's social cognitive theory has particular relevance for motivation and self-directed learning. Students who come to school are all able, and often very willing, to imitate: A

CASE NOTES

Observation   One attempt by Mark Siegel to use a reward system with Karim Peterson to increase his work completion rate was reportedly unsuccessful.

Hypothesis   Given that external reinforcement methods have been found to be quite effective at increasing desired behaviors (such as work completion), it seems likely that the teacher may not have identified a reinforcer (that is, free time) for Karim or the implementation of the reward system was poor—possibly too delayed or too infrequent.

Possible Action   Discuss the use of external reinforcement methods with Mark and provide a detailed implementation and evaluation plan for using reinforcement with Karim to increase his work completion rate.

TIPS ON MOTIVATION
When Faced with an Unmotivated Student

PRINCIPLE   Students do a task because it is fun, it brings them some external contingency, or it is seen as an important and useful thing to do.

STRATEGY   Find a way to make the task more interesting and enjoyable; this will increase the intrinsic motivation value of the task for students.

STRATEGY   Associate an extrinsic reward with task participation and completion; this will increase the extrinsic motivation value of the task for students.

STRATEGY   Explain carefully to students precisely why the task is important, meaningful, and valuable to them; this should increase the identified value of the task and influence self-regulation by students.

stronger impression is made on students not by telling them what to do, but by setting an example for them to follow. Teachers should be models as much as possible since their behavior can be a powerful motivating force for student behavior.

Students' behavior can be significantly affected by observing their teachers and classmates. Six-year-old Sarah constantly calls out in class. Her teacher Ms. Gold continually reminds Sarah to raise her hand like her fellow students. Ms. Gold only calls on students with raised hands to answer questions. Sarah will eventually learn to raise her hand so that she can participate in class discussions. By observing her teacher and classmates, Sarah can learn new ways to respond to the environment (raising her hand), and at the same time negative behavior (disruptive calling-out) is weakened. In addition, observing models may cue the appearance of apparently forgotten responses.

If **modeling** is to be a motivational force, then students' self-knowledge is crucial. Bandura (1986) believes that self-knowledge is gained from information conveyed by either personal or socially mediated experiences. Four major sources of information are available to students: performance accomplishments, vicarious experience, verbal persuasion, and emotional arousal.

MODELING

A teaching technique in which the teacher or model performs an activity that the student has previously found difficult to perform and encourages it to be copied.

1.   *Performance accomplishments.* Bandura states that we acquire personal and effective information from what we do. Students learn from firsthand experiences how

successful they are in mastering classroom challenges. Their grades and the reactions of their classmates leave no room for doubt. When we realize the validity of Bandura's statement and combine it with conclusions from attribution theory, the necessity of arranging carefully planned schedules of positive reinforcement is clearly demonstrated. Teachers must be sure that students encounter challenges that they realistically have a chance of mastering.

2. *Vicarious experience.* This is Bandura's expression for watching "similar others" perform. If others can perform a task successfully, students usually feel more optimistic when they begin. Unfortunately, the opposite is also true. This source of information can be a major motivational device for teachers. If they are aware of the modeling power of their behavior, they can use it to urge students to improve their performance. Teachers will also be more alert to the need to provide reasonable tasks for their class. If students look around and see that everyone is struggling, even the brightest children, many students will simply give up.

3. *Verbal persuasion.* Here Bandura means that students can be led, through persuasion, into believing that they can overcome any difficulties and improve their performance. If the instructor is respected and admired by students, then the instructor's suggestions become a potent influence on the students' behavior.

4. *Emotional arousal.* By this expression Bandura means that stressful situations constitute a source of personal information. If students see themselves as inept and fearful in certain situations and with certain subjects, then the possibility of that fearful behavior appearing is enhanced.

The role of *imitation* in motivation and learning has direct classroom implications. Students' successful imitation of what they see and hear in the classroom is partially influenced by how the teacher—the model—responds to them. Effective modeling requires a learner to pay attention, show retention, and receive reinforcement. That is, students must attend if they are going to imitate; they must remember what they have imitated if they are to reproduce it in the future; and their imitating behavior must have been reinforced for them to remember and later use. We can conclude that students will imitate when teachers provide incentives for them to do so and when the teachers attend to what they have done.

Note the two-way influence process described here. Students attend to and imitate a teacher; the teacher then attends to and reinforces the students. Imitative performance reflects not only the competencies of students but the reactions of the model (teachers). If teachers respond equally to performances that are markedly different in quality, students will not imitate successfully. But if teachers attend to students' actual behavior and reinforce them appropriately, they will accurately reproduce behavior.

As students grow older and move through the grades, their intellectual abilities increase and they become capable of delayed imitation. They can witness a modeled performance and later perform that task without having practiced it. If you recall Piaget's discussion of cognitive development, the growth of cognitive structures permits students to cope with increasingly more abstract material, retain that material, conserve it, and finally use it. If you now apply these concepts to Bandura's work, you realize that students can mentally rehearse what they view. For example, after observing a teacher or other adult deal with a difficult problem, they may also show the ability to reflect, make notes, and then try to solve the problem independently. With increasing cognitive sophistication, students will soon escape the limitations of direct imitation and form new patterns of modeled behavior. This is especially true when students become comfortable with verbal symbols.

CASE NOTES

Observation Karim has strong models to imitate at home but does not appear to have a person or persons at school to model.

Hypothesis Karim would show more interest in learning and would be more likely to form a meaningful personal relationship if he had a salient model, either another student or a teacher, to imitate.

Possible Action Discuss possible peer models for Karim with Mrs. Peterson and Mark Siegel. Consider a slightly older student from another classroom in the school who would be willing to be a peer tutor or study buddy for Karim.

As we conclude a review of Bandura's work that is relevant to motivation, remember: Students who observe enthusiastic, knowledgeable teachers tend to imitate that behavior and become enthusiastic and knowledgeable themselves. Thus, they appear motivated!

WHAT AFFECTS STUDENTS' MOTIVATION?

As we have seen, several theorists have attempted to explain the nature of motivation with varying degrees of success. Table 9.1 summarizes these theorists and their fundamental contributions to understanding human motivation. In their speculations, each of the theorists has had to account for those individual motives that influence behavior. Given the importance of motivation to learning, it would be good for you to be aware of several of the most crucial of these motives. Among them would be anxiety, curiosity, locus of control, learned helplessness, self-efficacy beliefs, and students' environment.

Anxiety

Were you anxious before your last exam? How do you feel when you must speak in public? Are there certain situations in which you feel particularly anxious, regardless of your preparation? We are all alike in this regard: anxious in some conditions, not in others. Within the classroom setting, there are numerous sources of anxiety for students: teachers, examinations, peers, social relations, achievement settings, what girls think of boys, what boys think of girls, like or dislike of subjects, and distance from home for younger students. Whatever the cause, whatever the level of anxiety, you can be sure of one thing: Anxiety will affect student performance. Keep in mind, however, anxiety at relatively low to moderate levels can be constructive; anxiety at relatively high levels can be destructive and nonadaptive.

Since our concern is primarily with anxiety's effect on achievement, you should realize that extremely intense motivation that produces high anxiety has a negative effect on performance. Moderate motivation seems to be the desirable state for learning complex tasks. This is the **Yerkes-Dodson law,** which states that ideal motivation for learning decreases in intensity with increasing task difficulty (see Figure 9.3). Note that increasing intensity improves performance only to a certain level, and then continued intensity results in a deteriorating performance. Think about some task that you generally do well; now think about your motivation for it. Would you characterize it as high or low? Usually as

YERKES-DODSON LAW

The principle that ideal motivation for learning decreases in intensity with increasing task difficulty.

Table 9.1 MOTIVATIONAL THEORISTS AND THEIR BASIC IDEAS

Name	Theory	Central Element of Theory	Explanation of Motivation
Maslow	Humanistic	Needs hierarchy	Need satisfaction
Bruner	Cognitive	Intrinsic processes	Mixed motives
Weiner	Attribution	Causes of behavior	Identifying perceived causes of behavior
Skinner	Operant conditioning	Reinforcement	Schedules of reinforcement
Bandura	Social cognitive	Imitation	Modeling

FIGURE 9.3

The Yerkes-Dodson law, explaining the relationship between motivation and task difficulty.

tasks become more difficult, students have fewer successes and subsequently become less motivated to continue the task. Anxiety may appear at any time, be confined to one situation, or generalize widely. *Anxiety* may be defined as an unpleasant sensation that is usually experienced as feelings of apprehension and general irritability accompanied by restlessness, fatigue, and various somatic symptoms such as headaches and stomachaches (Chess & Hassibi, 1978, p. 241).

Many classroom implications emerge from this general overview. One is the distinct possibility that anxiety may generalize from one subject or teacher to another. Older students may develop a distaste for school that affects their achievement. Younger students may develop school phobia, a psychological condition producing such physical manifestations as crying and vomiting before school in the morning, thus hoping to avoid school attendance. As we have noted, anxiety can affect students' classroom performance, especially their test taking.

TEST ANXIETY

Anxiety generated by planning for and taking tests.

The construct of **test anxiety** has been used for well over four decades to describe the behavior and emotions of students who find preparing for and taking tests stressful. Sarason's (1980) summary of the main characteristics of test anxiety includes the following: (a) the test situation is seen as difficult, challenging, and threatening, (b) students see themselves as ineffective or inadequate in handling the task, (c) students focus on undesirable consequences of personal inadequacy, (d) self-deprecatory preoccupations are strong and interfere with task-relevant cognitive activity, and (e) students expect and anticipate failure and loss of regard by others.

Researchers have documented that test anxiety first appears in children at an early age—perhaps as early as age 7—and persists well into high school (Hembree, 1988). Estimates are that as many as 30% of schoolchildren suffer from debilitative test anxiety (Hill & Wigfield, 1984). This translates into a figure of eight to nine million children in American schools who may experience debilitating anxiety in academic performance situations. Approximately 20% of all test-anxious children will drop out of school because of repeated academic failure (Tobias, 1979).

In a comprehensive meta-analytic study of test anxiety research, Hembree (1980) concluded the following major points:

- Test anxiety and academic performance are significantly inversely related at grade 3 and above.

- Test anxiety occurs in students from all sociocultural groups in our society.

- Females exhibit more test anxiety than males, but as a group females are more likely to admit and self-report test anxiety.

- Average students, as measured by standardized tests, experience higher levels of test anxiety compared with both higher and lower ability students.

- High test-anxious students perform better under conditions that include low-stress instructions, provisions for memory supports, performance incentives, and minimal classroom distractions.

- Worry components of test anxiety (for example, negative self-talk and cognitions) appear to be stronger than emotional components (for example, heartbeat, sweaty palms, and upset stomach).

- Test anxiety is directly related to fears of negative evaluation, dislike of tests, cognitive self-preoccupation, and less effective study skills.

- High test-anxious students hold themselves in lower esteem than do low test-anxious students.

- Finally, high test-anxious students spend more time than low test-anxious students attending to task-irrelevant behaviors such as negative self-statements, attention toward physical discomfort, and watching others in the classroom, and as a result, their performance suffers.

In summary, moderate levels of anxiety frequently have been found to be part of successful students' motivational "makeup." Too much anxiety, however, can be counterproductive for all students. The challenge for educators is to recognize when anxiety, particularly test anxiety, becomes problematic for students and to teach students effective ways for controlling or reducing anxiety.

Curiosity and Interest

If students are relatively relaxed and willing to work, then you could reasonably expect them to have some interest in their environment. Curiosity can be one of a teacher's best friends because it signals a motivated student, eager to learn. The task of a teacher, then, is to capitalize on students' interest by further stimulating them and maintaining an optimal level of curiosity. But first it is necessary to explain what we mean by curiosity.

What is **curiosity?** Curious behavior is often described by other terms, such as exploratory, manipulative, or active, but all have a similar meaning. To identify the origin of curiosity is difficult. Explanations have focused on the external (something in the student's

CURIOSITY

Explorative behavior that occurs when a learner recognizes a discrepancy or conflict between what he or she believes to be true about the world and what turns out actually to be true.

Curiosity is a meaningful component of motivation for many learners.

environment is attractive) or the internal (human beings need stimulation). Current interpretations include both aspects. According to Loewenstein (1994), *curiosity* is a cognitively based emotion that occurs when a student recognizes a discrepancy or conflict between what he or she believes to be true about the world and what turns out actually to be true. Students are believed to feel curious about events that they can neither make sense of nor explain fully. In addition, curiosity occurs when students encounter unexpected, novel, and unpredictable objects. Curiosity is a prime motivational ingredient in Bruner's discovery learning approach to instruction for it appears that curiosity motivates exploratory behavior.

The cognitive-developmental theory of Jean Piaget addressed the importance of curiosity in the acquisition of information and cognitive growth. For Piaget (1969), if you expect one thing but find another, such as "I expected more water, but found the same amount," this can create cognitive disequilibrium that in turn can lead to curiosity. That is, the theory goes something like this: Cognitive conflicts (the unexpected) produce disequilibrium (confusion, wonderment), which then stimulates an emotional desire or curiosity to resolve the conflict (to understand). This curiosity initiates attempts to assimilate new information into existing cognitive structures (to make the new thing fit into what you know) or to accommodate existing cognitive structures to new ways of understanding the world (to expand your knowledge to take into account something new). Thus, learning is "motivated" or stimulated by a desire to resolve cognitive conflicts. Curiosity is an important emotional and information state in Piaget's theory of cognitive development.

Curiosity appears to be a natural phenomenon that should be encouraged within the limits that you establish for your class. A relaxed atmosphere, freedom to explore, and an acceptance of the unusual all inspire curiosity. The development of curiosity should be encouraged as soon as possible—during the preschool and elementary years. The early years are a time for the formation of cognitive structures that furnish a basis for future cognitive activity. Students not only acquire knowledge, but they also learn about learning. They become curious if their environment is stimulating.

Youngsters are naturally curious, and if their curiosity is encouraged, it will probably last a lifetime. Here are some suggestions for engaging curiosity:

- Enthusiasm for a subject should be discernible to students. By using questions related to the material, teachers can tease students into exploring this new vista.

- Depending on a student's level of sophistication, teachers can stimulate cognitive conflicts, causing some apparent confusion and simultaneously providing clues to the solution.

CASE NOTES

Observation   Karim Peterson seems to be most interested in his family and cultural heritage; he has exhibited little interest in the subject matters studied in Mark Siegel's classroom.

Hypothesis   The more connections that Karim's school work has to his life outside of school, the more he is likely to be interested in it. In addition, giving him a major role in evaluating his own work may also increase his interest in the work.

Possible Action   Share knowledge about classroom structure and activities that increase students' interest with Mr. Siegel. Also discuss ideas with Mrs. Peterson about ways that Karim's cultural interests can be connected to classroom studies.

- When possible, allow students to select topics that they are curious about. Give them the freedom and the direction to explore for themselves.

- Model curious, inquiring behavior. Tell students the things you are curious about and model some of the resourceful behavior that curious people use to solve problems.

Interest is similar and related to curiosity. **Interest** is an enduring characteristic expressed by a relationship between a person and a particular activity or object. By comparison, curiosity is more fleeting. Interest occurs when a student's needs, capacities, and skills are a good match for the demands offered by a particular activity (Deci, 1992). That is, the tasks students find more interesting are the ones that provide opportunities to satisfy their needs, challenge skills they have and care about developing, and demand that they exercise capacities that are important to them. Thus, the interest students show in an activity or in an area of knowledge predicts how much they will attend to it and how well they process, comprehend, and remember it.

Classroom techniques to facilitate curiosity, such as those already listed, can help to stimulate students' motivation to learn, but a distinction must be made between catching students' interest and maintaining their interest. Curiosity-oriented strategies mainly catch interest. Holding students' interest is a long-term, developmental process. To facilitate the development of interest, teachers should structure their classroom around goals such as (a) inviting students to participate in meaningful projects with connections to the world outside of the classroom, (b) providing activities that involve students needs and provide them developmentally appropriate challenges, (c) allowing students to have a major role in evaluating their own work and in monitoring progress, (d) facilitating the integration and use of knowledge, and (e) learning to work cooperatively with other students.

> **INTEREST**
> *An enduring characteristic expressed by a relationship between a person and a particular activity or object.*

Locus of Control

Did you do well in your last test in this course? Why? Were you well prepared? Or does the instructor like you? Or were you just plain lucky? If you think about your answers to these questions, and consider how other students might answer them, you can discern possible patterns that identify your locus of control.

Some students' answers to these questions suggest that anything good that happens to a person is caused by chance; the replies of other students indicate that if anything good happens, it was deserved. For most of us, our responses follow a definite form: If we

"I'd like to dedicate this day to all my students who complain that nothing interesting ever happens in school."

©Randy Glasbergen.

LOCUS OF CONTROL

The cause of behavior; some individuals believe it resides within them, while others believe it resides outside them.

EXTERNAL LOCUS OF CONTROL

Individuals attribute the causes of their behavior to factors outside of themselves.

INTERNAL LOCUS OF CONTROL

Individuals attribute causes of their behavior to themselves.

attribute responsibility to ourselves, we are called *internals*. If we attribute the causes of our behavior to somebody or something outside ourselves, we are called *externals*.

Parents, peers, and a student's total environment subtly interact to produce these feelings of confidence or uncertainty about life's challenges. Using more refined and sophisticated versions of this basic theme, Rotter (1975) analyzed individuals to determine their **locus of control.** If students believe they have little control over the consequences of their actions, they are said to have an **external locus of control;** if they believe they can control what happens to them, they are thought to have an **internal locus of control.** For example, if students believe that success and rewards come from skill and not luck, they then assume that they have control over their own destinies. On the other hand, if students believe that rewards come from luck and not skill, they assume that they have little control over their own destinies.

What is significant about the locus of control concept is that it can be used as a personality characteristic or tendency that has implications for learning. Researchers have shown, for example, a positive relationship between externality and the use of extrinsic forms of motivation in experienced teachers. In one investigation, Wigfield (1994) found that age and past successes and failures have a significant effect on students' attributions of control. In general, as students become more mature and as they experience more success, their attributions about control become more internal.

Locus of control, however, can change under certain conditions, such as experiences that change the relationship between what a student does and its outcome. If students think they succeed at a task only because of their teacher's help, then there will be little change in their locus of control. It is only when they perceive that *their* actions were instrumental in achieving success that real change may occur.

A review of many studies of locus of control in school settings suggests the following (Dacey, 1989b):

- Teachers tend to attribute more negative characteristics to external students than internals, and external students describe their teachers more negatively than do internals.

- External students perform better when they receive specific comments about teachers' expectations.

- Internal students are more effective than external students in recognizing and using available information.

- External students do less well in competitive situations than internal students, which seems to be a result of their higher level of anxiety.

Regardless of a student's locus of control, consider these suggestions. First, present them with realistic challenges, which implies that you must know the students so that you can determine what is realistic for them. Second, carefully reward their accomplishments or at least their efforts. Reinforcement must be based on actual accomplishment; otherwise students will quickly identify it as a sham. Also reinforce their effort; be specific in noting that you realize that they took the responsibility. Finally, use any initial successes, and attempt to foster a habit of trying and taking responsibility for one's actions.

Learned Helplessness

For some students the best opportunity for change may be in the classroom, and if this chance is lost, they may experience a condition called **learned helplessness** (Seligman, 1975). What seems to happen is that after repeated failures, students become frustrated and simply stop trying. The evidence—both animal and human—strongly supports this conclusion. In a series of experiments by Seligman and Maier (1967), harnessed dogs encountered one of three conditions. An escape group learned to escape shock while harnessed by pressing a panel with their noses. A yoked group received precisely the same shocks as the escape group, but they could do nothing to reduce or escape the shock. A naive group received no shock while in the harness. After twenty-four hours all three groups were moved to a shuttle box where they could escape the shock by jumping over a barrier. Both the escape and naive groups quickly learned to escape the shock, but the yoked group showed little, if any, ability to learn how to avoid the shock. It could not have been the shock itself that made the yoked dogs unable to learn the escape response because dogs in the escape group had been equally shocked. It was the lack of control that sealed their fate when they were later in a position where they could control the shock.

The yoked group's response when presented with a situation that they could control—yet did not—is called learned helplessness. The animals refused even to try to escape and exhibited signs of stress and depression.

Learned helplessness also applies to humans, as seen in the work of Hiroto (1974). Hiroto subjected three groups to a loud, unpleasant noise. The escape group could stop the noise by pushing a button. The yoked group experienced the same noise with no way of reducing or eliminating it. The third group received no noise. In the follow-up condition, all groups could escape the noise by moving one of their hands in a shuttle box from one side to the other. Again, the escape and naive groups did well, but those who had experienced unavoidable noise simply sat and made no move to eliminate the noise.

If for noise we substitute failing grades, sarcasm at home and school, and ridicule, then it becomes possible to trace a possible developmental path of learned helplessness. Students who experience nothing but failure and abuse at home and school have little chance of obtaining positive reinforcement for their behavior. If you discover such students, though it may sound simple, make every effort to combat this habit of "giving up."

Investigating learned helplessness in fifth-graders, Dweck and Repucci (1973) had one teacher give solvable problems and another teacher give unsolvable problems to their students. Later when the teacher who had given the unsolvable problems instead gave students solvable problems (like those given by the other teacher), the researchers observed that many students could not solve the problems, even though they had previously done so with the other teacher.

In a follow-up study, Diener and Dweck (1978) investigated the differences in students' reactions to failure. They identified two groups of students, "helpless" and "mastery-oriented." When helpless students failed, they tended to dwell on the cause of their *lack* of success. In

LEARNED
HELPLESSNESS
*The reaction on the part of
some individuals to become
frustrated and simply give up
after repeated failure.*

contrast, when the mastery-oriented students failed, they focused on finding a *solution* to why they failed. Diener and Dweck also reported that the helpless students underestimated their number of successes and overestimated their number of failures. When the helpless students did have successes, they often reported that they didn't expect them to continue.

One of the practical outcomes of Dweck's research on learned helplessness is knowledge about training students to overcome learned helplessness by attributing their failures to a lack of effort rather than lack of ability. Dweck (1975) used an attribution training procedure that taught students to see that lack of *motivation* and *effort* (things they can control) as the primary determinants of failure, rather than lack of *ability* (something they cannot control).

In summary, the concept of learned helplessness has provided a meaningful way to understand the behavior of some students who have repeatedly, over several years, experienced many more failures than successes. It does not appear that simply increasing the number of their successes will significantly influence their outlook on learning. Teaching students to realistically assess their failures and to focus on increasing their effort or motivation are necessary components in overcoming feelings of helplessness.

Three components of learned helplessness have particular pertinence for the classroom: failure to initiate action, failure to learn, and emotional problems.

1. Failure to initiate action means that students who have experienced learned helplessness tend not to try to learn new material. Passivity becomes their predominant behavior.

2. Failure to learn means that even when new directions are given to these students, they still learn nothing from them.

3. Emotional problems seem to accompany learned helplessness. Frustration, depression, and incompetence occur frequently.

Self-Efficacy and Its Role in Motivation

SELF-EFFICACY

Individuals' beliefs in their abilities to exert control over their lives; feelings of competency.

Self-efficacy refers to persons' beliefs in their own capabilities to exert control over aspects of their lives. Self-efficacy theory suggests that efficacy beliefs are the product of one's own performances, vicarious experiences, verbal persuasion from others, and emotional arousal (Bandura, 1986, 1997). Students who believe they are not efficacious in coping with environmental demands tend to focus on their inefficiency and exaggerate potential difficulties. Students who have a strong sense of efficacy, however, tend to focus their attention and effort on the demands of tasks and minimize potential difficulties (Bandura, 1986).

Interest in self-efficacy and its role in motivation has grown immensely. Viewing motivation and efficacy as interacting mechanisms has important theoretical and practical implications for educators. As noted by Schunk, "A sense of efficacy for performing well in school may lead students to expend effort and persist at tasks, which promotes learning. As students perceive their learning progress, their initial sense of efficacy is substantiated, which sustains motivation" (Schunk, 1990, p. 33). Researchers have demonstrated that even when students have encountered prior difficulties, the students' belief that they are capable of succeeding can override the negative effects of prior performances and produce motivated behaviors (Schunk, 1989).

EFFICACY EXPECTATIONS

The belief that one can perform the behavior or behaviors required to produce a certain outcome.

OUTCOME EXPECTATIONS

The belief that a given behavior will lead to a specific outcome.

In self-efficacy theory, **efficacy expectations** are differentiated from **outcome expectations.** That is, an outcome expectation represents a person's estimate that a given behavior will lead to a certain outcome. In contrast, an efficacy expectation means that individuals believe that they can perform the behavior or behaviors required to produce certain outcomes. Outcome and efficacy expectations are differentiated because students

Persevering when others are playing is a sign of a highly motivated student.

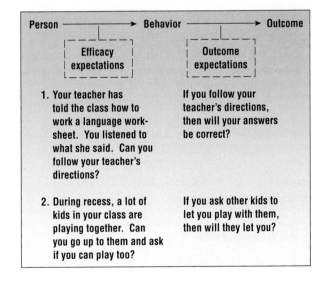

Person ──────▶ Behavior ──────▶ Outcome

```
          ┌─────────────┐          ┌─────────────┐
          │  Efficacy   │          │   Outcome   │
          │ expectations│          │ expectations│
          └─────────────┘          └─────────────┘
```

1. Your teacher has told the class how to work a language worksheet. You listened to what she said. Can you follow your teacher's directions?

   If you follow your teacher's directions, then will your answers be correct?

2. During recess, a lot of kids in your class are playing together. Can you go up to them and ask if you can play too?

   If you ask other kids to let you play with them, then will they let you?

FIGURE 9.4

Representation of the difference between efficacy expectations and outcome expectations within Bandura's (1977) theory of self-efficacy.

can believe certain behaviors will produce an outcome, but they may not believe that they can execute the behaviors that will produce the outcome. Figure 9.4 provides an illustration of this difference.

Individuals may possess low perceptions of efficacy in one skill domain (for example, academics) and high perceptions of efficacy in other skill domains (for example, social, physical). Moreover, self-perceptions of efficacy often vary as a function of setting. For example, it is a well-established finding that many handicapped children have higher self-concepts in self-contained special education classrooms than in regular education classrooms (Kaufman, Agard, & Semmel, 1985).

In the development of a scale to measure student's self-efficacy, Gresham, Evans-Fernandez, and Elliott (1988) found that the self-efficacy ratings of gifted, nondisabled, and mainstreamed students with mild disabilities consistently varied. Social, physical, and academic

> ## TIPS ON MOTIVATION
> ### *Facilitate Learners' Sense of Competence*
>
> **PRINCIPLE**   Competence is a psychological need that provides students with a source of motivation to seek out and master challenges that exist in the classroom.
>
> **STRATEGY**   Provide students "optimal challenges" to stimulate their competence needs. Optimal challenges involve some moderate level of risk-taking, choices in selecting tasks that vary in difficulty, a climate that tolerates errors, and opportunities to try again without punishment.
>
> **STRATEGY**   Provide students accurate, meaningful, and frequent feedback about their performances. The feedback should indicate whether a student's performance was or was not competent and be based on self and other evaluations.

variations were observed both intraindividually and interindividually. As expected, the students with disabilities rated themselves as less efficacious in the academic skill domain than the other domains and in comparison to the nondisabled and gifted students. The gifted students rated themselves on average highest in the academic domain and lowest in the social domain. In some cases, the gifted students also rated themselves as less efficacious in the social and physical domains than the nondisabled students. Thus, students' perceptions of their self-efficacy vary across skill domains and in comparison to fellow students who are known to function at different levels academically, socially, and physically.

Perceived self-efficacy affects a student's functioning by influencing an individual's choice of activities, effort expenditure, and persistence in the face of difficulties. The ramifications of self-efficacy for a student's classroom learning appear to be tremendous. Researchers interested in the role of self-efficacy in teacher-student interactions have recently reported some important findings about students' help-seeking behaviors and teachers' help-giving behavior. We examine several of these studies in the next section on classroom environments and motivation.

Classroom Environments

Students who ask questions and get help when they need it alleviate immediate learning difficulties and also acquire knowledge and skills that they can use for self-help later (Newman, 1990). Despite the obvious importance of help-seeking in the classroom, many students do not ask teachers for help or avail themselves of help when they need it.

Newman (1990) was curious about why children often are reluctant to seek academic assistance from teachers, so he designed a study with 177 third-, fifth-, and seventh-graders. Newman assessed the students' perceived academic competence, intrinsic orientation, and attitudes regarding help-seeking in math class. The data for these students were used to answer the question: How do students' efforts at academic help-seeking vary according to (a) characteristics of the students and (b) social-interactional conditions in the classroom? Here are some of the major findings from Newman's study:

- The influence of motivational factors on the children's intentions to seek help with an academic problem was stronger for the third- and fifth-graders than for the seventh-graders. The stronger the belief that help-seeking is beneficial and the

---

CASE NOTES

Observation   Mark Siegel frequently assists Karim Peterson when he is having difficulty with tasks; Karim, however, rarely asks for help.

Hypothesis   Karim may interpret the help-giving from his teacher as a sign that he is "dumb" or "incapable," thus the help is not appreciated and ineffective as presently done.

Possible Action   Discuss with Karim ways he can get help that he will feel comfortable with; consider a peer tutoring arrangement or study buddy. Also share information about help-giving with Mark so that he is sensitive to the possible negative side effects of help-giving to students with low self-confidence or esteem.

---

weaker the belief that it has associated costs, the greater the student's expressed likelihood of seeking help. For example, a fifth-grader, who believes his teacher is eager to help students and sees it as a good sign that students are able to ask for help, will generally be comfortable and willing to ask for help.

- For all grades, the greater the student's perceived competence, the less strongly the student felt there was a cost associated with seeking help. The implication regarding students with low perceived competence is the same as that regarding low achievers: Those most in need of help may be those most reluctant to seek help.

Newman concluded that his findings were consistent with a *vulnerability hypothesis* of help-seeking. According to this hypothesis, students with low self-esteem or efficacy have a greater need than students with high self-esteem to avoid situations in which they feel threatened by an admission of failure. Thus, students with low self-efficacy are less likely to seek help. Giving them help remains an important task of teachers.

Giving help to students is not always easy nor without some possible negative side effects for students. According to an investigation by Graham and Barker (1990) of children ranging in age from 4 to 12, they found that when teachers help students, it can be interpreted as indicating the student lacks ability. Specifically, Graham and Barker found that unsolicited teacher assistance signaled low ability to students. Compared with a non-helped peer, a student receiving teacher assistance was judged less smart, less proud of success, more grateful, less likely to be successful in the future, and less preferable as a work-mate. The cuing function of teachers' assistance was not present in the 4- and 5-year-olds, so it appears to emerge with the advent of schooling. This study has important implications for help-givers and alerts us to the potential negative side of help for students. In addition, it, along with the theoretical work on self-efficacy, emphasizes how instructional practices affect not only students' acquisition of skills but also their motivation and efficacy for learning.

Drawing heavily from the teacher expectancy literature, Alderman (1990) emphasized that teachers must show students that they want them to succeed and also that they expect students to achieve the major learning objectives for a class. Referring to her work as "the link model," Alderman stressed that students need to see a link between what they do and a given learning outcome.

Figure 9.5 illustrates Alderman's link model and highlights its four main linking components: proximal goals, learning strategies, successful experiences, and attributions for success. Let's briefly explore each of these components.

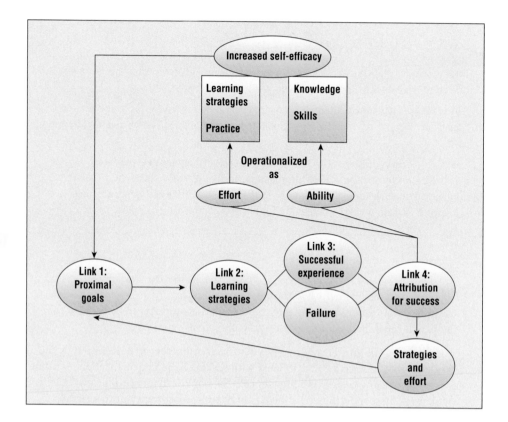

FIGURE 9.5

Motivational links to success.

(From M. K. Alderman, "Motivation for At-Risk Students" in *Educational Leadership, 48*(1):27–30. Copyright © 1990 Association for Supervision and Curriculum Development. Reprinted by permission. All rights reserved.)

- *Link 1: Proximal goals.* Goals play an important role in the development of self-motivation by establishing targets by which students can evaluate their own progress. To be effective, goals should be specific rather than general; attainable; and proximal, or close at hand, rather than long-term.

- *Link 2: Learning strategies.* Low achievers often are inefficient learners—that is, they fail to apply learning strategies that would facilitate their performance. In link 2, students are asked to identify effective learning strategies that will help them to accomplish their goals.

- *Link 3: Successful experiences.* A learning goal is the key to success in this component. Students measure their success using the proximal goals as the criteria. Teachers play a valuable role by creating opportunities for students to work on their goals and fostering effective learning conditions.

- *Link 4: Attributions for success.* Students are encouraged to attribute their success to their personal efforts or abilities. Teachers can help students make appropriate attributions; for example, they might ask, "What happened when you tried?" For difficult tasks, teachers' attributional feedback should begin with a focus on effort and then shift to students' abilities. The link model for fostering motivation goes "full circle." Students who have succeeded and attributed their success to their own effort and ability have concrete performance feedback that will lead them to increased self-efficacy, which in turn will lead to increased confidence about goal accomplishments. All students will not consistently experience success; some failures will always occur. When failure does occur,

---

TIPS ON COMMUNICATION
The Importance of Setting and Monitoring Goals

PRINCIPLE As students' goals increase in specificity and difficulty, their performance increases in a positive, linear fashion.

STRATEGY Help students set learning goals by (1) identifying the objective to be accomplished, (2) specifying how their performances will be measured, (3) defining goal difficulty, (4) specifying the conditions under which performances will be assessed, and (5) identifying materials needed to achieve goal.

STRATEGY Keep in mind that goal setting is not necessary for all tasks or activities; it is most likely to increase motivation when tasks are perceived to be uninteresting or of little intrinsic value.

---

students' attributions for it are important determinants of their future expectations for success. Students who attribute failure to the use of weak or inappropriate strategies are more likely to try again. Attributing failure to a lack of effort when students feel they have put forth a strong effort can be damaging. Working closely with students to assess their performance and helping them to make realistic attributions about their successes and failures is an important task for teachers and parents. The link model provides a useful organizer for working with students who are at risk for motivation problems.

Although not specifically designed to facilitate self-efficacy, instructional techniques based on cooperative learning principles have been used effectively with a wide range of students. Let us examine this popular methodology next.

Multicultural Background of Students

One of the major contributions teachers can make to the successful integration and accomplishments of multicultural students is to provide an understanding, supportive environment. Treating all students with respect and dignity is a vital first step. To be especially alert to the needs of students whose physical appearance, speech, and behavior may differ from those of other students, teachers must be familiar with their students' cultural backgrounds.

Discussing strategies that help to meet the needs of multicultural students, Gary and Booker (1992) suggested several techniques to empower African American students to achieve academic success. Help these students to establish goals early in life. Recognize and foster their early interests to help them engage in long-term thinking and avoid seeking immediate gratification. Recognize the need for racial pride. Be aware of distinct learning styles: Many African American students learn best in environments that encourage human interaction and verbal dialogue. Finally, try to foster in students a sense of self-control, and cultivate academic motivation as much as possible. Garibaldi (1992), in discussing the motivation of African American males to succeed, urged that teachers publicly recognize the successful academic experiences of young African American men, thus helping them to improve their self-concepts, self-esteem, and academic confidence.

Language can also be a serious obstacle to acceptance for many students. A practical technique for helping students overcome language barriers was described by First (1988). Called the English Plus program, it was developed for the Washington, D.C. schools, and

Current Issues & Perspectives

Will a Multicultural Curriculum Better Motivate Minority Children?

Is it important to give voice to the distinctions that exist within our schools and classrooms by revising curricula to include faces and ideas reflecting a multitude of colors, ethnicities, and cultures? Included in Jerome Bruner's *Acts of Meaning* is the following quotation, which argues for a multicultural approach to the school curriculum.

> *When someone with the authority of a teacher, say, describes the world and you are not in it, there is a moment of psychic disequilibrium, as if you looked into a mirror and saw nothing. (Bruner, 1990, p. 32)*

ISSUE

Students will better relate to and assimilate information that is meaningful to them.

Pro: Cognitive learning theory tells us that students learn by assimilating new information into already existing schemata. David Ausubel describes this process when he talks about *meaningful learning.* For Ausubel, meaningful learning takes place when the material to be learned is related to what the learner already knows. Making a concept or topic relevant to a student's previous experience sets the stage for the acquisition of new meaning, which is a good description of learning.

Con: Cognitive learning theory is only one way of explaining how we learn. There are many times when we are faced with information for which we have no reference point, but learn in spite of this. Behaviorists would attribute learning to positive reinforcement, to the positive consequences of similar behavior resulting in an enthusiastic repeat performance. This theory is not sensitive to the nature of the material itself, but rather to the circumstances in which it is presented. Consequently, a good teacher could motivate learners even if the students were all children of color learning to read from a basal text filled with stories and pictures of white suburban children.

ISSUE

A multicultural curriculum sends a message to the school community that all kinds of people are valued within the school. By modeling acceptable behavior in our culture, administrators and teachers can set an example that has a strong motivational influence on student behavior.

Pro: Modeling on the part of the teacher and other people of authority within a school can be an effective way to influence behavior. Teachers' enthusiasm for the material goes a long way to motivate student interest. Teachers who wholeheartedly embrace a multicultural curriculum send a strong message of endorsement for such a program.

Con: There is always the danger that a multicultural curriculum might not include all the learners in the classroom. To be left out of a program that promises to reflect everyone can be very damaging. Teachers who are less vigilant might not offer all students the opportunity to see themselves reflected in the material. A commitment to this curriculum that is less than enthusiastic, knowledgeable, and serious would do all learners a great disservice.

ISSUE

Once out in the world children must succeed in the mainstream culture, which is still predominantly white and Eurocentric. Doesn't a multicultural approach delude, if not ill serve, students of color?

Pro: Teachers already feel there is not enough time to accomplish all the work that needs to be done in any school year. To study minor writers, scientists, or historical figures would

continued

take even more time out of an already compromised schedule. While the major figures in Western history and culture are for the most part white, male, and of European descent, this doesn't change the fact that they are the people who have shaped our culture. Our young people, to be considered educated, must be aware of mainstream history and accomplishments.

Con: Only one part of a child's education consists of names and deeds and dates. The other part is the *process* that stands behind every thought and product of our culture. It is the discussion of the *how* that offers limitless opportunity to give reflection and voice to all of our citizens:

The Asian, the Hispanic, the Jew
The African, the Native American, the Sioux
The Catholic, the Muslim, the French, the Greek
The Irish, the Rabbi, the Priest, the Sheik
The Gay, the Straight, the Preacher
The privileged, the homeless, the teacher . . . .
(Angelou, 1993)

involves special strategies to supplement other language programs. For example, while multicultural students are learning English, the program uses peers and adults to work with those students in their native languages. This and similar strategies can motivate and improve learning by providing both subject-matter help and role modeling.

No class is completely homogeneous. Teachers learn to expect differences among their students and search for ways to best reach their multicultural students. Make sure these students experience immediate success by assigning tasks within their capability and rewarding them for successful performance. Individualize instruction as much as possible by sequencing and pacing the programs carefully for individual children. Consider using a classwide peer tutoring program or cooperative learning groups (Sleeter & Grant, 1988, p. 55).

What does all of this motivational work mean for teaching and learning?

Cooperative Learning

Cooperative learning has been defined as a set of instructional methods in which students are encouraged or required to work together on academic tasks (Slavin, 1987a; Stevens & Slavin, 1995). Slavin noted that such methods may include having students sit together for discussion, or help each other with assignments, and more complex requirements. He distinguished cooperative learning from peer tutoring by noting that all students learn the same material, that there is no tutor, and that the initial information comes from the teacher.

Motivation for cooperative learning is associated with the goal structures and potential rewards for group members. Group members can attain their personal goals only if the group as a whole is successful. Consequently, two conditions must be met if cooperative learning is to be effective. First, cooperating groups must have a group goal that is meaningful to them (a prize, recognition, free time). Second, the group's success must emerge from the individual learning of all group members (Slavin, 1988b). If these two conditions are met—group effort and individual accountability—then students are motivated to help each other learn.

Cooperative learning involves two aspects of classroom organization: task structure and reward structure (Slavin, 1987b). In cooperative learning, the task structures ensure that group members work with each other. Reward structures may depend on the performance of the total group (a product they produce), or on the sum of the individual learning performances.

COOPERATIVE LEARNING

A set of instructional methods in which students are encouraged or required to work together on academic tasks.

In a series of investigations, Johnson and Johnson (1987) introduced the concept of *goal structures,* which refers to the way that students relate to each other as they pursue similar goals (for example, understanding the causes of the American Revolution). Goal structures can be classified as follows:

- Cooperative, in which students work together to achieve a goal

- Competitive, in which students work against each other while pursuing an instructional goal

- Individualistic, in which students' activities are unrelated to each other as they work toward a goal

An example of a cooperative goal structure is, during an election, students in a high school political science or history class may poll different neighborhoods and combine their results to predict a winner (cooperative learning). An example of a competitive goal structure is when some instructors have the disconcerting habit of announcing to a class that "only four people in this class can get an A, and there will be only eight Bs"; this is a classic example of fostering competitive learning. Finally, "I do my work, you do yours; we receive grades based on how well we do individually" sums up the individualistic goal structure.

You can see how each of these goal structures establishes a specific learning atmosphere and different types of relationships in the classroom. Motivation also varies for these learning conditions. Each of these conditions can serve a definite purpose, but be aware of what you are trying to accomplish in a class and how you are doing it. There are circumstances best suited for each condition. A high school course in marketing techniques is obviously designed to teach students how to present their products in a manner superior to a competitor (competitive goal structure). A large middle school class in a core subject, for example, English or history, usually represents an individualistic goal structure: Attend the lectures, take the tests, pass in the assignments, receive the grade. Discussing social action or community involvement offers opportunities for cooperative learning in which students help each other to achieve goals.

In an attempt to develop techniques designed to further cooperative learning, Slavin (1987c) proposed the following:

- Students should work in small, mixed-ability groups of four members: one high achiever, two average achievers, and one low achiever.

- Students in each group are responsible for the material taught under regular classroom conditions but also for helping other group members to learn and to achieve a group goal.

One such technique is the *Student Teams-Achievement Division (STAD)* which consists of a definite cycle of activities. The teacher initially presents a lesson under regular classroom conditions. Students then attempt to master the material in their four-member group. For example, if the subject is math, after the teacher teaches the lesson students may work together on problems, compare their answers, and attack together any difficulties that arise. These students now take individual tests during which they cannot help each other. The teacher adds together the results of the four quizzes to obtain a team score. Since this is cooperative learning, however, the focus is on improvement, not on outright scores. Therefore, the teacher compares students' scores on the test with their average scores on previous tests. If a score is 10% above the average, that student earns three points for the group. An improvement of 5% to 9% earns two points, 3% above the average earns one point, and anything below 3% receives zero points.

CASE NOTES

Observation   Karim Peterson frequently isolates himself and does not work well with other students.

Hypothesis   If Karim and others are reinforced for working together, they will interact more positively during class and Karim will become more involved in learning.

Possible Action   Discuss the use of cooperative learning groups, such as STAD, with Mark Siegel to see what he thinks. If he is receptive, identify a couple of students who are most likely to work constructively with Karim and also discuss what the focus of the learning will be.

Stating that research supports the superiority of cooperative learning over other instructional methods, Slavin (1987a) warned that simply putting students together will not produce learning gains or motivation. Students need to work toward a group goal and all members must contribute, not just the smartest. Slavin stated that the most successful approaches to cooperative learning incorporate two key elements: group goals and individual responsibility. When these two features are used together, achievement effects are consistently positive. For example, thirty-seven of forty-four experimental/control studies (each at least four weeks long) found significantly positive results. These positive effects are about the same at all grade levels, in all major subjects, in urban, rural, or suburban schools, and for high, average, or low achievers. Positive effects also have been found on such outcomes as self-esteem, intergroup relations, acceptance of academically disabled students, and attitudes toward school (Slavin, 1991a).

Computer Technology

One increasingly popular way that classroom teachers and parents try to increase students' levels of motivation is to use educational software. The array of available types and levels of software is nothing short of staggering, ranging from action-oriented to problem solving to creating novel stories and artwork. The common belief seems to be that if the material is programmed, then students will be more interested and spend more time on the material, and learning will be enhanced.

Most studies assessing students' attitudes report positive changes when technology is used in classrooms; students seem to like using computers to learn (Martin, Heller, & Mahmoud, 1992; Todman & Dick, 1993). These results seem to hold for students of varying ages (K–12), though there is evidence that older students are less favorable toward computers than younger students (Krendl & Broihier, 1992). In a review of some of the early work on attitudes, Lawton and Gershner (1982) found that children generally had positive attitudes toward computers and computerized instruction, saying that computers had infinite patience, never got tired, never forgot to correct or praise them, were impartial to ethnicity, and were great motivators. Negative attitudes and fears about computers were found mostly among teachers rather than students.

Other researchers are not so convinced of the wonderful effects of computers on student attitudes. It could be that computer-based learning activities were relatively new to students and the highly positive attitudes were simply a novelty effect (Salomon & Gardner, 1986). It is a well-known finding in the literature that when a tool or program is new, it tends to get more attention and is often rated as being highly enjoyable and acceptable.

Interacting with a computer is a motivating task for many learners, young and old.

More recent work on attitudes toward computers shows mixed results. In one study spanning a three-year period, fourth- through tenth-graders were asked about three dimensions of learning with computers (preference, perceived learning, and perceived difficulty) (Krendl & Broihier, 1992). There was clear evidence of a *novelty effect* for preference and perceived learning, with ratings for these two dimensions declining each year. Students were more stable in their ratings of perceived difficulty, a finding that surprised the researchers. They had reasoned that the more familiar students became with computer technology across the three-year span, the easier they would find computer work to be, but this did not happen. Perceived difficulty remained the same across the three years, even though there was a vast increase in the number of students who gained computer experience during the time of the study. Other researchers do not find such clear-cut evidence of a novelty effect, though most of these are not of as long a duration as the Krendl and Broihier study just described.

So it seems that novelty plays some role in how favorable students are toward computers, though the existence and degree of novelty effect is probably related to how the technology is used in the classroom. What difference does this make for teachers using technology in their classrooms? It means that the high levels of interest and excitement students show initially will probably decrease as they become more used to technology. Technology-based teaching strategies may become less effective at creating and sustaining students' motivation.

It is likely that some of the initial excitement that most students feel when using educational technology is due to a novelty effect. But we think it is unlikely that interest in technology-based activities, and the motivation created by such activities, is due only to novelty. First, software is becoming increasingly better at providing students with their own, individual optimal level of excitement. As you read earlier in this chapter, motivation is clearly related to the level of anxiety a student experiences. The Yerkes-Dodson law indicates that if the difficulty of a task and its intensity are either too low or too high, motivation suffers. This lesson is not lost on software developers, who have become increasingly adept at designing educational programs that provide an optimum level of excitement and challenge for students. This is usually accomplished by having students (or their teacher) initially select a level of difficulty for the software. The software then adjusts (often automatically) the level of difficulty in future sessions. Although this strategy does not overcome problems of the novelty effect, it will help keep the challenge of software at an optimal level and may serve to motivate students longer than other instructional methods that often are directed at the group's average.

Second, software is often designed to allow students to ask for and receive help in private. Many programs don't allow a student to just get stuck if he or she cannot produce a correct response. The student is allowed a few attempts, often no more than three, then a hint is either automatically provided or the student is given the option of getting help. This kind of programming can help preserve a student's sense of esteem and capability by not forcing them to continually repeat one problem until they get it correct. A clear advantage of having help from the software is that it reduces any embarrassment that may come with asking for help, and it provides help in a timely manner.

A third reason that many students find computer software motivating is the wide range of characters and contexts in which learning can occur. The topics of software continue to grow, incorporating traditional themes from children's storybooks to pioneer travel and trips to Mars to an adventure with Madeline or Barbie. These characters and contexts are inviting and allow for constructive interactions for many learners.

A final reason that educational technology seems to motivate students is that it provides access to different kinds and levels of information than a typical teacher can provide. For example, when students in a class in one of our children's school were writing stories about planets they wanted to visit, they were able to "consult" with NASA experts and get close-up photos of planets like Mars and Saturn via the Internet at the NASA website. This experience stimulated a wide range of questions, much discovery learning, and numerous follow-up visits to the website weeks after the lesson on planets was completed.

EDUCATIONAL IMPLICATIONS OF MOTIVATIONAL THEORIES AND RESEARCH

Let's now examine how the theoretical and research-based information on motivation can be put into practice. In a perceptive analysis of motivation and teaching, Wlodkowski (1986) noted that for any learning to occur, motivational strategies exercise a decisive influence at the beginning of learning, during learning, and at the end of learning.

The Beginning of Learning

There are two key motivational factors involved at this stage: attitudes and needs.

Attitudes

What are students' feelings about themselves, their school, their teachers, and their subjects? As we discussed earlier in this chapter, the teacher as the communicator bears great responsibility for student attitudes—positive and negative. Teachers must identify what exactly is causing a student's negative attitude. Is the student uncomfortable with a subject because of its novelty or unsuccessful previous experiences? Has a student missed the fundamentals that are necessary for work in the class? Once teachers have located the problem, then they can precisely direct their efforts toward its solution.

For example, if some students believe that they simply lack the ability to succeed in a subject, the teacher's task will be to assess their level of competence and then construct a base from which they can experience success. If their difficulty seems to be mainly affective—they simply don't like the material—the teacher might assign them to a group that enjoys the subject.

Needs

Students behave to satisfy all of their needs, and the need that is predominant at any moment will be a student's primary concern. For example, you may have prepared an extremely stimulating lesson that is lost on the student who skipped breakfast and is ravenous by eleven o'clock. It is well to be guided by the indisputable fact that for most of us, physiological needs demand our immediate consideration.

Safety needs require a different type of response. Most students have had their fundamental safety needs met at home. This is not to say, however, that they are incapable of feeling anxiety. High anxiety does not correlate with high achievement; consequently, anything teachers can do to relieve this condition will help students.

Classroom work can help to combat the fears that accompany each developmental stage. For example, young children are afraid of the dark, the unknown, animals, and loud noises; from ages 9 to 18, fears relate to school failure and social relations. Probably the best advice to be offered with regard to students' needs is this: Make the classroom as physically and psychologically safe as possible.

During Learning

The key motivational processes involved during the middle stage of learning are stimulation and affect.

Stimulation

What are students paying attention to during the learning experience? Are there elements in the material or in the environment that attract—and distract—their attention? One of the most effective means of ensuring that students find a lesson stimulating is to involve their need for achievement. Working from the assumption that personal motives and increased individual effort can be stimulated in the classroom, de Charms (1976) asserted that motivation is tightly linked to students' identification of the origin of their actions.

Origins and *pawns* are terms used to distinguish the two motivational states that are basic to each individual's sense of who he or she is. Origins are those who believe that they control their own fate; pawns believe they are at the mercy of everyone and everything. A given person is not always an origin or a pawn, but one of these feelings usually predominates. (This concept is similar to that of locus of control, but de Charms believes that locus of control emphasizes reinforcement, whereas the origin-pawn concept stresses students' determination of their own goals and the courses of action needed to attain them.)

To enhance the motivation of teachers, the first step is to have them focus on their own motives. In his workshops, de Charms asked teachers to write imaginative stories in response to six pictures. This was intended to assess individuals' needs for achievement. The teachers were then asked to write essays in response to the question, "Who am I?" The teachers were encouraged to tell the group something about themselves: their goals, values, hobbies, lifestyles. As the group members became more comfortable with one another, discussion became more open.

While this was going on each teacher was asked to go into a nearby room to play a ring-toss game. A stake was set up at one end of the room, with three-foot distances marked off. Each participant was given four rings to toss from any distance desired. The only stipulation was that all the rings had to be thrown from the same distance. The objective of the game was to demonstrate the level of an individual's need achievement. Interestingly, those individuals who stood far from the stake and those who stood quite close had lower need achievement than those who selected intermediate distances. The rationale is that the intermediate group realistically decided that certain distances posed a challenge for them, indicating a high need for achievement.

Another technique used was the blindfold game. Here, one teacher was blindfolded and a partner was chosen to be the guide. The guide was responsible for taking the blindfolded member to dinner, where the blindfold was removed, and then back to the meeting room with the blindfold in place. The purpose of this exercise was to demonstrate individual differences in giving and receiving help, and to make the teachers aware of feelings of power and control.

Similar techniques were suggested to the teachers for use with their students. For example, the teachers were urged to have their students write stories with achievement themes that they elicited from the children. A class could be told that they were to think about a story that they would write on Friday. The discussion during the week would focus on a main character's efforts to do better (thus indicating the objective). The stories could then be used in a weekly essay contest and judged by the students.

Affect

How do students feel about their classroom work? If affect is a constant companion of learning, actually an integral part of the process, then student attributions have practical implications for the classroom. When students assign a cause to behavior, that assignment carries with it strong emotional overtones. For example, in one study, Weiner and his colleagues (1978) had participants read brief stories about success and failure that also contained the reasons for the successes and failures. Here is one of the stories:

> *Francis studied intensely for a test he took. It was very important for Francis to record a high score on this exam. Francis received a very high score on the test. Francis felt that he received this high score because he studied so intensely. How do you think Francis felt upon receiving this score?*

Participants were asked to give the emotional reaction of the person in the story by selecting affective words from a list presented to them. There were ten success stories, each with different reasons for success. Some words, such as *pleased* and *happy*, appeared in almost all of the attributions for success. But the reasons for the success influenced many of the words chosen. For example, if participants attributed success to an unstable effort, they chose words like *ecstatic* and *uproarious*.

There were also eleven stories of failure, which was attributed to luck, ability, and fatigue. When ability was mentioned, participants chose words such as *incompetent* and *inadequate*; when the cause was given as luck, their responses were *stunned* and *overwhelmed*. Thus it seemed possible to discriminate between participants' attributions by the affective words they chose.

These studies have direct implications for teachers: Different emotions are associated with different attributions for success and failure. If students think that they have succeeded at a task because they were lucky, they will have no feeling of pride at the outcome. Similarly, if their failure is attributed to lack of effort and not lack of ability, they may experience feelings of shame, but no loss of confidence.

When Learning Ends

The key motivational processes involved during the last stage of learning are competence and reinforcement.

Competence

If by competence we mean a feeling of controlling our environment, then competence is a powerful motive in our lives. A teacher can help students achieve competence by making sure that they have the skills necessary to attain desired goals. By doing this, the teacher also communicates to them that their classroom environment will support them in their work (Ford, 1992). In this way, teachers provide students with skill mastery and feelings of classroom acceptance.

Retention is aided by having pupils actually practice the behavior whenever possible: "Watch how I'm adjusting the microscope. Don't move it too quickly. OK, now you try it." Be sure that students have the capability of acquiring the behavior that is being modeled, and when they show the desired behavior, arrange for immediate reinforcement. A sense of competence not only reduces fear and anxiety for a task, but also increases the effort expended; thus, self-efficacy becomes a powerful motivating force (Bandura, 1977, 1986).

Reinforcement

Since the theoretical aspects of reinforcement are thoroughly discussed in Chapter 6, our focus here is on specific classroom use. Remember to reinforce as immediately as possible. Whenever possible, provide reinforcement while students are still learning. Reinforce with small amounts rather than large amounts. Use reinforcers—praise, stars, points, and so on—frequently, but in sufficiently small amounts to avoid having them become meaningless for students. Finally, reinforce small improvements in learning and motivation. A common mistake of teachers is to demand too much before they reinforce, thus discouraging students and interrupting the flow of learning.

CURRENT WISDOM: BALANCE THE INTERNAL AND EXTERNAL MOTIVATION METHODS

We have discussed a variety of approaches to understanding human motivation and a rather substantial list of variables that can influence a student's motivation to learn. Four conclusions from our examination of motivation should be clear:

1. Students differ in how they are motivated and what motivates them.

2. Differences in motivation can lead to important differences in learning.

3. No single theory of motivation adequately informs educators how to motivate students.

4. Over the course of development, students generally become more in control of and responsible for actions that influence their level of motivation for learning.

Current theories and research on motivation support the use of both external and internal motivational strategies for most learners. There is occasionally, however, concern voiced about the overuse of external reinforcement to motivate already motivated learners.

It is also well established that all learners have common needs, such as hunger, safety, and be-longingness, that serve to motivate some of their learning activity. Both young and older learners alike have the ability to be intrinsically motivated to learn. Situations that provoke curiosity and interest stimulate these internally oriented needs to learn. Learners also will find themselves in situations where learning is difficult and the perceived result is relatively unimportant. These learners will benefit from some external support to enhance their motivation. This may come in the form of some adjustment to the learning task, modeling of a successful outcome, and/or some form of external consequences, preferably one characterized as positive reinforcement.

Teachers control many aspects of instruction that can directly influence students' motivation to learn. In particular, students benefit when they have a clear understanding of the learning expectations and outcomes, work on tasks that are well matched with their abilities, receive frequent feedback about their work, and have opportunities to work with other students on common tasks.

Brophy (1987b) argued that no motivational strategies will succeed if certain classroom preconditions are not met:

- Classroom conditions must be supportive, warm, and encouraging so that students are sufficiently secure to take risks without fear of criticism.

- The challenges that students face are appropriate, which occurs only if teachers know and understand their students.

- Worthwhile, meaningful objectives that are clearly understood by the class can be powerful motivators.

- Motivational strategies should be moderate and monitored; that is, students can't be kept at too high or too low a level of motivation.

Teachers must adjust these preconditions, however, according to the developmental level of their students. For example, children enter school primarily attending to social feedback; their perception of their own competence remains positive. After the first few grades, objective feedback becomes more important and they learn that high academic performance is valued. They now begin to assess their performance more realistically. Often by the sixth grade they learn that ability is a stable factor in their performance and that differences in learning can be influenced by one's level of motivation (Stipek, 1984).

The more that teachers know about their students as individuals, and the more that they know about motivation, the more effective teaching will be and the more students will learn. To produce this condition in the classroom requires a judicious blending of intrinsic and extrinsic motivation and monitoring of students' reactions.

Case Reflections

This chapter on motivation provided several insights into the behavior of Karim Peterson, the fourth-grade African American student in Mark Siegel's class who was experiencing a variety of difficulties. In particular, Karim seemed uninterested in his schoolwork and was socially isolated from his classmates. Recall that there was some tension between Mark Siegel (Karim's teacher) and Kysha Peterson (Karim's mother), but both were concerned about Karim's lack of work completion and slow rate of academic progress.

The theoretical and applied research on motivation that was examined stimulated several possible hypotheses about Karim's lack of interest in his schoolwork and his limited social engagement with classmates. The chapter also provided information about the role that teaching and classroom structure can have on students' motivation to learn. First, with regard to Karim, it was noted that his strong interest in African culture was not an important part of life in Mark Siegel's classroom but could possibly be if more opportunities for discovery learning and personalized projects were possible. Second, it was noted that improving Karim's social interactions with classmates could be a key to meeting some belongingness needs, as well as advancing some of his academic needs. The use of peer tutors, study buddies, and cooperative learning groups were all brainstormed as possible actions. With regard to Mark Siegel's role in facilitating Karim's learning and social engagement, several possibilities were noted. First, he should be encouraged to again try using a reward system or reinforcement to increase Karim's work completion rate—it seemed like Mark's first efforts to implement a reward system were flawed. Second, based on research on help-giving, it was suggested that Mark reexamine ways he can provide Karim help; possibly offer assistance in a more private manner or by arranging for a peer, possibly an older African American student, who Karim is more likely to model. Finally, it was suggested that Mark Siegel should work with Mrs. Peterson to gain more information about (a) Karim's homework efforts and her involvement with his homework and (b) how more connections between the family's strong interest in African culture and Karim's classroom work could be forged.

CHAPTER HIGHLIGHTS

Motivation: Meaning and Myths

- Motivation arouses, sustains, and integrates behavior.
- Several myths have grown up around motivation that can obscure its actual meaning and cause classroom difficulty.
- Recognizing the distinction between intrinsic and extrinsic motivation can help teachers to devise techniques that improve learning in their classes.

Theories of Motivation: Explanations of Motivated Students

- Of the various attempts to explain motivation, Maslow's needs hierarchy has had a lasting impact, due to the appeal of its theoretical and practical implications.
- Bruner posited that educators use discovery learning as a means of stimulating students' interest in learning. One of Bruner's basic assumptions underlying discovery learning is that individuals behave according to their perceptions of their environment; that is, students see meaning in knowledge, skills, and attitudes when they themselves discover it.
- Students search for the causes of their behaviors just as teachers do. To explain this phenomenon, Weiner has been a leader in the development of attribution theory. Knowing whether students attribute their behaviors to ability, effort, task difficulty, or luck can help teachers to improve students' self-concepts, by realistically examining their abilities in light of the tasks, thus furthering learning.
- Skinner has long believed that the proper use of schedules of reinforcement (see Chapter 7) can improve motivation and, in general, enhance classroom performance.
- According to Bandura, the teacher's performance in the classroom can be a powerful model for students to imitate. Once teachers recognize desirable behavior in students, they must act swiftly to reinforce that behavior.

What Affects Students' Motivation?

- Among the most potent influences on motivation are anxiety, attitudes, curiosity, and locus of control.

- Anxiety, either situational or trait, affects classroom performance either positively or negatively. Increasing anxiety lessens performance as task complexity increases.

- A positive attitude toward school and learning increases achievement. Be particularly concerned with not only your students' attitudes toward you and the subjects you are teaching, but also their attitudes about themselves.

- All students possess a certain degree of curiosity that, if capitalized upon, can lead to richer and more insightful learning. Structured but relaxed classroom conditions that allow for an acceptance of students' ideas can encourage the creative use of curiosity.

- The locus of control concept can be useful in improving the achievement of students, especially the "externals." By carefully providing reinforcement for selected behaviors, teachers not only improve students' learning, but also help them to develop more positive self-concepts.

- Repeated criticism and failure can produce learned helplessness, a form of behavior that causes students to give up, just refusing to try. If you encounter such students, your first task will be to persuade them to make an effort so that you can begin to reinforce them for trying.

- Cooperative learning has been found to motivate student learning through group goal structures and rewards for group successes. The most effective methods for cooperative groups emphasize group goals and individual responsibility.

- Technology—in particular, computers in the classroom—has been found to have a positive impact on students' motivation to learn. Four reasons for this have been identified: novelty, individualized level of material, opportunities to receive help in privacy, and high interest material.

Educational Implications of Motivational Theories and Research

- Considering various stages of learning—the beginning, the middle, and the end—leads to the direct application of motivational theory and research in the classroom, for both teachers and their students.

WHAT DO YOU THINK?

1. Which of the myths of motivation do you believe? How has this belief affected your learning?

2. What motivational strategies do you use to get yourself to invest more time and energy in studying?

3. Distinguish between intrinsic and extrinsic motivation. Which form best characterizes your motivation for success in school?

4. Define the Yerkes-Dodson law. How does this apply to your learning in this course?

5. Describe cooperative, competitive, and individualistic goal structures. Which goal structure do you work best under?

Teachers' Case

A t the beginning of this section, "Learning Theories and Implications for Practice," you were introduced to Mark Siegel, a fourth-grade teacher who is puzzled by the learning problems of a student named Karim Peterson and challenged by this student's mother to do more for her son. As you read throughout the four chapters in this section, we have made numerous suggestions about instructional strategies that Mr. Siegel might consider to facilitate Karim's motivation to learn and enhance his ability to acquire more knowledge from class. Like most any instructional problem, there are a number of alternative perspectives that may prove fruitful. So let's now turn to a couple other "experts" on learning, Madonna Atwood and Erin DiPerna, and read what they would advise Mark Siegel to do to help Karim.

Madonna Atwood

A Former Principal, Now a Sixth-Grade Mathematics Teacher
Crestwood, Missouri

After reading the case study involving fourth-grade teacher Mark Siegel and his student Karim Peterson, one very large question seems to linger—why is the child's father not involved in this process? I feel this is a crucial point. The mother seems to be fully in charge of Karim's academic endeavors. Her level of frustration at his lack of progress has caused her to react in an almost obsessive manner, thereby, continually criticizing the teacher for responsive behavior or supposed lack of responsive behavior, finding fault with the curriculum and structure of classes, yet not offering any positive feedback from home. It seems that the mother perceives this lack of progress as a direct reflection on her abilities to raise an intelligent, well-educated child while she herself is an intelligent, well-educated parent. The harder she pushes, the more the child resists in that nonresponsive, apathetic manner he has perfected. He has developed his own response pattern. Personally, I feel this is Karim's attempt to involve his father in his school life or, hopefully, in "some," aspect of his life. Praise or rewards from the mother or the teacher receive no measurable response from the child; consequently, levels of frustration rise and Karim continues to be the center of attention. Blame, responsibility, and accountability for actions are directed at everyone but Karim. At this point I feel the child is waiting for his father to step in and assume the role of counselor, parent-in-charge, or activator.

Having been an elementary principal, I would recommend the following to Mr. Siegel. First, call a mandatory meeting involving both parents with principal/counselor also in attendance. Second, an established plan needs to be approved by the parents, in particular the father, for the completion of assignments, daily schoolwork, and an established time with one or both parents. Third, establish a program put together by the teacher and the student, with parental approval, that monitors and acknowledges positive behavior alterations by Karim, with appropriate rewards for accomplished goals. These rewards would be in the form of outings or special events/activities with his father, primarily. In addition to academic goals, there would be a small agenda to help deal with socialization issues and behaviors. Evaluation of this program would be monthly, with hopes of extension to six or eight weeks as the school year progresses.

Conference

Erin DiPerna

Third-Grade Teacher
Fitchburg, Wisconsin

As I was reading the case study of Mark Siegel's classroom, thoughts came to mind of previous students who brought me similar challenges. I remember feeling frustrated, unappreciated, and depleted of new ideas that I thought might work. But as I believe now, those challenges were a catalyst for me becoming a better teacher. Based on the information in the case study, I have three recommendations for Mark Siegel.

First, I think Mark would benefit from soliciting advice from other professionals within his school. I get the sense that Mark is mentally working overtime trying to "solve this puzzle" on his own. Collaborating with the school psychologist, guidance counselor, minority outreach coordinator, learning resource coordinator, and/or grade-level team members could give both Mark and Karim's mother new insights and ideas. Also, by collaborating with others, Mark's relationship with Karim's mother may not be as strained as it appears to be now. All of the people involved need to work together to show Karim that they care about him and his success in school.

Second, I would encourage Mark to look closely at his curriculum and his delivery of the curriculum. Does he give students opportunities to decide what they would like to learn about a theme? Does Mark offer choices in enrichment activities such as projects and presentations at the end of a theme? Students like Karim may not "thrive" during day-to-day lessons but they may feel very motivated to complete projects generated by their passions and interests, especially those linked to their cultural heritage.

Finally, I believe that Karim would benefit from additional support in reading. As we all know, reading comprehension is a positive indicator of students' academic success. Mark may want to contact individuals from the local high school or community who could serve as a reading tutor. Karim would not only learn to apply and use reading strategies in his various school subjects, but also have the opportunity to develop a positive relationship with another adult.

The insights and suggestions of Madonna Atwood and Erin DiPerna, combined with those that we noted throughout this section should provide you with many ideas for addressing challenging situations like those Mark Siegel is experiencing in his classroom. How would you use this information to help Karim Peterson?

Effective Teaching *and the* Evaluation *of* Learning

The Case of Melissa Williams

A first-year middle school teacher with many innovative ideas is feeling uneasy about her classroom management and assessment methods because several of her colleagues have different teaching styles and frequently warn her that she will be held responsible for how well students do on their end-of-year standardized achievement tests.

Melissa spent most of the summer eagerly preparing for her fall class. It was her first official teaching job—she had done a year of student teaching and had been a substitute teacher in the school district for the past two years—and she was excited to have her "own" students and the opportunity to help them learn. She had fond memories of her own middle school days, and after her daughter had started college, she decided to go back to school to get a teaching degree because she wanted to work with adolescents. Her experience at the university had been challenging but very rewarding, and now she was ready to really "test" herself to see if she could put all the pieces—effective instruction, sound classroom management, and meaningful assessments—together.

Her class of seventh-graders at Davis Middle School provided her the "test." Melissa was responsible for working with a heterogenous group of seventy-five seventh-graders in the DEW House. The DEW House was the group of students that Bill Drake, Sara Ellis, and Melissa Williams were responsible for teaching the core subjects of mathematics, science, language arts, and social studies. Melissa was the primary teacher for language arts and social studies and felt lucky to be working with Bill Drake and Sara Ellis, each of whom had more than ten years of teach-

ing experience, four of which were together at Davis Middle School. Bill was responsible for mathematics instruction and had a reputation among students and parents of being a no-nonsense guy. Sara was the science teacher and also had expertise in computer applications; students always seemed engaged during her lecture-style classes, but her laboratory sessions were noisy and often punctuated with minor "skirmishes" among students. Melissa replaced a social studies teacher who moved with her family to another state. Prior to Melissa's appointment, Bill and Sara had shared the responsibility for language arts instruction. They were really pleased Melissa was hired because they now could each teach their favorite subjects, and Melissa would teach both language arts and social studies.

Melissa liked her new colleagues, but felt their teaching approaches were different from hers, although they all shared high expectations for their students. These differences had come out in the interview she had before being hired, but all the teachers and the principal thought it was desirable to have teachers with different approaches working together. Specifically, Bill Drake liked to work systematically through his math text. He expected students to complete math worksheets daily and to take a weekly quiz on Friday. His room was highly organized and his rules and consequences well known, if not written down, because he reiterated them to the class almost every Monday as he laid out the week's instructional plan. Sara Ellis's class seemed less well organized and rule governed than Bill Drake's class, but she was every bit as demanding of her students. She had high expectations for her students and

had them write a two-page paper each week on a science concept or issue that was personally relevant to the topics they were reading about in their textbook. She also liked to give pop quizzes, especially if she thought students were not studying.

Bill and Sara enjoyed a positive reputation among their fellow teachers and also with many parents in the community. Their classes had a history of having some of the highest average test scores on the end-of-year achievement battery given to all seventh-graders in the district. In particular, their class averages in language arts and social studies had been among the highest in the state for the past three years and their mathematics and science scores, although not as stellar, had been well above the district and state mean scores. Bill and Sara were proud of their students' record on the annual achievement tests and had mentioned to Melissa that they were eager to help her continue the tradition of high scores in the language arts and social studies areas.

The first ten weeks of classes were just about over, and Melissa was feeling good about the progress that she and her students had made. She had, however, experienced some challenging days trying to establish a "friendly and fair" approach to discipline; Jim Watson, a very verbal and sometime aggressive student frequently created problems for her, as did two other male students Jim seemed to have a great influence on. Collectively, the three boys had a record of mild disruptive behaviors (for example, talking out of turn, teasing peers about their looks, and inattention) and poor work completion in language arts. All three of the boys had poor spelling and grammar skills, and consequently disliked the writing journal and topical papers Melissa used as primary instructional tools. Phone communications with their parents had begun on a weekly basis during the past month, but they did not seem to help. The boys' behavior was generally unacceptable, and the percentage of work they completed was less than half of what was assigned. The work that was completed often came in late and sloppy. Melissa had begun to worry about how she was going to grade these students' work. Her initial approach was to request them to do the work over again or to give them more time, but this seemed to result in the boys getting even further behind. In addition, Melissa had overheard a couple other students say it was unfair that Jim gets more time to do his assignments and gets chances at retakes.

When Melissa asked her colleagues about the boys, Bill Drake reported that they were doing fine in his math class, and Sara Ellis indicated that only Jim Watson was a concern because his lab reports were almost unreadable. When discussing these three boys, both Bill and Sara asked how they were doing in preparation for the annual achievement test. Melissa was pleased that they had listened to her concerns about the boys but was somewhat surprised that her colleagues were so focused on preparation for an achievement test. Melissa hadn't really spent any time directly preparing for an end-of-year test! Melissa thought to herself, "I need help managing these boys' behavior so they don't disrupt the learning of the other students and they can get more of their own work done, and all my colleagues can think about is an achievement test that is six months away!"

Melissa decided to redouble her efforts to get the boys' parents in-volved and planned to meet with the parents to develop a strategy to improve the boys' completion of homework and classroom behavior. She scheduled meetings with each of the parents for the upcoming week. Meanwhile, she decided to get more information about the school's annual achievement test. She had planned to look at the test information over her holiday break in December, but all the concern her colleagues continually expressed about student preparation for and performance on the end-of-year test had started her wondering about her own instructional efforts. She wanted to know what information was covered on the test, how students were tested, and what information she would get from the results.

Melissa had started the year thinking her most important goal was to get every student writing—regardless of what they wrote about—and thinking about clearly communicating their thoughts with others. She had shared with her students some examples of what she considered "excellent" and "good" papers for seventh-graders. She also had given them a general set of criteria by which she planned to evaluate most of their papers. These criteria concerned organization, sentence structure, spelling, punctuation, and legibility. Many students reported the scoring criteria and example papers were very helpful. Consequently, Melissa had recently decided to experiment with students self-assessing some of their own papers using the common scoring criteria. In addition, students were responsible for selecting three papers each ten weeks for inclusion in a writing portfolio.

Melissa's review of the end-of-year achievement test proved frustrating. The test manual was full of information, but most of it concerned the administration instructions and tech-nical evidence about the reliability and validity of the objective assessment instrument. There were some example items, but most of them were multiple-choice or short-answer items. The language arts subtest was separate from the social studies subtest; each required seventy-five minutes to complete and required only one answer where a student had to write an extended response.

Melissa's mind was racing; she began to worry that she was not preparing her students for this type of test. She valued critical thinking, problem solving, authentic types of problems where students had to impose order on information and then identify a viable solution. She believed the process of solving problems was every bit as important as the final answer. This test seemed to emphasize factual knowledge, comprehension of short stories, and the application of basic grammar and punctuation skills. Her students were receiving instruction in these areas, but not at the expense of critical thinking and written composition. Perhaps Melissa's most negative reaction about the test, however, concerned the fact that the results did not get returned to teachers until the last week of school, and they came in the form of total scale scores and percentile ranks. No diagnostic information was provided to her or the students, just numbers!

Melissa began to question her work—she was having some trouble managing three of her students, especially Jim Watson, and she was starting to feel pressure about the relevance of the end-of-year achievement test and her approach to instruction. She had started the year being very optimistic and excited about her work, but after only ten weeks she was having some concerns. She needed reassurance, or she needed to change.

Classroom Management:
Creating Effective
Learning Environments

Melissa Williams is a first-year middle school

teacher facing her first teaching experience.

Although she has many great ideas about

how to teach her seventh-grade class, she

does not have a great deal of self-confidence

about her classroom management skills. In

part, some of her shaken confidence comes

from her teaching colleagues who have

different teaching styles and have warned her

about the standards that she must uphold.

Look for information on this case throughout

the chapter.

Chapter Outline

Management Concerns
    in the Classroom
Life in the Classroom
Managing the
    Classroom
Methods of Control
Don't Cause Any
    Problems Yourself
Case Reflections
Chapter Highlights
What Do You Think?
Key Terms

To help you understand the importance of classroom management, we open this chapter by describing what most concerns teachers; we then turn to an analysis of life in the classroom—what really happens when you close the classroom door. Next, we examine models such as QAIT, to help identify critical classroom features that lead to successful classroom management. We then move to specific techniques for organizing the classroom, discussing rules that help, and what kinds of behavior teachers can expect at different age levels. Finally, we offer clear and specific suggestions for maintaining control in the classroom by analyzing three well-known methods. These techniques differ in philosophy and in efficiency. Teachers will want to select those that will give the most support for effective management of their unique classroom.

MANAGEMENT CONCERNS IN THE CLASSROOM

Many readers may believe that this is the most important chapter in the book. Managing a classroom means more than avoiding chaos; it means establishing a routine that enables learning activities to proceed smoothly. It also helps to prevent many unnecessary discipline problems.

Students must know what is expected of them. This circumstance is true from a practical standpoint: They must know what various signals mean and what they should do (this bell means a fire drill, that buzzer signals an assembly). It is true from an affective standpoint: Teachers who give the impression of knowing what they are doing and who act decisively establish that someone is in control, thus providing a sense of security.

And it is true from a pedagogical standpoint. Learning can occur only in an orderly classroom. "Orderly," however, does not imply quiet or rigid. The classroom whose hum and flow indicates youngsters engaged in meaningful activity can be more orderly than the classroom in which you can hear a clock tick. Students may be in various groups around the classroom, perhaps talking over projects, or moving to the library area for research materials, or reading or writing in the group area. An orderly environment is one in which everyone—teacher and students—knows exactly what is going on. Do not minimize the importance of routine: A smoothly running classroom can prevent discipline problems.

Although management issues most concern beginning teachers, they actually keep all teachers on the alert, regardless of our experience—and "management" is by no means confined to discipline alone. We can define *classroom management* as the use of rules and procedures to maintain order so that learning may result. In this light, *organizing the classroom is the first step in effective classroom management.*

Preventing Classroom Problems

Psychologists recently have begun to shift their focus from merely managing student behavior in the classroom to the *prevention* of behavioral problems by using instructional and managerial procedures. Increasingly, psychologists and educators have realized that the prevention of problems should be a national priority, not just in schools but across the life span in all types of community settings. Reflecting this perspective, the American Psychological Association commissioned a task force to examine existing prevention programs and identify those that could be considered outstanding (Price, Cowen, Lorion, & Ramos-McKay, 1988). The task force did identify fourteen programs as being outstanding.

In this chapter, we have adopted a dual focus: on strategies that teachers can use to respond to problems as they occur in the classroom, as well as techniques to prevent problems from occurring in the first place. A comprehensive classroom management program

Objectives

When you finish reading this chapter, you should be able to

- describe the significance of time in mastery of classroom material

- match developmental tasks with appropriate management techniques

- identify rules that are needed for a smoothly functioning classroom

- use methods that maintain productive classroom control

- apply the principles and techniques to the case of Melissa Williams

Proactive classroom management means that you should have a program that includes reactive responding to problems and a plan for productive learning.

PROACTIVE CLASSROOM MANAGEMENT
Classroom management including both reactive responding to problems and proactive planning for productive behavior.

includes both reactive responding to problems and proactive planning for productive behavior; the latter is an approach that has been labeled **proactive classroom management.** Proactive classroom management has three characteristics that distinguish it from other management techniques (Gettinger, 1988):

1. It is preventive rather than reactive.

2. It combines methods that help students behave correctly with procedures that promote achievement, using effective classroom instructional techniques.

3. It emphasizes the group dimensions of classroom management.

Maintaining sufficient order requires that the teacher has students enter the classroom and move to their seats with no disruption. Once they are seated, make sure that they have the materials they need, and they understand what they are supposed to do with them. The teacher's plan for any lesson must provide for **engaged time** for all students. Finally, students should leave the classroom in an orderly fashion. Let's use a general example here. Your students enter your room. They immediately check the board to see what they are supposed to do for the first part of the period. Two assigned students may move around the room collecting homework. Note: The students know what is expected of them; they know the rules (the classroom organization). While this is going on you may devote your time to individuals, checking on one or two students who could have problems. Notice how you are heading off potential trouble, a practice that in itself is a form of classroom control. At the same time, all of your students are productively engaged. Remember that engaged time is not the time allotted to any class; it is the time during which students are actively involved in their work.

ENGAGED TIME
The time during which students are actively involved in their work.

Thus, effective teaching and fruitful learning are tightly linked to classroom organization and management. Doyle (1986) noted that although *learning* is served by an *instructional* function, order is served by a *managerial* function: the forming of groups, establishment of rules and procedures, reaction to misbehavior, and in general, monitoring of classroom activities. Individuals learn; order applies to groups.

TIPS ON TIME
Proactive Classroom Management

PRINCIPLE Proactive classroom management can save teachers considerable time relative to management of disruptive behavior.

STRATEGY At the beginning of the academic year, establish rules and guidelines for classroom behavior.

STRATEGY Use effective instructional procedures that have been found to promote student achievement (for example, use interesting materials, teach at an effective pace).

STRATEGY Involve students in group activities that allow group reinforcement of individual student behavior.

Time and Teachers: The Carroll Model

In Chapter 13 we will mention the pervasive influence that John Carroll has exercised over recent research into the improvement of students' achievement. (His 1963 article, "A Model of School Learning," was the basis of Bloom's work on school learning.) Discussing classroom organization and management, Carroll noted that the primary job of the educational psychologist is to develop and apply knowledge concerning why students succeed or fail in their learning at school, and to assist in the prevention and remediation of learning difficulties (1963, p. 723).

Using this guideline, Carroll stated that a learner will succeed in learning a task to the extent that the needed time is spent for that student to learn the task. Time (actual time spent on learning) becomes the key feature. The Carroll model uses two categories to analyze time:

1. *The determinants of time needed for learning.* There are three important aspects in this category. (a) *Aptitude* refers to the amount of time any student will need to learn a task. Be on the watch for those students who do well, except perhaps in one subject (science, math, art, music); be sure to give them additional time in the subject that causes them difficulty. (b) *Ability to understand instruction* refers to the effects of general intelligence and verbal ability. (c) *Quality of instruction* refers to the teacher's ability to present appropriate material in an interesting manner. Teachers should not only be aware of a student's understanding, but also think of their own teaching: Was it clear? Was it to the point? How many failed to understand? Be honest.

2. *Time spent in learning.* Carroll focused on two important features of this category: (a) *the time allowed for learning,* which refers to the opportunity that individual schools allow for learning; and (b) *perseverance,* which refers to the amount of time students are willing to spend in learning.

We also may divide the five features included in these two categories by identifying those that reside within the student, those that stem from external conditions, and the one that results from the interplay of external with internal. The conditions over which a teacher has little control (the conditions that reside *within* the student) are aptitude and ability to understand instruction. Time allowed for learning and quality of instruction are both under the control of the instructor. Perseverance, or the motivational aspect, reflects both student characteristics and the classroom situation.

CASE NOTES

Observation   Bill Drake and Sara Ellis, Melissa Williams's colleagues, do not seem to have discipline problems in their classrooms.

Hypothesis   Both Bill and Sara may be using proactive classroom management strategies with their classes, especially the use of effective instructional tactics.

Possible action   Melissa Williams should take a close look at each of her colleagues' classes and review the elements of proactive classroom management operating. She should then consider implementing these strategies in her class.

If we now link Carroll's model of school learning to an effectively managed classroom, we can draw three conclusions. First is the inescapable link between learning and order. Simply put, learning rarely emerges from chaos. Second, a disorganized classroom substantially reduces time for learning; too much time is spent in trying to achieve order. Third, quality of instruction is tightly bound to efficiency of classroom management. In this instance, good intentions are not enough; teachers cannot teach effectively if students are out of control.

A strong relationship exists between the way in which teachers manage their classroom and the effectiveness of their teaching. Both these functions must be appropriate for the ages and levels of the children taught. Now we will discuss the developmental task model to review important developmental principles.

Developmental Tasks and Classroom Management

The developmental changes students experience will require teachers of different grade levels to adopt different types of management techniques. Stop for a moment to think of the developmental characteristics of the elementary school child that we discussed in Chapters 2 and 3; now, compare these with those of the adolescent. The developmental sequence alone dictates changing management techniques.

As we have seen in Chapter 9 on motivation, when natural motivators can be linked with educational requirements, tasks are more easily mastered. Examine Table 10.1 carefully to distinguish those tasks that are significant for the different age groups. (Note the appearance of developmental tasks in more than one category, emphasizing the integrated nature of development.) Now think about the classroom techniques you would use in teaching 5-year-olds to read, compared with those you would use in working with adolescents in a current events class.

Describing schools as different social contexts at the preschool, elementary, and secondary levels, Minuchin and Shapiro (1983) stated that they are organized differently, children perceive them differently, and different aspects of social behavior appear to meet students' changing needs. *Preschool experiences* are more protective and caring than educational, with children interacting with one or two teachers, perhaps an equal number of aides, and several peers. Socialization and communication needs are paramount and experiences are shaped by adults with two important, often unarticulated goals: desirable socialization (necessary conformity) and individuation (self-expression).

The *elementary school classroom* is more of a true social unit, with more intense interactions between teacher and student and among peers. Teachers, as authority figures, establish the climate of the classroom and the kind of relationships permitted. Peer-group relationships stress friendship, belongingness, and status. In *high school,* the entire school,

Table 10.1   DEVELOPMENTAL TASKS—GUIDELINES FOR TEACHERS

	Infancy-Early Childhood	Middle Childhood	Adolescence
Physical	Learning to walk Learning to take solid foods Learning to talk Learning to control eliminations	Learning physical skills necessary for games	Accepting one's physique
Cognitive	Learning to talk Acquiring concepts Preparing for reading Learning to distinguish right from wrong Learning sex differences	Building a healthy self-concept Learning an appropriate sex role Developing the fundamental skills—reading, writing, arithmetic Developing concepts for everyday living	Preparing for a career
Social	Learning to distinguish right from wrong Learning sex differences	Learning to get along with others Learning an appropriate sex role Developing acceptable attitudes toward society	Developing a satisfactory social role Achieving mature relations with both sexes Preparing for marriage and family
Personal-emotional	Learning to distinguish right from wrong Learning sex differences	Building a healthy self-concept Developing attitudes and values Achieving independence	Preparing for a career Achieving emotional independence from adults Preparing for marriage and family Acquiring systems to guide behavior Achieving socially responsible behavior

rather than a particular classroom, becomes the social context. Social relationships assume considerable importance, and social behavior becomes the standard of acceptance. Extracurricular activities now are a greater and more significant part of a student's life.

With a child's age, then, the school environment broadens in scope and complexity, producing changes in self-concept, gender differentiation, and interpersonal relationships. With these inevitable changes, it is little wonder that management techniques change accordingly. For example, during the kindergarten and early elementary school grades, students are being socialized—learning to respond to teachers and get along with their peers—and instructed in the basic skills. Discipline typically is not a major concern, since youngsters of this age usually react well to authority and seek teacher praise and rewards. Adjustment to the school as a major socializing agent and mastery of the fundamentals are the two chief tasks teachers should incorporate into their classroom management.

Students in the middle elementary school grades know a school's routine and have worked out their relationships with their peers. Teachers should be able to concentrate on curricular tasks, provided that they maintain a clearly defined classroom atmosphere. The upper elementary and lower high school years are times when peer pressure mounts, and most students are concerned with pleasing friends rather than teachers. The teacher's role as an authority figure is often challenged by students, and classroom control becomes more of an issue. Students should have mastered the basics and be able to function, to a certain extent, independently. Classroom procedures and rules should be distinct, understandable, and fair. Once students of these ages know the boundaries and what is expected of them, the teacher's major tasks include subject matter expertise and motivation.

In the upper high school grades, the teacher is working with more mature students, a majority of whom probably are beginning to think of college and/or careers. Thus, these

Table 10.2 MANAGEMENT AND DEVELOPMENT

Level	Desirable Qualities
Lower elementary	Patience Nurturance skills Socialization skills Instructional skills
Middle elementary	Patience Diagnostic skills Instructional skills Understanding Developmental awareness
Upper elementary–junior high	Motivating skills Firmness Management skills Patience Understanding of concerns of early adolescence
Senior high	Subject matter expertise Relationship skills Ability to have control yet give freedom

students are more responsible, and concern with management decreases after the beginning of the year, when the teacher informs students what is expected of them in the class. Wildly disruptive students (a small minority) often either have dropped out of school by these years or have been placed elsewhere.

The developmental characteristics that affect teacher management techniques should influence the decision as to the age group an individual would like to teach. Table 10.2 summarizes these features.

Classrooms are remarkably complex settings, and the activities that occur within them are subject to the likes and dislikes, feelings, and motivations of a large number of people. Many students have a tendency to "fool around" when their attention wavers; they require tasks to prevent classroom problems and loss of learning. What are some of these problems?

Management and Control of Problem Students

We have stressed that any analysis of classroom management cannot be confined to a discussion of discipline alone. Throughout the remainder of this chapter, we will mention a wide variety of factors that contribute to good classroom management; however, control remains central to our discussion. To help you put this issue in perspective, examples of student behavior problems (based on real life) will be identified. Thus, you will have a frame of reference to use in determining what kinds of management techniques may be most effective with each type of problem.

In thinking about managing classrooms, it is useful to know something about the kinds of students who will be exhibiting problem behaviors. Over the years researchers have used a variety of checklists and rating scales to measure the types of problems that parents and teachers report children experiencing. Table 10.3 displays some of the various patterns of child problems that have emerged. Remember, however, that although each category is presented separately, any one student may have more than one particular behavior problem. As you read through the categories, try to answer the following questions:

Table 10.3 DIMENSIONS OF BEHAVIOR ARISING IN MULTIVARIATE STATISTICAL ANALYSIS WITH FREQUENTLY ASSOCIATED CHARACTERISTICS OF EACH	

Conduct
   Fighting, hitting
   Disobedience, defiance
   Temper tantrums
   Destructiveness
   Impertinence, impudence
   Uncooperativeness, resistance
	Socialized aggression
	   "Bad" companions
	   Truancy from home
	   Truancy from school
	   Stealing in company of others
	   Loyalty to delinquent friends
	   Membership in a gang

Attention problems
   Poor concentration, short attention span
   Daydreaming
   Clumsiness, poor coordination
   Preoccupation, staring into space
   Failing to finish, lack of perseverance
   Impulsiveness
	Anxious-depressed withdrawal
	   Anxious, fearful, tense behavior
	   Shyness, timidity, bashfulness
	   Withdrawn, seclusive behavior
	   Depression, sadness, disturbance
	   Hypersensitivity, being easily hurt
	   Feelings of inferiority, worthlessness

Motor overactivity
   Restlessness, overactivity
   Excitability, impulsiveness
   Squirmy, jittery movements
   Overtalkativeness
   Humming and other odd noises
	Schizoid-unresponsive
	   Refusal to talk
	   Withdrawn behavior
	   Sadness
	   Staring blankly
	   Confusion

From *Contemporary Directions in Psychopathology,* edited by T. Millon and G. Klerman. Copyright © 1986. Reprinted by permission of Guilford Publications, Inc.

- What do you see as the core of each of these problems?

- How would this problem affect the rest of the class?

- How would you handle each of these problems?

- Would you need help in working with this student?

Remember your answers; we will return to them at the end of the chapter. Now let us examine what is actually going on in the classroom.

LIFE IN THE CLASSROOM

Much has been written about the necessity of adapting general management techniques for classroom use. Management, which is essential in all organizations for goal attainment, involves three basic functions: *planning,* by which objectives and procedures are selected; *communication,* by which information is transferred; and *control,* by which performance is matched to plans. Note how these three basic functions identify the major topics in the remainder of the chapter.

When You Close the Classroom Door

Philip Jackson, in his classic work *Life in Classrooms* (1968, updated in 1990), presented a charming and enduring essay on "life as it is" in the classroom. Noting that although schools are places where skills are acquired, tests are given, and amusing and maddening things

---

TIPS ON LEARNING
Managing the Instructional Environment

PRINCIPLE   Managing the classroom is more than managing student behavior.

STRATEGY   Plan the instructional day so as to create an organized student work environment.

STRATEGY   Establish classroom rules that provide clear expectations for student learning and behavior.

STRATEGY   Control the classroom environment by developing and implementing a behavior management plan for student disruptive behavior.

---

happen, they also are places where young people come together, make friends, learn, and engage in all sorts of routine activities. Jackson adds that if we total the number of hours that a youngster spends in kindergarten and elementary school, we obtain a figure of 7,000 hours. If you were to spend an equal amount of time at a house of worship, you would have to attend a one-hour service one day a week for 150 years!

Shouldn't this amount of time be translated into meaningful outcomes? Although the classroom is a stable environment and its activities are spin-offs of certain set procedures—seatwork, group discussion, teacher demonstration, questions and answers—we must also remember that young people are in school because they must be. Given the reality of time and coercion, Jackson turned to three features of classroom life not typically mentioned: *crowds, praise,* and *power.*

Spending time in a classroom means learning to live with others, which can entail delay, denial, interruptions, and social distraction. During this time, and in the presence of others, a student experiences the pain of failure and the joy of success, which then become part of that student's official record. Finally, there is a vast gulf between a powerful teacher and the students; how that teacher's authority is used tells us much about the atmosphere of any classroom.

It is difficult to determine how students react to classroom conditions. Realistically, everyone can be temporarily unhappy, including achieving, seemingly happy students. Jackson (1968) stated that students' attitudes toward school are complicated and puzzling. Summarizing data from previous studies, he demonstrated considerable negative feelings among basically satisfied students. Following are some of the negative terms students used to describe their feelings toward classroom life: bored, uncertain, dull, restless, inadequate, unnoticed, unhelped, angry, restrained, misunderstood, rejected.

Jackson summarized student feelings nicely in this way:

> *The number of students who become ecstatic when the school bell rings and who remain that way all day is probably very small, as is the number who sit in the back of the room and grind their teeth in anger from opening exercise to dismissal. One way of interpreting the data we have reviewed so far is to suggest that most students do not feel too strongly about their classroom experience, one way or the other. (Jackson, 1968, p. 60)*

Note how the adjectives students used reflected not only the material learned in the classroom, but also planning, communication, and control. For example, *bored* and *uncertain* probably related to poor planning and communication, as well as to uncertainty about what was expected of them.

Young people come together at school to learn, make friends, and engage in various routine activities. In reality, even achieving, happy students can be temporarily bored or unhappy.

Classroom Activities

In a more formal analysis of the classroom, classroom activities emerge as the basic unit of organization. Doyle (1986) described activities as relatively short blocks of classroom time (about ten to twenty minutes) during which students are arranged and taught in a particular way. For example, most activities involve seatwork, recitation, small groups, and/or presentations. Again we note the importance of engaged time. If students aren't "hooked" immediately, valuable learning time is lost.

Types of Activities

Berliner (1983), studying seventy-five classrooms from kindergarten to grade 6, identified eleven activities that consistently appear:

- Reading circle
- Seatwork
- One-way presentations
- Two-way presentations
- Use of media
- Silent reading
- Construction
- Games
- Play
- Transitions
- Housekeeping

You can probably determine at a glance that a few of these activities consume most of the time: About 60% of classroom time is spent in seatwork, and about 30% in recitation or whole-class presentations. These numbers vary because at any given time transitions and housekeeping may intrude.

Note that activities with different labels are similar in structure. All seatwork, for example, is alike, regardless of subject matter. Also, lectures, demonstrations, and audiovisual presentations share many similarities.

Doyle (1986) estimated that a teacher's involvement during a class seems to consist mainly of the following:

- Actual instruction (questions, feedback, imparting knowledge)—about 51%

- Organizing students—about 23%

- Dealing with deviant behavior—about 14%

- Handling individual problems and social tasks—about 12%

The findings we have been discussing are consistent with the emphasis placed on topics such as time on task and student engagement in the learning and teaching sections of this book. School outcome variables are not divorced from variables of "climate," the atmosphere to which students are exposed. From this brief glimpse of the varied and complex life of the classroom, you can understand the need for careful organization of its activities.

Organizing Classroom Activities

Recall the distinctions that have been made throughout the chapter thus far: Good classroom management entails more than gimmicks or entertainment devices to keep students under control. The first element to consider is classroom atmosphere. What is the "climate" of the classroom? Is it conducive to learning?

High work involvement with a minimum of deviant behaviors does not appear by accident. Laslett and Smith (1984) identified four "rules"—actually, skills—that should help classroom organization:

1. *Get them in.* Lessons should start on time, and teacher attention should not be diverted by routines that should have been attended to earlier. The authors believe that classwork begins smoothly when teachers are present before the class arrives and have checked to see that everything is in proper order. Teachers being there early simply reinforces their authority as they decide when they want the class to enter, assign seats, and have work available to occupy each student immediately.

2. *Get them out.* Laslett and Smith (1984) recommended that before teachers decide what they will teach, they consider the ideal method for concluding the lesson and dismissing the class. They argued that there is nothing strange about these priorities, since carefully won and maintained control can be quickly lost at the conclusion of a lesson. Such planning is only one factor ensuring the smooth transitional processes constantly needed. Control is not the only reason for thinking about concluding the lesson. If teachers do not provide time for some reinforcement at the end of the lesson, learning can be lost in the rush toward dismissal.

3. *Get on with it.* Here the focus should be on the lesson itself—its content, the teacher's manner, and the lesson's organization. To maintain motivation, ensure that class activities are complete, well structured, and as interesting as you can

make them. Balance your work by making your classes as varied as possible. Mix the familiar with the new, the interesting with what you know is necessary but might be boring, and seatwork with recitation. As these authors note, however, be sure that variety does not become confusion.

4. *Get on with them.* Classroom disruptions are infrequent when teacher-student interactions are positive. Your success as a teacher hinges on your relationships with your students. Several techniques to further these relationships are suggested throughout this chapter; for now, remember that you should know your students as well as you can, as they are both in and out of school. Constantly be aware of what is going on in your class.

Though these four "rules" will not guarantee the absence of discipline problems, following them carefully should help to eliminate misbehaviors that result from classroom disorganization. Let us now consider one technique for integrating the many ideas we have discussed. This is the QAIT model developed by Slavin (1987c).

The QAIT Model

Teachers must adapt instruction to students' levels of knowledge (and level of development), motivate students to learn, manage student behavior, group students for instruction, and test and evaluate students. These functions are carried out at two levels. At the (macro) school level, the principal and/or central administrators may establish policies concerning grouping of students (for example, tracking); provision and allocation of special education and remedial resources; and grading, evaluation, and promotion practices. At the classroom (micro) level, teachers control the grouping of students within the class, teaching techniques, classroom management methods, informal incentives, frequency and form of quizzes and tests, and so on. These elements of school and classroom organization are at least as important for student achievement as the quality of teachers' lessons (Slavin, 1987c, p. 90).

Building on Carroll's model of school learning (refer back to page 379), Slavin (1987e) proposed an instructional model focused on the alterable elements of Carroll's model. Called **QAIT,** the model encompasses four components: **Q**uality of instruction, **A**ppropriate levels of instruction, **I**ncentive, and **T**ime.

QAIT

An instructional model proposed by Slavin that emphasizes the quality of instruction, appropriate levels of instruction, incentive, and time.

Quality of Instruction

This component depends on both the curriculum and the lesson presentation. Slavin stated that when quality instruction occurs, the information presented makes sense to students, is interesting, and is easy to both remember and apply. Above all else, Slavin argued that *instruction must make sense to students.* For this to happen, the teacher must (a) present information in an orderly, systematic fashion; (b) provide smooth transitions to new topics; (c) use vivid images and concrete examples; and (d) ensure necessary repetition and reinforcement.

Appropriate Levels of Instruction

This concept implies that the teacher knows that the students are ready to learn new material. The lesson cannot be either too easy or too difficult. One of a teacher's most challenging tasks will be to accommodate teaching to the individual differences and needs of students. Though most of the methods that schools and teachers use to provide appropriate levels of instruction (remedial grouping, tracking, special education) have serious drawbacks, given the diversity of students, there can be no avoiding the issue. Slavin (1987c) identified the following methods as most common:

1. *Ability groups,* in which elementary students remain in heterogeneous classes most of the day but are grouped for certain subjects such as reading and mathematics, can be effective.

2. *Group-based mastery learning* (see Chapter 13) does not require permanent ability groups; students regroup after each skill is taught. The danger here is that in the traditional class period, corrective instruction can slow down the entire class.

3. *Individualized instruction* can be effective if coupled with personalized contact with an instructor and some group work.

Summarizing what is currently known about the results of grouping practices, Slavin (1988a) separated the results into two categories:

- *Within-class groupings.* The research suggests that the evidence for the value of mastery learning remains inconclusive, while analyses of cooperative learning methods indicate consistent gains in student achievement if properly managed.

- *Between-class groupings.* Such groupings (ability groups, special classes) have little effect on student achievement, although acceleration may possibly benefit some gifted students. Departmentalization at the upper elementary and middle school levels probably should be avoided, although regrouping strategies (for certain subjects such as math and/or reading) can be effective.

Incentive

Here we refer to the degree of student motivation. As much as we would like our students to be intrinsically motivated (see Chapter 9), not all students will be ecstatic about all subjects at all times. One of the best incentives a teacher can offer is to ensure that students be held accountable for what they do. Give them time to respond to questions; check their homework. Don't rely solely on individual praise and reward; cooperative learning methods in which groups are rewarded because of their learning consistently have shown increases in student achievement.

Time

There must be sufficient time for learning to occur. But don't be satisfied with "time" as a general concept. Remember the distinction between allocated time and engaged time.

The four elements of QAIT (quality, appropriateness, incentive, and time) share one critical characteristic: Each element must be adequate if instruction is to be effective (Slavin, 1987c, p. 92). Figure 10.1 illustrates the QAIT model.

Note the independent variables in Figure 10.1. Students bring certain variables to the classroom over which the school has little control. The alterable variables (the variables over which teachers *do* have control) are QAIT, and they influence achievement by two time-related variables: instructional efficiency and engaged time. Note how instructional efficiency in turn is related to quality of instruction, appropriate levels of instruction, and incentive.

Slavin argued that his model accounts for many of the variables through which classroom organization affects learning outcomes. The QAIT model is not bound by any particular theory, but can be adopted as a method for understanding instruction and learning in any classroom.

Classroom Contexts

We have identified several common classroom activities and examined ways to improve performance in many of them. Now let us consider two of these activities in greater detail.

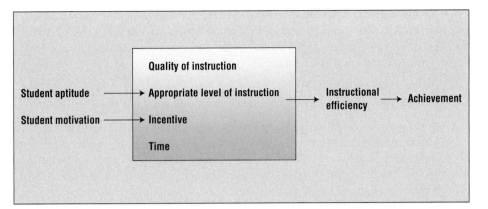

FIGURE 10.1

The QAIT model.

CASE NOTES

Observation   Jim Watson appears to be creating problems for Melissa Williams through his verbal and aggressive behavior.

Hypothesis   Jim's aggressive behavior may be related to the lack of a consistent instructional and management plan in Melissa Williams's classroom.

Possible Action   The QAIT model may be a very good option to adapt instruction to Jim, motivate him to learn, manage his behavior, group Jim and his friends, and evaluate their academic performance.

TIPS ON MOTIVATION
Reducing Behavior Problems

PRINCIPLE   Student motivation plays an important role in instructional activities and managing classroom behavior.

STRATEGY   Pick curriculum materials that are really interesting to students.

STRATEGY   Arrange for students to work in cooperative learning groups. This format will increase motivation.

STRATEGY   Use group contingencies (in addition to individual) in classroom management plans. For example, when all students complete their homework assignments, the class (group) watches a sports video.

Recitation

Recitation entails calling on individual students to give answers publicly before the rest of the class, usually for a brief time. Recitation has several purposes: review, introduction of new material, checking of assigned work, practice, and ensuring comprehension (Doyle, 1986). The purpose of the recitation dictates the type of question asked and opportunity for student participation.

Recitation involves the use of questions, and teachers should ask these questions in a way that will keep the whole class interested. Try to organize questions so that all students have the chance to participate. Think about the questions. Are they intended for review? Will you be satisfied with a yes or no answer, or are you looking for a thoughtful reply? Remember:

- *Ask your question of the entire class,* give them all time to think of the answer, and then call on an individual student. Do not indicate a student and then ask your question.

- *Wait for the answer.* Give the student time to think and respond. Use your best judgment; if the delay continues, rephrase the question, perhaps supplying prompts. If the student answers incorrectly, correct the answer impersonally, explaining as you do. Discourage any type of student calling-out behavior while another student is thinking of an answer. Such behavior can quickly produce chaos.

Seatwork

Two types of seatwork are used most commonly. The first is *supervised study,* during which all students are assigned *independent work* and the teacher moves around the room, monitoring each student's work. The second is independent work, when the teacher is busy with another task and does not monitor each student's work.

Estimates are that students in grades 1 through 7 spend from 50% to 75% of their time working alone on seatwork. Since students are generally less engaged during seatwork than they are in group or individual work with the teacher, you should be alert to techniques that improve engaged time. Here are several suggestions to guide seatwork:

- Teachers should spend sufficient time explaining, discussing, and even practicing before their students commence work on their own.

- Practice should immediately precede the seatwork.

- The exercises assigned to students should flow directly from the teacher's explanations and the practice.

- Teachers should guide students through the first few exercises.

A good clue to the success teachers can expect from assignments lies in the number of questions they receive during the actual seatwork. If you find yourself giving multiple explanations during the seatwork, you can anticipate multiple errors (Rosenshine & Stevens, 1986). Establish a set routine that students should follow any time they do seatwork. In this way, they will know what to do when they have questions and when they finish, and how to get help. Even if you are working with another group, arrange seating so that you can monitor both groups adequately. If possible, try to move around to check on the seatwork group. Teacher contact greatly increases engaged time, since feedback and follow-up are as related to achievement as praise or reward.

Although teachers can easily overuse seatwork, if the assignment is interesting, clearly explained, and not just busywork, seatwork can be a valuable classroom tool.

MANAGING THE CLASSROOM

The next two sections, on managing the classroom and methods of control, are actually subdivisions of one topic. They are separated here because of their individual importance and to give you both general and specific approaches to classroom control. Remember that initial meetings teachers have with their class during the first two weeks of school are probably the most important with regard to classroom control. During these sessions, teachers will set the classroom atmosphere by the rules and procedures they establish.

Rule Setting and Classroom Procedures

Any time people (adults or children) come together to achieve a particular goal, their behavior must be subject to rules. Otherwise, goal attainment is doomed. You may have had experience in attempting to learn in a setting where individual misbehavior constantly disrupted the class. If you were intent on learning, you probably became frustrated very quickly.

Many rules are explicit and openly discussed. Behaviors such as tardiness, fighting, and talking in class cannot be tolerated for the good of the entire group. Policies on other behaviors, such as leaving the room, sharpening pencils, or getting a drink of water are more implicit; that is, they are known and require little discussion once the rules are established. For a student to leave the room, a teacher may require hand-raising or some other routine, such as the student's walking to a chalkboard, writing his or her name on the board, leaving the room, and upon reentering, erasing the name from the board.

Good Managers

Emmer, Evertson, and Anderson (1980), after studying elementary school teachers designated as "good managers," stated that all these teachers made known their rules and procedures on the first day of class, and also quite deliberately integrated them into a system, which they taught. Their rules were explicit, concrete, and functional, and these teachers gave students examples of the signals they would use for various activities.

The "good managers" did not initially overburden their students with rules—a tendency of many beginning teachers—but began with those that they considered basic and then gradually introduced more as they were needed. They also periodically reminded their students of the rules. By monitoring their classes closely, they were able to notice any rule violations almost instantly and attempt to correct them before minor violations developed into major problems.

Effective secondary school teachers also clearly and unmistakably stated the desired behaviors for their classes, gave precise indications of the expected work standards in their classes, and acted immediately to check disruptive behavior (Evertson & Emmer, 1982). Soon after the opening of school, less effective managers experienced more talking out in class and unapproved movement around the room. The main difference between the elementary and secondary "good managers" was that the secondary school instructors spent less time teaching and rehearsing the rules and procedures. Remember these points:

- Decide on as few important rules as necessary.

- Make rules absolutely clear to all.

- Enforce rules for all.

- Avoid playing favorites.

Rules and Classroom Activities

Classroom activities run in cycles in which students' behaviors are defined by rules. Once the teacher and other students repeatedly perform and reinforce behaviors specified by the rules, the rules become a part of the regular classroom routine. When this routine happens, the pieces are in place for efficient teaching and learning. Medland and Vitale (1984) suggested that the following five steps will help formulate meaningful rules for many classroom activities:

1. *Define the class activity.* We have previously commented on general classroom rules (for example, no calling out), but specific activities require specific rules. When the teacher is working with one reading group, other group members must occupy

Good classroom management begins with a clear understanding of rules, preferably rules that are worded positively.

themselves with seatwork. Efficient laboratory sessions demand orderly retrieving and storing of equipment. Physical education classes necessitate proper dress, equipment, and warm-up, certainly requirements that need structure and rules.

2. *Determine the social behaviors necessary for activities.* What is it that the teacher wants students to accomplish during the activity? How should they go about it? Answering these two questions should help identify the needed behaviors. Also, consider what is inappropriate for the activity.

3. *Determine which activities need lists of rules.* Several guidelines can help here (Medland & Vitale, 1984):

   - Are there many social behaviors associated with the activity?
   - Does the activity require considerable time?
   - Are special classroom rules needed to cover the activity's behaviors?
   - Have misbehaviors been associated with this activity?

   Answering any of these questions in the affirmative would seem to suggest the need for appropriate rules.

4. *Make a set of rules for the selected activities.* Rules add structure to any activity and enhance learning by providing a means of coordinated movement. If you think for a moment about the rules that function when you are with one group, and the rules that apply to those doing seatwork, you can understand the necessity for coordination. Since rules describe the behaviors necessary to accomplish an activity, try these suggestions:

   - Keep rules short.
   - Phrase rules in a positive way.
   - Don't use too many rules.

5. *Be sure to formulate a set of general activity rules.* We have previously commented on the need for such rules, and you can understand the necessity for being certain

TIPS ON COMMUNICATION

PRINCIPLE Effective classroom management includes effective communication with students about classroom expectations.

STRATEGY Make a list of classroom activities that will be expected of all students, not too many, but just the four or five important ones (for example, grading, homework).

STRATEGY Make rules explicit by writing them on the board (for elementary students) or in a handout (for middle and high school students).

STRATEGY Review the classroom rules frequently and reinforce students that model and display adherence to the rules.

that specific activity rules are consistent with the general rules. Otherwise, students become confused, and any contradiction could lead to misbehavior.

From this discussion it should be clear that successful teachers establish a classroom work system with rules and procedures designed to keep the system in good order. Successful teachers set these rules at the beginning of the school year, even though their students previously have learned those general rules that apply to school behavior. Experience has shown that unless rules are reinforced, student behavior deteriorates. The quality of rule setting, even at the secondary level, determines the order that will prevail in any class for its duration (Doyle, 1986). Finally, although classroom order depends on a teacher's ability to have students understand classroom procedures, the teacher must also be ready to cope with rule violations.

Management and Control

Teachers should also take into account several developmental considerations in managing their classroom. Students exhibit a wide range of difficulties in development, but many problems are not serious enough to be of great concern. Kazdin (1988) stated that the following developmental issues are noteworthy in considering students' problems:

- Some behaviors that characterize maladjustment are relatively common in childhood. As most students mature, they do not experience severe problems.

- As students develop and undergo rapid changes, problem behaviors wax and wane at different ages. Such behaviors as lying and destructiveness are frequent from 4 to 9 years of age, but decline by 10 to 11 years of age.

- As a result of rapid changes as development continues, a problem of one type may be replaced by another problem at a later age.

There is probably no such thing as the "normal" youngster; usually all students exhibit some troublesome behavior during development. They may be anxious, insecure, or aggressive—but these characteristics bother teachers only when they persist and become severe. For most children, problems do not persist. Youngsters typically show decreases in such behavior and progress to more mature stages of development.

All children experience stress, and their reaction may be to exhibit maladaptive behavior. The teacher's role (shared with their parents) in helping students to master developmental crises is vital, because the manner in which they meet these difficulties shapes

"Heckuva day, wasn't it, Ms. Carpenter? No hard feelings?"
© *James Estes*.

the way that they will face future dilemmas. Adults are teaching students problem-solving behavior, and what they learn may last a lifetime. Be alert, however, to more serious or prolonged developmental problems, and know when and where to refer students. Constant failure, punishment, and ridicule destroy confidence and can cause a low self-concept that may result in a worrisome elementary school student who becomes a sullen, rebellious secondary school student. Estimates are that about 5% of all school-age youngsters show serious behavioral symptoms, and about 10% manifest milder behavioral disturbances. Thus, 85% of students proceed normally, perhaps causing teachers some anxieties with temporary maladaptive behavior (Travers, 1982). Students, then, will inevitably experience growth problems and bring these to the classroom. These problems usually pass fairly quickly; only when they persist should teachers become concerned.

Aggression in the Classroom

An aggressive student not only can be a classroom problem but also may require special treatment. You may find it helpful to consider this problem developmentally, so that you can identify those classroom situations that could trigger outbursts.

A completely satisfactory theory of aggression still eludes us, but research interest has turned recently to the social encounters of infancy and early childhood to discover the roots of aggression. (See Parke & Slaby, 1983, for a particularly thoughtful analysis of aggressive behavior.) Investigators have discovered that as early as 12 to 18 months, half of the interchanges among children in a nursery involved conflict. By the time children are 24 months, such disruptive interchanges had dropped to 20%, and by 42 months, they

Table 10.4 DEVELOPMENT AND AGGRESSION

Age	Type of Aggression	Cause
Birth–2 years	General upset	Possession of object
2–4	Physical Some verbal	Frustration
4–8	Verbal Physical	Hostility toward others
8–12	Verbal Some physical	Peers Authority Insecurity

dropped further to 5%. Between the ages of 2 and 4 years, physical aggression decreases and verbal aggression increases; by age 7, aggressive behavior becomes much more person-oriented. Aggressive students present behaviors that are typically classified as externalizing.

As students continue to age and greater cognitive ability develops, their understanding of other students' intentions becomes important. Clear developmental changes seem to be involved. Seven-year-olds respond aggressively to both accidental and intentional provocation, whereas 9- and 12-year-olds react less aggressively to accidental provocation. Twelve-year-olds also respond less aggressively to intentional verbal than to intentional physical provocations, in contrast to 7- and 9-year-olds. Table 10.4 illustrates a general developmental sequence of aggressive behavior.

There are clear sex differences in aggression, with boys generally being much more aggressive. Impressive evidence exists that aggression in males is remarkably stable. Studying individuals from 2 to 18 years of age, Olweus (1982) reported that male aggression and acting-out behaviors showed substantial persistence over long periods of time.

Some students who exhibit aggressive behavior may need professional services focused on the school and family (Horne & Sayger, 1990). In dealing with most cases of aggression, however, try these suggestions:

- *Stop trouble before it starts.* Knowing the right moment to interrupt behavior is a valuable asset; interrupting too soon makes a teacher appear fussy, while intervening too late may produce an uproar. If a youngster is not stopping voluntarily, then a teacher should act decisively.

- *Use signal interference.* A skillful teacher instantly notices the signs that lead to trouble: fidgeting in one youngster, rigidity in another. Watch youngsters and then act. Let the student know you are aware of them by moving closer, staring, coughing. Discover those mannerisms that signal difficulty. The results will make your time and efforts worthwhile.

- *Avoid the tribal dance,* which usually involves a dare. Trouble starts; the teacher acts; the student reacts, to protect status. The tribal dance has begun. The student dares the teacher to do something, and the teacher must accept the dare or retreat and lose status. Teachers must know which students are susceptible to the tribal dance and must act quickly to avoid the ritual, either by ignoring the behavior or by instantly suppressing it. The truly tough youngsters are not usually susceptible; they are not forced to prove their courage. The lesson here is that you should know the danger signals and not put yourself in an impossible situation.

- *Watch for hidden effects.* Though a student may do what you want, there are usually side effects, and the wise teacher will work with a youngster who must be disciplined to prevent feelings of hostility and isolation. We may have to live with aggression, but we should not breed it by exposing normal youngsters to classroom experiences that produce frustration.

- *Recognize your own aggression.* Though your hostility may be justified, your maturity and your professional obligation demand that your behavior reduce classroom tension and lessen the opportunities for student aggression.

- *Evaluate your classroom procedures.* Emmer, Evertson, Sanford, Clements, and Worsham (1984) suggested that teachers frequently check their classroom's organization and decide if they should make changes in their management procedures.

Searching for the Causes of Classroom Problems

Once teachers recognize that a problem exists, the next step is to identify its cause. If you answer these questions objectively, you may well discover significant clues:

- Is the room arrangement causing any problems, such as congestion, bumping, or limited visibility for some students?

- Are rules and procedures clear? Some disruptive behavior may not be included under your rules, or you may be forgetting to enforce one or more rules.

- Are you managing student work carefully? Be sure that directions are clear and understood by all and that students realize that they will be accountable for their work.

- Are you satisfied with your consequences for appropriate and inappropriate behavior? Review your own behavior to be sure that your rewards and penalties are still effective and that you are not punishing or praising students too freely.

- Are you detecting misbehavior in its early stages? You may need to work on your own monitoring ability for dealing with misbehaviors in their early stages, before they become major problems.

- Is your teaching effective? Check to be certain that students are not confused during your instruction and that transitions from one activity to another are smooth and uneventful.

METHODS OF CONTROL

You have now reached the point at which you can better understand specific suggestions about classroom control. All the topics discussed in this chapter point to one basic conclusion: *A smoothly running classroom blocks most problems before they can get started.* Teachers must always relate their present classroom situation to their students' needs and developmental changes. If the classroom is well organized and teachers have followed the management ideas presented here but are still not satisfied, they may want to adopt specific control techniques.

Misbehavior in the Classroom

The acts of school violence that you read or hear about in the news are infrequent and seldom occur in most effective schools. We do not wish to minimize, however, the growing concern in this country with crime and violence in the schools. The key to understanding misbehavior is to be alert to what students do while in the classroom. What may appear to be misbehavior may actually be helpful. For example, the student who talks out in eagerness may generate an enthusiasm and motivation that spreads to other class members. However, a student's refusal to do what you request or insistence on answering you back may constitute true misbehavior (Doyle, 1986).

Teachers must also be aware of any difference in their responses when different students demonstrate the same behaviors. Some students seem to be particularly skilled in irritating and frustrating teachers. These are not usually the overtly unruly, but those who walk the thin line between acceptable behavior and insolence. Others see any teacher as an authority figure who must be challenged.

Some teachers will ignore the insolent student and concentrate on any unruliness; others will see both types of behavior as inappropriate. Remember, however, that you and you alone will establish the rules of acceptable behavior in your classroom. As long as your students do not violate school codes, you are responsible for setting standards. You should never become a teacher who has to intervene frequently to check misbehavior. This practice characterizes the least effective teachers and is a clear signal that something is wrong.

Maintaining Classroom Control

Kounin presented a classic text on classroom control in 1970. While teaching a college mental hygiene course Kounin (1970) noticed a student reading a newspaper in the back of the room. He immediately and angrily reprimanded him. The discipline succeeded; the student's attention returned to the lecturer. But the reprimand had also affected other class members. Attention was rigid, and a depressing silence settled on the room. This was Kounin's first experience with the **ripple effect.** Punishment was not confined to one student; its effects spread to other class members. Kounin decided to study ripple effects and what he calls **desists:** a teacher's actions to stop misbehavior. To avoid experimental contamination, Kounin and his colleagues videotaped thirty actual classrooms. They analyzed the tapes and coded teachers' desist techniques for clarity, firmness, intensity, focus, and student treatment. They then attempted to relate the desist techniques to managerial success, which they defined as the degree of student work involvement in that teacher's class, the amount of student deviancy in that class, and the degree to which deviancy spread to other class members. They found that there was no relationship between the qualities of a teacher's desists and that teacher's success in handling deviant behavior.

Does this mean that misbehavior is insignificant and of no concern to others? Absolutely not; discipline heads any list of teachers', administrators', and parents' educational concerns. The problem is to isolate those techniques that can be used to contain misbehavior and prevent it from spreading. The question should be this: What is it that teachers do that makes a difference in how students behave?

RIPPLE EFFECT
The phenomenon in which punishment is not confined to one student; its effects spread to other class members.

DESISTS
A teacher's actions to stop misbehavior.

Effective Teacher Behaviors

Additional study convinced Kounin that some teachers' behaviors correlated highly with managerial success. These behaviors were effective not only with specific children, but also with entire classes. In this second study, Kounin videotaped fifty first- and second-grade classes for a full day each. Realizing that the clarity, firmness, intensity, and focus of

Teachers must have a clear
knowledge and
understanding of what is
happening in their classroom.

a teacher's desists are not critical in maintaining classroom control, Kounin searched for
other factors. From continued replaying of the tapes, certain characteristics emerged.

Withitness

WITHITNESS
*Teachers' knowledge and
understanding of what is
happening in their classrooms.*

The first was **withitness,** which means teachers' knowledge and understanding of what is
occurring in their classrooms. Some teachers clearly demonstrated that they knew what
was going on in their classrooms. These teachers selected the correct targets for their desists; that is, they knew who had misbehaved and how serious it was. They also timed their
interventions so that the misbehavior did not spread and become more serious.

Overlapping

OVERLAPPING
*A teacher's ability to handle
two or more classroom issues
simultaneously.*

Some teachers had no difficulty in attending to two issues simultaneously. For example, imagine what you would do in the following situation. You are with a group in which one youngster is reading aloud, when two other youngsters in another group, who are supposedly doing
seatwork, become noisy. Do you leave the reading group and attempt to check the noisy two-
some? Or do you tell the youngster to continue reading while simultaneously telling the other
youngsters to stop talking and get to work? Kounin refers to the latter technique as **overlapping:** a teacher's ability to handle two events simultaneously. As he notes, a learning event and
misbehavior simultaneously present a teacher with two issues; the two events overlap.

Although both withitness and overlapping are associated with managerial success,
Kounin believes that withitness seems to be more important. Teachers who demonstrate withitness can simultaneously handle two issues (overlapping). What can you learn from Kounin's
discussion of these two topics? Work at widening your attention; force yourself to try to be
aware of everything that is occurring in your classroom, so that you acquire withitness. When
this happens, you are almost compelled to use overlapping to attend to multiple events. Since
these teacher behaviors relate closely to managerial success, they are well worth the effort.

Transition Smoothness

TRANSITION
SMOOTHNESS
*Teachers have no difficulty in
handling activities and
movement in their classes.*

The next characteristic Kounin discovered was **transition smoothness.** Some teachers had
no trouble in handling activity and movement in their classes. The classes he videotaped
averaged 33.2 major changes in learning activities during the day. If such transitions are not
handled smoothly, chaos can result. Teachers must initiate, sustain, and terminate many ac-

tivities involving many materials. If you are to maintain smooth movement, you must avoid jerkiness and slowdowns, those teacher behaviors that abruptly introduce one activity by interrupting another: "Close your books, return to your desks, and do your arithmetic." There is no smoothness here; the youngsters are not ready to interpret and act on the teacher's directions. Also avoid "dangles"—leaving some direction unfinished—and changes from one activity to another and then back again.

A *slowdown* occurs when a teacher's behavior slows an activity's movement. Kounin identified two kinds of slowdown: *overdwelling,* when a teacher spends excessive time—beyond that needed for student understanding—on a topic; and *fragmentation,* when a teacher has individual students do something it would be better to have the group do—for example, have children come to the reading group one by one instead of as a group. Kounin concluded that avoiding jerkiness and slowdowns is a significant aspect of successful classroom management.

Group Alertness

For Kounin, **group alertness** refers to programming for "learning-related" variety. As mentioned previously, be honest with yourself: Am I an interesting teacher? Are my classes lively? Do I keep all of my students involved? To help you minimize misbehavior, remember to

- watch all of your students while one is responding.

- keep on the move; don't stay in one spot; let students know that you are interested in what they are doing.

- call on students randomly; avoid any set patterns.

- keep interest high by leading in to a question: "You haven't heard about this before, but I think you can answer it."

Finally, Kounin emphasized that teachers are not tutors; that is, they work with groups, either the class as a whole, or subunits within the class. How, then, can you keep your classes alert? Kounin observed teacher behaviors that he designated as *positive group alerting cues,* such as creating suspense before calling on a student, and consistently calling on different students. *Negative group alerting* cues included a teacher's concentration on only one student, designation of a student to answer before asking the question, and the practice of having youngsters recite in a predetermined sequence.

Using Behavior Modification

As we now focus our discussion on specific techniques for handling misbehavior, you must make a decision concerning the method with which you feel most comfortable. In a survey of teachers' classroom management techniques, Rosen, Taylor, O'Leary, and Sanderson (1991) found distinctions between teachers' responses to appropriate and inappropriate academic behaviors and their responses to comparable social behaviors. More teachers reported using management techniques to control inappropriate *social* behavior than reported their use for inappropriate *academic* behavior.

Although there were a few exceptions, the percentage of teachers using management techniques to address appropriate social behaviors was equivalent to the percentage using the same techniques for appropriate academic behavior. Moreover, verbal management techniques (for example, praise or reprimands) were used more than techniques based on concrete consequences (for example, a pat on the back or the sending of a note home). A second study by the authors using direct observations of the teachers also verified that the teachers used verbal techniques more than those based on concrete consequences. Interestingly, most of the interactions that teachers had with their students were

GROUP
ALERTNESS
Use of instructional methods that maintain interest and contribute to lively classes.

classified as neutral and were not designed to control behavior. The authors concluded that the choice of a management technique appears to depend greatly on the teacher's acceptance of the procedure.

In a sense, this chapter's discussion of control reflects many of the choices that you faced earlier (see especially Chapters 6 and 7). Which basic theoretical position should you follow: cognitive, behavioral, or some combination of both? Most of us are not bound by rigid adherence to a particular approach; nevertheless, we tend to favor one while incorporating material from others.

You may well believe that behavioral techniques are best suited for all aspects of the classroom, or decide that certain types of student behavior (perhaps hyperactivity or aggression) are best addressed by behavior modification. In fact, behavioral techniques are among the most widely evaluated procedures in psychology and education. Remember that behaviorism's basic assumptions are that both adaptive and maladaptive behavior are learned, and that the best means for treating problems is to structure a student's classroom environment so that you can reinforce desirable behavior. (You may want to reread Chapter 6 to refresh your knowledge of behaviorism.)

Definition of Terms

Although behavior modification is the general label that identifies those management techniques emerging from behavioral theory, certain distinctions should be made.

BEHAVIOR
INFLUENCE

The exercise of some control by one person over another.

- *Behavior influence.* **Behavior influence** occurs whenever one person exercises some control over another. It is a constant occurrence in home, work, politics, and schools where teachers are constantly involved with behavior.

BEHAVIOR
MODIFICATION

A deliberate attempt, using learning principles, to control student behavior.

- *Behavior modification.* **Behavior modification** is a deliberate attempt to apply certain principles derived from experimental research to enhance human functioning. Its techniques are designed to better a student's self-control by improving skills, abilities, and independence. One basic assumption guides the total process: *People are influenced by the consequences of their behavior.* A critical assumption is that the current environment controls behavior more directly than an individual's early experience, internal conflicts, or personality structure.

BEHAVIOR
THERAPY

An attempt to change behavior in a client-therapist relationship.

- *Behavior therapy.* Behavior modification and behavior therapy are often used synonymously, but behavior modification is the more general term. **Behavior therapy** usually applies to a one-to-one client-therapist relationship. So, technically, behavior therapy is only one aspect of behavior modification.

Teachers using behavior modification attempt to influence their students' behavior by changing the environments and the way that youngsters interact with their environments, rather than by probing into backgrounds, or referring the children for medical treatment (usually medications), or expelling them. To be successful, the teacher must clearly specify the problem behavior. What is it, precisely, that you wish a student to do, or not to do? Try to determine the consequences of children's behavior—that is, what they get out of it. Then decide what you are going to do. Will you ignore it, hoping for extinction; will you punish it; or will you reward some other form of behavior?

Decisions about how to manage behavior (for example, punishing an undesired behavior or reinforcing a desired one) and which behavioral techniques to use are important and often complex. Table 10.5 summarizes much of what was stated in Chapter 6 by highlighting the critical dimensions of applied behavioral techniques.

- *Positive reinforcement.* As we saw in Chapter 6, positive reinforcement can be defined as any event following a response that increases the possibility of recurrence of that

Table 10.5 SUMMARY OF BASIC PRINCIPLES OF OPERANT CONDITIONING	
Principle	**Characteristic Procedure and Its Effect on Behavior**
Reinforcement	Presentation or removal of an event after a response that increases the frequency of the response.
Punishment	Presentation or removal of an event after a response that decreases the frequency of the response.
Extinction	No longer presenting a reinforcing event after a response that decreases the frequency of the previously reinforced response.
Stimulus control and discrimination training	Reinforcing the response in the presence of one stimulus but not in the presence of another. This procedure increases the frequency of the response in the presence of the former stimulus and decreases the frequency of the response in the presence of the latter stimulus.

From *Behavior Modification in Applied Settings*, pp. 11, 26, by Alan E. Kazdin. Copyright © 1994, 1989, 1984, 1980, 1975 by Brooks Cole Publishing Company, a division of Thomson Publishing, Inc., Pacific Grove, CA 93950. Reprinted by permission of the publisher.

response. Good examples would be money, food, praise, attention, and pleasurable activities. Teachers must be careful in using positive reinforcement with their students; what may be pleasurable (providing positive reinforcement) for one student may not be for another. Rewards for secondary students will not be the same as those for elementary or preschool students. Table 10.6 provides examples of rewards that are effective with secondary school students. Here is the value of knowing students—what they like and dislike. Students will have different preferences for the items in the table. Positive reinforcement is a powerful tool in changing behavior; presenting youngsters with things they like can produce consistently desirable results if these things function as reinforcers.

- *Token economy.* The **token economy** technique has been widely used in managing groups. For example, students, patients, and other group members receive tokens when they exhibit desirable behavior; collect them; and when they have attained an accepted number, exchange them for something pleasurable. For example, talkative students may receive tokens for every fifteen or twenty minutes they are silent; when they have enough tokens, they may trade them for extra recreation or something else they like.

- *Shaping.* In **shaping,** the teacher first determines the successive steps in the desired behavior and teaches them separately, reinforcing each until students master it. The students then move to the next phase, where the procedure is repeated. Ultimately, they acquire the total behavior by these progressive approximations.

- *Contingency contracting.* In **contingency contracting,** a teacher and a student decide on a behavioral goal and what the student will receive after attaining the goal. For example, the goal may be successfully completing twenty division problems; the positive reinforcement may be an extra art period, if this is the child's favorite school activity. Contracts involve an exchange; both teacher and student agree on what each will do.

- *Aversive control.* Students maintain some undesirable behavior because the consequences are reinforcing. To eliminate the behavior, a teacher might apply an

TOKEN ECONOMY
A form of classroom management in which students receive tokens for desirable behavior. These may then be exchanged for something pleasurable.

SHAPING
A form of classroom management in which teachers determine the successive steps needed to master a task and then teach them separately, reinforcing each step.

CONTINGENCY CONTRACTING
Joint decision by a teacher and a student on a behavioral goal and what the student will receive when the goal is achieved.

> ### Table 10.6 INTERMITTENT REWARDS SUITABLE FOR SECONDARY STUDENTS
>
> · Writing a note to the student's parents
> · Writing a note to the student
> · Calling the student's parents
> · Calling the student
> · Complimenting the student in front of another staff member
> · Asking one of the administrators to reward the students' behavior
> · Privately praising the student's classroom performance in a nonclassroom setting such as in the hall after school
> · Give the student a responsibility
> · Tokens for a video arcade
> · Tickets to a school activity
> · Food
> · Coupon to rent a movie
> · Let the student choose an activity for the class
> · Check out a book the student might be interested in

From R. S. Sprick and V. Nolet, Prevention and Management of Secondary-Level Behavior Problems" in *Interventions for Achievement and Behavior Problems,* G. Stoner, et al. Eds. Copyright, © 1991 the National Association of School Psychologists. Reprinted by permission of the publisher.

AVERSIVE CONTROL

A technique to eliminate undesirable student behavior, either by introducing an unpleasant event or removing a pleasurable one.

OVERCORRECTION

A form of classroom management involving both restitution and positive practice.

aversive stimulus (for example, remaining after school). The removal of positive reinforcement is another example of **aversive control.** (Recall the definition of punishment: the introduction of aversive stimuli, or the withdrawal of positive reinforcement.) You have read about the possible negative consequences of punishment; use care in the selection of an aversive stimulus, and try to have students do something desirable so that you can positively reinforce them.

- *Overcorrection.* **Overcorrection** combines both restitution and positive practice. For example, a child may deliberately knock things off another student's desk while moving about the room. The teacher has the student not only remedy the situation (put the things back on the desk) as restitution, but also straighten all the other desks in the room, in positive practice.

Behavior Modification and the Causes of Behavior

As noted in previous chapters, behavioral techniques are often called *applied behavior analysis* when used in educational settings. Applied behavior analysis involves a "systematic performance-based, self-evaluative method of studying and changing socially important behavior" (Sulzer-Azaroff & Mayer, 1991, p. 4). Again, Table 10.7 provides a list of the characteristics of applied behavior analysis. As you examine this table, note the emphasis on the environment as the cause of behavior.

Why should teachers concentrate on student *behavior* and not on the *causes* of the behavior? Behavior therapists argue that teachers are not analysts. They are not trained to

---

Table 10.7 CHARACTERISTICS OF APPLIED BEHAVIOR ANALYSIS

· Focus on behaviors of applied (social or clinical) significance.

· Search for marked intervention effects that make a clear difference to the everyday functioning of the individual.

· Focus on overt behaviors.

· Focus on the behaviors of one or a small number of individuals over time.

· Assessment of behavior through direct observation, as in counting the frequency of responses.

· Assessment continuously over time for extended periods (hours, days, weeks).

· Use of environmental (and observable) events to influence the frequency of behavior.

· Evaluation and demonstration of the factors (for example, events) that are responsible for behavior change.

From *Behavior Modification in Applied Settings*, pp. 11, 26, by Alan E. Kazdin. Copyright © 1994, 1989, 1984, 1980, 1975 by Brooks Cole Publishing Company, a division of Thomson Publishing, Inc., Pacific Grove, CA 93950. Reprinted by permission of the publisher.

explore the special circumstances that influence behavior. Since the multiple and interactive causes of behavior can elude detection even by highly trained and skilled professional psychologists and counselors, busy teachers, who often do not have the required time, training, or experience, are less likely to detect them.

Even if teachers can identify the causes of maladaptive behavior, they frequently can do little about them. If the trouble lies in the home, a teacher's options are limited. Consequently, the teacher must focus on the child's behavior, and if necessary, obtain professional consultation. Occasionally, however, the causes of maladaptive behavior are discerned and treated, but the behavior remains. An example is a reading problem caused by poor vision; when the physical difficulty is corrected, the reading deficiency remains.

Noting the concern that all teachers share in maintaining discipline, Wielkiewicz (1986) suggested the need for several steps in any behavior management program:

■ *Identify the problem.* Usually a general problem is identified—this boy is hostile— and then additional assessment helps to identify the circumstances that trigger the problem (the hostility).

■ *Refine the target behavior.* A general label such as "hostility" is not much help. Recall that one of the major objectives of applied behavior analysis is the accurate presentation of reinforcement; you must identify precise behavior (the target behavior) if reinforcement is to be effective. What is the problem behavior? Under what circumstances is the behavior to be reinforced?

■ *Assess the baseline rate.* If you obtain a baseline rate before intervention, then you can assess the success of the program. What is the rate of occurrence when behavior management is not in effect? How does it compare to intervals when behavioral techniques are at work?

■ *Identify the reinforcer and the contingency.* You must know your students well to discover just what reinforces them; this task is not always easy with some students in a classroom setting. You may have to link tokens earned at school with reinforcement at home.

■ *Begin the program.* In a manner they can understand, tell students what they need to know.

TIPS ON ASSESSMENT
Functional Analysis

PRINCIPLE   Behavior is a function of the environment; functional assessment should help teachers understand classroom behavior.

STRATEGY   Use an ABC model to help assess student classroom behavior.

STRATEGY   Consider antecedents (the A) to some behavior (B) the student engages in. For example, are there specific things that you say to the class that increase disruptive behavior?

STRATEGY   Consider the consequences (the C) to some behavior the student engages in. For example, if you reprimand a student for not working at her desk, you may be reinforcing off-task behavior.

- *Modify the program when necessary.* If the program does not appear to be as successful as anticipated, step back to evaluate the steps. Perhaps more time is necessary, or some other element interferes, such as a brother or sister who attempts to subvert the program at home.

- *Fade out the program.* The good program puts itself out of business. The desired behavior appears at a steady rate with ever-increasing frequency between reinforcements.

- *Ensure generalization.* A good program includes procedures that will facilitate transfer and maintenance of behavior change over time and across settings.

Cognition and Behavior Change

Our third and final explanation of maintaining classroom control differs distinctly from that in Kounin's work, which focused on teachers' behaviors, and from behavior modification, which focuses on the careful application of the principles and procedures of behavior change. Here the search concentrates more on the cognitive than on overt behavior. The classic works of Dreikurs, Grunwald, and Pepper (1971) and of Redl and Wattenberg (1959) are good examples of this kind of analysis.

Social Discipline and Goal Seeking

Goal seeking, a frequent theme in motivational literature, is especially important for teachers, since a student seeking a positive goal is a joy in the classroom. Many years ago Dreikurs and his colleagues (1971) raised several provocative issues about discipline, and their discussion of goals is especially pertinent here. Their basic premise is that (1) behavior is purposeful, (2) correcting goals is possible, and (3) correcting deficiencies is impossible. They believe that the force behind every human action is its goal and that all our actions are efforts to find a place for ourselves. Students are not driven through life; they seek their own goals.

     The following assumptions are associated with Dreikurs' **social discipline** model:

- Students are social beings and desire to belong to social groups.

- Students are decision makers.

SOCIAL DISCIPLINE

A theory of classroom management based on the conviction that misbehavior can be eliminated by changing a student's goals.

Positive consequences for good behavior represent a strong influence in academic learning.

- All behavior is purposeful and directed toward social goals.

- Students see reality as they perceive it to be.

- A student is a whole being who cannot be understood by isolated characteristics.

- A student's misbehavior results from faulty reasoning on how to achieve social recognition (Wolfgang & Glickman, 1986, p. 190).

Once students establish goals, their behavior manifests a certain consistency and stability that is threatened by crises and frustrations. All youngsters want attention; when they do not receive it through socially acceptable means, they try other ways to obtain it. Punishment is preferable to being ignored: It reinforces one's presence. Some children feel accepted only when they do what they want to do, and not what they are supposed to do.

Parents and teachers who engage in power struggles with children are eventually doomed to failure. Once power struggles begin, youngsters want to get even with those who punish them. They seek revenge, and the turmoil they create provides feelings of satisfaction. If students experience constant struggle and failure, they finally withdraw, desiring only to be left alone.

Discipline should not be considered an either-or proposition (either students obey instantly or they rule the classroom, causing chaos). Discipline does not mean control by punishment. Dreikurs and associates believe that self-discipline comes from freedom with responsibility, while only forced discipline comes from the use of force, power, and fear (Dreikurs et al., 1971).

The classroom atmosphere must be positive, accepting, and nonthreatening. Students do need limits, however, and discipline means teaching them that certain rules exist that everyone must follow. Students and teachers should agree on the rules for classroom behavior; this agreement increases students' appreciation of the necessity for rules, especially when they have cooperated in formulating them. Discussing rules on borrowing, using equipment, name calling, or classroom manners is excellent training in discipline. (You can find further information on Dreikurs's social discipline model in Wolfgang & Glickman, 1986.)

Mutual Respect in the Classroom

Dreikurs and his colleagues believe that both teachers and students need inner freedom, which results from cooperating with each other, accepting responsibility for behavior, speaking truthfully, respecting each other, and agreeing on common behavioral rules. Here are some of their practical suggestions:

- *Do not nag or scold.* Frequently, this response gives students just the attention they want.

- *Do not ask a student to promise anything.* Children will agree to almost anything to extricate themselves from an uncomfortable situation. You just waste your time.

- *Do not reward good behavior.* The child may work only for the reward and stop immediately. Also, children come to expect something whenever they behave correctly. (Note how this differs from behavior modification techniques.)

- *Avoid double standards.* What is right for the student (politeness, punctuality) is right for the teacher. (Here, Dreikurs's work approximates the modeling of social learning theory.)

- *Avoid threats and intimidation.* Students cannot learn or acquire self-discipline in a tense, hostile environment.

- *Try to understand the purpose of misbehavior.* Why do students clown during arithmetic? Is it to get attention, or to demonstrate to peers that they are powerful by daring to defy adult pressure?

- *Establish a relationship based on trust and mutual respect.* If you treat your students as "nearly equal," they soon will respect you and believe that you truly want to help them. They often will discuss their problems with you, and help you devise ways to correct them.

- *Emphasize the positive.* Refuse to take misbehavior personally, to avoid causing a ripple effect to permeate the classroom. Try to make your behavior kind but firm.

These techniques of control reflect the theme of teacher-student cooperation that has been a continuous theme throughout our work. What happens between a teacher and student constitutes a relationship, one that must be positive if teaching and learning are to attain desired objectives.

Packaged Discipline Programs

Some school districts have adopted "packaged discipline programs," which are designed to give teachers and administrators comprehensive procedures for managing student behavior and addressing various discipline issues. Teachers are always looking for discipline programs that can be used in their classrooms. Yet selection of a program is not straightforward and requires consideration of a number of important issues. Chard, Smith, and Sugai

DISCIPLINE PROGRAM ANALYSIS FORM

FOUNDATION

Y N 1. Description of theoretical foundation stated?

2. Program's technical adequacy available to validate:

Y N a. problem diagnosis?
Y N b. treatment ?
Y N c. generalization?
Y N d. maintenance?

3. Social validity indicated for the program:

Y N a. in schools (that is, teachers, administrators)?
Y N b. in communities (that is, parents, public agencies)?
Y N c. among students?

FEATURES

Y N 1. Description of program's goals, outcomes, and focus?

2. Systematic approach to management at the:

Y N a. school level?
Y N b. classroom level?
Y N c. individual student level?

3. Definition of participants' roles for:

Y N a. teachers?
Y N b. students?
Y N c. parents?
Y N d. administrators?
Y N e. outside agencies (that is, public officials, police)?

Y N 4. Program's limitations of the behavior types that the program can effect described?

IMPLEMENTATION

Y N 1. Description of the environmental (that is, physical context, setting) prescriptions stated?

2. Effective instructional strategies for expected behavior explicitly addressed for:

Y N a. preskill assessment?
Y N b. effective teaching strategies?
Y N c. error correction procedures?
Y N d. adequate skill practice?
Y N e. generalization strategies?

Y N 3. Consequences strategies for inappropriate behaviors stated?

Y N 4. Description of summative and formative monitoring procedures stated?

STAFF AND SCHOOL DEVELOPMENT

Y N 1. Description of staff development model stated?

Y N 2. Empirical support for the model given?

Y N 3. Identification of the person to implement the training stated?

Y N 4. Description of the personnel and resources required for training stated?

Y N 5. Description of the orientation and training of students, parents, and community stated?

RESOURCES

Y N 1. Description of the amount of time required for implementation stated?

Y N 2. Description of the material resources to be provided by the school district stated?

Y N 3. Description of the required support personnel for implementation of the program stated?

FIGURE 10.2

Discipline Program Analysis Form.

(From D. Chard, S. Smith, and G. Sugai, "Packaged Discipline Programs: A Consumer's Guide" in J. Marr and G. Tindal (eds.), *The Oregon Conference Monograph*, 19–26, 1992. Copyright © 1992 University of Oregon, Eugene, OR.)

(1992) reviewed packaged discipline programs to provide a consumers' guide for selection of such programs. During their review, they found eight programs but had to exclude three from the list. Glasser's programs *Schools Without Failure* and *Control Theory in the Classroom* were excluded because Glasser's program is based on theoretical considerations rather than specific strategies. Algozzine's program *Behavior Management* is based on topic modules; because it was not considered an integrated program, it also was excluded.

The authors reviewed the discipline programs within the context of five general categories that appear in Figure 10.2: They include foundation, features, implementation, staff and school development, and resources. The presence of the critical features in each of the five programs that were reviewed is summarized in Figure 10.3.

FIGURE 10.3

Summary of results from the review of five discipline programs using the Discipline Program Analysis Form.

(From D. Chard, S. Smith, and G. Sugai, "Packaged Discipline Programs: A Consumer's Guide" in J. Marr and G. Tindal (eds.), *The Oregon Conference Monograph,* 19–26, 1992. Copyright © 1992 University of Oregon, Eugene, OR.)

Critical features \ Programs	Assertive discipline	Cooperative discipline	Positive discipline	Discipline with dignity	The solution book
Description of theoretical foundation	Present	Present	Present	Not present	Not present
Technical adequacy	Not present	Not present	Not present	Not present	Not present
Social validity	Present	Present	Partially present	Partially present	Not present
Description of program goals, outcomes, and focus	Present	Present	Present	Present	Present
Systematic approach to classroom management	Present	Present	Partially present	Present	Present
Systematic approach to schoolwide discipline	Not present	Present	Not present	Present	Present
Systematic approach to dealing with individual children	Present	Present	Partially present	Present	Present
Definition of participant's roles	Partially present	Partially present	Partially present	Present	Present
Program's limitations	Not present	Not present	Not present	Present	Present
Clear description of environmental prescriptions	Not present	Partially present	Partially present	Not present	Present
Effective instructional strategies for expected behaviors	Not present	Partially present	Not present	Partially present	Present
Consequence strategy for inappropriate behaviors	Present	Present	Present	Present	Present
Models and strategies for staff development	Partially present	Present	Partially present	Partially present	Partially present
Orientation for students, parents, and community	Not present	Partially present	Partially present	Not present	Partially present
Description of necessary resources	Not present	Not present	Not present	Not present	Not present

Present   Partially present   Not present

Current Issues & Perspectives

Do Discipline Programs Promote Ethical Behavior?

As we have noted in this chapter, classroom discipline is one of the major challenges facing American education. Virtually all teachers are faced with maintaining an effective instructional environment—on this issue there is general consensus. Yet the methods that are used to discipline students remain controversial. Some critics of behavior modification programs have argued that these programs (such as Cantor's Assertive Discipline) must do more than merely control behavior. Discipline programs, they argue, must also teach our children to be more responsible and engage in ethical behavior.

ISSUE

Should discipline programs teach the moral and ethical concepts that undergird appropriate behavior?

Pro: Discipline programs should include a focus that promotes moral and ethical behavior, so that our children grow up to be good citizens and not merely good students in school.

Con: Discipline programs are designed to control student behavior in schools and to promote effective instructional environments for students. They should not include curricula to teach moral and ethical behavior.

Pro: Children must be taught the concepts underlying the rules and behavior that they are to display in classrooms. That is, they must understand that some forms of inappropriate behavior are morally and ethically wrong. With this understanding they can leave our schools and become moral and ethical citizens.

Con: Discipline programs that focus on rules and control of behavior through contingencies, in effect, do teach appropriate ethical and moral behavior in children. When children behave in appropriate ways, they will receive feedback from significant adults and eventually learn the standards that guide our culture.

Pro: Children must develop internal consistencies during the school years that they take with them into our culture. Moral and ethical citizens have an understanding of the reasons behind their actions, not just a knowledge that they will be rewarded and punished for their actions.

Con: Discipline programs that rely on rules, standards, and contingencies for appropriate behavior do create a culture for the development of moral and ethical behavior. The real challenge is to generalize these standards to the greater culture when children leave the schools.

Where do you stand on these important issues? What focus do you think our discipline programs should take to create better moral and ethical individuals? Whatever your position, consider that you can do a number of things to promote student learning and control behavior in the classroom. Specifically, consider the following points:

1. Be alert to what your students are doing in the classroom. Watch your students carefully during class, and when you sense their attention is wandering, pose questions, stop and have students question each other, or suddenly become quiet to regain their attention.

   Involve the group: "Who'll get this first?" Look at one student, then another, and then another, creating the impression that you expect them all to be first. When you detect student restlessness or fading attention, act immediately; look at the student; use the student's name. Build a repertoire of these mild behavioral countermeasures to prevent, if possible, serious misbehavior.

continued

Make this repertoire a sequence of responses that ranges from less to more serious: standing next to the student, staring at the student, calling attention to the behavior by using the student's name, reprimanding more sharply, talking to the student after school, holding a conference with the parents (perhaps including the principal), making a referral, and finally, recommending formal school action.

Know your students well enough so that you can detect something outside the class that may be influencing a student's behavior in class. This strategy could include family financial problems, family illness, or a pending parental divorce. By talking to such students, you may be able to help them adjust to the stress and to prevent any emotional spillover to the classroom.

2. Certain teacher behaviors lead to a smoothly running classroom. Communicate with the entire class even while you are working with one student; use body language, facial expressions, and verbal statements and questions.

Be sensitive to your students' span of interest and when it's lost, shift to another medium (hold a discussion, watch a filmstrip, listen to a tape recording), or another activity ("OK, stand up and let's stretch"), or another subject. Don't overdwell; sometimes teachers are so concerned about learning that they continue to the point of boredom; watch for the signs.

Act immediately when you detect the first signs of misbehavior, no matter how small; be sure that your reaction is appropriate for the seriousness of the misbehavior.

Make sure that your behavior is consistent with what you expect from your students; in this respect you are a constant model: speech, dress, clarity, courtesy, promptness.

Don't be afraid to use humor; when appropriate, it can be an effective change of pace in the classroom. Be careful, however; don't let it become sarcastic, don't let any one student become the butt of jokes, and don't overdo it.

3. Use those control techniques that are best suited for you and a particular class.
Be natural; keep your voice and body movements as relaxed as possible. In this way, you can create a positive learning environment. Occasionally teachers, by the shrillness of their voices and tense, rapid movements, can overstimulate a class.

Use as much positive reinforcement as possible; identify desirable student behavior and respond to it immediately. If you "get along" with your students, most of them will want to receive similar recognition from you.

At times it may be difficult not to take misbehavior personally, but make every effort to understand why students respond as they do. Sometimes students can misinterpret your behavior and can't understand why they are punished.

Try to help your students to develop inner controls. After students have misbehaved and you have reacted, talk to them to discover why the misbehavior occurred. Do they know why they acted as they did? Were they angry for some reason? Did some classmates urge them on? Help them to recognize the signs of trouble and suggest ways of avoiding it: Remind them that they can always talk to you if something is bothering them; if you know your students well, you can use those whom they admire as models for handling difficult situations.

Rules, control measures, and appropriate disciplinary techniques all add up to good classroom management and a minimum of problems.

Some interesting trends emerged in the analysis of the five discipline programs. First, most programs embraced a behavioral perspective, although in some cases this philosophy was not made explicit in the materials. More important, none of the five programs included any data regarding the program integrity or its effectiveness. As in many traditional discipline approaches, the authors of these programs did not emphasize environmental or instructional prescriptions. With the exception of *The Solution Book,* generally, the programs did not include orientation and procedural guidelines for training individuals in the discipline systems. A more crucial omission was that none of the programs provided specific guidelines for how the program would be implemented and maintained in a schoolwide system of discipline. Where can a teacher obtain this kind of guidance? Perhaps the best option would be to talk to other school professionals who may have experience in establishing such programs. These individuals include school psychologists, school counselors, and sometimes special education program administrators or directors.

DON'T CAUSE ANY PROBLEMS YOURSELF

Your first task in establishing a desirable classroom atmosphere is not to cause any problems yourself. Your initial reaction undoubtedly will be to place all responsibility for discipline problems on students, but closer inspection may suggest that some responsibility falls "on the infallible side of the desk." Though experience may eliminate many of the self-generated problems, to be aware of them early is to minimize their repercussions. How would you honestly answer the following seven questions?

1. *Are you unfair?* Students probably react more intensely to this issue than to any other. You must treat all students equally, a task that may be difficult, because some students will seem to provoke you deliberately. But if you punish one student for disrespect, then you must punish all for disrespect. If you are not forthright, a student's attitude toward you will quickly degenerate into personal resentment, with serious consequences.

2. *Are you inconsistent?* You must react to similar conditions in a similar manner. If you scold or punish students for talking one day, then ignore this behavior the next, you are inconsistent. If you expect students to do papers or reports carefully in October and November, and then ignore these standards in January and February, you are inconsistent. Students are bewildered; they do not know how to act. Their behavior and work soon become erratic, and these conditions encourage trouble.

3. *Are you boring?* This is a blunt question that deserves a frank answer. If you maintain the same pace and procedure every day, students eventually will search for excitement. Break your routine: Use games, stories, the playground, audiovisual techniques, discussions, lectures, group work, guests, and any relevant source or technique that will make your classroom exciting and inviting.

4. *Have you established routine?* You cannot break routine unless you have established it. Make no mistake; routine is one of your best safeguards against discipline problems. Students must know what they should do, when they should do it, and where they should do it. If you show uncertainty about school rules, classroom procedures, location of materials, the meaning of bells, the function of machinery, or any aspect of daily planning, you only invite trouble. Master routine; when you break it consciously, your students will perceive the change as a real treat.

CASE NOTES

Observation   Some of the students in Melissa Williams's class are disrupting the learning of other students.

Hypothesis   Melissa Williams may not have established a desirable classroom atmosphere.

Possible Action   Answer the "seven questions" just listed to determine if Melissa Williams is causing problems through her own actions in the classroom.

5. *Do you know your subject?* Woe to the teacher who consistently cannot answer questions, who demonstrates a lesson only to arrive at the wrong answer. Students quickly sense incompetence and lose respect.

6. *Can you control your temper?* A common mistake is to interpret all challenges personally. Some problems are personal attacks, but these are usually infrequent; most arise from the daily give-and-take of the classroom. If you respond spitefully, you provoke a sharp personal confrontation. Although it is difficult not to see misbehavior as a personal challenge, work at this; eventually an objective perspective will serve you well.

7. *Have you considered how you should best respond?* If you require considerable personal control over the class, your disciplinary methods should focus on students' behavior, either rewarding, ignoring, or punishing it. If you are less concerned about control, you probably are more interested in a search for the causes of problems, in an understanding of the behavior. Adapt your techniques to your personality and beliefs; do what you do best.

If you are still concerned about classroom control and want to be certain that you are not responsible for any upsets, try the following exercise. First, identify a classroom problem. Next, evaluate your answers to the preceding seven questions to discover if you were the cause. If you honestly and objectively conclude that there was trouble, but that you did not cause it, then search elsewhere. What were you teaching? How were you doing it? What was the time of day? The problem could be a lack of specific control techniques, one or two particularly disruptive students, a topic that didn't interest students, or a restless class at a particular time of the day. Even if you're tired and unhappy after a class, try the exercise shown in Figure 10.4, being ruthlessly honest with yourself. You may want to do it for a full week, capturing all times and all classes.

List your classes (1–5 for secondary school subjects, subject name for elementary). Check the box that best describes students' behavior during each class. Now, focus on the class that you are concerned about. Use the second checklist to analyze your behavior objectively. You can use this technique for both classes and individual students.

Now return to Table 10.3 (on page 383) and reexamine the problem types discussed there. As a result of your reading, would you now handle any of these problems differently? Compare your answers now to those you gave when you first read about the problems.

CLASS	ON-TASK ENGAGED	ON-TASK NOT ENGAGED	OFF-TASK DISTRACTED	OFF-TASK DISRUPTIVE
One (Arithmetic)				
Two (Reading)				
Three (Social Science)				
Four (Art)				
Five (Music)				

After checking your students' behavior for each class, assess how much you contributed to that behavior.			
Your behavior	YES	NO	
Showed fairness			
Was interesting			
Had knowledge			
Controlled temper			
Required appropriate responses			
Established routine			

FIGURE 10.4

Classroom Management Reflection Form.

Teacher-Parent Collaboration

Virtually all of the management strategies that we have introduced in this chapter involve what teachers can do in the school setting. But students also spend a considerable amount of time at home and in the greater community. Parents still greatly influence students, and some parents have major roles in establishing effective management programs in the classroom. In fact, a considerable amount of research supports the successful outcomes that occur with students when parents are involved in academic and behavioral programs (Christenson & Conoley, 1992; Kramer, 1990).

What are some examples of the ways that parents can be involved? One illustration of how parent involvement can make a difference is a project by Sheridan, Kratochwill, and Elliott (1990). In the study, two forms of consultation with teachers for the purpose of establishing intervention programs for students demonstrating social withdrawal were implemented. In one form of consultation, the teacher and psychologist developed a program to improve social interaction skills in the school only. In the second form of consultation, the teacher met with the psychologist and the parent. The parent established the same program in the home setting as the teacher did in the classroom. What do you think the outcome of this study was? Results indicated that the students who received the teacher-only services improved only in the classroom. Students who received the services of both the teacher and the parent improved in both the home and the school. Also, the changes in the students in both home and school settings were maintained better in the dual teacher-and-parent program. Thus, there were direct benefits to the students in the intervention when it was implemented by the teacher, but the program had greater impact when both teacher and parent were involved.

Ongoing communication with parents is important to maintain high standards for achievement.

Similar programs have been established by teachers who make contact with parents in the hopes of improving behavior in school. Many of these programs involve home-based reinforcement delivered by the parent (Kelley, 1990; Kelley & Carper, 1988) or a combination of a home note system with back-up contingencies administered by the parent. Figure 10.5 provides an example of a home note for use with adolescents and older students. Such a note system is designed to be used by the teacher to monitor certain classroom behaviors and to communicate the information to the parents. Parents are responsible for establishing and delivering the consequences.

Here are several guidelines for implementing a school-home note system that will be useful to you:

- Plan a parent-teacher conference to communicate your concerns, agree on the nature of the problem, and secure the commitment of the parent.

- Define the problem behaviors that both you and the parent agree need to be changed, being as specific as possible.

- Set small goals to change the problem behavior.

- Design the school-home note (like the example in Figure 10.5).

- Establish responsibilities for you, the parent(s), and the student. The parent will complete the note, and it is the responsibility of the student to return the note to you.

- Collect baseline information to determine the nature of the problem.

- Establish the reward system and how consequences will be delivered.

- Implement the program with the stipulated consequences.

- Fade out the note system as the student's behavior improves.

Kelley and Carper (1988) suggested that cooperation is the key to success in any program when school-home notes are used. It is important for teachers to communicate with par-

SCHOOL-HOME NOTE

NAME _____   DATE _____

CLASS _____   **Assignment:**

Completed Classwork	Yes	So-So	No	NA
Obeyed Classroom Rules	Yes	So-So	No	NA
Handed in Homework	Yes	So-So	No	NA

Comments: Initials _____

_____

CLASS _____   **Assignment:**

Completed Classwork	Yes	So-So	No	NA
Obeyed Classroom Rules	Yes	So-So	No	NA
Handed in Homework	Yes	So-So	No	NA

Comments: Initials _____

_____

CLASS _____   **Assignment:**

Completed Classwork	Yes	So-So	No	NA
Obeyed Classroom Rules	Yes	So-So	No	NA
Handed in Homework	Yes	So-So	No	NA

Comments: Initials _____

_____

CLASS _____   **Assignment:**

Completed Classwork	Yes	So-So	No	NA
Obeyed Classroom Rules	Yes	So-So	No	NA
Handed in Homework	Yes	So-So	No	NA

Comments: Initials _____

_____

Parent Comments:

_____

FIGURE 10.5

To improve school-home relations and to keep parents informed of progress, many schools have adopted home notes as a neans of communication.

ents and urge them to assist with their child, since parents can be extremely helpful in a comprehensive classroom management program.

You Are Not Alone

In thinking about the task of managing a classroom, don't feel overwhelmed. In this chapter we have presented new information that can have a bearing on effective classroom management. You will need time, however, to think about the issues in classroom management, and you will need experience in putting the various techniques into practice. Here are some practices that will make the task of classroom management easier:

CASE NOTES

Observation   Melissa Williams has planned to meet with the parents of the boys who are having problems in her classroom.

Hypothesis   Melissa does not have a well-developed plan to work with the parents.

Possible Action   During the meeting with the boy's parents Melissa can review the procedures for a home note system.

CASE NOTES

Observation   Jim Watson's behavior appears to be quite serious and is interfering with the class.

Hypothesis   Jim may have a serious aggressive behavior disorder.

Possible Action   Consider professional assistance with management of Jim Watson's aggressive behavior. Contact the school psychologist for help.

- Read more about classroom management techniques.

- Take courses that focus on classroom management techniques. Typically, courses in classroom management are offered in schools of education through the departments of educational psychology or special education.

- Use your time in practice teaching to sharpen classroom management skills. Seek out effective teachers and visit their classrooms to observe skillful classroom management in action.

- Participate in preservice and in-service experiences that focus on developing successful classroom management skills.

- Discuss a student's problem with the parents when possible. Sometimes the parents can provide insights into the problem and may be able to assist in a discipline program (as noted previously).

- Consult other professionals who will be able to offer advice on solving specific discipline problems and suggest ways to improve classroom management tactics. Individuals in the school who may be able to assist you include lead teachers, special education resource teachers, school psychologists, and counselors.

Case Reflections

In this chapter we have pointed out that classroom management remains one of the most central concerns of all teachers from preschool through high school instruction. We also noted that one of the best strategies for a teacher is to establish proactive classroom management tactics that will reduce the emphasis on having to manage discipline problems that are already causing serious interference with the instructional routines in classrooms. We noted that some of Melissa Williams's colleagues did not seem to have discipline problems in their classroom. In fact, it appeared that both Bill Drake and Sarah Ellis were already using proactive classroom management tactics in their class and that Melissa Williams may want to review their strategies to deal with the significant issues she is facing in her classroom.

In the chapter we also noted the important linkage between student behavior and instructional activities. For example, Jim Watson appeared to be causing difficulties for Melissa Williams in terms of his verbal and aggressive behavior. We directed Melissa Williams to examine her instructional and management plans and consider Slavin's QAIT model as an option to adapt instruction to Jim Watson. We also know that classroom management is more than establishing rules and order. A desirable classroom atmosphere should be developed, and we

presented strategies for how Melissa Williams might develop a positive atmosphere in her classroom.

We also tried to make the point throughout the chapter that not all classroom management issues can be handled alone in the classroom. Sometimes it is desirable to work with parents. Although Melissa Williams had planned to meet with the parents of the boys who were having problems in her classroom, we thought that developing a linkage between the home and school, such as through a home note system, might be a desirable tactic to facilitate better student behavior in the classroom. Such a plan also helps parents take responsibility for their own children's behavior. Finally, we noted that despite the best efforts of teachers in managing classrooms, some students are going to have serious behavior problems. Under these conditions it is always a good idea to seek professional assistance from school-based professionals who are able to provide recommendations to teachers and parents.

Key Terms

Aversive control 402
Behavior influence 400
Behavior modification 400
Behavior therapy 400
Contingency contracting 401
Desists 397
Engaged time 378
Group alertness 399
Overcorrection 402
Overlapping 398
Proactive classroom management 378
QAIT 387
Ripple effect 397
Shaping 401
Social discipline 404
Token economy 401
Transition smoothness 398
Withitness 398

CHAPTER HIGHLIGHTS

Management Concerns in the Classroom

- Students' learning depends on the orderly routine established in the classroom. Remember that "orderly" does not imply an atmosphere of quiet terror. It means an atmosphere in which all students (and teachers) know exactly what is expected of them.
- Organizing the classroom in a way that satisfies the teacher and that students understand is the first step in providing effective teaching and learning.
- John Carroll's ideas on the use of time have had a significant impact on the way that teachers structure their classrooms. His basic thesis is that students will learn to the extent that time (that is, time on task) is available for learning.
- The developmental characteristics of students affect the management techniques teachers use and influence their decision about the age group they would like to teach.

Life in the Classroom

- Students' attitudes toward school seem to be a mixture of happiness and unhappiness. The causes of these mixed feelings seem to be rooted in the conditions of the individual classrooms, that is, how teachers manage their work.
- Student engagement (what students are doing at any time), is related to the teacher's activity. Student engagement seems to be highest when teachers lead small groups and lowest during student presentations.
- Teachers in "higher-achieving schools" spend more time in actual teaching and in academic interactions with their students than do teachers in "lower-achieving schools."

- As you decide how to organize your classroom, what to teach, and how to teach it, remember that you must adapt your techniques—both instructional and organizational—to the needs of students.

Managing the Classroom

- The rules teachers establish for organizing their classroom are critical, since these rules establish the conduct that teachers think is important. Unless students' behavior conforms to these rules, learning will be negatively affected.

- Good managers make their basic rules known on the first day of class and combine the teaching of the rules with a demonstration of the signals they would use for various activities.

- Good managers use as few initial rules as possible and then introduce others as needed. They also occasionally remind their students of these rules and act immediately when they see rule violations. Such action usually prevents minor difficulties from becoming major problems.

- When teachers understand the developmental characteristics of the students they are teaching, teachers can anticipate many of the sources of potential problems and formulate rules that will help prevent them.

Methods of Control

- Teachers alone can determine what is misbehavior, since individual differences apply to teachers as well as to students. What one teacher may judge to be misbehavior, another may ignore.

- Among teacher behaviors that contribute to the successful management of their classrooms are withitness, overlapping, transition smoothness, and group alertness.

- Behavior modification, as a means of classroom control, relies on changing the classroom environment and the manner in which students interact with the environment to influence students' behavior.

- Understanding the causes of a student's misbehavior requires that teachers realize that their students' behavior has a purpose. Consequently, if teachers can identify the goal that a particular behavior is intended to achieve, they can correct problem behavior.

- Most teachers are eclectic in the manner in which they manage their classes, selecting and choosing from all of the techniques discussed in this chapter as the need arises.

WHAT DO YOU THINK?

1. What age group would you like to teach? The developmental characteristics that affect teacher management techniques will influence your decision. Do you hold the desirable qualities of teacher management for your desired grade level?

2. Describe the four components of the QAIT model. Apply the model to a problem that you will face in the classroom.

3. What effective teacher behaviors did Kounin identify regarding maintaining classroom control? How could you use these procedures in your classroom?

4. Provide examples of how you could use these behavioral techniques in the classroom: token economy, shaping, contingency contracting, aversive control, and overcorrection.

5. Suppose seventh-grader Dale is late for school almost every day. Identify steps of a behavior management program that you could use to solve this problem.

eleven

Assessment of Students' Learning Using Teacher-Constructed Methods

This chapter provides some fundamentals about assessing student learning, a central issue for Melissa Williams and her colleagues in the case introduced at the beginning of this section. In particular, you will have a chance to apply information about performance assessment and writing portfolios to the instructional actions of Melissa in her quest to become an effective teacher.

Objectives

When you have completed reading this chapter, you should be able to

- **plan for tests that serve specific purposes**

- **understand what comprises appropriate test items**

- **assess the role of testing in a class**

- **evaluate how successfully students attained desired objectives**

- **evaluate instructional effectiveness by the results of an assessment program**

- **discuss the use of performance assessment methods to guide instruction and document students' learning**

Teachers are effective when they make good decisions that lead to actions that promote student responding and achievement. Good decision making involves (a) knowing which instructional procedures are effective under which conditions and (b) having good information about student performance. This is where assessment comes in. *The primary purpose of assessment is to gather information about students' performances to make decisions about how and where the students should be instructed.* Therefore, to the degree that teachers are knowledgeable about assessment, they increase the likelihood of making good decisions about the students in their classrooms. In essence, effective teaching boils down to good instruction, good assessment, and using each to do the other better (Witt, Elliott, Daly, Gresham, & Kramer, 1998). Before getting too far into an examination of effective assessment practices, let's take a look at a typical day in Melissa Williams's classroom, the teacher you were introduced to in the opening case for this section. As you will see, a classroom can be a very busy place where a teacher has to make dozens of assessment decisions daily.

Mrs. Williams had arrived at school, as usual, thirty minutes before the first bus arrived. She readied her room for the day's activities by writing the work schedule on an overhead transparency, briefly organized her lesson notes, and then went to meet her students as they came streaming into the building at 8:15. During the course of the day, she did the following:

- *Recommended Josh spend extra time each night this week reviewing his punctuation guidelines*

- *Called on Samantha twice even though she had not volunteered to answer questions about the social studies unit*

- *Scored and assigned grades to her students' spelling tests and writing journals*

- *Referred William to the school psychologist for evaluation because of the learning difficulties he was having in English and social studies*

- *Stopped her planned English lesson halfway through the period to review the previous day's lesson because several students seemed confused*

- *Assigned homework in social studies, but not English*

- *Changed the seats of two students who had been inattentive and disruptive for the third day in a row*

- *Reviewed learning objectives for the forthcoming state assessment in reading and then made some minor adjustments in her lesson plans to include two days to do some sample test items*

- *Held a conference with a parent of a new student who had been home-schooled for the past three years*

- *Gave a quiz in social studies covering two chapters and a field trip experience*

- *Listened to oral book reports from half of her students and then provided them feedback about each of their presentations*

- *Made notes to herself about some key words and important concepts in social studies that students were struggling with*

- *Wrote three short essay questions and outlined model answers to each question in preparation for an end-of-unit test in social studies that she planned to give next week*

The process of assessing students' learning is central to instruction and is most frequently accomplished with either teacher-made or commercially published standardized tests. To help teachers construct or select fair tests and at the same time to help students prepare for them, we'll explore the world of classroom testing in this chapter. The major theme in the chapter is that *good assessment facilitates communication.* Consequently, assessment and related activities, as illustrated in the vignette of Mrs. Williams's classroom, play a major role in the daily teaching-learning process in all classrooms. In other words, testing is not an isolated activity to be done because students "need a grade"; sound instruction requires sound classroom-level assessment of students' achievement and behavior.

As discussed in previous chapters, recent advances in instruction and our understanding of how students learn best have resulted in a greater emphasis on students' constructing and applying knowledge with authentic tasks typical of the world of work. These advances, in turn, have stimulated some exciting changes in educational assessment. Specifically, many teachers today are using performance assessment tasks and portfolios, in addition to more traditional multiple-choice or short-answer tests to evaluate students' learning and academic progress.

To understand these themes and integrate them into your thinking about testing, you'll need to examine terminology of testing and assessment, basic issues in measuring human performance, and issues that teachers face in constructing their own tests. You must plan assessments carefully and give thought to the kinds of tests and the kinds of items that will best sample students' learning. Finally, teachers also use test data to give marks, assign grades, and report on the progress of their students. Teachers report feeling much more comfortable discussing grades with students, parents, and school officials if their grades are based on well-constructed tests.

As you read through this chapter, think about the case of Melissa Williams, the new seventh-grade teacher who was struggling with behavior management of three boys and the overall alignment between what and how she was teaching in her language arts class and the expectations that others had for her to prepare her students to do well on an end-of-year standardized achievement test. As in the previous chapter in this section of the book, a series of observations and ideas for dealing with Melissa Williams's dilemma are offered in case notes throughout the chapter and summarized at the end of the chapter. Before we can begin to apply knowledge of good assessment practices with Mrs. Williams's classroom, however, some fundamentals and purposes of assessment need to be examined.

ASSESSMENT: TERMINOLOGY, ASSUMPTIONS, AND PURPOSES

Effective communication about tests and the assessment process requires us to distinguish between terms such as assessment, testing, tests, measurement, and grading. These are *not* synonymous terms. By **assessment** we mean the process of gathering information about a student's abilities or behavior for the purpose of making decisions about the student. There are many tools or methods a teacher can use to assess a student, such as paper-and-pencil tests, rating scales or checklists, interviews, observations, and published tests. Thus, assessment is more than testing.

Testing is simply one procedure through which we obtain evidence about a student's learning or behavior. **Teacher-constructed tests,** as well as commercially published tests, have and will continue to play a major role in the education of students. Such tests are assumed to provide reliable and valid means to measure students' progress. A *test* is a sample of behavior. It tells us something, not everything, about some class or type of behavior. Well-designed tests provide representative samples of knowledge or behavior.

Measurement means quantifying or placing a number on a student's performance. Not all performances demonstrating learning can or need to be quantified (for

ASSESSMENT
The process of gathering information about a student's abilities and using such information to make decisions about the student and future instruction.

TEACHER-CONSTRUCTED TESTS
Any number of tools designed by a teacher to assess student learning, usually not standardized or based on a normative sample.

MEASUREMENT
Quantifying or placing a number on a student performance.

Measurement, the quantification of an attribute, is a central aspect of good assessments.

example, art or musical exhibitions). The science of measurement in itself includes many important concepts—reliability, validity, standard scores—for teachers and others responsible for assessing students. We'll consider these psychometric concepts later in this chapter.

A final term that deserves definition is grading. *Grading* is the assignment of a symbol to a student's performance. Grading is not assessment; rather it is often an interpretation of the assessment process. As you well know, grading most frequently takes the form of a letter (A, B, C . . .) and indicates some relative level of performance to other students or stated criteria. Remember: Teachers can assess students' work, effort, attitude, and a host of behaviors without ever assigning a grade.

Now that we have defined key assessment terms, here are four assumptions that we believe are fundamental to the assessment of students. Read them carefully and think about the implications of each of these fundamental assumptions:

1. Tests are samples of behavior and serve as aids to decision making.

2. A primary reason to conduct an assessment is to improve instructional activities for a student.

3. The person conducting the assessment is properly trained.

4. All forms of assessment contain error.

These assumptions are rather straightforward; however, each deserves additional commentary. The first assumption stresses that tests do not reveal everything a student does or does not know; they provide snapshots of a student's knowledge or behavior. When a test is well constructed, it can give us representative and useful information about a student, which in turn can be helpful in making decisions about the student.

This information leads us to the second assumption, which emphasizes that the primary educational reason for using tests is to guide instructional activities. Good tests can furnish teachers with information about what to teach next and under what conditions the content might best be taught so that optimal learning can occur.

This point leads to the third assumption: A teacher must be properly trained to use tests and the information they yield. A poor test or the misuse of a well-constructed test can significantly damage the teaching-learning process.

The final assumption—all forms of assessment contain some error—is a cautionary note to all persons involved in assessing human performance and stresses the need for frequent assessment of students with a variety of methods. This final assumption also emphasizes that teachers are entrusted to make important and difficult decisions about all of their students.

Uses and Users of Classroom Assessment Information

Research suggests that teachers spend as much as a third of their time involved in some type of assessment. Teachers are continually making decisions about the most effective means of interacting with their students. These decisions are usually based on information they have gathered from observing their students' behavior and performances on learning tasks in the classroom (Witt et al., 1998).

Many individuals have a vested interest in student learning and assessment information about such learning. Clearly, teachers, students, and parents should have great interest in the results of student assessments. School administrators and community leaders also voice keen interest in assessment results that document students' performances. No single assessment technique or testing procedure can serve all these potential users of assessment results. Thus, the purpose of one's assessment must be clear, for it influences assessment activities and, consequently, the interpretation of any results.

Teachers have three main purposes for assessing students: (1) to form specific decisions about a student or a group of students, (2) to guide their own instructional planning and subsequent activities with students, and (3) to control student behavior. Teachers use assessment results for specific decisions, including diagnosing student strengths and weaknesses, grouping students for instruction, identifying students who might benefit from special services, and grading student performances.

Teachers can also use assessment activities and results to inform students about teacher expectations. In other words, the assessment process can provide students with information about the kind of performance that they need to be successful in a given classroom. Tests become a critical link in teaching when teachers provide students with clear feedback about results.

Teachers can also use tests and the assessment of students to facilitate classroom management. For example, the anticipation of a forthcoming assessment can serve to encourage students to increase their studying and classroom participation. Assessments likewise provide teachers valuable feedback about how successful they have been in achieving their instructional objectives and thus help teachers chart the sequence and pace of future instructional activities.

Students also are decision makers and use classroom assessment information to influence many of their decisions. For example, many students set personal academic expectations for themselves based on teachers' assessments of prior achievement. Feedback

Assessments should be a part of instruction so the results can be used to guide further instruction.

they receive from teachers about their performances on classroom tests directly affects other students' decisions about what, when, and with whom to study.

The assessment activities and decisions of teachers affect parents as well as students. For example, many parents communicate educational and behavior expectations to their children. Some parents also plan educational resources and establish home study environments to assist their children. Feedback from teachers about daily achievement, communicated via homework, classroom tests, annual standardized tests, report cards, and school conferences often significantly influences these parental actions.

Testing results also provide parents and others in the community with information about the school's performance. That is, does the school prepare students for the basic skills of reading, writing, and calculating? In sum, teachers' assessments of children greatly influence parents' attitudes about their children and schooling. Clearly, the enterprise of assessing students is crucial in the lives of teachers, students, and many parents.

Multicultural Students and Testing

Of all the topics discussed in this and the next chapter, none is more practically important than a teacher's ability to help students to take tests. Tests often scare students or cause them anxiety. Whatever the reason for test anxiety—parental pressure, their own anxieties, the testing atmosphere—merely taking a test can affect a student's performance. This is especially true for those students who find the classroom a different cultural experience. Language, reading, learning expectations, and behavior all may be different and influence test performance (Stigler et al., 1990). Many new immigrant students have experienced wars, political oppression, economic deprivation, and long, difficult journeys to come to the United States. Regardless, these students want to succeed. Interviews with many of these immigrant students show that almost 50% were doing one to two hours' homework every night (25% of the Southeastern Asian students reported more than three hours' homework each night). We have mentioned throughout this book the need for sensitive responsiveness. Here is an instance where being sensitive to the needs of multicultural students can aid both teaching and learning.

We commented earlier on the positive and receptive nature of the classroom environment. When students feel comfortable, they do better. When students are prepared adequately to take a test, they do better. Try to help any student who is uncertain about the test. Provide information about why the test is being given, when it is being given, what material will be tested, and what kinds of items will be used. These are just a few topics to consider. Teachers also want to be sure well in advance of the day of the test that language is not a barrier to performance. Take some time to explain the terms in the directions of the test. Tell students or illustrate what "analyze" means, what you are looking for when you ask them to "compare," what "discuss" means.

Helping all students, and in particular multicultural students, in this way will take some extra time and effort. But teaching students how to take tests is teaching, just like teaching English or history. As more and more multicultural students take classroom tests, you want them to do well and not be limited by the mechanics of the test. We say much more later in this chapter about helping students to become test-wise.

Integrating Learning and Assessment

Assessment of students' learning traditionally has been conducted with tests. Tests, however, don't exist in a vacuum. Good tests are designed and used to discover if instructional objectives have been met, if learning has occurred, and as a means of communication. They are a valuable and powerful tool, not only in assessing student progress, but also as a means of examining teaching efforts. Other techniques, such as teacher observation, student portfolios, and student exhibits also are frequently being used as a means of evaluating student performance (Airasian, 1994). This collection of techniques is now referred to as authentic/performance assessment.

Educators can defend the success of teaching, the value of curriculum, or the amount of learning only by some demonstrable evidence. In education, such evidence is obtained through assessment, often by testing. In this chapter we deal with a major part of effective instruction: assessing students' learning. Figure 11.1 illustrates the integrated nature of three critical aspects of effective instruction: identifying learning objectives, selecting teaching methods, and assessing learning.

Figure 11.1 graphically illustrates the key position of assessing students' learning in the teaching-learning process. Teachers must formulate desirable objectives, select methods and materials to attain these objectives, and use the results of assessment to indicate whether learning has occurred. If it has, students advance to more difficult materials; if it has not, then teachers should initiate review and repetition.

The preceding procedure, which is most commonly completed by using a classroom test, focuses on student achievement. What have students learned as manifested on the test? Have they achieved enough objectives to move on to the next level? The vital role of objectives is clear once more. That is, objectives must be sharply defined and stated in language that permits measurement and specifies behavioral change.

Testing, however, also has a guidance function. Depending on the nature of the test scores, the results will portray the specific type of remedial work required, or the kind of advanced material that would be most suitable for continued growth. Careful interpretation of test scores also furthers the diagnosis of learning difficulties, both for an individual and a class. If an individual, or class, has failed to attain objectives, teachers search for the cause. There are three immediate possibilities: *the student* (for example, physically ill at the time of testing, bothered by a personal problem), *the difficulty of the material,* or *the teacher's methods.* If the class as a whole is typical, if the material has been proven to be successful with other similar groups, then the teacher can consider several possibilities for class results: lack of background information, too rapid a presentation, or limited student activity when the material demanded more personal involvement. There is another lesson here: Professional teachers also will use test results as a form of self-evaluation; that is, testing results inform teaching!

FIGURE 11.1

The integration of teaching
and asssessment activities

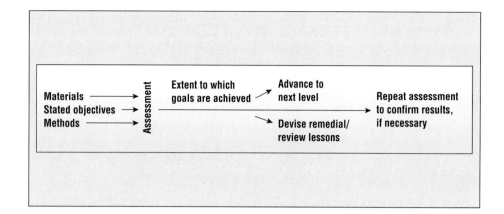

CASE NOTES

Observation   The teachers in the DEW House seem to value standardized achievement tests differently when considering what counts as evidence of successful teaching. Bill Drake and Sara Ellis value end-of-year, standardized achievement tests as important evidence of learning and successful teaching. Melissa Williams seems to value more authentic, teacher-constructed and scored forms of assessment as evidence of learning and successful teaching.

Hypothesis   Teachers tend to spend instructional time on what gets tested and use testing methods that most efficiently document what is taught.

Possible Action   As the teachers in the DEW House work more together they should have open discussions about the value of each type of assessment information and how they can use an array of assessment data to build a more comprehensive picture of students' learning and their own instructional efforts.

Testing can likewise help teachers and administrators in their search for appropriate subject matter. If students consistently fail, or experience difficulty, or score unusually high, you may question the nature of the subject matter. Objectives, methods, and materials all reinforce the belief that the assessment of students is at the vital core of education.

Tests and other assessment activities also provide information about the conditions of learning. What is known about the motivation of the class? Do students realize they are faced with a problem? Are teachers providing the opportunity for students to practice the desired behavior? Have they been given sufficient time? Are they deriving satisfaction from their work? How much direction is necessary? Are they getting feedback? Both learning and teaching become more efficient as teachers acquire additional knowledge about the conditions of learning.

Teachers and Testing

Some teachers feel that testing is an added burden that interferes with real teaching and learning. It frequently is, unless the tests are carefully constructed and the content is relevant! Can you assess the quality of materials, the effectiveness of teaching, and the worthiness of objectives without testing?

Assessment of what students know can be accomplished in many ways. Asking students to answer questions during lectures is often a time-efficient way to monitor learning of new material.

If teachers avoid, or merely tolerate testing, it is impossible to judge these issues without resorting to guessing. When one realizes that tests, both teacher-made and standardized, may alter a student's future, it is apparent that poorly made and questionably interpreted tests can cause lasting damage. Grades, promotion, college acceptance, and employment opportunities all reflect the results of testing. Why then are teachers frequently careless in the construction of tests and the interpretation of test results?

One reason may be that teachers are confident about their judgment of students (Marso & Pigge, 1989). They "know" what their students can do; in many instances they view testing as superfluous. Another reason is that a good test is extremely difficult and time consuming to construct. What are the objectives to be sampled? How are they related to this particular context? Will these items adequately measure the objectives? Still another reason is the dependability of the score: Was the student ill? Was there trouble at home? There may have been a discipline problem in class just before the test; the test itself may have left much to be desired.

Admittedly, each and all of these events can influence a test score. The primary purpose of this chapter is to alert you to these obstacles and to suggest techniques for limiting any negative effect they could have on students' performance. Let's now examine some of the various methods teachers use to assess students.

METHODS AND TECHNICAL ISSUES IN THE ASSESSMENT OF STUDENTS

The assessment of students' classroom performances can take many forms. Some assessment methods are formal, others informal; some are administered to an individual, others to a group; some are standardized (administered in virtually the same way for all students), others are designed for a specific classroom context. Typically, educators have used four primary methods for assessing students' classroom performances: paper-and-pencil tests, oral questions, performance tests, and standardized tests. The first three methods are teacher-constructed, whereas **standardized tests** usually are commercially constructed.

In this chapter, we focus on teacher-constructed tests, which are the most frequently used methods for assessing students. Chapter 12 is devoted to an analysis of standardized tests, behavior rating scales, and direct observations, which are all commonly used to identify students with potential learning or behavior problems and to conduct program evaluations. Before examining details of either teacher-constructed or standardized tests, note the major advantages of each as summarized in Table 11.1.

Teacher-Constructed Tests

Although teachers use many techniques in evaluating students, probably the most popular is the written paper-and-pencil test that they themselves construct. These usually consist of essay or multiple-choice items. The multiple-choice, pencil-and-paper test is probably the most frequently used test, with other types such as true-false, essay, and **performance tests** also quite popular with teachers. Good **multiple-choice items** are difficult to prepare but can be scored easily and objectively. **Essay tests,** on the other hand, are relatively easy to prepare but extremely difficult to score.

Individuals interested in constructing a test are confronted with challenges concerning *what* to assess, *how to* assess it, and whether they measure it in a *reliable* and *valid* manner. These are fundamental challenges to teachers who construct their own tests and to professionals who design standardized tests. Consequently, these topics now deserve our attention.

For teachers, the question of what to test implies that *the test must measure what was taught.* Tests will be reliable and valid to the same degree that test constructors are successful in relating test items to what was taught. For teacher-made tests, you may question whether there is any difficulty in testing what was taught. After all, students were exposed to the same teacher, methods, and materials. The answer is not that simple.

Temporarily ignoring the conditions of testing—classroom atmosphere, student health, and related factors—the test itself may fail to assess a student's learning. Were the test objectives stated in objective terms that permitted measurement? Did the test adequately sample the material that was taught? Did it stress the content that the teacher emphasized as important?

Teachers occasionally stress certain aspects of a subject and then test other sections. This strategy supposedly ensures broader coverage. Yet it is obviously unfair to the student. Did the teacher construct items that concentrated only upon a small amount of the material that was taught? Are the items comprehensible to students?

You should also be alert to other issues. The essay test, for example, allows students to express their own ideas in a creative fashion and permits them to demonstrate such elements as organization and grasp of a subject and its application to a particular problem. It also is deceptively easy to construct. But it samples only a limited amount of material, favors the articulate student, and is difficult to score. Conversely, an objective or multiple-

STANDARDIZED TESTS

Tests that are administered under a uniform set of conditions; they are usually commercially published and based on a large normative sample.

PERFORMANCE TESTS

An assessment method that requires students to construct a response or perform an action as an indication of their ability to apply knowledge and skills. Stronger performance assessments have explicit scoring criteria that students are aware of prior to performing.

MULTIPLE-CHOICE ITEMS

Questions or incomplete statements that are followed by several possible responses, one of which is the best answered and considered correct.

ESSAY TESTS

Teacher-constructed tests that allow an open-ended written response and require the development of criteria to reliably score.

Table 11.1 COMPARATIVE ADVANTAGES OF STANDARDIZED AND TEACHER-CONSTRUCTED TESTS OF ACHIEVEMENT

	Standardized Achievement Tests	Teacher-Constructed Achievement Tests
Learning outcomes and content measured	Measure outcomes and content common to majority of U.S. schools. Tests of basic skills and complex outcomes adaptable to many local situations; content-oriented tests seldom reflect emphasis or timeliness of local curriculum.	Well adapted to outcomes and content of local curriculum. Flexibility affords continuous adaptation of measurement to new materials and changes in procedure. Adaptable to various-sized work units. Tend to neglect complex learning outcomes.
Quality of test items	General quality of items high. Written by specialists, pretested, and selected on basis of effectiveness.	Quality of items unknown unless test item file is used. Quality typically lower than that of standardized because of teacher's limited time and skill.
Reliability	Reliability high, commonly between .80 and .95; frequently above .90.	Reliability usually unknown; can be high if carefully constructed.
Administration and scoring	Procedures *standardized;* specific instructions provided.	Uniform procedures favored but may be flexible.
Interpretation of scores	Scores can be compared with those of norm groups. Test manual and other guides aid interpretation and use.	Score comparisons and interpretations limited to local school situation.

Measurement and Assessment in Teaching 7th ed. by Linn/Gronlund, © 1995. Reprinted by permission of Prentice-Hall, Inc., Upper Saddle River, NJ.

choice test samples much more subject matter than the essay examination in the same amount of time, has greater objectivity of scoring, and reduces the verbal element in a student's response. Measuring problem solving and creative behavior, however, is difficult. These tests also emphasize factual information, frequently promote guessing, and are time consuming to prepare.

Determining what to measure and deciding how to measure it are genuine concerns for teachers. Avoid absolute standards. If most students receive an A on a test, or almost all fail another test, you can assume that the test is at fault. Often teachers postpone constructing a test until the last moment, with the result that the test is hastily written and inadequate to sample a student's attainment of objectives. Also be aware of the trivial and ambiguous.

Validity

When you test a student in arithmetic, you are testing a sample of that student's arithmetic knowledge. From the test score (for example, on subtraction), you infer that a student knows how to subtract or not. Your inference depends on the truthfulness or meaning of the test, its validity. **Validity** is the extent to which a test measures what it is supposed to measure. Of all the essential characteristics of a good test, none surpasses validity! If a test is not valid for the purpose used, it has little or no value. For example, if a test designed to measure academic achievement in geography or history uses questions that are phrased in difficult language, it probably does not test geography or history as much as it does reading. The test does not measure what it claims to measure. Validity is specific. A test may be valid for one purpose and no other. To administer a spelling test for the purpose of determining a student's achievement in grammar is very likely to be invalid.

VALIDITY

The extent to which a test measures what it says it does so that a meaningful inference can be made from a person's score on the test.

CASE NOTES

Observation Melissa's review of the content covered on the language arts section of the standardized achievement test indicated that it did not align well with what she covered in class or how she stressed the process of writing.

Hypothesis This mismatch between what and how language arts is taught in Melissa's class and how it gets assessed on the end-of-year achievement test may result in an inaccurate or invalid characterization of many students' skills, if the end-of-year test is considered the primary measure of student learning.

Possible Action To minimize the differences between what is taught and what is tested on the end-of-year achievement test, Melissa can change some of her instructional methods in language arts to focus on more discrete grammatical skills and factual comprehension methods. Alternatively, she can work with fellow teachers to select a better, or more valid method of assessing students' language arts skills, which would also align more closely with what and how she teaches. Finally, she can consider communicating with parents and students that the end-of-year test is only one of the methods that help her evaluate student learning and should not be weighed more than the many hours of classroom work and teacher-constructed assessments.

CONTENT VALIDITY

Type of validity based on a test's ability to adequately sample behavior that has been the goal of instruction; the material tested is representative of the material covered on the test.

CRITERION-RELATED VALIDITY

Type of validity of a test based on its results' similarity to some other external criteria (often another test that purports to measure the same behavior or skill).

CONSTRUCT VALIDITY

Type of validity of a test based on its actually measuring the knowledge domain or behavior it claims to measure.

Traditionally, test developers have tallied about three major kinds of validity: content validity, criterion-related validity, and construct validity. A test has **content validity** if it adequately samples behavior that has been the goal of instruction. Does the test adequately represent the material that was taught? Testing a minor portion of a unit on Hamlet after stressing the unity of the total play violates content validity. Determining whether a test has content validity is somewhat subjective. It usually is established when subject-matter experts agree that the content covered is representative of the tested domain of knowledge. Content validity also is referred to as *face validity* because judgments about content are based on reading or looking at the content.

A test has **criterion-related validity** if its results parallel some other, external criteria. Thus, test results are similar or not similar to another sample of a student's behavior (some other criterion for comparison). If students do well on a standardized reading test that measures all aspects of reading, they should likewise do well in completing and understanding geography and history assignments. Some authors refer to this type of validity as *predictive validity*. You can understand how this kind of validity is valuable for the teacher, particularly in assessing the validity of teacher-made achievement tests. Some other measure is taken as the criterion of success.

A test has **construct validity** when the particular knowledge domain or behavior purported to be measured is actually measured. For example, a teacher may claim that his or her test measures understanding and not facts. If the results of the test agree with ratings of students on understanding, then the test is, indeed, measuring the construct of understanding. If a test claims to measure anxiety, then its results should match judgments of people identified as anxious. Construct validity is a complex issue and is increasingly coming to refer to the entire body of research about what a test measures (Lyman, 1998).

It makes no sense to prepare or select a classroom test designed to measure something other than what has been taught. We don't measure height by using a bathroom scale. Therefore, teachers and others should work hard to ensure that a test does the job it's designed to do.

Evidence for the validity of a test or other assessment instrument generally takes two forms: (a) how the test or assessment instrument "behaves" given the content covered and (b) the effects of using the test or assessment instrument. Questions commonly asked about a test's "behavior" concern its relation to other measures of a similar construct, its ability to predict future performances, and its coverage of a content area. Questions about the use of a test typically focus on the test's abilities to differentiate individuals into groups reliably and to guide teachers' instructional actions with regard to the subject matter covered by the test. Some questions also arise about unintended uses of a test: Does use of the test result in discriminatory practices against various groups of individuals? Is the test used to evaluate others (for example, parents or teachers) not directly assessed by the test?

Criteria for evaluating the validity of tests and related assessment instruments have been written about extensively (Linn & Gronlund, 1995; Witt et al., 1998). A joint committee of the American Educational Research Association, the American Psychological Association, and the National Council on Measurement in Education (American Psychological Association, 1985) developed a comprehensive list of standards for tests that stresses the importance of construct validity and describes a variety of forms of evidence indicative of a valid test. These standards are currently undergoing revision and are being broadened to take into consideration a much wider range of assessment tools, many of which educators frequently use.

Many test users and consumers of test-based information struggle with the relative abstract concept of validity and its importance to the meaningful use of tests. Rest assured, it is the single most important characteristic of good assessment information. Keep in mind the following key aspects of validity nosed by Airasian (1994, p. 21):

1. Validity is concerned with the general question, "To what extent will this assessment information help me make an appropriate decision?"

2. Validity refers to the decisions that are made from assessment information, not the assessment approach or test itself. It is not appropriate to say "This assessment information is valid" unless you also say what decisions or groups it is valid for. Keep in mind that assessment information valid for one decision or group of students is not necessarily valid for other decisions or groups.

3. Validity is a matter of degree; it does not exist on an all-or-nothing basis. Think of assessment validity in terms of categories: highly valid, moderately valid, and invalid.

Reliability

A test is reliable to the extent that a student's scores are nearly the same on repeated measurements. A test is reliable if it is consistent (Frisbie, 1988). **Reliability** concerns questions such as: Do two forms of a test yield similar results? If the test is repeated after a certain interval, how consistent are the results? Some error always exists in any test since fluctuations in human behavior are uncontrollable, and the test itself may contain possibilities of error (Matarazzo, 1990). As errors in measurement increase, the reliability of a test decreases.

Carefully note the relationship and distinction between reliability (consistency) and validity (meaningfulness). A valid test must be reliable, but a reliable test need not be valid. In other words, *reliability is a necessary but not sufficient condition for validity.* For example, a test may have an error built into it. Giving an algebra test to first-graders will produce consistent results (most all children will fail the test), but the results are not meaningful for 6-year-olds who have not studied algebra. Thus, the test would be reliable (consistent), but would not be valid (meaningful).

R E L I A B I L I T Y

Characteristic of a test for which a student's scores are nearly the same in repeated measurements, and of a test that consistently measures what it says it measures.

Suppose, for instance, Mrs. Williams had just given an achievement test to her students. How similar would the students' scores have been if she had tested them yesterday, or tomorrow, or next week? How would the scores have varied had she selected a different sample of equivalent items? If it were an essay test, how much would the scores have differed had a different teacher scored it? These are the types of questions with which reliability is concerned.

The reliability of a test is often characterized by a correlation statistic. Correlations can range between $+1.0$ and -1.0, where $+1.0$ indicates perfect agreement between the magnitudes of the scores for the same individual. The case of a test-retest approach to reliability is illustrated in Table 11.2. Given that most teachers do not repeatedly administer a test, alternative methods of estimating the reliability of a test, such as internal consistency, must be used. The latter method uses a slightly different formula for calculating a reliability coefficient (referred to as *coefficient alpha*). Regardless of the method for quantifying the reliability of a test, most experienced users of teacher-constructed tests consider reliability coefficients in the $+.80$ or higher range to be essential. Many published tests have reliability coefficients in the $+.90$ range.

We conclude, then, that unless a test is reasonably consistent on different occasions or with different samples of the same behavior, we can have very little confidence in its results. A variety of factors, some concerning the individual taking the test and others inherent in the design and content of the test itself can affect the reliability of a test. Student characteristics affecting a test's reliability include guessing, test anxiety, and practice in answering items like those on the test (Witt et al., 1998). Characteristics of the test that can influence reliability include its length (longer tests are generally more reliable), the homogeneity or similarity of items (more homogeneous tests are usually more reliable), and time to take the test (speed tests are typically more reliable than unbound tests).

In conclusion, when thinking about the reliability of any test or assessment process, keep the following three points in mind:

1. Reliability refers to the stability or consistency of assessment information, not the appropriateness of the assessment information collected.

Table 11.2   TEST-RETEST RELIABILITY OF A KINDERGARTEN SCREENING TEST

Student	Number of Answers Correct	
	Test	*Retest*
1	9	10
2	7	6
3	5	1
4	3	5
5	1	3

$$r_{xy} = \frac{N\Sigma XY - (\Sigma X)(\Sigma Y)}{\sqrt{N\Sigma X^2 - (\Sigma X)^2][N\Sigma Y^2 - (\Sigma Y)^2]}}$$

$$r_{xy} = \frac{150}{\sqrt{(200)\,(230)}}$$

$$r = .70$$

From J. C. Witt, S. N. Elliott, J. J. Kramer, and F. M. Gresham (1998). *Assessment of Children: Fundamental Methods and Practices.* Dubuque, IA: McGraw-Hill, 1998.

2. Reliability is a matter of degree; it does not exist on an all-or-none basis. It is expressed in terms of degree: high, moderate, or low reliability.

3. Reliability is a necessary, but not sufficient, condition for validity. An assessment that provides inconsistent, atypical results cannot be relied on to provide information useful for decision making.

PLANNING A TEACHER-CONSTRUCTED TEST

With the fundamentals of validity and reliability in mind, we turn now to the process of constructing tests devised to assess students' learning. The first step in the process is planning. Constructing a "good" test remains a challenge, one that demands time and effort. Teachers are busy and may well be tempted to ask, "Why bother?" Nitko (1983) summarized the importance of developing skill in test construction:

- Developing a test helps you to identify more precisely those behaviors important for students to learn.

- As you develop a test, your perspective on both teaching and learning broadens as you distinguish conditions and sequences of learning.

- As you gain skill in constructing tests, you usually become more critical of published testing material.

- A carefully constructed test furnishes fair and objective information for the evaluation of students.

Assessing learning can be fun.

Test Planning and Objectives

The first step in planning the test is to review the objectives of the unit or subject. A clear understanding and statement of the specific instructional objectives will significantly improve the quality of the tests that teachers construct (Gentry, 1989). Some of the questions that teachers should answer in this planning stage include the following: What exactly is the purpose of this test? Is it a pretest to discover weaknesses and strengths, or will the results be used as a basis for evaluating a student's academic achievement? Will the test give evidence of the degree to which the students have achieved these goals? How many and what kind of questions should be used? Does the test reflect the emphasis of instruction?

As teachers plan tests, they should be guided by several considerations:

- Be sure you know why you are testing, that is, the purpose of your test. For example, "giving a test" merely because you need marks for your students lacks a clear rationale for testing.

- What type of item will best serve your purposes? Should you use essay or objective items?

- Devote time to preparing relevant items.

In Chapter 8, the importance of teaching thinking skills was stressed. It logically follows that the assessment of a student's knowledge should be sensitive to the various levels of thinking skills that can be used to solve problems. Both multiple-choice and essay test items can be written to assess recall, analysis, comparison, inference, or evaluation skills. By carefully wording questions, teachers can influence the level of thinking skills needed to answer the question. Table 11.3 illustrates action words to consider when you want to assess various levels of thinking skills in students.

Selecting Test Items

Teachers should consider carefully those aspects of testing that need pretest attention. Once teachers have determined the purpose of a test and identified those behaviors that are critical for mastery, they should give thought to those items that will best serve their purpose.

What type of test item should be used? Although some teachers will use performance items (such as a project or paper written over the course of a week) or interviews, most will be concerned with either objective or essay items. We'll discuss these in some detail, but here are a few distinguishing characteristics of each:

- Objective test items are usually separated into two classes: **supply items** that require students to give an answer, and **selection items** that require students to choose from among several alternatives. Selection items are more highly structured and restrict the type of response students can make.

- Essay questions permit students greater latitude of expression and are divided into two types. The **extended response** type furnishes students with complete freedom to make any kind of response they choose. The **restricted response** type asks for specific information, thus restricting students' responses somewhat.

Teachers need to be careful of the number of items they use. How much time has been allotted for testing? Here a teacher faces a rather delicate issue since an increase in the number of items increases a test's reliability. But students should have enough time to answer each item. These are decisions teachers have to make. Also, be conscious of the difficulty of the items since complexity obviously affects time and number of items that can reasonably be completed.

Table 11.3 USING ACTION WORDS TO ASSESS THINKING SKILLS

Thinking skill	Action words		Example
Analysis	Subdivide Break down Separate	Categorize Sort	Break the story down into different parts.
Comparison	Compare Contrast Relate	Differentiate Distinguish	Compare the two approaches to government.
Evaluation	Evaluate Judge Assess Appraise Defend	Argue Recommend Debate Critique	Evaluate this picture. Is it well-drawn?
Inference	Deduce Predict Infer Speculate	Anticipate What if Apply Conclude	If there were twice as many people, how might they change the shape of the room to accommodate them?
Recall	Define Identify Label List Name	Repeat What When Who	List the names of three states that produce wheat.

From Witt et al. (1998).

Before we consider the specifics of writing objective test items and essay questions, examine Table 11.4. This table provides a comparative summary of teacher-constructed tests and may help you to decide which type of item would best suit your purposes.

Writing Essay Tests

Teachers have long claimed advantages for the essay examination that are not subject to either proof or disproof. Whether they evaluate higher thought processes more effectively than the objective test is an unanswered question. Essay tests have both advantages and disadvantages. Since many teachers place significant value on essay tests, they remain the most widely used classroom test and deserve careful study and thought. Here are some general considerations teachers may find helpful:

- *Determine the level of thought you want the students to use.* For example, if a political science teacher wants students to think critically about election processes, then an essay question should force students to weigh TV commercials against fact, to question emotional appeals to an electorate, and to examine conflicting interpretations of issues. Responses should reflect these criteria.

- *Phrase questions so that they demand some novelty in students' responses.* Students often complain that essay questions make them reproduce material. Novel questions enable them to integrate and apply their knowledge. If teachers begin questions with action verbs such as "compare, contrast, predict, illustrate," they are asking students to select, organize, and use their knowledge.

Table 11.4　CHARACTERISTICS OF TEACHER-CONSTRUCTED TEST ITEMS

	Objective Test	Essay Test
Learning outcomes measured	Is efficient for measuring knowledge of facts. Some types (for example, multiple-choice) can also measure understanding, thinking skills, and other complex outcomes. Inefficient or inappropriate for measuring ability to select and organize ideas, writing abilities, and some types of problem-solving skills.	Is inefficient for measuring knowledge of facts. Can measure understanding, thinking skills, and other complex learning outcomes (especially useful where originality of response is desired). Appropriate for measuring ability to select and organize ideas, writing abilities, and problem-solving skills requiring originality.
Preparation of questions	A relatively large number of questions is needed for a test. Preparation is difficult and time-consuming.	Only a few questions are needed for a test. Preparation is relatively easy (but more difficult than generally assumed).
Sampling of course content	Provides an extensive sampling of course content because of the large number of questions that can be included in a test.	Sampling of course content is usually limited because of the small number of questions that can be included in a test.
Control of a student's response	Complete structuring of task limits student to type of response called for. Prevents bluffing and avoids influence of writing skill, though selection-type items are subject to guessing.	Freedom to respond in own words enables bluffing and writing skill to influence the score, though guessing is minimized.
Scoring	Objective scoring that can be quick, easy, and consistent.	Subjective scoring that can be slow, difficult, and inconsistent.
Influence on learning	Usually encourages student to develop a comprehensive knowledge of specific facts and the ability to make fine discriminations among them. Can encourage the development of understanding, thinking skills, and other complex outcomes if properly constructed.	Encourages students to concentrate on larger units of subject matter, with special emphasis on the ability to organize, integrate, and express ideas effectively. May encourage poor writing habits if time pressure is a factor (it almost always is).
Reliability	High reliability is possible and is typically obtained with well-constructed tests.	Reliability is typically low, primarily because of inconsistent scoring.

Reprinted with the permission of Simon & Schuster, Inc. from the Macmillan College text *Measurement and Evaluation in Teaching,* 7th ed. by Norman E. Gronlund and Robert L. Linn. Copyright © 1995 by Macmillan College Publishing Company.

- *Write essay questions that clearly and unambiguously define the students' task.* For example, "Discuss the organizations that contribute to the health of the community" is poorly phrased. What does "discuss" mean? Does it mean list, criticize, or evaluate? What kind of organizations? What type of contributions? This and similar items force students to guess.

- *Be certain that a question specifies the behavior desired.* If you phrase questions accurately, you will help students to display what they really know, and make scoring of the answers easier and more exact. The pertinence and phrasing of the question is critical in an essay test, which is one of the reasons that the construction of such a test may seem to be simple, but really takes much thought.

Suggestions for Scoring Essay Tests

Teachers can increase the reliability of a test before they actually administer it by giving thought to the scoring of the responses. We have previously touched on several important, but general considerations: Are you assessing objectives? How wide a range of responses will you accept? Specifically, you might consider the following:

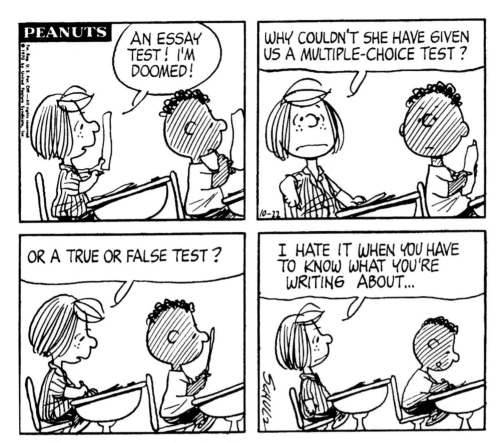

PEANUTS reprinted by permission of United Feature Syndicate, Inc.

TIPS ON ASSESSMENT
Writing Essay Test Questions

PRINCIPLE   Clear and purposeful essay questions enable teachers to assess students' factual knowledge and their ability to organize, interpret, and apply their learning.

STRATEGY   Be sure that questions reflect the material that was taught and that students have read.

STRATEGY   Be precise in wording so that students clearly understand what is expected of them. Vague, ambiguous questions are not only unfair to students, but they can only add to the difficulty of scoring.

STRATEGY   Use questions, when possible and when you deem advisable, to have students explain new situations or to solve problems; do not restrict them to purely factual material.

STRATEGY   Avoid optional questions. If alternative questions are provided—for extra credit or whatever reason—not all students take the same test, so it is almost impossible to compare the students.

STRATEGY   Write sensible questions that permit students to read, interpret, and answer them in the allotted time.

- Decide what major points must be in an answer for full credit. Must they all be there? If not, how many? How many points will you assign to each? How much weight will you give to each question?

- Read all answers to one question; do not read all the answers on a single student's test. By reading all answers to a single question, you increase the reliability of your scoring. You are more accurately comparing students' responses, thus giving you a sense of how a class achieved as a group. If all or most students—bright, average, slow—failed one question, then you can be quite sure that either the question was at fault, or the teaching was misinterpreted or not understood at all.

- Do not associate a name with a test, since one's previous knowledge and feelings about a student could possibly bias scoring. If possible, have students use an identification number instead of their names. You can match names to numbers after you have finished scoring the tests.

Finally, remember that essays are a good means of obtaining more than factual material from students: How do they organize, interpret, and apply data? Can they use data they know to solve problems? But also remember that scoring can be unreliable unless you're careful.

Writing Objective Tests

Objective tests are better suited than the essay examination for some purposes. Objective tests' range of coverage in a relatively brief period and the objectivity of their scoring make them an attractive tool, although you must consider the time and care that go into the construction of the items.

One of the major criticisms consistently directed at the objective test is its apparent emphasis on fragmented, factual knowledge. Consequently, psychologists and educators have labored to devise test items that sample a student's depth and understanding of knowledge. Objective items fall into two general categories: *supply type* (free response, simple recall, completion), and *selection type* (alternative response, multiple-choice, matching).

Suggestions for Writing Supply Items

Simple recall and completion items are fundamentally the same. In both instances, the test taker responds with either one or a few words. The simple recall type usually takes the form of a direct question, while the completion item normally uses a sentence with one or several key words missing. For example:

1. Who is the present president of the United States? (simple recall)

2. The next election for president of the United States will be held in the year
    _____ . (completion)

A teacher needs to take care to make directions sufficiently clear so that students know exactly what is expected without "leading" them. Remember: Avoid textbook language, phrase questions to offer only one possible correct answer, and avoid excessive blanks in completion items. Although supply items appear to be easy to write, you must be sure that the items serve the purpose for which they are intended. Here are guidelines to follow for writing supply items:

- *Don't be fancy or ambiguous with the wording of items.* Since only one response can be correct, phrasing must be sufficiently precise so that students understand its intent.

Good tests generally have a variety of items—short answer and extended-response type of items.

- *Avoid using the exact wording from a text in the item* since it often becomes vague when removed from context.

- *Avoid giving clues.* Giving clues is almost always inadvertent because of phrasing, answers from preceding questions, or the format of the item (using the exact number of blanks as letters in the correct response).

Suggestions for Writing Selection Items

The selection type (alternative response, multiple-choice, matching) restricts the student's answers to those that are presented in the item. The more common alternative response item is the true-false, right-wrong, yes-no variety. A declarative sentence is the usual form of a true-false item, and the subject indicates whether the statement is T (true) or F (false). Here are some examples of items:

> *Directions: Mark each of the following statements true or false. If the statement is true, circle the T; if it is false, circle the F.*

> *T   F   Jimmy Carter became president of the United States in 1977.*

As you can see, you are asking students to judge the correctness of a statement. Try to avoid opinion statements since students are unaware if it is your opinion or not. Attribute the opinion to a definite source.

> *T   F   Bill Clinton supported aid to the Contras.*

The multiple-choice item presents students with a question or incomplete statement and several possible responses, one of which is correct (unless more than one response to each item is permitted, which is the multiple-response type). The typical multiple-choice item reads as follows:

TIPS ON ASSESSMENT
Writing True or False Test Items

PRINCIPLE   True or false items must be stated in clear and unambiguous terms.

STRATEGY   Be certain that the statement is definitely true or definitely false.

STRATEGY   Avoid using negative statements.

STRATEGY   Avoid textbook phrasing.

STRATEGY   Avoid using terms such as *always* and *never*.

STRATEGY   Keep the length of true statements about the same length as false statements.

Directions: For each of the following questions, there are several possible answers. Select the response that you think is correct for each question, and write the number of that answer in the blank space to the right of the question.

1. Who is considered to be the "founder" of operant conditioning? _____

     a. Lewin   *b. Watson*   *c. Skinner*   *d. Thorndike*

Teachers present students a problem followed by several solutions. Note in the preceding, there is one correct answer (c) and three distractions. The manner in which the problem is stated (called the *stem*) may be either a question or an incomplete statement. The multiple-choice item is thought to be the best of the objective items. When it is used, the direct question is the preferred form. At least four possible responses are needed (all of which should be plausible); all answers require consistency and equal length.

The matching item usually utilizes two columns, each item in the first column to be matched with an item in the second column. Here is a typical matching item.

Directions: Below are two lists, one containing the names of individual psychologists, the other the names of schools of psychology. Match the individual with a school of psychology by writing the number of the school before the name of the appropriate individual in the space provided.

_____ Watson	1. Gestalt
_____ Skinner	2. Functionalism
_____ Thorndike	3. Dynamic psychology
_____ Koffka	4. Behaviorism
_____ Woodworth	5. Topological
	6. Connectionism
	7. Programming
	8. Structuralism
	9. Contiguity

In writing matching items, the instructions should be simple, clear, and precise; otherwise they can confuse students. Also include more than the required number of responses, keep homogeneous material in both columns, and keep the list of responses fairly short. The matching item is best suited for a test of factual material that is similar in nature.

TIPS ON ASSESSMENT
Writing Multiple-Choice Test Items

PRINCIPLE   Multiple-choice items allow for the assessment of a wide range of information involving facts, concepts, and application of knowledge.

STRATEGY   The item stem should present the problem in a clear and definite manner.

STRATEGY   Avoid negative statements where possible.

STRATEGY   Be sure that all distracters are plausible.

STRATEGY   The correct answer should be clearly distinguished from the incorrect distracters.

STRATEGY   Be sure that the correct answer appears in a different position from item to item.

STRATEGY   Infrequently use "all of the above" or "none of the above" responses.

STRATEGY   Avoid clues, that is, words such as *always* or *never*.

Current Issues & Perspectives
Subjectivity in the Assessment of Students' Achievement

Students and parents want teachers' assessments to be fair and the decisions they make from the results unbiased and objective. Yet as we have noted elsewhere, all measurements have some error, even those where the scoring method is a basic correct or incorrect decision. Many individuals favor multiple-choice, matching, and true-false type of test items because these forms of assessments are perceived to be more objectively scored, and subsequently less prone to error than open-ended or performance-type tasks. The scoring of these later types of assessment tasks are often characterized as subjective. And to many consumers of assessment information, subjective scoring methods are believed to result in biased, error-prone results. None of us want assessments that are biased and unreliable. It is important to realize, however, that essay questions and complex performance assessments can be scored reliably by experienced teachers using detailed scoring criteria. Thus, the issue is not really one of subjectivity; rather, it is one of taking time to develop well-defined scoring criteria and then using the criteria carefully, preferably with two or more raters who periodically compare their scoring on some common tasks. In other words, the scoring of students' work is an important task and should be taken seriously by teachers just as scientists take seriously the task of research.

   The comparison of teachers' work to that of scientists is relevant because scientists must also deal with the issue of subjectivity. Interestingly, it is a common perception among non-scientists that science is a highly objective, precise endeavor. Scientists are perceived as unusually impartial in their approach to their subject matter and are able to put their personal and professional biases aside in the interest of discovery. Scientists and those who study how science works know better! Scientists almost always have well-established biases about what they are looking for, and it unavoidably colors their perception of what they find. Although it is true that science is a way of learning about the world that is demonstrably more effective than any alternative, it is far from objective. Why then does it work so well?

continued

First, scientists (like teachers) are indeed framed to identify and acknowledge their prejudices. They are encouraged to put them aside to some extent or at least to limit the impact their prejudices have on experimental and interpretative decisions. This training helps a lot, but it hardly produces neutral observers of nature. In fact, preconceptions about the subject matter or the topic of an experiment (lesson) are not only inevitable, they are desirable. If, in preparing to study a phenomenon, an experimenter (teacher) does not learn enough to understand what previous investigators (teachers) have discovered and to develop some educated guesses about what to look for, then he or she is probably not ready to conduct the study (teach the lesson).

Second, although this subjectivity is indulged by the flexibility of the experimental method (instructional techniques), it is also constrained by another important characteristic of science (teaching)—its public nature. Although the conduct of experiments (assessments) is a relatively private exercise, experimental outcomes (assessment results) must be shared publicly for all to see. The publication of experimental data (scores with criteria) and conclusions (assessment results and feedback) means that everyone else is welcome to examine the data (scores with scoring criteria) and draw their own conclusions about the results. Researchers (teachers) can even repeat the study (assessment) to see if they obtain the same results. Replication of research (assessment) results provides an important limit on the impact of personal bias, and it helps to correct any erroneous findings.

In summary, the methods of science permit subjectivity because it is not only unavoidable but valuable. However, research methods, like well-developed assessment methods, protect against the possibility of excesses by arranging social contingencies for either ignorant misjudgment or intentional dishonesty. These contingencies are effective in encouraging scientists and teachers to be as objective as is possible and appropriate, while ensuring that improper actions are either rejected or eventually corrected.

When writing matching items, use more possible responses than items to be matched, thus reducing the likelihood of successful guessing and arrange the list of responses logically.

Objective items should be selected for a particular purpose, carefully written to suit the appropriate reading level of a class, and free from ambiguity. Teachers must rely on their own judgments, based on their knowledge of a class, to allot sufficient time for an objective test. There is no hard and fast guide, although a rule of thumb is that one hundred true-false items or seventy-five multiple-choice items are usually appropriate for a fifty-minute period for students in middle and high schools or older.

PERFORMANCE AND PORTFOLIO ASSESSMENT METHODS

During the past decade we have witnessed an immense growth in educational assessment methods that are curriculum-relevant and require students to apply their knowledge. These methods emphasize observation techniques to characterize a student's overt behavior and are useful in linking assessment results (how a student does) to interventions (how to improve learning) (Witt et al., 1998). Progress in the application of behavioral assessment methods in psychology, along with the school restructuring movement, have fostered the development of new assessment methods for evaluating students' learning. These techniques are referred to as **authentic/performance assessment** and **portfolio assessment.** These two methods are highly related and are examined here in some detail.

AUTHENTIC/PER-FORMANCE ASSESSMENT

The use of real-world tasks to gain information about a student's abilities to integrate and apply knowledge.

PORTFOLIO ASSESSMENT

Assessment of a student's behavior or skills based on a collection of the student's work that the teacher and the student both believe represents evidence of learning.

Recall watching the summer Olympics on television, in particular, the diving competitions. Try to visualize one of your favorite competitors *performing* a dive. Remember what the diver did: She slowly walked to the end of the board or platform, stood still for a few seconds to compose herself and visualize the dive she was about to do, then she launched into the dive, twisting and turning through the air, and finally entering into the water with almost no splash. The crowd applauded, the diver swam to the side of the pool, and then the camera focused on a group of expert judges who each, in a matter of seconds, provided a score for the dive. In most cases, the judges' scores were nearly identical. This is an amazing result given that the dive took less than three seconds from beginning to end, and the dive itself was a complicated series of physical maneuvers.

The description of the Olympic diving competition, although different from a typical classroom activity, serves as a useful illustration of many of the important features of a performance assessment. First, the diver, like a learner in a classroom, must *demonstrate* she can apply her knowledge and skills *by actually doing or creating something* (for example, a backward double somersault) that is valued and purposeful. Second, the diver's performance is *observed* by judges, or in the case of a classroom, by a teacher. Third, these judges use preestablished *criteria to score* the diver's performance, which in turn, provide the diver with feedback. These criteria are based on a set of *performance standards* developed by experts in diving and increase the likelihood that the judges' scores will be consistent or reliable. Finally, the scores are used to determine how well the diver does in comparison to other divers who compete in the same competition.

Our diving example highlights essential features of any formal performance assessments. We envision performance assessment as an important supplement to other types of assessment. Performance assessment is defined as "testing methods that require students to create an answer or product that demonstrates their knowledge or skills" and can take many forms, including conducting experiments, writing an extended essay, or doing mathematical computations (Office of Technology Assessment [OTA], 1992). Performance assessment is best understood as a continuum of assessment formats ranging from the simplest student-constructed responses to comprehensive demonstrations or collections of work over time. Whatever format, common features of performance assessments involve (a) students' construction rather than selection of a response, (b) direct observation of student behavior on tasks resembling those commonly required for functioning in the world outside school (c) illumination of students' learning and thinking processes along with their answers, and (d) the use of predetermined scoring criteria to score the student's performance and provide him or her feedback.

The term *performance* emphasizes a student's active generation of a response and highlights the fact that the response is observable, either directly or indirectly via a permanent product, whereas the term *authentic* (which perhaps is used as often as is performance) refers to the nature of the task and context in which an assessment occurs. The authenticity dimension of assessment has become a very salient issue for at least two reasons. First, most educators assume the more realistic or authentic a task is, the more interesting it is to students. Thus, students' motivation to engage in and perform a task is perceived to be much higher than on tasks where they have trouble seeing the relevance to real-world problems or issues. Second, for educators espousing a competence-based or an outcomes-oriented approach to education, it is important to focus assessments on complex sets of skills and conditions that are like those to which they wish to generalize their educational efforts.

Portfolio assessment is an approach to documenting students' skills and competencies by assembling previously completed work samples and other permanent products (for example, classroom tests, standardized tests, videotaped presentations, pictures of projects, audiotapes of reading) produced by the students. In many cases, products resulting from performance assessments are collected in portfolios.

The term *performance* is consistently used by most authors discussing statewide, on-demand assessments where students must produce a detailed response; the term *authentic* is used more often by educators to describe teacher-constructed or teacher-managed classroom assessment tasks that students must perform. We prefer to use the term *performance assessment* rather than *authentic assessment* because the term *authentic* suggests all other assessments are inauthentic, which is not accurate. However, any serious discussion of educational assessment must consider the key dimensions implicit to both terms.

Figure 11.2 illustrates the relationship among performance and authenticity, and the classroom curriculum in educational assessment tasks (Elliott, 1994). It also indicates that a common third dimension of a valid assessment task is that the content assessed is based on the content taught. Figure 11.2 synthesizes three key dimensions that educators manipulate in their assessments of students' achievement: *student response, nature of the task,* and *relevance to instruction.* As indicated in the figure, assessment tasks can be characterized as varying in the degree to which they are the following:

- *Performance in nature* (for example, low performance: filling in a bubble sheet or selecting the best answer by circling a letter; high performance: writing and presenting a report of research or conducting a scientific experiment in a lab)

- *Authentic* (for example, low authenticity: reading isolated nonsense words or writing a list of teacher-generated spelling words; high authenticity: reading a newspaper article or the directions for installing a phone answering system or writing a letter to a friend using words that are important to the student)

FIGURE 11.2

The relationships among performance, authenticity, and the classroom curriculum in an assessment task

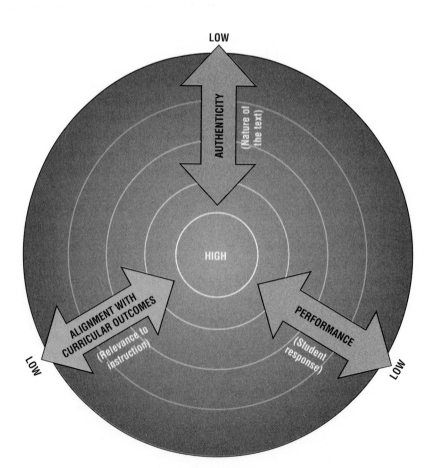

■ *Aligned with curriculum outcomes* (for example, low alignment: facts and concepts are taught, but application is assessed; high alignment: application of facts and concepts are taught and assessed)

Many educators are searching for assessments that are relatively high on all three dimensions. That is, they want highly authentic or real-world tasks that clearly are connected to their instructional curriculum and require students to produce, rather than select, a response. Conceptually, such tasks would lie within the High circle in Figure 11.2.

Performance assessment of students' achievement is not entirely new to many educators. For example, educators in the areas of physical education, art, music, and vocational and technological arts all use, to a large extent, students' products or performances to determine whether the learning objectives of a class have been met. What is new is (a) the use of this form of assessment in the core curricular areas of math, science, language arts, and social studies; (b) the use of scoring criteria, or rubrics, as many teachers call them, to influence and interpret performances; and (c) the encouragement of students to conduct self-assessments. Thus, many educators already use some "weak" forms of performance assessment; that is, they ask students to apply their knowledge and skills by producing a product and provide students feedback about their performances in the form of grades. Besides these two traditional elements of performance assessment, the new, instructionally "stronger" forms of performance assessment take steps to influence students' performances by doing the following:

1. Selecting assessment tasks that are clearly aligned or connected to what has been taught

2. Sharing the scoring criteria for the assessment task with students prior to working on the task

3. Providing students clear statements of standards and/or several models of acceptable and exemplary performances prior to their attempting a task

4. Encouraging students to complete self-assessments of their performances

5. Interpreting students' performances by comparing them with consensus standards that are developmentally appropriate, as well as possibly comparing them with other students' performances

As conceptualized here, the stronger forms of performance assessment interact in visible ways with instruction that precedes *and* follows an assessment task. This approach to assessment emphasizes the point that the central purposes of most educational assessments are to facilitate communication among key educational stakeholders—teachers, students, and parents—and to guide instruction!

Examples of Classroom Performance Assessments and Guidelines for Use

During the past several years, numerous books and manuals have been published that provide examples of performance assessment materials and guidelines for developing these assessments (for example, Blum & Arter, 1996; Herman, Aschbacher, & Winters, 1992). There are not published sets or kits of performance assessment tasks at this time, nor should there be. The power of alternative assessments, like performance assessment, lies in their ability to be constructed by individual teachers (or other professionals) so they correspond to specific instruction and provide information to learners and teachers about the learners' accomplishment of important competencies or outcomes. In effect, performance assessments are a method or means for collecting information about and judging the proficiency of students' learning. Thus, the pieces of a good performance assessment should include the following: an authentic task, a set of objective scoring criteria that can be used to describe the performance, and/or products resulting from the performance, a set of performance standards that provide information about the overall quality of the performance and products, and an opportunity to work on and complete the task under conditions that are as realistic as possible. To illustrate these components, let's examine performance assessment that was designed by a fourth-grade teacher to evaluate students' spelling competencies.

Performance Spelling

Performance spelling was designed to increase students' use of spelling words to communicate and to advance their writing skills (Elliott & Bischoff-Werner, 1995). This approach to spelling is individualized to each student, encourages active parent involvement in selecting words and studying, has public scoring criteria that all students know and use, and has a scoring and progress monitoring system that students manage. This system has been used by many elementary and early middle school teachers and requires each student to select five target words and their teacher to select five target words for a total of ten words per week (Olson, 1995). The selected words (actually the number of which is arbitrary) should be words the student is interested in using in written communications with others and for schoolwork assignments. Students study these words from Friday, over the weekend if they wish, until the next Thursday, when they are tested by writing each spelling word and a sentence correctly using the word. Students work in pairs, taking turns reading their words to each other and then returning to their own desks to privately write sentences using each word. All students have a copy of the scoring requirements for this weekly test; these requirements focus on four areas of spelling and writing as illustrated in Figure 11.3.

FIGURE 11.3

Performance spelling scoring
criteria and standards
(Courtesy Stephen N. Elliott.)

SPELLING: SCORING CRITERIA AND STANDARDS		
Accuracy	(0-1)	0 = incorrect spelling 1 = correct spelling
		Exemplary 90-100%, Satisfactory 70-89%, Inadequate 0-69%
Usage	(0-2)	0 = not used or used incorrectly 1 = acceptable basic use 2 = elaborative use (enriched vocabulary and language use, adjectives, etc.) Example: ate (0) He had ate books. (1) My dog ate his food. (2) She ate the delicious meal her father prepared.
		Exemplary 90-100%, Satisfactory 50-89%, Inadequate 0-49%
Punctuation	(0-3)	0 = no beginning capital letter or ending mark 1 = either beginning OR ending 2 = both beginning and ending 3 = both, plus additional punctuation (quotation marks, commas, etc.)
		Exemplary 90-100%, Satisfactory 67-89%, Inadequate 0-66%
Legibility	(0-2)	0 = generally illegible (majority) 1 = acceptable 2 = cursive, no trace overs
		Exemplary 90-100%, Satisfactory 50-89%, Inadequate 0-49%

As indicated in the figure, students' spelling tests focus on accuracy, usage, punctuation, and legibility of writing. Each of these areas of functioning has a set of prespecified scoring criteria, and in turn, the scoring criteria are used to establish performance standards. For example, with regard to the area of usage, students are required to compose a sentence using the target word appropriately. Usage is evaluated using a three-point scale, where 0 = not used or used incorrectly, 1 = acceptable basic use, and 2 = elaborative use (that is, enriched vocabulary and language use, adjectives). After each of ten sentences are scored, an overall usage score can be determined and characterized using the following performance standards: Exemplary = 90–100%, Satisfactory = 50–89%, and Inadequate = 0–49%. A similar logic, although varying in criteria and scales, is used to score the students' accuracy, punctuation, and legibility areas.

Students use a progress-monitoring graph to record their own scores for each week in each of the four areas (see Figure 11.4). Over the course of a year, students progress from writing ten separate sentences to writing a paragraph with the five words they picked and another paragraph with the five words selected by the teacher. Eventually, students are required to use all ten words in a thematically focused paragraph. These paragraphs are still scored using the accuracy, usage, punctuation, and legibility criteria. Olson (1995) reported that students at all skill levels could successfully participate in performance spelling, and when compared with students in other spelling programs (such as basal series), those in the performance spelling program, on average, actually (a) spelled more words and more difficult words and (b) wrote much more on a weekly basis. Teachers familiar with the performance spelling approach see it as more than a weekly spelling test; rather they commonly characterize it as a language arts program with opportunities for students to apply their knowledge of spelling and English grammar.

This example of performance spelling highlights several important characteristics of strong performance assessments. First, they are connected to the curriculum and are authentic with regard to the work they require students to create. Second, preestablished scoring criteria are available to and understood by students prior to participating in the task. The scoring criteria in this example represent an *analytic approach* to scoring, where a skill area is broken down into parts. Third, the scoring criteria can be used to build performance standards that help students see their level of proficiency in a skill or content area. Finally, teachers can use the results of the test to plan the next week's instructional focus, and students can monitor their own progress within specific skill areas over time.

Let's next examine another example of a performance assessment and focus on the development of scoring criteria. Good scoring criteria are critical to successfully scoring and communicating with students about their work.

Oral Classroom Presentation

Oral presentations or speaking skills are part of many learning activities and projects in classrooms grades 1 through 12, and yet there are no formal tests of oral presenting skills. What you say in a presentation is always important, and in some classes, *how* you say it is also highly valued. How would you evaluate an oral presentation? What behaviors or skills make an excellent presentation?

The first step in developing a performance assessment is to have a clear instructional purpose and vision of the desired outcome(s) of the assessment. Once you have this picture or model of an excellent performance or product, you need to identify the subcomponents or subparts of the outcome and describe them in objective terms so they can be observed by two or more people. Some typical aspects of a good presenter include speaking clearly and at an appropriate rate, making eye contact with the audience, understanding the topic, answering questions, and presenting information in an organized manner. These typical

FIGURE 11.4

Performance spelling progress graph

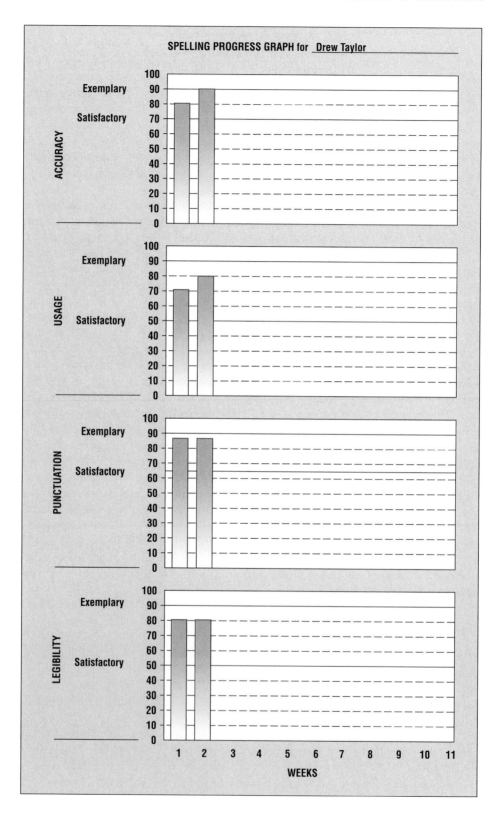

ORAL PRESENTATION SCORING CRITERIA

Each of the behaviors or skills listed below will be evaluated using a 4-point scale, where 4 = Mastered, 3 = Competent, 2 = Minimally Acceptable, and 1 = Poor. These ratings will be the basis for a written summary of your presentation.

I. **Physical Expression**
　　_____ A. Maintained eye contact with audience
　　_____ B. Positioned so everyone can see you and materials on board/screen

II. **Vocal Expression**
　　_____ A. Spoke in a steady, clear voice
　　_____ B. Spoke loudly to be heard by entire audience
　　_____ C. Paced words and varied tone to emphasize points

III. **Verbal Expression**
　　_____ A. Used precise words to convey meaning
　　_____ B. Avoided unnecessary repetition
　　_____ C. Organized information logically
　　_____ D. Summarized main points at conclusion
　　_____ E. Answered questions directly

IV. **Knowledge of Subject Matter**
　　_____ A. Presented and used facts accurately
　　_____ B. Integrated information meaningfully
　　_____ C. Demonstrated understanding of the problem or topic
　　_____ D. Explained the conclusions or results clearly
　　_____ E. Critically evaluated study

V. **Time Management**
　　_____ A. Materials and setting organized
　　_____ B. Used time well

VI. **Support Materials**
　　_____ A. Used materials to support major points
　　_____ B. Provided materials that supplemented presentation

Notes: _____

_____

FIGURE 11.5

Oral presentation scoring criteria

aspects can be more generally characterized as physical expression, vocal expression, verbal expression, and knowledge of the subject matter. In addition, some teachers piece importance on time management skills and the use of materials to support an oral presentation.

Assuming you agree that these are reasonable characteristics or dimensions of an oral presentation, how would you develop scoring criteria that are objective and meaningful to students? In Figure 11.5 we have listed each of these major components of an oral presentation along with various subcomponents that can be directly observed while students give their presentation. Do you agree that these six components and the related subcomponents can be used to directly observe and describe a student if he or she were given an opportunity to do a brief presentation in front of a class? If not, how would you modify these descriptions so they could be used as scoring criteria?

Once a set of knowledge or behavioral components is determined for a given performance task, the teacher or evaluator must decide on which dimension(s) to use to evaluate each component. Most human behavior can be described by dimensions of frequency (for example, never–sometimes–very often–almost always–always) and quality (for example, poor–fair–good–excellent). Table 11.5 lists examples of dimensions that educators commonly use to characterize gradations in students' performances or work products.

FIGURE 11.6

Examples of completed oral
presentation rating scale with
narrative feedback summary
(Courtesy Stephen N. Elliott.)

ORAL PRESENTATION SCORING CRITERIA

Each of the behaviors or skills listed below will be evaluated using a 4-point scale, where
4 = Mastered, 3 = Competent, 2 = Minimally Acceptable, and 1 = Poor. These ratings will be the
basis for a written summary of your presentation.

I.   **Physical Expression**
     __4__ A. Maintained eye contact with audience
     __4__ B. Positioned so everyone can see you and materials on board/screen

II.   **Vocal Expression**
     __4__ A. Spoke in a steady, clear voice
     __4__ B. Spoke loudly to be heard by entire audience
     __4__ C. Paced words and varied tone to emphasize points

III.   **Verbal Expression**
     __4__ A. Used precise words to convey meaning
     __4__ B. Avoided unnecessary repetition
     __3__ C. Organized information logically
     __2__ D. Summarized main points at conclusion
     __4__ E. Answered questions directly

IV.   **Knowledge of Subject Matter**
     __4__ A. Presented and used facts accurately
     __3__ B. Integrated information meaningfully
     __4__ C. Demonstrated understanding of the problem or topic
     __4__ D. Explained the conclusions or results clearly
     __NA__ E. Critically evaluated study

V.   **Time Management**
     __4__ A. Materials and setting organized
     __1__ B. Used time well

VI.   **Support Materials**
     __4__ A. Used materials to support major points
     __4__ B. Provided materials that supplemented presentation

Notes: __65/72 pts. = "Competent" with room for improvement. Please see summary.__

In the case of an oral presentation, we often use a combination of frequency and
quality to provide students comprehensive feedback about their performances. We use
four levels of proficiency (for example, 1 = poor, 2 = minimally acceptable, 3 = competent, and 4 = mastered) to indicate overall performance for each skill. Figure 11.6 is a
completed example of Figure 11.5, illustrating the use of the oral presentation scoring criteria and the narrative feedback summary that was provided to a specific student about
his oral presentation.

This example of a performance assessment of an oral presentation illustrates several
key aspects about the development and use of scoring criteria. First, it is possible to break
down a task into many specific behaviors or characteristics. However, there is a point at
which the list of behaviors or characteristics becomes too long and cumbersome to use.
Teachers rarely have the time to observe a large number of performance criteria for each student. Detailed performance criteria are useful only when the observer has the time to carry
out focused observations of a single student and when each criterion is essential for successfully completing a larger task. Thus, for classroom performance assessments to be manageable and meaningful, a balance must be established between specificity and practicality of

PRESENTATION FEEDBACK

Presenter: Joe
Date: February 27, 1999
Topic: The Relationship Between Observations and Ratings
Time limit: 15 minutes

Comments:
I enjoyed listening to your presentation on Tuesday – you were well organized and clearly
understood the thesis you presented. The attached rating scale documents my analysis of
your presentation according to six categories. You will note that you achieved top ratings for
14 of 19 skills (no rating for "Critically evaluated study" because it was not appropriate for this
presentation). The two skill areas where I believe you could improve the most are: Used time well
and Summarized main points at conclusion. I realize time constraints played some role in limiting
what you could say, but you spent too much time on the Method and too little time on the Results
and Discussion, and because you ran out of time, you could not provide a good summary of the
main points. Perhaps the entire issue here is the limited time you had, but you knew the time
constraints well in advance of the presentation. You spoke quite clearly, used your support
materials very well, and provided a clear context for understanding the study.

Recommendations
1. Provide a handout or overhead with a graphic or flowchart documenting the Method. The details
of the Method are not as important as the Results, so feature Results information and let the audience
question you about how you got them.

2. Consider starting with an orienting question that engages the audience, for example "What is the
relationship between direct observations and ratings of a child's behavior?" or "How can we increase
the agreement between observations and ratings of students' behavior?"

3. Monitor your own time throughout the presentation so you are not surprised to learn you have
only 5 minutes left.

4. Provide a handout with a concise summary of your Results and Conclusion. (By the way, I know
you had a handout, but I did not get one. Please provide me a copy at your convenience.)

OVERALL SCORE = 65/72 (92%) Grade = AB   Rater: S.N. Elliott

FIGURE 11.6

Continued.

Table 11.5 QUANTITATIVE AND QUALITATIVE DIMENSIONS
COMMONLY USED TO CHARACTERIZE STUDENTS'
PERFORMANCES OR PRODUCTS

Frequency (Never–Sometimes–Very Often–Almost Always–Always)

Quality (Poor–Fair–Good–Excellent)

Development (Not Present–Emerging–Developing–Accomplished–Exceeding)

Usage (Unused–Inappropriate Use–Appropriate Use–Exceptional Use)

Amount (None–Partially–All)

Percentage (0%–25%–50%–75%–100%)

Accuracy (Totally Incorrect–Partially Correct–Totally Correct)

Effort (Not Attempted–Minimal Effort–Acceptable Effort–Outstanding Effort)

From Witt et al. (1998).

TIPS ON COMMUNICATION
Developing Performance Criteria

PRINCIPLE   Well-developed performance criteria, or rubrics, provide a learner clear expectations about what aspects of a task a teacher values before the student does the task and also serves to facilitate detailed personal feedback once the learner completes the task.

STRATEGY   Identify the steps or features of the task to be assessed by (a) observing others do the task or by imagining yourself completing it and/or (b) inspecting an excellent example of a finished product.

STRATEGY   List the important criteria that you would ideally use to judge the performance or product.

STRATEGY   Keep the number of performance criteria small enough so they can be observed and judged in a reasonable time period.

STRATEGY   Express the criteria in terms of observable student behavior or product characteristics. Avoid vague and ambiguous terms such as "correctly" or "appropriately."

STRATEGY   Arrange the criteria in the order in which they are likely to be observed, to facilitate recording and communication.

STRATEGY   Select dimensions on which each criterion will be rated. Consider dimensions such as frequency, amount, quality, or accuracy, and develop descriptions for three to five anchor points (see the text discussion of anchor points).

---

the scoring criteria. The key to accomplishing this balance is an ongoing process whereby the criteria are evaluated and refined to ensure only the essential criteria are used. This usually results in a shorter, more clearly defined set of criteria.

General Guidelines for Developing Performance Criteria

Scoring criteria are perhaps the most instructionally relevant aspects of a performance assessment because teachers can use them to signal important skills and competencies to students prior to their work and use them to communicate feedback to them once they have completed their work.

Written Communication Scoring Guide

An example of an evolving analytic rubric for scoring students' written products is provided in Figure 11.7. As you can see, it covers five characteristics of writing (that is, organization, sentence structure, usage, mechanics, and format) and uses a five-point quality scale ranging from a score of 1 (generally poor quality work) to a score of 5 (generally high quality work). Descriptions are used to "anchor" rating points 1, 3, and 5. Raters are encouraged to compare a student's work on each dimension with the description that best characterizes the work, and thus assign a rating from 1 to 5 for each dimension. Descriptive anchors have yet to be developed for points 2 and 4. As this type of scoring rubric is used, a teacher typically can select a couple of examples of students' work that represent various levels of performance such as "poor" (should have ratings of 1 on all five dimensions),

CRITERIA FOR ANALYTICAL SCORING						
	1	**2**	**3**	**4**	**5**	
ORGANIZATION	Little or nothing is written. The essay is disorganized, incoherent, and poorly developed. The essay does not stay on the topic.		The essay is not complete. It lacks an introduction, well-developed body or conclusion. The coherence and sequence are attempted, but not adequate.		The essay is well-organized. It contains an introductory supporting and concluding paragraph. The essay is coherent, ordered logically, and fully developed.	
SENT. STR.	The student writes frequent run-ons or fragments.		The student makes occasional errors in sentence structure. Little variety in sentence length or structure exists.		The sentences are complete and varied in length and structure.	
USAGE	The student makes frequent errors in word choice and agreement.		The student makes occasional errors in word choice or agreement.		The usage is correct. Word choice is appropriate.	
MECHANICS	The student makes frequent errors in spelling, punctuation, and capitalization.		The student makes an occasional error in mechanics.		The spelling, capitalization, and punctuation are correct.	
FORMAT	The format is sloppy. There are no margins or indentations. Handwriting is inconsistent.		The handwriting, margins, and indentations have occasional inconsistencies— no title or inappropriate title.		The format is correct. The title is appropriate. The handwriting, margins, and indentations are consistent.	

FIGURE 11.7

Analytic scoring criteria for a written communication

(From Adams County School District #12, 11285 Highline Dr., Northglenn, CO 80203.)

CASE NOTES

Observation   Melissa Williams presented her students with some models of good and excellent writing and also a general sense of the criteria she planned to use to evaluate their language arts papers.

Hypothesis   The more specific the scoring criteria and examples of work scored using the criteria given to students prior to a test or an assignment, the clearer the communication and more likely students are to perform at a high level.

Possible Action   Melissa's efforts can be improved slightly by providing more-detailed scoring criteria and talking with students about how she uses the criteria. She can also invite them to each "blindly" score one or two of the papers she has already scored and then discuss how their scores compare with her own scores and what the scores mean.

"acceptable" (should have ratings of 3 or 4 on all five dimensions), and "outstanding" (should have ratings of 5 on all five dimensions). These papers serve as models or anchor papers that other raters can use to practice scoring and to calibrate their scoring to increase the likelihood for agreement among raters.

Scoring, Interpreting, and Reporting Results of Performance Assessments

Stiggins (1994) asserted that there are three critical issues in developing scoring criteria: (1) the level of detail needed in assessment results, (2) the manner in which results will be recorded, and (3) who will do the observing and evaluating. Your choice of scoring approach should be decided by how you plan to use the results. If you need a rather precise detailed account of functioning, you would develop an analytic set of scoring guidelines. If you are interested in a general picture of how a student is functioning, then a holistic approach will serve your purpose. Although there is no consensus on this, Stiggins recommends that when a holistic score is needed "it is best obtained by summing analytical scores, by simply adding them together." Or, if your vision of "academic success suggests that some analytical scales are more important than others, they can be assigned a higher weight (by multiplying by a weighting factor) before summing" (p. 196). It may also be acceptable to add a rating scale that reflects an "overall impression" to a set of analytical score scales, if the user can define how the whole is equal to more than the sum of the individual parts of performance.

With regard to recording results from performance assessments, we have emphasized the use of rating scales that characterize performances or products on a continuum of frequency or quality. This approach allows scorers to record their observation of a skill or dimension and at the same time indicate their judgment of the quality of it. A simpler, but often less informative, approach to recording results is the use of a checklist. As the name indicates, scorers are simply required to check whether a skill or dimension of a performance or product was observed. To illustrate the difference between a checklist and rating scale approach to recording, look back at the oral presentation scoring criteria illustrated in Figure 11.5. This set of criteria could be used as a simple checklist or, when the four-point scale of proficiency is applied, as a rating scale recording method. The checklist version of the criteria would be quicker to complete, but some qualitative information would be missing. For example, even in a poor oral presentation a speaker might make eye contact with the audience when he or she is first introduced and when finished. Thus, using a checklist approach, the criterion of "Maintained eye contact with the audience" would most likely get checked as observed. But if the rating scale were applied, it probably would get scored a 2 to indicate a "minimally acceptable" level of the skill.

A final approach to recording performance assessment results is to use an anecdotal record. This involves writing some detailed descriptions of a student's performance or the product he or she produced. This allows for richer portraits of the student's achievement but requires more time. The use of anecdotal records is a good adjunct method to either checklists or rating scales and should be encouraged when the purpose of the assessment is primarily to provide students feedback about an important set of skills that soon will be "exercised" again in learning activities. Anecdotal records are particularly helpful during the early stages in the development of a performance assessment task because they allow a scorer to note a wide range of skills and qualities of students' performances. By examining their notes, scorers often discover important skills or dimensions of functioning that should become part of a more formalized set of criteria with rating scales.

The interpretation of any performance or product involves *subjective judgments*. Professional judgments should guide every aspect of the design and development of any assessment, performance assessments in particular. For years, many experts in the assessment

TIPS ON ASSESSMENT
Enhancing the Objectivity of Results

PRINCIPLE   Maximizing the objectivity of decisions made from an assessment is valued by learners and other test result consumers because it enhances the sense of fairness and clarity of the results.

STRATEGY   Clearly state the purpose for an assessment.

STRATEGY   Be explicit about the assessment target and the key elements of a sound performance.

STRATEGY   Describe the key elements as scoring criteria.

STRATEGY   At the start of the process, and throughout, share the scoring criteria with students in terms they understand.

STRATEGY   Practice using the scoring criteria and then monitor the consistent use of the criteria with actual student products or performances.

STRATEGY   Double-check (using other raters) to ensure bias does not enter into the assessment process.

community have looked at performance assessments with skepticism because of the potential impact of scorer subjectivity. The possibility of bias or inaccurate scores has rendered this approach to assessment too risky or unreliable for some users. Recently, however, assessment experts and educators have realized that carefully trained performance assessment users can use this method effectively. (Interestingly, behavioral psychologists have used observation-based assessment methods for decades and have demonstrated high levels of reliability and validity for many observation systems.) In many cases where educators are interested in collecting evidence on complex achievement outcomes, assessors may have no choice except to use performance assessments. Therefore, it is very important that they work to make performance assessments as objective as possible.

The last strategy in the TIPS on Enhancing Objectivity of Results box—the use of other raters to monitor scoring for bias or inaccurate judgments—is very important and is a practice that most educators probably do not routinely do and often openly resist. With explicit scoring criteria that, in many cases, have been preestablished and the assessment of permanent products (for example, written reports, mathematical solutions to story problems, audio and videotapes of performances), it is convenient to invite other people such as teachers, parents, and students themselves to score an assessment. In the performance spelling approach discussed earlier in this chapter, all the students' weekly spelling tests were scored first by parent volunteers and then double-checked by the students themselves. Few discrepancies in scores were ever reported, so the scoring criteria were deemed highly objective and could be used with high reliability. In addition to the confidence gained from having others score an assessment, the learner appears to benefit from scoring his or her own work. First, more students seem to internalize or understand the characteristics of good work, as defined by their teacher, if they are involved in discussing performance criteria and in scoring. Second, students gain a more personal sense of their strengths and weaknesses, especially when analytic scoring criteria are used. Finally, getting students to be responsible for evaluating their own work with established scoring criteria provides them the opportunity to review and reflect on their work—something that does not routinely happen in busy classrooms or in the homes of many students.

In conclusion, many teachers are finding that by using the scoring criteria (that they produced with the express purpose of scoring students' work) as part of their preinstruction expectations about good work, they are effectively improving their instruction and aligning their curricular activities with their assessments. They are also having more conversations with students about what it means to produce good work. Thus, explicit scoring criteria developed for performance assessments have, in many cases, stimulated curriculum-instruction-assessment (CIA) connections in the classroom.

Portfolio Assessment

Portfolios are another common feature of an authentic/performance approach to assessment. A *portfolio* is a revealing collection of a student's work that a teacher and/or a student judges to be important evidence of the student's learning (Paulson, Paulson, & Meyer, 1991). A portfolio often serves the two purposes of documentation and **evaluation.** Some teachers, particularly those involved with language and communication arts, already use writing portfolios as a means of collecting and analyzing students' growth in written communication skills. As illustrated by Figure 11.8, portfolios can help "frame a picture" of learners' work and provide valuable information about the patterns of their work.

Portfolios are flexible assessment tools that are being used in many subjects and with students of all ability levels. For example, in schools throughout Michigan, high school students are responsible for developing an Employability Skills Portfolio (Stemmer, Brown, & Smith, 1992) that documents skills in three domains: academic skills (for example, understands charts and graphs, uses mathematics to solve problems, uses scientific method to solve problems), personal management skills (for example, attends school or work daily and on time, works without supervision, pays attention to details), and teamwork skills (for example, actively participates in a group, sensitive to the group members' ideas and views, be a leader or a follower to best accomplish a goal). See Table 11.6 for the complete listing of skills focused on in the Employability Skills Portfolio. This portfolio assessment tool encourages students to recognize their successes and to seek opportunities to fill in gaps in skills and to connect what they do in school to the world of work.

Exhibitions are one of the most frequently discussed components of an authentic assessment system. Exhibitions require integration of a broad range of competencies and ever-increasing student initiative and responsibility. Gibbons (1974, 1984) is credited with stimulating educators to apply to schooling the philosophy of the "Walkabout," an Australian aborigine rite-of-passage to adulthood. In many cases, the educational application of the Walkabout has been the development of rite-of-passage or exit exhibitions where students are required to demonstrate the integration and application of knowledge and skills

EVALUATION

The summative interpretation of data obtained from tests or other assessment instruments.

EXHIBITIONS

A form of authentic/performance assessment in which students are required to demonstrate the integration of the knowledge and skills they have acquired.

Good portfolios contain material that students are proud of and can show to others.

Painting PORTRAITS with PORTFOLIOS

Look for patterns which allow you to discover . . .

* what students are attempting to achieve
* if students are being successful
* what changes students may need to make
* what students have learned
* how students view learning
* how students approach learning
* what skills and strategies students use
* what kind(s) of judgments students make
* what type(s) of learning students value
* what expectations exist for future learning
* what conditions enhance learning
* what instructional factors influence or alter learning

You may also discover clues as to students' . . .

* interests	* habits	* independence
* persistence	* curiosity	* creativeness
* cooperativeness	* initiative	
* confidence	* willingness to take risks	

FIGURE 11.8

Painting "pictures" of learners with portfolios

(Courtesy Stephen N. Elliott.)

TIPS ON ASSESSMENT
Implementing a Portfolio

PRINCIPLE   Well-managed portfolios provide learners opportunities to communicate with samples of their actual work—what they have learned, how they have progressed over time, and how well they are doing in comparison to teachers' expectations.

STRATEGY   Find a focus for the portfolio and determine the key instructional goals in the subject matter.

STRATEGY   Establish ownership of the portfolio; think about what you already do instructionally to help children progress toward identified goals and how you determine progress.

STRATEGY   Decide on the contents of the portfolio; brainstorm evidence that might be included in a portfolio to show progress and accomplishment of instructional goals.

STRATEGY   Manage the input into the portfolio by sharing learning goals and scoring criteria with students. Also, whenever possible, share a successful model of a portfolio with students before they start working on their own portfolio.

STRATEGY   Use the development of a portfolio as a time to communicate with students about their best work and aspects of their work that need improvement.

Table 11.6 THE EMPLOYABILITY SKILLS PROFILE FOR ORGANIZING PORTFOLIO EVIDENCE

Academic Skills	Personal Management Skills	Teamwork Skills
Read and understand written materials	Attend school/work daily and on time	Actively participate in a group
Understand charts and graphs	Meet school/work deadlines	Know the group's rules and values
Understand basic math	Develop career plans	Listen to other group members
Use mathematics to solve problems	Know personal strengths and weaknesses	Express ideas to other group members
Use research and library skills	Demonstrate self-control	Be sensitive to the group members' ideas and views
Use specialized knowledge and skills to get a job done	Pay attention to details	Be willing to compromise if necessary to best accomplish the goal
Use tools and equipment	Follow written and oral instructions	
Speak in the language in which business is conducted	Follow written and oral directions	Be a leader or a follower to best accomplish the goal
	Work without supervision	
Write in the language in which business is conducted	Learn new skills	Work in changing settings and with people of differing backgrounds
Use scientific method to solve problems	Identify and suggest new ways to get the job done	

From Stemmer et al. (1992). *Educational Leadership, 49,* 78–81. (pub. ASCD).

CASE NOTES

Observation Melissa was having each of her students create a writing portfolio by selecting three papers from all that they had written during a ten-week period.

Hypothesis Students can develop a portfolio of their own work that illustrates their strengths and weaknesses, if their work has been scored using common scoring criteria and they have some clear sense of what "excellent" work looks like. Unless teachers communicate their performance expectation to students, the work they select for their portfolios may look like nothing more than a collection of interesting work.

Possible Action During the early stages in the development of a portfolio, teachers should provide students feedback about work samples that nicely communicate some of their strengths and weaknesses and how they can be used in a portfolio to "tell a story" or "paint a picture" about learning. Students should be encouraged to change their selections in their portfolios when a better work sample is found. Encourage students to think of a portfolio as a "living document" that shows change and improvement in effort and performance.

in specific areas. In some school systems, rite-of-passage exhibitions serve as gateways to the next level (that is, an exhibition of essential skills must be demonstrated to move to junior high school; another exhibition of even more sophisticated skills must be passed to earn a diploma). Figure 11.9 illustrates the content and activities required in a twelfth-grade exhibition referred to as a ROPE, or Rite-of-Passage Experience.

All seminars must demonstrate mastery in fifteen areas of knowledge and competence by completing a portfolio, a project, and six other presentations before a ROPE committee consisting of staff members (including the student's homeroom teacher), a student from the grade below, and an adult from the community. Nine of the presentations are based on the materials in the portfolio and the project; the remaining six presentations are developed especially for the presentation process.

THE PORTFOLIO. The portfolio, developed during the first semester of the senior year, is intended to be "a reflection and analysis of the graduating senior's own life and times." Its requirements are:

> To graduate from Walden III you must complete a portfolio, a written project, and fifteen oral presentations before two teachers, a peer, and an outside adult.

1. *A written autobiography*, descriptive, introspective, and analytical. School records and other indicators of participation may be included.

2. *A reflection on work*, including an analysis of the significance of the work experiences for the graduating senior's life. A resumé can be included.

3. *Two letters of recommendation* (at minimum) from any sources chosen by the student.

4. *A reading record*, including a bibliography, annotated if desired, and two mini-book reports. Reading test scores may be included.

5. *An essay of ethics* exhibiting contemplation of the subject and describing the student's own ethical code.

6. *An artistic product* or written report on art and an essay on artistic standards for judging quality in a chosen area of art.

7. *A written report analyzing mass media:* who or what controls mass media, toward what ends, and with what effects. Evidence of experience with mass media may be included.

8. *A written summary and evaluation of the student's course work in science/technology; a written description of a scientific experiment* illustrating the application of the scientific method; an *analytical essay* (with examples) on social consequences of science and technology; and *an essay on the nature and use of computers* in modern society.

THE PROJECT. Every graduating senior must write a library research-based paper that analyzes an event, set of events, or theme in American history. A national comparative approach can be used in the analysis. The student must be prepared to field questions about both the paper and an overview of American history during the presentations, which are given in the second semester of the senior year.

THE PRESENTATIONS. Each of the eight components of the portfolio, plus the project, must be presented orally and in writing to the ROPE committee.

Six additional oral presentations are also required. For these, however, no written reports or new products are required by the committee. Supporting documents or other forms of evidence may be used. Assessment of proficiency is based on the demonstration of knowledge and skills during the presentations in each of the following areas:

1. *Mathematics knowledge and skills* is demonstrated by a combination of course evaluations, test results, and worksheets presented before the committee, and by the ability to competently field mathematics questions asked during the demonstration.

2. *Knowledge of American government* should be demonstrated by discussion of the purpose of government; the individual's relation to the state; the ideals, functions, and problems of American political institutions; and selected contemporary issues and political events. Supporting materials can be used.

3. The *personal proficiency* demonstration requires the student to think about and organize a presentation about the requirements of adult living in our society in terms of personal fulfillment, social skills, and practical competencies; and to discuss his or her own strengths and weaknesses in everyday living skills (health, home economics, mechanics, etc.) and interpersonal relations.

4. *Knowledge of geography* should be demonstrated in a presentation that covers the basic principles and questions of the discipline; identification of basic landforms, places, and names; and the scientific and social significance of geographical information.

5. Evidence of the graduating senior's successful *completion of a physical challenge* must be presented to the ROPE committee.

6. A demonstration of *competency in English (written and spoken)* is provided in virtually all the portfolio and project requirements. These, and any additional evidence the graduating senior may wish to present to the committee, fulfill the requirements of the presentation in the English competency area.

The above is drawn from the 1984 student handbook, "Walden III's Rite-of-Passage Experience," by Thomas Feeney, a teacher at Walden III, an alternative public school in Racine, Wisconsin. Preliminary annotations are by Grant Wiggins.

FIGURE 11.9

Walden III's Rite-of-Passage Experience (ROPE)

(Courtesy Charles Kent, Principal, Walden III, Racine, Wisconsin.

Performances, portfolios, and exhibitions can be rich sources of information about a student and the teaching-learning process. To interpret the results of these assessment methods, an evaluation scheme is required that provides meaningful feedback about a student's academic and behavioral strengths and weaknesses. In an authentic assessment approach, evaluative schemes are referred to as *profiles*. Meaningful profiles are developed by expert teachers and provide clearly articulated criteria that allow reliable judgments about the student's demonstrated level of proficiency. The development of profiles to evaluate and score students' performances is perhaps the most challenging implementation aspect of portfolio assessment.

A final common component of a performance-oriented assessment system is student self-assessment. In theory, self-assessments by students could be part of any approach to assessment. In practice, they are infrequently used because the evaluation criterion and the expected learning outcomes rarely are explained to students. In a performance-oriented assessment system, learning outcomes are made explicit, and students are encouraged to review and analyze their performances, exhibitions, portfolios, or other activities that provide feedback about their learning. Thus, understanding one's own strengths and weaknesses is an important outcome of this form of assessment and schooling.

In conclusion, authentic/performance assessment is an ambitious approach to both assessing and teaching students that places heavy emphasis on teachers' judgments. Few teachers will use all the procedural components reviewed here for any given class, yet some of the procedures are very useful and easily can be integrated into almost any class—elementary through high school.

USING TEST DATA AND TEACHERS' ROLES AND RESPONSIBILITIES FOR STUDENT ASSESSMENT

So far, we have covered some of the purposes of classroom testing and assessment. Specifically, we have examined assessing ability, measuring achievement, determining the degree to which objectives have been attained, and guiding educational decisions. But teachers also use test data in marking, grading, and reporting. **Marking** refers to one's assessment of a test or an oral or written report; **grading** refers to the evaluation of tests, reports, essays; **reporting** refers to the manner in which teachers communicate these results to children and parents. Let's examine each of these in detail.

Marking

A mark, no matter what the educational level, is a judgment of one person by another. Sometimes your judgment may be informal, as when you discuss an oral report with a student, or mark and comment on an essay examination. Occasionally a teacher's mark may be quite mechanical, as when one simply totals the number of correct items in an objective test and assigns marks on the basis of number right. A certain percentage of a class receives an A, B, C, D, F or 70, 80, 90.

What can teachers do to improve their marking techniques?

- *Be sure to mark (or somehow indicate) all assigned work.* Nothing frustrates students more than spending substantial time on a project and not having teachers react to it. Assignments are quickly labeled "busywork" and, if done at all, contribute little to learning.

MARKING

The summary assessment of a test or an oral or written report.

GRADING

Assigning a symbol to a student's work or performance to provide general feedback about the quality of the work or performance.

REPORTING

The summary feedback provided to consumers of assessments; can be either quantitative or qualitative.

- *Return work promptly or as soon as possible.* Unless students receive feedback, they often forget, or worse, remember error. Giving a test one day and not returning it for a week or two is poor teaching. If teachers delay furnishing test results, students find it difficult to use feedback or corrections; too much has happened since the tests.

- *If possible, personally comment on the test.* If it is an objective test, students will appreciate some remark, even if only "You did quite well on this test." Essay tests provide more freedom to comment.

- *Provide specific comments about students' work.* Telling students they are wrong has little positive effect. Teachers' comments should indicate precisely where an error is and, if necessary, how to correct it. Tell students exactly where their answers are superior so that they can capitalize on their strengths.

- *Mark the student's work, not the student.* In this chapter, we have consistently cautioned against using tests for personal reasons, which is especially dangerous for objective marking.

- *Avoid sarcasm and belittling or ridiculing remarks.* Teachers have the experience, the authority, and the power in the classroom. A successful teacher works with students, so be careful of your remarks; they can hurt and discourage sensitive, developing personalities.

- *Teachers must make a personal decision,* which is often based on available time, whether to have students repeat their work and correct errors. Merely mentioning mistakes does not remedy them. If possible, have students actually rework their errors after they have determined where they blundered.

In a basic, but now famous study, Page (1958) conducted a study of marks and the effects of teachers' comments on students. He asked the fundamental questions: Are teachers' comments effective at improving students' performance? If so, which comments are effective? Seventy-four teachers randomly selected one of their classes as an experimental group. The total student group consisted of 2,139 secondary school students. The teachers initially administered whatever test came next in the course and were asked to split their classes into three groups: a No Comment group, a Free Comment group, and a Specified Comment group. The No Comment group received a mark and nothing else on their test, the Free Comment group received whatever comment a teacher deemed appropriate, and the Specific Comment group received uniform comments previously designated for each mark (that is, A = Excellent! Keep it up; B = Good Work. Keep it up; C = Perhaps try to do still better? D = Let's bring this up; F = Let's raise this grade). The teachers returned the tests with no unusual attention. The effects of these comments were judged by the scores the same students achieved on the next scheduled test. The results were as follows:

- The Free Comment group of students achieved higher scores than the Specified Comment group, who did better than the No Comment group.

- The results were consistent across all the schools in the sample.

- Although teachers had expected the better students to profit more from their comments, no evidence supported their expectations.

Page concluded that when secondary school teachers write truthful but encouraging remarks on student papers, they have a measurable and potent effect on students so that learning improves.

Grading

Most schools insist that teachers periodically grade their students, which means that they must judge a student's work for two or three months and decide on A or B, 90 or 72. What contributes to the grade? Is it the mere average of all test scores, or should it also include students' attitude, improvement, or participation? Only teachers can answer this question by determining the purpose of grading.

If a grade is intended to indicate competence in algebra, then it should probably consist essentially of marks assigned to subject matter: tests, reports, final examination. Specialized schools or programs can then strictly interpret a grade and judge a student's readiness for a course or program. Such grades characterize most secondary schools, while elementary school grades often represent some combination of competence, effort, and general attitude. A combination is difficult to interpret, and even at the elementary level it is better to assign a competence grade and to report on attitude, interest, or comprehension in some other way.

One danger in assigning grades, both at the elementary and secondary levels, is using grades to discipline or punish the unruly student. It can be more subtly done in grading than in marking. If a teacher marks harshly on a test, it is obvious that he or she is not marking content. Something else is influencing the mark. But unless a grade strictly represents competence—and students, parents, teachers, and administrators have agreed on this—many other forces will affect the final grade.

As you can see from this brief discussion, the more variables that are included in a grade, the less effective it is as an indication of achievement. Grades will represent true achievement to the extent that they reflect instructional objectives and satisfactory test construction. Teachers should decide specifically what the grade is to represent and have it firmly in mind when they assign grades. Teachers are advised to share this information, or whatever criteria they use, with students.

Reporting

Parents wish to be informed of their children's educational progress, which is one rationale for report cards. Teachers know how their students are progressing. Students and parents, however, need extra communication. You can use reports to strengthen the link between home and school, which is the main benefit of any reporting system. Schools and teachers should know how much support they will receive from parents, what advantages

Communicating the results of an assessment is a very important part of effective instruction.

or disadvantages the child has, and what the parents' attitude is toward education. Parents should know what the objectives of teachers and schools are, how their child meets these objectives, and what they should reasonably expect their child to attain.

Other than informing parents and students of progress, a reporting system should bring together parents and teachers so that they can combine efforts to encourage and help children. Unfortunately, most new teachers dread these conferences. They often report feeling insecure and defensive, especially if the child has earned poor grades. To evade or to be vague can be disastrous. Honest and hopeful evaluation, based on student work and observation of behavior, is the only rule. To portray an average child as superior in both ability and performance frustrates everyone. Parents' expectations are unduly heightened; children quickly sense adult dishonesty; teachers avoid a crucial task. If home and school are to work together, there must be honesty, tempered by mature judgment.

No reporting system is completely satisfactory. Either the report of academic progress is slighted (John is doing very nicely), or there is excessive emphasis upon a grade (John—C—). For example, the traditional report card supplies letter or numerical grades with little interpretation—A, B, C, 95, 85, 75. There may be a column where teachers check attitudes as satisfactory or unsatisfactory. Such cards are more typical of elementary than secondary schools.

TIPS ON COMMUNICATION
Grading and Reporting Achievement

PRINCIPLE   Students and their parents like frank and frequent reports of academic progress that provide information to guide future studying.

STRATEGY   Know exactly what constitutes your evaluation of a student. If you assign a C or 75, or satisfactory, or progressing normally, be sure that you specify exactly what contributes to the grade: tests, homework assignments, class participation, library research, and reports.

STRATEGY   Beware of personal opinion in any objective reporting. When you judge a student's work unsatisfactory, or nonprogressing, or even C, avoid any personal prejudices. Separate the subjective from the objective, even if the report is just a comment. For example, state precisely what the student has accomplished, and then relate it to ability or aptitude.

STRATEGY   Use any subjective evaluation cautiously but honestly. Whether it is a written comment, or an attitude checklist, make your judgment as fair as possible, but tell parents exactly what you think. For example, if a student is not working up to ability, tell the student; if a student's classroom behavior is damaging achievement, tell the student.

STRATEGY   Use a parent-teacher conference wisely. Here teachers have a unique opportunity to improve home-school cooperation. If they can justify their grades and provide specific corrective feedback, then a conference becomes a tool to help students. But teachers must be able to produce test scores, marks, or essays and reports, and a record of completed assignments to support objective grades. They must be prepared to furnish detailed reasons for their personal evaluation and suggestions for ways to help the student improve.

A less rigid system may use two categories: satisfactory or unsatisfactory, which provides a less rigid classification. Doubts persist about such reports. Satisfactory or unsatisfactory—compared with what? How much realistic information is conveyed to parents in this system?

A third, equally unsatisfactory, technique is to use even broader categories. For example, "John is progressing," "John has shown marked improvement since the last report," or "John is struggling, please schedule a conference with me."

Gronlund (1985) suggested that schools and teachers adopt guidelines for their grading and reporting practices and then follow these procedures. For example, a grading and reporting system functions effectively when it results from the efforts of students, parents, and school personnel. The system itself should be sufficiently detailed to be helpful in diagnosis, yet not overly complicated. It should also reflect those educational objectives that guide learning, grading, and reporting.

Evaluating and reporting students' academic progress is a challenging endeavor and one that evokes high interest from teachers and students alike. Although many people have questioned teachers' ability to accurately evaluate students' achievement, recent research indicates that teachers are highly accurate judges! We examine this important area more closely in the next section.

Research on Teachers' Judgments of Students' Achievement

In 1989, Hoge and Coladarci published a data-based review of research examining the match between teacher-based assessments of student achievement levels and objective measures of student learning. As a rationale for their work, they noted (a) that many decisions about students are influenced by a teacher's judgments of the student's academic functioning and (b) historically there seems to be a widespread assumption that teachers generally are poor judges of the attributes of their students.

Hoge and Coladarci (1989) identified sixteen studies that were methodologically sound and featured a comparison between teachers' judgments of their students' academic performance and the students' actual performance on an achievement criterion. They found generally "high levels of agreement between teachers' judgmental measures and the standardized achievement test scores" (p. 308). The range of correlations was from a low of .28 to a high of .92, with the median being .65. (Note: A perfect correlation would be 1.00.) The median correlation certainly exceeds the validity coefficients typically reported for psychological tests.

In a recent replication of this research on the accuracy of teacher judgments, Demaray and Elliott (1998) found that teachers accurately predicted 79% of the items that a diverse sample of students actually completed on a standardized achievement test of reading and mathematics. The teachers in this study were virtually equally adept at predicting the achievement of students with high ability and students with below average ability.

This research on teachers' ability to judge the academic functioning of students has an important practical implication: Teachers, in general, can provide valid performance judgments of their students. This result is comforting and shouldn't be surprising given the number of hours that teachers have to observe their students' performances. This research also reminds us of the following humorous, but meaningful story created by Anthony Fredericks, a Professor of Education at York College, York, PA. The story is titled "The Latest Model." Please read it and reflect on its message:

> *It was time once again to assess student performance, so I gathered up my catalogs and headed down to the local showroom of Ernie's Evaluation Emporium and spoke to the manager, Norm Reference.*

"I'm in the market for a new assessment tool," I said.

"Have I got a hot little number for you!" He pulled me over to one of the showcases.

"This little baby here not only gives you percentiles, grade equivalents, stanines, raw scores, means, medians, Z scores, and instructional reading levels, but plots the market value of the dollar on the Gold Exchange as well as the prime lending rate of 10 major banks for the next 6 months."

"I don't think that's what I had in mind," I replied.

"Well, this model over here not only graphs, calibrates, plots, scores, and interpolates all your students' scores, but also sends a four-color report home to parents every 3 weeks listing the colleges their youngsters will be eligible for after graduation."

"But these are elementary kids we're talking about," I said.

"I know, but there's no time like the present for parents to start saving up for those outlandish tuition bills."

"Perhaps I could look at something else," I said.

"Certainly. This sleek model here provides grade equivalent scores to 6 decimal places, is renormed every other Tuesday, and the publisher guarantees that every child scoring over the 90th percentile will receive a simulated gold bracelet with his or her score etched on the back.

"Or how about this flashy number. Not only does it provide an accurate assessment of each child's reading growth, but also charts their height and weight over the next 20 years, their individual horoscope, and their predicted income bracket by age 40.

"And this model here has been used extensively by a school district in Iowa. Their scores were so high last year that the taxpayers overwhelmingly voted in favor of building a new school, erected a statue of the principal in the town square, and sent the entire student body to Hawaii for 2 weeks."

"All these sound exciting," I said, "but I'm really not quite sure…"

"Well, you do look like the selective type. Perhaps we can fix you up with something from the back room. You realize, of course, that we can only show these models to our most discriminating customers."

I nodded and followed him behind a black curtain in the rear of the store.

"If you're not familiar with this model you should know that they provide a daily evaluation of student performance, chart growth and progress during the course of the entire school year, make full and complete reports to administrators and parents, structure reading groups according to interest and ability, and guide instruction on an individual basis. In fact, I know of several principals who use these extensively."

"These do seem interesting, but I wonder how long they'll be effective," I said.

"Several administrators have reported that they last forever and consistently give accurate diagnostic and evaluative information on students. And, believe me, the price is right!"

"Well, I think you've sold me. By the way, what do you call this model?"

He motioned me over and in a low voice he said, "Teachers."

(Fredericks, 1987, pp. 790–791)

Helping Students Take Tests

TEST-WISENESS

Knowing how to take tests; skills that can be learned and refined to improve test performance.

Let's turn now to the concept of **test-wiseness,** which refers to teaching students how to take tests. Don't confuse test-wiseness with coaching. Coaching means preparing students to take a specific test, that is, familiarizing them with the content of a particular test. Test-wiseness, however, means helping students to develop their test-taking skills. When you think of test-wiseness as providing an opportunity for students to demonstrate what they know, you become more sensitive to the importance of testing. Students can help to improve their test-taking skills by considering the following suggestions (Dobbin, 1984):

- Find out what the test is like beforehand. There is a lot of information and practice material available about such exams as the Scholastic Aptitude Test or the Iowa Test of Basic Skills. If it is a teacher-made test, students can ask the teacher any questions they may have and to supply them with a list of the types of items on the test and the topic areas they cover. For example, a student may ask: What will the test cover? Where will it begin? Where will it end? Will it be multiple-choice or essay? How long will it be? Should I guess? (Some tests penalize students for guessing.) Will anything else other than content be scored? Students have a right to know if handwriting and spelling will count.

- Students should decide how to study for the test. What are they going to study? If they have a good idea of what the test will be like, then they should concentrate on that content and any needed skills. They can gather relevant material and try to remember what the teacher emphasized in class. They can even make an outline of these topics. They can combine reading notes with reading the text, underlining anything they think is critical. As Dobbin (1984) noted, if you are going to cram, cram with a plan!

- Students should make sure they are physically prepared to take the test. This includes physical condition: They need plenty of sleep, they shouldn't take any stimulants, and they should not eat too much before the test because it can make you drowsy. They should give themselves plenty of time, and try to get to the test early. They should also take a few minutes while sitting in their seat before the exam to relax by taking a few deep breaths, closing their eyes, and tensing and releasing their muscles in their hands.

- When taking essay tests, before writing an answer, students should take time to formulate or outline their answer. As they read each question, they can jot down next to the question the ideas they think about immediately. Then writing as clearly as possible, using complete sentences, they can explicitly indicate how they have organized their answer, and restate the focus or purpose of their answer in the opening paragraph. Students should reread what they have written, making corrections in spelling and minor additions to the text by signaling inserts. Readability is important, but a comprehensive answer is more important in most cases so they should be prepared to write fast.

- When taking multiple-choice tests, students should remember: (a) to read the instructions or directions carefully and complete identifying information accurately before reading any items, (b) to read all the possible answers to each question before selecting an answer, (c) to go through the test quickly, answering those items they are sure about and then go back to those they are doubtful about, (d) on items giving them trouble, try to eliminate any response they know is wrong and then use any clues, such as wording or contradictions, to eliminate any other false responses, and (e) true-false items that use such terms as "always" or "never" are usually false and true-false items that are lengthy are usually true.

Teachers' Roles and Responsibilities for Student Assessment

We have covered a substantial body of information in this chapter on classroom assessment. It should be very evident that teachers should understand a variety of assessment tools. They should be capable of using several different techniques to describe students' learning and to communicate with students, parents, and others about such learning. Accordingly, the American Federation of Teachers (1990, p. 1) believes that "assessment competencies are an essential part of teaching and that good teaching cannot exist without good student assessment." As a result of these beliefs, educators representing the American Federation of Teachers, the National Council on Measurement in Education, and the National Education Association wrote a set of seven standards for teacher competence in student assessment. These standards are as follows:

Standard #1: Teachers should be skilled in *choosing* assessment methods appropriate for instructional decisions.

Standard #2: Teachers should be skilled in *developing* assessment methods appropriate for instructional decisions.

Standard #3: Teachers should be skilled in *administering, scoring, and interpreting the results* of both externally-produced and teacher-produced assessment methods.

Standard #4: Teachers should be skilled in *using assessment results* when making decisions about individual students, planning teaching, developing curriculum, and improving schools.

Standard #5: Teachers should be skilled in *developing valid pupil grading procedures* that use pupil assessments.

Standard #6: Teachers should be skilled in *communicating assessment results* to students, parents, other lay audiences, and other educators.

Standard #7: Teachers should be skilled in *recognizing unethical, illegal, and otherwise inappropriate assessment methods and uses of assessment information.*

The enactment of these standards requires a range of activities by teachers prior to instruction, during instruction, and after instruction. For example, assessment activities *prior to instruction* involve teachers (a) clarifying and articulating the performance outcomes expected of students, (b) understanding students' motivations and creating connections between what is taught and tested and the students' world outside of school and (c) planning instruction for individuals and groups of students that is aligned with what will be tested. Assessment-related activities occurring *during instruction* involve (a) monitoring student progress toward instructional goals, (b) identifying gains and difficulties students are experiencing in learning and performing, (c) adjusting instruction to better meet the learning needs of students, (d) giving contingent, specific praise and feedback, and (e) judging the extent that students have attained instructional outcomes. Finally, the assessment-related activities occurring *after instruction* that involve teachers include (a) communicating strengths and weaknesses

CASE NOTES

Observation   One aspect of using a standardized test of achievement that concerned Mrs. Williams the most was that she would not have an opportunity to use the results to improve instruction for her current students because the information would not be available until the last days of the school year.

Hypothesis   Test results will have little impact on instruction if they are not provided in a timely manner and in a form that provides details about strengths and weaknesses of students.

Possible Action   Melissa can use the results from the end-of-year test to influence her instructional planning for the following year for a new class of students. In addition, the results should be shared with her colleagues in eighth grade who will be working with her current students.

based on assessment results to students and parents, (b) recording and reporting assessment results for school-level analysis, evaluation, and decision making, (c) analyzing assessment information before and during instruction to understand each student's progress and to inform future instructional planning, and (d) evaluating the effectiveness of instruction and related curriculum materials.

As you can see, the professional expectations for teachers are high: Teachers must be competent and proactive in the assessment of their students! Study and guided experience beyond the knowledge acquired in this chapter is essential for the competent practice of educational assessment.

A COMPARATIVE SUMMARY OF TEACHER-CONSTRUCTED ASSESSMENT METHODS

This chapter focused on teacher-made tests, both essay and objective, and introduced several new suggestions for assessing students, particularly performance assessments. After the basic elements of each were identified, suggestions were made to help teachers write, mark, grade, and report assessment results. To determine the real purposes of a unit of work, teachers may want to write them out to aid teaching and testing. They can then decide what specific kinds of behavior can be measured to indicate attainment of these objectives.

You were asked to familiarize yourself with the different types of test items and with the principles of test construction. This can help one to decide what kind of test would be best suited for students. Table 11.7 provides an integrated summary of the various types of assessments available to use daily in most classrooms.

Don't throw away your tests. Look at the results and decide what items worked. Teachers can then begin a collection of items that measure what is taught and that do a good job of discriminating between students who know a subject matter and those who don't. Finally, keep an open mind about the first form of the test. There is no way of telling how easy or difficult a test is until it has been used. Constructing a good test is not an easy task; it is time-consuming, often difficult, and occasionally frustrating. But teachers cannot obtain an accurate appraisal of students without accurate measurement tools. Thus, we believe the information covered in this chapter is essential to effective teacher-student interactions!

Table 11.7 COMPARISON OF VARIOUS TYPES OF ASSESSMENT

	Objective Test	Essay Test	Oral Question	Performance Assessment
Purpose	Sample knowledge with maximum efficiency and reliability	Assess thinking skills and/or mastery of a structure of knowledge	Assess knowledge during instruction	Assess ability to translate knowledge and understanding into action

Typical exercise	Test items:
	
	    Multiple-choice
	    True/false
	    Fill-in
	    Matching
		Writing task	Open-ended question	Written prompt or natural event framing the kind of performance required

Student's response	Read, evaluate, select	Organize, compose	Oral answer	Plan, construct, and deliver original response
Scoring	Count correct answers	Judge understanding	Determine correctness of answer	Check attributes present, rate proficiency demonstrated, or describe performance via anecdote
Major advantage	Efficiency—can administer many items per unit of testing time	Can measure complex cognitive outcomes	Joins assessment and instruction	Provides rich evidence of performance skills
Potential sources of inaccurate assessment	Poorly written items, overemphasis on recall of facts, poor test-taking skills, failure to sample content representatively	Poorly written exercises, writing skill confounded with knowledge of content, poor scoring procedures	Poor questions, students' lack of willingness to respond, too few questions	Poor exercises, too few samples of performance, vague criteria, poor rating procedures, poor test conditions
Influence on learning	Overemphasis on recall encourages memorization; can encourage thinking skills if properly constructed	Encourages thinking and development of writing skills	Stimulates participation in instruction, provides teacher immediate feedback on effectiveness of teaching	Emphasizes use or available skill and knowledge in relevant problem contexts
Keys to success	Clear test blueprint or specifications that match instruction, skill in item writing, time to write items	Carefully prepared writing exercises, preparation of model answers, time to read and score	Clear questions, representative sample of questions to each student, adequate time provided for student response	Carefully prepared performance exercises; clear performance expectations; careful, thoughtful rating; time to rate performance

From: R. J. Stiggins, "Design and Development of Performance Assessments," *Educational Measurement: Issues and Practice,* 1987, p. 35. Copyright © 1987 by National Council on Measurement in Education. Reprinted with Permission.

Case Reflections

The case notes in this chapter on Melissa Williams and her class covered a range of possible actions designed to address her concerns about (a) the use of an end-of-year standardized achievement test as a primary method for documenting student achievement and (b) the role of other assessment methods in providing students feedback about their development in language arts and social studies. The role of the end-of-year achievement test provided an immediate values clarification test for Melissa and her teaching colleagues, Bill Drake and Sara Ellis. Bill and Sara clearly accepted, and maybe even celebrated, the importance of the achievement test. Melissa, however, was skeptical of its value because it did not appear to align well with her instructional objectives and it came so late in the year to be almost useless for guiding her instructional efforts with her current students. It was recommended that Melissa consider some compromise and change some of her instructional methods to increase the match between what was tested on the achievement test and what she emphasized in class on a daily basis. In addition, it was noted that the achievement test is only one form of evidence about student learning; in fact, more evidence about students is provided daily in the performance tasks and language arts portfolios Melissa had each student develop.

With regard to the use of performance assessments, it was noted that Melissa could probably improve her efforts by providing students with detailed scoring criteria in addition to the successful models she presently used to communicate her performance expectations. It was also noted that Melissa should occasionally use an additional scorer of students' performances to ensure high interrater agreement and fair judgments.

The writing portfolios that students are required to develop provide an excellent opportunity for students to showcase what they have learned *and* the process of writing. Melissa was encouraged to use portfolios as "living" documents where students can update their work over the course of a semester to show progress with early examples and more well developed examples. This form of assessment can help "paint the big picture" for a student and others who want to understand his or her accomplishments in a manner that gets beyond a number or test score.

Melissa's concern about the timing of feedback from the end-of-year test was addressed less successfully because the scheduling of the test is a system issue that she has little control over in the short term. It was noted that not all is lost just because the test results come at the end of the year. The test data, in fact, could be useful in providing her insights into what she might do differently next year to help students perform better, and they may also suggest what areas of instruction should continue without much change.

In summary, this chapter provided several suggestions for improving and using teacher-constructed tests and assessment data to evaluate student achievement. It should be clear there are a variety of assessment methods and no single method can address all the purposes for evaluating students. Therefore, it is expected that most teachers, like Melissa Williams, will need to use traditional multiple-choice objective tests, essay tests, performance assessments, portfolios, and standardized achievement tests. Then they will need to devise ways to effectively communicate the results of these assessments to students and others interested in helping students learn.

CHAPTER HIGHLIGHTS

Assessment: Terminology, Assumptions, and Purposes

- Assessment refers to the process of gathering pertinent information to help make decisions about students.

- Testing is one means of obtaining evidence about a student's learning or behavior.

- Measurement means placing a number on a student's performance.

- Grading is the assignment of a symbol to a student's performance.

- Careful analysis of testing results aids educators in improving instruction, revising curricula, guiding students to realistic decisions, judging the appropriateness of subject matter, and assessing the conditions of learning.

- Educators today are sensitive to the needs of multicultural students in taking tests. In giving tests to these students, teachers should be aware of students' test-taking skills, such as language comprehension, that could influence the test results.

- All forms of assessment contain error, which implies that we must assess students frequently and with a variety of methods.

- Assessment techniques should help teachers to determine if their objectives have been met.

- If objectives remain unmet, then teachers must search for the cause and attempt to discover whether it is in the student(s), the material, or the teachers' methods.

- The evidence provided by assessment enables teachers and administrators to present appropriate materials that serve the needs of their students.

Methods and Technical Issues in the Assessment of Students

- Assessing classroom performance typically entails four methods: pencil-and-paper tests, oral questions, performance tests, and standardized tests.

- Teacher-constructed tests usually consist of essay questions or multiple-choice items.

- Validity refers to a test's meaningfulness, that is, its ability to measure what it is supposed to measure.

- Reliability refers to a test's consistency, which can be affected by an individual's characteristics and by the design of the test.

Planning a Teacher-Constructed Test

- Test items should reflect the objectives of the subject or unit.

- Think about the test; take time to construct relevant items. Avoid the habit of hastily throwing a few questions together. This isn't fair to you, given the amount of time you have spent teaching, and it certainly isn't fair to your students, who deserve a thoughtful assessment of their achievements.

- Next you must decide what kind of test best serves your purpose—essay or objective—both of which have strengths and weaknesses. Consider carefully which type of test is better suited to obtain the information needed to evaluate students' achievement.

- Writing essay questions is more difficult than it initially appears. Clarity, level, and a necessary degree of objectivity are required.

- Scoring the answers to essay questions requires a clear understanding of the major points in the answer. Try to ensure that you do not know which student's paper you're marking. Also read all answers to one question rather than reading all of a student's answers at one time.

- Objective tests sample a wide range of material and, if carefully formulated, can also assess comprehension as well as knowledge.

- Be sure students are ready for an objective test: Are there any mechanics they should be familiar with? Do they have a strategy for taking the test? What clues does the item furnish? What are the rules for guessing?

Performance and Portfolio Assessment Methods

- Advances in behavioral assessment and the school restructuring movement have led to the development of two new assessment approaches: authentic/performance assessment and portfolio assessment.

- Performance assessment is a collection of assessment techniques (that is, portfolios, performances, exhibitions) and interpretative tools (that is, profiles and self-ratings) that are designed to link teaching and assessment.
- Authentic assessment focuses on authentic classroom performances rather than typical multiple-choice or pencil-and-paper essays. The integration of real-world skills is stressed.
- Authentic/performance assessment places a heavy emphasis on teacher judgments of students' performance.
- Portfolios of students' work samples and performance assessments provide powerful feedback to students and parents about achievement.

Using Test Data and Teachers' Roles and Responsibilities for Student Assessment

- If you assign work, mark it and return it as soon as possible with appropriate remarks.
- When you grade students (that is, judge their work over a period of time) be sure that your grade represents their work, not their behavior.
- One of the main reasons for reporting, if not the main reason, is to strengthen the association between home and school.
- Test-wiseness refers to familiarity with test-taking procedures that students can learn which will help them perform better on most tests. These include finding out what will be covered and the type of item format to be used, being physically prepared to take the test to ensure optimal alertness, reading instructions carefully, outlining an answer before responding to essay questions, and reading all parts of multiple-choice items before selecting the best answer.
- Professional organizations that represent teachers and educational assessment specialists in this country have established standards for teacher competence in assessment. Such competencies are considered an essential part of effective instruction.

WHAT DO YOU THINK?

1. From your perspective as a student, what are the most important reasons for giving a test?
2. If you were responsible for assessing a student with a primary language other than English and who was from a different culture than your own, what if any adjustments in your assessments would you make?
3. Based on your own experience with tests, what are two sources of error in the scores you have received?
4. Given your understanding of reliability, what steps can teachers take to ensure the reliability of their tests is high?
5. If you could select the method by which you would be assessed in this class, what would it be like?

C H A P T E R

twelve

Standardized Tests
and Behavior Rating Scales

This chapter concerns the use of

standardized achievement tests,

focusing on the central issue creating

tension for Melissa Williams in her

first year in the DEW House. As you

know from reading the case presented

at the beginning of this section,

Melissa is in a school that places a

high value on standardized test

results. While reading through this

chapter you should be able to develop

several ideas on how Melissa can

reduce her concerns about "teaching

to the test" and the meaningfulness

of test results.

ASSESSMENT

*The process of gathering
information about a student's
abilities and using such
information to make decisions
about the student.*

With the basics of classroom assessment and teacher-constructed tests behind us, we turn now to the world of standardized tests. Hundreds of test and **assessment** procedures can reasonably be characterized as standardized; that is, they were developed by professionals, to be administered in a uniform or standard fashion for the purposes of collecting and interpreting results about learners' knowledge or behavior. Tests commonly considered as standardized include individual and group achievement tests, measures of cognitive or intellectual abilities, and behavior rating scales used to evaluate the frequency of students' behaviors. Although teachers occasionally may have the responsibility of selecting standardized tests for particular purposes, the chances are that teachers' major responsibilities with regard to these tests will be as advisers in the selection process.

Standardized tests are a major part of many schools' testing programs, and teachers must be informed professionals. It should be noted, however, that today some school systems are questioning the value of standardized testing—it can be expensive, time-consuming, and it can lead to some negative consequences for educators. Yet, at state and national levels, many educational leaders are urging the use of achievement batteries to assess student academic progress. Thus, it is important to examine the advantages and disadvantages of standardized tests and rating scales.

Standardized tests have become "big business." When you consider that about 45 million students are enrolled in kindergarten through grade 12, you begin to sense the enormous dimensions of "testing." Standardized tests used as classroom tests must be appropriate for the educational purposes of the system, the school, and the students. Giving tests simply because "it's the thing to do" is an expensive and ineffective exercise. The best, and perhaps the only, safeguard against such a practice is knowledge: knowledge of test construction in general, of specific tests, of students, and of the educational goals of a school.

In this chapter, we discuss the objectives of a school's testing program and begin an examination of standardized tests with a description of major features of these tests. Next we examine how the results of standardized tests can help teachers in the classroom. As with most topics in education, some controversy exists about these tests, so both pros and cons are presented. Since there are several types of standardized tests, we identify and discuss a wide range of tests, including achievement tests, intelligence tests, and behavior rating scales. Finally, we examine several current issues concerning the use of standardized tests.

A SCHOOL'S TESTING PROGRAM

Before beginning a specific analysis of standardized tests, let us again recall how important the relationship is between learning objectives and testing. Schools are designed to change students' behavior; that is, increase knowledge, refine thinking skills, and cultivate social skills. The ideal means of accomplishing this change largely determines the choice of administrative structure (for example, self-contained classroom vs. team teaching), methods, materials, and curriculum. We can't make reliable decisions about these matters unless they are based on an accurate assessment of student capacity. All these issues—administration, assessment, counseling, teaching, and learning—involve educational objectives.

What do we need to know about a student, and how can we acquire this knowledge? Once we have the needed information, what does it mean? Little value is derived from a series of achievement tests unless the results can be used to improve the instruction offered students. Unless teachers and administrators understand what a test score does and does not mean, tests are of little value, and may, in fact, be detrimental.

The use of group intelligence testing during World War I, the more-sophisticated selection tests developed during World War II, and both state and federal legislation (such as P.L. 105-17, the 1997 reauthorized Individuals with Disabilities Education Act) have combined to establish an important place for testing at all levels of education. The selection,

Standardized tests often require students to work under time lines and to answer a wide range of questions.

CASE NOTES

Observation   The teachers at Davis Middle School administer their annual achievement test late in the spring to monitor students' learning and to provide accountability data for the school system.

Hypothesis   The timing of any test has an impact on students and teachers. Melissa Williams's concerns about the school's annual test would be greatly reduced if it were scheduled so she received feedback about students' performances in time for her to work with them to improve their knowledge and skills.

Possible Action   Melissa, and other teachers, should talk with the evaluation specialists in their school district about the instructional advantages to scheduling the annual achievement test earlier in the school year to allow more opportunities to use the test results to guide reteaching and to provide students and parents with detailed feedback about the test results.

---

administration, and interpretation of standardized tests should be linked closely to the educational objectives of a particular school system. A given testing program usually involves readiness tests before school entrance; subject matter achievement tests at all levels; occasional cognitive tests for students with special needs or disabilities; and other tests, such as interest inventories, personality questionnaires, and academic diagnostic tests, as needed in individual cases. See Table 12.1 for a list of school testing programs. In some cases, these tests are administered to individual students by specialists such as school psychologists or counselors. In other cases, teachers administer tests under the auspices of an evaluation specialist.

The choice of an appropriate testing program depends on one's knowledge about the nature of standardized tests and how they aid in the attainment of educational objectives. Testing programs generally have three major purposes: *instructional, guidance,* and *administrative.*

1. Instructional: Achievement tests administered in the fall help teachers to commence instruction at a point where students can logically expect both

challenge and success. In other words, some achievement tests answer these questions: Where are students right now? Where should instruction begin?

2. Guidance: The results of some testing programs enable instructors to adapt the curriculum more efficiently to individual students and to aid students in choosing specialized courses, thus serving a guidance function. These tests help to answer such questions as: What does this student need? Is this student exceptional in some way? Are special services needed, such as gifted/talented programs, remedial reading programs, or special education programs?

Table 12.1 SCHOOL TESTING PROGRAMS

Level	Type of Test
Preschool	Psychomotor and readiness
Primary	Basic skills Reading
Elementary	Achievement Basic skills Personality/behavior
Junior high	Aptitude Achievement Basic skills Personality/behavior
Senior high	Aptitude Achievement Basic skills Personality/behavior Vocational/interest College entrance

---

TIPS ON ASSESSMENT
The Primary Purpose of Assessment Is to Improve Student Learning

PRINCIPLE Assessment systems, including classroom and large-scale assessments, are organized around the primary purpose of improving student learning.

STRATEGY Teachers should be consulted about the alignment between what they teach and the content assessed by a test. To ensure reasonable alignment, a sample of experienced teachers should examine representative items from a test that is purported to test students at specific grade levels and these teachers should reach consensus about the appropriateness of the item content for their students.

STRATEGY Assessment results are provided in a form that provides feedback about specific areas of student performance. These results also must be provided in a timely manner so that the results are still relevant to the focus of instruction.

STRATEGY Teachers can explain how their assessment practices and instruments help improve teaching and how they provide useful information for working with students.

3. Administrative: Administrators are often interested in how groups of students are performing. Good tests can help them to make suitable decisions about curriculum and placement, based on substantial data comparing their students with others in the region or the nation.

STANDARDIZED TESTS

Standardized tests are commercially prepared and sample behavior under uniform procedures. Procedures clearly are uniform when the same fixed set of questions is administered to all students, the directions are the same for all, the time requirement is the same for all, and the scoring procedure is the same for all. Testing experts usually administer the test to a norm group (usually a large national sample) so that any one student's performance can be compared with those of others throughout the country. Standardized tests are usually classified according to what they measure. There are two general categories: **aptitude tests** and **achievement tests.**

1. Aptitude tests are intended to assess students' general or specific abilities; for example, an intelligence test supposedly assesses a student's total ability. (The current controversy over what intelligence tests really measure is discussed later in this chapter.) There are other, more specific aptitude tests that measure mechanical, musical, artistic, and many other aptitudes.

2. Achievement tests measure accomplishment in such subjects as reading, arithmetic, language, and science. Carefully constructed standardized achievement tests possess the following characteristics: The test items are of high technical quality, developed by test specialists, pretested, and selected according to precise requirements; directions for administering and scoring are rigidly controlled to ensure uniformity; norms are provided to help interpret test scores; equivalent forms of the test are typically available; and a variety of materials, including a test manual, are included to aid in administering, scoring, and interpreting scores.

STANDARDIZED TESTS
Tests that are commercially constructed and administered under uniform conditions.

APTITUDE TESTS
Tests that assess students' general or specific abilities.

ACHIEVEMENT TESTS
Measures of accomplishment in such specific subjects as reading, arithmetic, etc. Developed by testing specialists; concern today is that these tests may not reflect what is actually taught in the classroom.

Joe Heller, *Green Bay Press Gazette.* Used by permission of Joe Heller.

You can see, then, that uniformity is a critical element in these tests to ensure that legitimate comparisons can be made. How does a fourth-grade student in Maine compare with a fourth-grade student in California? Standardization is the degree to which the observational procedures, administrative procedures, equipment and materials, and scoring rules have been fixed, so that exactly the same testing procedure occurs at different times and in different places. With the increasing participation of students with disabilities in standardized assessment programs, however, we are seeing the use of testing accommodations that modify some of the standardization procedures, such as amount of time to complete a test or the use of an assistant to transcribe answers (McDonnell et al., 1997). The use of testing accommodations is another topic that deserves further examination later in this chapter.

Many standardized tests allow the teacher to compare a given student with a representative group (referred to as a **norm group**) of students. Such tests are called **norm-referenced tests.** A norm-referenced test (NRT) yields a score that can be compared with the scores of others who have taken the same test. When you grade an essay test, you might compare each student's answers with those of other students and decide that a student's answers, compared with the others, warrant a B. You have given a norm-referenced test at the classroom level. A score on a standardized achievement test informs you how a student compares with some national group that has taken the test. A norm-referenced test has several advantages:

1. It can assess a broad range of knowledge and understanding.

2. It reflects common goals for learning.

3. It can assess achievement at all levels of attainment: high, medium, or low.

4. It reflects the belief that achievement is "more or less," not "all or nothing."

5. It often furnishes a single score that summarizes a student's general level of achievement.

6. It provides summative evaluation information.

Another type of test that provides scores informing teachers of the extent to which students have achieved predetermined objectives is called a **criterion-referenced test** (CRT). Criterion-referenced tests are increasingly popular because of renewed emphasis on individualized instruction, behavior objectives, and mastery learning. They focus on providing information about students' performances in the context of an objective standard of performance. For example, tests used to diagnose mathematics skills or adaptive behaviors typically have used a criterion-referenced framework. Figure 12.1 illustrates the differences in the interpretations of a norm-referenced test and a criterion-referenced test.

Typically, skills within a subject are hierarchically arranged, so that the skills that are learned initially are tested first. In math, for example, addition skills are taught and evaluated before multiplication skills. These tests are usually criterion referenced, because a student must achieve competence at one level before being taught at a higher level. Thus, criterion-referenced tests help teachers to determine if a student is ready to move on to the next level. The major characteristics of criterion-referenced and norm-referenced tests are presented in Table 12.2.

Developing a Standardized Test

The term *standardization* implies consistency or sameness in the administration and format of a test. If students' scores are to be easily compared, the test and the testing circumstances ideally should remain uniform during all test administrations. Standardized tests contain detailed directions that a test administrator must follow. If test administrators vary the testing conditions, they introduce an unaccountable source of error, and comparison of these scores with others could become less meaningful or invalid.

NORM GROUP

A comparison group usually used to establish the scaled scores for a standardized test.

NORM-REFERENCED TESTS

Standardized tests that allow comparison of a score for a given student with a representative group of students.

CRITERION-REFERENCED TEST

A type of testing used to determine if a student has achieved predetermined behavioral or instructional objectives. A student's performance is interpreted by comparing the performance to a set of objective criteria.

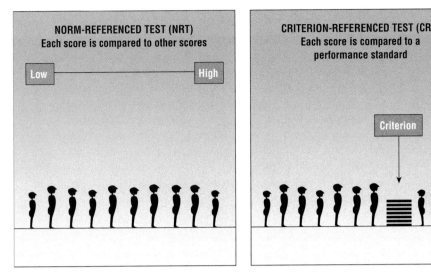

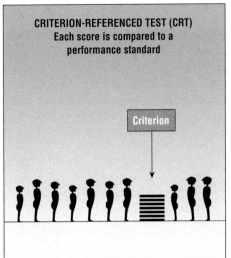

FIGURE 12.1

Simplified illustration of the nature of norm-referenced and criterion-referenced test scores (From F. L. Finch, Ed., *Educational Performance Assessment.* Copyright © 1991. Reproduced with permission of The Riverside Publishing Company, Chicago, IL.)

Table 12.2 COMPARISON OF NORM-REFERENCED TESTS (NRTs) AND CRITERION-REFERENCED TESTS (CRTs)

Common Characteristics of NRTs and CRTs

1. Both require specification of the achievement domain to be measured.

2. Both require a relevant and representative sample of test items.

3. Both use the same types of test items.

4. Both use the same rules for item writing (except for item difficulty).

5. Both are judged by the same qualities of goodness (reliability and validity).

6. Both are useful in educational measurement.

Differences between NRTs and CRTs (but it is only a matter of emphasis)

1. NRT—Typically covers a *large* domain of learning tasks, with just a few items measuring each specific task.
   CRT—Typically focuses on a *delimited* domain of learning tasks, with a relatively large number of items measuring each specific task.

2. NRT—Emphasizes *discrimination* among individuals in terms of relative level of learning.
   CRT—Emphasizes *description* of what learning tasks individuals can and cannot perform.

3. NRT—Favors items of average difficulty and typically omits easy items.
   CRT—Matches item difficulty to learning tasks, without altering item difficulty or omitting easy items.

4. NRT—Used primarily (but not exclusively) for *survey* testing.
   CRT—Used primarily (but not exclusively) for *mastery* testing.

5. NRT—Interpretation requires a clearly defined group.
   CRT—Interpretation requires a clearly defined and delimited achievement domain.

MEASUREMENT AND ASSESSMENT IN TEACHING 7th ed. by Linn/Gronlund, © 1995. Reprinted by permission of Prentice-Hall, Inc., Upper Saddle River, NJ.

Current Issues & Perspectives

High Standards for All Students and Testing Accommodations for Students with Disabilities

In communities across the nation many educational stakeholders want educators to be more accountable and to emphasize "high standards for all students." Assessment programs administrated in many states continue to be part of the evidence used to document what students are learning and how well they are learning it. Unfortunately, not all students have been included in many of the statewide or schoolwide assessment efforts. Participation rates for students during the past several years in statewide assessments have ranged from a low of 41% to a high of 95%. Many of the students who did not participate were students with disabilities or with limited English proficiency. There are several possible reasons for these varying participation rates. However, if educators and other educational stakeholders who aspire to high standards for all students are to have a meaningful picture of how well students are learning and applying valued content knowledge and skills, all students need to be assessed periodically. Ideally, the assessment should be with reliable and valid tests that cover content they have had opportunities to learn!

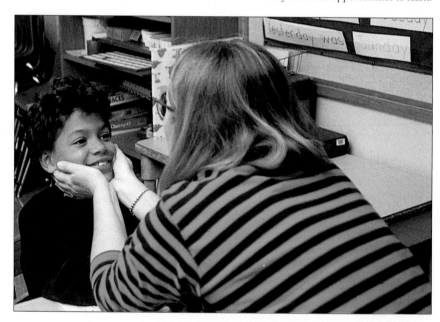

Students with disabilities are now required to be involved in state and districtwide achievement testing programs.

Testing students, making decisions about including students with disabilities in assessment programs, and implementing assessments fairly require teachers' active involvement and can be challenging. Many of the desired skills and much of the information that educators value today are part of content standards that have been developed in the areas of reading, mathematics, language arts, writing, and social studies. The use of results from tests that validly assess what all students know and can do in these content areas is a major component to a common accountability system for all students. Yet compliance with the delivery of required educational services specified on a student's individualized education plan (IEP) has been the major accountability indicator for students with disabilities. Information about all students' educational performance lies at the core of any educational accountability system, and only with public reporting on these performances can policymakers and educators make informed decisions to improve education for all students. At this point in time, results of students' performances on achievement tests have become the most frequently used indicator for accountability purposes. Therefore, when students do not participate in tests used for accountability purposes, there may be less incentive for schools to try to enhance their educational offerings

continued

and improve their performance. Involving all students in assessments is an important aspect of an inclusive education and essential to educational accountability.

One of the most common steps for increasing the meaningful participation of students with disabilities in assessments is allowing testing accommodations. Teachers are very familiar with instructional accommodations, for example, extra time to complete work or a quiet location to minimize distractions, but perhaps teachers are less familiar or comfortable with testing accommodations. *Testing accommodations* are changes in the way a test is administered or responded to by a student. Testing accommodations are intended to offset distortions in test scores caused by a disability, without invalidating (that is, changing what the test measures) the test. Many testing accommodations are allowable, although these differ somewhat across states because of different regulations. However, according to federal legislation, a student's IEP team plays the major role in selecting appropriate testing accommodations for a student with disabilities. Since the passage of federal and state legislation in the 1970s students with disabilities have been guaranteed access to a "free, appropriate, public education." Therefore, when tests and assessment systems are designed to serve as indicators of progress in the subject matter content of a school's curriculum and used to make decisions about future educational services, all students are expected to participate in the assessments as part of their free, appropriate, public education. The legal basis for this position has been established in numerous court cases under the Americans with Disabilities Act of 1990 and, most recently with regard to children with disabilities in the reauthorized version of the Individuals with Disabilities Education Act or IDEA (P.L. 105-17). In the 1997 amendments to IDEA, there are requirements concerning (a) the participation of children with disabilities in general state and districtwide assessment programs, with appropriate accommodations when necessary, (b) documenting in a student's IEP any individual modifications in the administration of state or district tests that measure achievement, (c) documenting in a student's IEP a justification for exclusion from a test and indicating how the student will be assessed with an alternative method, and (d) reports to the public about the participation and performance of children with disabilities with the same details as reports for nondisabled children.

Tests and assessment programs can be altered in a variety of ways to facilitate the participation of students with disabilities. As increasing numbers of students with disabilities are included, it is likely that teachers and other members of IEP teams will need to consider the use of testing accommodations. It is important to understand that accommodations are intended to maintain or facilitate the measurement goals of an assessment, not to modify the actual questions or content of the tests. Accommodations usually involve changes to the testing environment (for example, Braille or large print materials, the amount of time a student has to respond, the quietness of the testing room, assistance in reading instructions) or the method by which a student responds to questions (for example, orally with a scribe, pointing to correct answers). Testing accommodations are legally allowable under all state guidelines and should be determined on a case-by-case basis for each student. Accommodations generally result in some minor changes in the administrative procedures upon which a test was standardized. And consequently, because many educators have been taught to follow standardization procedures exactly, there may be some reluctance to use accommodations. The keys to the appropriate use of accommodations are twofold: (1) recognize that accommodations are intended to make the test a fairer measure of what a student knows or can do and (2) select accommodations that are not likely to invalidate the meaning of a resulting test score or scores. To date, there is not a comprehensive research basis to guide educators' decisions about which accommodations result in invalidating test results. However, if one has a clear understanding of what a test or subtest measures, then many of the decisions about appropriate accommodations become straightforward. For example, having a teacher read to a disabled student questions and answers on a reading test that was designed as a measure of sight vocabulary and comprehension would certainly invalidate the resulting score. Conversely, reading a complex story problem on a test designed to be a mathematics reasoning and calculation test could be appropriate for some students with disabilities.

The construction of a standardized test is an involved and complicated process. Unlike the teacher-made test, a standardized test is usually fashioned by a team of measurement and subject matter experts. Considerable care is taken to ensure comprehensive coverage of a subject (content validity) and to avoid ambiguity and bias in the writing of the individual items. Initially, the test is given experimental trials with representative groups of students to ascertain its suitability, reliability, and validity. As a result of these trials, revisions are made that should result in a highly accurate instrument. Authors of high-quality tests may spend from four to five years developing and refining the test, involving hundreds of subject matter consultants, most of whom are teachers.

Probably the most desirable feature of standardized tests for many consumers is the **norms** supplied with them. Norms enable teachers to interpret the test scores of a class of students or an individual student by comparing them with many other scores derived from a national sample. In the process of standardizing a test, researchers give it to large numbers of subjects who represent the population of students for whom it is ultimately intended. These norm groups should represent the total population with regard to age, sex, race, socioeconomic status, and disability status.

If a test is intended as a fifth-grade arithmetic achievement instrument, it is tried out with as many girl and boy fifth-graders as possible who represent the age range of the typical fifth-grade population, and who also represent urban and rural populations, children with and without disabilities, multicultural students, and the like. Norms, then, provide the normal range of scores for a given population. If a test consists of one hundred items, and the typical 12-year-old correctly answers sixty of these items, the 12-year-olds' average on this test is sixty.

Standardized tests are classified according to what they measure. Teachers generally are concerned with two overall test categories: achievement and aptitude. As we have mentioned, an achievement test measures accomplishment in a specific subject such as reading, arithmetic, language, or science. Aptitude tests are designed to assess students' general and specific cognitive and physical abilities. We examine both achievement and aptitude tests in some detail.

NORMS

Scores on a given test that are derived from an identified sample and are then used as a basis for comparison (and therefore interpretation) of scores on the same test.

Standardized Achievement Tests

Achievement tests attempt to assess the knowledge and skills taught by the school. A standardized achievement test has certain distinctive features, including a fixed set of test items designed to measure a clearly defined area of achievement, specific directions for administering and scoring the test, and norms based on representative groups: groups containing individuals like those for whom the test was designed (Gronlund, 1985, p. 264). Thus, the same content and procedure permit the identical testing of individuals in different places at different times. Students tested in Madison, Wisconsin, can be compared on the same test with students in Austin, Texas, or Newark, New Jersey, or a small rural town in Iowa. Norms, then, enable us to compare an individual's score with those of members of known groups who also have taken the test.

Achievement tests have one main objective: to discover how much individuals have learned from educational experiences. They may be prepared for use throughout the entire school system (for example, everyone studying American history in a particular school district would take the same examination, most likely at the end of the school year), or be prepared by specialists and standardized for national use. Some achievement tests (actually, batteries of tests) cover a number of subjects, like reading, mathematics, and social studies; and others cover specific subjects, such as American history or French.

When achievement tests fit the goals of learning and really measure what students have learned with acceptable accuracy, these tasks have many desirable uses. Probably the most important use is to assess the accomplishment of learning objectives by individual learners. Once teachers have determined students' potential and decided on the objectives of instruction, they should check students' learning progress, usually with teacher-made tests and occasionally with standardized tests.

Standardized achievement tests aid both in the academic guidance of students and in planning curriculum changes. Standardized achievement tests also help in decisions about promotion and admission, since they yield additional evidence from objective sources. The value of a standardized achievement test usually resides in the fact that it samples an extensive range of subject matter and provides norms that enable school systems to compare their students with a comparable sample of students. If such tests are selected in accordance with learning objectives, they can be helpful tools for any school system because they can stimulate an analysis of the effectiveness of the curriculum, materials, and instruction.

Two types of standardized achievement tests currently are popular: multilevel survey batteries, which assess separate curricular topics over a wide range of grades and are group administered, and those designed to measure specific subjects (for example, reading or mathematics) in order to provide detailed diagnostic information about an individual learner. We now examine an example of a multilevel achievement survey battery with the intent of introducing you to some of the important aspects that make for a useful standardized test.

TerraNova Assessment Series

TerraNova (CTB McGraw-Hill, 1997) is the name given to a series of editions (that is, survey, battery, and multiple assessments) of achievement tests designed to assess kindergarten through twelfth-grade students' knowledge in the broad subject matter domains of reading/language arts, mathematics, science, and social studies. Each of these subject matter areas is broken down into subdomains. For example, reading/language arts is comprised of nine subdomains (oral comprehension, basic understanding, analyze text, evaluate and extend meaning, identify reading strategies, introduction to print, sentence structure, writing strategies, and editing skills), as is mathematics (number and number relations; computation and numerical estimation; operation concepts; measurement; geometry and spatial sense; data analysis, statistics, and probability; patterns, functions, and algebra; problem solving and reasoning; communication). Like all high-quality achievement tests, each of these subdomains represents one or more learning objectives and a set of corresponding test items that measure the acquisition of knowledge and skills. Table 12.3 illustrates the various learning objectives and the corresponding subskills assessed within each of the reading/language arts subdomains on TerraNova. Table 12.4 provides a listing of abbreviated objectives and related subskills purportedly measured by the mathematics subtest and the science subtest.

Excellent achievement tests, such as TerraNova, will have multiple test items designed to primarily test each of the objectives within a domain. For example, in Figure 12.2 there are three items all of which are designed to measure problem solving and reasoning. As you can see, two of the items require a student to select the correct response (that is, multiple-choice) from a list of four choices, and one item requires a student to construct a response. The survey editions of the test use only the selected response item format to save administration and scoring time. The multiple assessment edition of TerraNova uses both types of item formats and thus covers more objectives with a greater sample of items.

The items on all the TerraNova tests besides measuring knowledge or skills in a subject matter area were also designed to provide evidence about thinking skills and thinking or problem-solving processes. Specifically, the authors of the test used the Rankin-Hughes Framework of Thinking Skills (Hughes & Rankin, 1987) as a basis for selecting and classifying all test items. This framework identifies skills that make up seven major thinking

Table 12.3 TERRANOVA READING/LANGUAGE ARTS OBJECTIVES
AND SUBSKILLS

01   **Oral Comprehension**
      Subskills: literal; interpretive

02   **Basic Understanding**
      Subskills: sentence meaning; vocabulary; stated information; sequence; initial understand-
      ing; stated information graphics

03   **Analyze Text**
      Subskills: main idea/theme; supporting evidence; conclusions; cause/effect; compare/con-
      trast; story elements—plot/climax/character/setting; literary techniques; persuasive tech-
      niques; nonfiction elements

04   **Evaluate and Extend Meaning**
      Subskills: generalize; fact/opinion; author—purpose/point of view/tone/bias; predict/hy-
      pothesize; extend/apply meaning; critical assessment

05   **Identify Reading Strategies**
      Subskills: make connections; apply genre criteria; utilize structure; vocabulary strategies;
      self-monitor; summarize; synthesize across texts; graphic strategies; formulate questions

06   **Introduction to Print**
      Subskills: environmental print; word analysis; sound/visual recognition

07   **Sentence Structure**
      Subskills: subject/predicate; statement to question; complete/fragment/run-on; sentence
      combining; nonparallel structure; misplaced modifier; mixed structure problems; sentence
      structure

08   **Writing Strategies**
      Subskills: topic sentence; sequence; relevance; supporting sentences; connective/transi-
      tional words; topic selection; information sources; organize information; writing strategies

09   **Editing Skills**
      Subskills: usage; punctuation; capitalization; proofreading

From CTB/McGraw-Hill *Teacher's Guide to TerraNova*. Copyright © 1997. Used by permission of The McGraw-Hill
Companies.

FIGURE 12.2

A sample item from
TerraNova that requires
problem-solving and
reasoning skills (Copyright ©
1997 CTB/McGraw-Hill. All
rights reserved.)

6 Nick wants to send postcards to as many friends of his friends as he can. He has $3.00.
For every postcard he buys, he also needs to buy a stamp. Check the prices above. What is
the greatest number of postcards with stamps that Nick can buy?

     A 3
   ✓ B 4
     C 5
     D 6

Table 12.4 TERRANOVA MATH AND SCIENCE OBJECTIVES AND SUBSKILLS

Mathematics Objectives and Subskills

10   **Number and Number Relations**
Subskills: counting; read, recognize numbers; compare, order; ordinal numbers; money; fractional part; place value; equivalent forms; ratio, proportion; percent; roots, radicals; absolute value; expanded notation; exponents, scientific notation; number line; identify use in real world; rounding, estimation; number sense; number systems; number properties; factors, multiples, divisibility; odd, even numbers; prime, composite numbers

11   **Computation and Numerical Estimation**
Subskills: computation; computation in context; estimation; computation with money; recognize when to estimate; determine reasonableness; estimation with money

12   **Operation Concepts**
Subskills: model problem situation; operation sense; order of operations; permutations, combinations; operation properties

13   **Measurement**
Subskills: appropriate tool; appropriate unit; non-standard units; estimate; accuracy, precision; time; calendar; temperature; length, distance; perimeter; area; mass, weight; volume, capacity; circumference; angle measure; rate; scale drawing, map, model; convert measurement units; indirect measurement; use ruler

14   **Geometry and Spatial Sense**
Subskills: plane figure; solid figure; angles; triangles; parts of circle; point, ray, line, plane; coordinate geometry; parallel, perpendicular; congruence, similarity; Pythagorean theorem; symmetry; transformations; visualization, spatial reasoning; combine/subdivide shapes; use geometric models to solve problems; apply geometric properties; geometric formulas; geometric proofs; use manipulatives; geometric constructions

15   **Data Analysis, Statistics and Probability**
Subskills: read pictograph; read bar graph; read line graph; read circle graph; read table, chart, diagram; interpret data display; restructure data display; complete/construct data display; select data display; make inferences from data; draw conclusions from data; evaluate conclusions drawn from data; sampling; statistics; probability; use data to solve problems; compare data; describe, evaluate data

16   **Patterns, Functions, Algebra**
Subskills: missing element; number pattern; geometric pattern; function; variable; expression; equation; inequality; solve linear equation; graph linear equation; solve quadratic equation; graph quadratic equation; model problem situation; system of equations; use algebra to solve problems

17   **Problem Solving and Reasoning**
Subskills: identify missing/extra information; model problem situation, solution; formulate problem; develop, explain strategy; solve nonroutine problem; evaluate solution; generalize solution; deductive/inductive reasoning; spatial reasoning; proportional reasoning; evaluate conjectures

18   **Communication**
Subskills: model math situations; relate models to ideas; make conjectures; evaluate ideas; math notation; explain thinking; explain solution process

Table 12.4 (CONTINUED)

Science Objectives and Subskills

19   **Science Inquiry**
      Subskills: abilities; understanding

20   **Physical Science**
      Subskills: properties; magnetism; motions and forces; light, heat, electricity; structure of
      atoms; energy; chemical reactions

21   **Life Science**
      Subskills: characteristics of organisms; structure and function; reproduction and heredity;
      population and ecosystems; diversity and adaptations; regulation and behavior; the cell; life
      cycles; organisms and environments

22   **Earth and Space Science**
      Subskills: properties of Earth materials; objects in the sky; changes in Earth/sky; Earth's his-
      tory; Earth in the solar system; Earth system; the universe; geochemical cycles

23   **Science and Technology**
      Subskills: natural/synthetic; abilities of technological design; understanding science/tech-
      nology

24   **Personal and Social Perspectives in Science**
      Subskills: personal/community health; population; natural resources; environmental qual-
      ity; risks/benefits; science/technology in society

25   **History and Nature of Science**
      Subskills: science as a human endeavor; nature of science; history of science

From CTB/McGraw-Hill, *Teacher's Guide to TerraNova.* Copyright © 1997. Used by permission of The McGraw-Hill
Companies.

FIGURE 12.3

A Sample Item from
TerraNova That Requires
Idea-Generating Skills
(Copyright © 1997
CTB/McGraw-Hill. All rights
reserved.)

> **Read the story and then choose the best answer to the question. (Student reads a story.)**
>
> **How would the tiger most likely behave if he were a student in school?**
>
> **A He would make fun of the teacher.**
> **B He would ignore unpopular students.**
> ✔ **C He would be friendly when he needed a favor.**
> **D He would force classmates to help him pass a test.**

processes: focus, gather information, organize information, analyze information, generate
ideas, synthesize elements, and evaluate outcomes. These thinking skills cut across the various subject matter domains and provide another way to examine the content of Terra-
Nova. Examples of a test item that primarily represents the thinking skill of generating
ideas are illustrated in Figure 12.3, and an item that primarily involves the thinking skill of
evaluating outcomes is displayed in Figure 12.4.

A Spanish version of TerraNova called Supera is also available. We will revisit the
TerraNova test later in this chapter when we discuss the scoring, interpretation, and
communicating results of achievement tests. Let's now examine standardized aptitude
tests and compare them with achievement tests.

Read the question and then choose the best answer.

Which of these would help you determine whether a plant is pollinated by the wind or by insects?

A Grow the plant indoors.
B Bring the plant indoors at night.
✔ C Tie insect netting around the plant outdoors.
D Tie a clear plastic bag around the plant outdoors.

FIGURE 12.4

A Sample Item from TerraNova That Requires Outcome Evaluation Skills (Copyright © 1997 CTB/McGraw-Hill. All rights reserved.)

CASE NOTES

Observation Melissa Williams values critical thinking and problem-solving skills in her students and has designed her classes in English and social studies to emphasize such skills.

Hypothesis Melissa would value an achievement test, like the TerraNova, that provides an interpretative framework for analyzing students' responses in skill areas such as critical thinking and problem solving. Such a test would be more closely aligned with her instructional approach and the content of her English and social studies classes.

Possible Action Consider reviewing the test manual for the standardized achievement test that the district administers each year to determine if an interpretive framework like that devised by Hughes and Rankin (1987) is available with it. If not, consider meeting with the district's evaluation specialists and test selection committee to share concern about the limitations of the existing test.

Standardized Aptitude Tests

Aptitude tests are used to predict what students can learn. Aptitude tests do not measure innate capacity or learning potential directly; rather, they measure performance based on learning abilities (Gronlund, 1985, p. 295). Intelligence tests are perhaps the best example of aptitude tests commonly used in schools. It is interesting to note some differences between aptitude and achievement tests. An aptitude test predicts an individual's performance in a certain task or in a particular job by sampling the cumulative effect on the individual of many experiences in daily living, including specific educational experiences. Make no assumption, however, that aptitude tests measure only innate capacity, while achievement tests measure only the effects of learning. Any psychological test reflects the influence of past experience on present performance.

While research supports the relationship between intelligence and achievement (general measures of ability predict learning performance quite well), specific abilities (such as an aptitude for mathematics) vary within each individual. Personal experience testifies to specific strengths and weaknesses within one person. Some readers of this chapter undoubtedly freeze at the sight of numbers, while others possess little, if any, artistic ability. It is the totality or pattern of performance on measures of general ability that is significant for understanding the achievement-intelligence relationship.

TIPS ON MOTIVATION AND ASSESSMENT
Creating Fair Assessments for All Students

PRINCIPLE   Assessment instruments and uses of assessment results should be fair to all students. Assessments are fair when every student has received equitable and adequate schooling, including sensitive curriculum, instruction, and assessment. When students perceive assessments to be unfair, they are less motivated to participate, and their performances will not represent what they really have learned.

STRATEGY   Educators should select tests that have been developed by professionals to reduce or eliminate insensitive content or language. Usually a representative panel of teachers, with knowledge of and sensitivity to the array of individual differences characterizing the students who will take the test, should review the content of the test.

STRATEGY   Educators should review research on standardized tests, specifically noting the performances of students of different race, gender, and ethnic backgrounds. Differences in the performances of groups of students are not always indications of bias, but they are signs that further examination of the test content and format needs to be studied carefully to determine the source of the differences.

STRATEGY   Educators should consider testing accommodations for students with disabilities that allow a student to participate but do not invalidate the intended purpose of the test. The instructional accommodations used by teachers are a good place to look for possible appropriate testing accommodations. Fair accommodations are adjustments in the testing procedures or format, not in the content, that allow a student to demonstrate knowledge or a skill.

Intelligence, IQ Tests, and Fundamental Assessment Issues

Intelligence tests have been one of the most frequently used tests to understand children's cognitive functioning and are administered to nearly 20% of all schoolchildren each year. But is IQ testing a worthwhile exercise? There is a wide range of opinion among educators and psychologists about the value of intelligence testing. Here is what some noted scholars have said about the construct of intelligence and the use of tests to measure it:

> *The IQ test has also played an important part in the American school system especially in assigning lower class and minority children to dead-end classes for those with mild mental disabilities. (L. Kamin, 1981)*

> *IQ is a questionable measure of general intelligence and a minor determination of success. (Robinson, 1973)*

> *IQ jointly with scholastic performance predicts more of the variance among persons in adult occupational status and income than any other known combination of variables, including race and social class or origin. (Jensen, 1980)*

> *If . . . the impression takes root that these tests really measure intelligence, that they constitute a sort of last judgment on the child's capacity, that they reveal "scientifically" his predestined ability, then it would be a thousand times better if all the intelligence testers and all their questionnaires were sunk without warning in the Sargasso Sea. (Lippmann, 1976)*

Intelligence is a very general mental capability that, among other things, involves the ability to reason, plan, solve problems, think abstractly, comprehend complex ideas, learn quickly and learn from experiences. It is not merely book learning, a narrow academic skill, or test-taking smarts. Rather, it reflects a broader and deeper capability for comprehending our surroundings—"catching on," "making sense" of things, or "figuring out" what to do. (Gottfredson, 1997)

The outstanding success of scientific measurement of individual differences has been that of the general mental test. Despite occasional over enthusiasm and misconceptions and the fact that the established tests are rendered obsolescent by recent conceptual advances, the general mental test stands today as the most important technical contribution psychology has made to the practical guidance of human affairs. (Cronbach, 1970)

Who is correct? Should these tests that purport to measure cognitive abilities and general intelligence be abolished or are they useful tools for understanding people? Although there is much debate among experts about the value of intelligence tests, the general public appears to believe that intelligence does play a role in the behavior and decision making of individuals, and intelligence testing has gained widespread acceptance in most places in the United States because it plays a central role in the classification of individuals with cognitive disabilities (that is, learning disabilities and mental retardation). There still are, however, many misconceptions about what intelligence is and what IQ tests measure. This is true among not only measurement experts, many psychologists, and educators but also the general public. For example, parents have become increasingly concerned with providing the optimal environment for their infants and preschoolers to maximize intellectual potential, and as children grow older teachers and parents often want to know their child's IQ score. A trip to your favorite bookstore is likely to reveal a number of books concerned with "increasing your child's IQ" or computer software for "testing your own intelligence in 15 minutes by asking yourself only five simple questions." This fascination with IQ measurement has not occurred without concern. A few of the most critical issues associated with the measurement of intelligence have involved its stability, bias measurements, and poor instructional utility or validity. Each of these issues are examined after we look at one of the most popular intelligence tests, the *Wechsler Intelligence Scale for Children-III.*

The Wechsler Intelligence Scale for Children-III: An Example of an Aptitude Test

In recent years the most widely administered test of cognitive ability with school-age children has been the Wechsler Intelligence Scale for Children-Revised (WISC-R) (Wechsler, 1974). The original WISC was designed as a downward extension of the adult intelligence scale that David Wechsler developed (the Wechsler Bellevue Intelligence Scale) while working at Bellevue State Hospital in New York. The general format and item content on the WISC-III remain similar to earlier editions of this test. The WISC-III is administered individually by a qualified examiner (who is usually a psychologist) and requires sixty to ninety minutes. The WISC-III is designed for children from 6 to 17 years of age and aims to provide a global measure of intelligence that taps "many different mental abilities, which all together reflect a child's general intellectual ability" (Wechsler, 1991, p. 1). The test is comprised of thirteen subtests, six in a Verbal Scale and seven in a Performance Scale. All instructions are given orally and all subtests on the Verbal Scale require oral responses. Performance subtests have time limits, and in some cases bonus points are provided for quick, accurate responses. Arithmetic is the only timed subtest on the Verbal Scale.

The Verbal Scale is composed of the following subscales: Information (thirty questions requiring general knowledge of facts), Similarities (nineteen pairs of words requiring

Intelligence tests require individualized conditions and highly trained examiners to ensure meaningful results.

an indication of how the items are similar), Arithmetic (twenty-four arithmetic problems requiring a response without the aid of paper and pencil), Vocabulary (thirty words requiring definitions or synonyms), Comprehension (eighteen problem situations requiring solutions or an understanding of social rules), and Digit Span (forward and backward repetition of digits).

The Performance Scale is composed of the following subscales: Picture Completion (thirty drawings of common objects, all of which require the identification of a missing essential element), Coding (symbols such as vertical lines and circles are to be matched to specific numbers according to a key available for the individual to review and examine), Picture Arrangement (a series of pictures requiring placement in a logical, ordered sequence), Block Design (twelve abstract designs to be copied using two-colored blocks), Object Assembly (five jigsaw puzzles of common objects requiring assembly), Symbol Search (a series of paired groups of symbols with the child scanning each group to assess whether or not a target symbol appears in the search group), and Mazes (eight mazes requiring a child to mark the way out without being blocked).

Not all items on the WISC-III are administered to each child. Each subtest has specific rules about where to begin and end, depending on the age or assumed ability of the child. The specificity of administration and scoring directions provided in the manual generally are considered assets of the WISC-III. Wechsler originally divided his tests into verbal and performance sections based on his conceptualization of intelligence, and he placed subtests that he believed involved primarily verbal or performance abilities into each domain. Many subsequent studies (see, for example, Kaufman, 1979) have generally supported the verbal/performance organization of the test.

The WISC-III remains a model of standardization procedures. It was standardized on 2,200 children selected to be representative of the U.S. population based on data gathered in 1988 by the U.S. Bureau of the Census. The sample was stratified on the basis of geographic region, age, gender, parent education, and race/ethnicity. Data were gathered in thirty-one states. Two hundred children (a hundred boys and a hundred girls) were tested at each of eleven different ages, with the median age at each age level being the sixth month of that age range. Raw scores on each subtest are first changed into normalized standard scores (scaled scores) with a mean of 10 and a standard deviation of 3. The scaled subtest scores are then added and converted into deviation IQs (standard scores) for the Verbal, Performance, and Full Scales. Verbal Scale IQ, Performance Scale IQ, and Full Scale IQ each have a mean of 100 and a standard deviation of 15. A child's "test age" for each subtest can be obtained, and a mean or median test age for each of the scales can be calculated. With this revision, the examiner is also able to calculate four "factor-based scores," including Verbal Comprehension, Perceptual Organization, Freedom from Distractibility, and Processing Speed. These scores also have a mean of 100 and a standard deviation of 15.

From a technical perspective, the WISC-III is a sound instrument. Although recently revised, preliminary information suggests that it will be widely used and that obtained scores will be moderately related to school achievement. The Wechsler tests are the standard against which other measures of cognitive abilities have been judged for the last three decades. Revised and restandardized in 1974 and again in 1991, the format and many items on the WISC-III are unchanged from the original WISC published in 1949. Pictures and some items have been updated and new norms provided. Much has been learned about the nature of cognitive abilities in the last thirty years, yet the design and purpose of the WISC-III has changed little. Many of the problems associated with earlier editions do not seem to have been addressed with the current revision of this test.

Stability of IQ

As a result of the popularization of intelligence tests and the intelligence testing movement, numerous misconceptions about the nature of intelligence developed and were fed by overzealous testers and a misinformed public. One of the most pervasive ideas, which became solidly entrenched in public opinion, was the notion that an infant was born with a certain amount of "intelligence" that did not change as the child grew older. As with many myths, this one was supported with a grain or two of truth. In general, most research has suggested that IQ tests do tend to yield scores that are fairly stable. However, this same research indicates that IQs are more stable over shorter as opposed to longer periods and more stable for older children and adults than for children under 6 years of age. A good deal of evidence indicates that IQ scores obtained before children enter kindergarten or first grade are not highly reliable. No one knows exactly to what extent intelligence scores can be altered through environmental manipulation. Although studies in the late 1960s and early 1970s (for example, the Milwaukee Project) reported that intensive early intervention in children's lives (such as Head Start programs) was capable of producing incredible increases in measured IQ, such studies have been severely criticized (Sommer & Sommer, 1983). Despite this criticism, most experts would agree that enriched environments are better than impoverished ones for fostering intellectual development.

Data on the relative stability of IQ can be deceiving and must be interpreted with care. When looking at the IQ scores of large groups of individuals, we can make the general statement that most of those within the group would receive similar scores if retested. However, it is not at all unusual for particular individuals to show a great deal of variability in their scores. Changes of 8, 10, 15, or even 30 IQ points are not unheard of, and authors of this text have tested children who exhibited these types of changes. This potential for intraindividual difference in IQ scores during different testing sessions means that when examining test results, we must not assume that a child who obtained an IQ in a certain range of intelligence will always remain in that range.

Table 12.5 DIFFERENT TYPES OF BIAS IN TESTS	
Type	**Definition**
Mean differences	Average scores for various groups (such as black, white, and Hispanic or rich and poor) are different.
Item/content bias	Portions of test content are biased in a manner that differentially affects the performance of certain groups (such as black and white, or men and women).
Factor analysis	The factors (for example, verbal abilities or attention) being measured are different for various racial, cultural, or economic groups.
Predictive validity	Scores predict with varying levels of confidence for different groups.
Social consequences	Tests are misused or misinterpreted to justify restrictive social policies.
Selection ratios	Test results are used in ways that cause particular groups to be over- or underrepresented in special classes or certain diagnostic categories (for example, mentally disabled).

Source: Witt et al. (1998).

Bias in Testing

No issue related to the assessment of intelligence has generated as much or as heated debate as the question of whether IQ tests are biased against individuals from minority cultures or different racial groups. Discussions in the popular press have vehemently assailed most aptitude and achievement tests as being unfair to children from backgrounds that are different from those of most middle-class white Americans. Numerous researchers have investigated the issue of bias in mental tests, with the greatest amount of attention focused on the differences between the performance of black and white students (Gottfedson, 1997; Neisser et al., 1996). Some people have turned to the courts for help in determining whether IQ tests are biased and whether they should be used in the assessment of minority children, but the courts have not been consistent in their findings (see for example, *Larry P. v. Riles,* 1986; *PASE v. Hannon,* 1980).

Many different types of test bias have been identified, and these have been discussed at length by both proponents and opponents of cognitive ability testing. Table 12.5 lists and defines the most common types of test biases that have been studied. As indicated by this table, there is no universally accepted definition of bias. However, most definitions hold that a test can be considered biased if it differentiates between members of various groups (for example, between men and women or between blacks and whites) on bases other than the characteristic being measured. That is, a test is biased if its content, procedures, or use results in a systematic advantage or disadvantage to members of certain groups over other groups *and* if the basis of this differentiation is irrelevant to the test purpose.

An examination of the research and writings related to bias in cognitive ability testing reveals that the issues are very complex, not easily resolved, and complicated by the emotional intensity with which individuals have advanced their arguments in this area. Given society's attention to the issue of equality, the different performances on IQ tests by different groups, and the fact that the developmental history of these tests has been dominated by whites, it is not surprising that so many people believe so strongly that these tests must be biased against minorities and in favor of whites. In fact, little evidence supports the belief of bias in intelligence tests. First, although it is true that blacks average lower intelligence scores than whites, this is not enough information to conclude that the tests are biased, especially when socioeconomic status is considered. The tests may be biased, but first we must determine if the differences in scores reflect true differences in the ability being measured. Tests are designed to discriminate, that is, to identify good spellers from poor ones, to predict success or failure in graduate school or in a job as a bank teller, and to determine those who have learned the material in history class and those who have not. Simple differences in average scores alone do not prove that bias exists. The fact that you may consistently obtain lower scores than a friend in history class does not mean that the instructor or the tests are biased. Other factors must be studied to reach that conclusion.

In the case of intelligence tests, one must investigate their content, construct, and predictive validity. That is, you have to examine whether the test items are biased in favor of one group, whether the test measures the same abilities for all groups, and whether the test predicts equally well for all groups. The technical evidence overwhelmingly indicates that the vast majority of items used on tests such as the Wechsler and Binet are not biased, that these tests tend to measure the same factors (verbal, perceptual, performance, quantitative, or the like) and predict success equally well for all racial groups (Reynolds, 1992). *This last point is critical. It is important to remember that IQ tests do not measure the amount of some innate, immutable ability that we all possess but do provide a general measure of expected school achievement,* just as they were designed to do in the early 1900s. The evidence on predictive validity suggests that whether someone is African American, Caucasian, Latino, or Asian does not really matter: An individual with an IQ score of 60 from a reliable test is at risk of failing in most every public educational system, and an individual with a score of 140 is likely to do well in that same system. The research indicates that these tests, although not perfect predictors, are not biased and that race has little to do with the accuracy with which these tests predict. Therefore, when we say that the difference in the average IQ scores of blacks and whites is not due to test bias, we are not asserting that blacks are less intelligent than whites, but that they are more likely to experience problems in our educational system. Nor does the failure to find bias in these tests explain why one group obtains higher scores than another, and whether that difference is due to a biased school system, cultural deprivation (or advantage), or as some have asserted, genetic differences. We only know that in general the tests do a fair job of what they were designed to do—*predict school achievement.*

Although we have concluded, based on a comprehensive review of the research literature, that most intellectual or cognitive ability tests are not biased, it is very evident that these instruments have occasionally been used in a biased fashion. *While it may be true that most intelligence tests are free of bias; it is also true that these tests have been used to discriminate.* To see that these tests are used fairly and judiciously, they must be revised frequently to make sure that they reflect the most-advanced understanding of the nature of cognitive abilities, that they utilize appropriate methodologies for assessing cognitive skills, and that the norms are representative of the groups of students one wishes to serve. In addition, individuals using the test must be well trained and able to administer them appropriately.

Instructional Validity and Applications of Results

Our review of the measurement of intelligence revealed that some commonly held beliefs about negative aspects of IQ tests can be called into question. We have concluded that most measures of intellectual or cognitive ability yield reliable results, that they are reasonably good predictors of achievement levels, and that they are essentially free of bias. This last factor has been especially satisfying to those who have suggested that most of these tests validly estimate the cognitive abilities of minority populations. One cannot help but wonder, however, if there is not a more subtle, more damaging problem in how these tests have been used in educational, clinical, and vocational settings. We are specifically speaking of the question of instructional validity, or the ability of a test to lead to better treatments, such as more effective educational programs or better counseling or teaching strategies (Gresham, 1992). Although many educators

Much can be learned by observing teachers and learners interacting.

and researchers have tried, there simply is no clear evidence that test results yielded by general measures of intelligence can be directly translated into effective educational or clinical programs (Kramer, Henning-Stout, Ullman, & Schellenberg, 1987).

It is important to remember that these types of tests were developed to provide educators with general predictions of success in the educational system, not to enable educators or psychologists to design effective remedial strategies for individual children. Although we can be relatively confident that children who score in the superior (or gifted) range of intelligence will do better in school than those who score in the intellectually disabled range, we are challenged to design individualized educational programs for either gifted or mentally disabled children based on their particular pattern of scores or their overall intelligence test performance. *Intelligence tests were not created for the purpose of designing prescriptive instructional interventions, and attempts to make them into tools for specific instructional planning have failed miserably.*

The Intelligent Use of Intelligence Tests

Given the previous examination of IQ tests, one may reasonably ask, "Why would anybody use an intelligence test?" The answer is because the concepts of intelligence and intellectual or cognitive functioning (however ill-defined) are central elements in the definition of several Individuals with Disabilities Education Act categories of disabilities, in particular specific learning disabilities and mental retardation (McDonnell et al., 1997). Thus, for many school psychologists and members of multidisciplinary teams who are required to make decisions about disability classifications and eligibility for special education, the results of an IQ test seem to be useful indicators of a child's intellectual functioning level. As long as classifications of disability are required for special education, it is likely that many service providers will feel the need to use IQ tests. Currently, there aren't well-validated alternative assessment tools for measuring cognitive functioning with the goal of classification in mind. Therefore, when IQ tests are used, it is important to remember that they *should only be used after* (a) there has been a detailed assessment of classroom functioning and (b) it is proven that placement in the regular classroom will not help a student. In addition, it should always be noted that IQ tests provide only *one piece of evidence* about how a child learns and the

TIPS ON COMMUNICATION
Best Practices in Reporting Intelligence Test Results

PRINCIPLE   A "Surgeon General's" warning should be formulated to protect children and youth from unwarranted inferences about their intellectual abilities and to remind everyone involved of the developmental nature of measured abilities.

STRATEGY   Educators must be aware and communicate that it is *inappropriate* to conclude that (a) intellectual abilities are determined by genetic factors, (b) IQ scores reflect all of intelligent behavior, and (c) performance on intellectual measures is fixed and unchanging.

STRATEGY   Educators should prepare a written statement that appears on test reports and in students' permanent folders:

> *IQ tests measure only a portion of the competencies involved in human intelligence. The IQ results are best seen as estimates of likely performance in school and reflections of the degree to which children have mastered the middle class cultural symbols and broad culturally rooted facts, concepts, and problem-solving strategies. This information is useful but limited. IQ tests do not reflect innate genetic capacity and the scores are not fixed. Some persons do exhibit significant increases or decreases in their measured intellectual abilities. (Reschly, 1979, p. 224)*

nature of any disability he or she may exhibit. This evidence is of limited value in the best of circumstances, and of *no value when the goals of special education services are to determine effective instructional methods and improve achievement.* Intelligence tests have not been designed to facilitate these goals—remember that (a) no evidence exists that supports the use of intelligence tests to design instructional interventions, and (b) intelligence tests are general measures of cognitive functioning, not curriculum-sensitive indicators of specific academic skills.

BEHAVIOR RATING SCALES: SUMMARIZING OBSERVATIONS OF STUDENTS' BEHAVIOR

Up to this point in our examination of testing and assessment, we have focused on the evaluation of children's academic and cognitive skills. As you know, however, children's social skills and emotional characteristics also influence their schooling. Teachers and parents, given their many opportunities to observe and interact with children, have often played a significant role in the assessment of children's inter- and intra-personal skills. Behavior rating scales have become one of the most popular and efficient assessment methods for gathering input from teachers and parents about a child's social-emotional functioning. Rating scales such as the Child Behavior Checklist (Achenbach & Edelbrock, 1986) and the Social Skills Rating System (Gresham & Elliott, 1990) are used in many schools with students from kindergarten through twelfth grade. Both these instruments are well developed, focus on a wide range of behaviors, and provide normative information about the social-emotional functioning of students. Many other rating scales that are used in schools focus on specific areas of functioning (for example, adaptive behavior, self-concept, motivation) or problems (for example, depression, anxiety, fears, hyperactivity) (Witt et al., 1998).

A typical behavior rating scale includes a list of items that clearly describes particular behaviors (for example, Shares materials with friends willingly; Follows directions; Teases other children) and ask a respondent to indicate how frequently the child exhibits the behaviors (for example, 0 = Never; 1 = Sometimes; 2 = Very Often; 3 = Always). Table 12.6 illustrates two items from a social skills rating scale. In addition to requesting information about the frequency of the described behavior, this rating scale asks the teacher-respondent to provide information about "how important" the behaviors are to functioning in that person's classroom. Most rating scales provide norms, so the results for a child can be compared with those of a sample of students of a similar age and the same sex. Well-constructed rating scales have the potential to facilitate communication among individuals interested in the assessment of particular children and to provide useful diagnostic information. Although rating scales appear straightforward, a closer look is required, to ensure that their strengths and weaknesses are understood.

Behavior rating scales have proliferated during the past ten years. This growth in objective rating scales seems to have been fueled by their ease of use, the need for more teacher and parent involvement in assessment and intervention activities, and generally improved reliability and validity information (Edelbrock, 1983; Wilson & Bullock, 1989).

Uses of Rating Scales

Traditionally, rating scales have been used primarily as part of the screening and identification process for children referred for possible special education services. Secondarily, rating scales have been used, albeit often inappropriately, to monitor behavior changes as a result of an intervention. Rating scales also have played a central role in the classification of childhood social-emotional disorders (for example, Achenbach & Edelbrock, 1983; Elliott & Gresham, 1989) and the validity of teachers' judgments of students' achievement (for example, Hoge & Coladarci, 1989). In addition to these well-established uses of behavior rating scales, they can have other uses, depending on the scale and the approach to service delivery. Practitioners who emphasize a prereferral intervention and/or consultation approach to service delivery should find rating scales to be a primary assessment tool (Witt et al., 1998). A rating scale can be used to facilitate a prompt reaction to a referral from a teacher or parent. For example, a rating scale that assesses hyperactivity can be a starting point for discussion with the child's parents. This practice of having a rating scale completed and interpreted before a meeting with a teacher or a parent often has several positive effects. These include precise, behavior-specific discussions and time-efficient interviews that focus more on problem analysis than on problem identification. When the rating scale used has sound, representative norms, it also facilitates understanding of the **social validity** of the referral problem. A fi-

SOCIAL
VALIDITY

The applied, or social, importance of exhibiting certain behaviors in particular situations.

Table 12.6 EXAMPLE OF ITEMS AND RATING FORMAT ON A BEHAVIORAL RATING SCALE

	How Often?			How Important?		
	Never	Sometimes	Very Often	Not Important	Important	Critical
Shows empathy for peers.	0	1	(2)	0	(1)	2
Asks questions of you when unsure of what to do in schoolwork.	0	(1)	2	0	1	(2)

This student *very often* shows empathy for classmates. Also, this student *sometimes* asks questions when unsure of schoolwork. This teacher thinks that showing empathy is *important* for success in his or her classroom and that asking questions is *critical* for success.

From Gresham and Elliott, *Social Skills Rating System.* Copyright © 1990 American Guidance Service, Circle Pines, Minnesota.

nal use is for purposes of documentation and accountability regarding regular teacher and parent involvement in the identification of a child's problem. In some cases, the child also is able to play an active role in the problem identification process through self-ratings.

Rating scales, of course, have some limitations or disadvantages, of which all users should be aware. McConaughy's list of disadvantages (1993) represents a good summary that deserves some comment and elaboration. She accurately noted that rating scales are measures of current or recent functioning, but they do not provide information on causes of problems. She also noted that scores on existing problem-focused rating scales do not dictate choices for intervention. Although this latter disadvantage generally is characteristic of rating scales, there are some published rating scales (for example, the *Social Skills Rating System*) that have direct conceptual and practical links to interventions. A third disadvantage that McConaughy indicated as characteristic of rating scales is that they involve perceptions of problems rather than truly "objective" measures of such problems. The practical ramification of this distinction is that one must confirm any rating scale results with an additional form of assessment, such as direct observation and/or clinical interviews. Multiple assessment methods and sources are always recommended best practices in addressing social-emotional difficulties.

In summary, rating scales have many potential positive uses in the delivery of psychoeducational services in schools. Primarily, these uses involve primarily the enhancement of problem-identification activities involving teachers and parents. The use of any rating scale is influenced by its particular characteristics and by some basic interpretive issues. Hence, we explore these next.

Characteristics and Interpretation Guidelines

Most rating scales have an appearance of simplicity due to the ease with which they can be administered and scored. But in terms of reliability and validity characteristics and of interpretation, rating scales are decidedly complex instruments. To conclude this section on behavior rating scales, we focus on four issues influencing the use and interpretation of behavior rating scales:

1. Ratings are summaries of observations of the relative frequency of specific behaviors. In reality, for example, one student may exhibit turn-taking behavior three times a day, whereas a second student may exhibit the same turn-taking behavior one time a day. These students exhibit different rates of turn-taking behavior, yet their teacher, when asked to complete a three-point rating scale

---

CASE NOTES

Observation   Melissa is concerned about the classroom behavior of Jim Watson and two other male classmates. This concern is manifested in attempts to alter classwork and to hold a meeting with her colleagues to discuss their experiences with these students. She has also spoken with the boys' parents.

Hypothesis   Melissa believes in open communication and seeks others' perspectives when she is confronted with a problem. An examination of behavior across environments (that is, classes and home) also can provide insights into possible variables that influence the behaviors of concern.

Possible Action   Consider using a behavior rating scale, like the Social Skills Rating System, to collect information from the other teachers, the boys' parents, and themselves. This information can be collected efficiently and provide some ideas for interventions that might be effective at increasing work completion and decreasing classroom disruptions.

(0 = Never; 1 = Sometimes; 2 = Very Often), is likely to characterize both students with a rating of 1. As illustrated, the precision of measurement with rating scales is relative, not exact, and needs to be supplemented by more direct methods if specific frequency counts of a given behavior are necessary.

2. Ratings of social behavior are evaluative judgments affected by the individual's environment and the rater's standards for behavior. Researchers and laypersons alike are aware that an individual's social behaviors may change depending on the situation in which the person is functioning. Such variability in behavior highlights the role one's environment (that is, people and places) plays in determining behavior. This has led researchers to characterize many social behaviors as situationally specific behaviors rather than traits (Achenbach, McConaughy & Howell, 1987; Kazdin, 1979). In addition to environmental influences, the standards of behavior established by the adults who regulate the settings largely determine the social behaviors deemed more important in one setting than in another.

3. Multiple assessors of the same child's social behavior may agree only moderately. This guideline is based on the facts that many social behaviors are situationally specific, that all measures of behavior have error in them, and that rating scales use rather simple frequency scales for quantifying behaviors that actually may vary widely in frequency, intensity, and duration. The work of Achenbach and his associates (1987) and McConaughy (1993) provides empirical support for this position of moderate agreement among raters of the same behaviors.

4. Many personal characteristics may influence the child's social behavior; however, the student's sex is a particularly salient variable. Researchers interested in children's social competence and social-emotional functioning have identified variables such as physical attractiveness, athletic abilities, language skills, family background, and gender as variables that can influence the judgments of others when evaluating social behaviors (Halle, 1985; Hops & Finch, 1985). Of all these characteristics, a student's gender is the one that consistently appears to be associated with differences in social behavior.

INTERPRETING STANDARDIZED TEST SCORES

Let us assume that students in an elementary school recently have taken a standardized achievement test, and a copy of the results is sent to you as their teacher. The students could receive several kinds of scores: raw scores, percentiles, grade equivalents, or standard scores. Since these scores are probably unfamiliar to most readers, we examine the meaning of the various scores and the uses to which they can be put. If test results are to provide the best information possible, then you must have some means of telling whether a score is good or poor. You usually cannot do this by looking at the raw score (the number of correct items on each of the subtests), although this gives some information, as we will see. Raw scores are converted into derived scores, which often are more meaningful and tell you more about a student's performance (Lyman, 1998).

Kinds of Scores

RAW SCORE
Uninterpreted data; often, the number of correct items.

A raw score may be difficult to interpret. If an arithmetic test contains 50 items and a student scores 32, that student's **raw score** is 32. What does this tell you? You probably think immediately that this student knew more than half the answers. But how did the other students do? You don't know. Was it an easy or difficult test? You don't know unless you can compare scores.

To help you make sense of the raw scores of all your students, you could rank them from highest to lowest. This ranking would enable you to interpret a score in relation to other scores.

Assume that the score of 32 is the average raw score for the group taking this test. These are fifth-grade students. The month is September. Thus, 32 is the **grade equivalent score** of 5.0 for that test. It is a mistake to assume that a student who has a grade equivalent score of 7.2 on this test should be working at a seventh-grade level. The score means that this student's performance on fifth-grade material is equal to the performance of a student in the second month of the seventh grade on fifth-grade material (Bloom, Madaus, & Hastings, 1981). It tells you that your fifth-grade student knows this subject thoroughly. It does not say that this same student has mastered seventh-grade or even sixth-grade material. These scores seem easy to interpret, but they are just as easily (and often) misinterpreted. Of greater interpretative value are derived standard scores, which we will examine shortly.

You probably are comfortable with a scoring system that assigns the highest score a rank of 1, the second-highest a rank of 2, and the like. **Percentiles** work in a way similar to this, except that the lowest percentile rank appears at the bottom of the scores. For example, a percentile score of 74 means that this student has done as well as or better than 74% of all the other students taking the test. If the student's raw score of 32 mentioned earlier placed her 40th from the bottom in a class of 50, her percentile rank would be computed like this:

$$\tfrac{40}{50} \times 100 = 80$$

This student would be at the 80th percentile, having done as well as or better than 80% of the students. Be careful how you use this score with parents who may interpret it as a grade of 80%.

Working with many numbers is cumbersome, time-consuming, and prone to misinterpretation. Consequently, we should search for techniques to organize our data. We often want to organize and summarize data. The first step usually entails constructing a **frequency distribution,** which indicates the frequency with which a particular score appears in a score category. In the preparation of a frequency distribution, the scores typically are grouped by intervals, and each test score is assigned to the proper interval. Table 12.7 illustrates this procedure; here, the scores range from a low of 10 to a high of 21, and the number of individuals achieving each score is provided in the frequency column.

Now that we have grouped the data, we want to use the groupings. A basic way of describing the scores is to give the average score. Are you of "average height"? Although most people understand the meaning of "average," there are three **measures of central tendency** (or average): mode, median, and mean.

The **mode** is that score obtained by the largest number of students. Once you have finished a frequency distribution, you can determine the mode simply by looking at the frequency column. In Table 12.7, the mode is 11, which 36 individuals earned.

The **median** is that point in the distribution above which exactly 50 percent and below which exactly 50 percent of the cases lie. In Table 12.7, look up the frequency column until you find half the scores accounted for. What is the median score? (Answer: 15.5.)

The **mean** is the average of the raw scores, arrived at by adding all the scores and dividing by the number of scores. The formula for calculating the mean is

$$\overline{X} = \Sigma X / N$$

where $\overline{X}$ is the mean score, Σ is the sum of all the scores, and N is the total number of scores. Table 12.8 illustrates the process using a sample data set.

These measures of central tendency provide a good idea of how any student has done in relation to the average score of the group. When the scores are normally distributed, all three measures of central tendency are equal. When the distribution of scores is skewed or unbalanced (for example, when there are two or three very high scores and the remainder of the scores in a typical class are much lower), the median is a more representative score than the mean.

GRADE EQUIVALENT SCORE

A standardized test score that describes a student's performance on a scale based on grade in school and month in grade; most commonly misinterpreted score; actually indicates student's level of performance relative to students in his or her own grade.

PERCENTILES

A score that tells the percentage of individuals taking a test who are at or below a particular score; a percentile rank of 74 means that this student did as well or better than 74% of those taking the test.

FREQUENCY DISTRIBUTION

A record of how often a score appears in a score category.

MEASURES OF CENTRAL TENDENCY

The mean, the median, or the mode are all a score that represents a distribution of scores.

MODE

The score obtained by the largest number of individuals taking a test.

MEDIAN

That point in the distribution above which 50 percent and below which 50 percent of the scores lie.

MEAN

The average of the raw scores.

Table 12.7 A TYPICAL FREQUENCY DISTRIBUTION

Scores	Frequency
21	2
20	1
19	6
18	10
17	20
16	19
15	16
14	22
13	5
12	27
11	36
10	27

Source: Witt et al. (1998).

Table 12.8 CALCULATING THE MEAN

$$9$$
$$4$$
$$4$$
$$3$$
$$3$$
$$3$$
$$1$$
$$9$$
$$7$$
$$\underline{7}$$
$$50$$

Using the formula for the mean:

$$\Sigma \frac{X}{N} = X$$

then $\quad X = \dfrac{50}{10} = 5$

Source: Witt et al. (1998).

To further an understanding of any particular score, we need a method that will provide constancy, that is, a score not affected by the length of the test or the difficulty of the items. Glasnapp and Poggio (1985) defined standard as constant across different times and situations. **Standard scores** have this quality; they offer a constant definition and interpretation. How is this possible? Standard scores relate to the normal curve, a theoretical mathematical model based on the assumption that most human characteristics are distributed normally. The **normal curve** is a representation showing the normal distribution of a particular trait. Figure 12.5 illustrates the normal curve.

Look at the baseline of the normal curve. You see a series of numbers ranging from +1 to +4 and from −1 to −4. Each number represents a **standard deviation unit.** These tell us how much a score varies from the mean. Look again at Figure 12.5: Note that over 68% of the scores fall between +1 and −1 standard deviation units from the mean; over 95% of the scores fall between +2 and −2 standard deviation units from the mean. Once the mean and standard deviation are computed, we can use them to derive several standard scores: z-scores, t-scores, and stanine scores.

A **z-score** is the fundamental standard score, which tells us the distance of a student's raw score from the mean in standard deviation units. Here is an example: The raw score on a reading test was 78; the mean was 72; the standard deviation was 24. The raw score minus the mean equaled 6; it was divided by a standard deviation of 24 to equal +.25. This student

STANDARD SCORES
Any of several derived scores (any score other than a raw score) based on the number of standard deviations between a specified raw score and the mean of the distribution.

NORMAL CURVE
A representation showing the frequency distribution of a particular trait or ability for a particular group.

STANDARD DEVIATION UNIT
Measure of how much a score varies from the mean.

Z-SCORE
A score that tells the distance of a student's raw score from the mean in standard deviation units; has a mean equal to 0 and a standard deviation equal to 1.

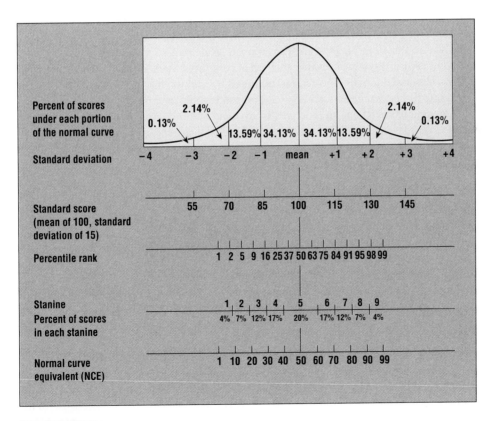

FIGURE 12.5

The Normal Curve and Its Relationship to Various Derived Scores

Normal Distribution
For many kinds of tests, developers often make the assumption that individual test scores have an approximately bell-shaped, or normal, distribution. The figure above illustrates, for a normal distribution, the relationship between standard scores and other derived scores: percentile ranks, stanines, and normal curve equivalents.

> ### CASE NOTES
>
> **Observation**   The average test performance for the students in the house headed by Bill Drake and Sara Ellis over the past three years has been among the highest in the state.
>
> **Hypothesis**   The students in these classes compared with other students in the district and state have strong competencies in the areas of language arts, social studies, mathematics, and science, yet we do not actually know what students know and don't know, nor at what level of proficiency they performed. If one wants to know this type of information, one would be wise to use a criterion-referenced test.
>
> **Possible Action**   Concerns about what the general results actually mean for individual students and for teachers working with them are well founded given the lack of specific mean scores, standard deviations, and normative group. In addition, the lack of a clear criterion of performance also limits the interpretation of the test results to norm-reference comparisons to groups of other students. Consumers of test results need specific information about the performances of the students taking the test and the comparison group.

had a z-score of $+.25$. The z-score informs us that the raw score was a little above average (one-fourth of a standard deviation unit). Thus, by looking at a z-score, you can tell quickly how a student has done on a test and can compare students across classes.

T-SCORE

A standard score with a mean of 50 and a standard deviation of 10.

STANINE SCORES

A standard score that classifies those taking a test into one of nine groups.

The **t-score** offers an alternative method of computing standard scores that avoids negative z-scores and decimals. T-scores are computed by multiplying the standard score by 10 and adding 50. Let us take a z-score of -1.5. The result would be this: $10 \times (-1.5) + 50 = 35$.

Stanine scores (the term is derived from "standard nine") were devised during World War II to classify pilots as quickly as possible. Those taking the tests would be classified into one of nine groups. A stanine has a mean of 5 and a standard deviation of 2. Stanine 5 includes the middle 20% of the scores. The ideal percentage for each stanine is as follows (Lyman, 1998):

	Lowest 4%	Next 7%	Next 12%	Next 17%	Middle 20%	Next 17%	Next 12%	Next 7%	Highest 4%
Stanine	1	2	3	4	5	6	7	8	9

As you can see, this is a quick means of classification and is easily understood. If you tell parents that their child is in the ninth stanine, with nine as the highest, they can readily grasp the meaning. Figure 12.5 illustrates how these various scores relate to one another.

Assume that one of your students has a raw score of 300 on a particular test and that the mean for the test is also 300. This can be transformed into a percentile rank of 50, a z-score of 0.00, a t-score of 50, and a stanine of 5. You would be wise to familiarize yourself with these scores, since almost all standardized tests use one or more of them.

STANDARD ERROR OF MEASUREMENT

An estimate of the standard deviation that would be found on the distribution of scores for a specified person if that person were to be tested repeatedly on the same or similar test.

Before leaving the topic of scores, it is critical for all consumers of test results to remember that tests are only samples of behavior and that all scores possess some error. Since a student's score from a single test may not represent the student's true ability, it is useful to get a sense of how accurate the score may be. The **standard error of measurement** (SEM) is an estimate of the amount of error you can expect in a test score. This statistic provides a range within which a student's true score is likely to fall. A student's score on any test, therefore, should be regarded as an estimate within a range that probably includes the student's true score, rather than an exact value. It is expected that 68% of the time a student's score obtained from a single test would fall within one SEM of that student's true score and that 95%

Teachers often can learn a lot about their students if they examine test data closely.

TIPS ON ASSESSMENT

Interpreting Test Results

PRINCIPLE Test users must understand what a test measures and how to correctly interpret the resulting scores, keeping in mind that some error exists in all scores.

STRATEGY Test users must obtain information about the scale used for reporting scores, the characteristics of any norms or comparison group(s), and limitations of the scores. Avoid using grade equivalent scores.

STRATEGY Interpret scores taking into account any major differences between the norm group and the actual test takers.

STRATEGY Avoid using tests for purposes not specifically recommended by the test developer unless evidence is obtained to support the intended use.

STRATEGY Test users should be able to explain how any passing scores were set and gather evidence to support the appropriateness of the scores. Ideally, the standard error of measurement will be taken into consideration when setting passing scores.

of the time the score would fall within two SEMs of the true score. The smaller the SEM, the more accurate or reliable the test score. The SEM should always be taken into account when interpreting test scores. The use of SEMs is illustrated in the next section when we examine the reporting practices for TerraNova, the achievement test we examined earlier.

Reporting Test Results

Let's now examine how some of the types of scores we have been talking about get used to communicate students' performances on tests. We will use the reporting forms from the TerraNova achievement battery introduced earlier in this chapter to illustrate the type and range of information communicated with teachers, students, and parents. Figures 12.6 and 12.7 provide examples of an Individual Profile Report (IPR) and an Objectives Performance Index (OPI), respectively. These report forms are commonly the types most scrutinized by teachers.

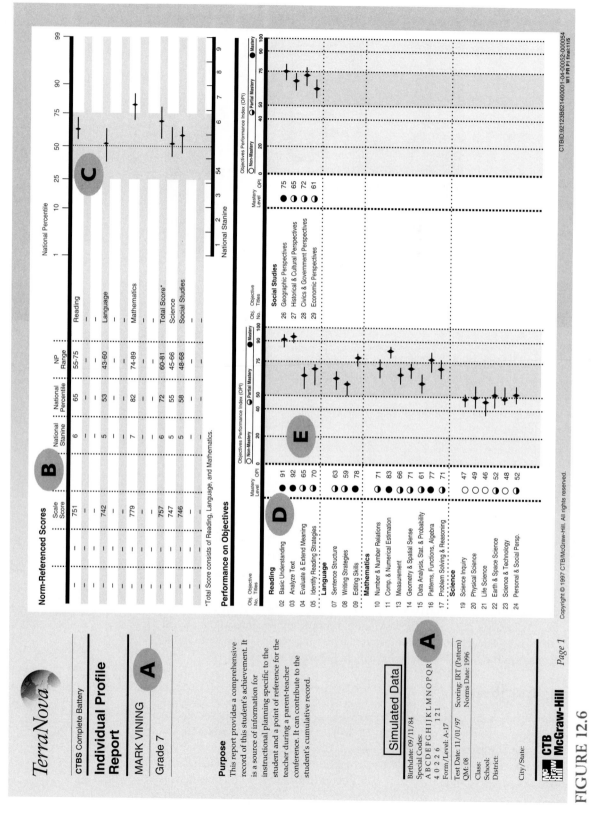

FIGURE 12.6

From CTB/McGraw-Hill, *Teacher's Guide to TerraNova.* Copyright © 1997. Used by permission of the McGraw-Hill Companies.

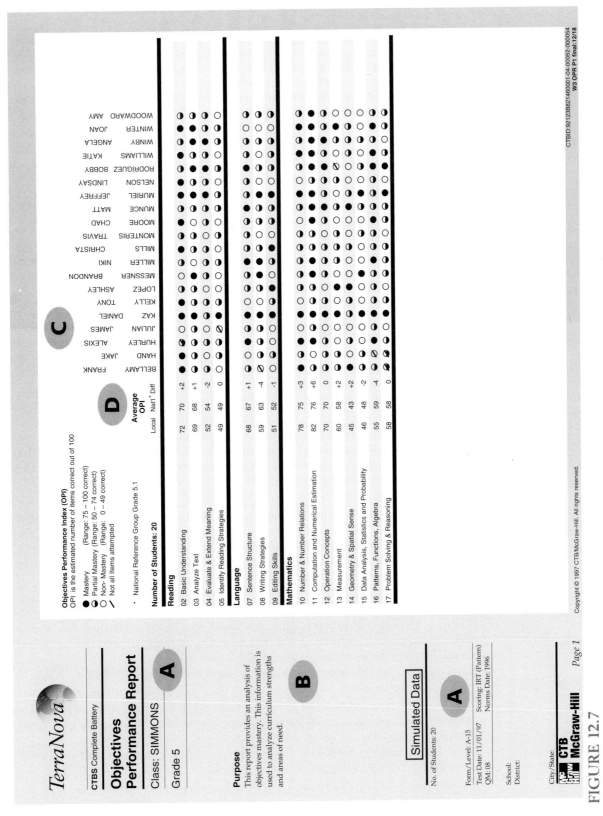

FIGURE 12.7

From CTB/McGraw-Hill, *Teacher's Guide to TerraNova.* Copyright © 1997. Used by permission of the McGraw-Hill Companies.

The IPR provides a complete record of a student's test performance, including general information about the student's strengths and needs in major content areas and specific information about the student's mastery of objectives. Consequently, it is a useful tool for general curricular planning and for organizing feedback about a student for a parent-teacher conference. The letter areas A–E in Figure 12.6 indicate several aspects of the IPR worth noting. The student's name and grade are listed prominently (see point A) along with a summary of the various norm-referenced scores for each subject matter area (see point B). Note that the SEM has been used to create a range for the national percentile scores (NP range) and these are translated into a graphic picture of the student's performance (see point C), where the diamond figure represents the student's observed score and the horizontal line indicates the range of scores representing $\pm$ 1 SEM. Note also that scores on this graph can be transformed easily into national stanines by using the line graph running along the bottom of area C. In the lower part of the report, specially areas D and E, the student's performance is characterized in terms of the objectives measured by TerraNova. This results in an OPI for each subject matter area. This index estimates the number of items that a student could be expected to answer correctly if there had been 100 such items for the objective. For example, Mark Vining had an OPI of 91 on Reading Objective 02: Basic Understanding. This indicates that Mark could be expected to answer correctly ninety-one out of one hundred items for that knowledge/skill area, had there been that many items of that type. In actuality, there were only 10 items measuring that knowledge/skill area. The graphic portrayal of the OPI again uses a SEM to indicate the range of probable functioning and characterizes performances at one of three levels of mastery: nonmastery, partial mastery, or mastery (see point E). An OPI of 75 or higher indicates mastery, an OPI between 50 and 74 indicates partial mastery, and an OPI of 49 or less indicates nonmastery. Note that each knowledge/skill area is accompanied by an icon (small circle) indicating the student's mastery level: a fully shaded circle represents mastery, a half-shaded circle shows partial mastery, and an unshaded indicates circle nonmastery. According to Mark's IPR, he has mastered six of the TerraNova objective areas. To identify skills and concepts on which to focus instruction and review, his teacher might consider the areas for which he demonstrated partial mastery (fourteen areas) and nonmastery (four areas).

Building on the IPR, a summary of the objectives mastered by an entire class is possible. Figure 12.7 provides an OPI for a fifth-grade class taught by Ms. Simmons. Of particular importance in this figure is information highlighted as points C and D. The information under point C is a listing of individual student's educational strengths and weaknesses as characterized according to levels of mastery. By reading across the rows of the report (extending from the content area objectives) one can identify potential instructional priorities. For example in Ms. Simmons's class of twenty students, it looks like many students would benefit from more mathematics instruction in the content areas of measurement; geometry and spatial sense; and data analysis, statistics, and probability. This report also shows the average OPI on each objective for the students in the local group and in the national norm group (see point D). The difference between the two groups is shown as a positive or negative number. A positive difference indicates that the performance of the local group was higher than that of the national group. The average OPIs for the local group provide a frame of reference for interpreting each individual student's OPI.

Parents usually get a copy of a test score report. In some cases, they will be provided a detailed report, such as the IPR. In other cases, they will be given more general information, such as that illustrated by the TerraNova Home Report (see Figure 12.8).

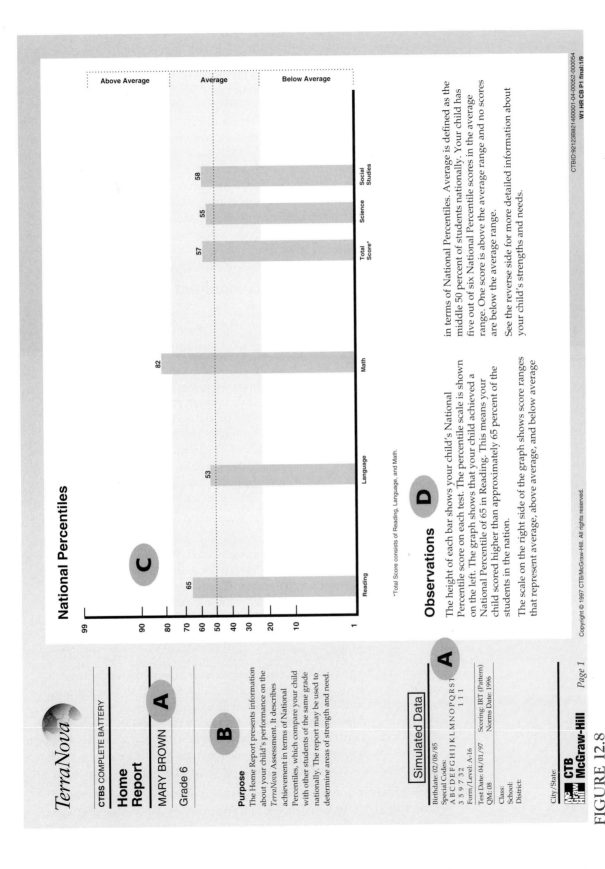

FIGURE 12.8

From CTB/McGraw-Hill, *Teacher's Guide to TerraNova.* Copyright © 1997. Used by permission of the McGraw-Hill Companies.

USING STANDARDIZED TESTS

A major concern about standardized tests is how to obtain the most helpful information from them to aid students. One way of accomplishing this is to compare the results with the learning objectives of your school or classroom. Understanding the potential uses of test results is a major step in actively applying their results to the classroom.

We have all heard reports about how standardized tests such as the California Achievement Test (now TerraNova) or Scholastic Aptitude Test (SAT) are used to form opinions about the state of education. The SAT recently was revised to include longer reading passages, vocabulary testing in the context of reading, interpretation of mathematical data, and the opportunity to work out mathematical problems rather than select options from a multiple-choice format, among other changes (Moses, 1991). Yet, in general, standardized tests have changed very little, in spite of widespread usage, continuing controversy about usage and interpretation, advances in statistical techniques, and improved test construction (Linn, 1986; Wiggins, 1993).

Educational Applications of Standardized Testing

Institutional concerns about efficiency, tracking, and selection mainly have been responsible for the popularity of standardized tests. One of the major reasons standardized tests have been widely accepted has been their educational application. Five major uses have been identified (Linn, 1986):

1. *Special education placement.* Tests that predict academic achievement (IQ tests) have played central roles in decision making about student placement. Many questions have been raised about this policy, and a particular concern has been expressed about the large numbers of minority children placed in special education classes. Do these tests lead to bias in decision making about minorities? Court decisions have both affirmed (*Larry P. v. Riles,* 1979/1986) and denied (*PASE v. Hannon,* 1980) that IQ tests are biased; the question is still unanswered.

2. *Student certification.* At one time, a high school diploma was a sign that, based on teacher grades and the satisfaction of course requirements, the school testified to a student's ability to perform adequately at a satisfactory level. Now, more and more states are turning to minimum competency tests (MCTs) to provide evidence for certification. Here, our interest lies in the ability of these tests to furnish convincing evidence concerning students' minimal satisfactory performance. Although student scores in those states using MCTs have risen rather dramatically, several questions remain. Would other tests of the same content produce the same results? Have thinking skills improved similarly? Are teachers teaching for the tests?

3. *Teacher testing.* Recently, national concern has been expressed over teacher competency, with regard not only to initial certification but also to continued employment. Heated political debates have emerged in the wake of questions about teacher competency. Our interest focuses on the *means* used to judge a teacher's instructional ability. Should the means be a national test or the judgment of others? In both instances, the key requirement must be that the knowledge and skills assessed are actually those required for competent job performance.

4. *Educational assessment and accountability.* This idea—making decisions about schools based on testing students—is far from new. The comparison of students from a particular school to national norms traditionally has appealed to many

educators. Though student scores may seem a fragile foundation on which to make judgments, sophisticated item analysis techniques have greatly enhanced and lent support to such a use of test scores.

5. *Instructional guidance.* As testing technology has improved, standardized tests more frequently have been used as diagnostic guides. When a combination of tests providing more detailed information is enriched with insights derived from cognitive psychology (see Chapter 7), sharper diagnostic distinctions are possible.

Common Criticisms of Standardized Tests

Though we have emphasized the positive aspects, standardized testing has had its share of criticism. The most common criticisms of standardized tests come from classroom teachers. These criticisms seem to focus on the pressure that tests exert on the curriculum, the danger of labeling students, and the accompanying side effects of worry and anxiety. Criticisms of standardized academic and cognitive tests in the classroom can be summarized by the following eight statements (Kellaghan, Madaus & Airasian, 1980; Wiggins, 1994):

1. Testing limits teaching, in the sense that instructors teach for the test, thus restricting students' experiences.

2. Testing produces rigid grouping practices. Students are assessed, and the resulting label causes an inflexible classification.

3. Testing lowers student achievement. Testing takes time away from instruction, especially if time is taken to practice for the test. Some teachers also have a tendency to concentrate on bright students, since their scores appear easier to raise.

CASE NOTES

Observation   Melissa is concerned that her colleagues are placing too much emphasis on the district's end-of-year achievement test and, consequently, are encouraging her to do the same. This makes her feel as if the test publishers have more to say about what she should teach than she does.

Hypothesis   When teachers believe that the content covered on a standardized test is more important than the material in class, they become frustrated with the test and the testing process. In fact, they may not even use the test results to guide future instructional efforts because they do not believe it is a valid indicator of achievement.

Possible Action   Consider exploring the test's content closely to determine the current extent of overlap between what is tested and what is taught. In fact, teachers are encouraged to "take" the test as a means of familiarizing themselves with the content and the kinds of decision-making skills required to be successful. They also are encouraged to examine the performances of some of their students on each item of the test to get a better sense of what they are learning and what they are struggling to understand. These types of interactions with a well-developed test usually result in some newfound appreciation for the test and some adjustments in the alignment between what is taught and what is tested.

Tests can arouse anxiety or fears in some students, but the majority of students readily engage in tests that are extensions of what they have worked on in class.

4. Tests lead to labeling students. This common danger can easily influence teacher expectations and leads to the difficulties posed in statement 2.

5. Testing arouses negative emotional feelings. We have commented frequently on such test related feelings as fear, anxiety, and competitiveness.

6. Testing may negatively affect a student's self-concept. Given the reality of students who "freeze" during testing, test results may not reflect actual ability. Yet students will believe "the score," causing lowered self-esteem, with all its attendant consequences.

7. Test scores do not directly influence teaching. Test scores provide little relevant information about individual students, revealing only how they compare with other similar students. We have mentioned this previously, when noting the efforts of test publishers to provide more penetrating diagnostic tools.

8. Tests often do not measure what was taught. This statement, which is a common criticism by teachers and students, reinforces statement 1: Teachers frequently feel compelled to teach for the test.

Given the advantages and disadvantages of standardized tests, it is now time to focus on the resulting "best practices." We believe that standardized tests have a significant role in educational psychology and effective teaching. As with almost anything else, however, one must be cautious and use good judgment to achieve maximum results from the use of standardized tests.

Best Practices

Standardized tests have generated concerns on the part of many educators. We believe, however, that (1) many of these concerns are the result of poor testing practices or misunderstanding the purposes of tests and that (2) standardized tests will continue to have a central place in students' education. Recognizing this, a joint committee on testing practices from major educational and psychological associations developed the *Code of Fair Testing Practices in Education* (American Educational Research Association, 1988). The code contains standards for educational test developers and users in four categories: developing/selecting tests, interpreting scores, striving for fairness, and informing test-takers.

The code is meant for the general public and is limited to educational tests. It supplements the more technical *Standards for Educational and Psychological Testing* (American Psychological Association, 1985). We have reprinted the four sections of the code in their entirety in the appendix to this chapter. It serves as an appropriate conclusion to this chapter on standardized testing, for it reminds us that tests affect everybody (developers, users, and students), and that their use requires significant knowledge and skill on the part of educators.

CONCLUDING THOUGHTS ABOUT THE VALUE OF STANDARDIZED TESTS

This chapter has focused on the development, use, and interpretation of standardized assessment instruments. Achievement tests, intelligence tests, and most behavior rating scales are representative examples of standardized tests frequently used in schools. Most of these tests have been designed by test experts and allow users to compare scores of a given student or group of students to a normative group of students. Thus, most standardized tests are considered norm-referenced tests. There are, however, some standardized tests that have been designed to allow users to compare a student's score to a preestablished criterion of performance. Such tests are referred to as criterion-referenced tests.

Most standardized tests yield a variety of scores that are based on a normal distribution of scores. Consequently, knowledge of the normal curve and measures of central tendency (mean, median, and mode) are very helpful when it comes to interpreting the general performance of a student on a test that uses scale scores and percentiles as the primary method of summarizing results.

Tests can be useful educational tools if used wisely. When misused, however, they can cause many problems for both teachers and students. Intelligence tests are perhaps the most frequently criticized type of standardized test because of concerns about bias, stability of IQ, and limited instructional utility. Today there is much disagreement about the value of intelligence tests. Consequently, we have seen an increase in the use of large-scale achievement batteries and behavior rating scales and checklists. These assessment instruments are seen as being more curriculum relevant and content valid.

Although teachers have been shown to be highly accurate judges of students' academic and social behavior, standardized tests of students' abilities will continue to play an important role in education because of increasing demands for accountability and communication about students' achievements. Professional associations of educators and psychologists have developed guidelines to encourage fair testing practices and standards to guide the development of high-quality tests. Clearly, knowledge of tests and test interpretation is an important aspect of being an effective teacher and consumer of research on the effectiveness of education.

Case Reflections

The five notes summarizing possible actions with regard to Melissa Williams and her seventh-grade class in the DEW House all concerned assessment and the use of either a large-scale achievement test or a behavior rating scale. Melissa seems to have several concerns about the school's annual achievement test. These include the time of administration of the test, the alignment between what she teaches (both the content and thinking skills) and what is covered on the test, and the meaningfulness of the resulting scores. It was recognized that she is only one teacher and she is working in a school system that seems to value the use of an annual group achievement test. Although all of Melissa's concerns are reasonable, she is unlikely to single-handedly change the system given its history of "successes" on the norm-referenced test. She, however, could be encouraged to pursue several actions to try to improve her situation. First, she needs to truly be informed about what is on the test so she can get an accurate sense of the alignment between what she emphasizes in her classes and what is covered on the test. Just because a test uses a multiple-choice or selected response format does not mean that it cannot do a reasonable job of assessing higher-

level thinking skills that require the integration and application of knowledge and skills. Melissa was encouraged to study the test's manual and to actually take a form of the test as a means of fully informing herself of the content knowledge and cognitive processes required to be successful. She was also encouraged to go beyond summary test scores and actually review some of her students' item level responses so she can understand how they performed. After becoming more familiar with the test, it was recommended she speak with the district's evaluation specialists or test selection committee, if she still has concerns about the test. Her concerns about the late spring administration of the test and the reporting of only group mean scores are common concerns of educators who want to use test results to guide instruction. The current testing time frame and reporting practices seem to serve administrators' accountability needs but have limited value for teachers who are directly working with students.

With regard to Melissa's ongoing concerns about Jim Watson and his two classmates who are misbehaving and not completing a high percentage of their work, it was suggested that she consider using a behavior rating scale to formalize input from her teaching colleagues and the boys' parents. Some rating scales also can be completed by students themselves. The use of rating scales can facilitate communication and focus attention on objectively defined behaviors of concern. This ideally will lead to a better understanding of the potential problem behaviors and provide documentation of the concerns should a more formal evaluation become necessary.

Standardized tests and testing practices are part of the communication and accountability systems in schools. Thus, teachers like Melissa need to understand these assessment tools and what they can and cannot do to facilitate their job of teaching. If Melissa follows up on some of the recommended actions, she will in all likelihood improve her understanding of testing and its important role in effective teaching.

CHAPTER HIGHLIGHTS

A School's Testing Program

- The use of standardized tests is integral to the educational purposes of the entire school system and should serve the needs of its students at all levels.

- A well-designed standardized testing program serves three purposes: instructional, guidance, and administrative.

- The value of standardized tests lies in their consistency or sameness, which provides a means of comparing students.

- The norms that accompany standardized tests enable teachers, counselors, and other educators to interpret test scores by comparing them with the scores of other students, taken from a comparison sample.

- A norm-referenced test enables the teacher to compare a student with a representative group of students who have already taken the test.

- A criterion-referenced test enables the teacher to determine if a student has achieved competence at one level of knowledge or skills before moving on to the next higher level of content.

Standardized Tests

- Standardized achievement tests are designed to assess the knowledge and skills taught by schools. The value of these tests is in their assessment of the development of individual learners at different ages and in different subjects.

- Standardized aptitude tests are used to predict what students can learn; they provide assessments of performance based on learning abilities.

- Although a clear definition of intelligence has remained elusive, attempts to measure it have produced some of psychology's most colorful, damaging, and useful insights into human behavior.

- Three important issues concerning the use of intelligence tests involve the stability of IQ test results, bias results for different ethnic groups, and the instructional validity or the usefulness of results. In general, researchers have found that well-constructed IQ tests yield stable results for children older than 7 years old, are generally relatively free from bias, and have limited instructional utility for educators. They are most useful in the process of classifying a student as mentally retarded or learning disabled, given current classification criteria.

- In spite of the problems that have been encountered in attempts to measure intelligence, several reasonable suggestions have been made as to fruitful uses of the results of intelligence testing. Properly interpreted, these scores can help teachers to improve their instruction; IQ scores are a good guide for initial efforts at grouping students; several of these tests can be used to identify students' needs; teachers can use test results to monitor school progress to determine if these students are doing as well as possible, given what the tests indicate about their abilities.

Behavior Rating Scales: Summarizing Observation of Students' Behavior

- Behavior rating scales are commonly used to identify potential problem behaviors in students referred for special services. Teachers and parents are frequently asked to complete scales concerning a wide range of intrapersonal and interpersonal behaviors exhibited by children in situations at school and in the community.

- A behavior rating scale provides information about the frequency of potential problem behaviors and often compares the ratings of a student to those of a group of students of the same age and sex. Thus, some behavior rating scales are used to classify children's problems.

Interpreting Standardized Test Scores

- To utilize the results of standardized testing as fully as possible, the teacher must have some means of interpreting students' scores. Several meaningful techniques are available that can help to analyze scores and organize data so that the results of testing can be applied to classroom work. These include standard scores, percentile ranks, and knowledge of the normal distribution.

Using Standardized Tests

- The possible uses of standardized tests include student certification, special education placement, the testing of teachers, assessing the success of a school, and instructional assistance.

- Clear standards as guides to the best practices in test construction have been proposed for test developers.

WHAT DO YOU THINK?

1. What do you see as the advantages of a criterion-referenced test compared with a norm-referenced test?

2. Intelligence is a complex and controversial construct. What is your definition of intelligence and what is the best way to measure it?

3. From your perspective, what is the most salient criticism of standardized tests?

4. What kind of information would you need to use the results of a standardized achievement test to inform your teaching of students?

5. From your perspective, what are the major limitations in using behavior rating scales to evaluate students?

APPENDIX:

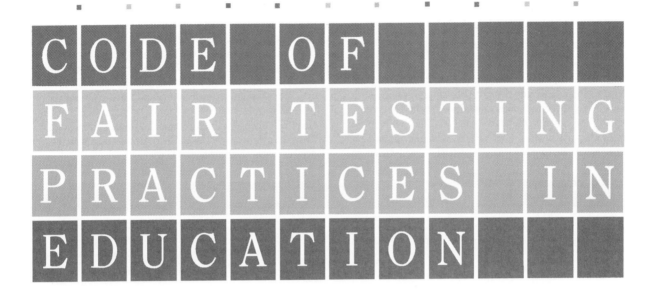

Prepared by the Joint Committee on Testing Practices

The Code of Fair Testing Practices in Education states the major obligations to test takers of professionals who develop or use educational tests. The Code is meant to apply broadly to the use of tests in education (admissions, educational assessment, educational diagnosis, and student placement). The Code is not designed to cover employment testing, licensure or certification testing, or other types of testing. Although the Code has relevance to many types of educational tests, it is directed primarily at professionally developed tests such as those sold by commercial test publishers or used in formally administered testing programs. The Code is not intended to cover tests made by individual teachers for use in their own classrooms.

The Code addresses the roles of test developers and test users separately. Test users are people who select tests, commission test development services, or make decisions on the basis of test scores. Test developers are people who actually construct tests as well as those who set policies for particular testing programs. The roles may, of course, overlap as when a state education agency commissions test development services, sets policies that control the test development process, and makes decisions on the basis of the test scores.

The Code has been developed by the Joint Committee on Testing Practices, a cooperative effort of several professional organizations, that has as its aim the advancement, in the public interest, of the quality of testing practices. The Joint Committee was initiated by the American Educational Research Association, the American Psychological Association and the National Council on Measurement in Education. In addition to these three groups, the American Association for Counseling and Development/Association for Measurement and Evaluation in Counseling and Development, and the American

Speech-Language-Hearing Association are now also sponsors of the Joint Committee.

This is not copyrighted material. Reproduction and dissemination are encouraged. Please cite this document as follows:

Code of Fair Testing Practices in Education. (1988) Washington, D.C.: Joint Committee on Testing Practices. (Mailing Address: Joint Committee on Testing Practices, American Psychological Association, 750 First Avenue, NE, Washington, D.C., 20002-4242.)

Code of Fair Testing Practices in Education

The Code presents standards for educational test developers and users in four areas:

- **A.** Developing/Selecting Tests
- **B.** Interpreting Scores
- **C.** Striving for Fairness
- **D.** Informing Test Takers

Organizations, institutions, and individual professionals who endorse the Code commit themselves to safeguarding the rights of test takers by following the principles listed. The Code is intended to be consistent with the relevant parts of the *Standards for Educational and Psychological Testing* (AERA, APA, NCME, 1985). However, the Code differs from the Standards in both audience and purpose. The Code is meant to be understood by the general public; it is limited to educational tests; and the primary focus is on those issues that affect the proper use of tests. The Code is not meant to add new principles over and above those in the Standards or to change the meaning of the Standards. The goal is rather to represent the spirit of a selected portion of the Standards in a way that is meaningful to test takers and/or their parents or guardians. It is the hope of the Joint Committee that the Code will also be judged to be consistent with existing codes of conduct and standards of other professional groups who use educational tests.

A   Developing/Selecting Appropriate Tests*

Test developers should provide the information that test users need to select appropriate tests.	Test users should select tests that meet the purpose for which they are to be used and that are appropriate for the intended test-taking populations.

Test Developers Should:

1. Define what each test measures and what the test should be used for. Describe the population(s) for which the test is appropriate.

2. Accurately represent the characteristics, usefulness, and limitations of tests for their intended purposes.

3. Explain relevant measurement concepts as necessary for clarity at the level of detail that is appropriate for the intended audience(s).

4. Describe the process of test development. Explain how the content and skills to be tested were selected.

5. Provide evidence that the test meets its intended purpose(s).

6. Provide either representative samples or complete copies of test questions, directions, answer sheets, manuals, and score reports to qualified users.

7. Indicate the nature of the evidence obtained concerning the appropriateness of each test for groups of different racial, ethnic, or linguistic backgrounds who are likely to be tested.

8. Identify and publish any specialized skills needed to administer each test and to interpret scores correctly.

Test Users Should:

1. First define the purpose for testing and the population to be tested. Then, select a test for that purpose and that population based on a thorough review of the available information.

2. Investigate potentially useful sources of information, in addition to test scores, to corroborate the information provided by tests.

3. Read the materials provided by test developers and avoid using tests for which unclear or incomplete information is provided.

4. Become familiar with how and when the test was developed and tried out.

5. Read independent evaluations of a test and of possible alternative measures. Look for evidence required to support the claims of test developers.

6. Examine specimen sets, disclosed tests or samples of questions, directions, answer sheets, manuals, and score reports before selecting a test.

7. Ascertain whether the test content and norms group(s) or comparison group(s) are appropriate for the intended test takers.

8. Select and use only those tests for which the skills needed to administer the test and interpret scores correctly are available.

---

*Many of the statements in the Code refer to the selection of existing tests. However, in customized testing programs test developers are engaged to construct new tests. In those situations, the test development process should be designed to help ensure that the completed tests will be in compliance with the Code.

Interpreting Scores

| Test developers should help users interpret scores correctly. | Test users should interpret scores correctly. |

Test Developers Should:

9. Provide timely and easily understood score reports that describe test performance clearly and accurately. Also explain the meaning and limitations of reported scores.

10. Describe the population(s) represented by any norms or comparison group(s), the dates the data were gathered, and the process used to select the samples of test takers.

11. Warn users to avoid specific, reasonably anticipated misuses of test scores.

12. Provide information that will help users follow reasonable procedures for setting passing scores when it is appropriate to use such scores with the test.

13. Provide information that will help users gather evidence to show that the test is meeting its intended purpose(s).

Test Users Should:

9. Obtain information about the scale used for reporting scores, the characteristics of any norms or comparison group(s), and the limitations of the scores.

10. Interpret scores taking into account any major differences between the norms or comparison groups and the actual test takers. Also take into account any differences in test administration practices or familiarity with the specific questions in the test.

11. Avoid using tests for purposes not specifically recommended by the test developer unless evidence is obtained to support the intended use.

12. Explain how any passing scores were set and gather evidence to support the appropriateness of the scores.

13. Obtain evidence to help show that the test is meeting its intended purpose(s).

 Striving for Fairness

| Test developers should strive to make tests that are as fair as possible for test takers of different races, gender, ethnic backgrounds, or handicapping conditions | Test users should select tests that have been developed in ways that attempt to make them as fair as possible for test takers of different races, gender, ethnic backgrounds, or handicapping conditions. |

Test Developers Should:

14. Review and revise test questions and related materials to avoid potentially insensitive content or language.

15. Investigate the performance of test takers of different races, gender, and ethnic backgrounds when samples of sufficient size are available. Enact procedures that help to ensure that differences in performance are related primarily to the skills under assessment rather than to irrelevant factors.

16. When feasible, make appropriately modified forms of tests or administration procedures available for test takers with handicapping conditions. Warn test users of potential problems in using standard norms with modified tests or administration procedures that result in non-comparable scores.

Test Users Should:

14. Evaluate the procedures used by test developers to avoid potentially insensitive content or language.

15. Review the performance of test takers of different races, gender, and ethnic backgrounds when samples of sufficient size are available. Evaluate the extent to which performance differences may have been caused by inappropriate characteristics of the test.

16. When necessary and feasible, use appropriately modified forms of tests or administration procedures for test takers with handicapping conditions. Interpret standard norms with care in the light of the modifications that were made.

Code of Fair Testing Practices in Education . . . .

 D **Informing Test Takers**

> Under some circumstances, test developers have direct communication with test takers. Under other circumstances, test users communicate directly with test takers. Whichever group communicates directly with test takers should provide the information described below.

Test Developers or Test Users Should:

17. When a test is optional, provide test takers or their parents/guardians with information to help them judge whether the test should be taken, or if an available alternative to the test should be used.

18. Provide test takers the information they need to be familiar with the coverage of the test, the types of question formats, the directions, and appropriate test-taking strategies. Strive to make such information equally available to all test takers.

> Under some circumstances, test developers have direct control of tests and test scores. Under other circumstances, test users have such control. Whichever group has direct control of tests and test scores should take the steps described below.

Test Developers or Test Users Should:

19. Provide test takers or their parents/guardians with information about rights test takers may have to obtain copies of tests and completed answer sheets, retake tests, have tests rescored, or cancel scores.

20. Tell test takers or their parents/guardians how long scores will be kept on file and indicate to whom and under what circumstances test scores will or will not be released.

21. Describe the procedures that test takers or their parents/guardians may use to register complaints and have problems resolved.

■   ▫   ■   ■   ■   ▫   ■   ■   ■   ▫   ■

Note: The membership of the Working Group that developed the Code of Fair Testing Practices in Education and of the Joint Committee on Testing Practices that guided the Working Group was as follows:

Theodore P. Bartell
John R. Bergan
Esther E. Diamond
Richard P. Duran
Lorraine D. Eyde
Raymond D. Fowler
John J. Fremer
   (Co-chair, JCTP and Chair,
     Code Working Group)

Edmund W. Gordon
Jo-Ida C. Hansen
James B. Lingwall
George F. Madaus
   (Co-chair, JCTP)
Kevin L. Moreland
Jo-Ellen V. Perez
Robert J. Solomon
John T. Stewart

Carol Kehr Tittle
   (Co-chair, JCTP)
Nicholas A. Vacc
Michael J. Zieky
Debra Boltas and Wayne
   Camara of the American
   Psychological Association
   served as staff liaisons

Additional copies of the Code may be obtained from the National Council on Measurement in Education, 1230 Seventeenth Street, NW, Washington, D.C. 20036. Single copies are free.

■ ■ ■ ■

Effective Teaching Strategies and the Design of Instruction

This final chapter provides many ideas that can help Melissa Williams enhance her instructional and assessment practices, thus maximizing the learning of her students. As you recall, she is experiencing a challenge in her first year at Davis Middle School, a school with high standards and a history of students scoring highly on annual objective tests.

Objectives

When you finish reading
this chapter, you should be
able to

- identify the common
  features of teaching

- distinguish between
  direct and inquiry
  teaching

- describe the effective use
  of praise

- apply some of the
  research on effective
  teaching to improve
  instructional efforts with
  students or other learners

- distinguish instructional
  theory from instructional
  design and apply the
  appropriate features of
  both to teaching

- write clear and concise
  learning objectives and
  understand their role in
  the design and
  management of
  instruction

- cite examples of how you
  could adapt teaching to
  the needs of students

To help you understand the intricacies of teaching, we examine various theories and designs of instruction that reveal how teaching can be analyzed. This should help those of you who want to become teachers to adopt and adapt different strategies for your purposes. But these adaptations should be made in light of the individual differences of students and evidence of effective instruction.

WHAT MAKES A TEACHER EFFECTIVE?

Have you ever been a babysitter? If so, you probably gave directions, explained a word, showed a child how to do something. Have you ever coached? If so, you instructed, explained, demonstrated, and evaluated. Have you ever been a summer camp counselor? If so, you managed, directed, lectured, demonstrated, and led group discussions. Have you ever held a job? If so, at some time you undoubtedly explained procedures to a fellow employee. Consequently, you have experience with the four "common features" of teaching: teachers, learners, subject matter, and context (Posner, 1989).

Reflecting on outstanding teachers that he had in school, Ernest Boyer (1990), a respected commentator on American education, stated that there were several characteristics that made them great. First was the way in which they used language. Think about it for a moment; the use of symbols is a constant in classrooms. A teacher's writing and use of oral language helps students to learn, while a teacher's ability to communicate effectively shapes the relationships with students. Boyer next mentioned the knowledge that these teachers possessed. Being well informed and able to move freely in the disciplines is essential if a teacher is to prepare students to succeed in a complex world. Finally, effective teaching implies that a teacher meaningfully relates what is known to the students so that they become aware of the power of knowledge.

In a similar, but more specific analysis, Borich (1992) reviewed recent research on teaching effectiveness and concluded that key behaviors characterizing effective teachers include lesson clarity, instructional variety, task orientation and engagement in the learning process, and student success:

- *Lesson clarity* refers to how clear teachers make their presentations to a class: Do students understand the teacher's message? Once you have decided on objectives (which will be discussed later in this chapter), step back and ask yourself, as if you were a student, if you could understand what it is you are asking a class to do. Some "dos and don'ts" are helpful here. Don't be vague, don't talk over the heads of students, and don't be too complicated. Do organize material carefully, do be precise in your directions, do use easily comprehended speech, do link the present lesson to past work, and do use instructional strategies that are appropriate to the material and to the ages and cognitive levels of your students. All of these practices will help to maintain clarity.

- *Instructional variety* means that one's teaching techniques remain flexible during the presentation of a lesson. Use different materials; switch from a recitation to a discussion technique; be precise in the use of reinforcement of student behaviors. Work hard to become a skilled questioner so that you can integrate questions into your lesson; this helps to keep student interest high. Vary the use of reading materials, audiovisual aids, reference tools, and any other learning resources.

- *Task orientation and engagement in the learning process* refer to the time spent in learning academic subjects. When students' academic learning time is increased,

Clarifying instructional objectives through personal communications is part of good instruction.

their achievement improves; this is especially true for low-achieving or at-risk students (Berliner, 1988). Students must be engaged in appropriate academic activities with a good probability of success. For example, the **beginning teacher evaluation studies (BTES)** inspired by John Carroll's model of school learning (1963) represented an effort to identify a mediating variable between teaching behavior and student performance (Shulman, 1986). Carroll's model shifted the research emphasis from teacher behavior to student activities: What were students doing with their tasks? Explanations of student achievement that focused solely on teachers seemed lacking in predictive power. For example, how could the number and quality of teacher praise statements in the fall influence student achievement in spring examinations? Researchers raising such questions turned their attention to a more meaningful subject: the time that a student spent on particular content. Figure 13.1 illustrates the various times—allocated time, instructional time, engaged time, and academic learning time—that teachers need to be aware of and manage. Is there anything you can do to improve the academic learning time of students? To encourage the efficient use of time, Borich (1992) suggested that teachers make sure students know the classroom rules, so that they don't have to ask each time they want to do something. Monitor seatwork carefully to be sure that students remain engaged. Independent assignments should be interesting and worthwhile so that you don't have to spend time in constantly giving directions. The time you devote to these matters will actually provide more time on task for students.

- *Success rate* means the rate at which students understand and correctly complete their work. As you would expect, if instruction produces a moderate to high success rate, students' achievement must increase. Time is a major contributor here. If students spend more than an average amount of time working toward high success, their achievement scores will rise and retention improves—both changes that are accompanied by a more positive attitude toward school.

BEGINNING TEACHER EVALUATION STUDIES (BTES)

A research program that evaluated beginning teachers by focusing on students' activities.

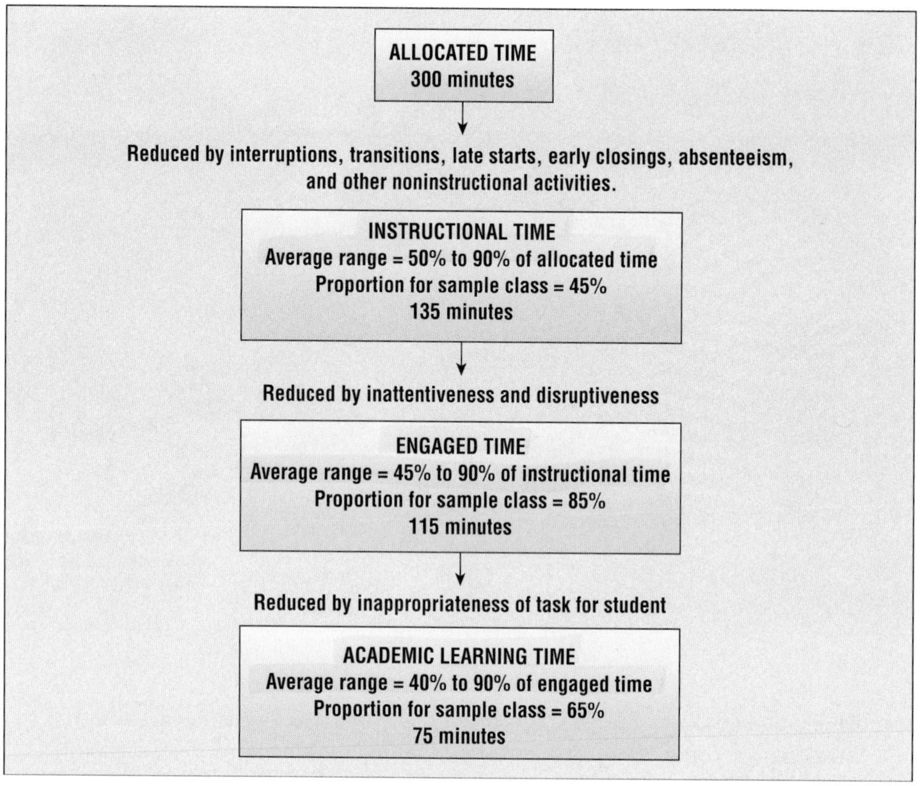

ALLOCATED TIME
300 minutes

Reduced by interruptions, transitions, late starts, early closings, absenteeism, and other noninstructional activities.

INSTRUCTIONAL TIME
Average range = 50% to 90% of allocated time
Proportion for sample class = 45%
135 minutes

Reduced by inattentiveness and disruptiveness

ENGAGED TIME
Average range = 45% to 90% of instructional time
Proportion for sample class = 85%
115 minutes

Reduced by inappropriateness of task for student

ACADEMIC LEARNING TIME
Average range = 40% to 90% of engaged time
Proportion for sample class = 65%
75 minutes

FIGURE 13.1

Components of Academic Learning Time

(From Maribeth Gettinger, *Best Practices.* Copyright © 1990 the National Association of School Psychologists. Reprinted by permission of the publisher.)

CASE NOTES

Observation   Melissa Williams is a conscientious teacher who is trying to be a success, both in the eyes of her students and her teaching partners. However, she is perplexed and frustrated because she does not define effective teaching as "teaching to a standardized test," yet it seems that her teaching colleagues place a high value on standardized test results as an indicator of teaching effectiveness.

Hypothesis   Melissa, like most new teachers, is challenged by the many new things she needs to get command of during her first few years of teaching. Until she feels more successful with class management and clarifies what the school's achievement test measures, she will remain frustrated and perplexed.

Possible Action   Melissa can reprioritize her time for reviewing the content of the school's achievement test to determine how well the content of her class aligns with what is tested. Once she has reviewed the test, she might want to meet with other language arts teachers to seek information about how they try to align their instruction with the assessment. Finally, she might want to share what she learns with her DEW House teaching colleagues, to assure them that she is working hard to be an effective teacher and has begun to understand the relationship between what she is teaching and the end-of-year achievement test. All these actions are intended to open up communication and facilitate the development of a first-year teacher.

TIPS ON COMMUNICATION
Using Praise Effectively

PRINCIPLE Praise, although conceptually a simple technique and easy to implement, can be a powerful tool for maintaining or improving student performance because praise can function as a reward and as feedback.

STRATEGY Praise is most effective when it is delivered contingently, that is, when it is offered immediately after a student exhibits a desired behavior. Under these conditions, praise often functions as a reinforcer for desired behavior.

STRATEGY Praise that specifies particular aspects of an accomplishment, such as effort or accuracy, focuses the attention of the student on behaviors that are valued and functions as feedback about the quality of task-relevant behavior.

STRATEGY Use praise judiciously, but not sparingly. Frequent and general praise (for example, "You're doing well," "Keep it up," "Great") may help keep students on task or attentive but doesn't provide specific, individual feedback and often is not perceived as being contingent or genuine.

Praise is often associated with student success, but teachers must be careful how they use praise. Teacher praise, as a function of teacher effectiveness, has recently received mixed reviews as a means of facilitating student achievement. Praise is different from feedback, conveying an affective commitment by the instructor. Examining the praise research, Brophy and Good (1986) found that teacher praise usually is infrequent, noncontingent (not always based on a student's appropriate behavior), global rather than specific, and determined more by students' personal qualities than by students' achievement. To help you to use praise as a teacher or parent, consider the TIPS box (Using Praise Effectively).

A final aspect of effectiveness we wish to mention involves *reflection*. Effective teachers report stepping back occasionally to think about what they are doing—not to evaluate test scores or the maintenance of an orderly environment (both desirable accomplishments, by the way), but to ask themselves if what they are doing is worthwhile. Try to assume the perspective of an objective observer of your own actions; this is a form of "knowing-in-action" (Schon, 1988). Reflective and mindful teachers are aware of the workings of their own minds as they engage in the practice of instruction, whether it be direct or indirect.

APPROACHES TO INSTRUCTION
Direct Instruction

Students achieve at a higher level in classes where they are directly taught by their teachers rather than working on their own (Blair, 1988). With direct instruction, teachers tell, demonstrate, explain, and assume the major responsibility for a lesson's progress, and they adapt the work to their students' age and abilities. Student achievement seems to be superior with direct instruction, particularly with regard to factual information. Table 13.1 summarizes many of the activities involved in direct instruction. These include giving class presentations, guiding practice, grading work, providing feedback, and monitoring students' work. An example of direct instruction can be found in the work of Madeline Hunter, which we examine next.

Many teachers spend time in front of their classes "orchestrating" learning.

CLINICAL THEORY OF INSTRUCTION (CTI)

Hunter's theory that features the teacher as a decision-making professional.

Working on the assumption that the teacher is a decision-making professional, Hunter, in her **Clinical Theory of Instruction (CTI)** (Hunter, 1991; Hunter & Russell, 1981), claimed universal application—regardless of content, school organization, learner's age, or socioeconomic status. CTI is derived from research on human learning and is based on the notion that instructional decisions are made consciously or by default. The careful design of lessons continues to be one of the most important elements in successful teaching, and the CTI model suggests the following steps to achieve your objectives:

Step 1: Anticipatory Set. Here Hunter was chiefly concerned with readiness and attention and suggested using a brief period to practice previous learning, then focusing students' attention on what is to be learned. Teachers should not continue this activity beyond the time needed to "set" students, that is, to make sure that they are ready for the new learning.

Step 2: The Objective and Its Purpose. Hunter asserted that teachers must clearly inform students up front of what they should be able to do by the end of the instruction, and why it is important that they master the lesson's content. Step 2 reflects our previous discussion of classroom objectives.

Step 3: Instructional Input. Teachers must decide just what information students need to attain the lesson's objective. How can this be done? The content of this chapter should be helpful: Determine the readiness of students, the reinforcements needed, the degree of understanding required, the necessary design, and any specific steps.

Step 4: Modeling. We discussed modeling in Chapter 6 sufficiently for you to realize its value to students in allowing them to see actual examples of an acceptable finished product. Whenever you model, be sure to combine both visual and verbal stimuli, so that students will concentrate on the essential features that you wish them to learn.

Step 5: Checking for Understanding. To make accurate adjustments in your instruction, you must continuously assess students' level of understanding.

Step 6: Guided Practice. Be alert to students' efforts in their initial attempts at new learning. Circulate among students to be sure that they are performing satisfactorily. Students must practice their skills, but they require monitoring in case clarification or remediation is needed.

Step 7: Independent Practice. Once students have eliminated major errors, they can apply the skills in some appropriate task: homework, research papers, reading assignments.

Table 13.1 INSTRUCTIONAL FUNCTIONS

1. Daily Review and Checking Homework
   Checking homework (routines for students to check each other's papers)
   Reteaching when necessary
   Reviewing relevant past learning (may include questioning)
   Review prerequisite skills (if applicable)

2. Presentation
   Provide short statement of objectives
   Provide overview and structuring
   Proceed in small steps but at a rapid pace
   Intersperse questions within the demonstration to check for understanding
   Highlight main points
   Provide sufficient illustrations and concrete examples
   Provide demonstrations and models
   When necessary, give detailed and redundant instructions and examples

3. Guided Practice
   Initial student practice takes place with teacher guidance
   High frequency of questions and overt student practice (from teacher and/or materials)
   Questions are directly relevant to the new content or skill
   Teacher checks for understanding (CFU) by evaluating student responses
   During CFU teacher gives additional explanation, process feedback, or repeats explanation—where necessary
   All students have a chance to respond and receive feedback; teacher ensures that all students participate
   Prompts are provided during guided practice (where appropriate)
   Initial student practice is sufficient so that students can work independently
   Guided practice continues until students are firm
   Guided practice is continued (usually) until a success rate of 80% is achieved

4. Correctives and Feedback
   Quick, firm, and correct responses can be followed by a question or a short acknowledgement of correctness ("That's right")
   Hesitant correct answers might be followed by process feedback (that is, "Yes, Linda, that's right because . . .")
   Student errors indicate a need for more practice
   Monitor students for systematic errors
   Try to obtain a substantive response to each question
   Corrections can include sustaining feedback (that is, simplifying the question, giving clues), explaining or reviewing steps, giving process feedback, or reteaching the last steps
   Try to elicit an improved response when the first one is incorrect
   Guided practice and corrections continue until the teacher feels that the group can meet the objectives of the lesson
   Praise should be used in moderation, and specific praise is more effective than general praise

5. Independent Practice (Seatwork)
   Sufficient practice
   Practice is directly relevant to skills/content taught
   Practice to overlearning
   Practice until responses are firm, quick, and automatic
   Ninety-five percent correct rate during independent practice
   Students alerted that seatwork will be checked
   Student held accountable for seatwork
   Actively supervise students, when possible

6. Weekly and Monthly Reviews
   Systematic review of previously learned material
   Include review in homework
   Frequent tests
   Reteaching of material missed in tests

Adapted with permission of American Educational Research Association from *Handbook of Research on Teaching*, 3/e edited by Merlin C. Wittrock. Copyright © 1986.

Note: With older, more mature learners, or learners with more knowledge of the subject, the following adjustments can be made: (1) the size of the step in presentation can be larger (more material is presented at one time), (2) there is less time spent on teacher-guided practice and (3) the amount of overt practice can be decreased, replacing it with covert rehearsal, restating and reviewing.

Some Dos and Don'ts for Direct Instruction

Properly used, direct instruction can be very effective, especially if the information it conveys is not easily available elsewhere. Direct instruction can also be preferable to textbook readings, workbook exercises, and the like as a way to maintain student interest. Students can see your enthusiasm for material that you are presenting in an exciting manner (Borich, 1992). It is a good idea to begin your teaching by using an advance organizer. (This is a summary of the ideas that will be presented, in which the teacher attempts to link new concepts with prior knowledge; read the discussion of meaningful learning in Chapter 7.) Be sure students understand any new words that they need. Present ideas in a carefully

TIPS ON LEARNING
Asking Questions of Students during Instruction

PRINCIPLE　Questions are an important teaching tool that facilitate communication, stimulate thinking, and serve as an ongoing assessment of both the effectiveness of instruction and student learning.

STRATEGY　Use a question or two at the outset of a lecture or lab session to pique students' interest and to focus attention on a central issue or concept. Ask all students to jot down their answers on a sheet of paper, then solicit responses from several students in the spirit of "brainstorming" possible answers.

STRATEGY　When asking questions during expository instruction, remember to allow students time to process the question and to formulate an answer. A *wait time* of ten seconds is often necessary to get a majority of students to volunteer answers.

STRATEGY　Avoid using questions to punish a student or to indicate he or she was not attending.

CASE NOTES

Observation　Jim Watson and two male classmates frequently misbehave and are performing poorly in the language arts class. Mrs. Williams has tried to accommodate them by giving them more time to redo the work, but this has not resulted in improved academic or behavior functioning.

Hypothesis　These three students have some significant skill deficits in written communication and possibly poor study skills. Their misbehavior is more of an attempt to avoid doing work they find difficult than it is to be mean or disruptive to Mrs. Williams.

Possible Action　These students would benefit from more intense, direct instruction where Mrs. Williams provides strong models of acceptable writing, detailed guidance during the writing process, and feedback about their writing skills and products. In addition, the level of material they work on may need to be lowered to increase the likelihood of successes.

prepared and logical sequence that is appropriate for their level. As you proceed, use questions to keep the class motivated and to check their understanding. Give students immediate feedback so that they know if their comprehension of the ideas being discussed is right or wrong. Be alert for any signs of wandering attention or boredom, and engage these students immediately. Finally, follow up a presentation with activities designed to help retention and transfer. A good rule to remember for direct instruction is this: *Tell students what you're going to tell them; tell them; and then remind them of what you've told them* (Callahan, Clark, & Kellough, 1992).

Guard against talking too much, a habit easily acquired in direct instruction. If you think this is happening, stop, ask questions, or pose a relevant problem. Another danger inherent in direct instruction is to assume that just because a teacher has told his or her students something, they have learned it. Constantly check for misinterpretations. Finally, as one reviews the content of the lesson that is being taught, be sure that the material lends itself to direct instruction. For example, assume that in a biology class you want students to comprehend the extent and possible application of the discoveries of the Human Genome Project. Simply lecturing them is probably not the most productive way to accomplish this. Rather, you would want them to read, explore, discuss with one another, and suggest creative possibilities. If you want students to integrate subject matter that is fairly complex for their level, you may well decide to turn to more indirect methods, which we examine next.

Indirect Instruction

Given the complexities of a modern society, teachers are aware that their students need to be adaptive and creative as they adjust to their changing environments. Consequently, the acquisition of facts and knowledge as the sole tools of teaching and learning is not enough. Teaching that encourages inquiry learning (let us call this indirect teaching or **inquiry teaching**) is less structured and more informal. Teachers using indirect instructional methods find themselves arranging classroom conditions in a way that encourages students to think about the means of solving problems, and teachers work from the assumption that students should actively seek information rather than passively accepting it in lectures, recitation, or demonstrations (Callahan et al., 1992).

INQUIRY
TEACHING
Bruner's term for teaching that permits students to be active partners in the search for knowledge, thus enhancing the meaning of what they learn.

To assist students in such active exploration, provide advance organizers and conceptual frameworks that can serve as "pegs" on which to hang key points that guide and channel thinking to the most productive areas. Teachers practicing indirect methods often use questions to guide the search and discovery process: raise contradictions, probe for deeper-level responses, pass responsibility for learning to each individual learner. These teachers also encourage students to use examples and references from their own experience, to seek clarification, and to draw parallels and associations that aid understanding and retention. They also encourage students to relate ideas to past learning and to their own sphere of interests, concerns, and problems. Finally, they provide learners cues, questions, or hints as needed to call their attention to inappropriate responses. Discussion is used to encourage critical thinking and help students to examine alternatives, judge solutions, make predictions, and discover generalizations. The teacher's task during discussion is to orient students, provide new content, review and summarize, alter the flow of information, and combine areas to promote the most productive discussion (Borich, 1992).

An example of indirect instruction can be found in the work of Jerome Bruner. In a wide-ranging series of essays written from a cognitive perspective, Bruner (1960, 1966a, 1966b, 1971) provided penetrating insights into both inquiry teaching and learning. Examining the classroom functions of the instructor, he noted three sources of teacher behavior. First, teachers are *communicators of knowledge;* this implies mastery of both the knowledge to be communicated and the effective methods of its communication: You must know what to teach and how to teach it. Second, teachers are *models;* they should be competent and exciting individuals who will inspire in students a love of learning. A teacher's behavior in the classroom is an important source of knowledge, guidance, and motivation for students. We saw this clearly demonstrated in Bandura's work on modeling in Chapters 6 and 9. Third, teachers are *symbols,* the immediate representatives of "education," and can be particularly persuasive figures in shaping students' attitudes, interests, opinions, and values, not to mention their intellectual achievement.

Bruner noted that learning is closely linked to cognitive structures, readiness, motivation, and interaction with the environment. He raised this question: Since psychology already contains theories of learning and development, why is a theory of instruction needed? His answer was that theories of learning and development are *descriptive* rather than prescriptive; that is, they tell us what has happened, rather than what should happen. For example, from Piaget's theory we know that a child of 6 usually has not achieved the cognitive ability of reversibility. A theory of instruction *prescribes* how teachers can help a child acquire this. It outlines the materials and the methods best suited to help these students move to a higher cognitive level.

Bruner developed four major themes in analyzing learning: structure, readiness, intuition, and motivation. Understanding a subject's structure is central in Bruner's thinking. The first object of any act of learning, over and beyond the pleasure it may give, is that it should serve us in the future. Learning should not only take us somewhere but also allow us later to go further more easily (Bruner, 1960, p. 17).

As Bruner noted, grasping a subject's structure is understanding it so that many other things can be related to it meaningfully: To learn structure is to learn how things are related. Students can grasp a subject's structure only if they understand its basic ideas. The more basic the idea that students learn, the more they can apply it to other topics. If students understand a subject's fundamental structure, the subject itself becomes more comprehensible, aids memory, facilitates transfer, and helps to build the **spiral curriculum.** For example, learning to identify and understand the causes of the Civil War can help students to look beyond the mere names of the battles in any other war they study.

The spiral curriculum, an excellent example of an attempt to develop structure, is closely linked to Bruner's second theme: readiness. For example, World War II has become a major topic in contemporary history. Using the principles of the spiral curriculum, it is taught at successively higher grade levels in an increasingly abstract manner. Figure 13.2 illustrates the process. Note the increasing abstraction and complexity of the presentation. Completing their study, students should have a good grasp of the subject.

Bruner's famous statement that any subject can be taught effectively in some intellectually honest form to any child at any stage of development implies that the basic ideas of science, mathematics, and literature are as simple as they are powerful. If teachers begin teaching the foundations of these subjects in an appropriate manner consistent with pupils' intellectual levels, as described by Piaget, pupils can learn important basics at any stage of mental development. Then, by applying the principles of the spiral curriculum, they can steadily proceed to more complex forms of the subject.

SPIRAL CURRICULUM

Bruner's term for teaching a subject in an ever more abstract manner; tied to his interpretation of readiness.

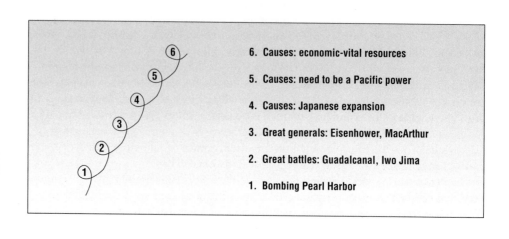

FIGURE 13.2

The Spiral Curriculum Illustrated with an Example: Content Concerning World War II

Once students obtain a detailed knowledge of a subject, they can begin to expand their hypothetical abilities; that is, they can make informed guesses. Knowing a topic deeply and widely enables them to proceed by implicit perception; they can grasp something without detailed analysis. They can make their informed guesses and then subject them to critical scrutiny, thus fostering both problem-solving and creative behavior. For example, an understanding of the geography and history of the countries of Eastern Europe can help students speculate about the reasons for their independence movements.

Motivation is Bruner's final indispensable learning ingredient. He questions the value of excessive emphasis on examinations, grades, and promotions with respect to a desirable lifetime commitment to learning. Children always have mixed motives for learning: pleasing parents and teachers, competing with peers, and acquiring a sense of self-mastery. Inspiring intrinsic motivation is difficult in children; Bruner realistically stated that if teachers teach well and if what they teach is worth learning, forces at work in our society will augment teachers' efforts with an external prod, with the combined result that students will become more involved in their learning processes.

Modes of Representation

How can Bruner's ideas help anyone who wants to teach others something new? Bruner believes that if teachers understand the mental stages that a person passes through, they can adapt their teaching accordingly. He calls these stages **modes of representation.** The first level is the **enactive mode of representation.** The infant knows the world only by acting on it; otherwise, the object does not exist for the child. As Bruner noted, even in an adult's life, there are times when words simply cannot express an experience. For example, how can you tell someone about the "feel" of a golf or tennis swing? The second level is the **iconic mode of representation,** Bruner's term for perceptual organization. For an individual faced with a series of apparently unrelated tasks, the discovery of a pattern makes the work easier. Word problems are a good example. Once students see the steps (the pattern) necessary to solve the problem, it then becomes more realistic and easier to solve. The third level is the **symbolic mode of representation.** At this level, the child engages in symbolic activities such as language and mathematics. Bruner (1966a) believed that when children translate experience into language, they enter the world of possibilities, enabling them to solve problems and engage in creative thinking.

Students learn according to their mode of representation. For Bruner, learning a subject involves three almost simultaneous processes: acquisition of new information, transformation, and evaluation. *Acquisition of new information* that replaces or expands what the pupil already knows is the initial phase. Here the child incorporates environmental stimuli according to the existing mode of representation: by physical action; by forming images; or by abstracting, comparing, and judging. For example, as mentioned earlier, before students can understand the surge toward freedom and independence among the countries of Eastern Europe, they must know the history of these countries, especially since World War II.

Transformation is the second phase. Once youngsters or adults acquire new information, they must manipulate or change it to meet new tasks. Bruner often uses the illustration of going beyond the information given. For example, your friend passes by the door and says, "Hi, Janie." You do not see her, but immediately think, "There goes Liz." You have manipulated verbal stimuli to form the idea of your friend.

Evaluation is the final phase. Students ask themselves if they have successfully manipulated the information. Was it adequate? Was it correct?

Bruner joins cognitive growth, modes of representation, and learning processes to support his model of the spiral curriculum. He believes that if teachers respect a student's thinking process and translate material into meaningful units (that is, if they match the

MODES OF REPRESENTATION
Bruner's term for the mental stages a child passes through.

ENACTIVE MODE OF REPRESENTATION
Bruner's term for the mental stage of knowing the world by acting on it; usually refers to the infancy period.

ICONIC MODE OF REPRESENTATION
Bruner's term for the perceptual organization of the world; a mode of representation.

SYMBOLIC MODE OF REPRESENTATION
Bruner's term for the ability to represent information, to consider possibilities.

subject matter to a student's mode of representation), they can introduce great ideas to children at different times and with increasing abstractness. For example, a discussion of freedom in the first grade differs from a junior high school discussion of slavery, which differs from a high school discussion of the meaning of the Constitution—hence, the spiral curriculum.

Bruner also made specific teaching recommendations, especially related to the continued use of discovery teaching and learning (Wilcox, 1987). He noted that despite the many technological aids for teachers, the chief facilitator of learning is still the teacher.

If you believe in cognitive learning principles, consider the following. First, if you desire to teach effectively, you must master the material to be taught. (There probably is no better way to learn a subject than to teach it.) Second, remember that you are a model. Unimaginative, uninspiring, and insecure teachers are hardly likely to spark a love of learning, especially since students quickly sense a lack of commitment. Recognize that students will identify with a teacher as a model, and they often compare themselves to the teacher. This is a sobering thought, but it can motivate a teacher to search for ways to better teaching and furnish a stimulating classroom atmosphere.

Some Dos and Don'ts for Indirect Instruction

Indirect (inquiry) instruction has a distinctive place in the classroom, since it helps students not only to learn concepts, but to move beyond memorization to draw conclusions and form generalizations. The knowledge that is acquired by this process may be more meaningful for students because of their self-involvement, which aids them in discovering the structure of the subject they're studying. They can also see how this topic relates to others. Both motivation and retention seem to be better with this type of instruction.

Remember, however, that there are also disadvantages with this method. The content and situation must be appropriate; devising a strategy to bring relief to a beleaguered nation requires a different process from mastering the vocabulary of a language. Considerable time and effort is required, and the results may be totally unexpected. For example, students will be much more noisy and active; this may lead to control problems unless a teacher monitors their activities closely. Also, as a consequence of their independent work, students may reach conclusions totally at odds with the teacher's goals (which may not be bad!).

There are several "dos" to remember when using indirect teaching techniques. Perhaps most important, be supportive. Students inevitably will make false starts, make incorrect assumptions, and reach sometimes startling conclusions. As a teacher works with students, the teacher should reinforce what they do correctly (but don't give general praise; you might reinforce an incorrect response). Since students will be working independently, be sure that adequate clues have been provided to help them structure their learning. By "adequate" we mean directions, reading, and materials that are suited to students' abilities. Encourage students to work cooperatively, which helps them to discover new ideas and also fosters positive relationships.

Both direct and indirect instruction are needed in the classroom, since pupils need to acquire facts before they attempt to solve problems. Creating learning environments that foster the learning of all students requires a flexible array of instructional tactics.

THE DESIGN OF INSTRUCTION

Students are supposed to learn specified content, which must be clearly understood by both teachers and their students. When students don't know what is called for, their performance suffers. Likewise a teacher's effectiveness in the classroom can falter when the focus of instruction is unclear. What precisely do we want students to accomplish in a particular lesson, a unit, a course, and under what conditions? These concerns take us into the world of objectives and instructional design.

Students benefit from seeing a good model of what they are to produce or learn.

Effective teachers interact on a personal level with students.

Effective instruction often requires students to work together to "dig" for information.

Technology is an important part of effective instruction for many students.

Classroom Objectives

To achieve and maintain a higher level of instruction, you must continually decide exactly what students need to accomplish. Thus, teachers need to formulate specific objectives that encompass their daily concerns and communicate with students what it is they are accountable to learn and under what conditions. If there is one indispensable guideline for formulating objectives, it is this: Be precise. Learning will improve because students will know exactly what is expected of them and, consequently, will understand the basis of their marks and grades.

In an excellent analysis of objectives, Bloom, Madaus, and Hastings (1981) noted that statements of educational objectives describe, in a relatively specific manner, what students should be able to produce or do, or what characteristics students should possess after the learning. In short, teachers should have clearly defined instructional objectives that form an integrated whole to guide all aspects of teaching: planning, teaching, and testing of students' learning. As Airasian (1994) noted, the intent of stating an educational objective is to identify student outcomes in order to select appropriate instructional methods and resources, to communicate to others the purposes of instruction, and to help plan assessments.

Why Bother with Objectives?

To write good objectives is a time-consuming, absorbing task. Why should teachers or managers bother? Before considering specific reasons, you should be aware that given the current decrease in dependence on textbooks and curriculum guides for the identification of objectives (particularly in such subjects as language arts), teacher planning is assuming greater importance. This is just one example of a deeper teacher involvement in the decision-making process. Although positive, this trend could cause conflict within a school system unless it is carefully handled. Everyone involved—parents, teachers, students, and administrators—must recognize the need for both individual and collective decision making. Teachers must make decisions based on the needs of the individual learners in their classrooms.

Many reasons exist for writing thoughtful objectives. One of these is that many students simply don't know what teachers expect. By writing clearly stated objectives, teachers keep their instruction focused and students quickly learn what is expected of them. They also recall more information (Muth, Glynn, Britton, & Graves, 1988).

Many school districts have established **expected learner outcomes (ELOs)** or **academic content standards.** ELOs or academic standards are used to communicate a school district's learning expectations to parents, teachers, and students. Well-written ELOs list curriculum-referenced cognitive and behavioral objectives that can be empirically assessed. Many school districts use their ELOs in making decisions about school entry and grade retentions. Ideally, preschool screening tests should be highly congruent with a school's kindergarten ELOs. Thus, those selecting preschool screening measures can assess their content validity by systematically comparing them with the ELOs developed by the schools the children will attend. A representative set of kindergarten ELOs for reading, writing, and mathematics is illustrated in Table 13.2.

One specific method of linking objectives to content is called **task analysis.** This method breaks down a body of material into distinct attainable tasks. For example, in a unit on American history, after students had studied about the American presidents, a teacher might say, "This week we're going to see how some former presidents led the country in times of peril. We'll discuss Washington, Lincoln, and Franklin Roosevelt."

Task analysis would require this teacher to decide first how these lessons related to the unit's objectives. Next, the teacher would have to be sure that the pupils had the skills to carry out any assignments. Did students have the necessary reading skills? Did they know how to do independent research? Had they been taught outlining skills? Could they write research papers? Next, the teacher would have to decide on materials and methods. Different stimuli would be used (pictures, stories, movies), in both direct teaching and group activities. Finally, the teacher would determine what kinds of pupil behavior would be accepted as evidence of learning.

If a component task has some hierarchical order, students should understand the logical sequence, and the necessity to integrate all components for achievement of the completed task. The teaching of the separate elements requires constant reference to the whole task to furnish direction and meaning to the learning. In a geography class, for example, a student needs to know fundamental facts about a country, but the teacher should relate these to an ultimate objective: determining the causes of the country's foreign policy, for example, and attempting to predict future action.

Questions like these can help a teacher identify and evaluate component tasks. Exactly what is it that we wish students to achieve? (For example, knowledge of the actions of presidents in troubled times.) What tasks must students undertake to gain these goals? (For example, reading, writing, outlining, research.) What stimuli must be provided to en-

EXPECTED
LEARNER
OUTCOMES
(ELOS)

Cognitive and behavioral objectives used to express learning expectations to students, teachers, and parents.

ACADEMIC
CONTENT
STANDARDS

A description of what teachers and schools consider to be important content knowledge and skills that all students should learn.

TASK ANALYSIS

Breaking down complex behaviors into their basic elements and sequencing them from first to last in a response chain.

Table 13.2 KINDERGARTEN ELOs

Subject	Expected Learner Outcomes
Reading	1. Identify common objects or pictures in the environment.
	2. Identify these positions: above–below, behind–in front, top–bottom, and left–right.
	3. Distinguish likenesses and differences.
	4. Identify lowercase manuscript letters.
	5. Identify uppercase manuscript letters.
	6. Identify rhyming pictures.
	7. Match upper- and lowercase manuscript letters.
	8. Sequence pictures.
	9. Select pictures that show story endings.
	10. Recognize words that begin with the same sound.
Writing	1. Identify these positions: above–below, behind–in front, top–bottom, and left–right.
	2. Distinguish likenesses and differences.
	3. Identify lowercase manuscript letters.
	4. Identify uppercase manuscript letters.
	5. Match upper- and lowercase manuscript letters.
	6. Sequence pictures.
Mathematics	1. Identify elements of a set.
	2. Identify the smaller or larger object.
	3. Identify these simple closed figures: circle, triangle, and square.
	4. Compare the number of elements in two sets and indicate which is greater.
	5. Classify objects or pictures according to color and shape.
	6. Count concrete objects.
	7. Count to ten by ones.
	8. Identify one-half of a concrete object.
	9. Identify these coins: penny, nickel, dime, and quarter.
	10. Identify sets with an equal number of elements.
	11. Identify the cardinal number of a set of not more than ten elements.
	12. Identify the primary colors.

Source: Modeled after the New Orleans' Public Schools Kindergarten ELOs, Fall 1984.

sure the necessary knowledge and skill to complete these tasks? (For example, books, films, group discussion.) When teachers use current information about varied curricula, techniques of grouping, assessment of capacity, and the like, students can progress by a graded series of discernible stages.

TIPS ON ASSESSMENT
Conducting a Task Analysis

PRINCIPLE   To teach complex behaviors it is necessary to "break down" a problem or task into small parts and sequence the steps into teachable components.

STRATEGY   Identify a competent example of the behavior you wish to teach, then examine the subparts or steps in exhibiting the behavior by observing or listening to a person demonstrating the behavior. Decide the "best" sequence of the various subparts and which are most difficult to do.

STRATEGY   Teach students how to do a simple task analysis so, when they are confronted with a complex task, they can break it down into several achievable parts.

What Are Good Objectives?

Once teachers have determined the type of objectives needed, they must express them in such a way that they are clearly understood by all. Objectives should also be expressed in behavioral terms that can guide teaching and enable the teacher to assess whether students have or have not attained them. Teachers should be cautious that their teaching and testing does not focus on one type of objective. Typically educators focus on the cognitive outcomes (especially knowledge of facts) that are most familiar to them. Don't forget those affective outcomes that can be so important to the total learning environment, as well as any essential psychomotor skills.

INSTRUCTIONAL OBJECTIVE

Learning outcomes deemed worthy of attainment; well-stated objectives are explicitly specified behaviors, conditions of performance, and criteria for evaluating the performance.

An **instructional objective** is an intent communicated by a statement describing a proposed change in the learner: a statement of what the learner is to be able to do upon completion of the learning experience (Kim & Kellough, 1991). Thus an instructional objective requires a demonstrable behavioral change in the learner. Consequently, we can tell that learning has occurred only when we observe a change in behavior.

Note the essential ingredients of this description: An objective is student centered and involves learning outcomes and observable behavior. In other words, an instructional objective states what a student is expected to accomplish, the products of that learning (not the activities), and clearly defined student levels of performance.

Evaluating and Writing Objectives

Your reading thus far should help you to be aware of the characteristics of good objectives. How would you evaluate the following four objectives according to the criteria just discussed?

1. To appreciate the insights offered by educational psychology.

2. To present to you, the reader, several examples of clearly stated objectives.

3. To study the "Chapter Highlights" summary at the end of the chapter and refer back to the appropriate parts of the chapter.

4. To write ten instructional objectives that reflect the content of educational psychology described in this book.

Let us look at each of these "objectives."

TIPS ON COMMUNICATION
Objectives Clarify Expectations

PRINCIPLE   Instructional objectives provide students a clear picture of the content to be learned and the product or performance to be generated.

STRATEGY   Students need to know what they are expected to learn and how they will be asked to demonstrate their knowledge. Use objectives to communicate (a) the behavior or product they need to show, (b) the conditions under which they will be asked to show the behavior or product, and (c) the criteria that will be used to evaluate the behavior or product.

STRATEGY   Select terminal behaviors that are observable. Use verbs that specify observable behaviors (for example, *write, compute, list, recite, select, orally state*). Avoid using verbs such as understand, appreciate, know, be aware of, or remember—these are not directly observable and make assessing the student unreliable.

STRATEGY   When indicating the criteria that will be used to evaluate whether a student has met the objective, consider characteristics communicating about *accuracy, quality,* and *time.*

STRATEGY   The ABCD format provides a useful organizer for thinking about important components of an instructional objective. A = audience, B = behavior to be observed, C = conditions for performing the behavior, and D = degree of competency needed to pass.

1. This objective is so vague as to be meaningless. What is meant by "appreciate"? What insights?

2. Here we have an objective for the teacher and not for students.

3. This objective tells students what to do (a learning activity), but it does not refer to a learning outcome. Be careful of objectives like this; although they are student-centered, they lack any reference to performance.

4. This meets the criteria of the good objective: It is student centered, identifies a learning outcome, and is observable.

As you turn your attention to the actual writing of objectives, consider Robert Mager's (1975) reminders that desirable objectives address three questions. First, what is the *behavior* that should result? Here you are concerned with identifying the specific behavior that signals that the learner has achieved the objective. Remember that a statement of the desired behavior also should specify an acceptable level. For example, if you give students ten problems, you might decide that seven correct solutions is an acceptable performance level. This description is sometimes called performance-based or outcome-based instruction (Kim & Kellough, 1991). Second, what are the *conditions* under which the specific behavior should occur? For example, calculating with paper and pencil differs from calculating by a computer. Mager also strongly urged that you describe enough conditions for the objective to write appropriate test items. Third, what are the *criteria* that inform a teacher that students have achieved an objective at the proper level? In other words, how well must a student perform to be judged successful? Is the criterion the number of items correct? Is it time? Be sure that students understand all criteria for a minimally acceptable level of performance.

Table 13.3 DESIRED CHARACTERISTICS OF OBJECTIVES

Characteristic	Meaning
Specified content	Content should be precisely stated in behavioral terms.
Specified outcome	Students' behavior as a result of learning, should be stated as observable outcomes.
Specified level of performance	Not only should expected student behavior be specified, but the exact degree of attainment should be clear to both teacher and students.
Specified outcome in clear, exact terms	Verbs such as *name, identify, classify, order, avoid,* and *understand* should be used.

The characteristics of appropriately stated instructional objectives as suggested by Bloom, Madaus, and Hastings (1981) and Gronlund (1985) are summarized in Table 13.3.

As you translate these ideas into action, remember to use precise terminology. As Gronlund (1985) noted, the action verbs teachers use should satisfy two criteria: They should convey clearly the instructional intent, and they should state precisely the behavior and level of performance expected of pupils (use action verbs such as *identify* and *name*).

Writing objectives can become more focused by following the suggestions offered by Armstrong and Savage (1983). Their ABCD format includes four elements:

A   **A**udience for which the objectives are intended

B   **B**ehavior that indicates learning

C   **C**onditions under which the behavior is to appear

D   **D**egree of competency that will be accepted

Although these elements are similar to those already discussed, the familiar ABCD format provides a helpful reminder. For example, in the following objective—"Each student will be able to define 8 of the 10 items in the reading passage of the unit test"—**A** is "each student," **B** is "will be able to define," **C** is "in the reading passage of the unit test," and **D** is "8 of 10 items," or 80%. The order in which these elements appear can vary; the important thing is that all four elements must be present.

Table 13.4 illustrates the manner in which an objective, by the use of an action verb, can specify a student response.

Sources of Objectives

As you begin to consider the importance of good objectives for teaching, you may want to turn to established sources of objectives and then commence writing your own. Many sources are available to use in guiding your own work. Published materials such as classroom textbooks and the instructor manuals that accompany them are a good place to begin. They usually contain a wealth of valuable materials. You might also consider the annual yearbooks published by the national associations of teachers in the various subject matter areas. You may also find specialized sources, such as the Taxonomy of Educational Objectives, extremely valuable. Finally, you may want to consult with your state department of education or public instruction to find out if they have published a list of academic standards for students; if so, these standards can be useful in stimulating many good instructional objectives.

Table 13.4 HOW VERBS SPECIFY RESPONSES

Action Verb	Types of Response	Sample Test Task
Identify*	Point to, touch, mark, encircle, match, pick up.	"Put an X under the right triangle."
Name*	Supply verbal label (orally or in writing).	"What is this type of angle called?"
Distinguish	Identify as separate or different by marking, separating into classes, or selecting out a common kind.	"Which of the following statements are facts (encircle F) and which are opinions (encircle O)?"
Define	Supply a verbal description (orally or in writing) that gives the precise meaning or essential qualities.	"Define each of the following terms."
Describe*	Supply a verbal account (orally or in writing) that gives the essential categories, properties, and relationships.	"Describe a procedure for measuring relative humidity in the atmosphere."
Classify	Place into groups having common characteristics, assign to a particular category.	"Write the name of each type of pronoun used in each of the following sentences."
Order*	List in order, place in sequence, arrange, rearrange.	"Arrange the following historical events in chronological order."
Construct*	Draw, make, design, assemble, prepare, build.	"Draw a bar graph using the following data."
Demonstrate*	Perform a set of procedures with or without a verbal explanation.	"Set up the laboratory equipment for this experiment."

Reprinted with the permission of Simon & Schuster, Inc. from the Macmillan College text *Measurement and Evaluation in Teaching*, 7/E by Norman E. Gronlund and Robert I. Linn. Copyright © 1995 by Macmillan College Publishing Company.

*Sullivan states that these six action verbs (and their synonyms) encompass nearly all cognitive learning outcomes in the school. See H. J. Sullivan, "Objectives, Evaluation, and Improved Learner Achievement," in *Instructional Objectives*. AERA Monograph Series on Curriculum Evaluation, No. 3 (Chicago: Rand McNally, 1969).

Benjamin Bloom (1913–), Professor Emeritus of Education at the University of Chicago, has long been interested in taxonomies of educational objectives. Bloom and his colleagues devised the Taxonomy of Educational Objectives, which is an endeavor to clarify some of the vague terminology often used in the social sciences (Bloom, 1956). The main purpose of the taxonomy is to provide a classification of the goals of our educational system (Bloom, 1956, p. 1). There are three taxonomies: cognitive, affective, and psychomotor. The cognitive taxonomy, which has greatly influenced American education, is divided into six major classes:

Knowledge. The recall of pertinent facts when needed (Who were the first astronauts to reach the moon?)

Comprehension. Understanding the meaning of what is presented (Can you explain the causes of World War II?)

Application. Use of ideas and rules where needed (Does final *e* make the preceding vowel long?)

Analysis. Separating a unit into its parts (How many subfields make up educational psychology?)

Synthesis. Constructing a whole from parts (Write a paper about a topic combining classwork, films, and a field visit)

Evaluation. Making judgments (Can you justify—or not—a particular nation's aggressive policies?)

Each category is further subdivided into other, more specific objectives. These six classes represent an hierarchical order of the different classes of objectives. The objectives of each class usually depend on the preceding classes.

The great value of the taxonomy is its general application. Experts in curriculum construction can study it to refine the objectives of any school. Inexperienced teachers can turn to the taxonomy as a guide to the kinds of objectives for which pupils should be striving. Both expert and neophyte can profit by the wide range of test items that the authors offer to ascertain if students are actually achieving these goals. The taxonomy (often referred to as **Bloom's taxonomy**) is a remarkably flexible tool. Not only does it offer reliable insights into the formation of acceptable objectives, but it also can be used as the basis for teaching thinking skills (see Chapter 8). Combining your knowledge of development and learning, remember those basic principles that can guide the selection and formulation of specific objectives suited for students. Table 13.5 illustrates these features.

It is time now to introduce the work of individuals who have concentrated on instructional designs and the specific steps needed to achieve particular learning objectives. Thus, next we examine the instructional design contributions of B. F. Skinner, Susan Markle, and Robert Gagne.

Skinner and the Technology of Teaching

As featured in Chapter 6, B. F. Skinner is best known for his theoretical and applied work operant learning, but during his lifetime he also contributed significantly to schooling and the technology of teaching. Specifically, he applied principles of operant conditioning to both learning and teaching, in a procedure called **programmed instruction.**

Recall that Skinner believed teachers depend too heavily on punishment while neglecting their use of positive reinforcement and antecedent control methods. Insisting that special techniques can arrange contingencies of reinforcement—resulting from the relationship between behavior and the consequences of that behavior—Skinner stated that teachers should be able to effectively control behavior. This assumption about contingency management is the basis of operant conditioning and one of the cornerstones of effective teaching and behavior management (see Chapter 10 for a more in-depth discussion of classroom behavior management).

One of Skinner's favorite subjects was the teaching of arithmetic. In arithmetic, the primary behaviors of concern are speaking and writing figures, words, and signs. It is necessary to bring these responses under stimulus control. How do teachers accomplish this? According to Skinner, they should use reinforcers. Traditionally, this has meant reliance on negative consequences. Skinner noted that although yesterday's physical punishment is mostly gone, teachers still rely too much on sarcasm, ridicule, and low marks. So arithmetic, like most subjects, has become mired in a maze of dislike, anxiety, and ultimately, boredom.

Improvement is possible, since there are general characteristics of teaching that, if practiced, cultivate both teaching and learning. For example, Skinner urged teachers to define the **terminal behavior:** They must decide what students should be able to do after having been taught. Statements like "be a good citizen" are both inadequate and unworthy; they

Table 13.5 GUIDELINES FOR ACHIEVING EDUCATIONAL OBJECTIVES

Knowledge of the Learner	Educational Importance
1. The learner possesses a unique capacity for achievement.	Schools must recognize and provide for individual differences among students.
2. The learner's achievement is affected by the nature of the environmental contacts.	Learning experiences furnished by the school must enhance, or enrich, the learner's background.
3. The learner's developmental pattern should suggest classroom materials and methods.	A wide assortment of learning experiences should afford maximum opportunity for achievement at all ages.
4. The learner's intellectual level is not fixed and is capable of change.	Administrative procedures and organization should account for a variable expression of intellectual capacity.
5. The learner's emotions exercise a decisive effect, either positive or negative, upon learning.	The classroom atmosphere should be sufficiently stable to afford security and sufficiently stimulating to offer challenge.
6. The learner is a social being who requires satisfactory relations with other humans.	Emphasis upon the individual should not cause neglect of the interaction with peers, which is necessary to develop the mature personality.
7. The learner is an active, motivated individual who is capable of responses that range from the concrete to the abstract.	Self-activity in pursuit of an attainable goal is essential for learning. The learner should have educational experiences that require motor responses, thinking, problem solving, and creative thought.

do not describe behavior. "Knowledge" is another deceptive goal of education. Students have learned something when they behave. That is, they respond to stimuli differently than they did before instruction. Students "know" when teachers can specifically identify their behavior; that is, teachers have taught them to behave in certain ways. What they know is what they do; therefore, teachers must objectively and concretely state their objectives.

Once teachers have determined the terminal behavior (what they want students to do after teaching), they must strengthen it by reinforcement. But teachers cannot reinforce what does not appear. Thus teachers must also solve the problem of the *first instance*. The problem of the first instance means the need for pupils to exhibit some aspect of the desired behavior. One option is to induce it, as in physically taking a child's hand and guiding it to form letters or numbers. Another option is to have pupils imitate the teacher or some example of excellent work. Simply telling pupils what to do and then reinforcing them when they do it is yet another possibility. Learning, however, does not occur because the teacher has primed the behavior; it occurs, according to Skinner, only when behavior is reinforced. The preceding examples illustrate only the first step in the process.

Skinner also stated that teachers should decide what they will use to prompt behavior. One reinforcement will hardly free a response from priming stimuli. When do you stop priming students? If you continue too long, you are inefficient; if you stop too soon, you may cause error. Use only as much as is necessary. For example, you may wish students to be able to identify the midwestern states, their major cities, and their principal industries. You may begin by using maps and reading materials. Some cities may be near water and thus be port cities. Later, when students should know which cities do what, you may ask them to locate a city without using maps or texts. You thus have supplied various prompts as part of the original priming behavior.

Be sure that you program complex behavior. Priming and prompting evoke a behavior to be reinforced in the presence of required stimuli. Some behavior, however, is so complex that you cannot reinforce it as a unit. You must program (or structure) it, which does not mean teaching one thing at a time in an isolated manner and as a collection of responses. What a student does halfway through a program may not be a part of the terminal behavior. Small steps are needed to ensure constant reinforcement.

Finally, teachers must decide on not only the proper size but also the most effective sequence of steps for the program. They must ideally ensure proper student preparation for each step, as well as an orderly arrangement of steps. One cannot always depend on a subject to be inherently logical. A good example is our work with Piaget. Usually students are well advised to read original sources and trace the author's work. This may not work with Piaget, because his ideas are so complex and his writing so tortuous that students, trying to proceed logically, may become hopelessly confused. Instructors are better advised to select and test basic ideas (such as Piaget's notion of the functional invariants) before presenting the entire system (his theory of cognitive development).

An example that reflects many of these principles is the highly structured Bereiter–Englemann program, designed to prescribe teaching procedures for disadvantaged children. Bereiter and Englemann (1966) stated that new teachers like to work with "ideas." Good teaching, however, employs much smaller and more intricate units than ideas; it involves specific information modules and specific techniques. Teaching is the interplay between information, pace, discipline, rewards, and drama as they relate to curriculum (1966, p. 105).

Acquiring these techniques comes gradually—a motivational trick here, an attention-getting device there. According to Bereiter and Englemann, teachers are good not because of what they are but because of what they do. Good teachers do the "right thing" because they have learned to do so slowly—even painfully. They were not naturally proficient; they achieved proficiency through practice.

Bereiter and Englemann devised several teaching strategies to use in an intensive preschool program for disadvantaged children. Nevertheless, these strategies have broad applicability. One suggestion is to be careful when you vary your presentation methods. Variations may confuse the culturally disadvantaged child, who ordinarily experiences considerable language difficulty. Excessive variation bothers and bewilders all children, who need to feel psychologically secure in the classroom.

Still, youngsters, disadvantaged or not, must respond in a variety of situations and should be ready to respond to variation outside of the classroom. Although the authors' suggestion is pertinent, remember also to consider variation in relation to the readiness of students. Whatever you do, give children sufficient time to respond. Time has been a recurring theme in this text. You previously encountered it in Bloom's work on mastery learning. In their work, Bereiter and Englemann urged that a lesson's tempo be such that the youngster can respond thoughtfully.

They also suggested that teachers use questions liberally. Questions are important because they help students attend to relevant cues. Teachers must consider the question's difficulty and ask whether a student is capable of answering it. The value of questioning is clear from countless studies. Individuals tend to remember more about material on which they are questioned, and to retain it longer. The direct instructional effect of questioning is substantial.

Try using multiple examples. When presenting a new concept, avoid talking too much about it. We advise that you "stretch" the concept. For example, if you are teaching the concept of the color red, give numerous examples of different objects whose sizes, shapes, and other characteristics are all different, with the one exception of their shared color: red. Remember, however, to try to prevent incorrect responses. Helping children avoid error will help them to avoid mistake patterns. Always assume that children will repeat mistakes in similar situations, and try to forestall them. Use prevention techniques.

Finally, be clear in responding to correct and incorrect answers. If a child brings a blue crayon when asked to bring a red one, do not praise the youngster for bringing a crayon. Youngsters cannot understand the subtle distinction. Teachers should provide nonthreatening but clear feedback. This suggestion is similar to our earlier warnings about nonpertinent praise.

Bereiter and Englemann furnished several more suggestions that indicate the nature of their program: carefully controlled stimuli, judicious application of reinforcement, and the avoidance of error. The Bereiter–Englemann program is an example of behavioral principles put to action.

Recent work derived from the Bereiter–Englemann program has focused on curricular interventions and been applied to all students with great promise, especially with regard to higher-order thinking skills (Carnine, 1991). Table 13.6 presents research that may close the gap between special and regular education and, as Carnine (1991) argued, should encourage educators to teach higher-order thinking skills in reasoning, science, and problem solving through curricular interventions.

Markle and Programed Instruction

Adapting Skinner's technology of teaching while remaining faithful to the basic principles of operant conditioning, Susan Markle (1990; Tiemann & Markle, 1990) built her concept of "programed" (note the one *m*) instruction around the principle of active responding (the student learns what the student does—Markle, 1990, p. 1). Although the original programmed instruction movement (based on Skinner's operant conditioning) enjoyed great initial success, Markle believes that too rigid adherence to these early views—small steps, heavy prompting, verbatim student responses to oft-repeated sentences—all contributed to criticism of the system as excessively sterile. Three programing principles—active responding, errorless learning, and immediate feedback—form the basis of Markle's model of instructional design.

The Principle of Active Responding

Markle refers to meaningful responses that are covert, overt, psychomotor, or verbal as active responding. To indicate how meaningful activity can be incorporated into programed instruction, Markle used the following example. The symbol for "less than" is <, and the symbol for "greater than" is >. Which of the following questions is more meaningful, 1 or 2?

> 1. Write the symbol for "less than" _____. Write the symbol for "greater than" _____.
> 2. Make each of the following arithmetic statements true by writing the correct symbol:
> a. 8 ? 3   b. 2×2 ? 5   c. 3+7 ? 8

Most everybody selects number 2 as being more meaningful. Each of these items requires student activity, but in the second item, a student reads the instruction, examines the problems, decides which quantities are greater (making computations, if necessary), and writes the symbol in the blank space. Note that the amount of processing required and the amount of overt activity needed are not identical. Return to the two math items; you notice immediately that task 2 requires far more thought. What the student is asked to do determines what information the student will notice and retain. Information that isn't needed, that is not processed at a meaningful level, is likely to go unnoticed. *Telling* the student to process and *causing* the student to process are not the same things.

Must students respond overtly? Note: This does not call into question the necessity of responding, but that of responding overtly. No one questions the need for active responding,

Table 13.6 RESEARCH ON CLOSING THE GAP BETWEEN SPECIAL EDUCATION AND GENERAL EDUCATION STUDENTS

Reasoning

1. On a variety of measures of argument construction and critiquing, high school students with mild handicaps in a higher-order-thinking intervention scored as high as or higher than high school students in an honors English class and college students enrolled in a teacher certification program (Grossen & Carnine, 1990).

2. In constructing arguments, high school students with learning disabilities in a higher-order-thinking intervention scored significantly higher than college students enrolled in a teacher certification program and scored at the same level as general education high school students and college students enrolled in a logic course. In critiquing arguments, the students with learning disabilities scored at the same level as the general education high school students and the college students enrolled in a teacher certification program. All of these groups had scores significantly lower than those of the college students enrolled in a logic course (Collins & Carnine, 1988).

Understanding science concepts

1. High school students with learning disabilities were mainstreamed for a higher-order-thinking intervention in science. On a chemistry test that required applying concepts such as bonding, equilibrium, energy of activation, atomic structure, and organic compounds, the students' scores did not differ significantly from control students' in an advanced placement chemistry course (Hofmeister, Englemann, & Carnine, 1989).

2. Middle school students with learning disabilities were mainstreamed for a higher-order-thinking intervention in science. On a test of misconceptions in earth science, the students showed better conceptual understanding than Harvard graduates interviewed in Schnep's 1987 film, *A Private Universe* (Muthukvishna, Carnine, Grossen, & Miller, 1990).

Problem solving

1. On a test of problem solving in health promotion, high school students with mild handicaps in a higher-order-thinking intervention scored significantly higher than nonhandicapped students who had completed a traditional high school health class (Woodward, Carnine, & Gersten, 1989).

2. Middle school students with learning disabilities were mainstreamed for a higher-order-thinking intervention in science. On a test of earth science problem solving, the students scored significantly higher than nonhandicapped students who received traditional science instruction (Woodward & Noell, this series).

3. High school special education students were mainstreamed for a higher-order-thinking intervention in math. On a test of problem solving requiring the use of ratios and proportions, the students scored as well as nonhandicapped high school students who received traditional math instruction (Moore & Carnine, 1989).

4. Middle school students with mild handicaps were mainstreamed for a higher-order-thinking intervention in earth science. Most of the students with handicaps scored higher than the nonhandicapped control students in problem solving involving earth science content (Neidelman, 1991).

but if a response remains covert (that is, inside a student's head), how can you be sure that the student knows the correct answer? Programers are often split on this issue; what teachers decide will reflect their personal preference. Incidentally, this issue is by no means restricted to programed instruction; all instructional theories and designs face this question about the nature of the student's response.

To illustrate the problem, examine the following statements and decide if you would want your students to respond covertly or overtly:

1. The student is learning how to write numbers.

2. The student is learning to sing the notes of the scale.

3. The student is learning how to play first base.

Active responding is a central ingredient for effective learning.

4. The student is learning Spanish names for familiar objects.

5. The student is learning to distinguish the music of Handel from that of Mozart.

You may decide that all statements require an overt response. Most readers would agree that 1, 2, and 3 demand overt activity; most would agree that learning is probably enhanced by overt responses in number 4; there would be less agreement about number 5.

Active responding, yes; overt responding, maybe. Note that active, overt responding provides rich opportunities for feedback and reinforcement, which is particularly important in the beginning stages of acquiring new knowledge or skills.

The Principle of Errorless Learning.

The goal of instruction should be to reduce error as much as possible. If learners respond actively, they tend to remember the circumstances surrounding the learning: the teacher, the stimuli, the response, any feedback that was provided. If they give an incorrect response, what do they learn? They learn the error.

Markle questioned the manner in which we treat error. If we tell a student, "No, that's wrong," or make a red X on his or her paper, will the student suppress the mistake? No. The student will simply try some other response. However, nothing will have been done to reinforce the correct answers, in working toward errorless learning. If you say, "No, John, 9 × 7 is not 56; it's 63," then the student does not respond actively. Does it follow, then, that students should never be allowed to make mistakes? Not in this system. Errors serve many functions. They can be signals that instruction needs improvement; they are a reliable guide for diagnosis; they aid programers in shaping the final form of a program. There may also be good reasons for getting a mistake out in the open, such as diagnosing a lack of background information that is needed for a topic. Students should also be permitted to "mess around" with the subject matter, as in a lab or in simulated lab situations in computer-assisted instruction.

The Principle of Immediate Feedback

Markle linked the need for feedback to the manner in which the statement is framed. For example, in some instances, feedback would add nothing to the learning. If I ask you how much 2 + 2 equals, you don't need me or the text to tell you that you are right. You have

---

CASE NOTES

Observation   Jim Watson and two male classmates frequently misbehave and are performing poorly in the language arts class. Melissa Williams integrates language arts and social studies and emphasizes critical thinking and problem solving.

Hypothesis   Mrs. Williams's teaching approach assumes students have developed many of the basic writing skills (that is, spelling, grammar, punctuation) and are ready to apply these skills to the production of written reports that demonstrate critical thinking and problem solving. Students who are struggling to acquire and use basic writing skills are often overwhelmed by the expectations to produce reports where critical thinking and problem solving are evident.

Possible Action   Use instructional strategies like those emphasized by Skinner and Markle that provide students time to practice basic skills in an interactive context where corrective feedback and reinforcement for effort and accurate production are available. These approaches to instruction differ from Mrs. Williams's current approach and may require assistance from her teaching colleagues or parents to put them into action.

that information from your personal knowledge. Challenging situations, however, cause students to make more errors and learn less when feedback is lacking.

Gagne and Instructional Design

Robert Gagne has been a leader in the field of instructional design for nearly three decades (Gagne & Briggs, 1979; Gagne & Driscoll, 1988; Gagne, Briggs, & Wager, 1988). Gagne's influential work has been based on his views of five learning outcomes: verbal information, intellectual skills, cognitive strategies, attitudes, and motor skills. Each of these five learning outcomes demands a different set of conditions for optimizing learning, retention, and transferability. The "optimal conditions" refer to a particular set of external events surrounding the learner: the instruction that students receive.

Here we see the great value of Gagne's work: the close relationship between teaching and learning. In his view of teaching and learning, Gagne has identified several instructional events that he believes help students to learn meaningfully. First, teachers must *gain the attention of their students.* Instruction terminates immediately if attention falters. What you have read in Chapters 6, 7, and 8 on learning applies here. Watch the conditions of your class (time of the day, hunger, fatigue); use stimulating materials that are appropriate for students; appeal to as many senses as possible (read, listen, discuss, touch, manipulate); be sure that stimuli are biologically and psychologically appropriate. *Informing learners of the objective of the lesson* is another way of helping them focus their attention. What precisely is to be learned? Students should know the *criteria for mastery* and when they have achieved it.

Gagne recommends that you *stimulate recall of prerequisite knowledge,* that is, appeal to students' prior knowledge. Students may need a simple reminder of previous learning, or they might require detailed help. This will help teachers when they *present the stimulus material.* Use techniques that are as attractive and exciting as possible, whether verbal, demonstrative, or media-related. Make the material interesting and pertinent to facilitate attention and to spark inquiry.

Teachers may have to *provide learning guidance.* By this Gagne means the teacher must ensure that students acquire the details involved in the learning objective; if a series of steps is needed for mastery, then students must know what these steps are and how to master them. Learn the geography; learn the history; finally, speculate about politics. This guidance in turn helps to *elicit the performance.* Teachers cannot be certain that a student has learned unless he or she performs the behavior. (Recall the discussion at the beginning of the learning section concerning learning versus performance.)

Once students exhibit a response or performance, it is important that a teacher provides *appropriate feedback.* Good feedback means giving students accurate, detailed information about their performance, specifying what was done well and what needs improvement. Does your feedback match a specific response? Is it appropriate for the quality of the response? Finally, check to see if students understand the feedback and are able to use it to improve future performance. Closely associated with providing feedback is assessing a student's performance. *Assessment of student performance* can occur in several ways and was discussed in detail in Chapters 11 and 12.

A final step in creating optimal conditions for learning is to *enhance retention and transfer.* A teacher simply cannot assume that students will automatically transfer their learning from one class to another; instructional plans must make provisions for both review and the use of the material in novel situations.

Gagne believes that this nine-step model can function as a theory of learning and memory. It utilizes existing theory as a basis for designing instruction and attempts to include all types of learning outcomes that are typically the objectives of instruction. Finally, the model provides an instructional basis for analyzing the interaction of internal events with external events; this makes the model applicable to instruction of many forms in a wide variety of settings, while simultaneously appealing to the individual differences of learners. We agree with Gagne, and therefore as a summary, we provide the following checklist of key features that he proposes create optimal learning conditions for most people:

1. Gain the attention of the learner.

2. Inform the learner of the learning objective and criteria determining mastery.

3. Stimulate recall of prerequisite knowledge that connects to information being taught.

4. Present the task or material to be learned in an interesting manner.

5. Provide learning guidance by pointing out details or major steps in learning the material.

6. Elicit a performance or demonstration of what the individual has learned.

7. Assess the performance of the student.

8. Provide the learner with specific feedback about performance.

9. Enhance retention and transfer of what has been learned to new situations or related subjects.

A close reading of this list and the points Gagne generated will reveal that we believe assessment should precede feedback, not follow it. Good instructional assessment, as we discussed in Chapter 11, results in feedback to the learner and to the teacher. Other than this small difference in the sequencing of learning conditions, we believe Gagne's design of instruction is pedagogically strong.

TECHNOLOGY-BASED TEACHING STRATEGIES

More and more teachers are integrating technology into their instruction. Technology-based teaching strategies take advantage of the unique properties of educational technology to help students master material and skills. The technology involved varies depending on the teacher's instructional goals, the students' levels and instructional needs, and the available resources.

Technology-based strategies offer several advantages over more traditional methods of presenting material. Technology allows students to work on problems that would be difficult or impossible otherwise. A genetics simulation program, for example, allows students to specify an organism's genetic makeup, systematically test hypotheses about genetic principles, and see the results of many generations of "virtual offspring" within a single lab class (Stewart, Hafner, Johnson, & Finkel, 1992)! A computerized tutoring system lets students learn how to diagnose and repair problems in airplane engines, learning about expensive and dangerous equipment without harming themselves or the equipment (Lesgold, Lajoie, Bunzo, & Eggan, 1992). CD-ROMs and laser videodiscs let students not only read and hear about processes and changes but also see the dynamics of such changes. Unlike slides or videotapes, students can precisely control how quickly the changes progress so that they can carefully examine and understand the causes and results. Finally, students and teachers can use computer networks to communicate with others across town or across the world. Networks also offer high-speed access to resources and expertise that otherwise would not be available, giving up-to-date and accurate information about virtually any topic of interest.

Technology allows a wide world of information to be the topic of instruction.

Differences between Technology-Based and Traditional Teaching Strategies

Technology-based teaching strategies are often based on cognitive views of teaching and learning, especially on the constructivist view you read about in Chapter 7. As you'll recall, this view places both teachers and students in new roles. Teachers are viewed as facilitators and collaborators with students as they learn, rather than as experts imparting knowledge. Students take much more responsibility for their own learning, directing its pace, format, and sometimes even content. It is sometimes hard for teachers, students, and parents to adjust to these new roles. The type of classwork students do can also be quite different when technology-based teaching strategies are used. Student-developed projects are typical. These projects can be very complex, with students seeking information from a variety of different computer- and network-based resources and going into great detail. Such projects can take several months to complete and usually involve a lot of collaboration among students. There also tends to be a strong emphasis on the use of problem-solving and research skills as students take more active roles in defining, developing, and presenting their projects.

Finally, technology-based teaching strategies often require different kinds of assessments of student learning than more traditional teaching strategies. Like the class activities, assessments tend to be more project and/or performance oriented. Attempts are often made to assess not only the specific content learned but also the problem-solving, thinking, and research skills acquired. Though it can be difficult, assessments also sometimes include changes in students' motivation for learning and the degree to which students take responsibility for their own learning.

Teachers can use technology in many ways in their teaching. We will discuss several of the most common and most recent uses. As with most developments in technology, new tools and techniques are developed every day. This adds to the difficulty in keeping up with the field but is also what makes technology-based teaching strategies exciting!

Web-Based Instruction

Most of you are familiar with the term "World Wide Web." It is an organized system of computer networks that allows users to transmit and search information using many different branching pathways. In other words, you can find information quickly, without having to go through (too many) intervening websites. The World Wide Web (WWW) also allows you to easily "browse" through many different links among websites, which lets a user look up related topics quickly and easily (but which can also lead you to spend a lot of time looking through fascinating but irrelevant information!).

Web-based instruction (WBI) uses the information search and transmitting capabilities of the WWW and the vast array of resources available on it to provide instruction to students (Khan, 1997). Sometimes WBI is very structured, as when colleges offer entire courses on-line, complete with "virtual office hours" and "chat rooms" where instructors and students discuss material. WBI at the K–12 level is usually less integrated and less comprehensive. It often involves using the WWW as an information resource for student projects, experiments, and reports. But the WWW is also increasingly used at these levels as a way to allow students to collaborate with experts and other students in different locations, often working to develop solutions to a complex, "authentic" (that is, meaningful and real-world) problem. For example, KIDLINK (http://www. kidlink.org) links thousands of schoolchildren across countries in projects such as Blue Print Earth. In this project, students from around the world work together to discuss ways of improving Earth's living conditions (Owston, 1997). The WWW is also used to allow K–12 students to actively participate in activities that would otherwise not be possible. For example, the MayaQuest project allowed students from across the country to electronically participate in a real archaeological expedition through Central America in an effort to better understand the fall of the Mayan civilization (Relan & Gillani, 1997).

Advantages of WBI

One of the major advantages offered by WBI is the potential to increase the accessibility of learning (Owston, 1997). Students and teachers can access information, materials, experiences, and expertise that would be quite difficult to obtain, even for the best-funded school districts. The scope of education for students moves well beyond what is locally available and immediately affordable to include "virtual" world travel, world-class scientific experimentation and expertise, and international exploration.

A second advantage of WBI is the potential for increased interaction with students of different backgrounds and races. The WWW allows collaboration across classes, districts, even across nations on all kinds of projects. In working with students who come from different cultures, students can begin to understand the influence of culture and move away from an "ethnocentric" perspective. They learn to not only respect and learn from others' views and positions but also how to reflect on and coherently state their own views and positions. Thus, in addition to learning tolerance and respect for others, students can gain greater self-understanding.

WBI also can improve the quality of learning by encouraging the development of problem solving, information evaluation, and information search skills (Owston, 1997). WBI often emphasizes solving realistic, meaningful, and important problems either independently, in "local" groups, or in "distributed" groups. This emphasis may even change students' ideas of what it means to learn, encouraging the view that learning involves active and often collaborative framing and solving of interesting problems, rather than a memory and task completion orientation.

WEB-BASED INSTRUCTION (WBI)

Using the information search and transmitting capabilities of the WWW and the vast array of resources available on it to provide instruction to students. In some cases, WBI is highly structured; however, at the K–12 level, it is usually less integrated and fosters discovery learning.

WBI also allows much greater learner control of the learning process and products. For example, a student might be browsing for information on the current exploration of Mars. She types in a keyword (for example, "Mars") and within seconds finds a current article on the Sojourner project, complete with the most recent photos of the exploration. In reading the text, she finds that the first exploration of Mars was in the 1970s, clicks on this section of text, and within seconds has access to a summary of this earlier exploration and how it led to the current work. She can branch to information about exploration of other planets, the U.S. space program in general, or more detailed information about Mars (existence of ancient rivers, evidence of life forms, why it is called the Red Planet). She can also enter chat rooms to discuss Mars exploration with other interested individuals from across the globe. Such a high degree of learner control has the potential for much more detailed, thoughtful, and creative student learning and products.

Finally, WBI can allow for a greater accommodation of different learning styles than might be the case with more traditional forms of instruction. Typically, the learner controls the pace of learning, and the multimedia nature of much of the information on the WWW lets students often choose their preferred format for information (audio, video, text, graphs). Students can experience the information several times and in different ways, something that can improve memory and comprehension.

Problems and Prerequisites

WBI is usually more student centered and project oriented than more traditional forms of instruction. Different thinking, learning, and study skills are often emphasized. Teachers, students, and parents need to understand and communicate about the goals, skills, and assessments of WBI to make sure that everyone is clear about what is expected.

To effectively use WBI, students need to learn web-navigating skills so they do not get lost or too distracted as they work their way through websites. Some unfocused exploration can be useful to help students learn what the WWW has to offer, but too much can severely impede their progress in finding relevant information. Some instruction is probably necessary, along with simply allowing time to learn how to effectively "surf the net."

As always, money is an issue. To participate in WBI, schools must have computers with adequate amounts of memory, processing capacity, and modem speed. Slower computer systems lead to poor sound and picture quality, long waits to access websites, and student and teacher frustration. If used well, however, the savings in access to information and expertise can balance the initial investment required, especially for those schools which would have little hope of ever purchasing such instructional materials outright.

Some argue that WBI will increase the already existing "technology gap" between higher and lower socioeconomic status (SES) schools. The belief is that as higher SES schools get more and higher-level computers and perhaps more expertise from teachers, parents, and community volunteers, they will increase in their use of and effectiveness in using WWW information. Lower SES schools will have less money to acquire equipment and pay for WWW access, and perhaps less expertise to draw on to teach students how to utilize the WWW, and these students will become more disadvantaged than they already are for college entrance and job competition. The other side of the argument, however, is that WWW access will lead to a *decrease* in the gap between richer and poorer schools, because it will allow lower SES schools access to information, instructional materials, expertise, and experiences that would otherwise be impossible. Given better materials and educational experiences, these students may benefit from WBI even more than those in higher SES schools. At this point, there is not enough information available to know what the outcome will be.

Effectiveness of WBI

There are few studies that assess the effectiveness of WBI, especially for K–12 students. College students seem to perform as well or slightly better on web-based courses, and they seem to like them (Owston, 1997). But little systematic data exist on skills learned (or required) or on the comparative mastery of skills and material using WBI versus more traditional methods of instruction. As with any teaching tool, WBI can be used in exciting, innovative ways that can increase the quality of learning. But it can also be used in ways that make little difference in what and how well learning happens. The effect on learning quality will depend on how WBI is used (Owston, 1997).

Multimedia

Multimedia instruction is the integration and simultaneous use of several different types of technology to improve instruction. For example, a computer software program might be written using some specialized language (for example, Handy, Hypercard) that controls not only the presentation of text and graphics on the computer screen, but also controls the use of laser videodisc, audio compact disc, videotape, audiotape, voice synthesis, digitized voice, touch, or animated graphics (see Nix & Spiro, 1990, for examples). Many media are interactive in that the user does not just listen and view them but can manipulate them in some way. Multimedia programs are often designed to encourage students to integrate different types of content as well (for example, science, mathematics, history). Integration can encourage students to use their knowledge and skills to solve problems, rather than seeing knowledge as a collection of unrelated, often nonuseful collection of facts (see Bransford, Sherwood, Hasselbring, Kinzer, & Williams, 1990).

Laser Videodiscs

One example of a multimedia project designed to integrate several content areas is a series of laser videodiscs about a character named Jasper Woodbury (Cognition and Technology Group at Vanderbilt, 1990; Van Haneghan, Barron, Young, Williams, Vye, & Bransford, 1992). Jasper is shown in several complex, realistic problem situations (like looking over and deciding whether to buy a new boat). Students are challenged to identify his major goal, generate the subproblems that must be solved to meet the goal, find relevant information presented in the videodisc, and come up with strategies to solve the subproblems and achieve the major goal.

Several aspects of the videodiscs make it useful for learning content knowledge, general problem-solving skills, and encouraging integration of knowledge across content areas. First, the problem presented is quite complex, requiring students to generate and solve approximately fifteen subgoals. The authors argue that students need experience generating problems and solving complex problems, but they are often not given such opportunities in classrooms (Cognition and Technology Group at Vanderbilt, 1990). Second, the problems encountered are realistic, allowing students the opportunity to make decisions in realistic settings. Third, the videodiscs use an embedded data design in which students view the videodisc, generate the subproblems, then go back and find the relevant information that is embedded in the story. All necessary data are included but, as in many real-life situations, the students are not told that the information is relevant for solving a problem when they first encounter it. Students must learn how to search information sources (including their memories!) for potentially useful information. Finally, the video encourages students to integrate content areas like mathematics and science. For example, in one disc Jasper must determine whether he has enough gas in his boat to make it home. This requires using scientific information like wind speed, rate of current, whether he is going with or against the current, the effect of the boat's weight on travel time, and so on. It also requires that students be able to use mathematical information like ratios and probabilities. Probably most important, the videodisc encourages students to view these scientific and mathematical skills as tools to be used in the service of solving a problem, rather than just as facts and formulas to be memorized.

Effectiveness of Teaching with Multimedia

A number of multimedia research projects have been conducted, including some in which children design and develop projects about the Civil War (Lehrer, 1994), science (Brown & Campione, in press), Victorian England, and in which they write stories (Bransford, Vye, Kinzer, & Risko, 1990). A recent review of twenty-four studies indicated that multimedia instruction resulted in more creative problem solving than other instructional approaches, especially for students who knew little about the content areas to begin with, and for those who were high in spatial ability (Mayer, 1997). Other studies report positive effects of multimedia design projects on student comprehension, retention, and use of new knowledge. In addition, both academically successful and less successful students say they feel a greater sense of ownership of the projects and are more involved in the design and production process (Cognition and Technology Group at Vanderbilt, 1990; Lehrer, 1994).

Disadvantages of Multimedia Instruction

As with many forms of technology-based teaching strategies, the cost associated with multimedia instruction can be a problem. Teachers must have available a variety of different types of technology (computers, videodisc players, audiodisc players, and so on) and software capable of interfacing the different machines. A bigger disadvantage in many teachers' minds, however, is the loss of control over what students are learning. Allowing students to design their own multimedia projects turns over the control and responsibility for learning to the students themselves. This may result in students not covering the material the teacher (or school system) feels they ought to cover. Proponents argue that students may well cover much of the "required" material, but in a very different way. Finally, as you read about earlier, a potential problem is how to assess exactly what a student has learned.

CD-ROM

Compact Disc-Read Only Memory (CD-ROM) is one of the fastest growing forms of technology-based teaching strategies. CD-ROM is an optical disc technology that allows the storage of very large amounts of any type of digital data including text, digital sound and graphics, and digital movies. CD-ROMs have been used in school libraries for quite some time, providing fast and easy access to large databases. At the college level, you might be familiar with CD-ROM versions of Psychological Abstracts or the ERIC system, both of which contain listings of thousands of references on psychological or educational topics. One well-known CD-ROM system at the K–12 level is Compton's Multimedia Encyclopedia, which allows users to access any topic included in the entire encyclopedia within seconds. They also include both static and dynamic visual information and sound, often in the form of news footage or animation. These features give much richer information than a printed text is capable of, helping students visualize and comprehend information.

CD-ROMs focused on initial instruction of skills are being developed at an astonishing pace. They feature animation, music, narration that can be turned on or off, bilingual options, teacher/parent "edit pages" (where teachers can provide custom-designed sets of problems, words, or other data), and progress reports to let teachers and students know how many items a given student has completed correctly. Many CD-ROMs now also have the capability to allow students to use images, vocabulary, and audio features to develop their own creations, with the program then able to read aloud the child's work. Assessments of CD-ROMs so far show positive effects on such measures as reading achievement, comprehension, and enjoyment (Matthew, 1996; Miller, Blackstock, & Miller, 1994; Reinking & Bridwell-Bowles, 1991).

Intelligent Tutoring Systems

One of the newest technology-based teaching strategies is an **intelligent tutoring system (ITS).** Originally developed for training in industry and the military, ITSs are not widely used yet in K–12 instruction because of high equipment and development costs. The goal of these systems is to provide an individual tutor for each student for a given subject area. The system must present new material in a way that is understandable to each student, provide examples, and provide problems appropriate for that student. Most important, the ITS must be capable of tracking a student's performance, identifying errors and misconceptions, and providing appropriate guidance and feedback. This last aspect often proves to be the most difficult, because it involves programming into the system decision rules for when as well as how to intervene, and when to allow the student to continue to the next set of skills or concepts.

An ITS typically has three components (Barr & Feigenbaum, 1982). First, the system must contain an expert component that is able to solve the problems that will be presented to the student. Second, there must be a diagnostician, which tracks a student's performance and diagnoses the student's misconceptions and errors. Finally, there must be a tutorial component that provides appropriate feedback and guidance for the student. When well programmed, ITSs can individualize instruction to a degree not seen before in educational technology. They track students' performance, provide different problems and explanations of content based on students' current understanding, intervene and reinstruct when appropriate, and give immediate feedback. Suppes (1966) described the advantage this way "…millions of school children will have access to what Phillip of Macedon's son Alexander enjoyed as a royal prerogative, the personal services of a tutor as well-informed and responsive as Aristotle" (p. 207).

An ITS can often allow a type of instruction that would otherwise be difficult if not impossible, using examples that are either rarely occurring but important, or dangerous. For example, an avionics ITS was developed to help train air force mechanics for maintenance and repair of air force jets and fighters (Lesgold et al., 1992). The traditional training method includes intensive classroom work (lecture and workbook exercises) on the many systems in these planes (for example, electrical, mechanical, fuel). Classroom instruction is followed by on-the-job training, where students work under the guidance of experienced mechanics to diagnose and repair planes. The avionics tutor was developed to improve the training these students receive. It can present very rarely occurring, but catastrophic, problems in the planes so students learn to recognize warning signs of such catastrophes. The ITS can also allow students to make mistakes, even quite dangerous ones, while working the problems and provides them with appropriate feedback (ZAP! You just received a serious electrical shock!). In a series of studies, this ITS was quite effective for learning basic information and how to solve problems. It was also a tremendous time-saver. After four months of classroom instruction and using the tutor, students were solving problems on a par with students who had four years of traditional training. In some cases, the level of content expertise programmed into an ITS far exceeds what a classroom teacher can be expected to have in his/her repertoire. This becomes especially important when trying to identify students' misconceptions about content, that is, those underlying and enduring ways of understanding and knowing about a concept that make sense to the student but are not correct. It can be quite difficult to identify such misconceptions, but they have a tremendous impact on students' ability to understand, remember, and use new information (Roth, 1990). In some cases, teachers may share the same misconceptions, making it difficult to identify and change them. An ITS offers the opportunity to have a high-level expert for every content area, making it more likely that such misconceptions will be identified and corrected.

What are the disadvantages of this use of technology? Cost and availability are two practical problems. ITSs require a significant amount of time and effort on the part of a number of experts, which of course makes their development costs high. Another potential disadvantage of ITS has to do with the tutorial component. This component focuses almost exclusively on the cognitive aspects of the tutoring process, that is, identifying and programming the rules that govern when and how a tutor should intervene. Lepper and Chabay (1988) point out that motivational as well as cognitive components of tutoring must be considered to develop a truly personalized instructional system. They feel that an ITS must display not only intelligent tutoring, but empathetic tutoring as well. Finally, most ITSs are based on a cognitive theory of learning. Current theories of human cognition, as you read about in chapters 7 and 8, consider the social nature of human learning and thinking, emphasizing the importance of the social context of learning and the role of social interactions (Rogoff, 1990; Vygotsky, 1978). ITSs usually do not consider the importance of these social aspects of learning, which may limit their effectiveness (Becker, 1991).

There are few systematic evaluations of the effectiveness of ITSs. Those that are published indicate that ITSs accelerate the pace of learning without causing decreases in learner performance, result in changes in the roles of teachers and students in the classroom, and that ITS use is seen as enjoyable and motivating by students (Anderson, Farrell, & Saurs, 1984; Lesgold et al., 1992; Schofield, 1995; Shute, 1991; Shute & Glaser, 1991). Shute and Regian (1993) note, however, that "we are familiar with other (unpublished) tutor-evaluation studies that were conducted but were 'failures' (p. 246) and suggest that improvement in the design of evaluation studies is necessary to provide a fuller understanding of the effectiveness of ITSs.

Virtual Reality

Virtual reality (VR) is a computer-generated environment that is three-dimensional and involves the user in real-time, multisensory interactions (Ferrington & Loge, 1992). The user wears a special viewing helmet that generates three-dimensional visual and auditory experiences, and a wired glove or full-body data suit that allows him or her to "move about" in the virtual space. As the user moves, the computer updates the position in the virtual space and provides appropriate changes in the visual and sound information provided in the viewing helmet.

The exciting aspect of VR systems for learning is that students will be able to engage in interactive learning that combines cognitive, affective, and psychomotor skills (Walser, 1990). For example, students will not imagine what it is like to live on Mars, they will be able to experience it within a VR simulation of Mars's environment. Biology and medical students could perform operations on "virtual" patients to learn about various organ systems and the effects of different treatments, learning activities which are clearly not possible in "real" reality. However, few elementary and secondary schools have VR systems available as of yet. The military and higher education institutions continue to experiment with VR systems for training and education in areas like physics, chemistry, biology, and music (Larijani, 1994). Some of these research projects have expanded to include preliminary work with high school students. Data on mastery of skills and information, pace of learning, and student attitudes about this technology are not yet available for K–12 levels. As more information about VR's educational usefulness is gathered and as the cost of the VR systems decreases, it is likely that such systems will begin to be used in K–12 classrooms.

We have reviewed a significant number of technologies that have application to teaching. Table 13.7 provides a summary of these technologies and outlines some of their uses in advancing effective teacher-student interactions.

Table 13.7   TYPES OF TECHNOLOGY AND THEIR USES IN THE CLASSROOM

Category	Definition	Example
Administrative/managerial	Using technology to collect, analyze, and report information concerning students or instruction.	Computerized gradebooks Word processing used to record lesson plans, student goal attainment Spreadsheets used to graph student progress
Audiovisual aids	Using technology to present information in several formats (vision, audition). Usually supplements a teacher- or text-based presentation.	Overhead projectors Slide projectors Television
Teaching technology	Teaching students the basics of how to use the technology itself, particularly how to use word processing packages, spreadsheets, graphing programs, etc.	Computer literacy Teaching programming basics Teaching how to use word processing software Teaching how to use spreadsheets
Computer-assisted instruction	Using technology to present material to students initially and to assist them in mastering it. Included are programs with a predominantly behavioristic theoretical basis, emphasizing progressive shaping of behavior toward a final goal via small steps and positive reinforcement. More cognitively based programs are included in other categories.	Programmed instruction Drill and practice software
Teaching of thinking using technology	Using technology to foster the development, use, and transfer of students' general thinking and problem-solving skills.	Teaching programming (for example, Logo) Using word processing to improve writing and thinking skills (especially when computerized prompting systems are incorporated)
Intelligent tutoring systems	Using technology to provide an individualized tutor for each student. The system presents new material in a way that is comprehensible to each student, provides examples and practice problems, tracks student performance, identifies errors and misconceptions, and provides appropriate guidance and feedback.	Sherlock (an avionics tutor)
Multimedia uses	Using technology to integrate and simultaneously use several different types of technology. Often based on cognitive constructivist theory, and often involves students in collaborative, large-scale projects.	Laser videodisc series (for example, Jasper Woodbury) CD-ROM (for example, National Geographic Society series)
Other recent developments Networks	Connecting computers to one another through telephone lines or cables so that information and/or equipment can be shared. Includes local area networks (LANs), wide area networks (WANs), and the Internet.	WaterNet project Intercultural Learning Network National Geographic Kids Network
Virtual reality (VR)	A computer-generated environment that is three-dimensional and involves the user in real-time, multisensory interactions.	

Teaching the Big Ideas in Reading and Mathematics

In analyzing the basic data teachers need, our first consideration should be the knowledge base of teaching. In a thoughtful essay, Good (1990) identified several topics with which teachers should be comfortable enough to use them almost automatically in assessing their instruction. These include motivation, classroom management, learning strategies, and subject matter knowledge. We have already addressed issues of student motivation (Chapter 9), learning strategies (Chapters 7 and 8), and classroom management tactics (Chapter 10). Here we examine the topic of subject matter knowledge, and in particular knowledge that will facilitate instruction of fundamentals (that is, big ideas) in reading and mathematics.

Shulman (1986) distinguished three types of content knowledge: subject matter knowledge, pedagogical knowledge, and curriculum knowledge. *Subject matter knowledge* refers to a teacher's comprehension of a subject when compared with that of a specialist. How comfortable am I with this subject? Can I answer students' questions accurately and in a relaxed manner? *Pedagogical knowledge* refers to how the basic principles and strategies of a subject are best acquired and retained. Am I sufficiently prepared in this subject to know the best way to introduce it? What is the best way to teach its core elements? What is the best way to evaluate my students? *Curriculum knowledge* refers to the optimal manner in which knowledge of a subject can be organized and presented: in texts, programs, media, and workbooks. Am I aware of the supplementary materials that can broaden my students' knowledge of this subject?

How does your knowledge of a subject affect the manner in which you teach it? Subject matter knowledge cuts both ways. If you feel shaky about material, you may attempt to brush by it quickly. Conversely, if you have depth of knowledge, you may do too much with your students. Generally, though, research indicates that knowledgeable teachers can better detect student misconceptions and exploit opportunities for meaningful learning. Teachers who are less knowledgeable in subject matter may avoid presenting critical material if they are uncomfortable with it and may misinterpret students' learning (Dill, 1990).

In attempting to answer the question of how much and what teachers should know of the material they teach, researchers are just beginning the task of unraveling teacher cognition. Shulman's three categories help us to discover where teachers turn when students experience difficulty, and whether differences in the knowledge that teachers bring to a subject produce differences in how they organize that topic.

Nevertheless, it all comes down to one fundamental question: How much and what should teachers know of what they teach (Shulman, 1986, p. 26)? The best approach is to know as much as possible about a subject, to present it as dynamically as possible, and to be prepared to answer all kinds of questions. What does all of this mean for you as a teacher? You should remember one guiding principle: A teacher's task is to help students learn as much as their potential permits.

To effectively help students achieve their potential, teachers need to have command of pedagogical knowledge in the core areas of reading and mathematics. In the remainder of this section, we examine what has become known as *big ideas* in reading and mathematics instruction. Insights into these big ideas have grown out of the effective teacher research base (Carnine, 1994).

Reading

Researchers have long searched for the causes of reading problems. In the early 1970s, they focused on visual perceptual abilities; however, findings consistently failed to confirm that these nonlinguistic abilities caused reading delay (Vellutino, 1991). These results led researchers to examine language-based deficits of reading. Thus, throughout the 1980s researchers paid significant attention to the linguistic basis of reading delay (Stanovich, 1986). This research generally revealed that good and poor readers differed on virtually every dimension of language (that is, phonology, morphology, semantics, and syntax). Yet there emerged from this research a clear picture: The basis of early reading delay can be largely attributed to phonological processing difficulties (Wagner & Torgesen, 1987). *Phonological processing* refers to the use of phonological information, that is, the sounds of one's language. Numerous authors have identified the phonological causes and correlates of beginning reading (Ehri, 1991; Juel, 1991), and although they talk about their models of teaching reading somewhat differently, three critical features of early reading are quite apparent: phonological awareness, alphabetic understanding, and automaticity with the symbol code. Effectively designed reading instruction should consider each of these concepts.

Phonological Awareness

Phonological awareness training strategies and programs are plentiful and varied. For many students, gaining an awareness of the sounds of a language is not easy because the individual sounds in words are often merged and not pronounced as separate parts and require some abstractions and discriminations (Ball & Blachman, 1991). Researchers have suggested that the most powerful interventions to improve phonological awareness combine phonological awareness and letter-sound instruction. An example of a strategy for developing phonological awareness is learning to blend sounds to form words. Other strategies for developing phonological awareness include segmenting words into their component sounds, rhyming tasks, or transforming words by changing initial or ending sounds (Adams, 1990).

Alphabetic Understanding

Analyses of prominent beginning reading programs have revealed the absence of systematic procedures to teach students to translate letters to sounds and blend them into words (Stein, 1993). Consequently, it should not be too surprising to find that many children fail to make the connections between learning the letter code and reading words. The first step in teaching students the alphabetic code is to teach them individual letter-sound correspondences. Once students master several letter-sound sets, they should be taught to blend isolated sounds into meaningful words. In this step, the simple, but important goal is to establish the connection between sounds and letters.

Automaticity with the Code

Automaticity means a rapid recognition and performance of a skill. In a study of automaticity and reading, Stanovich (1991) concluded that word identification becomes less capacity demanding as experience with words increases. Thus, continuing with the blending strategy taught in phonological awareness and alphabetic understanding, students should be given frequent practice at blending words with patterns previously practiced in oral blending exercises and to sound blend words containing letter-sound correspondences that have been systematically taught.

    The three phonological processing skills that we have briefly defined are part of the repertoire of beginning successful readers, but not most poor readers. The instructional methods outlined to facilitate the development of these skills in young readers emphasize the importance of making letter-sound correspondences explicit and systematically practiced. In addition to these basic tactics, there are several other instructional methods for effectively teaching children to read.

Mathematics

In 1989, Porter reported on the state of instruction and students' opportunities to learn mathematics in the United States. He noted several weaknesses clearly related to difficulties in acquiring complex problem-solving skills. First, excessive amounts of time are spent on computational skills with little emphasis on concept understanding and application. Second, the amount of time allocated for instruction is not adequate for many students. Specifically with regard to instructional time, Porter reported that teachers devoted less than thirty minutes across the entire year to 70% of the topics they covered—thus, "teaching for exposure" rather than understanding and application. Finally, the rate at which students are taught new content as they proceed through grades is slow because of redundancy. That is, considerable overlap occurs in the content covered in consecutive grade levels. Under these types of instructional conditions, only the most proficient students master substantial skills; less able learners truly struggle and acquire a fragmented array of skills at best. What needs to be done to improve mathematics instruction and student performances?

The current mathematics standards (National Council of Teachers of Mathematics, 1989) suggest that instruction in mathematics needs to be characterized by more teacher and student interactions in meaningful contexts, with less attention to rote practice. Unfortunately, teachers do not seem to devote much time to the development of meaningful acquisition of math skills. For students to solve complex and realistic problems, they must acquire knowledge of the more important key mathematics concepts or big ideas with mathematics. Big ideas make it possible for students to acquire and generalize the most knowledge and skills as efficiently as possible. Commonly identified big ideas include proportions, estimation, and area. The value of organizing instruction so that students will be most likely to learn big ideas may have more support in math education than in most other domains of knowledge because the skill hierarchies seem more apparent in mathematics.

Instructional Principles for Improving Reading and Mathematics

To advance the development of reading and mathematics fundamentals, experts suggest that instruction should be characterized by four principles: a conspicuous strategy, strategically integrated training, scaffold activities, and structured reviews. For example, with reading this means: (1) a conspicuous strategy for teaching segmenting, blending, and other phonological awareness skills, (2) strategically integrated training on letter-sound correspondence activities and word recognition skills in connected text, (3) scaffolding (organized and related) activities within levels and cumulatively, to ensure student success, while increasing task complexity and learning outcomes to more toward independent reading, and (4) structured judicious review both within levels and cumulatively to ensure retention and, gradually, automaticity of lessons learned.

The role of structured review is a particularly important instructional principle in reading and mathematics instruction and deserves more elaboration. Practice activities should be designed and organized so that students develop greater fluency and understanding as rapidly as possible and maintain those skills and knowledge as long as possible. Carnine (1989) identified six guidelines for designing review and practice activities that are supported by instructional research. The guidelines are as follows:

1. *Introduce information into review activities cumulatively.* Students will be more successful if the concepts or skills they have to practice are limited to manageable amounts. Newly acquired skills should replace skills the student has developed to greater fluency. The notion of cumulative review means the material taught accumulates in review.

2. *Distribute practice to build retention.* Although massed or concentrated practice will facilitate acquisition, subsequent practice should be *distributed* to establish long-term retention and automaticity of knowledge. Two aspects of distributed practice to consider are that difficult skills should be practiced a day or two within their initial acquisition and periodically afterward, and such practice provides opportunities to make discriminations among similar concepts or skills.

3. *Emphasize relationships to make learning more meaningful.* One goal of a review is to facilitate understanding. Practice and review should not amount to unconnected exercises in rote drill. The skills students are working on should be clearly related to a larger concept or set of skills. Thus, new information must be related to familiar information.

4. *Reduce processing demands by preteaching components of a strategy.* Some students will find it difficult to learn and apply a strategy simultaneously. Thus, preteaching and practicing of components can facilitate mastery of complex operations, especially in mathematics.

5. *Require quicker response times.* Fluent responding is one of the goals of review and practice. To become more fluent, students must practice responding with information they already know well.

6. *Use varied examples for review.* With rare exception, the specific items or words that are reviewed should not be the same as used earlier in instruction. This approach promotes generialization. Be careful, however, to ensure that material is not so varied that it actually requires new knowledge or skills to complete.

The instructional principles and strategies we have outlined in this section are relevant to all learners. Teachers, however, will be confronted with the task of teaching many students who will need even more specialized instructional strategies. We examine some of these in the next section on adapting instruction for diverse learners.

ADAPTING INSTRUCTION TO THE INDIVIDUAL DIFFERENCES OF LEARNERS

Adapting instruction means attempting to "match the mix" between student aptitudes and the methods and materials you use. A good example of this can be seen in the work of Benjamin Bloom, whose ideas on learning have received the careful attention of psychologists and educators. Bloom (1981) identified several variables that influence the teaching-learning process, particularly time on task.

Time on Task

Time on task has always been recognized as a critical factor in learning, whether the term refers to years a subject appears in a curriculum, number of days in the school year, number of hours per day, or number of minutes per class. These are relatively fixed times, which tell us little about how much time students are actively engaged in learning. As Bloom observed, if one student is actively engaged 90% of the time while another is thus engaged only 30% of the time, we should not be surprised at their different achievement levels. As for teachers, studies of cues (what is to be learned), reinforcement (rewards for learning), and

Effective teachers manage time well and help students do the same.

participation (active student engagement in learning) provide valuable clues as to just what teachers are doing with their time. What is most important to remember, however, is that time on task can be altered. Using Bloom's work as a basis, Gettinger (1990) identified three aspects of learning time that could be increased. The first is the time used for instruction, the second is engaged time, and the third is productive learning time. The accompanying TIPS box (Methods for Increasing Academic Learning Time) provides a summary of strategies that have been found to increase the various aspects of learning time.

Bloom believed that we must make a distinction between intelligence and cognitive entry behaviors. Although researchers repeatedly have demonstrated a link between intelligence and aptitude tests and later achievement, Bloom reasoned that these findings do not determine a student's potential for learning. **Cognitive entry behavior,** which is knowledge essential for learning a particular subject (what we have referred to as "prior knowledge"), also shows a close relationship with achievement and can be altered. These characteristics are subject to change because they contain specific content and skills that can be learned.

The purpose and uses of assessment are crucial. Here, Bloom turned to summative versus formative testing. While the customary use of classroom tests has been to measure a student's achievement at the completion of a block of work (**summative evaluation**), tests have also been used to assess the quality of learning, as well as the quality of the learner. **Formative evaluation,** on the other hand, is primarily intended to aid in the formation of learning by providing feedback about what has been learned and what still remains to be learned. Bloom believes that when tests are used in this manner, the number of students who achieve mastery increases dramatically, chiefly because the necessary prerequisite skills have been identified for each student, student motivation intensifies, and more time is spent on task.

Mastery Learning

Mastery learning is probably the key element in Bloom's work, for it is this goal that all other means are intended to achieve. As Bloom noted (1981), most teachers begin a school year with the entrenched expectation that about one-third of the students will adequately learn, one-third will pass, and one-third will achieve a marginal pass or fail. Bloom found this condition one of the most wasteful in all of education, especially since he believed that about 90% of all students could learn to mastery if properly instructed.

COGNITIVE ENTRY BEHAVIOR

Bloom's term for the prerequisite learning skills needed before attempting new learning.

SUMMATIVE EVALUATION

Assessment of a student's achievement at the completion of a block of work.

FORMATIVE EVALUATION

Assessment intended to aid learning by providing feedback about what has been learned and what remains to be learned.

MASTERY LEARNING

Learning in which instructor and student decide on time needed and what is necessary for mastery, usually 90% of the possible achievement score.

TIPS ON TIME
Methods for Increasing Academic Learning Time

PRINCIPLE   As time for learning increases, the learning of children increases. Thus, teachers need to have command of strategies for increasing the amount of time children spend actively engaged in productive learning.

STRATEGY   To increase time used for instruction, (a) establish contingencies for attendance and punctuality, (b) minimize interruptions, (c) program for brief transitions, and (d) maintain an academic focus.

STRATEGY   To increase engaged time, (a) clarify instructions and expectations regarding performance, (b) keep instruction relatively fast paced, (c) maintain an interactive teaching style where students are asked to respond frequently, and (d) adopt seating arrangements to maximize attending.

STRATEGY   To increase productive learning time, (a) use seatwork effectively, (b) encourage review and practice sessions, (c) provide immediate feedback about work, (d) monitor student performance and help students to self-monitor their work performances, and (e) use homework wisely.

QUALITY OF INSTRUCTION

Bloom's term for the cues, practice, and reinforcement necessary to make learning meaningful for students.

A few students (1% to 5%) will show special talent for any subject; that is, they will show an aptitude for particular learning. Another small group (1% to 5%) will show a special disability for a given subject. This leaves the majority of 90%. Here is the basis for Bloom's belief that 95% of our students can achieve mastery, with some requiring more time, effort, and help than others.

Mastery learning is tied closely to the **quality of instruction.** We begin with the assumption that individual students need individual instruction to reach mastery. You may argue that teachers have always attempted to adapt their teaching to individuals. In a classroom of thirty students to one teacher, this goal often remains elusive, reinforcing Bloom's idea that the quality of instruction must be considered in light of individual learners. This leads us to a student's ability to understand instruction. Do your students understand what they are to learn and how they are to learn it? It is precisely here that student ability interacts with quality of instruction and curricular material. Since our schools are highly verbal, ability to understand is linked to language ability and reading comprehension. Modifying instruction by using a variety of techniques—tutorial, group, text, and media— can benefit students' comprehension.

Do your students show perseverance? How much time is a student willing to spend in learning? We know that student perseverance varies from subject to subject. Adapting instruction and using appropriate content has been shown to increase perseverance. Bloom emphasized the significance of perseverance by commenting on students' variability in the amount of time they are willing to spend on a task. Some students give up quickly on math problems but will work indefinitely on faulty automobile engines. Bloom also believed that the key to increasing perseverance is appropriate design in instruction and learning materials.

If aptitude determines the rate of learning, then the time allowed for learning can produce mastery. Bloom believed that some students spend as much as six times longer on homework than others—yet time spent on homework often has little relationship to final grades. Homework with the correct structure and conditions for learning, however, can be quite effective (see the section later in this chapter). The time spent on task can be altered by following mastery principles and allowing students the time they need to reach mastery in particular subjects. This in turn depends on aptitude, verbal ability, quality of instruction, and quality of help received outside of school.

If you are to help your students achieve mastery, first be certain what you mean by mastery, and know when students reach it. Use formative evaluation techniques as frequently as you think they are needed: Divide a subject into meaningful sections, and then construct diagnostic tests to discover if students have mastered the material. You will then know where specific weaknesses lie and what steps need to be taken to overcome any difficulties.

Not only does Bloom's work on mastery learning recommend itself for its obvious cognitive benefits, but students usually show an increased interest in subject matter, and, perhaps most important of all, an increased sense of self-worth. They do better on teacher-made tests, earn higher grades, and attain higher scores on standardized tests. Their retention and transfer of material learned under mastery learning conditions also improves substantially (Guskey, 1986).

Teachers also experience positive effects. When they see the improvement in their students' learning, they gain a sense of professional renewal; they feel better about themselves and their work. Teachers using this approach tend to see learning as a cooperative venture in which their role is that of facilitator in helping their students reach the highest level of learning possible (Guskey, 1986).

How can Bloom's basic ideas help to improve classroom learning? Individual differences in learning ability may not be alterable, but individual differences in learning can be predicted, explained, and improved. For example, much of the variation in school learning can be traced to environmental conditions in the home and school, both of which are subject to modification if teachers work closely with parents.

Three interdependent variables, which can be phrased as questions, form the foundation of Bloom's theory: (1) To what extent has a student learned the necessary prerequisites for the new learning to be attempted?, (2) To what extent can a student be motivated to engage in the learning process?, and (3) To what extent is instruction appropriate to the learner? The theory addresses student characteristics, instruction, and learning outcomes. The student characteristics deemed to be most significant for learning are cognitive entry behaviors (the necessary prerequisite skills) and affective entry characteristics (motivation to learn new material). Quality of instruction, as we have seen, refers to needed cues, practice, and reinforcement. Learning outcomes can be designated by level and type of achievement, rate of learning, and affective results. The interaction of these variables can be seen in Figure 13.3. By learning task Bloom means a learning unit in a course, a chapter in a textbook, or a topic in the curriculum. Such a task usually takes from one to five hours to master.

As mentioned, cognitive entry behavior is the prerequisite learning needed for mastery of new tasks, and, as such, represents one aspect of a student's history. Although it is possible that all the students have had an opportunity to acquire the prerequisite learning, and it is even possible that all the students have acquired it, the critical point is the availability of the prerequisite learning at the time it is required for the specific new learning task. That is, the student remembers and can use these prior learnings when and where they are required in a specific new task. How much of the background of the Eastern European countries does a student bring to an analysis of the independence movements there?

Cognitive entry behaviors fall into two categories: those that are specific to a subject (addition, subtraction, and multiplication are necessary prerequisites for division), and those that are general, such as verbal ability and reading comprehension. Both types of entry behaviors are alterable.

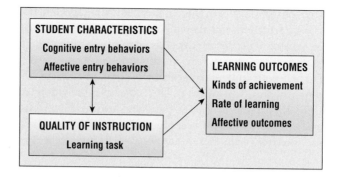

FIGURE 13.3

Bloom's Theory of School
Learning

AFFECTIVE
ENTRY
CHARACTERISTICS

*Bloom's phrase to describe a
student's motivation to learn
new material.*

Affective entry characteristics refer to the differences among students in what they are emotionally prepared to learn as expressed in their interests, attitudes, and self-views. All students have different histories that color their reactions to specific subjects and to school in general. A brother or sister may have been unhappy in school or disliked a particular teacher. Such feelings rub off on younger pupils.

Especially interesting in Bloom's analysis of affect is the notion of age change: The correlation between affect toward school and achievement in a particular subject is relatively low up to grade 5 but increases sharply at the junior and senior high levels. Bloom estimates that affect toward school accounts for as much as 25% of the variation in achievement. Again, affect toward both school and subject can be altered.

Bloom has focused on teaching and not on the teacher; thus, his analysis of quality of instruction focuses on the interactions that occur in the classroom. Cognitive entry behaviors and affective entry characteristics can account for about 65% of the achievement variation on a new learning task. The quality of instruction can do little to overcome the input of cognitive entry behaviors unless it is remedial, which is not usually the case. Affective entry characteristics can be altered by the quality of instruction; in spite of the significant contribution made by cognitive entry behaviors, quality of instruction can have a powerful effect on learning a particular task. We conclude Bloom's excellent analysis of school learning by noting that, with his approach, most students become quite similar with regard to learning ability, rate of learning, and motivation for further learning when provided with favorable learning conditions.

In this chapter, we have examined teaching from several theoretical perspectives. Each of them has much to offer; you probably would be well advised to take from each those aspects that are best suited to your beliefs and objectives. That is, you may analyze a task from a cognitive perspective, yet find much to use in the work of Skinner concerning the best means of using reinforcement, or in Bloom's concern with cognitive entry behavior. To help you compare the various components of these theories we have constructed Table 13.8.

Although our focus has been on teachers and teaching strategies, we should remember that adapting instruction can involve many techniques. Two important ways of accomplishing this goal are to help students develop efficient study skills and to actively complete homework. Let's look at these two activities next.

Study Skills

The ability to study effectively is important for any student's success in school. Many capable students at all grade levels may experience frustration and even failure in school not because they lack ability, but because they do not have adequate study skills. Good study skills benefit students beyond improving their academic performance. Children who have

Table 13.8 INSTRUCTIONAL THEORIES: A SUMMARY

Theorist	Basis	Emphasis	Application
Bloom	Educational research	Mastery learning Entry behaviors Time on task Learning outcomes	Prerequisite skills Learning tasks Achievement levels Instructional processes
Bruner	Cognitive development	Theoretical base Optimal sequence Modes of representation	Readiness, motivation, acquisition, transformation, evaluation
Gagne	Information processing	Instructional events Learning outcomes	Learning Retention Transfer
Hunter	Decision making	Adaptive teaching Instructional decisions	Formulating objectives Direct instruction Enhanced achievement
Markle	Operant conditioning	Active responding Errorless learning Immediate feedback	Programed instruction Behavior analysis
Skinner	Operant conditioning	Defined objectives First instance Sequential steps Controlled responses Reinforcement	Programmed instruction All aspects of behavior

developed good study skills are also more likely to experience an increase in their feelings of competence and confidence as they learn. They tend to approach their schoolwork with a positive attitude, rather than a negative and anxious one.

Study skills may be viewed as basic learning tools; they enable students to acquire and retain information presented in textbooks and classrooms. More specifically, study skills include listening and reading, notetaking, outlining, managing time, and taking tests. Study skills may be organized according to four general stages of learning that are common to all students. The first stage of studying involves taking in information from books, lectures, or presentations. Study behaviors that are associated with success at this stage include listening and reading. The second stage entails some organization of the information. Study behaviors that facilitate organization of the information include underlining, notetaking, outlining, making lists, and asking oneself questions about the material. Stage three involves practicing or rehearsing the organized material and requires some type of review or discussion on the part of the learner. The final stage is the actual remembering or application of information. Skills in taking tests, writing, and preparing reports are used in this stage.

Parents and teachers need to remember that there is no simple formula for improving study skills for all children. More important than following any one particular method are building good habits, developing a system that works for a given child, and using the system effectively and consistently. Learning styles vary from student to student. Study habits that work for one person may not work well for another person—even when both children come from the same family. Students need to discover how they learn and then work out study systems that fit in best with the way they learn. Here are some tips parents and teachers can pass on to their children for helping them develop good study skills:

- *Establish a study routine.* Children should pick a place, find a time, and build a routine. Studying should be a part of a daily routine. Students find that they learn more if they get into the habit of studying at the same time and in the same place each day. Of course, special family events or sudden demands will force them to break that routine from time to time, but they should try to stay in the routine as much as possible.

- *Make sure study surroundings allow children to concentrate.* To concentrate on studies, some children may require total quiet, whereas others may need a little background noise (such as music). Children should find the atmosphere that helps them focus on what they have to study without being distracted by other activities or being so relaxed that they fall asleep. Children may need some cooperation from the family to do this (not disturbing them, taking phone messages, etc.).

- *Keep assignments in one folder.* Students may have a separate notebook for each class, but they should keep all homework assignments in one folder. That way, they will be able to see all of the things they have to do and divide their study time accordingly.

- *Work out a study system.* Rather than just reading straight through an assignment, most students find that they learn more if they work out a systematic method. This may involve skimming the material, underlining or taking notes, reviewing major ideas, and so on. Two key elements are to read with a question in mind and take notes in the student's own words. One popular system, known as the SQ3R method, involves these steps: (a) Survey: Quickly scan the reading assignment (look at headings, graphs, summaries, etc.); (b) Question: Make up a question to keep in mind as they read (Manzo & Manzo, 1990); (c) Read: Read actively to answer the questions they have formulated; (d) Recite: Try to answer questions without looking at the reading assignment; and (e) Review: Immediately review the material to make certain notes are organized and major ideas are understood. The best way to begin using this method with students is to model it for them and then have the whole class try it before using it independently (Reutzel & Cooper, 1992).

- *Expand concentration time.* At first, children may be able to concentrate only for short time periods (ten minutes is typical, since it is the time between commercials on TV programs). Parents can help children work on building this up to longer stretches without breaks, so it will take less time to get through assignments. Most children need to work up slowly and steadily, just as one does in weight training or aerobics.

- *Develop time estimation skill.* One key to good studying is being able to estimate how long it will take to complete each assignment. Start by having children make an estimate for each assignment, then note how long it really took to do the work, and note how well they did on the assignment (or on the test for which they studied). Most students must keep adjusting and evaluating estimates until they become routinely accurate.

- *Plan ahead.* Athletes cannot get in shape in one or two nights; they need to "work out" for several weeks. Studying works the same way. Students should start working on major assignments or reviewing for major tests well ahead, planning their strategy for finishing the assignment on time.

- *Set goals.* Before they begin work on an assignment, help children decide how well they want to do on it and how much effort it will take to do that well. This will help them learn to divide study time effectively so they do not spend too much time on relatively unimportant assignments.

- *Reward achievements.* When children achieve one of their study goals, give them a little reward: make a snack, allow them to call a friend, and so on. Often children want someone (parent or friend) to congratulate them on their achievements and with whom they can share what they have learned.

Homework

Another means of adapting your instruction to the needs of your students is by the use of carefully assigned homework. Homework engenders many different responses from students, teachers, and parents. Many students hate it; still, a significant number think it's important. Some teachers think it is useless; others see it as essential. Some parents think it is just busywork, yet many think it is an indication of the quality of the school and is critical for their child. By homework, we mean "tasks assigned to students by school teachers that are meant to be carried out during non-school hours" (Cooper, 1989a, p. 86).

Homework facilitates connections between home and school and has the potential to increase the amount of time students are engaged in learning.

CASE NOTES

Observation Jim Watson and two other classmates' rate and quality of work completion was below Mrs. Williams's expectations. She has spoken with the boys' parents, but this has not helped.

Hypothesis Besides having some significant skill deficits, the boys also have poor study habits and infrequently complete homework. Thus, they are actively engaged in learning less time than most of their peers, and when they are engaged, their work is often incomplete, making it difficult for Mrs. Williams to provide corrective feedback and reinforcement. Their work will improve if they spend more time working on material that is developmentally appropriate.

Possible Action A face-to-face meeting with each boy, his parents, and Bill Drake and Sara Ellis (the other two teachers in the DEW House) should be arranged so that a detailed study plan can be developed. This plan should include a clear statement of the learning expectations, a description of a study routine that allows for concentrated study at school and at home, and a reward system initially focusing on work completion (probably at the 75% to 80% level, moving toward 100% as each boy demonstrates success) and then work accuracy. Each set of parents could also be provided with examples of acceptable work and how it is scored. In addition, the parents will be provided a description of each boy's weekly assignments every Monday and are encouraged to communicate each Friday with Mrs. Williams about their son's work effort.

In a thorough review of research on homework, Cooper (1989b) concluded that homework has positive effects on achievement, especially for junior and senior high school students. Several other authors, although with far less empirical evidence than that of Cooper, have touted the benefits of homework for children in the 1980s and 1990s. Books such as *Homework Without Tears* (Canter & Hausner, 1987) and *Hassle-Free Homework* (Clark & Clark, 1989) have been promoted in bookstores across the country to parents as guides for helping their children. Thus, homework currently seems to be perceived positively, as an important instructional adjunct that involves students, teachers, and parents. Homework deserves your attention, so let's scrutinize some of the points that Cooper (1989b) made in his synthesis of research on homework.

Cooper's review of the research literature identified numerous potential positive and negative effects of homework on students. Table 13.9 documents many of the suggested effects of homework. Note that homework is seen as having some important "side effects" on student-parent relations and self-management. Based on your own experiences with homework, can you add possible positive or negative effects to the list in Table 13.9?

In addition to examining the effects of homework, Cooper formulated a "model" of the factors that influence homework outcomes. He identified more than twenty specific factors (for example, student characteristics, home environment, testing of related work, parents' involvement) and organized these specific factors into six general factors. These general and specific factors, which influence the effects of homework, are displayed in Table 13.10. Of all the factors, grade level was perhaps the most significant one. Specifically, Cooper found the effect of homework on achievement to be only negligible for elementary students, moderately important for junior high students, and very important for high school students. Although the effects of homework on elementary students' achievement were

Table 13.9 SUGGESTED EFFECTS OF HOMEWORK

Positive Effects	Negative Effects
Immediate achievement and learning Better retention of factual knowledge Increased understanding Better critical thinking, concept information, information processing Curriculum enrichment	*Satiation* Loss of interest in academic material Physical and emotional fatigue
	Denial of access to leisure-time and community activities
Long-term academic effects Willingness to learn during leisure time Improved attitude toward school Better study habits and skills	*Parental interference* Pressure to complete assignments and perform well Confusion of instructional techniques
Nonacademic effects Greater self-direction Greater self-discipline Better time organization More inquisitiveness More independent problem solving	*Cheating* Copying from other students Help beyond tutoring
	Increased differences between high and low achievers
Greater parental appreciation of and involvement in schooling	

From Harris Cooper, *Homework.* Copyright © 1989 Longman Publications. Reprinted by permission of Harris Cooper.

Table 13.10 A MODEL OF FACTORS INFLUENCING THE EFFECTS OF HOMEWORK

Exogenous Factors	Assignment Characteristics	Initial Classroom Factors	Home-Community Factors	Classroom Follow-up	Outcomes or Effects
Student characteristics Ability Motivation Study habits Subject matter Grade level	Amount Purpose Skill area utilized Degree of individualization Degree of student choice Completion deadlines Social content	Provision of materials Facilitators Suggested approaches Links to curriculum Other rationales	Competitors for student time Home environment Space Light Quiet Materials Others' involvement Parents Siblings Other students	Feedback Written comments Grading Incentives Testing or related content Use in class discussion	Assignment completion Assignment performance Positive effects Immediate academic Long-term academic Nonacademic Parental Negative effects Satiation Denial of leisure time Parental interference Cheating Increased student differences

From Harris Cooper, *Homework.* Copyright © 1989 Longman Publications. Reprinted by permission of Harris Cooper.

small or nonexistent, Cooper still recommended some homework for elementary students. He believes it can help them to develop good study habits, fosters positive attitudes toward school, and communicates the idea that learning takes place at home as well as at school.

Cooper also concluded that in-class study supervised by a teacher was as good as or better than homework, especially for younger students. As noted by Cooper, however, the allocation of time for in-class study versus other learning activities becomes the issue.

In 1998, Cooper and colleagues (that is, Lindsay, Nye, and Greathouse) investigated the relationships among attitudes that students, teachers, and parents had about homework. In addition, the researchers studied the influence of amount of homework assigned and completed on attitudes and student achievement. They reported weak relations between the amount of homework assigned and student achievement, but positive relations between amount of homework completed and student achievement, especially at the upper grades (6–12). At the lower grades, teacher-assigned homework was related to negative student attitudes.

Several lessons concerning effective instructional practices can be learned from this recent study of homework. First, it indicates that the benefits of homework for young children may not be immediately evident, but they exist nonetheless. As early as second grade, the frequency of completed homework assignments predicts students' grades. Further, to the extent that homework helps young students develop effective study habits, Copper's results suggest that homework in early grades can have a long-term developmental effect that reveals itself as an even stronger relationship between completion rates and grades when the student moves into secondary school. The impact of early-grade homework is mediated, through time, by its facilitation of the development of proper study skills, which in turn, influences grades.

A second practical implication of the Cooper et al. (1998) study derives from its demonstration of the significant and stable role that parental attitudes play in shaping students' attitudes toward homework and the grades of older students. The lack of positive effect of homework for some students may be due, in part, to negative attitudes held by parents. Thus, educators are encouraged to make efforts to improve parents' attitudes toward homework. Improved parental attitudes about homework are likely to result from clear communications about the goals for homework and how parents can effectively help their children complete homework.

Multicultural Education

Multicultural education is a concern affecting every phase of effective teaching (Ramsey, 1987). In a multicultural curriculum, pupils learn about themselves and others as they study various cultures. They analyze the beliefs, attitudes, values, and behaviors that are characteristic of particular cultures. As they do, members of those cultures should have an increase in self-esteem and simultaneously develop an appreciation and understanding of other cultures. In this way, instruction that is dedicated to multicultural understanding can help raise the academic expectations of minority students and combat negative stereotypes. A good guiding principle here is this: Challenge minority students (Spencer & Dornbusch, 1990). Minority students are no different in this respect from any others; that is, they respond best to teacher support and warmth and to appropriate, challenging standards.

In presenting multicultural topics, teachers proceed exactly as they would with their other subjects. They establish the necessary knowledge base, utilize effective instructional methods, and base their instruction on their students' needs. As we have emphasized throughout this chapter, teaching is not telling—a warning that is particularly timely when you are attempting to further multicultural understanding. You must help your students construct their own positive attitudes toward people who appear different (Tiedt & Tiedt, 1990). Involve families as much as possible. Try to arrange school events (ac-

Current Issues & Perspectives

Can Homework Bring Home and School Closer Together?

Homework is a topic of interest for all involved, including teachers, students, and parents. When used effectively, it can enhance learning and send a strong message that learning also takes place outside of the classroom. It also offers parents the opportunity to participate in the education of their children (Schiefflin & Gallimore, 1993).

Parental involvement in a child's education is an increasingly provocative topic among educators and parents. Traditionally, parental involvement has been relegated to PTA social activities, but a closer look at successful schools shows a high level of parental involvement. One way parents can participate in their children's education is to support the schoolwork they do at home.

ISSUE

Homework offers parents a real opportunity to become involved on many different levels with their children's schoolwork—as coaches, tutors, and resource persons.

Pro: Through their working together, a student's skills improve and parental attention sends a strong message that schoolwork is valued.

Con: Parents can run the risk of becoming too involved in their child's school life. In some cases, they may become too critical; in other cases, they may actually do the child's work.

ISSUE

Teachers often complain that there aren't enough hours in the day to cover all they would like to accomplish. Homework is a good way to extend the day's learning time.

Pro: Homework, when used effectively, can offer opportunities to add depth and breadth to a topic, allowing learners to explore at length subjects that are of interest to them.

Con: Not all children have access to materials or an environment that allows them to concentrate on schoolwork. Depending on work outside of the classroom to acquire needed skills can put these students at a disadvantage.

ISSUE

Homework is a valuable adjunct to the curriculum. As to any other part of the curriculum, teachers must devote thought and creativity to their homework assignments.

Pro: Interesting homework can supplement skills and also challenge and excite students.

Con: Homework assignments are not always carefully planned by teachers. When they are used only for rote activities (memorizing math facts and spelling words), students can come to dislike not only homework but also the subject and school itself.

ademic and social) in a manner that enables parents to visit the school without major interruptions in their schedules (Comer, 1988).

This is actually a continuation of a theme initially presented in Chapter 1: Teachers must be sensitive to the unique needs of all students (Rogoff, 1990). Although the recognition of students' individual differences is not confined to cultural diversity, nevertheless, the classroom challenges of minority students may have quite different roots from those of your other students. Minority students may bring distinctive behavioral and communication styles to a classroom that a teacher must recognize if these students are to achieve as well as possible. For example, Shade and New (1993) noted that many African American students are movement oriented and appear less responsive to direct verbal questioning in the classroom. Yet these same students may be leaders on the playground and be able to explain the rules of a game in some detail.

Although teachers may not have the language skills to communicate fully with some of their students, they can nevertheless be sensitive to their origins and customs, help these students to see themselves as part of the larger society, encourage respect and appreciation for the ways of others, urge students to develop positive relationships with children of all cultures, and learn as much as possible about the heritage of all students.

Teachers' Expectations and How They Influence Interactions with Students

Can teachers' expectations for students influence their achievement? In 1968, Rosenthal and Jacobson reported the results of a study that fascinated both educators and psychologists to this day. Beginning in 1964, the authors had teachers in an elementary school administer an imposing test, the Harvard Test of Inflected Acquisition, that actually was a nonverbal IQ test. It was administered to youngsters who would return in the fall. Teachers were told that the test would predict which youngsters would show an academic spurt in the coming year. These would be the "intellectual bloomers." The tests had supposed predictive value, and the youngsters so identified were imaginary. Teachers believed that they were taking part in a study to validate a test predicting the likelihood that a child would show an inflection point or "spurt" in the near future. The test would predict which youngsters were most likely to show academic spurts. Teachers were told that students with scores on these tests in the top 20% (approximately) would probably be found at various levels of present academic functioning (Rosenthal & Jacobson, 1968, p. 66).

In the fall, the teachers were told which youngsters had scored in the top 20%, and the investigators suggested that these children would probably show remarkable progress during the year. Actually, there was no difference between these children and the control group. All the youngsters were retested at the end of the school year, using the same test. The experimental group (the "bloomers") all scored higher than the control group. The investigators interpreted the results to indicate that when teachers expected more of children, the youngsters met their expectations, in a **self-fulfilling prophecy** referred to as "Pygmalion in the classroom."

The news media and general public seized upon the results and the study received enormous publicity. Uncritically accepted, the results were interpreted as heralding a breakthrough in the classroom. Many educators and investigators remained skeptical, and their skepticism was confirmed when attempts to replicate the Rosenthal and Jacobson study produced conflicting evidence. Other critics attacked the study's methodology. Carefully controlled studies, in which teachers received varied information (IQ scores, no IQ scores, IQ scores inflated by 16 points, or designation of some students as academic bloomers) did not duplicate Rosenthal's findings. These findings cast serious doubt on the Rosenthal hypothesis.

Perhaps it is safest to conclude that teachers' expectations make a difference, but not as uniformly and in a much more complex manner than they were originally believed to by Rosenthal and Jacobson. Answering their critics, Rosenthal and Jacobson stated that expectations produced effects because teachers provided a favorable social and emotional atmosphere for the selected students. These students received more attention and thus were furnished carefully controlled reinforcement. Teachers spent more time with them, demanded more from these students, and usually received it.

If a teacher's expectations do influence a student's achievement, the process may be as follows. Because of what they have heard or read about these students, teachers de-

SELF-FULFILLING
PROADECY

The phenomenon that when teachers expect more of students, the students tend to meet the expectations, or vice versa.

velop certain expectations about them. Teachers then behave differently with these students. Students infer from a teacher's behavior that they are or are not good achievers, and frequently behave accordingly. If a student understands the meaning of the teacher's behavior, achievement may follow the direction of the teacher's expectations (Hamachek, 1987).

How do expectations translate into teacher behavior in the classroom? Teachers often tend to do the following:

- Seat low-expectation students farther from the teacher

- Pay less attention to low-expectation students in academic activities

- Call on these students less often to answer questions

- Wait less time and then interrupt students whom they perceive as less capable

- Criticize students for whom they have low expectations more frequently, praising them less often

- Provide lower-quality feedback to their low-expectation students

Not all teachers, of course, treat low- and high-expectation students differently. Yet the evidence continues to indicate the existence of expectations that influence teacher and student interactions. An effective teacher has a lot to think about!

THE ELEVEN BIG IDEAS IN EFFECTIVE TEACHING

Effective teachers must have a wide range of activities and strategies in their repertoire for interacting with students. Although teachers can use different approaches, direct or indirect, to deliver instruction, effective teaching has several features in common. Specifically, the research suggests that effective teaching has a clear focus and explicit learning outcomes that students understand and are held accountable for learning. Well-written learning objectives provide teachers and students this type of focus. Second, instruction is delivered under conditions like those described by Gagne as optimal. That is, students' attention is under the control of the teacher, relationships or connections between what is being taught and their prior knowledge is established, material is presented in a manner that elicits active inquiry and interest, guidance is provided by the teacher as students interact with the new material or tasks, students are asked to respond to demonstrate what they are learning, these responses are assessed and feedback is provided about the quality of the students' learning. Finally, review and practice sessions follow over the course of several sessions to help facilitate retention of the new material and transfer to new situations or more complex problems. To accomplish this sequence of interactions with students and to enhance the effects of instruction, students often benefit from direct instruction in how to study and complete homework. The recruitment of parent involvement in homework also provides enhanced effects on learning.

In addition to having command of the process of teaching and learning, effective teachers also have a strong understanding of the big content ideas, or fundamental concepts, in subject matter areas. In this chapter, we briefly examined some of the big ideas in reading and mathematics and outlined strategies for activating learning in these two subjects.

It is now time to summarize and to not only conclude this chapter, but the book. We do so with a list of eleven big ideas of effective teacher-student interactions.

Teachers Communicate Clear and High Expectations for Student Learning

- Learning goals and objectives are developed and prioritized according to district and building guidelines, selected or approved by teachers, sequenced to facilitate student learning, and organized or grouped into units or lessons.

- Teachers set high standards for learning and let students know they are expected to meet them. Standards are set so they are both challenging and attainable.

- All students are expected to attain the level of learning needed to be successful at the next level of education.

- Students are provided information about scoring criteria and grades before they start learning.

Standards for Classroom Behavior Are Explicitly Communicated

- Teachers let students know that there are high standards for behavior in the classroom. Classroom behavior standards are written, taught, and reviewed from the beginning of the year or the start of new courses.

- Rules, discipline procedures, and consequences are planned in advance. Standards are consistent with or identical to the building code of conduct.

- Consistent, equitable discipline is applied across all students. Procedures are carried out quickly and are clearly linked to inappropriate student behavior.

- Teachers stop disruptions quickly, taking care to avoid disrupting the whole class.

- In disciplinary actions, teachers focus on the inappropriate behavior, not on the student's personality.

Classroom Routines Are Smooth and Efficient

- Class starts on time and purposefully. The teacher has assignments or activities ready for students when they arrive.

- Students are required to bring the materials they need to class each day.

- Administrative matters are handled efficiently and class disruptions are kept to a minimum.

- Transitions between activities or classes are smooth and rapid.

Students Are Carefully Oriented to Lessons

- Teachers help students get ready to learn by explaining lesson objectives in simple, everyday language and refer to their objectives throughout lessons to maintain focus.

- Objectives may be posted or handed out to help students keep a sense of direction.

- The relationship of a current lesson to previous study is described. Students are reminded of key concepts or skills previously covered, thus connections are made between new material and students' prior knowledge.

- Students are encouraged to personalize learning by using information from their particular cultural backgrounds and lives outside of school to make connections with material they are studying in school.

- Students are challenged to learn, particularly at the start of difficult lessons. Students know in advance what's expected and are ready to learn.

Instruction Is Clear and Developmentally Appropriate

- Lesson activities are reviewed, clear written and verbal directions are given, key points and instructions are repeated, and student understanding is checked. In effect, an advanced organizer is used at the outset of each lesson.

- Presentations, such as lectures or demonstrations, are designed to communicate clearly to students; digressions are avoided.

- Students have plenty of opportunity for guided and independent practice with new concepts and skills.

- To check understanding, teachers ask clear questions and wait to make sure all students have a chance to respond.

- To ensure a high rate of student success, teachers select problems and other academic tasks that are well matched to lesson content and students' developmental level. Seatwork assignments also provide variety and challenge and opportunities for a teacher to monitor students' progress.

- Technology is used to stimulate high interest and to extend examinations of a wide range of topics. Using technology to facilitate structured review and practice session geared to a student's appropriate level of proficiency is also considered.

Instructional Groups Are Based on Instructional Needs of Students

- When introducing new concepts and skills, teacher-led, whole-group instruction is most effective.

- To maximize student learning, smaller groups are formed within the classroom as needed. Students are placed according to individual achievement levels based on subject matter assessments.

- As achievement levels change, teachers review and adjust groups.

Learning Progress Is Monitored Frequently

- Teachers frequently monitor student learning, both formally and informally.

- Teachers require that students be accountable for their academic work.

- Classroom assessments of student performance are aligned with learning objectives.

- Teachers know and use test-sound techniques to prepare valid, reliable assessment instruments.

- Routine assessment procedures simplify checking student progress. Students get results and constructive feedback quickly. Reports to students are simple and clear, help students to understand and correct errors, and are tied to learning objectives.

- Teachers use assessment results not only to evaluate students but also for instructional diagnosis and to find out if their teaching methods are working.

- Grading scales and mastery standards are set to promote excellence.

- Teachers also encourage parents to keep track of student progress.

Teachers Review and Reteach When Necessary

- New material is introduced as quickly as possible at the beginning of the year or course, with a minimum review or reteaching of previous content. Key prerequisite concepts and skills are reviewed thoroughly but quickly.

- Teachers reteach priority lesson content until students demonstrate competence.

- Regular, focused reviews of key concepts and skills are used throughout the year to check on and strengthen student retention.

- Computer software and peer tutors are often used effectively to facilitate meaningful and fun review sessions.

Learning Time Must Be Increased

- Teachers follow a system of priorities for using class time, allocating time for each subject or lesson. They use class time for learning and spend very little time on nonlearning activities after the first few days of class.

- Teachers set and maintain a brisk pace for instruction that remains consistent with thorough learning. New objectives are introduced relatively quick; clear start and stop cues help pace lessons according to specific time targets.

- Students are provided frequent opportunities to respond during class presentations. Use of wait time by teachers after asking a question is important to encourage as many students as possible to think about an answer and to generate an answer.

- Homework that students can complete successfully is assigned. It is typically in small increments and provides additional practice of content covered in class; work is checked and students are given prompt feedback. Homework extends the amount of learning time available.

- Teachers communicate to parents that homework is an important part of class and encourage parents to help keep students involved in learning and the completion of homework in a timely manner.

Personal Interactions Between Teachers and Students Are Positive

- Teachers show students they care about them by paying attention to students' interests, problems, and accomplishments in social interactions both in and out of the classroom.

- Students are allowed and encouraged to develop a sense of responsibility and self-reliance. Older students in particular are given opportunities to take responsibility for school-related matters and to participate in making decisions about important school issues.

Incentives and Rewards Are Used to Promote Excellence

- Excellence is defined by objective standards and not by peer comparison. Systems are set up in the classroom for frequent and consistent rewards to students for academic achievement and excellent behavior. Rewards are appropriate to the developmental level of students.

- All students know about class rewards and what they need to do to get them. Rewards are chosen because they appeal to students.

- Rewards are related to specific student achievements. Some rewards may be presented publicly, some should be immediately presented, while others are delayed to teach persistence.

- As students develop they are encouraged to set goals, evaluate their work, and to reward themselves.

- Parents are told about their children's successes and are encouraged to help students keep working toward excellence.

Case Reflections

In many ways, this chapter on effective teaching strategies is directed at the heart of the Melissa Williams's case. Melissa, a mature first-year teacher, wants to be effective and wants to have her seventh-graders excel in language arts and social studies. She also is eager to get along with her teaching colleagues, Bill Drake and Sara Ellis, and make a positive instructional contribution to the DEW House. But she feels two issues are limiting her effectiveness—the poor academic performance and behavior of three boys, in particular Jim Watson, and her teaching colleagues' "exaggerated" concern about preparing students for the school's annual achievement testing in the spring. In reading through the chapter, case notes were recorded on a range of possible actions to address these two sources of problems. First, it was suggested that Melissa make reviewing the content of the school's achievement test a top priority, given she intended to do so anyway in a couple of months. This action was designed to facilitate relations among the DEW House faculty and to enlighten Melissa about the specific alignment between her instruction and the annual achievement test. Second, after examining direct instruction strategies, it

was noted that such methods might be beneficial for Jim Watson and his two friends. In particular, it was hypothesized that each of the three boys had some significant skills deficits in written communication as well as poorly developed study skills. Direct instruction requires structured interactions between a teacher and student where successful models and detailed feedback are provided after each student performance. Continuing along these same lines, it was noted how the structured instructional methods advanced by Skinner and Markle also seemed very appropriate for Jim and the other two boys. In particular, these programmed instructional methods feature time to practice basic skills with reinforcement for effort and accuracy of responses. Because these are relatively time-consuming instructional methods, it was suggested that cooperation among the DEW House teachers and the boys' parents would be advantageous to get the students started. Finally, the cooperation of parents was also suggested to improve the study skills and engaged learning time of each of the boys. Thus, a face-to-face meeting designed to improve communications and clarify expectations was planned.

CHAPTER HIGHLIGHTS

What Makes a Teacher Effective?

- Effective teaching is characterized by identifiable behaviors: lesson clarity, instructional variety, task orientation and engagement in the learning process, praising students appropriately, and reflection.

Approaches to Instruction

- Direct and indirect, or inquiry, instruction must be compatible with both objectives and materials.
- A well-known example of direct instruction is Madeline Hunter's Clinical Theory of Instruction.
- A well-known example of inquiry instruction is Jerome Bruner's cognitive theory.
- Teachers' use of praise has been carefully analyzed in attempts to make it a more meaningful and forceful element in the classroom.

The Design of Instruction

- Clearly articulated objectives make learning more meaningful and useful by providing a structure for planning, delivering, and assessing instruction.
- A well-written objective specifies the behavior to be acquired or demonstrated, the conditions under which the behavior occurs, and the criteria for evaluating the behavior.
- B. F. Skinner applied the principles of operant conditioning to the classroom as he consistently advocated a technology of teaching. He encouraged teachers to first decide what their students should be able to do after instruction, carefully determine the steps needed to achieve that behavior, and skillfully use appropriate reinforcers.
- Susan Markle, using a programed instruction model ("programed" with one *m*) that featured three principles of instruction: a student's active responding, errorless learning, and immediate feedback.
- Robert Gagne formulated an instructional design technique that accounts for learning outcomes as they are related to specific conditions for that learning. Gagne outlined what he believed to be the "optimal conditions" for learning. These included: gaining the attention of a student, learning objectives, stimulating prior knowledge, presenting material in an interesting manner, providing learning guidance, eliciting a performance, providing feedback, assessing the performance, and enhancing retention and transfer.

Technology-Based Teaching Strategies

- Researchers indicate that using technology in classrooms can significantly improve instruction and students' learning. Educational technology offers a number of advantages for instruction, from providing simple audiovisual demonstrations of concepts to allowing students to interact with concepts and materials in a way that would otherwise be difficult, dangerous, or impossible, and to collaborate with students across the world.
- Computer-assisted instruction uses technology to present material to students or assist them in mastering it. Examples are computerized programmed instruction and drill and practice software.
- Multimedia uses technology to integrate and simultaneously use several different types of technology. Laser videodiscs and CD-ROMs are examples.
- Intelligent tutoring systems use technology to provide an individualized tutor for each student.
- Finally, the use of web-based learning and virtual reality are connecting learners with others across the world and exposing students to many subjects in a personal way that only five years ago was not possible. These advances are encouraging discovery learning for many students.

Teaching the Big Ideas in Reading and Mathematics

- Subject matter knowledge is one of the fundamental characteristics of an effective teacher.
- Pedagogical knowledge refers to how the basic principles and strategies of a subject are best acquired and retained.
- Fundamental concepts, or big ideas, are critical elements to stress in instruction. In reading, the big ideas are phonological awareness, alphabetic understanding, and automaticity with the code. In mathematics, big ideas include proportions, estimation, area, and fractions.
- Subject matter experts agree that effective delivery of the big ideas includes the use of a conspicuous strategy, strategically integrated training, scaffolding, and structured review sessions.
- High-quality review sessions involve introducing information into activities cumulatively, distributed practice that emphasizes relationships between new and old material, quick response times, and varied examples for practice and generalization.

Adapting Instruction to the Individual Differences of Learners

- Benjamin Bloom believes that studies of teaching must take into account the time pupils need for a task, their cognitive entry behaviors, and the proper use of testing, among other aspects. Bloom's concern with mastery learning led him to propose a model of school learning with such core concepts as cognitive entry behaviors, affective entry characteristics, and quality of instruction.
- Study skills and homework are part of effective instruction and help students improve their achievement.
- The "Pygmalion in the classroom" effect, that is, a self-fulfilling prophecy about students, although not as great an influence on students' learning as originally thought, still should be a concern for educators.

WHAT DO YOU THINK?

1. You have read a significant amount of information about effective teaching. In your own words, summarize what is an effective teacher. Identify at least five characteristics of an effective teacher you had when you were in high school.

2. What is the difference between an objective, a goal, and a standard? Many people seem to use these terms interchangeably. Do you?

3. Time on task has consistently been shown to be an important aspect of effective learning. What could you do as a teacher or parent that would increase the amount of time a learner spends actively engaged in learning?

4. What do you think about the use of praise? Do you like to be praised? If so, why? What effect does it have on your learning when somebody praises you?

5. Homework often stimulates many negative reactions from learners, yet it has consistently been shown to be part of effective teaching and learning, especially for middle and high school aged students. If it enhances learning, why don't more learners like homework? Why don't more parents stress it?

At the outset of this section, "Effective Teaching and the Evaluation of Learning," you were introduced to Melissa Williams, a mature first-year middle school teacher. Although full of innovative ideas, especially about the assessment of her students' learning, Melissa was uneasy with her classroom management skills and a bit concerned about the emphasis that her teaching colleagues seemed to place on an annual norm-referenced achievement test.

Throughout the last four chapters, we have made suggestions via Case Notes and Case Reflections to stimulate your thinking about ways Melissa could address some of her classroom concerns. It is now time to examine the perspectives of two expert teachers who don't "know" Melissa, but who have experienced some of the same challenges in their own classroom. Let's see what advice they have for Melissa.

Jayne Werner

Former Fourth- and Fifth-Grade Teacher; Now an Assessment and Curriculum Consultant for More Than Twenty Rural Schools in Northern Wisconsin.
Tomahawk, Wisconsin

The complexity for any teacher, much less a first-year teacher, to successfully balance classroom management, discipline, coherent instruction, and quality assessment issues is extremely challenging. I can definitely empathize with Melissa's frustration! Melissa could really benefit from the expertise of Bill and Sara (her teaching colleagues in the DEW House), and she should capitalize on the mentoring and professional relationship she can develop with them. Other resources in the building or district (curriculum coordinators, specialists, other teachers) might be accessible support for Melissa as well.

Classroom management and discipline techniques take lots of experience and persistence. I recommend Melissa try initiating classroom meetings. This democratic approach involves students in creating an agenda around issues for improvement, dialoguing openly, and then designing solutions. I've experienced students to be much more respectful and productive as the student-created solutions are implemented. Anything Melissa can do to facilitate the development of a trusting, community-of-learners environment will almost certainly have a positive impact on student behavior.

I presume that Melissa's district, perhaps with community involvement, has identified and agreed upon learning outcomes for students. This may be in the form of a curriculum document of some sort. As a first-year teacher, I went diving right for the teaching materials without first looking at the actual curriculum to guide my instructional planning! The curriculum framework for Melissa's class may include more specifics, too, about the content of the end-of-year standardized test. Melissa should continually strive to align her curriculum, instruction, and classroom assessments to best ensure students meet these expectations. Good luck, Melissa!

Joseph J. Malecki

Middle School Teacher (Social Studies and Religion)
Kuemper Catholic Grade Schools—St. Angela Center
Carroll, Iowa

This is my fifth year teaching middle school students, so I could relate to a lot of the difficulties that Melissa Williams is facing. Although Melissa may believe that her problems are unique to a first-year teacher, I have found that even seasoned teachers face similar challenges, especially regarding behavior management.

If I could tell Melissa how I would handle the situation, I would share the following thoughts and beliefs. I believe that the teacher's role is to be a mentor to students in the classroom. Acting as a model and a leader, teachers should encourage students to take ownership over their academic, social, and behavioral performances. I have had success with behavior management when promoting a sense of mutual respect in my room. That is, if the students feel that I respect their ideas and their individuality, they will show me respect as their teacher. While expectations are set high for each student, the level I expect from them may vary individually. That is, a teacher should meet the student at their level (academically *and* socially) and work up from there. When students of all abilities can experience success in my classroom, they will be more likely to cooperate behaviorally.

There are always exceptions to even my rules. In these cases, I involve the parents as soon as possible to ensure that we have similar goals and expectations for the students. With the parents, I try to devise a strategy that places the burden of change on the students. Especially at the middle school level, students need to start showing responsibility and ownership over their struggles. I try to find out what matters to these students (with parental input), and reinforce the positive attributes they already exhibit as much as possible.

I would encourage Melissa to seek the advice of other educators to see what works in their classroom and tailor their strategies to fit her personality and teaching style. Teachers have a wealth of knowledge up and down the halls around them; we should draw upon those resources. Finally, I have found that in general, if a teacher is well prepared and organized each day, 95% of the behavioral management difficulties can be avoided.

We hope the insights and suggestions of Jayne Werner and Joseph Malecki have added to your understanding of the Melissa Williams case. Many teachers in schools across the country will experience the kinds of challenges confronting Melissa, but unlike those teachers, you should have some clear strategies for addressing these challenges successfully after studying this case.

APPENDIX

RESEARCH METHODS AND THE PRACTICE
OF EDUCATION

Objectives

When you finish reading this appendix, you should be able to:

- identify the sources of knowledge that lead to educational decisions

- distinguish the various types of research methods

- describe the techniques used by educational researchers

- classify the various types of research methods according to the purposes for which they are intended

In this appendix you will discover the vital relationship between research and effective schooling. You also will explore the various methods used to obtain data and the specific purposes for which each method is intended. Finally, you will be asked to think about an issue that is becoming increasingly critical for those of us who work with other human beings: the ethical and legal aspects of research.

Research and Effective Schooling

Teachers are always concerned about the effectiveness of their methods, and they like to try different techniques. Teachers who are alert to the latest research and the methods that are appropriate to use become increasingly more skillful in their classroom instruction. This appendix is designed to acquaint you with the ways in which educational research is conducted and the ways in which it contributes to our understanding of schools, teaching, and learning.

Educational researchers have provided systematic guidelines for the teaching of mathematics.

Traditionally, educational research has had an "awful reputation" (see Kaestle, 1993), especially when compared with the physical sciences. Efforts to synthesize the outcomes of educational research and make the results relevant to answering policy questions may improve its reputation (Sroufe, 1997). Research answers questions. Most research is designed to answer questions about causation, relationships among variables, or effectiveness. Here are some examples of questions relevant to many educators: What effect does a teacher's oral questions have on students' attention and comprehension of material? What is the relationship between the amount of time spent on homework and classroom test performance? Which social skills program, Program A or Program B, is more effective with regard to increasing students' cooperation skills?

Sources of Knowledge

Much of the systematic knowledge we have about educational psychology has resulted from the application of scientific methods to the study of certain events. A major goal of scientific study is to explain, predict, and/or control these events. Yet the application of scientific procedures is relatively recent. It is also true that although scientific study has contributed greatly to understanding ourselves and others, knowledge is obtained from many different sources (see Table A.1).

Authority   Individuals in a position of status or authority have provided people or societies with the so-called truth. One prominent example was the belief that the earth is flat. Scholars and mapmakers proclaimed this fact with absolute confidence. As you can see, depending on this type of knowledge can lead to trouble if the authority is wrong. The information conveyed to others will be in error. Of course, authority may not be incorrect in all cases.

Tradition   Knowledge is also obtained from tradition. In the past, most children started school (either kindergarten or first grade) at age 6 because traditionally this was the appropriate age to begin formal schooling. Moreover, American schools had a tradition of closing for the summer for agricultural reasons. Such a rationale is no longer relevant, but tradition has prevailed. Knowledge based on tradition can also be inaccurate. Formal educational experiences often begin much earlier than age 6. In fact, many children in the United States begin some type of formal education by age 2 or 3. This example illustrates the considerable debate over tradition as a source of knowledge.

Expert Opinion   Another influential source of knowledge comes from the opinion of experts. Certain individuals may take positions that dramatically influence people's beliefs. Many readers of this book may have been reared according to the practices suggested by Dr. Benjamin Spock in his book *Baby and Child Care* (1957, and frequently updated). Many other popular books (for example, *How to Parent,* by Fitzhugh Dodson, 1970; *How to Raise Independent and Professionally Successful Daughters,* by Rita and Kenneth Dunn, 1977; *How Children Fail,* by John Holt, 1964) have influenced the thinking and behavior of parents and teachers. The thinking of many young Americans on the

Table A.1	COMMON SOURCES OF KNOWLEDGE ABOUT PEOPLE AND THE ENVIRONMENT
Source	**Example**
Authority	The earth is flat.
Tradition	Children should begin school at 6 years of age.
Expert opinion	Retention of student is unlikely to improve academic functioning.
Personal experiences	Mothers should breast-feed.
Documentation	More children attend school today than they did in 1900.
Scientific research	Some forms of mental retardation are genetic in origin.

birth process has been influenced by the writings of Lamaze and his followers on natural childbirth. Many attitudes now in vogue are the ideas of various experts and have had a tremendous impact on childrearing and social practices.

Personal Experience   Human beings gain a considerable amount of knowledge from personal experience, although not all of it is accurate. In many instances we may change our beliefs through knowledge from different sources. A teacher might adopt a classroom management program because personal experiences with the techniques suggest that it likely will be effective with students. However, the approach may have little or no research support. Some limitations of personal experience are that certain evidence may be omitted and that we may be too subjective in our beliefs.

Documentation   Another knowledge source is the documentation of events, in which records are kept of various events or phenomena. Today there is rather extensive documentation of data, easily accessible through the use of computer technology. For example, we can document that a specific number of children in a large city have received inoculations against a certain disease. Documentation is a relatively new source of information and knowledge. In many cases, we must speculate about certain events in history, because important documentation is incomplete or fragmented. Documentation is a good source of knowledge, but it has its limitations. People can be biased in providing certain information. Nevertheless, documentation is a step in the right direction: scientific data as a source of knowledge.

Scientific Research   The final source of information is scientific research. "Scientific research is the systematic, controlled, empirical, and critical investigation of hypothetical propositions about the presumed relations among natural phenomena" (Kerlinger, 1973, p. 11). This definition implies that scientific investigation is an orderly endeavor, so that the researcher can have confidence in the outcomes. Scientific research typically is carried out under controlled conditions. Educational researchers make available both the procedures and findings of research to outside evaluation or criticism.

      With procedures, findings, and conclusions available, other reviewers of a study may propose rival hypotheses or different interpretations of the data from those drawn by the original researchers (Huck & Sandler, 1979). In this appendix, we present a study as summarized by Huck and Sandler (1979), along with a rival hypothesis. After you have read the summary of the study, suggest an alternative interpretation; then read what the authors had to say about the research. (You will find this in the Current Issues & Perspectives box, under the section called "Rival Hypothesis.")

      Although the scientific form of investigation generally is regarded as an important method of generating knowledge, there is considerable disagreement over which forms are best. Scientific methods of investigation have evolved over a considerable period of time. In the next section, we review some of the historical features of scientific research.

Current Issues & Perspectives

Piaget's Modeling Clay Conservation Task

Jean Piaget is a well-known Swiss psychologist whose ideas have transformed the field of developmental psychology over the past few decades. You have read about his theories throughout this book. Many students associate him with conversation tasks, such as how a child learns that 200 cc of water is the same in a tall skinny glass as in a short fat glass, despite the difference in the water level. A similar task involving a clay ball and a clay cylinder (each with the same volume of clay) was one of a number of conservation tasks used in a study comparing modeling and nonmodeling instructions given to 6-year-olds.

In this study, a random sample of twenty-eight Chicano children was drawn from the first grade of a school located in a *barrio* area of Tucson, Arizona. The children were all from Spanish-speaking homes and were in the first few months of school, with a median age of 6.3 years. The children were randomly assigned to one of two groups. Each group included seven boys and seven girls. The children in the modeling group were allowed to watch the experimenter transform an object from one shape to another while listening to another child (the model) answer the experimenter's questions about the transformation. Those in the nonmodeling group were not shown the transformation process but were instead presented with "before" and "after" objects. The nonmodeling group was told that the objects were equivalent. Analysis of variance showed significant differences between the two groups, with the modeling group showing superiority on the conservation tasks. Furthermore, according to the authors, the nonmodeling instructions produced no reliable changes.

RIVAL HYPOTHESIS

Although we are generally sympathetic toward social learning theory and its methods (including modeling), we have difficulty accepting this study as evidence in its favor. Though the authors are to be commended for the design (true random selection and assignment) and analysis (appropriate use of variance analysis), we wonder about the effectiveness of English instructions being given to children for whom Spanish is a first language. We would have recommended that the entire experiment be conducted in Spanish to eliminate the plausible rival hypothesis that the nonmodeling instructional group received its instructions in a foreign language (English).

The Emergence of Research on Children

Long before researchers developed systematic experimental procedures to study children, an interest was evolving in the documentation of child behavior. Some of these procedures, such as baby biographies and individual case studies, were dominant forms of investigating aspects of child development. Although both of these techniques are still used in educational psychology, they generally have been replaced by more credible strategies based on principles of scientific research.

Baby Biographies

Many parents keep records of their children. This common practice has likely existed since written communication began. However, it was not until late in the eighteenth century that some individuals began to share formally and publicly their observations on children. For example, in 1774, Johann Pestalozzi, a Swiss educator, published observations on the development of his 3-year-old son, in which he affirmed the innate goodness of the child. In 1787, Dieterich Tiedeman published his observations of a baby during the first two years of life, in which aspects of sensory motor, language, and intellectual growth were reported.

Systematic observation of children continued into the nineteenth century. Two important publications were instrumental in promoting a long series of observational studies of children. In 1877, Charles Darwin published *A Biographical Sketch of an Infant,* an account of his infant son. Likewise, in 1882, William Preyer published a book on his son's first four years of life. The involvement of these professionals facilitated the proliferation of the baby biography as a method of child study. These biographies also focused attention on important aspects of child development and created interest in child study in general.

Despite the positive contributions of the baby biography in child study, the method is not held in high regard in the scientific community. There are several reasons for this conclusion. First, the biography represents a subjective description of events and cannot be independently evaluated and replicated by others. Second, typical observations made by individuals are unsystematic and may be made at irregular intervals. Third, the descriptions of behavior may represent the bias of the individual who holds certain conceptions about human development. Fourth, it is difficult to generalize data from biographies as a result of the aforementioned problems.

Case Studies

The case study is a tool of investigation that is characterized by uncontrolled reporting of some experience, treatment, or phenomenon. The typical case study lacks the usual controls that are a part of scientific experiments. Case studies have played an important role in research investigations throughout the history of psychology and education, and case studies are still used in psychology and psychiatry. As a form of research methodology, the case study evolved as individuals of various theoretical orientations began to treat people with personality and behavior problems. Case studies commonly are used in reporting therapeutic interventions with children and adults, and they have been used widely in psychology and education. Professional journals have often reported using case study methods (Kazdin, 1982, 1988), which remained a primary form of methodology of clinical investigations through the first half of this century.

Case study investigation has been useful in advancing knowledge, particularly in psychotherapy. Barlow and Hersen (1984) noted that case studies can (a) foster clinical innovation, (b) cast doubt on certain theoretical positions, (c) permit study of uncommon problems, (d) develop new technical skills, (e) support theoretical views, (f) promote refinement in various techniques, and (g) provide data that can be used to design more highly controlled research. For example, Dukes (1965) reviewed more than two hundred case studies over a twenty-five-year period from many areas of psychology, noting that in many instances the reports provided evidence of findings that changed the course of future study.

Despite positive features, case studies (like baby biographies) have many problems and generally are not regarded as reliable research procedures. Case studies typically are characterized by subjective impressions, bias, and inadequate description of the procedures used to treat a person. They are difficult to replicate, and replication is a key concern. Case study methods increasingly are being replaced by single-case time-series research strategies that are designed to make replication possible. These strategies are described later in this appendix.

Scientific Influences

Researchers embarking on the systematic study of education have many techniques to use. Contemporary research in educational psychology is guided by scientific methods. We use the plural term "methods" because there is no one scientific method. Scientific research generally is guided by the five steps shown in Figure A.1, which are used to study a particular topic or problem. We will examine these steps in the context of an applied educational problem that was investigated by researchers in a preschool setting more than twenty-five years ago (Twardosz, Cataldo, & Risley, 1974):

- Step 1: Research problem identification. A first step in conducting scientific research involves the identification of a problem or question. There is great interest in knowing how the physical environment influences behavior and learning of children (Dunn, 1987). One aspect of the problem identified in the study by Twardosz and her colleagues (1974) was determining how an open day-care environment influenced the sleep of infants and toddlers.

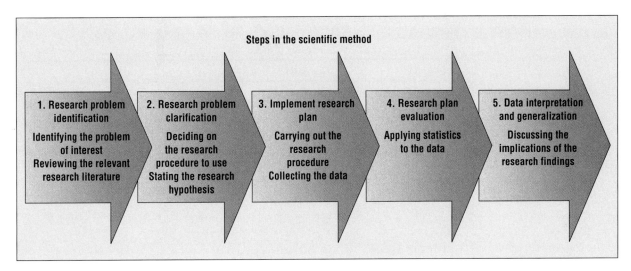

Steps in the scientific method

1. Research problem identification

Identifying the problem of interest
Reviewing the relevant research literature

2. Research problem clarification

Deciding on the research procedure to use
Stating the research hypothesis

3. Implement research plan

Carrying out the research procedure
Collecting the data

4. Research plan evaluation

Applying statistics to the data

5. Data interpretation and generalization

Discussing the implications of the research findings

FIGURE A.1.   The Scientific Method

- Step 2: Research problem clarification. Researchers must analyze the specific aspects of the problem and identify the nature, scope, and specifics of the situation. In the Twardosz study, there was the problem of how to examine the variables that might influence sleep. Any ideas? If you choose the conditions of noise and light versus quiet and darkness, you are on the right track.

- Step 3: Implement research plan. In this step, researchers state the problem and test the plan and program implemented to answer the question. The researchers measured the percentage of sleeping and crying children repeatedly over forty-seven days under the conditions of noise and light (door was left open and light entered the room) and quiet and darkness (door was closed and light was shut out).

- Step 4: Research plan evaluation. This step involves making decisions based on the data collected from the study. The data may or may not support the hunches (hypotheses) of the researchers. Any guesses as to how the Twardosz study turned out? The researchers found no differences in the effects of noise and light and quiet and darkness (for example, none of the children's sleep was adversely affected by noise and light).

- Step 5: Data interpretation and generalization. The final step involves interpreting and generalizing the researchers' findings into a larger body of knowledge related to the problem under study. Results may be integrated into existing knowledge, or it may suggest topics for future research. How would you explain the findings of the Twardosz study? Perhaps the conditions of noise and light were not strong enough to make a difference. Would you generalize the results of the study by telling people that noise and light have no effect on a child's sleep patterns? You may be "going beyond the data" to suggest this generalization; as you have seen in previous chapters, research data in educational psychology are sometimes misrepresented in just this way.

Major Research Methods

To a greater or lesser degree, all the preceding steps are involved in the major types of research conducted in schools and about schooling. These approaches to research include (a) historical, (b) descriptive, (c) correlational, (d) comparative, and (e) experimental research. Table A.2 summarizes these types of research.

Table A.2 CLASSIFICATION AND DESCRIPTION OF MAJOR RESEARCH METHODS

Classification	Description
Historical research	Involves studying, understanding, and explaining past events.
	Example: Factors leading to the development and growth of the use of teaching machines.
Descriptive research	Involves collecting data to test hypotheses or answers questions related to the current status of a problem.
	Example: How new parents share responsibilities in childrearing. New parents would be observed for a period of time and results could be reported as percentages (for example, Feeding: Mother 60%, Father 40%; Diaper changing: Mother 95%, Father 5%).
Correlational research	Involves determining whether, and to what extent, a relation exists between two or more variables.
	Example: The relation between intelligence and achievement. Scores on an intelligence test and an achievement test would be obtained from each individual in a certain group. The two sets of scores would be correlated, and the resulting correlation coefficient would indicate the degree of relation between intelligence and achievement.
Comparative research	Involves establishing a direct relation between variables that are compared, but not manipulated, by the researcher.
	Example: The effect of preschool attendance on achievement at the end of first grade. The independent variable (or presumed cause) is preschool attendance; the dependent variable (or effect) is measured achievement at the end of first grade. Groups of first-graders would be identified—some that had attended preschool and some that had not—and the achievement would be compared.
Experimental research	Involves actual manipulation by a researcher of at least one independent variable to observe the effect on one or more dependent variables.
	Example: The effect of positive reinforcement on the number of math problems completed by second-grade children. The independent variable is the reinforcement (praise statements by teachers); the dependent variable is the number of problems completed. Two groups would be exposed to essentially the same experiences, except for the reinforcement. After some time, their output on math problems would be compared.

Historical Research

As the name implies, historical research involves studying, understanding, and explaining past events. A major purpose of historical research is to formulate conclusions about causes, effects, or trends of past events that help to either explain current events or anticipate future events. Typically, individuals conducting historical research do not gather data by administering tests or observing behavior. Rather, they use data that are already available. For example, if educational researchers wanted to examine the factors that influence academic achievement of children in orphanages, they would conduct a search of the literature of follow-up studies of achievement of children in this type of institution.

Descriptive Research

In descriptive, or qualitative, research, the investigator examines and reports things the way they are in an effort to understand and explain them. In this type of study, the researcher collects data to test an hypothesis or answer questions concerning the status of some issue or problem. Instruments such as surveys, questionnaires, interviews, and observation may be developed for this type of investigation. The year-round school is an educational alternative being examined by many public school systems. If you were interested in studying the students, parents, and teachers participating in a year-round school, you might observe a select sample of children, their parents, and teachers. Such a study would be an example of qualitative research.

Correlational Research

In correlational research, the researcher attempts to determine if a relation exists between two or more variables. Variables can refer to a range of human characteristics, such as height, weight, sex, intelligence, and so forth. For example, a researcher may be interested in examining the relation between intelligence and creativity. But the finding that there is a relation between intelligence and creativity does not mean that intelligence causes creativity. A high positive correlation indicates only that most people with high intelligence have higher creative behavior, and that most people with lower intelligence have lower evidence of creativity. Thus, the finding that two variables are highly related (correlated) does not mean that one has caused the other; a third variable may cause or strongly influence both variables. Or, in our example, it may be that some degree of intelligence is necessary to, but not the only requirement for, creativity.

The degree of relation between two or more variables generally is expressed as a correlation coefficient (labeled r), represented by a number between .00 (no relation) and 1.00 (perfect relation). Of course, two variables can be negatively related, too, when a high score on one variable is accompanied by a low score on the other variable. The closer the coefficient is to 1.00, the better the researcher is able to make a prediction. Most correlations are less than 1.00; thus, prediction is far from perfect. Nevertheless, predictions based on known relations are useful in understanding the nature of behavior.

Comparative Research

In comparative research the investigator searches for causal relations among variables that are compared with each other. Comparative research shares many of the characteristics of correlational research, and some people do not distinguish between the two. Typically, comparative research involves the comparison of groups that are different before the study begins. For example, if researchers are interested in examining the effect of socioeconomic status (SES) on drug abuse in adolescents, they might form several different groups on the basis of different SES (that is, the nonmanipulated independent variable). Much research in educational psychology is conducted in this fashion, but the scientific community does not regard this type of research as being as reliable and credible as studies in which variables are manipulated directly. Since there is no manipulation of a critical variable or control over extraneous events, the causal relations established in comparative research must remain tentative. Thus, in the preceding example, we would have to consider that variables other than SES may account for different patterns of drug abuse. Although comparative research is not as predictable as experimental research, it has the following advantage: Many variables cannot be manipulated or controlled by the educational researcher, and the alternative might be no study at all.

Experimental Research

Experimental research involves the active manipulation of an independent variable to observe changes in the dependent variable. In experimental research, the independent variable frequently is manipulated in a condition called the experimental, or treatment, condition. The treatment condition is one level of the independent variable. Treatment conditions may be compared with each other or with a control condition, a condition in which no treatment is administered, although the group is the same as the treatment group in all other respects. The most important feature of experimental research is that researchers can manipulate variables and control sources of influence that can affect the results. Thus, researchers attempt to make the groups as equal as possible on all variables except the independent variable.

Experimental research is developed when an investigator forms two groups by randomly assigning participants. In random assignment, any individual going into one of the two groups has an equal chance of ending up in either group. No bias is introduced into the experiment by having more participants with specific characteristics, such as age or gender, in one group than in the other. For example, let's assume that you are the researcher, and you want to assess the effectiveness of a new method of teaching reading. You have decided that you are interested in discovering the effects of a new type of reading instruction for fifth-graders. You have selected the independent variable (the new reading method), so one of the criteria for a true experiment has been met. Next, you randomly assign each fifth-grader to one of two groups. The first group receives reading instruction according to the new method, while the second group continues with the traditional method. You have now met both of the criteria for experimental research: control of the independent variable and random assignment of participants. If the study is carefully done, by meeting these two criteria, the researcher can point to a cause-and-effect relationship. That is, the researcher can state that the new type of reading instruction did cause an improvement in pupils' reading scores, if the average scores for the students in the group that were taught by the new reading method were higher than those of the students in the group that were taught by the traditional method.

The variable (here, the reading method) that is manipulated or directly controlled is the independent variable. The experimental participants must perform some task (here, a reading test) that is selected to determine the effect of the independent variable. The way in which the participants respond (here, their test performance) is the dependent variable. The design is as follows:

$$E \quad O \times O$$

$$C \quad O \quad \ \ O$$

In this illustration, E is the experimental (new reading approach) group, C is the control (traditional reading approach) group, X is the independent (new reading program) variable and O is the observations or measures that are gathered. If the study has been carefully controlled, any differences on the reading test should be the result of X, the new method of teaching reading.

In experimental research, the investigator is interested in determining if a relationship exists between the independent and the dependent variable (in our example, between the new reading program and test performance), and how widely the relationship applies. Campbell and Stanley (1963) labeled these two criteria, respectively, as the internal validity and external validity of research. To determine if a relationship exists, internal validity is examined. To determine how widely the relationship applies, Campbell and Stanley (1963) refer to external validity, which represents the generality of the research findings. Consider our example of the reading experiment to understand both types of validity. To determine the internal validity, the investigator would be interested in ruling out variables that might link the new reading instruction to obtained improvements in reading. What variable might reduce internal validity? What would you expect if it were determined that the teachers in the new method didn't like it and used the procedure only occasionally during the study? Such a conclusion would surely reduce internal validity. In the case of external validity we could consider a number of criteria that might influence the degree to which we could generalize our findings. We conducted our reading experiment with fifth-grade participants. Would the same results be expected with third-grade children? Maybe not! Results may not generalize to this group.

Levin (1994) has argued that educational intervention research can be designed that is both credible and creditable. Research *credibility* refers to a study that is methodologically sound and is a function of internal validity characteristics. *Creditable* educational intervention research refers to work that addresses important issues and problems. Research that has creditability has what Levin calls "impact potential." Levin (1994) advocates that educational researchers design research that takes into account the best possible, or *optimal*, design and then proceed to the *best possible given certain constraints*, and then to the *next best possible* design, given constraints. This strategy is preferable to the "can't do" design philosophy that often pervades educational research.

Which type of research is best—historical, descriptive, correlational, comparative, or experimental? Many educational researchers believe that experimental research is the most useful form of scientific investigation. Since experimental research allows control of many factors that potentially bias results, it is preferred in the scientific world. However, determining which method of research is best for a particular study depends on numerous factors, such as the problem under investigation, persons to be studied, instruments used to collect data, and previous work in the field. The purpose of the research helps to determine if correlational/comparative or well-controlled experimental studies should be conducted. For example, if you are interested in reviewing historical events that led to some current school practice, historical research is the most appropriate. Many factors must be examined to decide which research method is best under which circumstances; no single research method is always the best.

Techniques Used by Researchers

Researchers in the field of educational psychology use many different approaches to gather data. In the following sections, we review some of the more common techniques and procedures used in research. These techniques include surveys, interviews, and observations, and the procedures to be highlighted are cross-sectional and longitudinal methods. Single-case research and cross-cultural research are also discussed.

Surveys

In survey research the investigator asks a group of individuals questions about a particular issue. Survey research often is used to study teachers, particularly their attitudes, beliefs, opinions, and behavior. Surveys actually are conducted through a variety of methods, such as questionnaires (called *direct administration*), the telephone, mail, and interviews (Fraenkel & Wallen, 1990). Regardless of the method, the heart of good survey research is the development of a meaningful survey tool—one that clearly communicates questions or concerns in an unbiased fashion, can be completed in a time-efficient manner, and can be scored or interpreted reliably. Each of these methods has various advantages and disadvantages, as can be observed in Table A.3.

Stinson, Whitmire, and Kluwin (1996) were interested in the perceptions of hearing-impaired and other disabled adolescents regarding social relationships with disabled and nondisabled peers in school settings. These researchers administered a social activity scale (that is, forty-seven items; for example, "In my mainstream classes, I talk with hearing-impaired students") to 220 mainstreamed hearing-impaired adolescents. What do you expect that the authors found from the survey? Generally, students reported participating in school activities more frequently with hearing-impaired than with hearing peers. However, reported participation with hearing-impaired peers decreased for the students who were mainstreamed for more classes, thereby qualifying the general finding. Furthermore, the students reported that they were more "emotionally secure" with hearing-impaired peers, and there appeared to be no increase in their emotional security with hearing peers as the hearing-impaired students experienced more mainstreaming.

What are the implications of this study in relation to the concept of mainstreaming discussed in Chapter 5? Some educators argue that hearing-impaired students should be mainstreamed. Such mainstreaming would promote contact and social relationships with hearing peers (for example, Kauffman, 1993). In the Stinson et al. (1996) study, students distinguished between participation and the quality of the peer relationship. Thus, the authors noted that the quality of the relationship may or may not be positive—positive relationships may need to be prompted by teachers and others. Teachers can have a big role in mainstreaming of students with disabilities.

Survey research like that performed in the Stinson et al. (1996) study has the advantage of wide scope, in that a great deal of information can be obtained from a large sample. Generally, survey research provides a good representation of sources of information. But survey research also has disadvantages. First, survey methods may not allow very detailed information on the issue being researched because the survey questions are so general. Second, survey research can be expensive and time-consuming. Third, one may introduce into the study sampling error that can bias the results. Fourth, survey research is subject to faking responses and bias in responding to questions. Even with these limitations, however, the survey method can provide useful information in research.

Table A.3	ADVANTAGES AND DISADVANTAGES OF SURVEY DATA COLLECTION METHODS			
	Direct	Telephone	Mail	Interview Administration
Comparative cost	Lowest	About the same	About the same	High
Facilities needed?	Yes	No	No	Yes
Require training of questioner?	Yes	Yes	No	Yes
Response rate	Very high	Good	Poorest	Very high
Group administration possible?	Yes	No	No	Yes
Allow for random sampling?	Possibly	Yes	Yes	Yes
Require literate sample?	Yes	No	Yes	No
Permit follow-up questions?	No	Yes	No	Yes
Encourage response to sensitive topics?	Somewhat	Somewhat	Best	Weak
Standardization of responses	Easy	Somewhat	Easy	Hardest

From J. R. Fraenkel and N. E. Wallen, *How to Design and Evaluate Research in Education.* Copyright © 1990 McGraw-Hill, Inc., New York, NY. Reprinted by permission of McGraw-Hill.

Interviews

Although interviews are used often in survey research, they are used in many other forms of research as well. Have you ever been interviewed by someone who was conducting a study on some problem or issue? If so, you were exposed to another common method of obtaining information for research purposes. The interview procedure involves a face-to-face situation in which an interviewer asks another individual questions designed to obtain answers relevant to the research problem. Of course, interview procedures are used for purposes other than research, such as those interviews usually conducted to fill job openings.

In research, interviews are typically categorized as either structured (also called *standardized*) or unstructured (also called *unstandardized*). In a standardized interview, the interviewer asks questions in which the sequence and wording are fixed. Thus, the interviewer has little freedom to depart from a prepared script. In contrast, unstandardized interviews are more flexible and open, in that the interviewer determines what will be asked. Thus, the unstandardized, nonstructured interview has an open format, whereas the standardized, structured interview has a closed format.

Interview strategies allow the researcher to obtain a great deal of information, particularly when the situation is open. The interview can also be made flexible, to meet the needs of the situation, problem, and person. This flexibility is an advantage with children, since questions can be reworded so that a child can understand the question. Interviews are often used as adjunct methods, to probe individuals after an experiment, or to follow up on written survey responses. On the negative side, interviewee responses can be faked, are subject to interpretation, and can take a lot of time.

Observation

One of the most common ways we obtain information is through observation. Systematic observation also has evolved as a basic scientific tool for gathering data in research on teaching (Boehm & Weinberg, 1997; McNeely, 1997). As noted previously, many early researchers made observations of their own children. A special branch of psychology called *ecological psychology* was developed out of naturalistic observational techniques used by Barker (1968, 1978). In this form of observation, teams of observers view children throughout a typical day's activities. The observers may literally follow the child for the entire day, recording virtually every event.

The observational form of research has opened many new possibilities in the field of educational psychology. It also has been useful for studying young children in their natural environments (Puckett & Block, 1994). But observational research is expensive and time-consuming, both in training observers and in conducting the observations in the natural environment.

Cross-Sectional and Longitudinal Research

Two broad, contrasting approaches are used to study students in schools: *cross-sectional* and *longitudinal*. A main feature of cross-sectional research is the selection of different groups of children at a variety of age levels for study. Typically, a researcher separates the children into different age levels and studies the problem of interest. Following is an example. Have you ever wondered when children are able to judge age accurately? In early research in this area, Kratochwill and Goldman (1973) noted that previous research had found that it is not until children are approximately 9 years old that they are able to judge age accurately. Kratochwill and Goldman believed that results in previous studies had been influenced by the ambiguity of the drawings used (cartoon characters were used in previous research); their study was designed to investigate children's judgments of age when more realistic stimuli (photographs) were used.

The primary focus of the study was evaluating a cross section of children (ages 3, 4, 5, 6, 7, 8, and 9 years) on developmental changes in judgments by relating people's ages with their physical sizes. The photographs consisted of males and females at four age levels: infant, child, adolescent, and middle-aged adult. Each photograph (and thus each human figure) was reproduced in two sizes. Using a paired-comparison procedure, experimenters presented a cross section of children from ages 3 through 9 years (there were sixteen children at each age level) with either the male or the female photographs. (See female photographs in Figure A.2 for one example of the paired comparison.) The authors found that the accuracy of children's judgments increased in a generally orderly fashion, improving from 47% at age 3 to 59% at age 6, and to 100% at age 9. In comparison to a previous study (Looft, 1971) that had used cartoon-like drawings, Kratochwill and Goldman's use of photographs improved the children's accuracy in age judgments. In contrast with previous research (Looft, 1971), the errors children made in the Kratochwill and Goldman study were primarily the result of basing age judgments on size.

A major advantage of cross-sectional research is that data can be collected across a wide age range in a relatively short time. Kratochwill and Goldman (1973) evaluated age judgments within a few days. They did not have to measure 3-year-olds at one-year intervals for six years to examine the same problem. The advantage is even more apparent when the comparisons involve longer age periods. The major disadvantage of cross-sectional research, however, is that it yields no information about the history of age-related changes. Thus, knowing how specific children in cross-sectional research would have responded at earlier ages is impossible.

A second form of educational research is called longitudinal research because the same participants are assessed repeatedly over a longer period of time. Technically, one could study the same individuals from birth to death, but this strategy would likely involve more than one team of researchers. An example of the longitudinal method of research is the Fels study, begun in 1929 at the Fels Research Institute in Ohio. Initially, eighty-nine participants (forty-four males and forty-five females) were enrolled in the study. In the Fels study, children repeatedly were weighed, measured, and assessed to identify various developmental changes. For example, at least twice a year, from each child's birth to age 6, a trained interviewer visited the parents' home for half a day. For the six years thereafter, researchers interviewed mothers annually to assess their attitudes toward their children. Most children between the ages of 2 and $2\frac{1}{2}$ also attended the Institute's nursery for two three-week

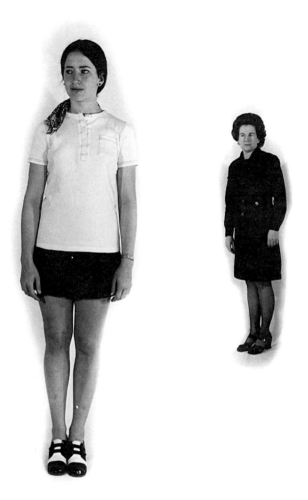

FIGURE A.2.

Actual Photographs from the Kratochwill and Goldman (1973) Study Depicting an Adolescent and an Adult in Two Sizes. Children under the age of 7 generally indicated that the adolescent on the left was older because she was taller.

sessions, and researchers observed peer interaction at the Fels day camp in children ages 6 to 10 years. Such measures as achievement, aggression, conformity, dependency, imitation, language, sex role, and sociability were rated repeatedly. This study was later followed up by Kagan and Moss (1962), who brought back seventy-one of the original eighty-nine Fels participants (who were then between 20 and 29 years old). Thus, longitudinal studies can extend for a long time, even beyond the period originally intended by the initial research team.

A major advantage of the longitudinal research approach over cross-sectional research is that the researcher can study the same participants at each stage or age interval, to record the patterns of an individual's behavior. In this way, a researcher can assess the influence of early events on later behavior. There are also some disadvantages. The longitudinal approach is very expensive and time-consuming. Participants also may leave the study as a result of such factors as moving, illness, death, and loss of motivation to participate. When the sample of participants changes dramatically, the researcher cannot be sure that those who have left the study are similar to those who remain. This problem could cause a bias in the results. Some of the major features of cross-sectional and longitudinal methods of educational research are summarized in Table A.4.

Cross-Cultural Research

Many of the studies cited in this text present research that took place within the context of American culture. Yet, as many educational researchers recognize, cross-cultural research should be conducted to determine which factors are related to a particular culture. For example, people from a

Table A.4 CROSS-SECTIONAL AND LONGITUDINAL DEVELOPMENT
RESEARCH STRATEGIES COMPARED

Characteristics	Design Type	
	Cross-sectional	Longitudinal
Research procedure	Measurement of several groups on different development dimensions (for example, age) simultaneously over a short time period	Repeated measurement of the same group over long periods of time
Time investment	Short time to conduct (that is, days, weeks, months)	Long time to conduct (that is, years, decades)
Expense	Typically inexpensive	Typically expensive
Resources	Relatively few researchers needed	Typically many researchers or research teams needed, depending on the time period
Major advantage	Relatively large amounts of data can be gathered on a large age span within a short time	Researchers can study individual developmental changes within groups
Major disadvantage	Analysis of individual change is obscured	Requires considerable time and resources; participants may leave study

traditional Euro-American culture differ considerably from people from Asian cultures in the way they behave, think, and approach problems. Consider our earlier example of children's judgment of age. From research conducted in the United States, researchers have found that children living in the United States become aware sometime during the first two or three years of life that there is a correlation between the physical size of people and their age. Looft, Raymond, and Raymond (1972) attempted to determine the characteristics of age judgments by children in a non-American culture: Sarawak, of the Federation of Malaysia. Children in the study made age judgments on cartoon drawings of four different male figures (infant, child, adolescent, and adult). The procedures were much the same as those described earlier in the Kratochwill and Goldman (1973) study.

Looft and his associates found that as in the American studies, the older children in the sample were more accurate than the younger children in determining the older of the two persons on each stimulus card. However, the children's explanations for their judgments varied greatly between the two cultures. Fifty-five percent of the Sarawak children used the word *stronger* in their explanations for their judgments; this rationale was never offered by U.S. children in comparable research (Kratochwill & Goldman, 1973; Looft, 1971). Also, 64% of the Malaysian children mentioned the degree of fatness or thinness in their responses, whereas in the U.S. research, descriptions almost always pertained to height. One must again use caution in the interpretation of these results since cartoon figures were used rather than actual photographs.

To account for these cultural differences, Looft et al. (1972) noted that they reflect the occurrence and status of obesity in Sarawak. A fat person was regarded as one who has accumulated considerable wealth—enough to allow that person to eat well and not work hard. In contrast to Americans, most people in Sarawak associate fatness with older individuals, since fat people would presumably live longer. Thus, a young child would commonly judge the infant, whose drawing showed a protruding belly, to be older than the adolescent figure, and explain that the infant was "bigger and fatter."

Single-Case Research

A research approach that is similar to the longitudinal methods discussed in the last section is called *single-case design*. Single-case designs incorporate some of the "control" features of the experimental research such as systematic manipulation of an intervention. Like the repeated measurement feature of the longitudinal design, single-case research emphasizes the repeated analysis of a group or individual participant over a definite time period. However, in the single-case research strategy, the repeated measurement is taken at more frequent intervals (hours, days, weeks) over a relatively short time (several weeks or months). At some point during the research period, an intervention or program is introduced and the researcher evaluates the effect. Single-case designs can involve any number of participants, ranging from one to one million.

Single-case designs are used most commonly in psychological research in behavioral or operant psychology (see Chapter 6). However, the designs are not limited to this orientation and are used currently in psychology, sociology, medicine, and education (Kazdin, 1998; Kratochwill & Levin, 1992). The major advantage of single-case research is that formal measurement takes place, some credible design is used to evaluate interventions, and reliable data are gathered.

Many single-case designs are used in applied settings where the researcher wishes to demonstrate that some intervention was effective with an identified problem. Single-case designs have often been recommended in evaluation of practice in educational settings (Barlow, Hayes, & Nelson, 1984). However, their most common application is in research. Narayan, Heward, and Gardner (1990) demonstrated the use of single-case methodology in their investigation of a strategy to increase active student responding in the classroom. Based on educational research that has shown a positive relationship between active student responding and academic achievement, the authors were looking for a time- and cost-efficient way to increase student responding. Traditionally, a teacher would call on one student at a time to respond. As an alternative, the authors devised a response card that can be held up simultaneously by every student in the class to respond to a question by the teacher.

To evaluate their strategy, Narayan and associates selected a regular fourth-grade classroom in an urban public elementary school. There were twenty students in the class and six were chosen to participate. The authors measured four dependent variables in the study: (1) teacher presentation rate, (2) number of student responses, (3) accuracy of student responses, and (4) daily quiz scores. The study consisted of two independent variables, hand raising and write-on response cards, that were alternated in a replication-type design. During the baseline, the teacher called on one student, who raised a hand in response to a teacher question. In the response-card condition, each student in the class was presented with a white laminated board on which to write one- or two-word answers in response to teacher questions.

The results of the study for each of the six selected students are presented in Figure A.3. As you can observe from the graphs, the rate of active student responses during instruction was higher with the use of response cards than with hand raising. Also, most of the students scored better on daily quizzes following the sessions in which the response cards were used than they did on quizzes following sessions that used hand raising. What do you think the students had to say about the procedure? Interestingly, nineteen of twenty students in the class preferred the response cards over hand raising.

Primary, Secondary, and Meta-Analysis

Have you ever wondered how educational researchers draw conclusions from a body of research evidence? The process of drawing conclusions is not as straightforward as you might think. After the researcher completes the data-gathering phase of the investigation, the data are analyzed in some manner. Typically, some form of statistical test is applied to the data. The first or original analysis of the data that takes place is called *primary analysis*. This primary analysis is usually done by the individual who designed and conducted the research. Following the analysis and discussion of the results, the researcher may share the findings with the scientific community. Once the results are published, they may influence future research, practice, or even educational policy.

Not all published research is accepted at face value. Sometimes other researchers wish to reexamine the original data analysis. This procedure is called *secondary analysis* (Cook, 1974). Secondary analysis refers to the reanalysis of data to clarify the original research questions with better

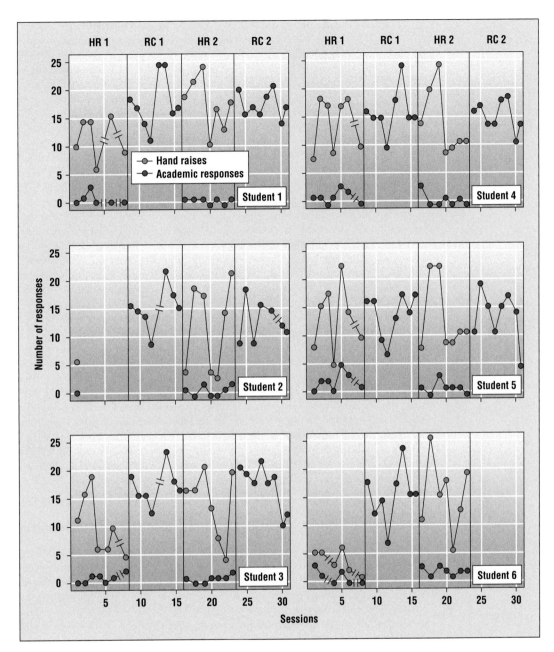

FIGURE A.3. Number of Academic Responses and Hand Raises by Students 1–6 During Hand-Raising (HR) and Response-Card (RC) Conditions. Breaks in data paths indicate student absences.

(From J.S. Narayan, W. L. Heward and R. Gardner, "Using Response Cards to Increase Student Participation in an Elementary Classroom," in *Journal of Applied Behavior Analysis, 23,* 483–490, 1990, Copyright 1990 JABA. Reprinted by permission of the authors.)

statistical procedures, or to answer new questions with old data. For example, a researcher may want to examine some early research data on the effect of class size on student achievement. Perhaps the reanalysis will pose some new issues or even different conclusions from those reached by the original researcher's data analysis. Secondary analysis depends greatly on the availability of the original data. Such data are not always easy to come by. Sometimes they are lost, or coded so that it is difficult to understand the original analysis scheme.

Another form of analysis is called *meta-analysis:* the analysis of analyses (Glass, McGaw, & Smith, 1981). Meta-analysis refers to the statistical analysis of a large collection of analysis results from individual studies, for the purpose of integrating the findings. Meta-analysis is a relatively recent procedure, first coming into prominence during the mid-1970s. It was designed to replace narrative review of research studies, something that most of us have done as students when writing term papers. Some authors have recommended that traditional narrative review be combined with meta-analysis (for example, Slavin, 1991), a strategy called *best-evidence synthesis.*

Applications of meta-analysis have been quite controversial. For example, Smith and Glass (1977) coded and integrated statistically the results of nearly 400 controlled evaluations of psychotherapy and counseling. Their findings provided convincing evidence of the effectiveness of psychotherapy. Specifically, the individual receiving therapy was better off than 75% of untreated individuals. In another study, Smith and Glass (1980) conducted a meta-analysis of research on class size and its relationship to attitudes. They found that advantages of reduced class size are greater in classes whose sizes range from one to fifteen than in classes of larger sizes (that is, only small differences occur in the attitudes of students whose class sizes range from twenty to sixty). Recently, several meta-analyses have appeared in the psychological and educational literature. These papers are reviews of individual meta-analyses in various areas. For example, Lipsey and Wilson (1993) reviewed the efficacy of psychological, educational, and behavioral treatments. The authors found that the effects were overwhelmingly positive for the interventions reviewed, including those with an educational focus.

Wang, Huertel, and Walberg (1993) reviewed the literature to identify and estimate the influence of various educational, psychological, and social variables on learning. Evidence was obtained from sixty-one research experts, ninety-one meta-analyses, and 179 chapters and narrative reviews. Thus, meta-analysis was combined with other literature review methods. The authors found that *proximal variables* (such as psychological, instructional, and home environment variables) exerted more influence on learning than *distal variables* (such as demographic, policy, and organizational variables). Despite such interesting findings, some researchers have been especially critical of meta-analysis, because in making general statements about a particular research topic, it does not discriminate between good and poor studies (Levin, 1994). The future, however, will likely see more of the meta-analysis research strategy used in educational psychology (Asher, 1990; Walberg, 1986; Wang et al., 1993). Research synthesis may help provide information on effective educational practices and improve the "awful reputation" of educational research (Sroufe, 1997).

Ethical and Legal Considerations in Research in Education

Research with human participants carries with it special responsibilities for the educational researcher. A major goal of research is to generate knowledge that will be useful in advancing the human condition and quality education. Increasingly, ethical and legal guidelines have been advanced for individuals conducting research with children and adults. The American Psychological Association (APA) undertook one such effort in its formulation of a code of *Ethical Standards for Research with Human Subjects* (APA, 1982). The guidelines provide researchers with direction when undertaking scientific investigation.

APPENDIX HIGHLIGHTS

Research and Effective Schooling

- One of the most important sources of knowledge about human behavior is scientific research.
- Research answers questions about the effectiveness of educational practices.
- Scientific research is systematic, controlled, empirical, and involves a critical study of some issue or problem.

- Scientific research has been subjected to many and varied influences.
- Scientific research typically follows a series of steps that consists of identifying, clarifying, implementing, evaluating, and interpreting procedures.

The Emergence of Research on Children
Major Research Methods

- Research into educational problems may be historical, descriptive, correlational, comparative, or experimental.
- Historical research involves studying, understanding, and explaining past events.
- Descriptive, or qualitative, research involves collecting data to test hypotheses or answer questions related to the current status of a problem.
- Correlational research involves the process of determining whether, and to what degree, a relation exists between two or more variables.
- Comparative research involves establishing a direct relation between variables that the researcher compares but does not directly manipulate.
- Experimental research involves a study in which the researcher actually manipulates at least one independent variable to observe the effect on one or more dependent variables.

Techniques Used by Researchers

- The more common research techniques used today are surveys, interviews, observations, and cross-sectional and longitudinal studies.
- Research can be conducted with large groups of subjects or with a single case.
- Cross-cultural research helps to explain differences in how individuals behave, think, and attempt to solve problems.
- Meta-analysis, the analysis of the results of a large number of individual studies, is increasingly popular today.
- No one research method is always best; the research question and issues investigated often determine the method that the researcher will use.

GLOSSARY

A

Academic Content Standards A description of what teachers and schools consider to be important content knowledge and skills that all students should learn.

Acceleration A change in the regular school program that permits a gifted student to complete a program in less time or at an earlier age than usual.

Accommodation Piaget's term that refers to a change in cognitive structures that produces corresponding behavioral changes.

Achievement Tests Measures of accomplishment in such specific subjects as reading, arithmetic, etc. Developed by testing specialists; concern today is that these tests may not reflect what is actually taught in the classroom.

Activity Reinforcers High-frequency behaviors used to reinforce low-frequency behaviors.

Adaptation Piaget's term for one of the two psychological mechanisms used to explain cognitive development (organization is the other); refers to the two complementary processes of assimilation and accommodation.

Advance Organizers Ausubel's term for an abstract, general overview of new information before the actual learning is expected.

Affective Entry Characteristics Bloom's phrase to describe a student's motivation to learn new material.

Animism Piaget's term for a child's tendency to attribute life to inert objects.

Aptitude Tests Tests that assess students' general or specific abilities.

Artificialism Piaget's term to describe a preoperational child's tendency to assume that everything is the product of human creation.

Artist A skilled performer.

Assessment The process of gathering information about a student's abilities and using such information to make decisions about the student and future instruction.

Assimilation Piaget's term to describe how human beings take things into their minds; one part of adaptation.

At risk A term used to describe those children who have a high probability of developing a disability.

Attachment Behavior intended to keep a child (or adult) in close proximity to a significant other.

Attention-Deficit/Hyperactivity Disorder (ADHD) A disorder usually appearing in childhood that is characterized by various symptoms of inattention and/or hyperactivity-impulsivity.

Attribution Theory A motivational theory that assumes people want to know the causes of their behavior.

Authentic/Performance Assessment The use of real-world tasks to gain information about a student's abilities to integrate and apply knowledge.

Autonomy Erikson's term for a child's growing sense of independence. Attained in stage 2 (autonomy versus shame and doubt).

Aversive Control A technique to eliminate undesirable student behavior, either by introducing an unpleasant event or removing a pleasurable one.

B

Beginning Teacher Evaluation Studies (BTES) A research program that evaluated beginning teachers by focusing on students' activities.

Behavior Disorders Any conditions in which environmental conflicts and personal disturbance persist and negatively affect academic performance.

Behavior Influence The exercise of some control by one person over another.

Behavior Modification A deliberate attempt, using learning principles, to control student behavior.

Behavior Therapy An attempt to change behavior in a client-therapist relationship.

Bilingual Education Programs designed to help students who have problems with the language of the school.

Biopsychosocial A model used to illustrate the influences on development.

Bloom's Taxonomy A classification of learner activities into cognitive, affective, and psychomotor domains. The cognitive domain has greatly influenced American education and focuses on six classes of cognitive functions: knowledge, comprehension, application, analysis, synthesis, and evaluation.

C

Causality Children distinguish their own actions as causes.

Centering Piaget's term to describe a child's tendency to concentrate on only part of an object or activity. Characteristic of preoperational children.

Cerebral Lateralization The extent to which a function is predominately controlled by one cerebral hemisphere.

Classical Conditioning Pavlov's explanation of conditioning in which a neutral (conditioned) stimulus gradually gains the ability to elicit a response because of its pairing with a natural (unconditioned) stimulus.

Classification Piaget's term for the ability to group objects with some similarities within a larger category.

Clinical Theory of Instruction (CTI) Hunter's theory that features the teacher as a decision-making professional.

Cognitive Entry Behavior Bloom's term for the prerequisite learning skills needed before attempting new learning.

Cognitive Research Trust (CoRT) de Bono's program that is intended to help students acquire thinking skills.

Cognitive Styles Strategies involved in thinking and problem solving.

Comer Schools Strategy advocated by James Comer by which a school-based management team runs the school.

Conditioned Reflex A response that is elicited by a conditioned stimulus when the unconditioned stimulus is not present.

Conditioned Stimulus A previously neutral stimulus that has acquired the power to elicit a response.

Connectionism Thorndike's explanation of learning (by selecting and connecting).

Conservation Piaget's term for the realization that the essence of something remains constant although surface features may change.

Construct Validity Type of validity of a test based on its actually measuring the knowledge domain or behavior it claims to measure.

Constructivism An approach to learning that holds that people actively construct or make their own knowledge and that reality is determined by the experiences of the knower.

Content Piaget's term for behavior.

Content Validity Type of validity based on a test's ability to adequately sample behavior that has been the goal of instruction; the material tested is representative of the material covered on the test.

Context For Hayes, the strategy of searching for relationships between new material and material that is already known.

Contextualized Instruction An approach to instruction that uses a student's personal experiences in a particular culture to introduce new material.

Contingency Contracting Joint decision by a teacher and a student on a behavioral goal and what the student will receive when the goal is achieved.

Conventional Thinking Kohlberg's second level of moral development when children desire approval both from others and society (from about 10 to 13 years of age).

Convergent Questions Questions that require specific material, that is, the right answer.

Cooperative Learning A set of instructional methods in which students are encouraged or required to work together on academic tasks.

Criterion-referenced Test A type of testing used to determine if a student has achieved predetermined behavioral or instructional objectives. A student's performance is interpreted by comparing the performance to a set of objective criteria.

Criterion-related Validity Type of validity of a test based on its results' similarity to some other external criteria (often another test that purports to measure the same behavior or skill).

Cues Techniques to help us recall; particularly effective if we generate them ourselves.

Cultural compatibility Compatibility of instruction with the cultural patterns of students.

Culture The customs, values, and traditions inherent in one's environment.

Curiosity Explorative behavior that occurs when a learner recognizes a discrepancy or conflict between what he or she believes to be true about the world and what turns out actually to be true.

D

Day Care A place where a child spends part of a day outside of his or her own home in the care of others.

Deaf A term describing a hearing disability so acute that an individual is prevented from processing linguistic information through audition, with or without a hearing aid.

Desists A teacher's actions to stop misbehavior.

Developmental Contextualism Analyzing and understanding development in the light of the multiple levels of interactions between individuals and their environments.

Dialect A variety of a language distinguished by vocabulary, grammar, and pronunciation that differs from a standard language.

Discovery Learning Bruner's term for learning that involves the rearrangement and transformation of material by a learner in a way that leads to insight.

Discrimination The process by which we learn not to respond to similar stimuli in an identical manner.

Divergent Questions Questions that require students to expand, explore, be creative.

Diversity Students representing many different kinds of cultural backgrounds.

DUPE An acronym for a problem-solving model: **D**etermine just what the problem is; **U**nderstand its nature; **P**lan for its solution; **E**valuate your plan.

E

Educational Psychology A discipline bridging two fields, education and psychology, that is primarily interested in the application of psychological methods to the study and practice of teaching and learning.

Efficacy Expectations The belief that one can perform the behavior or behaviors required to produce a certain outcome.

Egocentric Speech A form of speech in which children talk, whether anyone is listening or not.

Egocentrism Piaget's term for children's tendency to see things as they want them to be.

Elaboration The adding of information to what one is trying to learn so the material becomes more personally meaningful.

Enactive Mode of Representation Bruner's term for the mental stage of knowing the world by acting on it; usually refers to the infancy period.

Engaged Time The time during which students are actively involved in their work.

Enrichment A method of instruction for gifted students in which they are furnished with additional, challenging experiences.

Episodic Memory The recall of personal experiences within a specific context or period of time.

Equilibration Piaget's term for the balance between assimilation and accommodation.

Essay Tests   Teacher-constructed tests that allow an open-ended written response and require the development of criteria to reliably score.

Evaluation   The summative interpretation of data obtained from tests or other assessment instruments.

Exceptional   A term that refers to one or more kinds of special needs or characteristics in children.

Exhibitions   A form of authentic/performance assessment in which students are required to demonstrate the integration of the knowledge and skills they have acquired.

Expected Learner Outcomes (ELOs)   Cognitive and behavioral objectives used to express learning expectations to students, teachers, and parents.

Extended Response   A form of essay question that permits a student to make any kind of answer the student desires.

External Locus of Control   Individuals attribute the causes of their behavior to factors outside of themselves.

External Representation   A method of problem solving in which a person uses symbols or some other observable type of representation.

Extinction   Refers to the process by which conditioned responses are lost.

Extrinsic Motivation   Those rewards and inducements external to students.

F

Fast Mapping   Refers to a child's ability to quickly grasp the meaning of a word from the context in which it appears.

Fixed Interval   Term describing a schedule in which a response results in reinforcement only after a definite length of time.

Fixed Ratio   Term describing a schedule in which reinforcement depends on a definite number of responses.

Forgetting   The loss of previously acquired material from memory.

Formative Evaluation   Assessment intended to aid learning by providing feedback about what has been learned and what remains to be learned.

Frequency Distribution   A record of how often a score appears in a score category.

G

Gender Identity   The conviction that one belongs to the sex of birth.

Gender Role   Culturally acceptable sexual behavior.

Gender Schema Theory   A mental blueprint for organizing information about gender.

Gender Stereotypes   Beliefs about the characteristics associated with males or females.

Generativity   Erikson's term for productive and creative responsibility for the next generation. Attained in stage 7 (generativity versus stagnation).

Gifted   A term describing those with abilities that give evidence of high performance capabilities.

Grade Equivalent Score   A standardized test score that describes a student's performance on a scale based on grade in school and month in grade; most commonly misinterpreted score; actually indicates student's level of performance relative to students in his or her own grade.

Grading   Assigning a symbol to a student's work or performance to provide general feedback about the quality of the work or performance.

Group Alertness   Use of instructional methods that maintain interest and contribute to lively classes.

Grouper   Groupers prefer as wide a grasp of a subject as possible.

H

Hard of Hearing   A term describing those individuals with sufficient hearing potential (with hearing aids) to process linguistic information through audition.

Head Start   Intervention program intended to provide educational and developmental services to preschool children from low-income families.

Functional Invariants   Piaget's term for the cognitive mechanisms adaptation and organization.

Hearing Impairment   A term referring to any type of hearing loss, from mild to profound.

Hierarchy of Needs   A theoretical model of five needs that Maslow believed every human being had; the needs range from basic physiological and safety needs, to love and belongingness needs, to esteem, and finally at the top of the hierarchy the need for self-actualization.

I

Iconic Mode of Representation   Bruner's term for the perceptual organization of the world; a mode of representation.

Identity Achievement   Committing oneself to choices about identity and maintaining that commitment.

Identity Confusion   Those who experience doubt and uncertainty about who they are.

Identity Crisis   Erikson's term for those situations, usually in adolescence, that cause us to make major decisions about our identity.

Identity Diffusion   An inability to commit oneself to choices—the lack of a sense of direction.

Identity Foreclosure   Making a commitment under pressure, not as the result of the resolution of a crisis.

Identity Moratorium   Desiring to make a choice but lacking the ability to do so.

Imagery   The ability to visualize objects or events.

Individuation   Refers to the fullest development of one's self (self-esteem and self-control).

Industry   Erikson's term to describe a child's sense of being able to do things well and to win recognition in this way. Attained in stage 4 (industry versus inferiority).

Information Processing   A process of information gathering that encompasses such topics as attention, perception, thinking, memory, and problem-solving strategies.

Initiative   Erikson's term for children's ability to explore the environment and test their world. Attained in stage 3 (initiative versus guilt).

Inner Speech Vygotsky's name for that time in a child's life when speech turns inward and guides behavior.

Inquiry Teaching Bruner's term for teaching that permits students to be active partners in the search for knowledge, thus enhancing the meaning of what they learn.

Instantiation The strategy of furnishing an example.

Instructional Objective Learning outcomes deemed worthy of attainment; well-stated objectives are explicitly specified behaviors, conditions of performance, and criteria for evaluating the performance.

Integrity Erikson's term for the ability to look back and see meaning in life. Attained in stage 8 (integrity versus despair).

Intelligent Tutoring System (ITS) Use of technology to provide an individualized tutor for each student. The computer presents new material, provides examples and practice problems, tracks student performance, identifies errors and misconceptions, and provides appropriate guidance and feedback.

Interactions Exchanges between individuals.

Interest An enduring characteristic expressed by a relationship between a person and a particular activity or object.

Intermittent Reinforcement Reinforcement in which reinforcers occasionally are implemented.

Internal Locus of Control Individuals attribute causes of their behavior to themselves.

Internal Representation A mental model of how to solve a problem.

Internalization Transforming interpersonal processes into intrapersonal.

Interval Reinforcement Scheduled reinforcement, in which the reinforcement occurs at definite established time intervals.

Intimacy Erikson's term for the ability to be involved with another without fearing a loss of self-identity. Attained in stage 6 (intimacy versus isolation).

Intrinsic Motivation The desire of students themselves to learn, without the need for external inducements.

Irreversibility Piaget's term for children's inability to reverse their thinking.

L

Learned Helplessness The reaction on the part of some individuals to become frustrated and simply give up after repeated failure.

Learning Disabilities A term referring to a handicapping condition characterized by a discrepancy between ability and achievement, most commonly manifested in reading, writing, reasoning, and/or mathematics.

Learning Styles Preferences in learning and studying.

Least Restrictive Environment A learning environment or classroom situation that provides necessary support for a disabled student's continuing educational progress while also minimizing the time the student is removed from a normalized educational environment. In many ways, it has the same philosophical base as the practice of mainstreaming.

Legally Blind A term referring to those individuals with vision of 20/200 or less in the better eye (after correction).

Levels of Processing Describes analysis of memory focusing on the depth at which humans process information.

Locus of Control The cause of behavior; some individuals believe it resides within them, while others believe it resides outside them.

Long-Term Store The aspect of memory that holds both conscious and unconscious data for long periods of time; related to meaningfulness of material.

M

Mainstreaming Integrating physically, mentally, and behaviorally disabled students into regular classes.

Marking The summary assessment of a test or an oral or written report.

Mastery Learning Learning in which instructor and student decide on time needed and what is necessary for mastery, usually 90% of the possible achievement score.

Mean The average of the raw scores.

Meaningful Learning Ausubel's term to describe the acquisition of new meanings.

Measurement Quantifying or placing a number on a student performance.

Measures of Central Tendency The mean, the median, or the mode are all a score that represents a distribution of scores.

Median That point in the distribution above which 50 percent and below which 50 percent of the scores lie.

Mental Image A conscious representation of previous perceptions in any sense modality, less vivid and not finely detailed as a picture.

Mental Representation The coding of external events so they are retrievable in an internal form.

Mental Retardation Significantly subaverage general intellectual functioning.

Metacognition The ability to think about thinking.

Metacognitive Experiences Cognitive or affective experiences that relate to cognitive activities.

Metacognitive Knowledge An individual's knowledge and beliefs about cognitive matters, gained from experiences and stored in long-term memory.

Metalinguistic Awareness Children's ability to think and talk about their language.

Method of Loci The use of familiar locations to help one visually store things in memory and retrieve them more easily.

Mode The score obtained by the largest number of individuals taking a test.

Modeling A teaching technique in which the teacher or model performs an activity that the student has previously found difficult to perform and encourages it be copied.

Modes of Representation Bruner's term for the mental stages a child passes through.

Moral Dilemma Conflicts causing subjects to justify the morality of their choices.

Morpheme The smallest unit of language to have meaning, may be a whole word or part of a word (*old, er*).

Motherese That tendency to talk to infants in short sentences with a high-pitched voice.

Multiple Coding The process of representing information in more than one way.

Multiple Intelligences Gardner's eight relatively autonomous intelligences. These include linguistic, musical, logical-mathematical, spatial, bodily-kinesthetic, interpersonal, intrapersonal, and naturalistic intelligences.

Multiple-choice Items Questions or incomplete statements that are followed by several possible responses, one of which is the best answered and considered correct.

N

Naive Psychology Children explore the concrete objects in their world.

Negative Reinforcers Stimuli whose withdrawal strengthens behavior.

Negative Transfer When something a person learns at one time hinders their learning or performance at a later time.

Noncontingent Praise Praise that is not linked to specific behavior.

Norm Group A comparison group usually used to establish the scaled scores for a standardized test.

Norm-referenced Tests Standardized tests that allow comparison of a score for a given student with a representative group of students.

Normal Curve A representation showing the frequency distribution of a particular trait or ability for a particular group.

Norms Scores on a given test that are derived from an identified sample and are then used as a basis for comparison (and therefore interpretation) of scores on the same test.

Number Concept Piaget's term for children's understanding of the meaning of numbers; the oneness of one.

O

Object Permanence Piaget's term for an infant's ability to realize that an object or person not within sight still exists.

Operant Conditioning Skinner's explanation of learning, which emphasizes the consequences of behavior.

Operations Piaget's term for actions that we perform mentally to gain knowledge.

Organization Piaget's term for the connections among cognitive structures.

Out-of-School Influences Forces outside of the classroom that affect learning.

Outcome Expectations The belief that a given behavior will lead to a specific outcome.

Overcorrection A form of classroom management involving both restitution and positive practice.

Overlapping A teacher's ability to handle two or more classroom issues simultaneously.

P

Percentiles A score that tells the percentage of individuals taking a test who are at or below a particular score; a percentile rank of 74 means that this student did as well or better than 74% of those taking the test.

Perception The process or act of perceiving information and making sense of it.

Performance Tests An assessment method that requires students to construct a response or perform an action as an indication of their ability to apply knowledge and skills. Stronger performance assessments have explicit scoring criteria that students are aware of prior to performing.

Phonemes The distinctive, fundamental sounds of a language.

Phonology The use of sounds to form words.

Plasticity Resiliency or flexibility shown by humans.

Portfolio Assessment Assessment of a student's behavior or skills based on a collection of the student's work that the teacher and the student both believe represents evidence of learning.

Positive Reinforcers Those stimuli whose presentations increase the rates of responses.

Positive Transfer When something a person learns in one situation helps them learn or perform in another situation.

Postconventional Thinking Kohlberg's third level of moral development when individuals act according to an enlightened conscience.

Poverty Level Government-determined level of poor who need assistance ($16,036 for a family of four).

Pragmatics The ability to take part in a conversation, using language in a socially correct manner.

Preconventional Thinking Kohlberg's first level of moral development when children respond mainly to reward and punishment (about 4 to 10 years of age).

Preintellectual Speech Elementary processes that develop into speech.

Premack Principle The theory that states that access to high-frequency behaviors acts as a reinforcer for the performance of low-frequency behaviors.

Proactive Classroom Management Classroom management including both reactive responding to problems and proactive planning for productive behavior.

Programed Instruction A set of instructional materials that students can use to teach themselves about a particular topic, skill, or content area. Based on Skinner's theory of operant conditioning, programed instruction is designed so it progresses in small steps toward a well-defined terminal behavior, is sequenced so students give correct answers most of the time, and relies heavily on positive reinforcement of correct answers.

Punishment Refers to the presentation of an aversive stimulus or removal of a positive stimulus contingent upon a response that decreases the probability of the response.

Q

QAIT An instructional model proposed by Slavin that emphasizes the quality of instruction, appropriate levels of instruction, incentive, and time.

Quality of Instruction Bloom's term for the cues, practice, and reinforcement necessary to make learning meaningful for students.

R

Ratio Reinforcement Reinforcement occurring after a certain number of responses.

Raw Score Uninterpreted data; often, the number of correct items.

Realism Piaget's term for a child's growing ability to distinguish and accept the real world.

Reception Learning One part of meaningful learning that refers to using information in the form in which it was received without imposing a new order or meaning.

Reciprocal Interactions Process in which we respond to those around us and they change; their changed behavior then causes changes in us; emphasizes a student's active involvement in teacher-student interactions, that is, students are not merely passive recipients in any exchange.

Recognition The act of comparing an incoming representation with a representation already in memory.

Reflective Teachers Teachers who think about their teaching.

Regular Education Initiative (REI) A movement to include more of the mildly disabled in regular classrooms.

Reinforcement The use of a consequence to increase the frequency of a response.

Reinforcer A consequential stimulus that occurs contingent on a behavior and increases the behavior.

Reliability Characteristic of a test for which a student's scores are nearly the same in repeated measurements, and of a test that consistently measures what it says it measures.

Reminiscence The phenomenon that after rest, memory seems to improve.

Reporting The summary feedback provided to consumers of assessments; can be either quantitative or qualitative.

Resilient Children Children who, in spite of daunting hardships, manage to thrive.

Response Cost A form of punishment involving the loss of a positive reinforcer (for example, after misbehavior, a student may no longer be a classroom monitor).

Restricted Response A form of essay question that asks for specific information.

Retrieval The act of recognizing, recalling, and reconstructing what we have previously stored in memory.

Retrieving Ability to access information in stored memory.

Reversibility Piaget's term for children's ability to use cognitive operations "to take things apart," to reverse their thinking.

Ripple Effect The phenomenon in which punishment is not confined to one student; its effects spread to other class members.

S

Scaffolding Help, usually from adults, that enables a child to move to a higher level of accomplishment.

Schemata (pl. of schema) Hypothetical mental frameworks that modify incoming information so it fits a person's experiences and perceptions.

Schemes Piaget's term for our organized patterns of thought.

Scientist A logical investigator.

Selection Items Questions on objective tests that require students to choose from among possible answers.

Self Children's sense of who they are and what makes them different from everyone else.

Self-Actualization The full development or use of one's talents and potentialities.

Self-Efficacy Individuals' beliefs in their abilities to exert control over their lives; feelings of competency.

Self-esteem A feeling of confidence and self-satisfaction with one's self.

Self-Fulfilling Prophecy The phenomenon that when teachers expect more of students, the students tend to meet the expectations, or vice versa.

Semantic Memory Memory necessary for the use of language.

Semantics The meaning of words, the relationship between ideas and words.

Sensory Register The ability, which is highly selective, to hold information in memory for a brief period.

Seriation Piaget's term for the ability to arrange objects by increasing or decreasing size.

Sex Cleavage The tendency of children of the same sex to play together.

Shaping A form of classroom management in which teachers determine the successive steps needed to master a task and then teach them separately, reinforcing each step.

Short-Term Store The working memory; consciousness is involved.

Social Cognitive Learning According to Bandura's theory, the process whereby the information we glean from observing others influences our behavior.

Social Discipline A theory of classroom management based on the conviction that misbehavior can be eliminated by changing a student's goals.

Social Validity The applied, or social, importance of exhibiting certain behaviors in particular situations.

Socialization The need to establish and maintain relations with others and to regulate behavior according to society's demands.

Special Grouping A term that implies self-contained special classes or schools for the gifted.

Spiral Curriculum Bruner's term for teaching a subject in an ever more abstract manner; tied to his interpretation of readiness.

Standard Deviation Unit Measure of how much a score varies from the mean.

Standard Error of Measurement An estimate of the standard deviation that would be found on the distribution of scores for a specified person if that person were to be tested repeatedly on the same or similar test.

Standard Scores Any of several derived scores (any score other than a raw score) based on the number of standard deviations between a specified raw score and the mean of the distribution.

Standardized Tests Tests that are administered under a uniform set of conditions; they are usually commercially published and based on a large normative sample.

Stanine Scores A standard score that classifies those taking a test into one of nine groups.

Stimulus Generalization Transfer of a trained response to situations or stimulus conditions other than those in which training has taken place. The behavior generalizes to other situations. Contrast with *response generalization*.

Storage The act of putting information into memory.

Storing The ability to hold information in memory.

Stringer   Stringers prefer a systematic, methodical analysis leading to mastery of details.

Structures   Piaget's term for the psychological units of the mind that enable us to think and know.

Structuring   The strategy of searching for relations in learning materials.

Style   A strategy used consistently across a wide variety of tasks.

Subject Matter Knowledge   Basic content to be taught.

Summative Evaluation   Assessment of a student's achievement at the completion of a block of work.

Supply Items   Questions on objective tests that require students to give the answers as opposed to choosing from among possible answers.

Symbolic Mode of Representation   Bruner's term for the ability to represent information, to consider possibilities.

Syntax   The grammar of a language; putting words together to form sentences.

T

T-score   A standard score with a mean of 50 and a standard deviation of 10.

Task Analysis   Breaking down complex behaviors into their basic elements and sequencing them from first to last in a response chain.

Teacher-constructed Tests   Any number of tools designed by a teacher to assess student learning, usually not standardized or based on a normative sample.

Teaching (Pedagogical) Knowledge   How best to present a subject.

Teaching Subject Matter Knowledge   Principles and strategies applicable to a particular subject.

Telegraphic Speech   The use of two or three words to convey more sophisticated meanings ("milk gone" means "my milk is all gone").

Terminal Behavior   Skinner's term for what students should be able to do after instruction.

Test Anxiety   Anxiety generated by planning for and taking tests.

Test-Wiseness   Knowing how to take tests; skills that can be learned and refined to improve test performance.

Thinking Skills   Skills and strategies that enable students to adapt to constant change.

Time Out   A form of punishment in which a student loses something desirable for a period of time.

Token Economy   A form of classroom management in which students receive tokens for desirable behavior. These may then be exchanged for something pleasurable.

Transductive Reasoning   Piaget's term for a preoperational child's reasoning technique—from particular to particular in a nonlogical manner.

Transfer of Learning   Learning one topic may influence later learning.

Transition Smoothness   Teachers have no difficulty in handling activities and movement in their classes.

Triarchic Model of Intelligence   Sternberg's view of intelligence as consisting of three elements: componential, experiential, and contextual.

V

Validity   The extent to which a test measures what it says it does so that a meaningful inference can be made from a person's score on the test.

Variable Interval   Term describing a schedule in which the time between reinforcements varies.

Variable Ratio   Term describing a schedule in which the number of responses needed for reinforcement varies from one reinforcement to the next.

Verbal Processing   The encoding of a perceived stimuli into a word or words.

Visually Impaired   Those individuals subject to any type of reduction in vision.

Visually Limited   Those who have difficulty seeing under ordinary conditions but who can adapt with glasses.

W

Web-Based Instruction (WBI)   Using the information search and transmitting capabilities of the WWW and the vast array of resources available on it to provide instruction to students. In some cases, WBI is highly structured; however, at the K–12 level, it is usually less integrated and fosters discovery learning.

Whole Language   A technique in which all language processes are studied together in a natural context (as a whole, and not as a series of facts).

Withitness   Teachers' knowledge and understanding of what is happening in their classrooms.

Y

Yerkes-Dodson Law   The principle that ideal motivation for learning decreases in intensity with increasing task difficulty.

Z

Z-score   A score that tells the distance of a student's raw score from the mean in standard deviation units; has a mean equal to 0 and a standard deviation equal to 1.

Zone of Proximal Development   Vygotsky's concept of the distance between a child's actual developmental level and a higher level of potential development with adult guidance (between what children can do independently and what they can do with help).

Achenbach, T., & Edelbrock, C. (1983). *Manual for the child behavior checklist and revised child behavior profile.* Burlington: University of Vermont, Department of Psychiatry.

Achenbach, T., McConaughy, S., and **Howell, C.** (1987). Child/adolescent behavioral and emotional problems: Implications of cross-informant correlations for situational specificity. *Psychological Bulletin, 101,* 213–232.

Adams, M. J. (1990). *Beginning to read: Thinking and learning about print.* Cambridge, MA: MIT Press.

Ainsworth, M. (1979). Infant-mother attachment. *American Psychologist, 34,* 932–937.

Airasian, P. W. (1994). *Classroom assessment.* New York: McGraw-Hill.

Alberto, P., & Troutman, A. (1986). *Applied behavioral analysis for teachers.* Columbus, OH: Merrill.

Alderman, M. K. (1990, September). Motivation for at-risk students. *Educational Leadership,* Vol. 49, 27–30.

Alexander, P. (1996). The past, present, and future of knowledge research: A reexamination of the role of knowledge in learning and instruction. *Educational Psychologist, 31*(2), 89–92.

American Association of University Women (AAUW) Educational Foundation. (1992). *How schools shortchange girls: The AAUW report.* Washington, DC: Author.

American Association on Mental Retardation. (1992). *Mental retardation: Definition, classification, and systems of support* (9th ed.). Washington, DC: Author.

American Educational Research Association. (1988). *Code of fair testing practices in education.* Washington, DC: Author.

American Federation of Teachers. (1990). *Standards for teacher competence in educational assessment of students.* Washington, DC: Author.

American Psychiatric Association. (1994). *Diagnostic and statistical manual of mental disorders* (4th ed.). Washington, DC: Author.

American Psychological Association. (1982). *Ethical standards for research with human subjects.* Washington, DC: Author.

American Psychological Association. (1985). *Standards for educational and psychological testing.* Washington, DC: Author.

Anderson, J. (1985). *Cognitive psychology and its implications.* San Francisco: W. H. Freeman.

Anderson, J. R., Farrell, R., & Saurs, R. (1984). Learning to program in LISP. Cognitive Science, 8, 87–129.

Anderson, Spiro, and Anderson. *American Education Research Journal,* 17, 400–404.

Anglin, J. (1993). Vocabulary development: A morphological analysis. *Monographs of the Society for Research in Child Development,* Serial No. 238, Vol. 58(10).

Armstrong, D., & Savage, T. (1983). *Secondary education: An introduction.* New York: Macmillan.

Asher, W. (1990). Educational psychology, research methodology, and meta-analysis. *Educational Psychologist, 25,* 143–158.

Atkinson, R. C., & Shiffrin, R. M. (1968). Human memory: A proposed system and its control processes. In K. W. Spence & J. T. Spence (Eds.), *The psychology of learning and motivation.* New York: Academic Press.

Ausubel, D. (1960). The use of advance organizers in the learning and retention of meaningful verbal material. *Journal of Educational Psychology, 51,* 267–272.

Ausubel, D. (1968). *Educational psychology: A cognitive view.* New York: Holt, Rinehart & Winston.

Ausubel, D. (1977). The facilitation of meaningful verbal learning in the classroom. *Educational Psychologist, 12,* 162–178.

Ausubel, D., Novak, J., & Hanesian, H. (1978). *Educational psychology: A cognitive view.* New York: Holt, Rinehart & Winston.

Ayersman, D. J. (1996). *Effects of computer instruction, learning style, gender, and experience on computer anxiety.* Computers in the Schools, 12(4), 15–30.

Baddeley, A. (1990). Human memory: Theory and practice. Boston: Allyn & Bacon.

Baillargeon, R. (1987). Object permanence in 3 1/2 and 4-month-old infants. *Developmental Psychology, 23,* 655–664.

Baker, E. T. (1994). *Meta-analytic evidence for non-inclusive educational practices: Does educational research support current practices for special needs students?* Doctoral Dissertation: Temple University, Philadelphia.

Baker, E. T., Wang, M. C., & Walberg, H. J. (1994). The effects of inclusion on learning. *Educational Leadership,* December, 33–38.

Bales, J. (1990). Skinner gets award, ovations at APA talk. *The APA Monitor, 21* (10), 1, 6.

Ball, E. W., & Blachman, B. A. (1991). Does phoneme awareness training in kindergarten make a difference in early word recognition and developmental spelling? *Reading Research Quarterly, 24,* 49–66.

Bandura, A. (1997). *Self-efficacy: The exercise of control.* New York: Freeman.

Bandura, A. (1977). Social learning theory. Englewood Cliffs, NJ: Prentice-Hall.

Bandura, A. (1981). Self-referent thought: A developmental analysis of self-efficacy. In J. Flavell & L. Ross (Eds.), Social cognitive development. New York: Cambridge University Press.

Bandura, A. (1986). *Social foundations of thought and action: A social-cognitive theory.* Englewood Cliffs, NJ: Prentice-Hall.

Bandura, A., Ross, D., & Ross, S. (1963). Imitation of film-mediated aggressive models. Journal of Abnormal and Social Psychology, 66, 3–11.

Banks, J. (1993a). Multicultural education: Characteristics and goals. In J. Banks & C. Banks (Eds.), *Multicultural education: Issues and perspectives.* Boston: Allyn & Bacon.

Barker, R. G. (1968). *Ecological psychology.* Stanford: Stanford University Press.

Barker, R. G. (1978). *Habitats, environments, and human behavior.* San Francisco: Jossey-Bass.

Barkley, R. A. (1994). *ADHD in the classroom: Strategies for teachers.* New York: A Guilford Press Video.

Barkley, R. A. (1996). Attention-deficit/Hyperactivity disorder. In E. J. Mash & R. A. Barkley (Eds.), *Child psychopathology* (pp. 63–112). New York: Guilford Press.

Barlow, D. H., & Hersen, M. (1984). *Single case experimental designs: Strategies for studying behavior change* (2nd ed.). New York: Pergamon Press.

Barlow, D. H., Hayes, S. C., & Nelson, R. O. (1984). *The scientist practitioner: Research and accountability in clinical and educational settings.* New York: Pergamon.

Barnett, W. (1995). Long-term effects of early childhood programs on cognitive and school outcomes. In R. Behrman (Ed.) *The Future of Children.* Los Altos, CA: Center for the Future of Children.

Barr, A., & Feigenbaum, E. A. (1982). Applications-oriented AI research: Education. In A. Barr & E. Feigenbaum (Eds.), *The handbook of artificial intelligence* (Vol. 2, pp. 229–235). Los Altos, CA: William Kaufmann.

Bartlett, F. C. (1932). *Remembering: A study in experimental and social psychology.* London: Cambridge University Press.

Bartlett, S. (1997). No place to play: Implications for the interactions of parents and children. *Journal of Children and Poverty, 3*(1), 12–16.

Becker, H. J. (1993). How computers are used in United States schools: Basic data from the 1989 I.E.A. Computers in education survey. *Journal of Educational Computing Research, 7*(4), 385–406.

Bem, S. (1992). On the inadequacy of our sexual categories: A personal perspective. *Feminine Psychology, 2,* 435–437.

Bem, S. (1993). *The lenses of gender: Transforming the debate on sexual inequality.* New Haven, CT: Yale University Press.

Bereiter, C., & Englemann, S. (1966). Teaching disadvantaged children in the preschool. Englewood Cliffs, NJ: Prentice-Hall.

Berk, L. (1997a). *Child development.* Boston: Allyn & Bacon.

Berk, L. (1997b). *Infants, children, and adolescents.* Boston: Allyn & Bacon.

Berliner, D. (1983). Developing conceptions of classroom environments. *Educational Psychologist, 18,* 1–13.

Berliner, D. C. (1988). The half-full glass: A review of research on teaching. In E. L. Meyer, G. V. Vergason, & R. L. Whelan (Eds.), Effective instructional strategies for exceptional children (pp. 7–31). Denver, CO: Love.

Billingsley, A. (1992). *Climbing Jacob's ladder: The enduring legacy of African American families.* New York: Simon & Schuster.

Blair, T. (1988). Emerging patterns of teaching. Columbus, OH: Merrill.

Bloom, B. (1981). *All our children learning.* New York: McGraw-Hill.

Bloom, B. (Ed.). (1956). *Taxonomy of educational objectives. Handbook 1: Cognitive domain.* New York: McKay.

Bloom, B., Madaus, G., & Hastings, J. T. (1981). *Evaluation to improve learning.* New York: McGraw-Hill.

Blum, R. E., & Arter, J. A. (Eds.) (1996). *A handbook for student performance assessment in an era of restructuring.* Alexandria, VA: ASCD.

Boehm, A. E., & Weinberg, R. A. (1997). *The classroom observer.* Teachers College Press.

Borich, G. (1992). *Effective teaching methods.* New York: Merrill.

Borko, H. & Putnam, R. (1996). Learning to teach. In Berliner, D. & Calfee, R. (Eds.), *Handbook of educational psychology.* New York: Macmillan.

Bos, C., & Vaughn, S. (1988). Strategies for teaching students with learning and behavior problems. Boston: Allyn & Bacon.

Bowlby, J. (1969). *Attachment.* New York: Basic.

Boyer, E. (1990). Giving dignity to the teaching profession. In D. Dill (Ed.), *What teachers need to know.* San Francisco: Jossey-Bass.

Branch, R. M. (1997). *Educational technology frameworks that facilitate culturally pluralistic instruction.* Educational Technology, 37(2), 38–41.

Bransford, J., & Stein, B. (1993). *The IDEAL problem solver.* New York: Freeman.

Bransford, J. D., Sherwood, R. D., Hasselbring, T. S., Kinzer, C. K., & Williams, S. M. (1990). Anchored instruction: Why we need it and how technology can help. In D. Nix & R. Spiro (Eds.), *Cognition, education, and multimedia: Exploring ideas in high technology,* 179–201. Hillsdale, NJ: Erlbaum.

Bransford, J. D., Vye, N. J., Kinzer, C., & Risko, V. (1990). Teaching thinking and content knowledge: Toward an integrated approach. In B. F. Jones & L. Idol (Eds.), *Dimensions of thinking and cognitive instruction* (pp. 381–413). Hillsdale, NJ: Erlbaum.

Braswell, L., & Bloomquist, M. L. (1991). *Cognitive-behavioral therapy with ADHD children.* New York: Guilford Press.

Brislin, R. (Ed.). (1990). *Applied cross-cultural psychology.* Newbury Park, CA: Sage.

Brooks, D. & Kann, M. (1993). What makes character education programs work? *Educational Leadership, 51*(3), 19–21.

Brophy, J. (1983). Fostering student learning and motivation in the elementary school classroom. In S. Paris, G. Olson, & H. Stevenson (Eds.), Learning and motivation in the classroom. Hillsdale, NJ: Erlbaum.

Brophy, J. (1987, October). Synthesis of research on strategies for motivating students to learn. *Educational Leadership,* Vol. 46, 40–48.

Brophy, J., & Good, T. (1986). Teacher behavior and student achievement. In M. Wittrock (Ed.), *Handbook of research on teaching,* 315–347. New York: Macmillan.

Brown, A. (1990). Domain-specific principles affect learning and transfer in children. *Cognitive Science, 14,* 107–133.

Brown, A., & Campione, J. (1986). Psychological theory and the study of learning disabilities. *American Psychologist, 41,* 1059–1068.

Brown, A. L., & Campione, J. C. (1996). Psychological learning theory and the design of innovative learning environments: On procedures, principles and systems. In L. Schauble & R. Glaser (Eds.), Contributions of instructional innovation to understanding learning (pp. 289–325). Hillsdale, NJ: Erlbaum.

Brown, R. (1988). Model youth: Excelling despite the odds. *Ebony, 43,* 40–48.

Brown, R., & Lennenberg, E. (1954). A study in language and cognition. *Journal of Abnormal and Social Psychology, 44,* 454–462.

Bruer, J. (1994). *Schools for thought.* Cambridge, MA: MIT Press.

Bruner, J. (1960). *The process of education.* Cambridge, MA: Harvard University Press.

Bruner, J. (1966a). *Studies in cognitive growth.* New York: Wiley.

Bruner, J. (1966b). *Toward a theory of instruction.* New York: John Wiley & Sons.

Bruner, J. (1971). *The relevance of education.* New York: Norton.

Bruner, J. (1986). *Actual minds, possible worlds.* Cambridge, MA: Harvard University Press.

Bruner, J. (1990). *Acts of meaning.* Cambridge, MA: Harvard University Press.

Bruner, J. (1996). *The culture of education.* Cambridge, MA: Harvard University Press.

Bruner, J., & Goodman, C. (1947). Value and need as organizing factors in perception. *Journal of Abnormal and Social Psychology, 42,* 33–44.

Bruner, J., Goodnow, J., & Austin, G. (1956). *A study of thinking.* New York: Wiley.

Burke, J. (1991). Teenagers, clothes, and gang violence. *Educational Leadership, 49*(1), 11–13.

Caine, R., & Caine, G. (1990). Understanding a brain-based approach to learning and teaching. *Educational Leadership, 48,* 66–70.

Caine, R. N., & Caine, G. (1997). *Education on the edge of possibility.* Alexandria, VA: Association for Supervision and Curriculum Development.

Calderhead, J. (1996). Teachers: Beliefs and knowledge. In D. Berliner, & R. Calfee (Eds.), *Handbook of educational psychology, 21,* 709–725. New York: Macmillan.

Calfee, R., & Berliner, D. (1996). Introduction to a dynamic and relevant educational psychology. In D. Berliner & R. Calfee (Eds.), *Handbook of educational psychology, 1,* 1–14. New York: Macmillan.

Callahan, J., Clark, L., & Kellough, R. (1992). *Teaching in the middle and secondary schools.* New York: Macmillan.

Campbell, D. T., & Stanley, J. C. (1963). Experimental and quasi-experimental designs for research and teaching. In N. L. Gage (Ed.), *Handbook of research on teaching.* Chicago: Rand McNally.

Canter, L., & Hausner, L. (1987). *Homework without tears: A parents' guide for motivating children to do homework and to succeed in school.* New York: Harper & Row.

Carlberg, C., & Kavale, T. (1980). The efficacy of special versus regular class placement for exceptional children: A meta-analysis. *Journal of Special Education, 14,* 295–309.

Carnine, D. (1989). Designing practice activities. *Journal of Learning Disabilities, 22,* 603–607.

Carnine, D. (1991). Curricular interventions for teaching higher order thinking to all students: Introduction to the special series. *Journal of Learning Disabilities, 24,* 261–269.

Carnine, D. (1994). Educational tools for diverse learners. *School Psychology Review, 23*(3), 341–350.

Carroll, J. (1963). A model of school learning. Teachers College Record, 64, 723–733.

Casas, J., & Pytluk, S. (1995). Hispanic identity development: Implications for research and practice. In J. Ponterotto, J. Casas, L. Suzuki, & C. Alexander (Eds.), *Handbook of multicultural counseling,* 155–180. Thousand Oaks, CA: Sage.

Ceci, S. (1996). *On intelligence.* Cambridge, MA: Harvard University Press.

Chard, D., Smith, S., & Sugai, G. (1992). Packaged discipline programs: A consumer's guide. In J. Marr & G. Tindal (Eds.), *The Oregon Conference Monograph: 1992* (pp. 19–26). Eugene: University of Oregon Press.

Chess, S., & Hassibi, M. (1978). *Principles and practices in child psychiatry.* New York: Plenum.

Christenson, S. L., & Conoley, J. C. (Eds.). (1992). *Home-school collaboration: Enhancing children's academic and social competence.* Silver Springs, MD: National Association of School Psychologists.

Clark, F., & Clark, C. (1989). *Hassle-free homework: A six-week plan for parents and children to take the pain out of homework.* New York: Doubleday.

Clarke-Stewart, A. (1993). *Daycare.* Cambridge, MA: Harvard.

Clarke-Stewart, A., Allhusen, V., & Clements, D. (1995). Nonparental caregiving. In M. Bornstein (Ed.), *Handbook of parenting,* Vol. 3, 151–176. Mahwah, NJ: Erlbaum.

Clements, D. H., & Nastasi, B. K. (1992). Computers and early childhood education. In M. Gettinger, S. N. Elliott, & T. R. Kratochwill (Eds.), *Preschool and early childhood treatment directions: Advances in school psychology* (pp. 187–246). Hillsdale, NJ: Erlbaum.

Cobb, P., & Yackel, E. (1996). Constructivist, emergent, and sociocultural perspectives in the context of developmental research. *Educational Psychologist, 31,* 175–190.

Cobb, P. (1991). Reconstructing elementary school mathematics. *Focus on Learning Problems in Mathematics, 13*(2), 3–22.

Cognition & Technology Group at Vanderbilt. (1990). Anchored instruction and its relationship to situated cognition. *Educational Researcher, 19*(6), 2–10.

Cohen, R. (1992). *A lifetime of teaching: Portraits of five veteran high school teachers.* New York: Teachers College Press.

Colby, A., Kohlberg, L., Gibbs, J., & Liberman, A. (1983). *A longitudinal study of moral judgment. Monographs of the Society for Research in Child Development, 48,* Serial No. 200. Chicago: University of Chicago Press.

Cole, M. (1996). *Cultural psychology.* Cambridge, MA: Harvard University Press.

Cole, M., & Scribner, S. (1974). *Culture and thought.* New York: Wiley.

Coles, R. (1970). *Erik Erikson: The growth of his work.* Boston: Little Brown.

Collins, M., & Carnine, D. (1988). Evaluating the field test process by comparing two versions of a reasoning skills CAI program. *Journal of Learning Disabilities, 21,* 375–379.

Collins, W. A., Harris, M., & Susman, A. (1995). Parenting during middle childhood. In M. Bornstein (Ed.), *Handbook of parenting,* Vol. 1, 65–90. Mahwah, NJ: Erlbaum.

Comer, J. (1988). Educating poor minority children. *Scientific American, 259*(5), 42–48.

Cook, T. D. (1974). The potential and limitations of secondary evaluations. In M. W. Apple, H. C.

Cooper, H. (1989a). *Homework.* White Plains, NY: Longmans.

Cooper, H. (1989b, November). Synthesis of research on homework. *Educational Leadership,* Vol. 48, 85–91.

Cooper, H., Lindsay, J. J., Nye, B., & Greathouse, S. (1998). Relationships among attitudes about homework, amount of homework assigned and completed, and student achievement. *Journal of Educational Psychology, 90,* 70–83.

Cooper, J. J., Heron, T. E., & Heward, W. L. (1987). *Applied behavior analysis.* Columbus, OH: Merrill.

Corkill, A. J., Glover, J. A., Bruning, R. H., & Krug, D. (1989). Advance organizers: Retrieval hypotheses. *Journal of Educational Psychology, 81,* 43–51.

Costa, A. (Ed.). (1985). *Developing minds.* Alexandria, VA: Association for Supervision and Curriculum Development.

Craik, F. I., & Lockhart, R. S. (1972). Levels of processing: A framework for memory research. *Journal of Verbal Learning and Verbal Behavior, 11,* 671–684.

Cronbach, L. (1970). *Essentials of psychological testing.* New York: Harper & Row.

Cruickshank, D., Bainer, D., & Metcalf, K. (1995). *The act of teaching.* New York: McGraw-Hill.

CTB/McGraw-Hill. (1997). *TerraNova achievement battery.* Monterey, CA: Author.

Dacey, J. (1989a). Discriminating characteristics of the families of highly creative adolescents. *The Journal of Creative Behavior, 23,* 263–273.

Dacey, J. (1989b). *Fundamentals of creativity.* Lexington, MA: D.C. Heath/Lexington Books.

Dacey, J. (1989c). Peak periods of creative growth across the lifespan. *The Journal of Creative Behavior, 23*(4), 224–247.

Dacey, J. & Kenny, M. (1997). *Adolescent development.* Dubuque, IA: McGraw-Hill.

Dacey, J., & Travers, J. (1999). *Human development across the lifespan.* New York: McGraw-Hill.

Dale, E. J. (1993). Computers and gifted/talented individuals. In J. D. Lindsey (Ed.), *Computers and exceptional individuals* (2nd ed.), 108–127. Austin, TX: Pro-Ed.

Darling-Hammond, L. (1994). Performance-based assessment and educational equity. *Harvard Educational Review, 64*(1), 5–30.

de Charms, R. (1976). *Enhancing motivation: Change in the classroom.* New York: Irvington.

de Jong, T., & Ferguson-Hassler, M. (1986). Cognitive structures of good and poor novice problem solvers in physics. *Journal of Educational Psychology, 78,* 279–288.

de Bono, E. (1985). The CoRT thinking program. In A. Costa (Ed.), *Developing minds,* 81–97. Alexandria, VA: Association for Supervision and Curriculum Development.

Deci, E. L. (1992). The relation of interest to the motivation of behavior: A self-determination theory perspective. In K. A. Renninger, S. Hidi, & A. Krapp (Eds.), *The role of interest in learning and development* (pp. 43–70). Hillsdale, NJ: LEA.

Demaray, M. K., & Elliott, S. N. (1998). Teachers' judgments of students' academic functioning: A comparison of actual and predicted performances. *School Psychology Quarterly, 13,* 8–24.

Derry, S. J. (1989, December/January). Putting learning strategies to work. Educational Leadership, pp. 4–10.

Diener, C., & Dweck, C. (1978). An analysis of learned helplessness: Continuous changes in performance, strategy, and achievement cognitions following failure. *Journal of Personality and Social Psychology, 36,* 451–462.

Diener, C., & Dweck, C. (1980). An analysis of learned helplessness: 2. The processing of success. *Journal of Personality and Social Psychology, 39,* 940–952.

Dill, D. (Ed.). (1990). *What teachers need to know.* San Francisco: Jossey-Bass.

Dobbin, J. (1984). *How to take a test: Doing your best.* Princeton, NJ: Educational Testing Service.

Donnellan, A. M., & LaVigna, G. W. (1990). Myths about punishment. In A. C. Repp & N. N. Singh (Eds.), *Perspectives on the use of nonaversive and aversive interventions for persons with developmental disabilities* (pp. 33–57). Sycamore, IL: Sycamore.

Doyle, W. (1986). Classroom organization and management. In M. Wittrock (Ed.), *Handbook of research on teaching,* 407–461. New York: Macmillan.

Dreikurs, R., Grunwald, B., & Pepper, F. (1971). Maintaining sanity in the classroom. New York: Harper & Row.

Dreyfus, H. L. (1979). *What computers can't do: The limits of artificial intelligence.* New York: Harper & Row.

Dukes, W. F. (1965). N-1. *Psychological Bulletin, 64,* 74–79.

Dunn, R. (1987). Research on instructional environments: Implications for student achievement and attitudes. *Professional School Psychology, 3,* 43–52.

DuPaul, G. J., & Barkley, R. A. (1998). Attention-deficit hyperactivity disorder. In R. J. Morris and T. R. Kratochwill (Eds.), *The practice of child therapy* (3rd ed.) (pp. 132–166). Boston: Allyn & Bacon.

DuPaul, G. J., & Stoner, G. (1994). *ADHD in the schools: Assessment and intervention strategies.* New York: Guilford Press.

Dweck, C. S. (1975). The role of expectancies and attributions in the alleviation of learned helplessness. *Journal of Personality and Social Psychology, 31,* 674–685.

Dweck, C. S., & Repucci, N. D. (1973). Learned helplessness and reinforcement of responsibility in children. *Journal of Personality and Social Psychology, 25,* 109–116.

Dweck, C. S., & Elliott, E. S. (1983). Achievement motivation. In E. M. Hetherington (Ed.), *Handbook of child psychology: Vol. 4 Socialization, personality, and social development* (4th ed.), 215–239. New York: Wiley.

Ebbinghaus, H. (1885). *On memory.* New York: Teachers College Press.

Eby, J., & Smutny, J. (1990). *A thoughtful overview of gifted education.* New York: Longman.

Eccles, J., & Wigfield, A. (1985). Teacher expectations and student motivation. In J. B. Dusek (Ed.), *Teacher expectancies,* 93–117. Hillsdale, NJ: LEA.

Edelbrock, C. (1983). Problems and issues in using rating scales to assess child personality and psychopathology. *School Psychology Review, 12,* 253–299.

Ehri, L. C. (1991). Development of the ability to read words. In R. Barr, M. L. Kamil, P. B. Mosenthal, & P. D. Pearson (Eds.), *Handbook of reading research* (Vol. 2, pp. 383–417). New York: Longman.

Eisenberger, R., & Cameron, J. (1996). Detrimental effects of reward: Reality or myth? *American Psychologist, 51,* 1153–1166.

Elkind, D. (1994). *Understanding your child.* Boston: Allyn & Bacon.

Elliott, S. N. (1994). *Creating meaningful performance assessments: Fundamental concepts.* Reston, VA: Council for Exceptional Children.

Elliott, S. N., & Bischoff-Werner, J. (1995). *Performance spelling.* Madison, WI: University of Wisconsin-Madison.

Elliott, S. N., & Gresham, F. M. (1989). Teacher and self-ratings of popular and rejected adolescent boys' behavior. *Journal of Psychoeducational Assessment, 7,* 308–322.

Ellis, H., & Hunt, R. (1989). *Fundamentals of human memory and cognition.* Madison, WI: Brown & Benchmark.

Ellis, H., & Hunt, R. (1993). *Fundamentals of cognitive psychology* (5th ed.). Madison, WI: Brown & Benchmark.

Emmer, E., Evertson, C., & Anderson, L. (1980). Effective classroom management at the beginning of the school year. *Elementary School Journal, 80,* 219–231.

Erikson, E. (1950). *Childhood and society.* New York: Norton.

Erikson, E. (1968). Identity: Youth and crisis. New York: Norton.

Esveldt-Dawson, K., & Kazdin, A. E. (1982). *How to use self-control.* Lawrence, KS: H & H Enterprises.

Evertson, C., & Emmer, E. (1982). Effective management at the beginning of the school year in junior high classes. *Journal of Educational Research, 74,* 485–498.

Fagot, B. (1985). Changes in thinking about early sex role development. *Developmental Review, 5,* 83–98.

Fagot, B. (1995). Parenting boys and girls. In M. Bornstein (Ed.), *Handbook of parenting,* Vol. 1, 163–184. Hillsdale, NJ: Erlbaum.

Fagot, B., & Hagan, R. (1991). Observations of parent reactions to sex-stereotyped behaviors: Age and sex effects. *Child Development, 62,* 617–628.

Fagot, B., Leinbach, M., & O'Boyle, C. (1992). Gender labeling, gender stereotyping, and parenting behaviors. *Developmental Psychology, 28,* 225–230.

Fantz, R. (1961). The origin of form perception. *Scientific American, 204,* 66–72.

Fantz, R. (1963). Pattern vision in newborn infants. *Science, 140,* 296–297.

Ferrington, G., & Loge, K. (1992). Virtual reality: A new learning environment. *The Computing Teacher, 19*(7), 16–19.

Ferster, C. B., & Skinner, B. F. (1957). *Schedules of reinforcement.* New York: Appleton-Century-Crofts.

Finch, C. L. (Ed.). (1991). *Educational performance assessment: The free-response alternative.* Chicago: Riverside.

First, J. (1988). Immigrant students in U.S. public schools: Challenges with solutions. *Phi Delta Kappan, 70,* 205–210.

First, J. M., & Carrera, J. W. (Eds.). (1988). *New voices: Immigrant students in U.S. public schools.* Boston: The National Coalition of Advocates for Students.

Flavell, J. (1985). *Cognitive development.* Englewood Cliffs, NJ: Prentice-Hall.

Flavell, J. , Miller, P., & Miller, S. (1993). *Cognitive development.* Englewood Cliffs, NJ: Prentice-Hall.

Flavell, J. H. (1963). *The developmental psychology of Jean Piaget.* Princeton: Van Nostrand.

Ford, M. (1992). *Motivating humans.* Newbury Park, CA: Sage.

Fosnot, C. T. (1996). Constructivism: A psychological theory of learning. In C. T. Fosnot (Ed.), *Constructivism: theory, perspectives, and practice,* 45–69. New York: Teachers College Press.

Foster, S. (1986). Ten principles of learning revised in accordance with cognitive psychology: With implications for teaching. *Educational Psychologist, 21,* 235–243.

Fraenkel, J. R., & Wallen, N. E. (1990). *How to design and evaluate research in education.* New York: McGraw-Hill.

Frasier, M. (1989). Poor and minority students can be gifted, too. *Educational Leadership, 46,* 16–18.

Fredricks, J. (1987). The latest model. *The Reading Teacher, 46,* 790–791.

Fried, R. (1995). *The passionate teacher.* Boston: Beacon Press.

Frisbie, D. (1988). NCME instructional module on reliability of scores from teacher-made tests. Educational Measurement, 7, 25–33.

Fuchs, D., & Fuchs, L. S. (1994). Inclusive schools movement and the radicalization of special education reform. *Exceptional Children, 60,* 294–309.

Fuchs, D., & Fuchs, L. S. (1995). Sometimes separate is better. *Educational Leadership,* Vol. 52, 22–26.

Gagne, R., & Briggs, L. (1979). *Principles of instructional design.* New York: Holt, Rinehart & Winston.

Gagne, R., & Driscoll, M. (1988). *Essentials of learning for instruction* (2nd ed.). Englewood Cliffs, NJ: Prentice-Hall.

Gagne, R., Briggs, L., & Wager, W. (1988). *Principles of instructional design* (3rd ed.). New York: Holt, Rinehart & Winston.

Garbarino, J., & Benn, J. (1992). The ecology of childbearing and childrearing. In J. Garbarino (Ed.), *Children and families in the social environment,* 133–177. New York: Aldine.

Gardner, H. (1985). *The mind's new science.* New York: Basic Books.

Gardner, H. (1993). *Creating minds.* New York: Basic Books.

Garger, S. (1990). Is there a link between learning style and neurophysiology? *Educational Leadership, 48,* 63–65.

Garibaldi, A. (1992). Educating and motivating African American males to succeed. *Journal of Negro Education, 61*(4), 4–11.

Gary, L., & Booker, C. (1992). Empowering African Americans to achieve academic success. *Urban Education,* 51–55.

Gelb, M. (1996). *Thinking for a change.* London: Aurum Press.

Gelman, R., & Baillargeon, R. (1983). A review of some Piagetian concepts. In P. Mussen (Ed.), *Handbook of child psychology,* Vol. 3, 167–230. New York: Wiley.

Genshaft, J. (1991). The gifted adolescent in perspective. In M. Birely & J. Genshaft (Eds.), *Understanding the gifted adolescent: Educational development and multicultural issues* (pp. 259–262). New York: Teachers College Press.

Gentry, D. (1989). Teacher-made test construction. Paper presented at the annual meeting of the Mid-South Educational Research Association, Little Rock, AR.

Gettinger, M. (1988). Methods of proactive classroom management. *School Psychology Review, 17,* 227–242.

Gettinger, M. (1990). Best practices in increasing academic learning time. In A. Thomas & J. Grimes (Eds.), *Best practices in school psychology-II* (pp. 393–405). Washington, D.C.: National Association of School Psychologists.

Gibbons, M. (1974). Walkabout: Searching for the right of passage from childhood and school. Phi Delta Kappan, 9, 596–602.

Gibbons, M. (1984). Walkabout ten years later: Searching for a renewed vision of education. Phi Delta Kappan, 9, 591–600.

Giddings, L. (1992). Literature-based reading instruction: An analysis. *Reading Research and Instruction, 31*(2), 18–30.

Gilligan, C. (1977). In a different voice: Women's conception of self and of morality. *Harvard Educational Review, 47,* 481–517.

Gilligan, C. *In a different voice.* (1982). Cambridge, MA: Harvard University Press.

Gilligan, C., Ward, J., & Taylor, J. (1988). *Mapping the moral domain.* Cambridge, MA.: Harvard University Press.

Ginsberg, H. & Opper, S. (1988). *Piaget's theory of intellectual development.* Englewood Cliffs, NJ: Prentice-Hall.

Glaser, R. (1991). The reemergence of learning theory within instructional research. *American Psychologist, 45,* 29–39.

Glasnapp, D., & Poggio, J. (1985). *Essentials of statistical analysis for the behavioral sciences.* Columbus, OH: Merrill.

Glass, A., Holyoak, K., & Santa, J. (1987). *Cognition.* Reading, MA: Addison-Wesley.

Glass, G., McGaw, V., & Smith, M. L. (1981). *Meta-analysis in social research.* Beverly Hills: Sage.

Gleick, J. (1992). *Genius.* New York: Pantheon.

Glover, J. A., & Ronning, R. R. (1987). Introduction. In J. A. Glover & R. R. Ronning (Eds.), *Historical foundations of educational psychology* (pp. 3–15). New York: Plenum Press.

Golomb, C. (1974). *Young children's sculpture and drawing.* Cambridge, MA: Harvard University Press.

Good, T. (1990). Building the knowledge base of teaching. In D. Dill (Ed.), *What teachers need to know,* 54–76. San Francisco: Jossey-Bass.

Goodlad, J. I., & Lovitt, T. C. (Eds.). (1993). *Integrating general and special education.* New York: Merrill.

Goodman, Y. (1989). Roots of the whole language movement. *Elementary School Journal, 90,* 113–127.

Gottfredson, L. S. (1997). Mainstream science on intelligence: An editorial with 52 signatories, history, and bibliography. *Intelligence, 24*(1), 13–25.

Grady, M. (1984). *Teaching and brain research.* New York: Longman.

Graham, S., & Barker, G. (1990). The downside of help: An attributional-developmental analysis of helping behavior as a low-ability cue. *Journal of Educational Psychology, 82,* 7–14.

Grant, C., & Sleeter, C. (1993). Race, class, gender, and disability in the classroom. In J. Banks & C. Banks (Ed.), *Multicultural education: Issues and perspectives, 3,* 48–68. Boston: Allyn & Bacon.

Greenberg, J. (1990). *Problem-solving situations, Volume 1.* Grapevine Publications, Inc.

Greene, L. (1987). *Learning disabilities and your child.* New York: Fawcett Columbine.

Gresham, F., Evans, S., & Elliott, S. N. (1988). Self-efficacy differences among mildly handicapped, gifted, and nonhandicapped students. *The Journal of Special Education, 22,* 231–241.

Gresham, F. M., MacMillan, D. L., & Siperstein, G. N. (1995). Critical analysis of the 1992 AAMR definition: Implications for school psychology. *School Psychology Quarterly, 10*(1), 1–19.

Gresham, F. M., & Elliott, S. N. (1990). *Social skills rating system.* Circle Pines, MN: American Guidance Service.

Gronlund, N. (1985). *Measurement and evaluation in learning.* New York: Macmillan.

Gronlund, N. E., & Linn, R. L. (1995). *Measurement and evaluation in teaching* (7th ed.). New York: Macmillan.

Grossen, B., & Carnine, D. (1990). Diagramming a logical strategy: Effects in difficult problem types and transfer. *Learning Disability Quarterly, 13,* 168–182.

Grossman, H. (1990). *Trouble-free teaching.* Mountain View, CA: Mayfield.

Grossman, P. (1990). *The making of a teacher: Teacher knowledge and teacher education.* New York: Teachers College Press.

Guskey, T. (1986, Winter). Bloom's mastery learning: A legacy of effectiveness. *Educational Horizons,* pp. 80–86.

Hakuta, K. (1986). *Mirror of language: The debate of bilingualism.* New York: Basic Books.

Halford, G. S. (1989). Reflection on 25 years of Piagetian cognitive research: 1963–1988. *Human Development, 32,* 325–357.

Hallahan, D., & Kauffman, J. (1988). *Exceptional children: Introduction to special education.* Englewood Cliffs, NJ: Prentice-Hall.

Halle, J. W. (1985). Enhancing social competence through language: An experimental analysis of a practical procedure for teachers. *Topics in Early Childhood Special Education, 4,* 77–92.

Hamachek, D. (1987). *Encounters with the self.* New York: Holt, Rinehart & Winston.

Hammill, D., Leigh, J., McNutt, G., & Larsen, S. (1981). A new definition of learning disabilities. *Learning Disability Quarterly, 4,* 336–342.

Hammill, D. D. (1990). On defining learning disabilities: An emerging consensus. *Journal of Learning Disabilities, 23,* 74–84.

Haring, N., & McCormick, L. (1986). *Exceptional children and youth.* Columbus, OH: Merrill.

Hart, L. (1983). *Human brain and human learning.* New York: Longman.

Harter, S. (1993). Visions of self: Beyond the Me in the mirror. In J. Jacobs (Ed.), *Developmental perspectives on motivation.* Lincoln, Nebraska: University of Nebraska Press.

Hauser-Cram, P., Pierson, D., Klein Walker, D., & Tivnan, T. (1991). *Early education in the public schools.* San Francisco: Jossey-Bass.

Hayes, J. (1989). *The complete problem solver.* Philadelphia: Franklin Institute Press.

Hayes, L. (1992). Building schools for tomorrow. *Phi Delta Kappan, 73*(5), 412–413.

Hembree, H. (1988). Correlates, causes, effects, and treatment of test anxiety. *Review of Educational Research, 58,* 41–77.

Hendrick, J. (1992). *The whole child.* New York: Macmillan.

Hergenhahn, B. R. (1988). *An introduction to theories of learning.* Englewood Cliffs, NJ: Prentice-Hall.

Herman, J. L., Aschbacher, P. R., & Winters, L. (1992). *A practical guide to alternative assessment.* Alexandria, VA: ASCD.

Hetherington, E. M., & Parke, R. (1993). *Child psychology* (4th ed). New York: McGraw-Hill.

Hetherington, M., & Stanley-Hagan, M. (1995). Parenting in divorced and remarried families. In M. Bornstein (Ed.), *Handbook of parenting, 9,* 233–254. Hillsdale, NJ: Erlbaum.

Heward, W. L., & Orlansky, M. D. (1988). *Exceptional children.* Columbus, OH: Merrill.

Hill, K. T., & Wigfield, A. (1984). Test anxiety: A major educational problem and what can be done about it. *Elementary School Journal, 85,* 105–126.

Hiroto, D. S. (1974). Locus of control and learned helplessness. *Journal of Experimental Psychology, 102,* 187–193.

Hocutt, A. M., Martin, E. W., & McKinney, J. D. (1991). History and legal context of mainstreaming. In J. W. Lloyd, N. N. Singh, and A. C. Repp (Eds.), *The regular education initiative: Alternative perspectives on concepts, issues, and models* (pp. 17–28). Sycamore, IL: Sycamore Publishing Co.

Hodapp, R. M., & Dykens, E. M. (1996). Mental retardation. In E. J. Mash and R. A. Barkley (Eds.), *Child psychopathology* (pp. 362.–389). New York: Guilford Press.

Hofmeister, A., Engelmann, S., & Carnine, D. (1989). Developing and validating science education videodiscs. *Journal of Research in Science Teaching, 26,* 665–677.

Hoge, R. D., & Coladarci, T. (1989). Teacher based judgment of academic achievement: A review of the literature. *Review of Educational Research, 59,* 297–313.

Holmstrom, J. (1988). Perseverance in teaching children with CP helps them communicate through computers. *OTWeek, 2*(21), 6–7, 18.

Hops, H., & Finch, M. (1985). Social competence and skill: A reassessment. In B. H. Schneider, K. H. Rubin, & J. E. Ledingham (Eds.), *Children's peer relations: Issues in assessment and intervention* (pp. 24–40). New York: Springer-Verlag.

Horne, A. M., & Sayger, T. V. (1990). *Treating conduct and oppositional defiant disorders in children.* New York: Pergamon Press.

Howard, G. (1991). Culture tales: A narrative approach to thinking, cross-cultural psychology, and psychotherapy. *American Psychologist, 46,* 187–197.

Hubel, D. (1979). The brain. *Scientific American, 241,* 44–53.

Huck, S. W., & Sandler, H. M. (1979). *Rival hypotheses: Alternative interpretations of data based conclusions.* New York: Harper & Row.

Hughes, C. S., & Rankin, S. C. (1987). *Developing thinking skills across the curriculum.* Westland, MI: Michigan Association for Computer Users in Learning.

Hulit, M., & Howard, M. (1997). *Born to talk.* Needham Heights, MA: Allyn & Bacon.

Hulse, S., Egeth, H., & Deese, J. (1980). *The psychology of learning.* New York: McGraw-Hill.

Hunter, M. (1991). Hunter design helps achieve the goals of science instruction. *Educational Leadership, 48*(4), 79–81.

Hunter, M., & Russell, D. (1981). Planning for effective instruction: Lesson design. In *Increasing your teaching effectiveness,* 19–44. Palo Alto, CA: The Learning Institute.

Huston, A., McLoyd, V., & Gracia Coll, C. (1994). Children and poverty: Issues in contemporary research. *Child Development, 65*(2), 275–282.

Huttenlocher, J., Haight, W., Bryk, A., Seltzer, M., & Lyons, T. (1991). Early vocabulary growth: Relation to language input and gender. *Developmental Psychology, 27,* 236–248.

Hyden, H. (1985). The brain, learning and values. In J. Eccles (Ed.), *Mind and brain,* 78–102. New York: Pergamon.

Ingersoll, B. (1988). *Your hyperactive child.* New York: Doubleday.

Jackson, A., Fletcher, B. & Messer, D. (1988). *Effects of experience on microcomputer use in primary schools:* Results of a second survey. Journal of Computer-Assisted Learning, 4, 214–226.

Jackson, P. (1990). *Life in classrooms.* New York: Holt, Rinehart & Winston.

Jacobson, J. W., & Mulick, J. A. (Eds.) (1996). *Manual of diagnosis and professional practice in mental retardation.* Washington, D.C.: American Psychological Association.

Jennings, T. E. (Ed.). (1997). *Restructuring for integrative education: Multiple perspectives, multiple contexts.* Westport, CT: Bergin & Garvey.

Jensen, A. R. (1980). *Bias in mental testing.* New York: The Free Press.

Johnson, D., & Johnson, R. (1987). *Learning together and alone: Cooperative, competitive, and individualistic learning* (2nd ed.). Englewood Cliffs, NJ: Prentice-Hall.

Jonassen, D. H. (1991). Objectivism versus constructivism: Do we need a new philosophical paradigm? *Educational Technology Research and Development, 39*(3), 5–14.

Jones, J. (1994). The African American: A duality dilemma. In W. Lonner & R. Malpass (Eds.), *Psychology and culture, 1,* 17–22. Boston: Allyn & Bacon.

Juel, C. (1991). Beginning reading. In R. Barr, M. L. Kamil, P. B. Mosenthal, & P. D. Pearson (Eds.), *Handbook of reading research* (Vol. 2., pp. 759–788). New York: Longman.

Kaestle, C. (1993). The awful reputation of education research. *Educational Researcher, 22,* 23–31.

Kagan, J., & Moss, H. (1962). *Birth to maturity.* New York: Wiley.

Kalish, H. (1981). *From behavioral science to behavior modification.* New York: McGraw-Hill.

Kamin, L. (1981). Some historical facts about IQ testing. In H. J. Eysenck & L. Kamin (Eds.), *The intelligence controversy* (pp. 90–97). New York: Wiley.

Kassenbaum, N. (1994). Head Start: Only the best for America's children. *American Psychologist, 49*(2), 123–126.

Kauffman, J. (1993). How we might achieve the radical reform of special education. *Exceptional Children, 60,* 6–16.

Kauffman, J., Gerber, M., & Semmel, M. (1988). Arguable assumptions underlying the regular education initiative. *Journal of Learning Disabilities, 21,* 6–11.

Kaufman, M., Agard, J. A., & Semmel, M. I. (1985). *Mainstreaming: Learners and their environments.* Cambridge, MA: Brookline Books.

Kazdin, A. (1989). *Behavior modification in applied settings* (4th ed.). Pacific Grove, CA: Brooks/Cole.

Kazdin, A. E. (1998). *Research design in clinical psychology* (3rd ed.). Boston: Allyn & Bacon.

Kazdin, A. E. (1979). Situational specificity: The two-edged sword of behavioral assessment. *Behavioral Assessment, 6,* 57–76.

Kazdin, A. E. (1982). *Single-case research designs: Methods for clinical and applied settings.* New York: Oxford University Press.

Kazdin, A. E. (1988). *Child psychotherapy: Developing and evaluating effective treatments.* New York: Pergamon Press.

Kazdin, A. E. (1994). *Behavior modification in applied settings* (5th ed.). Pacific Grove, CA: Brooks/Cole.

Kellaghan, T., Madaus, G., & Airasian, P. (1980). *Standardized testing in elementary schools: Effect on schools, teachers, and students.* Washington, DC: National Education Association.

Kelley, M. L. (1990). *School-home notes: Promoting children's classroom success.* New York: Guilford Press.

Kelley, M. L., & Carper, L. B. (1988). Home-based reinforcement procedures. In J. C. Witt, S. N. Elliott, and F. M. Gresham (Eds.), *Handbook of behavior therapy in education* (pp. 419–438). New York: Plenum Press.

Kerlinger, F. (1973). *Foundations of behavioral research.* New York: Holt, Rinehart & Winston.

Kim, E., & Kellough, R. (1991). *A resource guide for secondary school teaching.* New York: Macmillan.

Kim, U. (1990). Indigenous psychology: Science and applications. In R. Brislin (Ed.), *Applied cross-cultural psychology,* Vol. 14, 142–160. Newbury Park, CA: Sage.

Kinsbourne, M. (1986). Systematizing cognitive psychology. *Behavioral and Brain Sciences, 9,* 567.

Klinger, L. G., & Dawson, G. (1996). Autistic disorder. In E. J. Mash and R. A. Barkley (Eds.), *Child psychopathology* (pp. 311–339). New York: Guilford Press.

Kohlberg, L. (1975). The cognitive-developmental approach to moral education. *Phi Delta Kappan, 56,* 670–677.

Kosslyn, S. (1980). Image and mind. Cambridge, MA: Harvard University Press.

Kounin, J. (1970). Discipline and group management in classrooms. New York: Holt, Rinehart & Winston.

Kozol, J. (1991). *Savage inequalities.* New York: Crown.

Kramer, J. J. (1990). Training parents as behavior change agents: Successes, failures and suggestions for school psychologists. In T. B. Gutkin & C. R. Reynolds (Eds.), *Handbook of school psychology* (2nd ed., pp. 683–702). New York: Wiley.

Kratochwill, T. R., & Goldman, J. A. (1973). Developmental changes in children's judgments of age. *Developmental Psychology, 9,* 358–362.

Kratochwill, T. R., & Levin, J. R. (Eds.). (1992). *Single-case design and analysis: New developments for psychology and education.* Hillsdale, NJ: Erlbaum.

Krendl, K. A., & Broihier, M. (1992). Student responses to computers: A longitudinal study. *Journal of Educational Computing Research, 8*(2), 215–227.

Kulik, C. C., & Kulik, J. A. (1991). Effectiveness of computer-based instruction: An upgraded analysis. *Computers in Human Behavior, 7,* 75–94.

Lahey, Benjamin B. (1989). *Psychology: An introduction* (3rd ed.). Dubuque, IA: Wm. C. Brown.

Larry P. v. Riles, 343 F. Supp. 1306 (N.D. Cal. 1972) (preliminary injunction). Aff'd 502 F. 2d 963 (9th cir. 1974); 495 F. Supp. 926 (N.D. Cal. 1979) (decision on merits). Aff'd (9th cir. no. 80-427 Jan. 23, 1984). Order modifying judgment, C-71-2270 RFP, Sept. 25, 1986.

Laslett, R., & Smith, C. (1984). *Effective classroom management.* New York: Nichols.

LaVigna, G. W., & Donnellan, A. M. (1986). *Alternatives to punishment: Solving behavior problems with non-aversive strategies.* New York: Irvington Publishers.

Lawton, J., & Gerschner, V. T. (1982). A review of literature on attitudes towards computers and computerized instruction. *Journal of Research and Development in Education, 16*(1), 50–55.

Leahey, D., & Harris, T. (1985). *Human learning.* Englewood Cliffs, NJ: Prentice-Hall.

Lehrer, R. (1994). Authors of knowledge: Patterns of hypermedia design. In S. Lajoie & S. Derry (Eds.), *Computers as cognitive tools* (pp. 197–227). Hillsdale, NJ: Erlbaum.

Lepper, M. R., & Chabay, R. W. (1988). Socializing the intelligent tutor: Bringing empathy to computer tutors. In H. Mandl & A. Lesgold (Eds.), *Learning issues for intelligent tutoring systems* (pp. 242–257). New York: Springer-Verlag.

Lerner, R. (January, 1991). Changing organism–context relations as the basic process of development: A developmental contextual perspective. *Developmental Psychology, 27*(1), 27–32.

Lesgold, A., Lajoie, S. P., Bunzo, M., & Eggan, G. (1992). A coached practice environment for an electronics troubleshooting job. In J. Larkin & R. Chabay (Eds.), *Computer assisted instruction and intelligent tutoring systems: Shared goals and complementary approaches* (pp. 201–238). Hillsdale, NJ: Erlbaum.

Levin, J. R. (1994). Crafting educational intervention research that's both credible and creditable. *Educational Psychology Review, 6,* 231–243.

Lewis, D., & Greene, J. (1982). *Thinking better.* New York: Holt.

Lewis, M., & Brooks-Gunn, J. (1979). *Social cognition and the acquisition of self.* New York: Plenum.

Lewis, R. B. (1993). *Special education technology: Classroom applications.* Pacific Grove, CA: Brooks/Cole Publishing Co.

Lickona, T. (1991). *Educating for character: How our schools can teach respect and responsibility.* New York: Bantam.

Lickona, T. (1993). The return of character education. *Educational Leadership, 51(3),* 6–11.

Lieberman, A. F., Wieder, B., & Fenichel, E. (1997). *DC: 0-3 casebook.* Richmond, VA: National Center for Infants, Toddlers, and Families.

Liebert, R. M., Sprafkin, J. N., & Davidson, E. (1988). *The early window.* New York: Pergamon.

Linn, R. (1986). Educational testing and assessment. *American Psychologist, 41,* 1153–1160.

Linn, R. L., & Gronlund, N. E. (1995). *Measurement and assessment in teaching,* (7th ed.). Englewood Cliffs, NJ: Merrill.

Lippmann, W. (1976). The abuse of the tests. In N. Block & Y G. Dwokin (Eds.). *The IQ controversy.* New York: Pantheon (originally published in 1922).

Lips, H. (1993).*Sex and gender.* Mountain View, CA.: Mayfield.

Lipsey, M. W., & Wilson, D. B. (1993). The efficacy of psychological, educational, and behavioral treatment: Confirmation from meta-analysis. *American Psychologist, 48,* 1181–1209.

Livingston, R. (1986). Visual impairments. In N. Haring & L. McCormick (Eds.), *Exceptional children and youth.* Columbus, OH: Merrill.

Lloyd, J. W., Singh, N. N., & Repp, A. C. (Eds.). (1991). *The regular education initiative: Alternative perspectives on concepts, issues, and models.* Sycamore, IL: Sycamore.

Lockard, J., Abrams, P. D., & Many, W. A. (1994). *Microcomputers for twenty-first century educators.* New York: HarperCollins.

Loewenstein, G. (1994). The psychology of curiosity: A review and reinterpretation. *Psychological Bulletin, 116,* 75–98.

Loftus, E. F., & Palmer, J. C. (1974). Reconstruction of automobile destruction: An example of the interaction between language and memory. *Journal of Verbal Learning and Verbal Behavior, 13,* 585–589.

Looft, W. R. (1971). Children's judgments of age. *Child Development, 42,* 1282–1284.

Looft, W. R., Raymond, J. R., & Raymond, B. B. (1972). Children's judgments of age in Sarawak. *Journal of Social Psychology, 86,* 181–185.

Lott, B. (1987). *Women's lives.* Monterey, CA: Brooks/Cole.

Lovinger, S. L., Brandell, M. E., & Seesdedt-Stanford, L. (1991). *Language learning disabilities: A new and practical approach for those who work with children and their families.* New York: Continuum.

Lowenbraun, S., & Thompson, M. (1986). Hearing impairments. In N. Haring & L. McCormick (Eds.), *Exceptional children and youth,* 92–119. Columbus, OH: Merrill.

Luria, A. (1980). *Higher cortical functions in man.* New York: Basic Books.

Lyman, H. B. (1998). *Test scores and what they mean* (6th ed.). Boston: Allyn & Bacon.

Lyons-Ruth, K., Yeanah, C. H., & Benoit, D. (1996). Disorder and risk for disorder during infancy and toddlerhood. In E. J. Mash and R. A. Barkley (Eds.), *Child psychopathology* (pp. 457–491). New York: Guilford Press.

Maccoby, E., & Jacklin, C. (1974). *The psychology of sex differences.* Stanford, CA.: Stanford University Press.

Madaus, G. (1994). A technological and historical consideration of equity issues associated with proposals to change the nation's testing policy. *Harvard Educational Review, 64(1),* 76–95.

Maddus, C. D., Johnson, D. L., & Willis, J. W. (1997). *Educational computing: Learning with tomorrow's technologies* (2nd ed.). Boston: Allyn & Bacon.

Mager, R. (1975). *Preparing instructional objectives.* Palo Alto, CA: Fearon.

Manning, M., & Baruth, L. (1996). *Multicultural education of children and adolescents.* Needham Heights: Allyn & Bacon.

Manzo, A., & Manzo, U. (1990). Content area reading: A heuristic approach. Columbus, OH: Merrill.

Marcia, James. (1966). Development and validation of ego identity status. *Journal of Personality and Social Psychology, 3,* 551–558.

Marcia, James. (1980). Identity formation in adolescence. In J. Adelson (Ed.), *Handbook of adolescent psychology,* 159–187. New York: Wiley.

Marin, G. (1994). The experience of being a Hispanic in the United States. In W. Lonner & R. Malpass (Eds.), *Psychology and culture, 2,* 23–28. Boston: Allyn & Bacon.

Markle, S. (1990). *Designs for instructional designers* (2nd ed.). Champaign, IL: Stipes.

Marso, R., & Pigge, F. (1989). *The status of classroom teachers' test construction proficiencies.* Paper presented at the annual meeting of the National Council of Measurement in Education, San Francisco.

Martin, C., Wood, C., & Little, J. (1990). The development of gender stereotype components. *Child Development, 61,* 1891–1904.

Martin, C. D., Heller, R., & Mahmoud, E. (1992). American and Soviet children's attitudes toward computers. *Journal of Educational Computing Research, 8(2),* 155–185.

Maslow, A. (1987). *Motivation and personality.* New York: Harper & Row.

Matarazzo, J. (1990). Psychological assessment versus psychological testing: Validation from Binet to the school, clinic, and courtroom. *American Psychologist, 45,* 999–1017.

McConaughy, S. H. (1993). Advances in empirically based assessment of children's behavioral and emotional problems. *School Psychology Review, 2,* 285–307.

McDonnell, L. M., McLaughlin, M. J., & Morison, P. (Eds.). (1997). *Educating one and all: Students with disabilities and standards-based reform.* Washington, DC: National Research Council.

McLaughlin, B. (1990). Development of bilingualism: Myth and reality. In A. Barona & E. Garcia (Eds.), *Children at risk: Poverty, minority status, and other issues in educational equity,* 65–75. Washington, DC: National Association of School Psychologists.

McNamara, E., Evans, M., & Hill, W. (1986). The reduction of disruptive behavior in two secondary school classes. *British Journal of Educational Psychology, 36,* 209–215.

McNeely, S. L. (1997). *Observing students and teachers through observation strategies.* Boston: Allyn & Bacon.

Medland, M., & Vitale, M. (1984). *Management of classrooms.* New York: Holt, Rinehart & Winston.

Menyuk, P. (1982). Language development. In C. Kopp & J. Krakow (Eds.), *The child, 6,* 282–331. Reading, MA: Addison-Wesley.

Menyuk, P., Liebergott, J., & Schultz, M. (1995). *Early language development in full-term and premature infants.* Hillsdale, NJ: Erlbaum.

Mervis, C. B., & Rosch, E. (1981). Categorization of natural objects. *Annual Review of Psychology, 32,* 89–115.

Messick, S. (1994). The matter of style: Manifestations of personality in cognition, learning, and teaching. *Educational Psychologist, 29(3),* 121–136.

Mischel, H., & Mischel, W. (1983). The development of children's knowledge of self-control strategies. *Child Development, 54,* 603–619.

Molnar, J., & Rubin, D. (1991). *The impact of homelessness on children: Review of prior studies and implications for future research.* Paper presented at the NIMH/NIAA research conference, Cambridge, Ma.

Moore, L., & Carnine, D. (1989). Evaluating curriculum design in the context of active teaching. *Remedial and Special Education, 10,* 28–37.

Morsink, C. (1985). Learning disabilities. In W. Berdine & A. E. Blackhurst (Eds.), *An introduction to special education,* 1–31. Boston: Little, Brown.

Moses, S. (1991). Major revision of SAT goes into effect in 1994. *The APA Monitor, 22*(1), 34–35.

Muir, M. (April, 1994). Putting computer projects at the heart of the curriculum. *Educational Leadership, 51*(7), 30–32.

Muth, D., Glynn, S., Britton, B., & Graves, M. (1988). Thinking out loud while studying text: Rehearsing new ideas. *Journal of Educational Psychology, 80,* 315–318.

Muthukvishna, N., Carnine, D., Grossen, B., & Miller, S. (1990). *Children's alternative frameworks: Should they be directly addressed in science?* Unpublished manuscript, University of Oregon at Eugene.

Myers, P. I., & Hammill, D. D. (1990). *Learning disabilities: Basic concepts, assessment practices, and instructional strategies* (4th ed.). Austin, TX: PRO-ED.

Narayan, J., Heward, W. L., & Gardner, R. (1990). Using response cards to increase student participation in an elementary classroom. *Journal of Applied Behavior Analysis, 23,* 483–490.

National Center for Clinical Infant Programs. (1994). *Diagnostic classification: 0-3. Diagnostic classification of mental health and developmental disorders of infancy and early childhood.* Arlington, VA: Author.

National Commission on Testing and Public Policy. (1990). *From gatekeeper to gateway: Transforming testing in America.* Chestnut Hill, MA: Boston College.

National Council of Teachers of Mathematics. (1989). *Curriculum and evaluation standards for school mathematics.* Reston, VA: Author.

Neidelman, M. (1991). Problem solving and transfer. *Journal of Learning Disabilities, 24*(6), 322–329.

Neisser, U. (1982). *Memory observed.* San Francisco: Freeman.

Nelson, J. R., Smith, D. J., Taylor, L., Dodd, J. M., & Reavis, K. (1991). Prereferral intervention: A review of the research. *Education and Treatment of Children, 14,* 243–253.

Newman, R. S. (1990). Children's help-seeking in the classroom: The role of motivational factors and attitudes. *Journal of Educational Psychology, 82,* 71–80.

Nieto, S. (1996). *Affirming diversity.* New York: Longmans.

Nitko, A. (1983). *Educational tests and measurement: An introduction.* New York: Macmillan.

Nix, D., & Spiro, R. (1990). *Cognition, education, and multimedia: Exploring ideas in high technology.* Hillsdale, NJ: Erlbaum.

Office of Technology Assessment. (1992, February). *Testing in the American schools: Asking the right questions.* (OTA-SET-519). Washington, DC: U.S. Government Printing Office.

Olson, A. (1995). *An evaluation of the effectiveness of different approaches to spelling.* Unpublished master's thesis, University of Wisconsin-Madison.

Olweus, D. (1982). Development of stable aggression reaction patterns in males. In R. Blanchard & C. Blanchard (Eds.), *Advances in the study of aggression (Vol. I).* New York: Academic Press.

Owens, R. (1996). *Language development.* Needham Heights, MA: Allyn & Bacon.

Owston, R. D. (1997). The World Wide Web: *A technology to enhance teaching and learning?* Educational Researcher, 26(2), 27–33.

Page, E. (1958). Teacher comments and student performance. *Journal of Educational Psychology, 49,* 173–181.

Paivio, A. (1974). Comparisons of mental clocks. *Journal of Experimental Psychology, 4,* 61–71.

Papert, S. (1993). *Mindstorms: Children, computers, and powerful ideas* (2nd ed.). New York: Basic Books.

Parasuraman, S., & Igbaria, M. (1990). *An examination of gender differences in the determinants of computer anxiety and attitudes toward microcomputers among managers.* International Journal of Man-Machine Studies, 32, 327–340.

Paris, S., Cross, D., & Lipson, M. (1984). Informed strategies for learning: A program to improve children's reading awareness and comprehension. *Journal of Educational Psychology, 76,* 1239–1252.

Parke, R., & Slaby, R. (1983). The development of aggression. In P. Mussen (Ed.), *Handbook of child psychology,* 44–81. New York: Wiley.

PASE *(Parents in Action on Special Education) v. Joseph P. Hannon.* U.S. District Court, Northern District of Illinois, Eastern Division, No. 74 (3586), July, 1980. Also 506 F. Supp. 831 (N.D. Ill. 1980).

Patrick, H. (1997). Social self-regulation: Exploring the relations between children's social relationships, academic self-regulation, and school performance. *Educational Psychologist, 32,* 209–220.

Paulson, F. L., Paulson, P. R., & Meyer, C. A. (1991, February). What makes a portfolio a portfolio? *Educational Leadership,* pp. 60–63.

Pavlov, I. P. (1927). *Conditioned reflexes.* London: Oxford University Press.

Pavlov, I. P. (1928). *Lectures on conditioned reflexes.* London: Oxford University Press.

Perkins, D. N., & Blythe, T. (1994). Putting understanding up front. *Educational Leadership, 51*(5), 4–7.

Petri, H. (1991). *Motivation: Theory and research.* Belmont, CA: Wadsworth.

Phye, G., & Andre, T. (1986). *Classroom cognitive learning.* New York: Academic Press.

Piaget, J. (1926). *The language and thought of the child.* New York: Harcourt, Brace, and World.

Piaget, J. (1952). *The origin of intelligence in children.* New York: International Universities.

Piaget, J. (1969). *Science of education and the psychology of the child.* New York: Viking.

Piaget, J., & Inhelder, B. (1969). *The psychology of the child.* New York: Basic Books.

Piersel, W., & Kratochwill, T. R. (1979). Self-observation and behavior change: Applications to academic and adjustment problems through behavioral consultation. *Journal of School Psychology, 17,* 151–161.

Pinker, S. (1994). *The language instinct.* New York: Morrow.

Pintrich, P. R., Marx, R. W., & Boyle, R. A. (1993). Beyond cold conceptual change: The role of motivational beliefs and classroom contextual factors in the process of conceptual change. *Review of Educational Research, 63,* 167–199.

Pipher, M. (1994). *Reviving Ophelia.* New York: Putnam.

Posner, G. (1989). *Field experience: Methods of reflective teaching.* New York: Longmans.

Premack, D. (1965). Reinforcement theory. In D. Levine (Ed.), *Nebraska symposium on motivation* (Vol. 13). Lincoln: University of Nebraska Press.

Pressley, M., & Harris, K. R. (1990, September). What we really know about strategy instruction. *Educational Leadership,* Vol. 48, pp. 31–34.

Price, R. H., Cowen, E. L., Lorion, R. P., & Ramos-McKay, A. (1988). *14 ounces of prevention.* Washington, DC: American Psychological Association.

Puckett, M. D., & Black, J. K. (1994). *Authentic assessment of the young child.* New York: Merrill.

Pullin, D. (1994). Learning to work: The impact of curriculum and assessment standards in educational opportunity. *Harvard Educational Review, 64*(1), 31–54.

Rafferty, M., and Shinn, M. (1991). The impact of homelessness on children. *American Psychologist, 46,* 1170–1179.

Rahman, R., & Bisanz, G. (1986). Reading ability and use of a story schema in recalling and reconstructing information. *Journal of Educational Psychology, 75,* 323–333.

Ramsey, P. (1987). *Teaching and learning in a diverse world.* New York: Teachers College Press.

Rauth, M. (1981). What can be expected of the regular teacher? Ideals and realities. *Exceptional Education Quarterly, 2,* 27–36.

Redl, F., & Wattenberg, W. (1959). *Mental hygiene in teaching.* New York: Harcourt, Brace and Jovanovich.

Reeder, G. D., Maccow, G. C., Shaw, S. R., Swerdlik, M. E., Horton, C. B., & Foster, P. (1997). School psychologists and full service schools: Partnerships with medical, mental health, and social services. *School Psychology Review, 26,* 603–621.

Reed-Victor, E., & Stronge, J. (1997). Building resiliency: Constructive directions for homeless education. *Journal of Children and Poverty, 3*(1), 67–91.

Reinking, D., & Bridwell-Bowles, L. (1991). *Computers in reading and writing.* In R. Barr, M. L. Kamil, P. B. Mosentahal, & P. D. Pearson (Eds.), *Handbook of reading research,* Vol. II (pp. 310–340). New York: Longmans.

Reis, S. (1989). Reflections on policy affecting the education of gifted and talented students. *American Psychologist, 44,* 399–408.

Relan, A., & Gillani, B. B. (1997). *Web-based instruction and the traditional classroom: Similarities and differences.* In B. H. Khan (Ed.), Web-based instruction. Englewood Cliffs, NJ: Educational Technology Publications.

Renyi, J. (1993). *Going public: Schooling for a diverse democracy.* New York: The New Press.

Repp, A. C., & Singh, N. N. (Eds.). (1990). *Perspectives on the use of non-aversive and aversive interventions for persons with developmental disabilities.* Sycamore, IL: Sycamore.

Reschly, D. (1979). Nonbiased assessment. In C. Reynolds & T. Gutkin (Eds.). *The handbook of school psychology.* (pp. 421–459). New York: John Wiley.

Reutzel, R., & Cooper, R. (1992). *Teaching children to read: From basics to books.* New York: Macmillan.

Robinson, D. Z. (1973). If you're so rich you must be smart. In C. Senna (Ed.), *The fallacy of IQ* (pp. 18–30). New York: The Third Press.

Rogoff, B. (1990). *Apprenticeship in thinking.* New York: Oxford.

Rose, S. (1987). *The conscious brain.* New York: Knopf.

Rosen, L. A., Taylor, S. A., O'Leary, S. G., & Sanderson, W. (1991). A survey of classroom management practices. *Journal of School Psychology, 28,* 257–269.

Rosenshine, B., & Stevens, R. (1986). Teaching functions. In M. Wittrock (Ed.), *Handbook of research on teaching* 81–206, (3rd ed.). New York: Macmillan.

Rosenthal, R., & Jacobson, L. (1968). *Pygmalion in the classroom.* New York: Holt, Rinehart & Winston.

Rosser, P. (1989). *Gender and testing.* Berkeley, CA: National Commission on Testing and Public Policy.

Roth, K. J. (1990). Developing meaningful conceptual understanding in science. In B. F. Jones & L. Idol (Eds.), *Dimensions of thinking and cognitive instruction* (pp. 139–175). Hillsdale, NJ: Erlbaum.

Rotter, J. (1975). Some problems and misconceptions related to the construct of internal versus external control of reinforcement. *Journal of Consulting and Clinical Psychology, 43,* 56–67.

Rourke, B., Bakker, D., Fisk, J., & Strang, J. (1983). *Child neuropsychology.* New York: Guilford.

Rutter, M. (1975). *Helping troubled children.* New York: Plenum.

Ryan, A. W. (1991). Meta-analysis of achievement effects of microcomputer applications in elementary schools. *Educational Administration Quarterly, 27*(2), 161–184.

Sadker, M., & Sadker, D. (1994). *Failing at fairness: How America's schools cheat girls.* New York: Scribners.

Salomon, G., & Gardner, H. (1986). The computer as educator: Lessons from television research. *Educational Researcher, 15*(1), 13–19.

Sarason, I. (1980). Introduction to the study of test anxiety. In I. G. Sarason (Ed.), *Test anxiety: Theory, research, and applications,* 1–36. Hillsdale, NJ: LEA.

Scarr, S. (1992). Developmental theories for the 1990s: Development and individual differences. *Child Development, 63*(1), 1–19.

Schab, F. (1991). Schooling without learning: Thirty years of cheating in high school. *Adolescence, 26,* 839–848.

Schacter, D. (1996). *Searching for memory.* New York: Basic Books.

Schiefflin, B., & Gallimore, P. (1993). *The acquisition of literacy: An ethnographic perspective.* Norwood, NJ: Ablex.

Schoem, D. (1991). *In separate worlds: Life stories of some young Blacks Jews, and Latinos.* Ann Arbor: University of Michigan Press.

Schofield, J. W. (1995). *Computers and classroom culture.* Cambridge: Cambridge University Press.

Schon, D. A. (1988). *Educating the reflective practitioner: Toward a new design for teaching and learning in the professions.* San Francisco: Jossey-Bass.

Schunk, D. (1989). Self-efficacy and cognitive skill learning. In C. Ames & R. Ames (Eds.), *Research on motivation in education: Vol. 3. Goals and cognitions,* 111–142. San Diego, CA: Academic Press.

Schunk, D. (1990, April). *Socialization and the development of self-regulated learning: The role of attributions.* Paper presented at the annual meeting of the American Educational Research Association, Boston.

Schunk, D. H., & Zimmerman, B. J. (1997). Social origins of self-regulating competence. *Educational Psychologist, 32,* 195–208.

Schunk, D., Hanson, A., & Cox, P. (1987). Peer model attributes and children's achievement behaviors. *Journal of Educational Psychology, 79,* 54–61.

Segall, M. H. (1994). A cross-cultural research contribution to unraveling the nativist/empiricist controversy. In J. Lonner & R. Malpass (Eds.), *Psychology and culture* (pp. 135–138). Boston: Allyn & Bacon.

Seligman, M. (1975). *Helplessness: On depression, development, and death.* San Francisco: Freeman.

Seligman, M., & Maier, S. F. (1967). Failure to escape traumatic shock. *Journal of Experimental Psychology, 74,* 1–9.

Selinske, J. E., Greer, R. D., & Lodhi, S. (1991). A functional analysis of the comprehensive application of behavior analyses to schooling. *Journal of Applied Behavior Analysis, 24,* 107–117.

Seppa, N. (1996). Rwanda starts its long healing process. *The APA Monitor,* August, 1996, p. 14.

Serbin, L., Powlishta, K., & Gulko, J. (1993). The development of sex typing in middle childhood. *Monographs of the Society for Research in Child Development, 58*(2).

Sheffield, C. J. (1997). *Instructional technology for teachers: Preparation for classroom diversity.* Educational Technology, 37(2), 16–18.

Shade, B., & New, C. (1993). Cultural influences on learning: Teaching implications. In J. Banks & C. Banks (Eds.), *Multicultural education: Issues and perspectives.* 271–304. Boston: Allyn & Bacon.

Shekerjian, D. (1990). *Uncommon genius: How great ideas are born.* New York: Viking.

Sheridan, S. M., Kratochwill, T. R., & Bergan, J. R. (1996). *Conjoint behavioral consultation: A procedural manual.* New York: Plenum Press.

Sheridan, S. M., Kratochwill, T. R., & Elliott, S. N. (1990). Behavioral consultation with parents and teachers: Delivering treatment for socially withdrawn children at home and school. *School Psychology Review, 19,* 33–52.

Sherman, L. (1978). Three dimensional art media and the preschool child. *Presentations in Art Education Research, 1,* 97–107.

Sherry, D., & Schachter, D. (1987). The evolution of multiple memory systems. *Psychological Review, 94,* 439–454.

Shuell, T. (1986). Cognitive conceptions of learning. Review of Educational Research, 56, 411–436.

Shuell, T. (1996). Teaching and learning in a classroom context. In Berliner, D. & Calfee, R. (Eds.), *Handbook of educational psychology.* New York: Macmillan.

Shulman, L. (1986). Paradigms and research programs in the study of teaching. In M. Wittrock (Ed.), *The handbook of research on teaching.* New York: Macmillan.

Shute, V. J., & Glaser, R. (1991). *An intelligent tutoring system for exploring principles of economics.* In R. E. Snow & D. Wiley (Eds.), *Improving inquiry in social science: A volume in honor of Lee J. Cronbach.* Hillsdale, NJ: Erlbaum.

Shute, V. J., & Regian, J. W. (1993). *Principles for evaluating intelligent tutoring systems.* Journal of Artificial Intelligence and Education, 4(2/3), 245–271.

Shweder, R. (1991). *Thinking through cultures.* Cambridge, MA: Harvard University Press.

Siegler, R. S. (1998). *Children's thinking* (3rd ed). Upper Saddle River, NJ: Prentice-Hall.

Silver, H., Strong, R., & Perini, M. (1997). Integrating learning styles and multiple intelligences. *Educational Leadership, 55*(1), 22–27.

Sindelar, P. T., Griffin, C. C., Smith, S. W., & Wantanabe, A. K. (1992). Prereferral intervention: Encouraging notes on preliminary findings. *The Elementary School Journal, 92,* 245–259.

Skinner, B. F. (1938). *The behavior of organisms.* New York: Macmillan.

Skinner, B. F. (1953). *Science and human nature.* New York: Macmillan.

Skinner, B. F. (1957). *Verbal behavior.* New York: Appleton-Century-Crofts.

Skinner, B. F. (1968). *The technology of teaching.* New York: Appleton-Century-Crofts.

Skinner, B. F. (1971). *Beyond freedom and dignity.* New York: Knopf.

Skinner, B. F. (1974). *About behaviorism.* New York: Knopf.

Skinner, B. F. (1984, September). The shame of American education. *American Psychologist, 39*(9), 947–954.

Skinner, B. F. (1986, March). Some thoughts about the future. *Journal of the Experimental Analysis of Behavior,* Vol. 22, 229–235.

Skinner, B. F. (1990). *Remarks after receiving a lifetime achievement award at the 98th Annual Convention of the American Psychological Association,* Boston. Cited in E. Scott Gieller, The Editor's Page. *Journal of Applied Behavior Analysis, 23,* 399–402.

Slavin, R. (1987). A theory of school and classroom organization. *Educational Psychologist, 22,* 90–99.

Slavin, R. (1988a, September). Synthesis of research on grouping in elementary and secondary schools. *Educational Leadership,* Vol. 45, 67–77.

Slavin, R. (1988b, October). Cooperative learning and student achievement. *Educational Leadership,* Vol. 45, 31–33.

Slavin, R. (1991). *Educational psychology* (3rd ed.). Englewood Cliffs, NJ: Prentice-Hall.

Slavin, R. E. (1989). Students at risk of school failure: The problem and its dimensions. In R. E. Slavin, N. L. Karweit, & N. A. Madden (Eds.), *Effective programs for students at risk,* 104–129. Needham Heights, MA: Allyn & Bacon.

Slavin, R. E., & Madden, N. A. (1989, February). What works for students at risk: A research synthesis. *Educational Leadership,* Vol. 46, 4–13.

Sleeter, C., & Grant, C. (1998). *Making choices for multicultural education.* Columbus, OH: Merrill.

Smith, M. L., & Glass, G. V. (1977). Meta-analysis of psychotherapy outcomes studies. *American Psychologist, 32,* 752–760.

Smith, M. L., & Glass, G. J. (1980). Meta-analysis of psychotherapy outcome studies. *American Psychologist, 32,* 752–760.

Snow, R., Corno, L., & Jackson, D. (1996). Individual differences in affective and conative functions. In D. Berliner & R. Calfee (Eds.), *Handbook of educational psychology,* 194–224. New York: Simon & Schuster/Macmillan.

Spaulding, C. L. (1992). *Motivation in the classroom.* New York: McGraw-Hill.

Spencer, M., & Dornbusch, S. (1990). Challenges in studying minority youth. In S. Feldman & G. Elliott (Eds.), *At the threshold: The developing adolescent.* Cambridge, MA: Harvard University Press.

Spencer, M., & Markstrom-Adams, C. (1990). Identity processes among racial and ethnic minority children in America. *Child Development, 61,* 290–310.

Speth, C., & Brown, R. (1988). Study approaches, processes and strategies. Are three perspectives better than one? *British Journal of Educational Psychology, 58,* 247–257.

Spring, J. (1997). *Deculturization and the struggle for equality.* New York: McGraw-Hill.

Sroufe, G. E. (1997). Improving the "awful reputation" of education research. *Educational Researcher, 26,* 26–28.

Stanovich, K. E. (1986). Matthew effects in reading: Some consequences of individual differences in the acquisition of literacy. *Reading Research Quarterly, 21,* 360–407.

Stanovich, K. E. (1991). Word recognition: Changing perspectives. In R. Barr, M. L. Kamil, P. B. Mosenthal, & P. D. Pearson (Eds.), *Handbook of reading research* (Vol. 2., pp. 418–452). New York: Longman.

Stein, M. (1993). *The beginning reading instruction study.* Washington, DC: U.S. Government Printing Office.

Steinberg, L. (1996). *Beyond the classroom.* New York: Simon & Schuster.

Stemmer, J. Brown, B. & Smith, S. B. (1992). The employability skills portfolio. *Educational Leadership, 49,* 78–81.

Sternberg, R. (1997). *Thinking styles.* New York: Cambridge University Press.

Sternberg, R., & Lubart, T. (1995). *Defying the crowd: Cultivating creativity in a culture of conformity.* New York: Free Press.

Sternberg, R. (1994). Allowing for thinking styles. *Educational Leadership, 52*(3), 36–41.

Sternberg, R. (1996). *Successful intelligence.* New York: Simon & Schuster.

Sternberg, R., & Davidson, J. E. (Eds.). (1986). Conceptions of giftedness. New York: Cambridge University Press.

Sternberg, R., Okagaki, L., & Jackson, L. (1990). Practical intelligence for success in school. *Educational Leadership, 48,* 35–39.

Stevens, R. J., & Slavin, R. E. (1995). The cooperative elementary school: Effects on students' achievement, attitudes, and social relations. *American Educational Research Journal, 32,* 321–351.

Stevenson, H., Lee, S., Chen, C., Lummis, M., Stigler, J., Fan, L., & Ge, F. (1990). Mathematics achievement of children in China and the United States. *Child Development, 61,* 1053–1066.

Stewart, J., Hafner, R., Johnson, S., & Finkel, E. (1992). Science as model building: Computers and high-school genetics. *Educational Psychologist, 27*(3), 317–336.

Stiggins, R. J. (1994). *Student-centered classroom assessment.* New York: Merrill.

Stigler, J., Shweder, R., & Herdt, G. (Eds.). (1990). *Cultural psychology.* New York: Cambridge University Press.

Stinson, M. S., Whitmire, K., & Klawin, T. N. (1996). Self-perceptions of social relationships in learning-impaired adolescents. *Journal of Educational Psychology, 88,* 132–143.

Stipek, D. J. (1984). Sex differences in children's attributions for success and failure on math and spelling tests. *Sex Roles, 11,* 969–981.

Stipek, D. J. (1998). *Motivation to learn: From theory to practice.* Englewood Cliffs, NJ: Prentice-Hall.

Stokes, T. F., & Baer, D. M. (1977). An implicit knowledge of generalization. *Journal of Applied Behavior Analysis, 11,* 285–303.

Sue, D., & Sue, D. (1990). *Counseling the culturally different.* New York: John Wiley.

Sue, S., & Okazaki, S. (1990). Asian-American educational achievements: A phenomenon in search of an explanation. *American Psychologist, 45,* 913–920.

Sullivan, H. J. (1969). Objectives, evaluation, and improved learner achievement. Instructional objectives. *AERA Monograph Series on Curriculum Evaluation,* (No. 3). Chicago: Rand McNally.

Sulzer-Azaroff, B., & Mayer, G. R. (1991). *Behavior analysis for lasting change.* Fort Worth: Holt, Rinehart & Winston.

Suppes, P. (1966). The uses of computers in education. *Scientific American, 215,* 206–221.

Tchudi, S. (1991). *Planning and assessing the curriculum in English Language Arts.* Alexandria, VA: Association for Supervision and Curriculum Development.

Tharp, R. (1989). Psychocultural variables and constants: Effects on teaching and learning in schools. *American Psychologist, 44,* 349–359.

Thorndike, E. (1913). *Educational psychology* (Vol. 1). New York: Teachers College Press.

Tiedt, P. & Tiedt, I. (1990). *Multicultural teaching.* Boston: Allyn & Bacon.

Tiemann, P., & Markle, S. (1990). *Analyzing instructional content: A guide to instruction and evaluation.* Champaign, IL: Stipes.

Tobias, S. (1980). Anxiety and instruction. In I. G. Sarason (Ed.), *Test anxiety: Theory, research, and applications,* 78–103. Hillsdale, NJ: LEA.

Todman, J., & Dick, G. (1993). Primary children and teachers' attitudes to computers. *Computers in Education, 20*(2), 199–203.

Travers, J. (1982). *The growing child.* Glenview, IL: Scott, Foresman.

Triandis, H. (1990). Theoretical concepts that are applicable to the analysis of ethnocentrism. In R. Brislin (Ed.), *Applied cross-cultural psychology.* Newbury Park, CA: Sage.

Tulving, E. (1972). Episodic and semantic memory. In E. Tulving & W. Donaldson (Eds.), *Organization and memory,* 64–89. New York: Academic Press.

Twardosz, S., Cataldo, M. F., & Risley, T. R. (1974). An open environment design for infant and toddler daycare. *Journal of Applied Behavior Analysis, 7,* 529–546.

Unger, R., & Crawford, M. (1996). *Women and gender.* New York: McGraw-Hill.

Unger, R. (1979). Toward a redefinition of sex and gender. *American Psychologist, 34,* 1085–1094.

University of Michigan Institute for Social Research. (1994). *Monitoring the future study.* Ann Arbor, MI: unpublished data.

U.S. Bureau of the Census. (1995). Statistical abstracts of the United States. Washington, D.C.: U.S. Government Printing Office.

U.S. Bureau of the Census. (1996). *Child and adult poverty rates, 1959 to 1995.* Washington, D.C.

U.S. Department of Education. (1993). *Fifteenth annual report to Congress on the implementation of the Individuals with Disabilities Education Act.* Washington, D.C.: Author.

Van Haneghan, J., Barron, L., Young, M., Williams, S., Vye, N., & Bransford, J. D. (1992). The Jasper series: An experiment with new ways to enhance mathematical thinking. In D. F. Halpern (Ed.), *Enhancing thinking skills in the sciences and mathematics* (pp. 15–38). Hillsdale, NJ: Erlbaum.

Vellutino, F. R. (1991). Introduction to three studies of reading acquisition: Convergent finding on theoretical foundations of code-oriented versus whole-language approaches to reading instruction. *Journal of Educational Psychology, 83,* 437–443.

von Glaserfeld, E. (1996). Introduction: Aspects of Constructivism. In C. T. Fosnot (Ed.), *Constructivism: Theory, perspectives, and practice,* 1–24. New York: Teachers College Press.

Vygoskaia, G. (1995). Remembering father. *Educational Psychologist, 30*(2), 57–59.

Vygotsky, L. (1962). *Thought and language.* New York: Wiley.

Vygotsky, L. (1978). *Mind in society.* Cambridge, MA: Harvard University Press.

Wagner, R., & Torgesen, J. (1987). The nature of phonological processing and it causal role in the acquisition of reading skills. *Psychological Bulletin, 101,* 192–212.

Walberg, H. J. (1986). Synthesis of research on teaching. In M. Wittrock (Ed.), *Handbook of research on teaching,* 108–147. New York: Macmillan.

Walker, H., & Sylvester, R. (1991). Where is school along the path to prison? *Educational Leadership, 49*(1), 14–16.

Walker, L. & Taylor, J. (1991). Stage transitions in moral reasoning: A longitudinal study of developmental processes. *Developmental Psychology, 27,* 330–337.

Walser, R. (1990). *Virtual reality: Theory, practice, and promise.* New York: Meckler Press.

Walsh, M. (1992). *Moving to nowhere.* New York: Auburn House.

Walsh, M. E., & Bibace, R. (1990). Developmentally-based AIDS/HIV education. *Journal of School Health, 60,* 256–261.

Wang, M. C., Reynolds, M. C., & Walberg, H. J. (1995). Serving students at the margins. *Educational Leadership,* Vol. 53, 12–17.

Wang, M., & Baker, E. (1985/1986). Mainstreaming programs: Design features and effects. *The Journal of Special Education, 19,* 503–521.

Wang, M. C., Huertel, G. D., & Walberg, H. J. (1993). Toward a knowledge base for school learning. *Review of Educational Research, 63,* 249–294.

Webster-Stratton, C. (1996). Early intervention with videotape modeling: Programs for families of children with oppositional defiant disorder or conduct disorder. In E. D. Hibbs and P. S. Jensen (Eds.), *Psychosocial treatments for child and adolescent disorders: Empirically-based strategies for clinical practice* (pp. 435–474). Washington, DC: American Psychological Association.

Wechsler, D. (1974). *The measurement and appraisal of adult intelligence* (4th ed.). Baltimore: Williams & Wilkins.

Weiner, B. (1990a). History of motivational research in education. *Journal of Educational Psychology, 82,* 616–622.

Weiner, B. (1990b). On perceiving the other as responsible. In R. Dienstbier (Ed.), *Nebraska symposium on motivation: Perspectives on motivation.* Lincoln, NE: University of Nebraska Press.

Weiner, B., Russell, D., & Lerman, D. (1978). Affective consequences of causal ascriptions. In J. H. Harvey et al. (Eds.), *New directions in attribution research.* Hillsdale, NJ: Erlbaum.

Weinraub, M., & Gringlas, M. (1995). Single parenthood. In M. Bornstein (Ed.), *Handbook of parenting.* Vol. 3. Mahwah, NJ: Erlbaum.

Weinstein, C., & Mayer, R. (1986). The teaching of learning strategies. In M. Wittrock, *Handbook of research on teaching,* 315–352. New York: Macmillan.

Weiss, L., Farrar, E., & Petrie, H. (1989). *Dropouts from school: Issues, dilemmas, and solutions.* Albany: State University of New York Press.

Weissbourd, R. (1996). *The vulnerable child.* Reading MA: Addison-Wesley.

Werner, E., & Smith, R. (1992). *Overcoming the odds: High risk children from birth to adulthood.* Ithaca, NY: Cornell University Press.

Wertsch, J., & Tulviste, P. (1992). L. S. Vygotsky and contemporary developmental psychology. *Developmental Psychology, 28*(4), 558–565.

White, O. R., & Associates. (1988). Review and analysis of strategies for generalization. In N. G. Haring (Ed.), *Generalization for students with severe handicaps: Strategies and solutions* (pp. 15–51). Seattle: University of Washington Press.

White, T. (1975). *Breach of faith: The fall of Richard Nixon* (1975.). New York: Atheneum.

Wielkiewicz, R. (1986). Behavior management in the schools. New York: Pergamon.

Wiggins, G. P. (1993). Assessing student performance: Exploring the purpose and limits of testing. San Francisco: Jossey-Bass.

Wigfield, A. (1994). Expectancy-value theory of achievement motivation: A developmental perspective. *Educational Psychology Review, 6,* 49–78.

Wilcox, R. (1987, October). Rediscovering discovery learning. *The Clearing House,* pp. 53–56.

Wilder, G., Mackie, D., & Cooper, J. (1985). Gender and computers: Two surveys of computer-related attitudes. *Sex Roles, 13*(3,4), 215–228.

Will, J. Self, P., & Datan, N. (1976). Maternal behavior and perceived sex of infant. *American Journal of Orthopsychiatry, 46,* 135–139.

Williams, J. (1986). Teaching children to identify the main idea of expository text. *Exceptional Children, 53,* 163–168.

Wilson, B. (1987). What is a concept? Concept teaching and cognitive psychology. *Performance and Instruction, 25,* 16–18.

Wilson, M. J., & Bullock, L. M. (1989). Psychometric characteristics of behavior rating scales: Definitions, problems, and solutions. *Behavioral Disorders, 14,* 186–200.

Witt, J. C., Elliott, S. N., Daly, E. J. III, Gresham, F. M., & Kramer, J. J. (1998). *Assessment of at-risk and special needs children* (2nd ed.). Boston: McGraw-Hill.

Wlodkowski, R. (1986). *Motivation and teaching.* Washington, DC: National Education Association.

Wolfgang, C. H., & Glickman, C. D. (1986). *Solving discipline problems: Strategies for classroom teachers* (2nd ed.). Boston: Allyn & Bacon.

Woodward, J., & Noell, J. (1991). Science instruction at the secondary level: Implications for students with learning disabilities. *Journal of Learning Disabilities, 24,* 277–284.

Woodward, J., Carnine, D., & Gersten, R. (1989). Teaching problem solving through a computer simulator. *American Educational Research Journal, 25,* 72–86.

Workman, E. A. (1982). *Teaching behavioral self-control to students.* Austin, TX: Pro-Ed.

Wright, J. L. (1992). *My father, Frank Lloyd Wright.* New York: Dover.

Wynne, E. (1988). Balancing character development and academics in the elementary school. *Phi Delta Kappan,* February, 424–426.

Yemma, J. (September 17, 1997). Assessing integration in hearts and minds. *The Boston Globe,* p. A18.

Yoshikawa, H. (1995). Long-term effects of early childhood programs in social outcomes and delinquency. In R. Behrman (Ed.) *The future of children,* 51–75. Los Altos, CA: Center for the Future of Children.

Young, B. (1991). The vital ingredients of self-esteem and how to develop them in your child. New York: Rawson Asssociates.

Ysseldyke, J. E., & Algozzine, B. (1990). *Introduction to special education* (2nd ed.). Boston: Houghton Mifflin.

Ysseldyke, J. E., & Algozzine, B. (1995). *Introduction to special education* (2nd ed.). Boston: Houghton Mifflin.

Ysseldyke, J. E., Algozzine, B., & Thurlow, M. L. (1992). *Critical issues in special education* (2nd ed.). Boston: Houghton Mifflin Co.

Ysseldyke, J. E., Christenson, S. L., Thurlow, M. L., & Bakewell, D. (1989). Are different kinds of instructional tasks used by different categories of students in different settings? *School Psychology Review, 18,* 98–111.

Yuochi, S., Mischel, W., & Peake, P. (1990). Predicting adolescent cognitive and self-regulatory competencies from preschool delay of gratification, *Developmental Psychology, 26*(6), 978–986.

Zigler, E., & Lang, M. (1991). *Child care choices: Balancing the needs of children, family and society.* New York: The Free Press.

Zigler, E., & Muenchow, S. (1992). *Head Start.* New York: Crown.

Zigler, E., & Styfco, S. (1994). Head Start: Criticisms in a constructive context. *American Psychologist, 49*(2), 127–132.